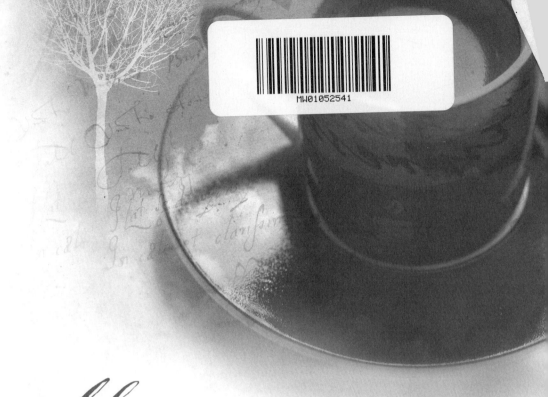

Morning
MANNA

A devotional help and Bible study guide
for the pulpit and the pew

R. CHRIS HANKS

Morning Manna: A devotional help and Bible study guide for the pulpit and the pew

© 2010 R. Chris Hanks

All Scripture quoted is from the Authorized King James Version.

Unless otherwise noted, all Greek and Hebrew word definitions given are from Strong's Exhaustive Concordance of the Bible. Access online at http://www.biblestudytools.com/concordances/strongs-exhaustive-concordance.

All italics in Scripture quotations have been added by the author for emphasis.

The author has chosen to spell "Saviour" with seven letters to represent the Lord's perfection.

Published by
Deep River Books
Sisters, Oregon
http://www.deepriverbooks.com

ISBN-10 1-935265-39-3
ISBN-13 978-1-935265-39-9

Library of Congress Control Number: 2010941290

Printed in the USA

Cover and interior design by Robin Black, www.blackbirdcreative.biz

DEDICATION

This book is first dedicated to my Lord and Saviour, Jesus Christ, for it is all about His precious and perfect Word.

To my wonderful wife and help meet, Alicia, and to my children, Kyle, Chelsie, Bethany, Caleb, and Connor, who supported me and sacrificed much in time and resources so this book could be written and published.

To my father, friend, counselor, and mentor, Roger Hanks, who taught me to love the Word of God as a child.

To Gospel Way Baptist Church, the precious church that God has called me to pastor. This book was begun to strengthen their love of the Word of God and help them in their Christian walk.

SPECIAL THANKS

To Shannon Fure and Rebekah Hanks, my sisters, for helping me prepare the whole manuscript. Thanks to Zena Spann, my secretary, for all of her hard work to make this a reality.

Thanks to Jan Kiemle, who made sure the verses and references were accurate throughout the book, and to my editor, Rachel Starr Thomson, who did an excellent job in bringing out my message in a clear, concise, and professional way.

Finally, my thanks to the many preachers and people who encouraged me to write this book: missionary Tony Howeth, Dr. Scott Hanks, Dr. Dean McNeese, Pastor Eric Brown, Pastor Stephen Henderson, Dr. Clay McNeese, Pastor Wayne Cofield, Dr. Mike Bagwell, Paw Paw Keever, and businessman Mark Farrington.

INTRODUCTION

*J*eremiah 15:16 says, "Thy words were found, and I did eat them; and thy word was unto me the joy and rejoicing of mine heart: for I am called by thy name, O Lord God of hosts." As a pastor, my desire is to connect people to the Word of God. There is no way that we can obey, grow, mature, serve, or worship without the Word of God in our lives. For some, studying Scripture has become a mundane chore rather than a pleasure. That is why some would rather watch television to receive their spiritual food than study the Bible for themselves.

God talks about His Word as milk, meat, honey, bread, and water. Job said, "I have esteemed the words of his mouth more than my necessary food" (Job 23:12). My desire for this book is to give readers a substantive study of one verse for each day's devotion. As you go through this systematic study, my prayer is that you will begin to crave more of the Word of God.

If you follow the schedule provided at the top of each devotion, you will read through the Bible in a year. The Bible says, "All scripture is given by inspiration of God, and is profitable" (2 Timothy 3:16). If all of the Word of God is profitable, we must read it all. I believe that you will find yourself understanding more of the Bible and becoming excited about reading through parts of the Book that you may never have read before.

Each single-verse devotion is broken down by phrase in outline form. This will be a help to any Bible student, from new babes in Christ to seasoned preachers. I hope that those in the ministry will find this book to be an invaluable tool and a great addition to any library. The topical index referenced at the bottom of each devotion and compiled at the back of the book will prove extremely helpful as you look for other thoughts and outlines on the same subjects. I have aimed to write a book that is easy to use, practical in its application, and profound in its truths, yet with a writing style that is easy and enjoyable to read.

Because of the depth of this devotional, you may find that you will be able to use it year after year. I pray that it will challenge you, reveal spiritual truths that you have never known, and draw your heart to worship as it exposes who God is. Start today, taste the manna, and experience God. As the psalmist said in Psalm 34:8, "O taste and see that the Lord is good: blessed is the man that trusteth in him."

—R. CHRIS HANKS

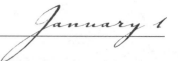

DAILY BIBLE READING: Genesis 1–3

TODAY'S VERSE: Genesis 2:15: "And the Lord God took the man, and put him into the garden of Eden to dress it and to keep it."

THERE IS SOMETHING SPECIAL about something new. I have always enjoyed new things. We cannot get any "newer" than the way Genesis 1 starts: "In the beginning." With the beginning of a New Year, we have great anticipation of what the Lord can do in us and through us. There will be new challenges and new victories. There will be new wounds and new healings. There will be new troubles, but also new triumphs. Thank God that Hebrews 13:8 says, "Jesus Christ the same yesterday, and to day, and for ever." We can still sing John Newton's powerful hymn"Amazing Grace," which says, "Through many dangers, toils, and snares/I have already come/Tis grace hath brought me safe thus far/And grace will lead me home."

We could have looked at many verses in these first three chapters, with tremendous doctrines contained in each of them, but in this verse we see God's choice to put man in the garden planted by the Great Farmer of the universe.

First, we see the **Pleasure of God** ("And the LORD God took the man"). Why did God choose man? We know that He breathed into man the breath of life and created him in His image, but why? Even David is confounded by God's concern for man: "What is man, that thou art mindful of him? and the son of man, that thou visitest him?" (Psalm 8:4). The only reason is because it pleased God to do so. Psalm 135:6 says, "Whatsoever the LORD pleased, that did he in heaven, and in earth, in the seas, and all deep places." God is still pleased to use man to bring glory to Himself.

Second, we see the **Placement of God** ("and put him into the garden of Eden"). In Hebrew, the words for "put him" mean "to deposit, to allow to stay." This word is not for Adam alone. It is the sovereign will of God that has placed you where you are. He gave you your family, your country, and even your neighbors. Instead of despising your placement, accept it as the will of God for your life and begin serving where God has you. This will honor Him and bless you at the same time.

Third, we see the **Purpose of God** ("to dress it and to keep it"). God did not make some eternal vacation for Adam to enjoy. God did something better—God gave him work! Yes, God gave Adam work even before he sinned in the garden! Two words are used here to describe God's purpose in Adam's life: "dress" and "keep." One has to do with preparation ("dress it"), and the other has to do with protection ("keep it"). Both of these purposes are desires that God still has for you. Be faithful in your work, labor for Him, and protect your work from any who would destroy it.

TOPICS: God's Pleasure, God's Purpose, Sovereignty, Work

January 2

DAILY BIBLE READING: Genesis 4-7

TODAY'S VERSE: Genesis 4:7: "If thou doest well, shalt thou not be accepted? and if thou doest not well, sin lieth at the door. And unto thee shall be his desire, and thou shalt rule over him."

WHAT A SAD VERSE and a sad story in the Bible! This story occurs between Cain's *bloodless sacrifice* before God and the *bloody slaying* of his brother. Before he committed this murderous act against his brother, Cain had a conversation with God about his sacrifice. God warned Cain against his anger and encouraged him to return to good fellowship, but he would have none of it! This verse is God's warning to Cain and to us as well. By letting our anger consume us, we hurt not only ourselves, but also everyone around us! God warns Cain against this sin in three different ways.

First, we see the **Danger of Sin** ("sin lieth at the door"). I don't know about you, but I don't have to go very far to find sin! As a matter of fact, it is usually waiting for me! It is encamped right outside my door. My anger becomes a homing device for sin to find me. Sin is a *present danger* (it is at the threshold). It is a *personal danger* (it is against me). It is a *patient danger* (it "lieth at the door"). It will wait for the right time to make its move to destroy each one of us.

Second, we see the **Desire of Sin** ("unto thee shall be his desire"). Sin will do whatever I tell it to do. Isn't this great? Sin is a servant that will obey me much more quickly than my own children will! There is no feeling like having your way in the selfish desires of your sin. I believe this is part of the pleasure that Hebrews 11:25 talks about when it describes some who "enjoy the pleasures of sin for a season." Sin will be there to do your heart's desire concerning evil. The Bible says in Genesis 6:5, "And God saw that the wickedness of man was great in the earth, and that every imagination of the thoughts of his heart was only evil continually." These evil people were served well! You will never be able to accuse sin of not doing what you want it to do. There is a pleasure that comes with getting your way in sin, but it is short-lived.

Third, we see the **Dominion of Sin** ("and thou shalt rule over him"). Sure, sin offers a kingdom that you can rule! Here is your chance to make a difference! All of the bitterness, murder, hate, and wrath (the list could go on much, much longer!) can be *your* kingdom—today! It is a *devilish kingdom,* a *destroying kingdom,* and a *defiling kingdom.* It's one of the only things today that you don't need a permit to build! Many have already started building this kingdom in their own personalities, homes, relationships, and spirits. Maybe you are one of them. But this is not the kingdom you want! This is no way for a child of God to live. This is no *dominion;* it is a *dungeon!* Jesus has come to set you free! Come and live in the palace of the King!

TOPICS: Anger, Bondage, Hatred, Sin

DAILY BIBLE READING: Genesis 8–11

TODAY'S VERSE: Genesis 8:1: "And God remembered Noah, and every living thing, and all the cattle that was with him in the ark: and God made a wind to pass over the earth, and the waters asswaged."

WHAT A BLESSED ACCOUNT we have here of the great flood and God's deliverance from it. The Hebrew word for "remembered" means "to mark so as to be recognized." God marked the end of the flood with a rainbow so that all would recognize that it was a work of God in His judgment as well as His restoration. Let's consider what God remembers in this passage.

First, we see **God's Remembrance of Mercy** ("And God remembered Noah"). While God was destroying the earth, God remembered Noah. What great love our Lord has for all of us! Just the fact that God was thinking about Noah during this time of punishment is a blessing to me. We see this illustrated again later, while God was destroying Jerusalem because of David's sin. God was moved with love for that city that was the "apple of His eye," and He told the Destroying Angel to stay his hand (2 Samuel 24:16). Even while He was commencing His judgment upon Jerusalem in wrath, He was moved by mercy! In Habakkuk 3:2, the prophet prays, "In wrath remember mercy." Even in the midst of God's punishment, there is the hope of His everlasting mercy!

Second, we see **God's Response of Peace** ("and God made a wind to pass over the earth"). The word used for "pass" means "to cross over, to cover." This same idea applies to our salvation. We have "crossed over" from His judgment and into His love. John 5:24 says that we have "passed from death unto life." I love it when God covers me up! What kind of a wind was this after the flood? I believe it was a move of the Holy Ghost! Genesis 1:2 says that the "Spirit of God moved upon the face of the waters." Only the Spirit of God can bring new life where there had been nothing but the judgment of God!

Third, we see **God's Reward of Deliverance** ("and the waters asswaged"). What a blessed time when God's judgment is over! What a renewed fellowship! What joy divine! Psalm 51:8 says, "Make me to hear joy and gladness; that the bones which thou hast broken may rejoice." We still experience this today. Some of the greatest joys in our lives will come immediately following chastisement. A little bit later, in verse 12, the psalm says, "Restore unto me the joy of thy salvation; and uphold me with thy free spirit."

I am glad that God remembered Noah!

TOPICS: Chastisement, God's Judgment, Mercy, Restoration

January 4

TODAY'S VERSE: Genesis 13:4: "Unto the place of the altar, which he had made there at the first: and there Abram called on the name of the LORD."

AFTER ABRAM LAPSED in faith by going into Egypt to run from the "grievous" famine in the land, he came out by way of Bethel, which means "the House of God." Isn't that a good place to get right with God? I love to go to church! I go expecting to hear or see something from God. I can say as David did in Psalm 84:10, "For a day in thy courts is better than a thousand. I had rather be a doorkeeper in the house of my God, than to dwell in the tents of wickedness."

First, we see that **God's House Is a Place of Reverence** ("unto the place of the altar"). Every time I visit the place of the altar, I am humbled in silent thought. Every time I remember Calvary, I feel I'm on holy ground. Even as I go to the altar to make decisions, I can't help but remember Christ's great sacrifice for my sinful soul. Abram could have passed by this special place, but his heart was full of reverence and worship, and he just had to stop and give glory to God. That place had special meaning. He could still feel the presence of God right there in Bethel. We should be moved by our worship and adoration of God! Bethel was the place where God had changed Abram, the first place he met with God.

Second, we see that **God's House Is a Place of Remembrance** ("which he had made there at the first"). Do you still have a sense of respect and love for the place and time where God changed you? The place I got saved is no longer what it once was, but oh, it has not lost its meaning for me! I am constantly amazed that an Almighty God would save a wretch like me! I remember the time that God called me to preach. I remember the time God called me to go to Colorado to start a church. What a blessed time of remembrance! God's house is full of precious memories in my life.

Third, we see that **God's House Is a Place of Renewal** ("and there Abram called upon the name of the LORD"). Abraham wanted to do it all again! Even after his failure, he wanted to serve God again! Aren't you glad today that God will take you back? Praise Him for His longsuffering! Praise Him for His renewing and reviving ministry! Have you lost your way? Come back to Him! Renew your love and service today! He is waiting for you. When you return, the house of the Lord will hold even greater meaning in your life.

TOPICS: Altar, Church, Rededication, Worship

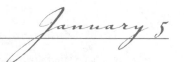

DAILY BIBLE READING: Genesis 16–18

TODAY'S VERSE: Genesis 18:14: "Is anything too hard for the Lord? At the time appointed I will return unto thee, according to the time of life, and Sarah shall have a son."

WHAT A WONDERFUL QUESTION for us to consider today: "Is anything too hard for the Lord?" As children we used to ask silly questions like, "Can God make a rock so big that even He cannot lift it?" Of course, those silly questions are based upon the faulty premise that God's character and abilities can be contradicted. Certainly, God cannot compromise or contradict Himself! This question in Scripture, however, is one that pertains to His ability and His power. Whatever comes our way, whatever problem we may face, we must never doubt the power of God, especially where His promises are concerned. No matter your situation today, whether it be one of fearful trepidation or just of nervous concern, you can be assured of Luke 1:37: "For with God nothing shall be impossible."

A Promise of Power in a Miracle ("At the time appointed I will return unto thee, according to the time of life"). Earlier, verse 11 said, "It ceased to be with Sarah after the manner of women." For her to conceive was going to take a work of God. Abraham and Sarah were looking at the physical limitations of man and of nature—but can you imagine telling the Creator what can and cannot happen? I would love to know exactly what miracle God performed in Sarah. Hebrews 11:11 tells us, "Through faith also Sara herself received strength to conceive seed, and was delivered of a child when she was past age, because she judged him faithful who had promised." I do not believe it was the strength God gave to her, but *the faith* to receive strength. Faith was the miracle. We need to pray as the father who asked Christ to heal his child in Mark 9:24: "Lord, I believe; help thou mine unbelief." Oh, for our Lord to increase our faith that we might believe! That is the true miracle.

A Promise of Pleasure to a Mother ("and Sarah shall have a son"). To capture this thought, let us look at verse 12: "Therefore Sarah laughed within herself, saying, After I am waxed old shall I have pleasure, my lord being old also?" Sarah did not think she would ever experience physical happiness with her husband and bear a son. She had lived her life barren. She had been the object of scorn and ridicule in that hard desert land for as long as she could remember. She had grown accustomed to it, comfortable in her life of contempt. Her urge to hold a little babe in her arms had been forsaken a long time ago. Now we hear the care of God as He promises her the one thing that had been missing for so long. A pleasure that was only dreamed about for decades would now become hers! What a blessing!

A Promise of Presenting the Messiah ("and Sarah shall have a son"). It's very important that we all understand what "son" this verse is talking about. This was "the son" who had the guarantee with him. This was the covenant son of promise! This was the son through whom the promised Messiah would come! Genesis 17:19 says, "And God said, Sarah thy wife shall bear thee a son indeed; and thou shalt call his name Isaac: and I will establish my covenant with him for an everlasting covenant, and with his seed after him." This was the promise they had that proved not to be "too hard for the Lord." Praise the Lord for His power in bringing the Messiah to us!

TOPICS: Blessing, God's Power, God's Promises, Miracles

January 6

DAILY BIBLE READING: Genesis 19-21

TODAY'S VERSE: Genesis 21:7: "And she said, Who would have said unto Abraham, that Sarah should have given children suck? for I have born him a son in his old age."

WHAT A GREAT TIME this was! God's promises were finally fulfilled. Abraham and his faithless relationship with Hagar, meant to help God fulfill His promises, had proven to be an immense failure. Whenever we do not wait upon God, our efforts are always an immense failure! But now, God's promise finally came in the package of a bouncing baby boy. I mean "bouncing" literally, for his name means "laughter." Isaac was named as a rebuke to Abraham and Sarah's lack of faith, but despite the reproof, his coming was a welcome and celebrated blessing. His birth was so much of a blessing to Abraham and Sarah that we must rejoice in it as well, for this was the child of promise. This was the one through whom God would bless all nations of the earth with the birth of the Messiah. We need to respect and rejoice in the promises of God, for they are the pillars of our faith.

The Possibilities of God's Promises ("And she said, Who would have said unto Abraham . . ."). Nobody would ever have thought this birth could have happened, but God's promises bring certainty to a situation. If need be, all creation will stand at attention and change its molecular structure to fulfill God's promises. This is something the young virgin Mary came to understand. Luke 1:35, 37–38a says, "And the angel answered and said unto her, The Holy Ghost shall come upon thee, and the power of the Highest shall overshadow thee: therefore also that holy thing which shall be born of thee shall be called the Son of God . . . *For with God nothing shall be impossible.* And Mary said, Behold the handmaid of the Lord; *be it unto me according to thy word.*" Natural law could not bind the spiritual promise and work of God. His promises bring infinite possibilities.

The Pleasures of God's Promises ("that Sarah should have given children suck"). Could it be that Sarah would become a mother? Would she really be able to experience the pleasure of nursing her own son at such an old age? God's promises bring pleasure to the child of His heart, for when they are accomplished, God's children can rest assured knowing that His will has been done. Sarah finally experienced what she had desired for so many years. What joy and excitement for her as she held that child to her bosom in amazement at what God's promises had wrought! Don't give up, Christian! God's promises are still true and will be done according to His will.

The Production of God's Promises ("for I have born him a son in his old age"). It was God's promise that produced this child. Everything in Sarah's body was working against this great miracle. Nothing but God's promise produced a babe in an old, barren woman who had no hope of conceiving. Not only was God's promise greater than Sarah's problems, but it was greater than Abraham's as well. You see, Abraham was as "dead" as Sarah was. Romans 4:19–21 says, "And being not weak in faith, *he considered not his own body now dead*, when he was about an hundred years old, neither yet the deadness of Sara's womb: he staggered not at the promise of God through unbelief; but was strong in faith, giving glory to God; *and being fully persuaded that, what he had promised, he was able also to perform.*" God's promises are able and capable of performing the desired fruit of God's will.

TOPICS: Faith, God's Promises, Joy, Hope

DAILY BIBLE READING: Genesis 22–24

TODAY'S VERSE: Genesis 24:65: "For she had said unto the servant, What man is this that walketh in the field to meet us? And the servant had said, It is my master: therefore she took a vail, and covered herself."

WE'VE BEEN GOING THROUGH tremendous chapters this past week. This chapter, although it talks about Rebekah and Isaac, holds much greater truth as you go past the surface and dig a little deeper in the Word. Isaac, the son of promise, has been patiently waiting and now gets to meet his future bride. Isaac is a type of Christ in this story, so let's look at our verse in that blessed light.

First, we see the **Gladness of the Son** ("What man is this that walketh in the field to meet us?"). Rebekah could not have known who the son was without revelation by the unnamed servant. The promised son was coming to meet his future bride in the field. This was a glad moment. As a bride, Rebekah had free choice to accept or reject the tremendous blessing of marriage to Isaac after speaking with the unnamed servant. (An unnamed servant in the Bible is always a type of the Holy Ghost.) Now, as she approached, the son could not contain himself any longer and walked "in the field" to receive her. After one of Christ's parables, He explained to His disciples that "the field is the world." I am looking forward to the day when our Promised Son will come with gladness to receive His future bride, a bride of free choice, in the field of the world. He is coming to take us to His home! He has been preparing "a place for you" (John 14:2)!

Second, we see the **Greatness of the Son** ("And the servant had said, It is my master"). Do you believe that Christ is our Master? He is the one of whom the Holy Ghost, unnamed servant, has been telling you! In Genesis, the unnamed servant was sent by Abraham to find a bride for his son. The heir of his master *was also his master!* In verses 34–35, this servant called Abraham his master. Here in verse 65, he calls the son his master. The son was heir to everything. He had as much right to it as the father did! So does our Lord and Saviour Jesus Christ. When the servant sat in Rebekah's father's house in verse 35, the very first thing he did was speak of his master's power, wealth, and greatness. We see this same concept of God the Father exalting His Son in Ephesians 1:22: "And [the Father] hath put all things under his feet, and gave him to be the head over all things to the church." Christ is as much God as the Father is!

Third, we see the **Glory of the Son** ("therefore she took a vail, and covered herself"). Rebekah covered herself out of respect and honor for the son. She was not trying to hide anything, unlike Leah many years later. She felt that she was not yet worthy for him to look at her uncovered. She had a glorious master and would show him humility. Once they were man and wife and had fully accepted one another, she would be "worthy" for him to behold. Notice, though, that she did not just "put on" a veil, but "she took a vail, and covered herself." This is the first time that the word "vail" is used in the Bible. The word comes from a root meaning "to wrap over." The time is coming when we will be taken to His place and will be face-to-face with the One whom we love. Then our veil will be taken away. That time is not too far away!

TOPICS: God's Glory, Holy Spirit, Respect

January 8

DAILY BIBLE READING: Genesis 25–26

TODAY'S VERSE: Genesis 26:25: "And he builded an altar there, and called upon the name of the LORD, and pitched his tent there: and there Isaac's servants digged a well."

IT IS AMAZING HOW many different ways the precious and perfect Word of God can speak to our hearts. In this passage, Isaac is in Beersheba right after God spoke to him. He responds to God's work in four ways.

First, **He Builds an Altar** ("And he builded an altar there"). Every time God meets with you, build an altar. Every time He speaks to you, build an altar. Every time He manifests Himself in your life, make a sacrifice. We are greatly lacking in altars that have been built from a heart of reverence and worship as a result of God's work in our hearts and lives. Isaac did not just raise a pillar or a statue commemorating God's presence, but an altar, a place to offer a sacrifice. God has always been honored by an altar. The altar is a testimony of something or someone given out of free will and love to honor God. After God speaks to your heart and moves in your life, this is the very first thing that needs to be done. Make sure your altar is built and built properly!

Second, **He Bids an Invitation** ("and *called* upon the name of the LORD"). The word translated "bid" means "to call." Instead of making demands upon God, why not request His presence? So many people give God an ultimatum and bribe Him with their worship and service. Some people say, "God, if you do this for me, then I will do this for you," as though they are enticing or manipulating God to work for them. God is not moved by the carrots you place before Him for selfish, carnal reasons. *Invite* God into your marriage, your home, your church, and you will see Him do great things that you never thought possible!

Third, **He Bows in His Dwelling** ("and pitched his tent there"). The Hebrew word for "pitched" means "to stretch or spread out; to bow down." God's followers will greatly enjoy dwelling where God has shown Himself to be! When was the last time you lay prostrate in His presence? We need to bow down before Him and remember that we are but dust. Your children need to see you "pitch a tent" at church or at home in the early morning hours! They need to see you bow down in the presence of God!

Fourth, **He Breaks up the Ground** ("and there Isaac's servants digged a well"). Isaac was the great well-digger of the Bible. The term used for "digged" means "to bore or open." The Christian life is not just sod work, it is *well* work! We need Christians who will not be satisfied with surface water, but who are willing to dig deeper to find springs of sweet, cool water. The best water I have ever tasted came from deep wells! Sometimes you might wonder why God has taken you down to great depths in sorrow or tribulation. God has placed blessings in those deep places of sorrow just for you!

TOPICS: God's Presence, Offering, Prayer, Tribulation, Work, Worship

DAILY BIBLE READING: Genesis 27–29

TODAY'S VERSE: Genesis 27:21: "And Isaac said unto Jacob, Come near, I pray thee, that I may feel thee, my son, whether thou be my very son Esau or not."

WHAT A SAD DAY in the life of Isaac! This story is about the destruction caused by sensualism. What we see here did not happen in a day but over time. Isaac did not lose his spiritual discernment suddenly, but slowly and steadily over the years.

First, Isaac was **Deceived by His Spouse**. Jacob received a blessing due to the deceitful work of his mother, Rebekah. Today, we need parents who are going to stand together in every decision they make. In the passage, we also see how easy it is to change stories quickly in the line of deceitful work. In verse 13, Rebekah says to Jacob, *"Upon me* be thy curse." Yet in verse 45 she says, " . . . until thy brother's anger turn away from thee, and he forget that which *thou* hast done to him." All of a sudden, it is Jacob's fault! Many have seen the parallelism between Jacob and his deceitful Uncle Laban. But in reality, Jacob was just like Rebekah, and his father was on the receiving end of a deceitful wife and son!

Second, Isaac was **Disappointed by His Sons**. Jacob presumed to deceive his father and steal from his own brother. Even though the blessing was his by right because of prophecy, he should have waited for God's timing. And what about Esau? This man of the world had no spiritual desire and wanted to receive spiritual satisfaction by satisfying his father's carnal appetites. After Jacob completed his act of deception, Esau became so angry and twisted in his mind that he unleashed his venom toward his parents by immediately marrying someone of whom they disapproved. Isaac lost both of his boys that he loved so much.

Third, Isaac was **Destroyed by His Senses**. Every sense failed him but one. First, his *taste* destroyed him. He asked Esau to make him "savoury meat, such as I love." But he couldn't even tell the difference between venison and mutton after Jacob deceived him. He must not have loved it like he thought he did! His sense of *touch* also failed him. He even told Jacob that he wanted to "feel thee, my son, whether thou be my very son Esau." Don't be governed by your feelings, for they will destroy you! The next verse says that he felt Jacob, but was deceived by the woolly skins of the sheep that Jacob had placed on his arms and his neck. His *sight* also failed him. Verse 1 says, "his eyes were dim, so that he could not see." The Bible instructs us in 2 Corinthians 5:7 to "walk by faith not by sight." The fourth sense that destroyed him was his sense of *smell*. Verse 27 says that as Jacob came to kiss his father, Isaac smelled his garments. Jacob was wearing Esau's clothing, the clothing of the world, and by that he deceived his own father.

The only sense that was not deceived was Isaac's *hearing*. Verse 22 says, "The voice is Jacob's voice." Isaac knew it was Jacob's voice he heard, but he was unwilling to trust his hearing. Have you heard the Word of God today? Do you believe it? Learn to hear God's voice now, for there will come a time when you will have every sense telling you something contrary, but the only thing that will matter is what God has told you. Isaiah 30:21 says, "And thine ears shall hear a word behind thee, saying, This is the way, walk ye in it, when ye turn to the right hand, and when ye turn to the left."

TOPICS: Deceitfulness, Flesh, Lying, Sensualism

January 16

DAILY BIBLE READING: Genesis 30–31

TODAY'S VERSE: Genesis 30:1: "And when Rachel saw that she bare Jacob no children, Rachel envied her sister; and said unto Jacob, Give me children, or else I die."

IN SOME WAYS, Rachel's situation is similar to Hannah's, a woman who also struggled in competition with her husband's other wife, Peninnah. Both Rachel and Hannah endured great mocking. Both of them were barren. Both greatly desired to be fruitful.

First, we see **Rachel's Problem** ("And when Rachel saw that she bare Jacob no children . . ."). This, by the way, was definitely *her* problem. There was no problem with Jacob. How helpless it is to feel that there is nothing you can do about a difficult circumstance! No doubt your heart is or has been disturbed about something over which you have no control, and you long for the peace of deliverance. You have read the Bible and other books looking for help. You have sought godly counsel, yet there is still a problem—**barrenness.** Jacob says in verse 2, "Am I in God's stead, who hath withheld from thee the fruit of the womb?" Then verse 22 says, "And God remembered Rachel." Hallelujah! Rachel went from barren to blooming. She never did have as many children as Leah, but the fruit of her womb blessed her future family, her nation, and her world. We later witness the blessing that Joseph was in his character and his faith even today!

Second, we see **Rachel's Plight** ("Rachel envied her sister"). In verse 8, Rachel says, "With great wrestlings have I wrestled with my sister." This was the same plight that Hannah had in 1 Samuel 1. The Bible called the other wife Hannah's "adversary" and says that she "provoked her." God does know the inner struggles in your life and the persecutions involved. He even knows the accusations you face and those who would say, "If you were right with God, then none of this would be happening to you." Yet if their arguments were true, then Christ would never have suffered, Paul would never have been on trial, and Hebrews 11 would never have been written. *Victory often comes with a lesson of perseverance!*

Third, we see **Rachel's Passion** ("and [she] said unto Jacob, give me children, or else I die"). Her desire was to be fruitful! She longed to produce for the one she loved! This ought to be our desire in the work of our Lord—to be fruitful. Our pastors and churches ought to have this same passion: "Give me children, or else I die." We must be consumed with this desire. It ought to lead us in our prayers and our love. Psalm 126:6 says, "He that goeth forth and weepeth, bearing precious seed, shall doubtless come again with rejoicing, bringing his sheaves with him." Just remember that *all is in God's hands.* Only God can bring life. Only God can make the child in the womb. Only God can make you fruitful. Because of that same truth, we must also beware "Leah Syndrome": if you are producing much, it doesn't make you better than others!

There is a story of an old country preacher who was confronted by his congregation because they had only gained one new member throughout the past year—and it was a little boy. The preacher was discouraged and felt like a failure. One day, however, the little boy came to the preacher and asked if he could preach or be a missionary. The preacher felt the Holy Ghost move as he spoke with the boy. That boy was Robert Moffat, who would become a great missionary! God had given that preacher a little Joseph! Not only did Robert Moffat lead many chiefs to the Lord, but his daughter also became the wife of missionary David Livingstone.[1] What fruit God gave to that old country preacher because of his faithfulness!

TOPICS: Barrenness, Perseverance, Prayer, Soul-Winning

---

1   Paul Chappell, *Fruit Grows Where The Stream Flows* (Lancaster, CA: Striving Together Publications, 2007), 126.

R. CHRIS HANKS

DAILY BIBLE READING: Genesis 32–34

TODAY'S VERSE: Genesis 32:25b–26: "And the hollow of Jacob's thigh was out of joint, as he wrestled with him. And he said, Let me go, for the day breaketh. And he said, I will not let thee go, except thou bless me."

THIS WAS A LIFE-CHANGING time for Jacob. He needed to be changed from being deceitful to being faithful. When the Great Wrestler showed up, Jacob was forced to come to the end of himself. We all need this kind of wrestling experience to pull us away from the deceitful life of self-reliance.

Three lessons in this wrestling match help us understand how to be a prince with God, as God called Jacob afterward.

The first is about **Leaning** ("and the hollow of Jacob's thigh was out of joint"). You will find that Jacob did not wrestle with God, but that *God wrestled with him* ("and there wrestled a man *with him* until the breaking of the day," says verse 24). What did God want from Jacob that He would wrestle him for it? God wanted his leaning! Everything that Jacob had done up to this point, he had done in his own carnal flesh. He had never trusted in God's ways yet! Jacob was used to manipulating every situation and getting his own way. God confronted Jacob with this in verses 27 and 28 when He asked him his name (God knew his name; He just wanted Jacob to admit what he was! He was a trickster and deceiver!). This was the very lesson that God wanted to teach the Israelites as they wandered in the wilderness, and it's the lesson God wants to teach you. God wants you to lean on Him! Quit trying to manipulate things to get your own way, and learn to trust God!

The second lesson is about **Latching** ("Let me go, for the day breaketh. And he said, I will not let thee go"). Instead of latching onto a hope or vision, why not latch onto hope itself? Once people find God, they do not ever want to let go of Him again! Song of Solomon 3:4 says, "It was but a little that I passed from them, but I found him whom my soul loveth: I held him, and would not let him go." This is how Jacob "prevailed," as verse 28 tells us. He latched onto God and would not let go!

The third lesson is about **Longing** ("except thou bless me.") What do you long for in your spiritual life? Isn't it time for something to change? Isn't it time to give up your own way? Isn't it time to let God change your world? Isn't it tiring trying to be something you're not? Why not let God change you and give you a new name, a new purpose, and a new life? If it is not a blessing from God, then it is no blessing at all! Such a change is not received by demanding, but by God's grace coming upon a longing servant. In the "prosperity gospel" age we live in, it is easy to get caught up in the name-it-and-claim-it mentality. Instead, wait, and let God bless you according to His will. Your longings will *push* you to your knees, *please* you to obey His Word, and *prepare* you be His servant!

TOPICS: God's Blessing, Prayer, Spiritual Desire, Trusting

January 12

DAILY BIBLE READING: Genesis 35–36

TODAY'S VERSE: Genesis 35:7: "And he built there an altar, and called the place Elbethel: because there God appeared unto him, when he fled from the face of his brother."

WHAT A BLESSED TIME this was for Jacob as he attended church. Let me remind you that the definition of "Bethel" is "house of God." In chapter 35 verses 1 and 6, we find that Jacob was going to "the house of God" to worship. We should be looking for the Lord to speak every time we come into His house. We should also come with a tender heart so that we can hear what He has to say. Jacob could not help but leave changed!

Four things about Jacob's visit to church changed him.

First, we see his **Response to Being in the House of God** ("And he built there an altar"). This response was one of immediate action. It was a *pressing* decision. Jacob didn't wait until he got home from church to make a decision about what the Lord had impressed upon him. It was a *pieced* decision. He built this altar piece by piece. It required effort and purpose to put together and construct this altar by God's command to honor Him. It was also a *parting* decision. He built an altar as a place of sacrifice. He parted with something that day and dedicated himself to the Lord.

Second, we see his **Recognition of Being in the House of God** ("and called the place Elbethel"). This was the place where Jacob's spiritual perception was changed. He did not just go meet at Bethel (the house of God), but at Elbethel (the *God* of the house of God). He didn't just go to church, but he met with God! How many people need to find the difference that Jacob did! Rather than just going to church, it will change your life to meet with God.

Third, we see his **Revelation from Being in the House of God** ("because there God appeared unto him"). When you meet with God, you will see God in His house as you never have, and you will hear things from His Word that you have never heard! The literal definition of the Hebrew word for "appeared" is "to denude." God just exposed some things to Jacob that he had never seen or known. Have you ever been to church or read your precious Bible only to say, "I have never seen that before"? What a blessing it is to have the Lord reveal things to us!

And fourth, we see his **Release after Being in the House of God** ("when he fled from the face of his brother"). What a release and deliverance! When Jacob met the Lord in His house, he was no longer afraid of Esau! He would never forget the fear that was in his heart and the peace that God gave him after being in the house of God! I cannot count how many times I have come into the house of God carrying the weight of the world upon my shoulders. Sometimes, within a few stanzas of a hymn or in the middle of the message, the Lord met with me and set me free from the cares of this world that had nearly destroyed my Christian joy. Enjoy the release that comes when you meet with God in His house!

TOPICS: Church, Deliverance, Liberty, Revelation, Spiritual Perception, Word of God

R. CHRIS HANKS

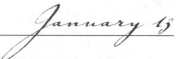

DAILY BIBLE READING: Genesis 37–39

TODAY'S VERSE: Genesis 39:9: "There is none greater in this house than I; neither hath he kept back any thing from me but thee, because thou art his wife: how then can I do this great wickedness, and sin against God?"

WHAT A TREMENDOUS TESTIMONY of Joseph! He feared God more than he wanted to fulfill the lust of his flesh. He identified exactly who this sin was against—God! There was no struggle with his flesh, though he had been separated from his family. His mind could have argued that no one would ever know. His heart could have argued that God didn't really care. His will could have argued that it didn't matter anyway. Maybe he could have even said, "When in Egypt, do as the Egyptians do." But Joseph knew that any sin was only and utterly against God.

A **Blessed Position** did not give him the right to sin ("There is none greater in this house than I"). Joseph knew that his position did not rival God's position. Power does not equal right. If God gives us a position, we should use the position to glorify God. Businessmen and women, your position is a God-blessed position demanding humility and honor from you. Official, your office is God-appointed and demands your honesty and righteous judgment. Pastor, yours is a God-called position and demands your devotion and compassion. No position ever justifies sin.

A **Bestowed Privilege** did not give him the right to sin ("neither hath he kept back any thing from me but thee"). Joseph recognized that his position was a privilege granted him by a greater authority than he. His was a freedom that required humility in knowing he had no right to accept anything as his own, especially that which had not been specifically granted concerning Potiphar's wife. His was a privilege that commanded innocence, transparency, and propriety. In other words, Joseph knew that he could not tamper with a grace extended to him.

A **Broken Promise** did not give him the right to sin ("because thou art his wife"). Joseph could have made the argument that Potiphar's wife had broken her vows to her husband first, so it would not be sin for him to follow her desires. Joseph had no vow or oath to keep him from this Egyptian woman. All Joseph had was his regard, respect, and love for God. He held to a life of moral purity that he knew God demanded. Because of this, her immoral desires did not justify his sin and wickedness before God. As Joseph did, we should dedicate ourselves to "glorify God in your body, and in your spirit, which are God's" (1 Corinthians 6:20).

TOPICS: Integrity, Moral Purity, Responsibility, Sin

January 14

DAILY BIBLE READING: Genesis 40–42

TODAY'S VERSE: Genesis 41:38: "And Pharaoh said unto his servants, Can we find such a one as this is, a man in whom the Spirit of God is?"

JOSEPH'S STORY IS ONE of sorrow and triumph. No one else in Scripture met such circumstances of turmoil and woe except for Christ, who was also destroyed by His own brethren. In today's reading, as Joseph is interpreting Pharaoh's dream, the Lord begins to touch the heart of Pharaoh about him, and before long, Joseph has been exalted to sit at the right hand of Pharaoh.

First, we see a **Search for a Man or Woman of God** ("Can we find?"). Pharaoh did not even know he was looking for a man of God until the man of God appeared. When Joseph came, Pharaoh knew he was exactly what was needed for this job. Maybe your friends and neighbors do not know it yet, but you are an answer to prayer for them. We are in great straits today. Psalm 12:1 says, "Help, LORD; for the godly man ceaseth; for the faithful fail from among the children of men." There is a search today for godly men and women who *show* the way of salvation, *see* the way of revelation, and *serve* in the way of consecration.

Second, we see the **Sign of a Man or Woman of God** ("such a one as this is"). Joseph did not come making promises and speeches or grandstanding spiritual things in an effort to "get out of prison." He did not say anything that was centered on himself, but only spoke about what God had revealed. This was refreshing for Pharaoh to see. I am sure that he was used to receiving the preferential treatment and lies others would give concerning his prosperity. Remember, Pharaoh was considered a god by all the people of Egypt. For Joseph to tell Pharaoh what God was going to do was demeaning to Pharaoh and could bring about a judgment upon Joseph's own life. Even so, he did not waver, but gave the Word of God without compromise. This dark world is in great need of men and women of God who will give proof of their relationship with God. The Christian life is not one of deceit that is lived by smoke and mirrors, but is lived consistently in the sight of all men. Integrity is the sign of a man or woman of God.

Third, we see the **Spirit of a Man or Woman of God** ("in whom the Spirit of God is"). This is the very thing that makes a difference—the Holy Spirit of God in your life! The Bible says of Stephen in Acts 6:5 that he was "a man full of faith and of the Holy Ghost." Stephen was just a layman, but he was full of the Holy Ghost. Only the Holy Ghost will make a lasting change in hearts that desire Him. Let the Spirit of God fill you, and then watch Him work Himself out! He will change you as well as others.

TOPICS: Boldness, Godliness, Holy Spirit

DAILY BIBLE READING: Genesis 43–44

TODAY'S VERSE: Genesis 43:34: "And he took and sent messes unto them from before him: but Benjamin's mess was five times so much as any of theirs. And they drank, and were merry with him."

AT THIS POINT, Joseph has been exalted in Egypt, has saved the excess harvest from the years of plenty, and has started to supply food to the region since the famine has begun. Joseph's brothers have previously bought food in Egypt and are returning to buy more. They have brought their youngest brother, as required by Joseph, and this day they are seated in his house to dine. In this story, Joseph is a type of Christ. Special things happen when we gather to "eat" at His house.

First, we see the **Good Things of His House** ("And he took and sent messes unto them from before him"). The word used for "messes" means "a present or tribute." Have you ever felt that God gave you something in a message that was just for you? These men were blessed collectively, but they were also blessed individually. This was not just food for "*all* of them," but for "*each* of them." I sure am glad Christ gives us each good things! Psalm 103:5 says, "[God] satisfieth thy mouth with *good things*"; Matthew 7:11 asks, "How much more shall your Father which is in heaven give *good things* to them that ask him?" We should come to His house expecting to receive the *good* things of His will.

Second, we see the **Gracious Things of His House** ("but Benjamin's mess was five times so much as any of theirs"). Joseph and Benjamin were the only sons of Jacob's beloved wife Rachel, and Joseph was the elder brother. The number five is a type of God's grace.[2] Isn't it beautiful that Benjamin received so much more grace from His elder brother? James 4:6a says, "But he giveth more grace." Our "elder brother" is Jesus Christ, and by Him we receive grace! There is no greater place to be than on the receiving end of God's grace!

Third, we see the **Glad Things of His House** ("and were merry with him"). When is the last time you were "happy" in the house of God? As a preacher, many times I see scowls in the pews, but other times I see smiles or a tear upon the face of a child of God. The Hebrew word for "merry" means "to become tipsy." I am not condoning the drinking of alcohol, but there is a Bible principle here that needs some attention. We should be a little "tipsy" in our love for God, in our joy in the Christian life, and in the merriment of God's house! Ephesians 5:18 says, "And be not drunk with wine, wherein is excess; but be filled with the Spirit." The word "drunk" in this verse means "intoxicated." You should not be intoxicated with wine and alcohol, but you should be intoxicated and filled by the Spirit. Get a little glad about the things of God. We should be sober in our duties, but merry in our worship. When is the last time either you or your church were accused of being "a little tipsy"?

TOPICS: God's Blessing, Grace, Holy Spirit, Joy

---

2   J. Edwin Hartill, *Principles of Biblical Hermeneutics* (Grand Rapids: Zondervan, 1947), 113.

January 16

DAILY BIBLE READING: Genesis 45–47

TODAY'S VERSE: Genesis 47:23: "Then Joseph said unto the people, Behold, I have bought you this day and your land for Pharaoh: lo, here is seed for you, and ye shall sow the land."

JOSEPH HAS NOW TAKEN all the people's money and cattle to give Egypt continued sustenance. Now he has bought the people and their land for Pharaoh. I find it very interesting that Joseph gave the people seed and told them to sow the land. Let's look at the significance of that.

First, **They Did Not Have a Good Problem**. Their problem was a famine, but even in the midst of those hard times, they still needed to sow the land. It does not matter how serious the famine is wherever you might be, the land still needs to be sown. The precious seed of the Word of God needs to be sown upon the barren hearts of unbelievers. You may say that the seed should only be sown on good ground. I would like to remind you of the parable in Luke 8. The Good Sower did not just put seed upon good ground, but upon all types of ground. This thought destroys the central idea of Calvinism: If only the elect were to be saved, then only the good ground would get the seed. That is not how God works! Seed has been sown generously to all types of people, whether or not they receive the word of God. There are mission fields that are spiritually starving today and are in desperate need for seed to be sown. It doesn't matter if they are in a famine, they need seed! Even in a famine, the land will yield a return when seed is sown, even if it is only enough to sow for the next year.

Second, **They Did Not Have a Good Prospect**. This was the second year of a grievous seven-year famine. But they kept sowing! Sometimes you may wonder if the famine will ever break—just keep sowing! I know that you weary of sharing the gospel with friends or family who have not responded to it for years— just keep sowing! It may take many more years, but when the famine ends, *it will be worth it all!* One reason the people kept sowing in the midst of the famine was so the land would not become desolate. If the Egyptians had stopped working the land in that dry, arid climate, it would have stayed barren all the time. When they worked the land, they had no immediate hope, but if they did not work it, they would *never* have hope!

Third, **They Did Not Have a Good Purpose**. The Egyptians were no longer working for their own profit. Now they belonged to someone else. However, they were willing for the sake of their lives and families to let Pharaoh buy them to preserve life. This is not a good purpose for their prosperity, but it was a great purpose for their lives. Don't serve God for your own profit, but rather serve God for His honor and glory. It will bring blessings beyond compare!

TOPICS: Gospel, Soul-Winning, Work

DAILY BIBLE READING: Genesis 48–50

TODAY'S VERSE: Genesis 48:21: "And Israel said unto Joseph, Behold, I die: but God shall be with you, and bring you again unto the land of your fathers."

IN THIS CHAPTER, Jacob blesses Joseph's sons, Manasseh and Ephraim, and speaks with Joseph. At the end of his life, Jacob only had thoughts concerning God's covenant and the Promised Land he had left years ago to sojourn in the land of Egypt. In his final breaths, he could not help but speak of the land God had given to Abraham and his seed after him.

First, Jacob speaks of the **Promise of God's Presence** ("but God shall be with you"). What a comfort to know that God is with us! If God is with me, I can climb the highest mountain, traverse the greatest distance, reach the lowest depth, and face the toughest foe. But I don't want to go anywhere without God! Exodus 33:15 says, "And he said unto him, If thy presence go not with me, carry us not up hence." This is perhaps the most heartening thought that Jacob could leave with his children—the certainty of the presence of God! There is great joy in a much-awaited reunion. Psalm 16:11 says, "Thou wilt shew me the path of life: *in thy presence is fulness of joy*; at thy right hand there are pleasures for evermore."

Second, Jacob speaks of the **Presence of God's Promise** ("and bring you again unto the land of your fathers"). Though he was in Egypt, Jacob never forgot the Promised Land. Joseph had been away from the Promised Land for most of his life, and his children, Manasseh and Ephraim, had never seen it. But Jacob faithfully passed on to his grandchildren the promise of their covenant relationship with God. After four hundred years in captivity, the children of Israel never forgot their land of promise. Even in the Babylonian captivity, the Hebrews never lost their love for the Promised Land. Psalm 137:4–6 says, "How shall we sing the LORD's song in a strange land? If I forget thee, O Jerusalem, let my right hand forget her cunning. If I do not remember thee, let my tongue cleave to the roof of my mouth; if I prefer not Jerusalem above my chief joy." O how we should long for the promises of God to be experienced in our lives! Don't quit, child of God! You may be weary and worn, troubled and tired, but keep your eyes fixed, for the Promised Land is on the horizon.

TOPICS: Death, God's Presence, Heaven

DAILY BIBLE READING: Exodus 1–3

TODAY'S VERSE: Exodus 3:14: "And God said unto Moses, I Am That I Am: and he said, Thus shalt thou say unto the children of Israel, I Am hath sent me unto you."

THESE CHAPTERS IN THE BEGINNING of Moses' life are powerful in their picture and their meaning. No verse is so powerful as this, in which God reveals Himself to Moses and commissions him to the great task of leading His people out of Egypt and into the Promised Land.

First, **God Declares Himself to Be the Self-Existent One** ("I Am That I Am"). There is no one else in the universe who can make this claim. "He is because He is." What a powerful word for all of us! Many commentaries have discussed the actual meaning of these words and this name that carries so much importance throughout Scripture. Whatever they may conclude, I believe it is safe to say that God's name means He is the *sum total of all!* He is the One and Only Original Being. Everything revolves around Him, for Acts 17:28 says, "For in him we live, and move, and have our being."

Second, **God Declares Himself to Be the Self-Explained One**. No other words are given here to Moses or even to Pharaoh about who God is. God's explanation of Himself is enough! You will find that once Moses and Aaron speak with Pharaoh, the very first words out of Pharaoh's mouth are, "Who is the Lord, that I should obey his voice to let Israel go? I know not the Lord, neither will I let Israel go" (Exodus 5:2). Pharaoh's ignorance was no excuse, for God had told him who He was. The day will come when people will look for many excuses as to why they did not believe in God or His way, but they will be without excuse. We are responsible for God's Word whether we believe it or not. Romans 3:3 says, "For what if some did not believe? shall their unbelief make the faith of God without effect?" God does not have to explain Himself, but when He does, it is enough!

Third, **God Declares Himself to Be the Self-Exalted One**. Nobody was going to call any shots over the head of Jehovah God. Since there was no one higher, God exalted Himself. There have been many different people through the millennia who have tried to exalt themselves above governments and enemies, and they have been put down because there was someone greater than they. The Bible says in Hebrews 6:13, "For when God made promise to Abraham, because he could swear by no greater, he sware by himself." We need to realize who God is and let Him be exalted in our lives, for He has exalted Himself over all the earth.

TOPICS: God, God's Glory, God's Power

DAILY BIBLE READING: Exodus 4–6

TODAY'S VERSE: Exodus 4:11: "And the LORD said unto him, Who hath made man's mouth? or who maketh the dumb, or deaf, or the seeing, or the blind? have not I the LORD?"

THIS VERSE IS A LESSON on disabilities—right? Actually, that's only half true. This verse is a lesson on the sovereignty of God. In verse 10, Moses was looking for a reason not to serve God. Romans 9:20 gives us an understanding of God's divine and sovereign will: "Nay but, O man, who art thou that repliest against God? Shall the thing formed say to him that formed it, Why hast thou made me thus?" Many have become bitter at God for the struggles and troubles that come with a disability. Instead of seeking for God to be glorified, they will question God's motives and even His righteousness because they reject God's will for their lives. Some are born with a disability, while others are disabled while heeding their country's call on a battlefield. Some are disabled from an accident, while others are disabled from a disease. Many are disabled as a result of someone else's fault. A recurring question is, "God, why did you allow this to happen to me?" There may be no answer other than that it was God's will. Here are a few thoughts to contemplate as we consider the hindrances and limitations in God's flawless plans.

There Is No Problem with God's Design ("And the LORD said unto him, Who hath made man's mouth?"). Moses did not like his mouth. He wanted something more "usable" than what he had. Surely if God intended for Moses to serve Him, then God would have blessed him with more ability. Basically, Moses thought God had forgotten how He made him. Psalm 139:14 declares, "I will praise thee; for I am fearfully and wonderfully made: marvellous are thy works; and that my soul knoweth right well." Even in the beginning of creation, God considered everything He had made, and Genesis 1:31a says, "And God saw every thing that he had made, and, behold, it was very good." God has made everything exactly as He meant to make it.

There Is No Problem with God's Determination ("or who maketh the dumb, or deaf, or the seeing, or the blind?"). Moses had to accept the fact that God had made him that way on purpose. No production line had malfunctioned. Each person is made perfectly in the fashion that God determines. God can heal anyone from a disability, but He may not. God could heal every hindrance of the flesh, but He may have a purpose to fulfill that you do not understand. John 9:1–3 says, "And as Jesus passed by, he saw a man which was blind from his birth. And his disciples asked him, saying, Master, who did sin, this man, or his parents, that he was born blind? Jesus answered, Neither hath this man sinned, nor his parents: *but that the works of God should be made manifest in him.*" There is a work that God wants to do through your disability that will show His power in your life.

There Is No Problem with God's Disposition ("have not I the LORD?"). God is not being despicably unkind and uncaring by allowing disabilities into our lives. Moses had not yet accepted the truth of God's kindness in his disability. In truth, Moses had to be taught that his disability pleased God! God is not ashamed at all of how He made you. Psalm 135:6 says, "Whatsoever the LORD pleased, that did he in heaven, and in earth, in the seas, and all deep places." Your disability does not please Him with sadistic glee, but rather with tender love. He knows that you can trust Him to meet your needs and glorify Him like no one else can. Our lives are not about our comfort, but about His glory. I could tell you of some of the sweetest and most spiritual Christians I have ever met and how they had to deal with painful and taxing disabilities every day of their lives. What a testimony they are to every person around them, as all they can do is talk about how wonderful God is and how He supplies every need and strengthens them to meet every challenge.

Thank God today for the blessing in your life that drives you to pray. Your disability is a grace that God alone has extended to you!

TOPICS: Disability, Strength, Trial, Trust

January 20

DAILY BIBLE READING: Exodus 7–8

TODAY'S VERSE: Exodus 7:5: "And the Egyptians shall know that I am the Lord, when I stretch forth mine hand upon Egypt, and bring out the children of Israel from among them."

AT THIS POINT in the Bible's narrative, the Israelites have been under slavery to the Egyptians for over four hundred years. Now, we finally hear the Word of God break through in power to confirm His deliverance to Moses and Aaron. This would not just be a blessing to Israel, but a judgment upon Egypt. Pharaoh and his hard heart would finally receive their just rewards! Moses knew that this was the time Israel was anticipating! In our verse, we find three works that God was going to do in His deliverance of Israel.

God's Vindication over Egypt ("And the Egyptians shall know that I am the Lord"). God desires to prove Himself righteous in the eyes of mankind. Though He is not in a hurry, the prospect of justifying Himself with all of creation as an audience is something that thrills Him. God will indeed be vindicated in the eyes of all mankind. Revelation 1:7 tells us of this joy upon His return: "Behold, he cometh with clouds; *and every eye shall see him, and they also which pierced him:* and all kindreds of the earth shall wail because of him. Even so, Amen." We see this same principle again in Philippians 2:10–11 as God will make every created being bow before Christ and worship Him: "That at the name of Jesus every knee should bow, of things in heaven, and things in earth, and things under the earth; and that every tongue should confess that Jesus Christ is Lord, to the glory of God the Father."

God's Vengeance over Egypt ("when I stretch forth mine hand upon Egypt"). God's outstretched arm is an image that should strike fear into every heart. Though God wants all people to respond to His love and mercy, He will still judge them in His holiness. Proverbs 16:4 says, "The Lord hath made all things for himself: yea, *even the wicked for the day of evil.*" Finally, the God of the Israelites will set things straight! God will now take up their cause and fight their battle! God has given a warning to all concerning the day of His vengeance. The wrath of Almighty God is nothing to trifle with or dismiss. Hebrews 10:31 says, "It is a fearful thing to fall into the hands of the living God."

God's Victory over Egypt ("and bring out the children of Israel from among them"). God is not just willing to flex His muscle so that the wicked will respect Him; He also wants to deliver His people so that they might glorify Him. Luke 18:7–8a reads, "And shall not God avenge his own elect, which cry day and night unto him, though he bear long with them? I tell you that he will avenge them speedily." It is not in vain to trust in God, for He has never let His people down nor left one promise empty. As Luke testifies, there are times when God will "bear long" concerning answers to prayer and giving the victory; but do not worry, victory will come! First Corinthians 15:57 says, "But thanks be to God, which giveth us the victory through our Lord Jesus Christ."

TOPICS: God's Judgment, God's Promises, Victory

R. CHRIS HANKS

DAILY BIBLE READING: Exodus 10–12

TODAY'S VERSE: Exodus 12:22-23: "And ye shall take a bunch of hyssop, and dip it in the blood that is in the bason, and strike the lintel and the two side posts with the blood that is in the bason; and none of you shall go out at the door of his house until the morning. For the LORD will pass through to smite the Egyptians; and when he seeth the blood upon the lintel, and on the two side posts, the LORD will pass over the door, and will not suffer the destroyer to come in unto your houses to smite you."

THERE ARE CHAPTERS in the Bible that some would call "watershed moments" in Christian doctrine: Genesis 1 with its account of creation, Genesis 12 with Abraham's calling, Genesis 22 with Isaac's sacrifice, and Exodus 12 with the Passover. The blood of the Passover is one of Scripture's most significant symbols.

I Am Surrounded by the Blood. ("And ye shall take a bunch of hyssop, and dip it in the blood that is in the bason, and strike the lintel and the two side posts with the blood that is in the bason"). If I am to be safe from the judgment of God, I need the blood all around me. This reminds me of the view of Calvary, with the precious head of the Son of God on the "lintel" and the two "side posts" of His hands that were nailed to the cross. Some might say the picture is imperfect because Christ's feet were nailed as well and no blood was upon the threshold at the Passover. I beg to differ. The word rendered "bason" is *sap,* an old Egyptian word for the step before a door, or the threshold of a house.[3] The animal had been killed on the threshold and the blood was already there, so it did not have to be applied.

Since the blood was there as a result of the sacrifice, we see another picture that awaits us: The blood, though it is there by sacrifice, was not to be ceremonially placed upon the ground, for it is never to be trodden upon! Hebrews 10:29 says, "Of how much sorer punishment, suppose ye, shall he be thought worthy, who hath trodden under foot the Son of God, and hath counted the blood of the covenant, wherewith he was sanctified, an unholy thing, and hath done despite unto the Spirit of grace?" Many today would tread upon the blood of Christ and count it an unholy thing! There are many who believe that the blood of Christ went into the ground and has since wasted away. We know differently. We have been saved by incorruptible blood! We have been surrounded by the precious blood of the perfect Lamb of God!

I Am Staying with the Blood ("and none of you shall go out at the door of his house until the morning"). Psalm 30:5 says, "Weeping may endure for a night, but joy cometh in the morning." When Christ returns in the morning in the eastern sky, Lord willing, I will be found "staying with the blood." No matter how dark the night, no matter how sorrowful the pain, no matter how insecure I feel—I'm staying with the blood! I am so thankful that the blood doesn't go anywhere! Had I been there that fateful night in Egypt, I believe I would have left everything where it was until morning. I don't believe I would have left the security of the blood to find a tool, pick up a needed object, or secure an animal in the barn! When it comes to the blood, stick with it!

There are some who have heard of God's eternal salvation, but have not yet put their trust in Jesus Christ. If that is you, put your faith in Him today! Once you trust in Jesus Christ as your Saviour, the blood goes with you everywhere you go.

I Am Safe with the Blood. ("when he seeth the blood . . . the LORD will pass over the door, and will not suffer the destroyer to come in unto your houses to smite you"). What a safe place to be! There is no place I would rather be than in the midst of the blood of Christ! The wrath of God cannot touch me there. The devil cannot harm me there. My own sin cannot cause me to fail there! Hebrews 9:12 says, "Neither by the blood of goats and calves, but by his own blood he entered in once into the holy place, *having obtained eternal redemption for us.*" There is wonder-working power in the blood of the Lamb!

TOPICS: Blood Atonement, Calvary, Passover, Sacrifice

---

3   W. Pink, *Gleanings in Exodus* (Chicago: Moody Press, 1981), 93.

DAILY BIBLE READING: Exodus 13–14

TODAY'S VERSE: Exodus 14:14: "The Lord shall fight for you, and ye shall hold your peace."

THIS IS ONE OF THE SHORTEST verses in our reading today, but one of the most wonderful in its truth.

First, it was a **Preeminent Promise** ("*The Lord* shall fight for you"). Wouldn't it be comforting to know that Jehovah God will be the one to fight your battles? I remember growing up, we kids would fight over which captain would pick his team first. It was important. It would likely affect the outcome of the game. Adults play that same game today through fantasy football, in which they pick their own players and play them against others in a fantasy football league. What a blessing it is to be on the same team as God! Let's huddle up for our game plan today.

Second, it was a **Powerful Promise** ("The Lord *shall fight* for you"). Don't ever forget what God is capable of doing. He is all-powerful. Genesis 18:14 says, "Is any thing too hard for the Lord?" What a comfort it is to know that God can do anything! Mark 10:27 says, "And Jesus looking upon them saith, With men it is impossible, but not with God: for with God all things are possible." Philippians 4:13 encourages us, "I can do all things through Christ which strengtheneth me." God has blessed us with powerful promises!

Third, it was a **Personal Promise** ("The Lord shall fight *for you*"). This promise was made to the Israelites themselves. God has made promises to *us* today! There are over three thousand promises given to the believer to enjoy the wonders and the truth of God. Quit acting like the promises are for everybody else! The promises are there for whoever will accept them. As you receive the Word of God, the Holy Ghost will change your life to receive the blessings of God. Even the Holy Spirit's working in your life is a promise from God to you!

Fourth, it was a **Peaceful Promise** ("and ye shall hold your peace"). This phrase is often used in the Bible and means, "be quiet, rest, keep silent." We need a settling in our spiritual lives. The uneasiness and unsettled hearts of God's people amaze me as they flutter about like a bird with a broken wing. Once you see the Lord move in your life, you will have peace. What a blessing it is to know that He cares about me! What an encouragement to see Him work on my behalf! The word "peace" is used over four hundred times in the Bible. There are people today, even Christians, who would give all they have to obtain peace. When you see God move on your behalf, accept the peace that comes with His presence!

TOPICS: God's Power, God's Promises, Peace

DAILY BIBLE READING: Exodus 15–17

TODAY'S VERSE: Exodus 17:12: "But Moses' hands were heavy; and they took a stone, and put it under him, and he sat thereon; and Aaron and Hur stayed up his hands, the one on the one side, and the other on the other side; and his hands were steady until the going down of the sun."

TODAY, I WOULD LIKE to focus on laymen and women. The Israelites were fighting with Amalek in a hotly contested battle. Moses went up a hill with the rod of God in his hand and found that when he lifted his hands, the people of God prevailed, but when he dropped his hands, Amalek prevailed. Moses did much greater work with his hands outstretched to God than he did with a sword in his hand. He was fighting on a spiritual front that was *more physically exerting than the battle on the field.* I am thankful for Aaron and Hur, who were willing to do what was necessary to help the man of God. Let's look at their ministry and how it applies to our lives.

First, **They Had a Sustaining Ministry** ("stayed up his hands"). One reason preachers do not stay long in certain ministries is that no one is sustaining them. Most people in churches today demand that the pastor work for them. When is the last time you found a way to sustain your preacher's hands while he did the work of the Lord? I am reminded of the two main pillars of the temple that we read about in 1 Kings 7:21: "And he set up the pillars in the porch of the temple: and he set up the right pillar, and *called the name thereof Ja'chin:* and he set up the left pillar, and *called the name thereof Boaz."* We know that our church is not a physical building, but a spiritual building. What are the names of those who support your pastor, not just with money, but in his work and vision for the Lord?

Second, **They Had a Synergistic Ministry** ("the one on the one side, and the other on the other side"). These words in this phrase means "united, one." *Synergy* is a buzz word in today's business world, and here is what it means: "Cooperative action of discreet agencies such that the total effect is greater than the sum of the effects taken independently."[4] Aaron and Hur had a common goal, and the result of their united action was greater than what they could have done independently! Too many people in church today are trying to do their own thing rather than catch the vision of the pastor. When God's people come together behind the man of God and unitedly put their hands to the plow, there is no business in this world that can rival the church in effectiveness, profit, results, and efficiency.

Third, **They Had a Steadying Ministry** ("his hands were steady until the going down of the sun"). The Hebrew word for "steady" means "firm, secure, stable." Your pastor is not supposed to do everything himself. As a matter of fact, the early church voted in deacons so the pastors could give themselves "continually to prayer, and to the ministry of the word" (Acts 6:4). These apostles felt an unsteadiness in their ministry and took steps to correct it. The truth is that the people of the church have a definite part in the steadiness of their pastor and their church.

Some may think their pastor has changed, that preaching has changed for the worse, or that the church doesn't have the impact it once did. More than likely, their preacher needs some sustaining, synergistic, steadying hands upon him. How is this done practically? First, you must *pray* for him. Take this seriously. Beg for God's mercy and power upon your preacher. Second, *encourage* him. Tell him how his messages touch your heart, or send him a letter of encouragement. Third, *catch the vision* that God has given him. Aaron and Hur were willing to do more, but the preacher wanted to lift his hands before the Lord for his people, so they enabled him to do just that. Fourth, *volunteer.* These men were willing to do what was needed to help their preacher, which, in turn, glorified God. God will reveal many other things to you as you take these beginning steps to support the man of God in your life and church.

TOPICS: God's Man, Service, Support, Unity

---

4   *Webster's School Dictionary* (New York: American Book Company, 1980), 944.

January 24

DAILY BIBLE READING: Exodus 18-20

TODAY'S VERSE: Exodus 19:5: "Now therefore, if ye will obey my voice indeed, and keep my covenant, then ye shall be a peculiar treasure unto me above all people: for all the earth is mine."

BEFORE WE LOOK at the main thought of this verse, notice that the beginning of the verse is preparatory. We must obey. This is a classic "if . . . then" statement. To obey God's voice and keep His covenant, we must do three things: First, there must be an *acknowledgment* of the will of God. Then there must be an *acceptance* of the will of God. How can we obey if we never accept the Word as authoritative? Third, there must be an *attention* to the will of God. The word "keep" in "keep my covenant" means, "to hedge about as with thorns; to guard." Obedience never happens by accident.

Now, let us look at the thought of being a "peculiar treasure" to the Lord.

First, it is a **Safe Treasure**. The Hebrew words translated "peculiar treasure" mean "to shut up." People always have a safe place for their things of value. In whom has God placed His most valuable possessions? In you! Second Corinthians 4:7 says, *"But we have this treasure in earthen vessels,* that the excellency of the power may be of God, and not of us." Again the Bible says in Colossians 1:27, "To whom God would make known what is the riches of the glory of this mystery among the Gentiles; which is *Christ in you,* the hope of glory." No one has access to this place but Him! Only He has the code! Once we have believed in Christ, we are protected against any tampering. Once the treasure is there, it will never change or be rewritten in our hearts.

Second, it is a **Special Treasure**. The word used also has the meaning of being special. Some things are more special and valuable than others because of their rarity. As mineral experts look at rocks and stones and gems, they are automatically drawn to those things that are uncommon. They will look at the colors and the densities of diamonds that make those particular gems "precious." The Bible says that when we trust in Christ, we are a "new creature" (2 Corinthians 5:17). A new creation—how rare is that?

Third, it is a **Significant Treasure**. What makes this treasure significant? Our verse says, "ye shall be a peculiar treasure unto me above all people." We are so significant to God that He is coming to take us home one day! The Bible says in Malachi 3:17, "And they shall be mine, saith the LORD of hosts, in that day *when I make up my jewels;* and I will spare them, as a man spareth his own son that serveth him." The word for "peculiar treasure" in our main verse is the same Hebrew word used in Malachi for "jewels." And when God comes to make up His jewels, He will take us home to be with Him!

TOPICS: God's Will, Safety, Security, Value

R. CHRIS HANKS

DAILY BIBLE READING: Exodus 21–23

TODAY'S VERSE: Exodus 23:29: "I will not drive them out from before thee in one year; lest the land become desolate, and the beast of the field multiply against thee."

THIS AND THE SURROUNDING verses talk about God driving out the enemy from the Promised Land and giving it to Israel. Let's see how the Lord works in giving the Promised Land to the people.

First, we see **His Patience** ("I will not drive them out from before thee in one year"). Though God desires to bring us to the Promised Land, He is not in a hurry! The very next verse explains how God was going to do this in Moses' day: "By little and little I will drive them out from before thee." That is the way the Christian life works—little by little. Why doesn't God just do it all at once? His desire is for us to keep *trusting!* If we were to receive those things He has promised without recognizing His work and His patience to get us there, we would stop trusting in Him and begin trusting the arm of flesh. His desire is for us to keep *trying!* We need incentive to see the Lord at work in our lives. His desire is for us to keep *telling!* Every little victory is all part of God's divine plan. It sure is good to know that God is still working in our lives! Though we want ultimate victory, His patient plan is confirming His presence and His power in our lives, and we must share that with others!

Second, we see **His Preservation** ("lest the land become desolate"). God was taking care to preserve His people for the future. Deuteronomy 6:11 describes the bounty of the land this way: "And houses full of all good things, which thou filledst not, and wells digged, which thou diggedst not, vineyards and olive trees, which thou plantedst not." Earlier, we learned that Joseph gave out seed in the midst of the famine so the land of Egypt would not become desolate. This is God's desire. What good would it be if God gave you land that was good for nothing? God desires fruit from the great land that He is preparing to give to you.

Third, we see **His Protection** ("and the beast of the field multiply against thee"). I remember my brother-in-law, an evangelist, saying that it was God's mercy to leave Israel's enemies in the land to protect them from the evil beasts. But God will reverse this too. The verse just before our text says that God will actually use wild beasts to drive the enemy away: "And I will send *hornets* before thee, which shall drive out the Hivite, the Canaanite, and the Hittite, from before thee." God will not only protect us from the evil beasts, but will actually use the evil beasts on our behalf when it is time to drive out our enemies.

TOPICS: God's Power, God's Promises, Patience, Preservation, Protection

January 26

DAILY BIBLE READING: Exodus 24–26

TODAY'S VERSE: Exodus 25:22: "And there I will meet with thee, and I will commune with thee from above the mercy seat, from between the two cherubims which are upon the ark of the testimony, of all things which I will give thee in commandment unto the children of Israel."

THE TOPIC OF THIS VERSE, as well as the previous five verses, is the mercy seat. The mercy seat was the lid of the ark of the covenant. Its only function was to cover the broken law (the commandments that were kept in the ark) with the blood atonement that was applied by the High Priest.

Blood is fundamental in the biblical doctrine of salvation. Hebrews 9:22 says, "And almost all things are by the law purged with blood; and without shedding of blood is no remission." The book of Hebrews tells us very plainly that the Old Testament sacrifices could not take away our sin, but could only cover it. The only way our sins could be taken away was with the perfect sacrifice and shed blood of our Saviour, Jesus Christ. Hallelujah for the blood that Jesus shed for us! The blessing of the mercy seat was nonexistent without blood atonement. This is the only place where God would come to meet with man! It is also the only place that man could come to meet with God. God does several things as a result of the blood.

There Is a Blood Presence ("And there I will meet with thee"). God says, "And *there* I will meet." There is no other place God will come but to the place where the blood was applied! The word for "meet" here carries a very interesting definition: "to meet (at a stated time), to summon (to trial), to direct (in a certain quarter or position), to engage (for marriage)." It contains a *summons,* a *service,* and a *ceremony.* Because the blood is present, all those things will happen in our favor!

There Are Blood Precepts ("and I will commune with thee from above the mercy seat"). Without the blood, we would have no Bible, no Scriptures, no perfect Word of God through which we can hear God speak. All of Scripture flows from Calvary! Our Bible is wringing wet with the blood of Christ! Every time the Book is opened, the fountain filled with blood is flowing and attesting of Jesus: His truth, His power, His love, and His sacrifice. There is no part of Scripture that is not associated with Golgotha's lonely hill and the shed blood of Christ.

There Is a Blood Praise ("from between the two cherubims which are upon the ark of the testimony"). The cherubim in the Bible were to guard the holiness of God. It was between these cherubim that the *shekinah* glory of God would appear, accept the offering, and speak to the people. The Bible is quick to tell us that the angels are forever praising God, for He is worthy! From the mercy seat, God praised the future work of the blood atonement of Jesus Christ.

There Are Blood Promises ("of all things *which I will give thee* in commandment unto the children of Israel"). The phrase "I will give thee in commandment" is interesting since it means "to constitute, enjoin." God is promising to bring His people in and enjoin them to His cause. We have the same promise in the New Testament. First Corinthians 3:9 says, "For we are labourers together with God." In every promise God has given me, He is enjoining me to His cause! All these promises are based on the blood atonement and the sacrifice of our Saviour.

TOPICS: Blood, God's Presence, God's Promises, Salvation, Word of God

R. CHRIS HANKS

DAILY BIBLE READING: Exodus 27–28

TODAY'S VERSE: Exodus 27:20: "And thou shalt command the children of Israel, that they bring thee pure oil olive beaten for the light, to cause the lamp to burn always."

THIS VERSE OCCURS WITHIN the preparation of the tabernacle. This is interesting because all of the tabernacle materials and furniture were mentioned in the preceding chapters. From Exodus 27:20 through chapter 29, we have verses on the light, the garments for the priests and Levites, and the priest's handling of the offerings. Then chapter 30 begins talking about the furniture and materials of the tabernacle as if nothing has changed. It's no coincidence that these verses come before the work of the priest is discussed in chapters 28 and 29. Christ had to meet the demands of God's holiness and purity before He could qualify to be our High Priest. In looking at this verse in particular, we are reminded of Christ and what He has done for us. However, it was the people who were to bring this olive oil to be used in the service of the sanctuary. We have here a picture of Christ that we are to follow in our lives for His glory.

The Picture of Purity ("And thou shalt command the children of Israel, that they bring thee pure oil olive"). The word for "pure" means "clear." If there is an area where many of us are greatly lacking, it is in clarity. Christ was pure in His life, ministry, and motivations. Can that be said of you as Christ's follower? God has always desired to use something that is pure and righteous in His sight. Yes, man has defiled himself and become impure, but that is why Christ came—to make man the partaker of His righteousness! God still desires to use something that is clean and holy for His honor and glory. Today, our churches have failed in doctrinal purity, our society has failed in moral purity, and our leaders have failed in ethical purity. God is looking for someone who might bring Him pure olive oil that He can use. Will you be pure for Him?

The Picture of Preparation ("pure oil olive beaten for the light"). The word "beaten" talks about the bruising process in which the olive would freely offer up its purest oil. This process was much different than the dreg-filled process of putting the olives in an olive press. Isaiah 53:5 uses the word "bruised" in speaking of Christ: "He was bruised for our iniquities." Yet Isaiah 42:3 carefully tells, "A bruised reed shall he not break." A great work was done in the bruising process! The outpouring of the pure oil of the Holy Ghost began in the preparation of the bruising of our Saviour upon Calvary. God will do a work of preparation in your life also so that the Holy Spirit will be manifested in you.

The Picture of Purpose ("to cause the lamp to burn always"). There was a reason for all of this to happen—light. The verb for "to cause to burn" literally means "to ascend." As we burn and shine for the glory of God, our light ascends to Him as something that is most pleasing. Isn't that how Jesus described John the Baptist in John 5:35? "He was a burning and a shining light: and ye were willing for a season to rejoice in his light." Our light should issue in the form of the living sacrifice that Romans 12:1 discusses: "I beseech you therefore, brethren, by the mercies of God, that ye present your bodies a living sacrifice, holy, acceptable unto God, which is your reasonable service." The word for "always" demands our quick acknowledgment. It means "to stretch properly, continuance (as indefinite extension)." Our purpose in burning should continue until the day we meet our Saviour face-to-face!

TOPICS: Perseverance, Preparation, Purity

January 28

DAILY BIBLE READING: Exodus 29-30

TODAY'S VERSE: Exodus 29:43: "And there I will meet with the children of Israel, and the tabernacle shall be sanctified by my glory."

AS WE LOOK at this verse, I would like us to keep in mind that it is part of the law God was giving Moses concerning the consecration of the tabernacle to the Lord. This meeting with God was essential for the people of Israel in their work and their worship.

It Is Based upon His Pardon ("And there I will meet with the children of Israel"). God would meet with the people in this place because of a sacrifice. The altar where it was offered was the place where God would be glorified. God has always been glorified by the freewill offering upon a place of judgment. Don't ever think that you will glorify God without a sacrifice. So many people today are trying their best to attain salvation without kneeling at Calvary's hill, but there is no salvation without the proper sacrifice. That sacrifice was placed upon the altar of the old rugged cross and lifted up to heaven, given of Christ's own free will, and accepted by God for all those who would trust in Him.

It Is Based upon His Presence ("And there *I will meet*"). It would do us well to accept the fact that we have absolutely nothing to do with God's glory in the church. We need to understand that our churches today are not sanctified by our *programs,* our *preachers,* our *power,* or even our *plans.* They are sanctified by God's glory! How I long for the presence of God to be manifested in our services! God's glory is wherever He is. Too many places are operating much too efficiently without the presence of God.

It Is Based upon His Pleasure ("shall be sanctified by my glory"). The question comes, "Well, then, how do we get His glory?" Many preachers will throw their "sanctified actions list" upon your back for you to bear so God might send His glory upon you. However, truly receiving God's glory is purely a work of divine grace. His glory is not defined by what we do. It is not demanded by our works. It is given by the grace of God. Yes, I believe in holy living, but our living does not demand the glory of God in our lives. This truth is given to us in Romans 11:6a: "And if by grace, then is it no more of works: otherwise grace is no more grace." It is a kindness and blessing of God to shed His grace upon us that we might behold His glory! It is His glory that will change our hearts, our churches, our homes, our service, our walk, and our ministries.

TOPICS: God's Glory, God's Presence, Grace

DAILY BIBLE READING: Exodus 31–33

TODAY'S VERSE: Exodus 33:21: "And the Lord said, Behold, there is a place by me, and thou shalt stand upon a rock."

THIS CHAPTER IS ONE of the most precious to me in the entire Bible. The wrath of God is seen, the judgment of God is felt, the mercy of God is experienced, and the love of God is restored. By the end of this short chapter, there is a new and precious relationship between Moses and God to the point that God will show Moses His glory as He had never shown it to anyone else. Moses is standing in a new place.

First, we see that it is a **Prepared Place** (*"Behold, there is a place* by me"). It is almost as if God is saying, "Hey look, there is a place right beside me that I have prepared just for you!" God has prepared a place for all of us, not just in heaven, but right here upon earth, so we can be close to Him. Moses desired to see the glory of God. God told Moses that he would not be allowed to see His face, for no man had seen Him and lived. But God did not end there! He said, "I'll tell you what I'll do. You can come and stand right by me!" Let me tell you something, child of God: you will see more of God's glory being close to God than you will in trying to have a spiritual encounter with God!

Second, we see that it is a **Perpetual Place** ("Behold, there *is* a place by me"). The keyword in this phrase is the word "is." This place is always available for the Christian who desires fellowship with God and His Word. There is no perpetual place in God's presence for an unsaved person who has not trusted in Christ as Saviour, for the Bible says in Isaiah 55:6, "Seek ye the Lord while he may be found, call ye upon him while he is near." If you are not saved, you need to be saved *today!* Do not wait! If one rejects the conviction of the Holy Spirit, there will be a time when God's opportunity for salvation will be removed; but for the child of God, there is always the opportunity to come back to the Lord in fellowship. Nothing can destroy my relationship with God! No matter how far I am away, I can always return to His wonderful embrace.

Third, we see that it is a **Promoted Place** (*"and thou shalt stand upon* a rock"). There is no higher place to be than with God. Even in my privacy with God, there have been times when He has swept me away and carried me to greater heights in His *glory,* His *goodness,* and His *grace!* Every time you meet with God, you can rest assured that you have met with the King! What a place of promotion! Second Samuel 22:34 says, "He maketh my feet like hinds' feet: and *setteth me upon my high places.*" Again, Psalm 40:2 says, "He brought me up also out of an horrible pit, out of the miry clay, and *set my feet upon a rock,* and established my goings."

Note that this place is not considered a promoted place because of its height, but because of its spiritual depth. This was not Mount Everest they were upon in Israel. However, there was no higher place Moses could have gone! The place where Moses was beside God dwarfed every mountain in the region and the world in spiritual reality and significance.

Fourth, we see that it is a **Powerful Place** ("and thou shalt stand *upon a rock*"). What great power there is in the presence of God! It is a place protected from those who desire to destroy you. This was about Moses' *foes.* It is a place of security, for Moses' feet were founded upon a rock! This was about Moses' *falls.* It is a place of confidence, for Moses could serve God as never before, for he had seen God as never before! This was about Moses' *faith.* What a powerful place for us to be!

TOPICS: God's Glory, God's Presence, Victory

January 30

DAILY BIBLE READING: Exodus 34–35

TODAY'S VERSE: Exodus 35:21: "And they came, every one whose heart stirred him up, and every one whom his spirit made willing, and they brought the Lord's offering to the work of the tabernacle of the congregation, and for all his service, and for the holy garments."

THIS IS A VERY CHALLENGING verse for all Christians today. I love how the verse begins: "And they came." The verse before said that they "departed from the presence of Moses." This verse says that they came. What a blessed time it is when there is a return to the Lord!

First, **There Was a Stirring** ("every one whose heart stirred him up"). This was a limited number of people. Not everyone was stirred! Thank God for those who were! Collectively, we are living in a very dead time in churches across the country. Preachers have to try to get up before their people and tell them how good their church is, how good the revival was, and how great a love their church has. If God would move and the people would stir, there would not be any preachers trying to convince their people about what God has done. Allow yourself to be stirred about godly things. What is it that stirs your heart today? Work? Some hobby? Friends? When is the last time you were stirred to serve the Lord in a ministry, stirred to give a witness to a lost soul, stirred to praise the name of the Lord in the midst of the congregation, or stirred to seek God's face in a decision? As Paul told Timothy to "stir up the gift of God, which is in thee," so we should stir our love for God in worship, service, devotion, and love.

Second, **There Was a Willing** ("everyone whom his spirit made willing"). This word actually means "to volunteer." Where has our spiritual desire gone to serve our Lord? This phrase says that the people's spirit made them willing. The motivating factor was their spirit! It is so sad when our spirit will not receive the truth of God's Word or respond to the Holy Spirit's conviction in our hearts, because that means that we will never be willing to do anything. The Bible tells us plainly that "stubbornness is as iniquity and idolatry" (1 Samuel 15:23). Let your spirit make you willing.

Third, **There Was an Offering** ("and they brought the Lord's offering to the work of the tabernacle") This offering did not make the people good. It was the natural progression of God working in their lives! God worked in them, they were stirred, they were willing, so they offered. When is the last time your offering was an act of worship to the Lord and not an act of duty? I am not necessarily talking about your financial giving. You can offer many things, not just your money. Judges 5:2 says, "Praise ye the Lord for the avenging of Israel, *when the people willingly offered themselves.*" As you grow as a Christian, you will learn the glory of giving God *everything!*

TOPICS: Offering, Revival, Will

DAILY BIBLE READING: Exodus 36–38

TODAY'S VERSE: Exodus 36:8: "And every wise hearted man among them that wrought the work of the tabernacle made ten curtains of fine twined linen, and blue, and purple, and scarlet: with cherubims of cunning work made he them."

THOUGH THE WORDS at the beginning of the verse, "every wise hearted man," have to do with intelligence, ability, and skill, let's look at what defined the wisdom of these men. We need some wise-hearted men and women who are cunning about the work of the Lord!

First, we see that their **Wisdom Was Defined by Their Action** ("*that wrought* the work of the tabernacle"). This was what they did for a living. The book of James speaks of our faith and that "faith without works is dead" (James 2:20). These wise-hearted men were not dead in their faith, but their faith caused them to "do." Some today feel that their little work has no real meaning and no real substance. Don't get caught in the trap of feeling that your works are only good for the present! I would like to remind you of the martyr Jim Elliot, who gave his life in Ecuador as he sought to reach a murderous tribe. Some may look at his life as a waste, but after his death, the Lord brought revival to that savage people! The Bible says in Revelation 14:13, "And I heard a voice from heaven saying unto me, Write, Blessed are the dead which die in the Lord from henceforth: Yea, saith the Spirit, that they may rest from their labours; *and their works do follow them.*" Labor on! Keep serving the Lord! Keep praying for your family! Keep witnessing to the lost! You may not see results, but your wisdom will make a difference through your actions.

Second, we see that their **Wisdom Was Defined by Their Attempt** ("that wrought *the work* of the tabernacle"). "Work" is used here not as a verb, but as a noun. It is actually a thing, much as some would call a piece of art a "work." In other words, these people did *the job!* You may be guilty of many things, but don't be guilty of not trying! It is God's work! Here is a verse for you from 1 Corinthians 15:58:"Therefore, my beloved brethren, be ye stedfast, unmoveable, always *abounding in the work of the Lord*, forasmuch as ye know that your labour is not in vain in the Lord." Don't quit! Don't give up! You might think that what you do is not worthwhile, but God can change everything and use our feeble attempts to His honor and glory.

Third, we see that their **Wisdom Was Defined by Their Adoration** ("that wrought the work *of the tabernacle*"). Everything you do must be connected to your worship! Their actions and their attempts were all focused on their adoration. This was what made everything worthwhile. This was not just an act of nobility. We need to go beyond our silly little way of thinking that we deserve every little pat on the back. This is not just an act of novelty. They were not just doing this so that forty years down the road they would be able to look at that tabernacle and say, "Yeah, I did that!" This was a necessity! This was something they had to do in their hearts, for it was connected to their worship. What is it that defines you as a Christian? If there is anything that ought to define us in spirit, it should be our adoration!

TOPICS: Dedication, Wisdom, Work, Worship

DAILY BIBLE READING: Exodus 39–40

TODAY'S VERSE: Exodus 39:43: "And Moses did look upon all the work, and, behold, they had done it as the LORD had commanded, even so had they done it: and Moses blessed them."

THIS PASSAGE SHOWCASES the end of the building of the tabernacle. It has been a long and hard preparation, but now it is ready to be raised. In chapter 40, the glory of the Lord will fill the tabernacle so that Moses cannot even enter into it to serve the Lord. In this verse, though, it is time for an inspection from God's man, the one to whom God gave the plans, the one who has been the foreman upon this holy project.

First, the work had to be **Approved** ("And Moses did look upon all the work"). Tensions were high as the people watched, the men stood by their work, and the man of God inspected what had been done. What was he going to say? What was he going to think? Would it be approved and accepted by the one who mattered? I am sure you can identify with this feeling of fear as they waited to hear that all had been done in the right and proper way. There is only one right way to go in this Christian life, and, like Moses, you must follow the Word of God. Second Timothy 2:15 says, "Study to shew thyself *approved unto God, a workman that needeth not to be ashamed, rightly dividing the word of truth.*" God has not hidden His perfect way from you. He has told you plainly in His Word how you are to live! If you desire the ultimate approval from God, follow the plan in the Word of God!

Second, it had to be **Accomplished** ("they had done it as the LORD had commanded"). This is where many people fail. There are many who have great plans for their service to the Lord, their dedication and faithfulness to His house, and the protection and blessing of their homes, but they never accomplish their plans. What a time of rejoicing, of confidence, of encouragement, when you know that you have done it just like God said! That is how Noah did the work of the ark. Proverbs 13:19 says, "The desire accomplished is sweet to the soul." There is a sweetness in doing God's work just like He has said!

Third, it was **Applauded** ("and Moses blessed them"). Applause awaits us one day if we are faithful to our Lord. Matthew 25:21 ends of one Jesus' parables with the words, "His lord said unto him, Well done, thou good and faithful servant: thou hast been faithful over a few things, I will make thee ruler over many things: enter thou into the joy of thy lord." We do not serve God to get applause or acclamation, but to honor and glorify Him. However, "God is not unrighteous to forget your work and labour of love, which ye have shewed toward his name, in that ye have ministered to the saints, and do minister" (Hebrews 6:10). One day, life will be over, and God will commend us for our service to Him if we have served Him according to His Word. God sees and notices your dedication and commitment and will bless you for your labor for Him!

TOPICS: Preparation, Work

DAILY BIBLE READING: Leviticus 1–4

TODAY'S VERSE: Leviticus 1:3: "If his offering be a burnt sacrifice of the herd, let him offer a male without blemish: he shall offer it of his own voluntary will at the door of the tabernacle of the congregation before the LORD."

LEVITICUS TAKES US into the depths of the work of the tabernacle and its ministers. God was very detailed and specific about the law of the offerings. Each offering was a picture of the future perfect sacrifice of Jesus Christ, showing us how He met every divine requirement to satisfy the payment for sin. Many would deny the importance of these details, and some might even call them petty laws from a petty God. However, the details only show the plan of God as He contemplated the perfect sacrifice of His Son.

It was to be a **Consumed Sacrifice** ("If his offering be a burnt sacrifice of the herd"). The words for "burnt offering" mean "a holocaust (as going up in smoke)." Nothing was to be left after the sacrifice. It was to be completely given over to the Lord with nothing left for self. Just a few sentences later in Leviticus 1:9, we read this: "But his inwards and his legs shall he wash in water: *and the priest shall burn all on the altar.*" We must be completely dedicated to the Lord in order for Him to consume us as He pleases.

It was to be a **Clean Sacrifice** ("let him offer a male without blemish"). It is no secret that God has always used sacrifices that were clean. This sacrifice was to be without blemish; David used five smooth stones out of the brook; Mary was a virgin when she was with child of the Holy Ghost. Psalm 73:1 says, "Truly God is good to Israel, even to such as are of a clean heart." The only truly clean sacrifice we can have is found in Christ, but there is a principle here that declares to us that God is a holy God and demands purity of heart and of life.

It was to be a **Controlled Sacrifice** ("he shall offer it of his own voluntary will"). This sacrifice was no whim! It was not an impulse gift! It was carefully thought, planned, and purposed. Second Corinthians 9:7 explains to us the purpose of a willing heart in spiritual giving: "Every man according as he purposeth in his heart, so let him give; not grudgingly, or of necessity: for God loveth a cheerful giver."

It was to be a **Committed Sacrifice** ("at the door of the tabernacle of the congregation before the LORD"). It was at the door that the priest would take the lamb and begin its ceremonial preparation for the offering. The door is a very important place for us. God warned Cain after his failure in his sacrifice that "sin lieth at the door" (Genesis 4:7). Let us make sure that our offering is committed to the Lord all the way.

TOPICS: Commitment, Holiness, Offering, Purity, Sacrifice

DAILY BIBLE READING: Leviticus 5-6

TODAY'S VERSE: Leviticus 5:5: "And it shall be, when he shall be guilty in one of these things, that he shall confess that he hath sinned in that thing."

WHENEVER WE TALK about offering, we must also talk about sin. Our sin has not helped us to mend our relationship with our Creator. Isaiah 59:2 says, "But your iniquities have separated between you and your God, and your sins have hid his face from you, that he will not hear." It is our sin that brings death, makes us fall short of the glory of God, and makes us want to disguise its ugliness in the sight of God, just as Adam and Eve did when putting on their biodegradable fashion show. God relates to our sin in several ways in this verse.

God's Strategy for Our Sin ("And it shall be"). This portion of the verse is a statement of fact. Though God knows of man's failures and faults, He also has a plan for our sin. We saw this evidenced in the garden when God came to visit Adam, exposed his sin, and then gave both he and his wife hope in the first promise of the Messiah in Genesis 3:15: "And I will put enmity between thee and the woman, and between thy seed and her seed; it shall bruise thy head, and thou shalt bruise his heel." This was the same plan God had from eternity past. He was prepared!

God's Certainty of Our Sin ("when he shall be guilty in one of these things"). It does not say "if he shall be guilty," but "when he shall be guilty." Many times, this chapter uses the word if in referring to a particular sin, but this verse shows God's knowledge that all men will be guilty of sin sometime. Romans 5:8 shows us that God did not come because we are good, but because we are bad! "But God commendeth his love toward us, in that, while we were yet sinners, Christ died for us."

God's Stipulation for Our Sin ("that he shall confess that he hath sinned in that thing"). God demands our acknowledgment of our sin. No sinner will see the need to trust in Christ if he never views himself as a sinner in need of salvation. The word for "confess" means "to use (i.e. hold out) the hand." Isn't that the picture of true confession? Proverbs 28:13 says, "He that covereth his sins shall not prosper: but whoso confesseth and forsaketh them shall have mercy." Admission of sin is mandatory in the eyes of God. Romans 10:9 tells us the same thing: "If thou shalt confess with thy mouth the Lord Jesus, and shalt believe in thine heart that God hath raised him from the dead, thou shalt be saved." We must agree with God about our wickedness and sinful failures before we can accept His gift of salvation.

TOPICS: Confession, Salvation, Sin

DAILY BIBLE READING: Leviticus 7–8

TODAY'S VERSE: Leviticus 8:12: "And he poured of the anointing oil upon Aaron's head, and anointed him, to sanctify him."

THE ANOINTING OIL was very important for the priest. It is also very important for us today, as it is a type of the Holy Ghost. The Holy Ghost is actually the presence and power of God in our lives!

First, we see the **Pouring of the Oil** ("and he poured of the anointing oil"). This was a *purposeful* pouring. It was not an accident, but was poured on purpose! What a testimony of the Lord's blessing as the Holy Spirit is poured on purpose on the life of a believer. This was also a *plentiful* pouring. When God pours out the Holy Spirit, it is enough! It covered the priest's whole body and soul. It is also a *passionate* pouring. Every time God starts pouring something, it goes all over the place! Psalm 23 says, "My cup runneth over." Somebody wanted to make sure the oil was everywhere. What a blessing when the Holy Spirit is flowing freely! Second Corinthians 3:17 says, "Now the Lord is that Spirit: and where the Spirit of the Lord is, there is liberty."

Second, we see the **Placing of the Oil** ("upon Aaron's head"). Psalm 133:2 recounts to us the pouring of the oil upon the head of the High Priest: "It is like the precious ointment upon the head, that ran down upon the beard, even Aaron's beard: that went down to the skirts of his garments." The Bible teaches us that the Holy Spirit was poured out upon Jesus Christ, our High Priest, without measure! Colossians 1:18 says, "And he is the head of the body, the church." Just as with Aaron, when the Holy Spirit was poured upon Jesus Christ, it ran down upon His beard, upon His priestly garments, and all the way down to His skirts, to the bottom of His garment. The anointing upon the head, Christ, has now flowed upon the rest of the body (the church). When He got it all, we got it all!

Third, we see the **Purpose of the Oil** ("to sanctify him"). The whole purpose of the oil was to set the priest apart to do the work that God had called him to do. That is what the Holy Spirit does to all of us! Acts 13:2 says, "As they ministered to the Lord, and fasted, the *Holy Ghost said, Separate me Barnabas and Saul for the work whereunto I have called them.*" God has separated you for His honor and glory to do a work you may not know about yet. When God sanctifies us, we must be patient and willing to do the will of the Lord in whatever way necessary. First Corinthians 6:19 says, "What? know ye not that your body is the temple of the Holy Ghost which is in you, which ye have of God, and ye are not your own?" Yield to the will of God in your life, and let Him use you as He sees fit. Then you will be fulfilled in your spirit as you yield to His anointing.

TOPICS: Blessing, God's Will, Holy Spirit, Sanctification, Work

DAILY BIBLE READING: Leviticus 9–11

TODAY'S VERSE: Leviticus 10:1: "And Nadab and Abihu, the sons of Aaron, took either of them his censer, and put fire therein, and put incense thereon, and offered strange fire before the Lord, which he commanded them not."

IN THE VERSE AFTER this one, the Lord consumes Nadab and Abihu with His fire of judgment. What was the problem, if they were just trying to serve the Lord? There are many problems if we do not serve God according to His plan! The end does *not* justify the means before a thrice-holy God! The fire offered by Nadab and Abihu was a testimony of their rebellion and disobedience.

It Was a Proud Fire ("And Nadab and Abihu, the sons of Aaron, took either of them his censer, and put fire therein"). Nadab and Abihu thought quite a lot of themselves to be able to offer this proud fire before the Lord! It was not God's fire in their eyes, but their own! Romans 12:3 deals with this thought for us today: "For I say, through the grace given unto me, to every man that is among you, not to think of himself more highly than he ought to think; but to think soberly, according as God hath dealt to every man the measure of faith." We know what pride does in the heart of a man. We also know that "God resisteth the proud but giveth grace unto the humble." Nothing we have and nothing we do is worthy of our Lord! If we are standing here by grace, then we have nothing of which we can boast!

It Was a Profane Fire ("and offered strange fire"). The word for "strange" means "a foreigner, strange, profane, to commit adultery." Many today are prostituting the old-time religion for new, sleek, contemporary worship. Many do not even understand that this is "strange fire" before the Lord. We need to let the Holy Ghost set our hearts aflame with *His passion, His purity,* and *His power.* In returning to the old-time fire, there will be no need and no desire to profane that which is heaven-sent! One problem today is that we have not allowed God to set the revival fire in our lives. We think, teach, and preach that this holy fire is developed by our own good works and our own desire in prayer. Nothing could be further from the truth! Our teaching proves that we are looking to a false fire to satisfy our spiritual desires.

It Was a Presumptuous Fire ("which he commanded them not"). Nadab and Abihu took it upon themselves to create a fire. Did a fire need to come? Yes! But it needed to come God's way! Usurping the authority of God's Word and God's plan is wrong and will not be blessed. In many ways, we have presumptuously placed ourselves above God's Word in order to make our religious experience "right." What an arrogant way to live as we dare the Lord to back up His Word! This is the same sin as tempting God. This behavior concerned the heart of David greatly, as we see in his prayer in Psalm 19:13: "Keep back thy servant also from presumptuous sins; let them not have dominion over me."

TOPICS: Disobedience, Passion, Pride, Rebellion, Sin, Worship

DAILY BIBLE READING: Leviticus 12–13

TODAY'S VERSE: Leviticus 13:45: "And the leper in whom the plague is, his clothes shall be rent, and his head bare, and he shall put a covering upon his upper lip, and shall cry, Unclean, unclean."

IN SCRIPTURE, LEPROSY is a type of our sin. Leprosy was a terrible scourge among the Jewish people, and it had no known cure. It was so easily passed from one person to another that lepers had to separate themselves and live in leper colonies outside the town. They lived in a *bad compound*. Separated from the tabernacle and the people of God, their worship and fellowship were destroyed. They lived in a *bad company*. Every contact they had was as bad or worse than they were. They lived in a *bad condemnation*. They had no hope of relief or healing without divine help. Here are a few thoughts about leprosy and the spiritual plague of sin.

First, it was a **Plague of Concern** ("his clothes shall be rent"). This was the same way the Israelites acted when they were to repent of their sins. Have you ever seen someone walk down the street with ripped clothes? It strikes a different chord in your heart than the usual dirt, grime, and dishevelment that you might see more often. When clothes are torn, they draw more attention and more pity than anything else. Rent clothes in Moses' time were a testimony of utter sorrow, sadness, and grief. Many in the Bible "rent their clothes" out of sorrow and repentance. The plague of leprosy defiled even the wearer's clothing. Even their clothes were to be burnt in fire. This reminds me of the terrible nature of sin as we are commanded in Jude 23: "And others save with fear, pulling them out of the fire; *hating even the garment spotted by the flesh.*"

Second, it was a **Plague of Calamity** ("and his head bare"). There are few things so powerful as embarrassment and shame. No doubt, the leprous person could hear the "tsk, tsk!" and the "he was so nice: what a shame!" of so many people who saw his bald head as he walked by. And what about the leprous woman? The Bible says in 1 Corinthians 11 that a woman's hair is her glory! This was of greater shame to her. The bald head brought much shame upon both as they walked down the street bearing the shame of their affliction.

Third, it was a **Plague of Concealment** ("and he shall put a covering upon his upper lip"). So many times we try to mask our problems and hide them from others. Nobody desires his sin to be exposed and laid bare for all to see. God has ways of exposing our sin with the Word of God, as we read in Hebrews 4:12–13: "For the word of God is quick, and powerful, and sharper than any twoedged sword, piercing even to the dividing asunder of soul and spirit, and of the joints and marrow, and is a discerner of the thoughts and intents of the heart. Neither is there any creature that is not manifest in his sight: but *all things are naked and opened unto the eyes of him with whom we have to do.*"

Fourth, it was a **Plague of Confession** ("and shall cry, Unclean, unclean"). This cry was a constant reminder of their affliction. It was with sufferers every moment of every day. There was no relief from the constancy of their shame and disease. But such crying out is also the first step of a person toward salvation. After we are convicted of our sin by the Holy Spirit, we have to admit our sin, which is paramount in receiving Christ as Saviour. Romans 10:10 says, "For with the heart man believeth unto righteousness; and *with the mouth confession is made unto salvation.*" The cry was also for the security of those nearby, to keep them from the same destruction the lepers were facing! Confession for the saved must take place in the daily Christian walk in addition to fellowship with God. Thank God for 1 John 1:9, which says, "If we confess our sins, he is faithful and just to forgive us our sins, and to cleanse us from all unrighteousness."

TOPICS: Confession, Guilt, Repentance, Sin, Shame

DAILY BIBLE READING: Leviticus 14–15

TODAY'S VERSE: Leviticus 14:35: "And he that owneth the house shall come and tell the priest, saying, It seemeth to me there is as it were a plague in the house:"

IN THIS CONTINUED ADDRESSING of leprosy, God deals with the problem of the plague being in the house itself. We have many problems in our homes today that have tremendous plagues within them. Our houses and homes need help! God has given us instruction on what to do in case the plague has consumed our house. He even goes so far as to break it down: throw all the timber, bricks, and mortar away and start over (see verse 45).

Someone Has to Take Responsibility ("And *he that owneth* the house shall come"). This has to do with **action.** We need the men in our homes to step up and take responsibility when something is happening that is hurtful to the family. It is not the woman's place to handle this. It is not the child's place to handle it either. The verse calls for "he" to step up. Men, it is our job to *protect* the home. It is our job to *provide* for the home. It is our job to *pray* for the home. It is our job to *preserve* the home. It is our job to *purify* the home.

Someone Has to Make a Request ("and tell the priest"). This has to do with **assistance.** It may be hard for some, but we would all do well to know that there is no shame in asking for help! As a matter of fact, these men went to their Old Testament preacher! The priest sat down with the man of the house and asked him to describe what was happening. He then laid out the plan for attacking this problem in the home. As was mentioned earlier, the family always had the opportunity to tear the house down and begin again. It amazes me today how many people know they need help, say they want help, but won't accept the help that is given to them or do what they are told. They still want to do it their way.

Someone Has to Use Reason ("saying, It seemeth to me. . ."). This has to do with **assessment.** For the most part, our spiritual perception is dead today. Parents allow and make fleshly concessions to their children, never taking into consideration the wickedness and destruction contained in the Pandora's Box that has just been opened. They are oblivious to the telltale signs of the leprosy that is beginning in their children's hearts. They are even unwilling to admit that their failure has allowed seeds of discontent in their marriage. Where are the people with spiritual understanding who say, "It seemeth to me"? Such people might not be able to put their finger on it, but they know in their hearts that something is wrong! They are not willing to sit on the sidelines and watch uncleanness take over their homes and their lives without doing something to try to correct it!

Let us learn this verse for our homes' sake, our marriages' sake, and our children's sake!

TOPICS: Discernment, Flesh, Leadership, Men, Pastor, Sin

DAILY BIBLE READING: Leviticus 16–18

TODAY'S VERSE: Leviticus 17:11: "For the life of the flesh is in the blood: and I have given it to you upon the altar to make an atonement for your souls: for it is the blood that maketh an atonement for the soul."

TALKING ABOUT THE BLOOD starts this day off right! To see the work of the blood centers my heart upon God. To think of its worth humbles my soul before Him. God takes great care to tell us exactly what we need to know about the blood. Don't stop with this devotional. Study in your Bible the blessing of blood atonement. Many verses support these few simple thoughts about the blood, but I will only give a few.

First, we see its **Vitality** ("For the *life* of the flesh is in the blood"). Vitality is that which distinguishes the living from the nonliving. There is no doubt that the healthier your blood is, the healthier you are. According to scientific study, everything that is needed to live comes from the blood. Adam Clarke says in his commentary, "The blood possesses a living principle, and that the life of the whole body is derived from it, is a doctrine of Divine revelation, and a doctrine which the observations and experiments of the most accurate anatomists have served strongly to confirm."[1]

Here is a little thought for you this morning: could there be something in our blood that is a gift from God to us? Genesis 2:7 says that God "breathed into [Adam's] nostrils the breath of life, and man became a living soul." Yet according to today's verse, the life of the flesh is in the blood. There are many differences between man's blood and an animal's blood. The breath of God is in man, and I personally believe that it is the blood of man that testifies that fact.

Second, we see its **Vicariousness** ("and *I have given it to you* upon the altar to make an atonement *for your souls*"). "Vicarious" means "Made or performed by substitution; suffered or done in place of another."[2] God gave His own blood on Calvary's altar as a substitute for our hell-bound souls! He took my place on the cross! He gave His blood for the cleansing of my sin and the purification of my soul in His sight. First John 1:7 tells us, "And the blood of Jesus Christ his Son cleanseth us from all sin." This is a *selfless* deed! This is a *saving* deed! This is a *sacrificial* deed!

Third, we see its **Victory** ("it is the blood that maketh an atonement for the soul"). Nothing else brings us to the Lord and "covers" our sin. Nothing else has been provided by God to cleanse us from all unrighteousness. He has told us plainly what will make atonement for our sin, and we can rejoice in it: the Bible says in Hebrews 9:12, "Neither by the blood of goats and calves, but by his own blood he entered in once into the holy place, *having obtained eternal redemption for us.*" Hallelujah for the blood! God drew this picture back in the Levitical law and gave it to us today to remember His great gift of salvation.

TOPICS: Blood, Life, Sacrifice, Victory

---

1   Adam Clarke, *Holy Bible with Commentary and Critical Notes*, Vol 1. (New York: B. Waugh and T. Mason for the Methodist Episcopal Church, 1846), 542–543.

2   *Webster Comprehensive Dictionary: International Edition.* Vol. 1. Edited by Albert H. Marckwardt, Frederic G. Cassidy, and James B. McMillan. (Chicago: J.G. Ferguson, 1992)

DAILY BIBLE READING: Leviticus 19–20

TODAY'S VERSE: Leviticus 20:24: "But I have said unto you, Ye shall inherit their land, and I will give it unto you to possess it, a land that floweth with milk and honey: I am the LORD your God, which have separated you from other people."

THOUGH JACOB'S FAMILY REMAINED in Egypt for over four hundred years and the Israelites wandered in the desert another forty years after that, they never forgot the promise of God to bring them into a wonderful land. When the time finally came for Israel to prepare to possess the Promised Land, God had to give them some ground rules. First, He reminded them of the failure of the people who already inhabited the land before them and of their wicked ways. Second, He told them how they were to honor Him and obey His commands. And third, He told them that He had chosen them to be different from all other nations in order to glorify Himself.

The Promise of God's Land ("But I have said unto you, Ye shall inherit their land"). In this verse, the word for "inherit" is the same word used for "possess" that we will discuss a little later. The point for now is that somebody gave the Israelites this land. It was God! The verse begins, "But I have said unto you." There is much discussion about whose land it really is over in the Middle East. The answer cannot be "whoever was there first." Psalm 24:1 tells us, "The earth is the LORD's and the fulness thereof; the world, and they that dwell therein." Very plainly, the earth is God's, and God very plainly gave that plot of land to the nation of Israel. Argument over!

The Present of God's Land ("and I will give it unto you"). Before they received the land, the people of Israel looked to it with great anticipation and excitement. It was God's gift to them, the fulfillment of God's promise to Abraham in Genesis 12:7. Abraham never went out and got his own land, but waited for the Lord to provide and present it to him. Now God was confirming the same promise to the people of Israel. God would not be found a liar to His people, but would bless them in His integrity and prove that His promises are true.

The Possession of God's Land ("to possess it"). The word used for "possess" means "to occupy (by driving out previous tenants, and possessing in their place)." With this was a promise of war. What they were sure to understand was that this was also a promise of victory! Israel had only to claim the land God had already given to them.

The Pleasantness of God's Land ("a land that floweth with milk and honey"). The land would be watered and lush so the cattle could grow and make the land flow with milk. The field would receive much water to produce many flowers for the bees who would, in turn, be able to make much honey. In that dry and arid climate, God's favor and blessing was shown upon the land by giving it rain. God even gave the people a promise of His healing even after His punishment for their disobedience in 2 Chronicles 7:13–14: "If I shut up heaven that there be no rain . . . If my people, which are called by my name, shall humble themselves, and pray, and seek my face, and turn from their wicked ways; then will I hear from heaven, and will forgive their sin, and will heal their land." We hear the same thing in a spiritual context from Hosea 10:12, where God tells His people, "For it is time to seek the LORD, till he come and rain righteousness upon you." O Lord, send the rain! Let it flow from your hand, and bless us with rain from heaven.

The Partition of God's Land ("I am the LORD your God, which have separated you from other people"). The word for "separated" means "to divide, separate, distinguish, differ, select." We are different from the world. Great confidence comes when you embrace the separation from the world rather than trying to prove to the world that you are really no different from them! The separation that God has placed upon His people is not a cross to bear, but a tremendous blessing to wear!

TOPICS: Battle, Promises, Promised Land, Separation, Victory

DAILY BIBLE READING: Leviticus 21–23

TODAY'S VERSE: Leviticus 22:32: "Neither shall ye profane my holy name; but I will be hallowed among the children of Israel: I am the LORD which hallow you."

GOD IS VERY JEALOUS of His name. He has given very serious commands concerning the way in which His name is to be used. Exodus 20:7 tells us, "Thou shalt not take the name of the LORD thy God in vain; for the LORD will not hold him guiltless that taketh his name in vain." His name should be most precious to those who have tasted of the heavenly gift of salvation. We should use His name with the utmost respect and reverence as we contemplate the One whom that name represents.

It Is a Holy Name ("Neither shall ye profane my holy name"). The word for "profane" means "to bore, to wound, to dissolve." I shudder to think that I could bore or carve into the heart of God and wound Him by using His name in a way that is not right. God's name is the embodiment of holiness. Yet, instead of using God's name to identify holiness, we often use it flippantly to show forth some silly thought, or even worse, to blaspheme and curse out of anger and bitterness. Our God is a holy God, and His name is pure. Without His name, we would have no help! Psalm 54:1 says, "Save me, O God, by thy name, and judge me by thy strength." And Romans 10:13 tells us the importance of the Lord's name in our salvation: "For whosoever shall call upon the name of the Lord shall be saved."

It Is a Hallowed Name ("but I will be hallowed among the children of Israel"). Even Jesus Christ said that His Father's name was hallowed: "After this manner therefore pray ye: Our Father which art in heaven, hallowed be thy name" (Matthew 6:9). His name is to be consecrated and honored in the most sincere of ways! God desires His children to acknowledge Him as holy and to set Him apart from all others so they might love and worship Him in the sweetest love! If we would hallow God, then we would not serve Him emptily, and we would not speak of Him flippantly! There is a ceremonial gravity attached to our Lord that is only shown from a heart of respect and devotion. Though this gravity exists in heaven in the highest order, it only resides upon this earth in the hearts of those who deem Him worthy and reverence Him in deepest love.

It Is a Heavenly Name ("I am the LORD which hallow you"). The name we are given here is "LORD" in all capitalized letters. Whenever that form is used in the English Bible, it denotes the Hebrew name "Jehovah." Jehovah means "Self-Existent, Eternal." That can only be a name from heaven! There is no one above Him! It is Jehovah who dwells in the heavens! David knew that Jehovah was the highest; for in Psalm 8:1 he said, "O LORD our Lord, how excellent is thy name in all the earth! who hast set thy glory above the heavens." "LORD" capitalized early in the verse tells us that David was naming Jehovah. Praise the Lord for a heavenly name that we can worship and adore!

TOPICS: God's Name, Holiness, Reverence, Worship

February 11

DAILY BIBLE READING: Leviticus 24–25

TODAY'S VERSE: Leviticus 25:10: "And ye shall hallow the fiftieth year, and proclaim liberty throughout all the land unto all the inhabitants thereof: it shall be a jubile unto you; and ye shall return every man unto his possession, and ye shall return every man unto his family."

THIS VERSE HAS GREAT spiritual meaning for us today as it announces freedom in the Year of Jubilee. I've also chosen this verse for a patriotic reason: in its entirety, it is inscribed on the Liberty Bell, which currently sits in Liberty Bell Center in Philadelphia, Pennsylvania. I remember the awe I felt when I was able to see the Liberty Bell. Don't tell anyone, but I even touched it! The Hebrew word for "liberty" comes from a word meaning "to move rapidly; freedom; hence, spontaneity of outflow, and so clear:—liberty, pure." What a powerful word for us to ponder this morning! We should share our freedom and liberty with others so they can also hear the sound of the gospel.

First, we see it was a **Purified Liberty** ("And ye shall *hallow* the fiftieth year"). The word for "hallow" means "to make clean." Our lives should be purified and hallowed for the Master's use. Let me address an important topic here: It is not purity that demands liberty, but liberty that demands purity. This is a very important doctrinal principle for us today. Some people think their "good living" demands that God save them, yet the Bible makes it very clear that even "our righteousnesses are as filthy rags" (Isaiah 64:6). But our salvation does demand our "good living." The Holy Spirit inside us will bring about the fruit of purity in the Christian life and hallow us unto our God.

Second, we see it was a **Published Liberty** ("and proclaim liberty throughout all the land unto all the inhabitants thereof"). This word "proclaim" means "to call out to." What a day it was when the Lord called out to me! Now, the Lord desires to use you and me to call out to those who are without hope and share the blessed gospel of Christ with them. It is a blessing to watch a parent with a little child. The parents will "call out to" the child to come for protection from harm, to share a joy, to comfort in pain, and to bless in fellowship. God is calling out to you today to hear His Word, keep Him first, and enjoy the fellowship of walking with Him each and every day.

Third, we see it was a **Powerful Liberty** ("it shall be a jubile unto you"). The Hebrew word "jubile" means "the blast of a horn, the instrument itself and *the festival thus introduced*." When the gospel horn is sounded and the sinner hears and responds to its glorious melody, a celebration begins in heaven that causes even the angels to rejoice and celebrate. The Jubilee horn was to be blown when the Festival of Jubilee began. When the time comes for us to be called away, there will be a blowing of a horn to begin a heavenly Jubilee for the glory of the Lord!

It was a **Pardoned Liberty** ("and ye shall return every man unto his possession, and ye shall return every man unto his family"). This liberty has introduced a new way of living, a new heart of serving, a new joy in hearing, and a new passion in worshiping! It has brought us into a new world! What a blessing not to be in the old world any longer! When the Jubilee sounded, slaves were freed, lands were returned to the original owners, and debts were wiped clean. Family members returned, rejoiced, and sang the praises of Jehovah God for freeing them from their problems and giving them new freedom. Can you hear the Liberty Bell ringing in your heart today?

TOPICS: Freedom, Liberty, Pardon, Rejoicing

DAILY BIBLE READING: Leviticus 26–27

TODAY'S VERSE: Leviticus 26:44: "But I will for their sakes remember the covenant of their ancestors, whom I brought forth out of the land of Egypt in the sight of the heathen, that I might be their God: I am the LORD."

THIS VERSE DESCRIBES beautifully the restoration of God's people and the mercy of God upon them. It always blesses my heart to speak of the mercy of God and the new opportunities that He allows us to have in spite of our stumbling and faults. God's mercy affects not only us, but Him as well.

God's Mercy Makes Him Remember His Promises ("But I will for their sakes remember the covenant"). What a blessed day when God remembers His promises and His covenants with His people! His promises are *powerful*. Hebrews 6:13 says, "For when God made promise to Abraham, because he could swear by no greater, he sware by himself." The wonderful thing about God's promises is just that: they are the promises of *God!* Not only are the promises of God powerful, but they are also *precious*. Second Peter 1:4 says, "Whereby are given unto us exceeding great and precious promises." Every time I hear or remember a promise of God, I am touched by its value and its honor! His promises are also *perfect*. Second Corinthians 1:20 says, "For all the promises of God in him are yea, and in him Amen, unto the glory of God by us." There are no failures, no flaws, and no faults associated with the promises of God!

God's Mercy Makes Him Remember the Parents ("the covenant of their ancestors"). This blesses my heart because it tells me there is no expiration date upon His promises! Romans 15:8 says, "to confirm the promises *made unto the fathers,"* and Galatians 3:16 says, "Now to *Abraham* and his seed were the promises made." You might wonder why it's so important that God remembers the parents—well, because it also means He won't forget me! I stand here redeemed because of a covenant God made with His own Son Jesus Christ. Because of salvation, I have been included in the eternal blood of the new covenant of God!

God's Mercy Makes Him Remember Their Parade ("whom I brought forth out of the land of Egypt in the sight of the heathen"). God never forgot the day that He led the Hebrews out from the land of Egypt. He made quite a parade of it! All the Egyptians watched as the people of God took everything and walked away. Numbers 33:3 says, "The children of Israel went out with an high hand in the sight of all the Egyptians." God loves to do things openly in the sight of all and put His power and might on display to the awe of those who do not believe. God loves to parade the answers to your prayers. Matthew 6:4 says, "And thy Father which seeth in secret himself shall reward thee openly." God had a parade in paradise. Ephesians 4:8 says, "Wherefore he saith, When he ascended up on high, he led captivity captive, and gave gifts unto men." Christ brought the captives out and led them to heaven with His glory and His presence. He will give a parade for His faithful servants at the great promotion. Matthew 25:21 says, "His lord said unto him, Well done, thou good and faithful servant: thou hast been faithful over a few things, I will make thee ruler over many things: enter thou into the joy of thy lord." I have always enjoyed a good parade! How about you?

TOPICS: Honor, Promises, Victory

DAILY BIBLE READING: Numbers 1–2

TODAY'S VERSE: Numbers 2:2: "Every man of the children of Israel shall pitch by his own standard, with the ensign of their father's house: far off about the tabernacle of the congregation shall they pitch."

THE "STANDARD" IN THIS VERSE is a banner or a flag. Our standard in America is the red, white, and blue, Old Glory, the Star-Spangled Banner. Our flag is meaningful. Even our national anthem, Francis Scott Key's "The Star-Spangled Banner," was based upon the placement of our flag: "And the rocket's red glare/ The bombs bursting in air/Gave proof through the night/That our flag was still there." Back in the Hebrew encampment, God gave orders concerning the flags and banners of each tribe and their meanings to the people. God has also blessed us with a beautiful banner for us to enjoy His blessing. Song of Solomon 2:4 says, "He brought me to the banqueting house, and *his banner over me was love.*" What can we learn from the banners of Israel about our own banner in Christ?

First, we see it is a **Fine Banner** ("Every man of the children of Israel shall pitch by his own standard"). This has to do with **individuality**. Every man has to make the standard his own! It cannot be anybody else's! You must find it suitable and choose it yourself. No one can do it for you. What a banner has been given to us today through our Lord and Saviour Jesus Christ: it is a *blood-stained* banner, a *blood-borne* banner, and a *blood-blessed* banner! Psalm 60:4 says, "Thou hast given a banner to them that fear thee, that it may be displayed because of the truth. Selah."

Second, we see it is a **Family Banner** ("with the ensign of their father's house"). This has to do with **identity**. We have quite a family! Our elder brother, Jesus Christ, has claimed and formed the banner. Now all of our brothers and sisters in Christ share that banner as well! This banner tells all others exactly who we are. There should be no doubts about whose we are in this world in which we live: there is too much at stake for our title not to be clear and our mission not to be plain. If you have not trusted Jesus Christ as your personal Saviour, you do not yet have a family banner with which you can identify. Trust in Him, and enjoy the identity of Christ. I would still rather be identified with my wonderful Saviour in the midst of persecution than be identified with the world and its praise!

Third, we see it is a **Focused Banner** ("far off about the tabernacle of the congregation shall they pitch"). This has to do with **integrity**. Chapter 2:17 and 34 say that as the tribes pitched around the tabernacle, they were to set the tents *forward*. Every bit of their attention was to be completely focused upon the tabernacle and the presence of God! As they walked out of their tent doors every morning, they would see the column of smoke of God's presence as it rested upon the tabernacle. Isn't His presence all that matters? All that we do should be sharply focused on Him. What a wonderful thing for us to do—focus on our worship of God. As God moves, so we move! Let us focus all of our worship and adoration upon Him.

TOPICS: Banner, Blood, Decision, Focus, Identity

R. CHRIS HANKS

DAILY BIBLE READING: Numbers 3-4

TODAY'S VERSE: Numbers 4:49: "According to the commandment of the Lord they were numbered by the hand of Moses, every one according to his service, and according to his burden: thus were they numbered of him, as the Lord commanded Moses."

THIS VERSE TELLS US all about the numbering and the work of the children of Israel, especially the Levites and the priests. The Levites were numbered in three ways.

First, they were numbered **According to the Commandment** ("According to the commandment of the Lord they were numbered by the hand of Moses"). This has to do with **appointment.** What a joy divine to be given a commandment from God to do His bidding! This was not something conjured up in the mind of Moses, but decided by God Himself. Doing God's will in our lives ought to be more enjoyable than a hot fudge sundae! Matthew 26:19 says, "And the disciples did as Jesus had appointed them." What a testimony that they were obedient and willing! It is common today to see so many people, whether at work or at home, complaining and unsatisfied with what has been appointed for them to do. This should never be our attitude. We have the opportunity to do the will of God!

Second, they were numbered **According to Their Service.** ("every one according to his service"). This has to do with **assistance.** Not only were they numbered by the will of God, but they were also numbered according to the work of God. They were actually numbered according to the service they were performing before God. God willed it, they performed it, and others were blessed by it. We are yoked together with Christ in this service and labor. Matthew 11:29 says, "Take my yoke upon you, and learn of me; for I am meek and lowly in heart: and ye shall find rest unto your souls." A yoke is built for two! We are working with our blessed Saviour!

Third, they were numbered **According to His Burden.** ("and according to his burden: thus were they numbered of him, as the Lord commanded Moses"). This has to do with **affliction.** The word for "burden" means "load, weight." The Levites had been designated a weight to carry for the Lord. God may have called you to carry certain weights for His glory as well. Some are called to carry a physical burden. Some are called to carry a family burden. Some are called to carry a church burden. Paul spoke of this last burden in 2 Corinthians 11:28: "Beside those things that are without, that which cometh upon me daily, *the care of all the churches.*" God has called you, Pastor, to have a special burden for your people. God has called you, Evangelist, to have a burden for the church and the man of God you are serving. God has called you, Missionary, to have a burden for another people and another culture. We are all called in Galatians 6:2 to "bear ye one another's burdens, and so fulfil the law of Christ." We are also called to carry a burden for the lost and their salvation from the eternal punishment of God. Whatever burden you may have today, let me remind you of what Jesus said in Matthew 11:30: "For my yoke is easy, *and my burden is light.*"

TOPICS: Burdens, God's Will, Service, Work

 *February 15*

DAILY BIBLE READING: Numbers 5–6

TODAY'S VERSE: Numbers 6:24–26: "The Lord bless thee, and keep thee: The Lord make his face shine upon thee, and be gracious unto thee: the Lord lift up his countenance upon thee, and give thee peace."

TODAY'S VERSES SHARE the priestly blessing that was given by Aaron to the people of Israel. Three times, "the Lord" is used in these verses. That is neither chance nor a mistake. Every time you find the all-capitalized "Lord" in the Bible, it is the Hebrew name "Jehovah" for which the English word is being used. Many study books indicate that each time "Jehovah" is used in these three verses, it has a different accent mark upon it, stating its difference from the other two. This threefold blessing upon the people is a testimony of our thrice-holy God, a perfect picture of the Trinity in Scripture. Second Corinthians 13:14 says, "The grace of the *Lord Jesus Christ*, and the love of *God*, and the communion of the *Holy Ghost*, be with you all."

The first of today's verses says, "The Lord bless thee, and keep thee." This is witness of **God the Father and His Faithfulness.** He blesses us and keeps us. Every blessing is from God our Father. James 1:17 says, "Every good gift and every perfect gift is from above, and cometh down from the Father of lights." His blessing is a result of His pleasure. His keeping is a result of His protection. The Bible says in Psalm 68:19, "Blessed be the Lord, who *daily loadeth us with benefits*, even the God of our salvation." God has been so faithful to keep me. He watches over me every day and protects me from evil. Even Jesus, in His model prayer, asked God to "deliver us from evil." My, how many times He has heard and answered that prayer in my life! Lamentations 3:23 proclaims, "Great is they faithfulness."

The second of these verses says, "The Lord make his face shine upon thee, and be gracious unto thee." I believe that this is witness of **God the Son, Jesus Christ, and His Favor.** Psalm 31:16 says, "Make thy face to shine upon thy servant: save me for thy mercies' sake." God's grace came to me through Jesus Christ and Calvary's cross! Grace—what a word! What a sound! What a thought! One of our most well-known and blessed hymns says, "Amazing grace, how sweet the sound/That saved a wretch like me! I once was lost, but now am found/Was blind but now I see!"[3] Grace is seen all through the Bible in both the Old and the New Testaments. It has a continuing ministry during this church age. First Corinthians 1:4 says, "I thank my God always on your behalf, *for the grace of God which is given you by Jesus Christ.*"

The third of these verses says, "The Lord lift up his countenance upon thee, and give thee peace." I believe that this is witness of **God the Holy Spirit and His Fullness.** In speaking to His disciples about the Comforter, the Holy Spirit, Jesus says in John 14:27, "Peace I leave with you, my peace I give unto you: not as the world giveth, give I unto you. Let not your heart be troubled, neither let it be afraid." What a day when He sent the Holy Spirit to indwell the believer! The word used for "peace" in Jesus' words means "prosperity, quietness, peace." The fullness and prosperity of God is experienced in the peace of God in every part of our lives. That is the ministry of the Holy Ghost! What a work and what a blessing the Godhead has unto us, manifesting each office with such splendor and mercy! What a priestly blessing we have to rejoice in today!

TOPICS: Blessing, Faithfulness, Fullness, God the Father, Grace, Holy Spirit, Jesus Christ, Trinity

---

3   These lyrics, of course, come from John Newton's "Amazing Grace."

DAILY BIBLE READING: Numbers 7

TODAY'S VERSE: Numbers 7:11: "And the Lord said unto Moses, They shall offer their offering, each prince on his day, for the dedicating of the altar."

THIS CHAPTER TELLS US about the establishing of God's house in the wilderness. Each tribe came with a gift and an offering to honor God. Some of the gifts were to help in the sanctuary and service; others were to dedicate the altar in sacrifice. Though each tribe gave the same offering, each offering is explained and accounted in greatest detail. Don't think that God does not pay attention to the offerings you give!

It Was a Drawing Offering ("And the Lord said unto Moses, They shall offer their offering"). The word for "offer" means "to approach (causatively, bring near)." Our greatest desire should be to draw near to God as we give Him our offering. There are many who are satisfied with just giving. They think they are doing God a favor. That kind of an offering is a failure! God warns against prideful giving in Matthew 6:2: "Therefore when thou doest thine alms, do not sound a trumpet before thee, as the hypocrites do in the synagogues and in the streets, that they may have glory of men. Verily I say unto you, They have their reward." The point of giving is to draw nigh to Him! Our giving is connected to our worship. As your heart is connected to worship in giving unto Him, He will approach and draw nigh to you as well.

It Was a Dignified Offering ("each prince on his day"). It was the leader of each tribe who was responsible to give the offering. We need our leadership today to take their place and honor God in the sight of the people. Our preachers need to take the lead in offering themselves to the Lord. Church leadership and teachers need to show the church the right way to give. Our fathers need to dedicate themselves and their homes to the Lord in the sight of their families. It was David who danced with all his might and offered himself before the ark of the covenant as they brought it to Jerusalem. This was not done in a spirit of pride or self-exaltation, but in humility, showing the people how to worship in their offerings and their giving.

It Was a Dedicating Offering ("for the dedicating of the altar"). This was a special time as God's people dedicated the altar. The word for "dedicating" means "initiation, consecration." This was a special time. Even though churches should beware of too much formalism of the sort that has wreaked havoc in worship, there are special dedications that demand sobriety, sincerity, and also great respect in their observance. For instance, the Lord's Supper or the dedicating of a new building or ministry may require a special dedication. This was the introduction of the tabernacle to the people of the congregation. They were going to "break in" a brand new altar. It was time for it to be done right. Later, we see the same honor given on a much larger scale when Solomon dedicated the temple. Find times to dedicate your home and ministry to the Lord. A brand-new marriage, a new baby, a new home, or a call to the ministry are all great opportunities for the most sincere dedication.

TOPICS: Dedication, Giving, Leadership, Offering, Worship

February 17

DAILY BIBLE READING: Numbers 8–10

TODAY'S VERSE: Numbers 10:2: "Make thee two trumpets of silver; of a whole piece shalt thou make them: that thou mayest use them for the calling of the assembly, and for the journeying of the camps."

THESE SILVER TRUMPETS were very interesting works and also had an important ministry in the camp of Israel. The sound of the trumpet is a very distinct sound. It was used in celebration to herald or crown a king; it is used in battle to give directions; and it will be used to call us to heaven.

The Trumpets Were a Complete Work ("Make thee two trumpets of silver; of a whole piece shalt thou make them"). Some suppose that these trumpets were made differently in size, for they did have different sounds. Only one was to be used to call the princes together. If they had the same sound, how could the people know if it were one or two trumpets being sounded? They were trumpets of silver. Silver is always used in the Bible as a type of redemption and atonement.[4] Both silver trumpets were used at the same time to signal all the people, whether in journey or in battle. Can you see the picture shown here? The trumpet is used to sound out the gospel of Jesus Christ! Even a preacher was to lift up his voice like a trumpet (Isaiah 58:1). Doesn't that sound like the Bible to you? We have an Old and New Testament that carry the message of one gospel to be sounded for all the people to hear!

The Trumpets Gave a Call to Worship ("that thou mayest use them for the calling of the assembly"). Whenever the congregation needed to be assembled, the trumpeters blew the trumpets. Isn't that the meaning of the word *church*—"a called-out assembly"? There is a call to worship for us today. We must gather together to glorify our Lord and Saviour.

The Trumpets Gave a Call to Walk ("and for the journeying of the camps"). There had to be a way to accomplish the great task of moving this many people through the desert. Who was to go and when? How was this supposed to happen? By the sound of the trumpet! Many today are looking for direction in their lives. Why not listen to the sound of the trumpet, the Word of God? It will tell you when to walk, where to walk, and how to walk! We must listen to the Word of God to direct our lives.

The Trumpets Gave a Call to War ("of the camps"). The word for "camps" means "an encampment (of travellers or troops)." First Corinthians 14:8 says, "For if the trumpet give an uncertain sound, who shall prepare himself to the battle?" Are we not in the army of the Lord? There is a call to battle that we can hear from the trumpet of God's Word. First Timothy 6:12 tells us to "fight the good fight of faith." Listen to the sound of the trumpet, and prepare yourself for the battle.

TOPICS: Battle, Christian Walk, Church, War, Word of God, Worship

---

4   M.R. DeHaan, *The Tabernacle* (Grand Rapids: Zondervan, 1955), 42.

R. CHRIS HANKS

DAILY BIBLE READING: Numbers 11–13

TODAY'S VERSE: Numbers 11:23: "And the Lord said unto Moses, Is the Lord's hand waxed short? thou shalt see now whether my word shall come to pass unto thee or not."

THAT IS A GOOD QUESTION for us today. "Is the Lord's hand waxed short?" I have heard people say that God cannot do what He used to do in the Bible days. I have heard some say that "God just doesn't work that way anymore!" I beg to differ! God is working the same way He always has—according to His own sovereign and divine will! Here are a few thoughts about the way God works.

First, we see the **Example of God's Hand** ("And the Lord said unto Moses, Is the Lord's hand . . ."). The word for "hand" is very interesting: Strong's definition says "a hand, the open one (indicating power, means, direction, etc.), in distinction from . . . the closed one." Did you get it? This is an open hand! This tells me a few things. God is not trying to *hide* anything from me! His hand is open! Have you played the guessing game with children in which you hide something in your hand and they have to guess where it is? God is offering what you desire with an open hand. This also tells me that God is not trying to *hurt* me. His hand is not clenched. It is a hand, not a fist! The definition also says that God is not trying to *hinder* me by withholding something. This hand is "the open one (indicating *power, means, direction*)."

Second, we see the **Extent of God's Hand** ("waxed short"). God's reach is great. There is no place that His hand cannot reach you! As a matter of fact, His hand reached way down for me: "He brought me up also out of an horrible pit, out of the miry clay, and set my feet upon a rock, and established my goings." No matter where you are, God can reach you. The question asks, "Is the Lord's hand waxed short?" The word for "waxed short" means to "dock off, curtail, cut down." God can reach as far today as He ever could! Not only can God reach you, but God can reach others. Maybe you are concerned about a wayward son or daughter who is miles away from you. God can reach them wherever they might be. Those who have needs on the other side of the world can still feel the hand of God rest upon them.

Third, we see the **Expectation of God's Hand** ("thou shalt see now whether my word shall come to pass unto thee or not"). When God asks this question, He is asking Moses if he thought that God could not do what He needed to do. Just because God has chosen to wait to answer your prayer, you still must live with an expectancy that God will answer it! Matthew 21:22 says, "And all things, whatsoever ye shall ask in prayer, *believing*, ye shall receive." Doesn't it sound to you like God is asking Moses, "So you don't think that I can do this? You don't think I can help? You don't think that I am strong enough?" When I hear God ask those questions, I can almost hear the following words: "Just watch and see!" I believe that we miss many blessings in our lives because we do not believe that God will do them. Believe on!

TOPICS: Expectancy, Faith, God's Ability, Hope, Prayer

DAILY BIBLE READING: Numbers 14–15

TODAY'S VERSE: Numbers 14:3: "And wherefore hath the LORD brought us unto this land, to fall by the sword, that our wives and our children should be a prey? were it not better for us to return into Egypt?"

WE HAVE ALL HEARD many statements such as this from people throughout the years. It saddens my heart greatly to see people so discouraged in their lives. And in fact, this is a dangerous place for us to be. We actually need to protect ourselves against coming to this place in our spiritual lives. Here are three conclusions the Israelites arrived at before they could ask these questions.

First, we see a **Lack of Truth.** They called God a liar ("And wherefore hath the LORD brought us unto this land"). They were still in the wilderness, yet they said that the "LORD brought us unto *this* land." This was not a land that flowed with milk and honey: it was a barren land. Since they were not yet where God had told them they would be, they concluded God must be a liar. This shows a lack of patience in their hearts. Because they were frustrated, they began to accuse. They said, "I tried the church thing, and it didn't work for me!" or even, "I did what God said in the Bible, and He never did what He said." Such statements are the sign of someone who will not wait upon God. Numbers 23:19 says, "God is not a man, that he should lie." God has not broken one promise to His people. God will not let one word fall to the ground from His precious Word and promises.

Second, we see a **Lack of Trust.** They did not believe that God would take care of them ("to fall by the sword, that our wives and our children should be a prey"). They presumed God had evil intentions toward them. They did not learn from Pharaoh that it is never good to harden your neck after seeing God's judgment. If you trust God, then let Him have His way with you! Although God had kept them safe in the wilderness, they felt it was now up to them to survive. They were still unhappy with God's judgment upon them for their disobedience. Galatians 3:1–3 says it all: "O foolish Galatians, who hath bewitched you, that ye should not obey the truth, before whose eyes Jesus Christ hath been evidently set forth, crucified among you? This only would I learn of you, Received ye the Spirit by the works of the law, or by the hearing of faith? Are ye so foolish? *having begun in the Spirit, are ye now made perfect by the flesh?*" As John Newton wrote in "Amazing Grace," "'Tis grace hath brought me safe thus far, and grace will lead me home."

Third, we see a **Lack of Thought.** They didn't think God knew what He was doing ("were it not better for us to return into Egypt?"). Many people struggle with this and wonder, "Well, why doesn't God just defeat the devil?" or even, "If God really knew what I needed, then He would . . ." Don't quit believing! God does know all things! He does know how you feel! He desires your well-being! You must believe that He alone knows the way. The Bible says in Job 23:10, "But *he knoweth the way that I take:* when he hath tried me, I shall come forth as gold." God knows exactly what you need and where you need to go. God said in Isaiah 55:9, "For as the heavens are higher than the earth, so are my ways higher than your ways, and my thoughts than your thoughts." God knows best!

TOPICS: Faith, Patience, Trust

DAILY BIBLE READING: Numbers 16–18

TODAY'S VERSE: Numbers 17:8: "And it came to pass, that on the morrow Moses went into the tabernacle of witness; and, behold, the rod of Aaron for the house of Levi was budded, and brought forth buds, and bloomed blossoms, and yielded almonds."

AARON'S ROD IS A FASCINATING tool that God used for His honor and glory throughout the Exodus from Egypt and the wanderings in the wilderness. Aaron's rod was a priestly rod and signified the power of God Himself. It was with Aaron's rod that Moses and Aaron went into the presence of Pharaoh, casting the rod down to see it become a serpent. As it consumed the other rods, it signified the *ruling* power of God. It was Aaron's rod, in Numbers 17, that budded and blossomed. It signified the *resurrection* power of God. It was also Aaron's rod that was placed in the mercy seat and signified the *redemptive* power of God. Here are a few thoughts from our verse this morning that might help us see Aaron's rod in a new light.

First, we see the **Possibility of Fruit Bearing** ("and brought forth buds"). Budding is a very important step in the fruit-bearing process. God thought it important to put these little buds in here for a reason. Some would just be satisfied that the rod brought forth almonds, but that is not all that God did. He also had it bring forth buds! The almonds it bore were not the end of the process: the picture of God sending buds on the rod tells us that this is just a beginning! God's work would continue. Philippians 1:6 says, "Being confident of this very thing, that he which hath begun a good work in you will perform it until the day of Jesus Christ." God has done a work in your life to bring forth fruit, but it is not a one-time thing! God has done that work and produced buds in your life as well, buds that will continue to bring the possibilities of God's continued miracles. The buds are the first steps of spiritual fruit.

Second, we see the **Promise of Fruit Bearing** ("and bloomed blossoms"). Not all buds are for fruit, but all blossoms are! Some buds are just for leaves. Every flower, however, is a little piece of fruit. As a matter of fact, if you eat the blossoms of some fruit trees, you can actually taste the fruit of that tree! Yes, something may happen to that flower to cause it not to bring forth fruit. A storm may destroy it. A frost may kill it. A pruner may pluck it in order to give the other fruit a chance to grow more fully. But every blossom is in all actuality a God-given promise of future fruit. One of our favorite pastimes in the spring is to ride through the orchards here in the Grand Valley. They are so beautiful while they are in bloom. The word in this passage translated "bloomed" means, "to twinkle, a radiance." Start twinkling and radiating the glory of God in your life! The blooms themselves are the telltale sign of the crop the farmer can expect to yield.

Third, we see the **Production of Fruit Bearing** ("and yielded almonds"). This fruit had absolutely nothing to do with Aaron or Moses. If you remember, Aaron's rod was just a rod. He and Moses hadn't planted it, watered it, or sheltered it. God brought forth the fruit! It would do you well to allow God to bring forth the fruit in your life. You cannot produce it! That is why it is called the Fruit of the Spirit. The word for "yielded" means "ripen." This fruit was exactly what it should be to bring satisfaction to the One who desired it! There is nothing so disappointing as fruit that is green and not yet ready, but here we find that God will make it ready! God can ripen fruit instantly in your life, but usually, it takes time. Let God have His way, and allow Him the time to work in your heart.

TOPICS: Blessing, Fruit, Maturity

February 21

DAILY BIBLE READING: Numbers 19–21

TODAY'S VERSE: Numbers 21:8: "And the Lᴏʀᴅ said unto Moses, Make thee a fiery serpent, and set it upon a pole: and it shall come to pass, that every one that is bitten, when he looketh upon it, shall live."

THE STORY OF THE FIERY SERPENTS and the brazen serpent carries a great and powerful picture of what God planned to do one day upon Calvary.

The Symbol of the Serpent ("And the Lᴏʀᴅ said unto Moses, Make thee a fiery serpent, and set it upon a pole"). This symbol of judgment and healing was easily seen by the people as the brazen serpent was placed upon a pole. Brass is always a symbol of God's judgment in the Bible, yet this story includes a twist on that theme. Even today, that brazen serpent is a symbol for us: an ambulance, almost without exception, will have a picture or symbol of a serpent upon a pole. That symbol refers to this biblical story of Moses and the fiery serpents. It is a symbol of *honor*. Paramedics are heroes to the many people whose lives they have saved. It is also a symbol of *health*. The serpent on a pole indicates dedication to full and complete healing. And it is a symbol of *help* to those who are in need. What a blessing to those in an emergency situation to hear the siren, see the lights, and behold that wonderful symbol!

The Sight of the Serpent ("and it shall come to pass, that every one that is bitten, when he looketh upon it . . . "). The bitten people had to look on the serpent. That was an act of faith. No doubt there were some who thought they might get better on their own. Maybe a salve or a compress might work, they hoped. Yet nothing but an obedient look of faith upon that which God had provided would save them from certain death. This was also a "whosoever will" opportunity! Jesus is asking you today, "Wilt thou be made whole?"

The Saving of the Saviour ("when he looketh upon it, shall live"). Jesus was placed upon a pole, the old rugged cross, in judgment for man's sin. John 3:14 speaks of the symbol of Moses' serpent and of Christ: "And as Moses lifted up the serpent in the wilderness, even so must the Son of man be lifted up." It is Christ upon the cross, or pole, that defeats the serpent's bite. I would like to remind you of the promise made by God in Genesis 3:15: "Thou [the serpent] shalt bruise his heel." Only Christ can heal the bite of the old Serpent!

TOPICS: Faith, Healing, Help, Hope, Salvation

R. CHRIS HANKS

DAILY BIBLE READING: Numbers 22-23

TODAY'S VERSE: Numbers 22:5: "He sent messengers therefore unto Balaam the son of Beor to Pethor, which is by the river of the land of the children of his people, to call him, saying, Behold, there is a people come out from Egypt: behold, they cover the face of the earth, and they abide over against me."

THESE CHAPTERS TELL of a wicked spiritualistic mercenary named Balaam and of King Balak of Moab. Balak had never seen, met, or spoken with the children of Israel, yet he hated them. He was willing to do anything to curse them and get them away from his country. You will find that some will hate you though they have never seen, met, or spoken with you before. Today's passage may help you understand their anger a little better.

Balak Did Not Like Them Because of Where They Came From ("Behold, there is a people come out from Egypt"). This was a problem with their **pardon**. Many people do not like Christians just because God has delivered them. As with the Israelites, the very thing that has brought you out is the death of the Firstborn and the safety of the blood upon you. Enemies of God hate anything about you that might show that you are one of God's chosen people. They hate to see the testimony of the cross upon any heart and life. Don't let that stop you! Thank God for pulling you out of that horrible pit and setting your feet upon a rock. Remember when God brought you out of Egypt with "an high hand," and thank God for His mercy and grace!

Balak Did Not Like Them Because of God's Blessing in Their Lives ("behold, they cover the face of the earth"). This was a problem with their **prosperity**. God had blessed the Israelites and multiplied them greatly. Here they were on a journey, and all Balak could see was their testimony! Look around at God's blessings in your life and thank Him today! Do not be surprised if others become angry at the work of the Lord and His blessing in your life. They are ruled by their own anger and jealousy. They try to satisfy their envy by buying things. Yet, as they accumulate material possessions, they are still tormented by the life you live in *peace* and *joy* in the Holy Ghost!

Balak Did Not Like Them Because of What He Was Reminded of Every Time He Saw Them ("and they abide over against me"). This was a problem with their **pleasure**. Balak did not like their being so close. He did not like their camping right outside his back window. Every time he looked at them, he was reminded of God and His care for His people. Every time they stood at their cubicles and he saw their smiling faces, he hated it. Every time he passed them in the break room with a cup of coffee and he overheard their witness and testimony, his anger built. Every time he came to a stoplight and heard the music from their car singing the praises of Jehovah God, it afflicted both his mind and spirit. Of course, you can see the facts of the biblical story—but I sure do believe this Scripture carries great application for us in our world today!

TOPICS: Blessing, Conviction, Joy, Pardon, Prosperity, Testimony

February 23

DAILY BIBLE READING: Numbers 24–26

TODAY'S VERSE: Numbers 24:11: "Therefore now flee thou to thy place: I thought to promote thee unto great honour; but, lo, the Lord hath kept thee back from honour."

BALAAM WAS A PROPHETIC MERCENARY who would hire himself out to the highest bidder to make a buck. He is best known for holding a conversation with his own donkey in which it was proven that the donkey had more spiritual perception than he did! Balaam was an enemy of Israel. If he could have cursed them for Balak, he would have—but God would not allow him to do so. Since he could not curse Israel outright, Balak counseled with Balaam in how to pull them away from God. When the Israelites finally caught up with Balaam, they killed him as an enemy. Our verse shows us the frustrations of Balak with Balaam because he would not curse the people of God. I believe it holds some important thoughts for us today so that we might discern the ways of the wicked world and the means they use to fight their battles.

He Tried to Assign Shame in Obeying God ("Therefore now flee thou to thy place"). This was King Balak pitching a fit because he did not get his way. He tried to shame Balaam by telling him, "Since you won't do it my way, you can just leave, because I am the one in charge." Balak had brought Balaam to himself with great honor and fanfare; now the prophet could leave in shame and disgrace. For a real child of God, there is no embarrassment or humiliation in taking a stand and obeying God's Word. Moses determined that he desired the "reproach of Christ" more than the "treasures in Egypt" (Hebrews 11:26). Paul said it like this in 2 Timothy 1:12: "For the which cause I also suffer these things: nevertheless *I am not ashamed:* for I know whom I have believed, and am persuaded that he is able to keep that which I have committed unto him against that day."

He Tried to Assign Sorrow in Obeying God ("I thought to promote thee unto great honour"). This was Balak's bargaining chip and manipulation tool. The devil has used the carrot of promotion many times to get his way and destroy people in the process. This goes to the baseness of our fleshly desires, for it presumes on man's greed. How many times have we given in to the temptations of, "You don't know what you are missing! Everybody's doing it! You would like it! You'll be glad you did it!" Paul said in Philippians 3:7, "But what things were gain to me, those I counted loss for Christ." I don't know about you, but there is not anything I miss about living a life without God! I am not disappointed that God pulled me out of the pit and the miry clay to set my feet upon a rock and establish my goings (Psalm 40:2).

He Tried to Assign Shortcomings to Obeying God ("but, lo, the Lord hath kept thee back from honour"). This argument hurts sometimes because it appeals to our pride. The Balak in your life is saying, "God doesn't even love you! If He did, He would honor you, treat you better, and bless you more than others!" But our blessing will come in heaven. We see this problem plainly in Psalm 73 when the psalmist pines for the way of the wicked in verse 3: "For I was envious at the foolish, when I saw the prosperity of the wicked." We hear the inner struggle of his thoughts, and finally he comes to himself when he enters the house of God in verses 17 and 18: "Until I went into the sanctuary of God; then understood I their end. Surely thou didst set them in slippery places: thou castedst them down into destruction." When he beholds their end and discerns that their prosperity is nothing but a house of cards, he says again in verse 22, "So foolish was I, and ignorant: I was as a beast before thee." We must be looking for something far greater than what the wicked have embraced as their hope, for it will consume them in the end.

TOPICS: Manipulation, Perseverance, Reward, Wicked

R. CHRIS HANKS

DAILY BIBLE READING: Numbers 27–28

TODAY'S VERSE: Numbers 27:20: "And thou shalt put some of thine honour upon him, that all the congregation of the children of Israel may be obedient."

IN TODAY'S READING, we read of the ceremony of transferring power from Moses to Joshua. Moses would die in Mount Nebo, but Joshua and the people of Israel would push on and possess the Promised Land. This verse is God's instruction to Moses as to how he should make the transfer to give the people a sense of security and delight in seeing and respecting their new leader. This was a great principle of leadership, shown by Moses in passing the torch to the new Director of Operations. God was the One who determined how this should be done and how it would affect both Joshua and the people.

It Was an Incredible Honor ("And thou shalt put some of thine honour upon him"). We are talking here about Moses' honor. This was the man who received the commandments that were carved out of the rock by the finger of God. This was the man who spoke with God face-to-face. This was the man who had to wear a veil on his face as he talked with the people because God's glory shone so brightly from him. This was the man whom God used to bring judgment upon Pharaoh by many different miracles and plagues. This was the man who raised his rod and brought the people through the Red Sea on dry ground. This was the man who smote the rock, and water came out to satisfy the nation of Israel. All of these things were not done by the power of Moses himself, but by the power of God upon him. What an honor to stand by Moses and receive *his* honor in the sight of the people!

It Was an Inclusive Honor ("that all the congregation of the children of Israel"). The transfer of leadership was not done in a private ceremony, but before the congregation. They needed to witness it themselves. There are times for private ceremonies, and there are times for public ceremonies. This needed to be done publicly so there could be no false accusations, no misunderstood action or situations, and no false allegations of self-exaltation. The people of Israel were to observe the transfer and participate in Joshua's honor. Isn't that the picture we have with Christ? The Old Testament name for the New Testament *Jesus* is the Hebrew name *Joshua!* We will be allowed to see Christ receive His honor and glory, and then we will enjoy it with Him for eternity! We can hear it in John 17:24: "Father, I will that they also, *whom thou hast given me, be with me where I am; that they may behold my glory, which thou hast given me:* for thou lovedst me before the foundation of the world." Hallelujah!

It Was an Instructed Honor ("may be obedient"). God always has a reason for everything He does. God's reason for Moses giving honor to Joshua was the good of the people that they might be obedient. Even today, God has provided His Word to be read by all and delivered by His pastors and preachers for the obedience of His people. Christ in John 15:10 gives us the encouragement to obey God: "If ye keep my commandments, ye shall abide in my love; even as I have kept my Father's commandments, and abide in his love." Everything that God does is for us, so that we might hear His Word and do it with all our might.

TOPICS: Honor, Leadership, Obedience

DAILY BIBLE READING: Numbers 29–31

TODAY'S VERSE: Numbers 31:16: "Behold, these caused the children of Israel, through the counsel of Balaam, to commit trespass against the Lord in the matter of Peor, and there was a plague among the congregation of the Lord."

THE KEY TO UNDERSTANDING today's verse is the one just before it, which said, "And Moses said unto them, Have ye saved all the women alive?" Moses could not believe what was going on! What were they thinking? Were they going to allow the enemies of the Lord to continue to live? These were the people who had stolen away their hearts and perverted their minds away from the Lord. We need to get serious about our Christian life and see sin through the eyes of God. Here is what the Bible says about dealing with sin and evil in our lives.

We must understand that **Sin Has a Plan for Our Lives** ("Behold, these caused the children of Israel, *through the counsel of Balaam . . .*"). Don't think for a minute that temptation is a happy-go-lucky fellow who just happens to show up at different times by chance. This is all part of a grand plan that the devil has for your life. It is not always a *devilish* influence, but it can also be a *selfish* influence. So many times we think that only God has a plan for our lives. If you do not follow God's plan and obey His will and His Word, then you are following sin's plan for your life. God has made this truth evident by many Scriptures, including Romans 14:23: "For whatsoever is not of faith is sin."

Second, we must understand that **Sin Has a Purpose for Our Lives** ("to commit trespass against the Lord in the matter of Peor"). In other words, sin has a reason for you to commit sin against God. Sin *always* desires your defilement! This is an assault upon your relationship with God! Isaiah 59:2 says, "But your iniquities have separated between you and your God, and your sins have hid his face from you, that he will not hear." The devil does not like your fear of God, your reliance upon God, or your trust in God. He wants to cut off God's power in your life, and the only way he can do that is to separate you from God by sin.

Third, we must understand that **Sin Has a Punishment for Our Lives** ("and there was a plague among the congregation of the Lord"). Rather than being surrounded by the blessing and the favor of God, sin desires your life to be littered and destroyed by the punishment it will bring upon you. The word for "plague" here means, "pestilence, to defeat." Rather than you being the victor, sin will be the victor over you. Second Peter 2:19 articulates this truth very well: "While they promise them liberty, they themselves are the servants of corruption: *for of whom a man is overcome, of the same is he brought in bondage.*" So much more awaits the one who will obey the Lord and receive His blessings!

TOPICS: Defilement, Destruction, Judgment, Sin, Warfare

DAILY BIBLE READING: Numbers 32–33

TODAY'S VERSE: Numbers 32:7: "And wherefore discourage ye the heart of the children of Israel from going over into the land which the LORD hath given them?"

TODAY'S VERSE ASKS a question in response to Reuben and Gad, who had asked for their portion of the land to stay on this side of the Jordan River. They were asking for permission not to enter the Promised Land! Eventually, this arrangement was allowed, but they had to commit to fight for the Promised Land even though they would not live in it. It amazes me when children of God just reject His promises. For God to give and offer them His best and then for them to say to Him, "No, I don't want that" is the epitome of *ingratitude toward the gift of God, iniquity against the grace of God,* and *indignation against the glory of God.* Verse 6 ended with the question, "Shall your brethren go to war, and shall ye sit here?," telling a great deal about many people. They don't want the war, but they also don't want the Promised Land! In our churches today, however, many have chosen not to participate in the war, but they still want the Promised Land! They want the good things of God but do not want to obey the Lord and join the fight. This kind of disobedience affects others as well as ourselves.

Their Disobedience Would Bring Discouragement to God's People ("And wherefore *discourage* ye the heart of the children of Israel?"). The word for "discourage" means "to refuse, forbid, dissuade, or neutralize." Sadly, we don't have much need of neutralizing God's people today! We are living in an impotent day concerning the power of our homes and our churches. We have been neutralized by our own *selfish lusts,* our own *savorless living,* and our own *sinful labors.* Let us not bring discouragement to the hearts of God's people by not obeying His Word. Israel was discouraged by being made to believe that their enemies were bigger and better than either they or their God. Deuteronomy 1:28 says, "Whither shall we go up? our brethren have discouraged our heart, saying, The people is greater and taller than we; the cities are great and walled up to heaven; and moreover we have seen the sons of the Anakims there." New converts need to see our unwavering obedience. Children need to see our reckless abandon in following the Word of God. Church members need to see our commitment to godliness. Our commitment to God's way is also a commitment to one another! Let's encourage one another in obeying His Word!

Their Disobedience Would Battle the Desires of God's People ("And wherefore discourage ye *the heart* of the children of Israel?"). If Israel's heart grew too discouraged, they might never have had the desire to go into the Promised Land. Seeing Gad and Reuben staying behind, it would have been easy for them to say, "We can't do it without them." When people are discouraged from serving the Lord, it will affect their desire to serve the Lord. Psalm 73:25 should be our motto: "Whom have I in heaven but thee? and there is none upon earth that I desire beside thee." Don't allow your desire toward God to be discouraged from serving Him, and don't defeat the desire of other Christians by discouraging them by your disobedience.

Their Disobedience Would Bring the Defeat of God's People ("from going over into the land which the LORD hath given them"). That is all the devil wants: to keep you out of the Promised Land. You might think there is nothing the devil can do to you now that you are saved, but let me tell you something: he might not be able to keep you out of heaven, but he can keep you from living the victorious Christian life and from experiencing the promises God has given to those who will obey His word! Isn't that in itself defeat? To keep me from the promises and blessings that God has prepared for me and desires me to have is a great form of defeat. Don't allow the devil to keep you from experiencing the blessing of the Lord in your life!

TOPICS: Defeat, Discouragement, Disobedience, Rejection, Victory

DAILY BIBLE READING: Numbers 34–36

TODAY'S VERSE: Numbers 35:9: "And the Lord spake unto Moses, saying."

THIS PHRASE IS FOUND word for word in the books of Exodus, Leviticus, and Numbers, for a total of seventy-two verses. Sometimes we bypass the simplest of thoughts in our meditations, and we miss the significance of things so easy and common, even taking them for granted. But there is more here than may immediately meet the eye.

First, we see the **Grace of God's Arrangement** ("And the Lord *spake*"). Just the fact that God spoke at all to man is an act of His divine grace. The word for "spake" has a root meaning of "to arrange." An almighty thought process went into arranging things in such a way as to speak to the heart of man. God has arranged His word in a certain way, and it should not be tampered with in even the simplest form! In other words, *how* God said a thing is just as important as *what* He said! It was the same for me growing up in my home. *How* my dad told me to do something was just as important as *what* he told me to do! Don't study the Bible just to learn trivia. Trivia is concerned only with the "what"; if you learn "how" God said it, you will begin to see the mind of God, His plan, and the arrangement of His own precious Word!

Second, we see the **Grace of God's Acceptance** ("And the Lord spake unto *Moses*"). God spoke to Moses! God accepted Moses! Some might think that was normal. Some might even think that it was expected. It was not. It was *grace!* God did not have to speak to anybody. God accepted Moses because of His own plan and His own pleasure. Ephesians 1:6 says it like this: "To the praise of the glory of *his grace, wherein he hath made us accepted in the beloved.*" We can and do have the same grace that was afforded to Moses. We can hear the Word of God. We can feel the breath of God in our services as His word is both preached and taught.

Third, we see the **Grace of God's Answer** ("And the Lord spake unto Moses, *saying*"). The word for "saying" has the root meaning of "to answer." When God answers, you can count on three things. It will be a *definite* answer. God does not walk the fence on anything. God's answers are clear and plain. His way and His Word are not of vagueness and obscurity. Psalm 119:105 says, "Thy word is a lamp unto my feet, and a light unto my path." God's answer will also be a *doctrinal* answer. Mark 4:2 says, "And he taught them many things by parables, and *said unto them in his doctrine.*" Everything Jesus said was connected to His doctrine. God will never tell you anything that goes against His own Word. God's answer will also be a *divine* answer. Think about that: it will be an answer from God! And it will even be an answer that can impart to us His divine nature and way. Second Peter 1:4 says, "Whereby are given unto us exceeding great and precious promises: that by these *ye might be partakers of the divine nature,* having escaped the corruption that is in the world through lust." Hear the answer of God today in a new light, a new fervor, and a new desire!

TOPICS: Doctrine, Grace, Inspiration, Word of God

DAILY BIBLE READING: Deuteronomy 1–2

TODAY'S VERSE: Deuteronomy 1:33: "Who went in the way before you, to search you out a place to pitch your tents in, in fire by night, to shew you by what way ye should go, and in a cloud by day."

AS MOSES IS SPEAKING in this second giving of the law, he shares with the people all that God has done for them. We all need to know that God cares about us and all that we do. This verse tells us that God went to great lengths in order to care for the children of Israel. We have seen the same in our lives in the many times God acts in our behalf.

First, we see that God goes to **Search You a Place** ("Who went in the way before you, to search you out a place to pitch your tents in"). The word "before" in this verse means "face." God has already stared every adversary you will ever have in the face. Every bit of suffering you will endure, God already knows about. Job 23:10 says, *"But he knoweth the way that I take:* when he hath tried me, I shall come forth as gold." Not only does God know the way that I take, but it is the way that He prepared for me to take! God brought Israel into a place where they could *rest*. It was a place that they could *recline*. It was a place that they could *refresh*. Psalm 23:5 says, "Thou preparest a table before me in the presence of mine enemies." On your journey, you will find that God will take you to a place for a period of time to learn a specific lesson. That place has been well thought and well sought by God for your life.

Second, we see that God goes to **Show You a Path** ("to shew you by what way ye should go"). He doesn't just have a place where He wants you to end up and it is up to you to get there. No, He will show you the path that will allow you to make it to the destination of His will. Isaiah 30:21 says, "And thine ears shall hear a word behind thee, saying, This is the way, walk ye in it, when ye turn to the right hand, and when ye turn to the left." He will walk with you every step and every mile along the rugged way. In the time of trouble, God does not go inside for lemonade while He watches you struggle through every trial and heartache. One thing to remember is that God really does want you in the center of His will, and He will show you the way you are to go. I remember when we went camping as youth. While we were walking, whether in the day or at night, I had no idea where I was or where I was going. The leader knew how to get to the campsite, and he showed us the way. All we had to do was follow! Some of you may be struggling with direction in your life, not knowing where to turn or where to go. Wait on the Lord, for He will surely show you the way!

Third, we see that God wants to **Show You His Presence** ("in fire by night . . . and in a cloud by day"). God's whole purpose in leading them this way was to confirm to His people His presence in their lives. How often we fail to see the presence of God at work in our lives! Even if Israel was not traveling, what a blessing it was to look at the tabernacle, see the cloud of smoke or pillar of fire, and say, "God's presence is still here!" The key to our relationship with God is not just in trying to get somewhere, but in being with Him! Enjoy His presence today.

TOPICS: Direction, Guidance, Preparation, Presence of God, Trust

DAILY BIBLE READING: Deuteronomy 3–4

TODAY'S VERSE: Deuteronomy 4:7: "For what nation is there so great, who hath God so nigh unto them, as the Lord our God is in all things that we call upon him for?"

THERE IS NO DOUBT that God's people are dear to His heart. The greatness of Israel is purely dependent upon God's goodness to them. Certainly, the greatness of America can only be attributed to God's goodness as well. In this verse, Moses is recognizing God's blessings on Israel and connecting the dots back to the Lord in the sight of the people. It is so easy for man to think that all good things have come as a result of his own efforts and plans. Before our pride carries us away in vanity and senseless self-praise, let us look for the hand of God in every blessing. James 1:17 says, "Every good gift and every perfect gift is from above, and cometh down from the Father of lights, with whom is no variableness, neither shadow of turning." As we ponder this verse, may we acknowledge the goodness of God to us as citizens of a "holy nation" (1 Peter 2:9) and identify the blessings of His faithfulness.

God Has Blessed Us with His Power ("For what nation is there so great?"). The word for "great" in this verse can be used for time, height, length, sound, and might. God has blessed us in each of these areas for His honor and glory. Truly, our "greatness" is dependent upon *His* greatness. This greatness was evident to Moses, and he wanted others to see it for themselves. Not only was it evident to Israel, but it was evident to others as well. Every other nation despised Israel because of God's blessing upon them. Jealousy will cause others to despise the blessing of God upon someone's life. True greatness is not man-made, but God-given.

God Has Blessed Us with His Presence ("who hath God so nigh unto them"). This is the greatest of God's blessings. An old preacher used to say, "The blessings of God are not necessarily proof of the presence of God." Many churches are caught up in the numbers they have in attendance or the activities they perform. They think God is more interested in what they do than He is in giving them His presence. Many people in the Bible had God's blessing, but it was not until later that they had God's presence. Don't believe me? Why not take a long look at the lives of Abraham and Jacob? They had God's blessing early on, but they did not enjoy the presence of God until many years later. It was not until then that they realized that the real blessing was in His presence and not just in prosperity.

David knew he desired God's presence more than God's blessing, for he said in Psalm 84:10, "For a day in thy courts is better than a thousand. I had rather be a doorkeeper in the house of my God, than to dwell in the tents of wickedness." He said again in Psalm 16:11, "Thou wilt shew me the path of life: *in thy presence is fulness of joy; at thy right hand there are pleasures for evermore.*" Instead of praying for God's blessing upon your home, why not pray for God to be in your home? We do not need God's blessings upon our churches, because we have, as a whole, lost His presence. We should not be looking for "good things," but for God Himself.

God Has Blessed Us in Our Prayers ("as the Lord our God is in all things that we call upon him for"). If God's presence is with us, then we can ask for things according to His will. Notice that the point of this verse was not that God was answering Israel's prayers, but that God was with them in their prayers! Hear the verse again: "*Who hath God so nigh unto them, as the Lord our God is* in all things that we call upon him for?" If God is with us in our prayers, we will most certainly receive answers. Too often, we ask God for things in which He has no particular interest. James 4:3 tells us, "Ye ask, and receive not, because ye ask amiss, that ye may consume it upon your lusts." If God's desires would become our desires, we would begin receiving answers to our prayers!

TOPICS: Blessing, God's Presence, Jealousy, Prayer

R. CHRIS HANKS

DAILY BIBLE READING: Deuteronomy 5–7

TODAY'S VERSE: Deuteronomy 7:8: "But because the Lord loved you, and because he would keep the oath which he had sworn unto your fathers, hath the Lord brought you out with a mighty hand, and redeemed you out of the house of bondmen, from the hand of Pharaoh king of Egypt."

I LOVE THIS VERSE because it tells me that God loves me! Perhaps the most loved of all songs in the world is the children's song, "Jesus Loves Me." Doesn't it lift your spirit to know that God loves you today?

I once heard of a preacher who told children and teens in a Christian school chapel that God did not love them anymore. He said that John 3:16 said, "For God so *loved* the world." Since "loved" is past tense, the verse meant He did not love them anymore. This preacher said that God loved them all that He could love them while He was on Calvary. To some nitpicky theologian, this argument might seem to have critical merit; however, it is completely opposed to Scripture and is a lie from the pit of hell! God said in Malachi 3:6, "For I am the Lord, I change not." If God ever did love us, my friend, He still loves us today! First John 4:8 says, "He that loveth not knoweth not God; for *God is love.*" If God ever stops loving, then He will stop being God. Love is not just a character trait for God, but is the essence of His being!

There are two aspects to God's love for us. First there is how God feels about us (He loves us). Second, there is how God feels about Himself (He will not let His name fall to the ground). My friend, don't ever forget that whatever God has done in your life, He has done because of His love for you. Moreover, He will be found true to every promise that He has made!

He Will Convincingly Promote ("hath the Lord brought you out with a mighty hand"). Moses reminds the people of Israel of the time when God brought them out of the land of Egypt. Exodus 14:8 says, "And the Lord hardened the heart of Pharaoh king of Egypt, and he pursued after the children of Israel: and the children of Israel went out with an high hand." Did your life change when you got saved? What a promotion! Psalm 40:2 says, "He brought me up also out of an horrible pit, out of the miry clay, and set my feet upon a rock, and established my goings."

He Will Completely Pardon ("and redeemed you out of the house of bondmen"). Do you remember how God redeemed His people out of Egypt? God brought the judgment of the death of the firstborn in the land of Egypt, and God redeemed Israel that same night by the Passover sacrifice. It was in the Passover that God told His people in Exodus 12:13, "And when I see the blood, I will pass over you, and the plague shall not be upon you to destroy you, when I smite the land of Egypt." God has redeemed us out of the house of sin by His own blood, paid the entire debt, and pardoned us with the offering of His own blood!

He Will Clearly Prevail ("from the hand of Pharaoh king of Egypt"). What a blessing to know the hand from which God has delivered us! God wanted Israel to know without a doubt whom He had defeated! God has done the same thing for us. Revelation 12:9 says, "And the great dragon was cast out, that old serpent, called the Devil, and Satan, which deceiveth the whole world: he was cast out into the earth, and his angels were cast out with him." God wants us to know that He has the victory over every foe and has vanquished every enemy!

TOPICS: Blood, Deliverance, Devil, Pardon, Redemption, Salvation, Victory

DAILY BIBLE READING: Deuteronomy 8–10

TODAY'S VERSE: Deuteronomy 8:16: "Who fed thee in the wilderness with manna, which thy fathers knew not, that he might humble thee, and that he might prove thee, to do thee good at thy latter end."

TODAY, WE LOOK at the ministry of manna. I hope that your heart will be touched as you receive manna from this devotion—a piece of bread from God to help you throughout the day.

First, we see the **Privilege of the Manna** ("Who fed thee in the wilderness with manna, *which thy fathers knew not*"). The manna was a gift that God gave just for Israel! The Hebrew word *manna* means "whatness." They had no idea what it was! The last part of Jeremiah 33:3 says, " . . . and shew thee great and mighty things, which thou knowest not." Manna was a privilege for them in its *availability*. All the people had to do was gather it! It was a privilege for them to *see*. The Bible says the color was beautiful and likened to the color of bdellium, a fragrant gum that was extracted from a tree.[1] It was a privilege for them to *taste*. The Bible says it tasted like wafers made with honey, or like fresh oil. In speaking of the manna, Psalm 78:25 says, "Man did eat angels' food." What a privilege God had given them!

Second, we see the **Purpose of the Manna** ("that he might humble thee"). God wanted to teach the Israelites about trust. We all need to be humbled, for it is when we are humbled before Almighty God that we realize that our abilities and efforts are not enough. God is willing to go to great lengths to humble us so that we may rest and trust in Him. Deuteronomy 8:3 says, "And he humbled thee, and suffered thee to hunger." Part of God's reason for humbling His people was to make them hunger. It was a mercy of God to send them through the hard time in order to teach them reliance upon Him. What do you hunger for today? Let that hunger drive you to God. Matthew 5:6 says, "Blessed are they which do hunger and thirst after righteousness: for they shall be filled."

Third, we see the **Proving of the Manna** ("and that he might prove thee"). Manna was not the end result of what God was doing in the people's lives; it was just the beginning. Manna was the test. Deuteronomy 8:2 says the reason God proved the people was "to know what was in thine heart, whether thou wouldest keep his commandments, or no." This testing was not for God, "for he knew what was in man" (John 2:25). This test was for the people. Job 23:10 says, "But he knoweth the way that I take: *when he hath tried me, I shall come forth as gold.*" This is a purifying trial, a purging trial, though it may be a painful trial. God's desire is to prove you and your worth and make you better.

Fourth, we see the **Pleasure of the Manna** ("to do thee good at thy latter end"). God wanted so much more for the people of Israel. There was so much He wanted to do for them following the work of the manna. There are great things that God wants to do in the latter end. I know that it is hard to wait. Patience may be a virtue, but it's not *my* virtue! God has a finished plan for your life "to do thee good." Wait on the Lord, and you will see that His way is greater than you ever imagined!

TOPICS: Privilege, Proving, Provision, Testing, Word of God

---

1   Merill F. Unger, *Unger's Bible Dictionary* (Chicago: Moody Press, 1985), 733.

DAILY BIBLE READING: Deuteronomy 11–13

TODAY'S VERSE: Deuteronomy 11:10: "For the land, whither thou goest in to possess it, is not as the land of Egypt, from whence ye came out, where thou sowedst thy seed, and wateredst it with thy foot, as a garden of herbs."

NOTICE THE BEGINNING of today's verse: "For the land, whither thou goest in to possess it, *is not as the land of Egypt, from whence ye came out.*" Things are different now than they were before we got saved! Life isn't, nor should it be, the same! Everything has changed.

First, there was a land from which they were **Commanded to Depart** ("from whence ye came out"). They were sent out of that land by the Word of God. *God's blessing* would not rest there. *God's battles* would not be fought there. And *God's beauty* would not be seen there. Galatians 5:17 reads, "For the flesh lusteth against the Spirit, and the Spirit against the flesh: and these are contrary the one to the other: so that ye cannot do the things that ye would." We must leave the land of worldly desires and fleshly lusts that we might serve the Lord in freedom.

Second, there was a land they were **Commissioned to Defeat** ("whither thou goest in to possess it"). God had already promised them victory as they went into the Promised Land, and all they had to do was fight the battle! The same is true for us. God has promised us victory; we just need to fight the battle! In this verse, Moses told the people that the spiritual life was not one of ease and luxury. The Christian life has never been about sitting under a fanning servant while eating grapes and having a pedicure! The picture God paints for us is one of a faithful soldier with a bloodstained sword, following the Captain of his faith into a great battle that is certain to be a great triumph!

Third, there is a land we are **Compelled to Desire** ("is not as the land of Egypt"). This is a land that God has promised to us. God has something much better for me and you, and it is a place of His own choosing and design. I believe that God is preparing us a place in heaven, but I also believe that He has a place of blessing for us here upon this earth as we serve Him. We can live the victorious Christian life right now and experience the many blessings of the promised land of God's blessings upon this earth!

TOPICS: Battle, Desire, Victory, War, World

DAILY BIBLE READING: Deuteronomy 14–16

TODAY'S VERSE: Deuteronomy 15:15: "And thou shalt remember that thou wast a bondman in the land of Egypt, and the LORD thy God redeemed thee: therefore I command thee this thing to day."

THIS REMINDER ABOUT the children of Israel being bondmen in Egypt is used a number of times in Scripture. We all need to be reminded of what God has done for us through the blood of Christ. The word for "remember" in this verse means "to mark." Let us mark some things so as never to forget them.

We Should Never Forget Our Plight ("And thou shalt remember that thou wast a bondman"). We were without hope and without help. When you belong to someone else, you are completely at his or her mercy. I don't know about you, but I would say my sin had no mercy upon me. My own Pharaoh was a hard taskmaster. It dominated my heart and my life. This was not just a life of *servitude,* but of *slavery.*

We Should Never Forget Our Place ("in the land of Egypt"). Have you forgotten the "horrible pit" from whence God took you? Yes, the world goes down to fleshly Egypt and is enamored by its trappings and ornamented, selfish ways of living. They are mesmerized by its mantra of "Pleasure, Passion, and Plenty, to All Who So Desire." Yet they do not recognize that the dead are there, nor do they sense the regrets of experiencing its delicate dainties. They do not see that every piece of lace will become a noose, every branch of every tree an arrow, and all of its fine silks and linens a shroud.

We Should Never Forget Our Pardon ("and the LORD thy God redeemed thee"). Jehovah God Himself has bought us back and paid the price of our pardon. Thank God for Jesus and His ministry to buy back that which is unlovely for His honor and glory. Now that He has set me free, I have a new hope and a new view of God and His love. John 8:36 says, "If the Son therefore shall make you free, ye shall be free indeed." How can I ever forget the price that my loving God has paid for me? I am greatly indebted to Him for His wonderful work of mercy and grace.

TOPICS: Deliverance, Remembrance, Salvation, Slavery

R. CHRIS HANKS

DAILY BIBLE READING: Deuteronomy 17–20

TODAY'S VERSE: Deuteronomy 20:4: "For the LORD your God is he that goeth with you, to fight for you against your enemies, to save you."

SOMETIMES I STARE my foes in the eye and wonder if I have a chance! What a comfort to know that God has committed His strength and dedicated His resolve to fight for us and promise us victory! Here are a few principles from this verse about what it means to a child of God.

He Has Become My Companion ("For the LORD your God is he that goeth with you"). What a thought—to have God with you! This has always been in the mind of God; He has always had a desire to be with us. How do we know that? God prophesied in Isaiah that when Christ was born, they would call Him "Immanuel," which means "God with us" (Isaiah 7:14). As we follow the Lord in salvation, we now receive the gift of the Holy Ghost to indwell our hearts. Colossians 1:27 says, "To whom God would make known what is the riches of the glory of this mystery among the Gentiles; *which is Christ in you,* the hope of glory." We now have a *common bond—a family bond.* We now have a *common blood—a freeing blood.* We now have a *common battle—a fighting battle.* This is not just about God going *before* me, but going *with* me. Amos 3:3 says, "Can two walk together, except they be agreed?" What a blessing to know that God is walking with me!

He Has Taken Up My Cause ("to fight for you against your enemies"). God has taken it upon Himself to fight and defeat our enemies for His glory. It sure is good to know that God will fight the battle and give us victory! A wonderful verse is Psalm 56:9: "When I cry unto thee, *then shall mine enemies turn back: this I know; for God is for me.*" So many people think that God is against them, but even God's punishments are to bring us back into His fellowship! All that God has done in your life has happened to increase your faith and to draw you closer to Himself.

He Has Become My Champion ("to save you"). God did not come to help us; He came to save us! He did not come just to give us a little push and relieve a little pressure so we could save ourselves. We were so far down and without hope that He had to come all the way down to save us from certain destruction and complete desolation! Psalm 55:16 says, "As for me, I will call upon God; and the LORD shall save me." To show His love for you and His commitment to give you full and complete victory, I would like to share this verse as well: Psalm 54:7 says, "For he hath delivered me out of all trouble: and mine eye hath seen his desire upon mine enemies."

TOPICS: Battle, Cause, Companionship, Friendship, Victory

DAILY BIBLE READING: Deuteronomy 21–23

TODAY'S VERSE: Deuteronomy 23:5: "Nevertheless the Lord thy God would not hearken unto Balaam; but the Lord thy God turned the curse into a blessing unto thee, because the Lord thy God loved thee."

THOUGH BALAAM WAS SENT to hurt and destroy the children of Israel, God had other plans and blessed them instead. In the midst of a great trial and certain backsliding (for Israel had defiled themselves with the daughters of Moab and shamed themselves among the inhabitants of the land), God still loved them and had a plan for them. Here are a few thoughts about what God did for Israel and what He does for us all the time.

First, we see **God's Choice in Blessing Israel** ("Nevertheless the Lord thy God would not hearken unto Balaam"). Though there were others who desired the ultimate demise of God's people, God chose to bless them instead. There were some setbacks along the way because of their disobedience, but the Lord still chose to bless them because they were His chosen people. Deuteronomy 7:6 says, "For thou art an holy people unto the Lord thy God: the Lord thy God hath chosen thee to be a special people unto himself, above all people that are upon the face of the earth."

Second, we see **God's Change in Blessing Israel** ("but the Lord thy God *turned the curse into a blessing* unto thee"). God can change anything in your life. God had to change some things before He could bless Israel, for they were a cursed people. We have all known many people who have gone through great trials and heartaches, but who will tell you that the hardship became the greatest blessing they have ever received. God has a future glory that He desires to give us. Second Corinthians 4:17 says, "For our light affliction, which is but for a moment, worketh for us a far more exceeding and eternal weight of glory." God has turned the curse of our sin into blessing by promising us a home in heaven with Him!

Third, we see **God's Charity in Blessing Israel** ("because the Lord thy God loved thee"). This is the source and the reason for all that is good for the child of God! God's blessing us always boils down to His love. Romans 8:38–39 says, "For I am persuaded, that neither death, nor life, nor angels, nor principalities, nor powers, nor things present, nor things to come, nor height, nor depth, nor any other creature, shall be able to separate us from the love of God, which is in Christ Jesus our Lord." There is no reason for God to love us; He just does! That is a testimony of His grace. Why has He offered us a pardon, forgiveness, and a home in heaven? Because He loves us! Enjoy the blessing of God, and worship Him because of His love for you today.

TOPICS: Blessing, Care, God's Love, Protection

DAILY BIBLE READING: Deuteronomy 24–27

TODAY'S VERSE: Deuteronomy 25:18: "How he met thee by the way, and smote the hindmost of thee, even all that were feeble behind thee, when thou wast faint and weary; and he feared not God."

THIS STORY IS ABOUT a nation named Amalek. In the prior verse, God said, "Remember what Amalek did unto thee by the way, when ye were come forth out of Egypt." Amalek's actions stirred up the anger of God as He saw the pain and suffering of His people as a result of the destructive nature of this wicked nation. Maybe you think that God has forgotten about the trials you have endured or the sacrifices you have made for His name's sake. Rest assured, God will make things right! Even if you never see it on this side of death's river, you will receive a reward in glory in His presence, and you will enjoy those fruits for eternity. First Peter 3:12 and 14 say, "For the eyes of the Lord are over the righteous, and his ears are open unto their prayers: but the face of the Lord is against them that do evil . . . But and if ye suffer for righteousness' sake, happy are ye: and be not afraid of their terror, neither be troubled." All Israel did to deserve persecution was obey the Lord and follow Him in the wilderness en route to the Promised Land. There may be times when the only thing you do is obey the Lord and trust His Word, and all that seems to find you is trouble and adversity. Let us meditate on today's verse in light of enduring persecution in our Christian lives.

It Was a **Confrontational Act** ("How he met thee by the way"). Israel had not provoked anybody. They were not looking for a fight. They were just following the Lord to the Promised Land. There are times when the fight will be brought to you. No gift, no apology, no attempt to avoid this trouble will help. It is in your enemy's heart to destroy you. What are we to do in this situation, when we have done all we can to avoid conflict? Trust in God and His Word! Psalm 119:95 says, "The wicked have waited for me to destroy me: but I will consider thy testimonies."

It Was a **Consuming Act** ("and smote the hindmost of thee"). Amalek's desire in smiting the hindmost of Israel was to consume all of them. They did not attack the front, for then those behind would have been warned. By the time the front knew about the attack, destruction would be inevitable. The devil and spiritual enemies are not only trying to hurt you, but are looking for a way to consume you.

It Was a **Cowardly Act** ("even all that were feeble behind thee"). Amalek even tried to kill those who had no strength to fight at all. Bullying has been around for millennia. Attacking and intimidating those who cannot defend themselves is one of the greatest acts of cowardice known to man. The devil is after those who are the most innocent and the most fragile. When the devil is ready to fight, he will not fight fairly. He will often attack those who are most feeble, so that he might divide and conquer. That is why a husband and wife are to "cleave" together. That is why a church is to be of one mind and one accord. You have enemies who are willing to fight a coward's war.

It Was a **Compassionless Act** ("when thou wast faint and weary"). None of us have much respect for someone who will kick a man when he is down. That was exactly the action of Amalek to the people of Israel. You will find that many of your greatest spiritual battles will happen when you are physically exhausted. The greatest illustration of this is the devil's temptation of our own Saviour in the wilderness after He had fasted for forty days. It is often in fatigue that the devil will afflict you with various temptations, because he knows your resistance to your flesh is low. Draw your strength from the Lord in those exhausting times, and He will lift you up.

It Was a **Conceited Act** ("and he feared not God"). The epitome of pride is found in this phrase. A proud man has no limits. There is no height that he does not think is rightfully his, and there is no depth he will not go to satisfy his desires. Proverbs 26:12 says, "Seest thou a man wise in his own conceit? there is more hope of a fool than of him." Again, James 4:6b says, "God resisteth the proud, but giveth grace unto the humble."

TOPICS: Battle, Enemies, Pride, Satan, War

DAILY BIBLE READING: Deuteronomy 28

TODAY'S VERSE: Deuteronomy 28:2: "And all these blessings shall come on thee, and overtake thee, if thou shalt hearken unto the voice of the LORD thy God."

THIS CHAPTER IS FULL of blessings and cursings. In it, we see motivations given concerning God's rewards, and then warnings given concerning God's judgment. I surely don't want to be one of those who miss God's blessings! This particular promise of God's blessing is one of extreme measure. There are a few verses in the Bible that tell of God's blessings getting out of control. Psalm 81:10b says, "Open thy mouth wide and I will fill it." And again, "If I will … open you the windows of heaven, and pour you out a blessing, that there shall not be room enough to receive it" (Malachi 3:10b). Psalm 23:5b reads, "My cup runneth over." Let's let our minds run wild as we think of God's blessings today!

The Endowment of God's Blessing ("And all these blessings shall come on thee"). This was a promise of God's action. Is there anyone in his or her right mind who would not desire a gift such as this? I love the part that says the blessings "shall come on thee." This gives me some important information! First, it tells me of *the blessing's positive certainty.* God has never made a promise that is only a possibility! Even God's conditional promises, such as this one, are true and guaranteed. It also tells me of *the blessing's personal connection.* It will be on me, not just around me! This is not a blessing around a particular place, but around a particular person. David said it like this in Psalm 23:6: "Surely goodness and mercy *shall follow me* all the days of my life." Everywhere I go, God's blessing goes!

The Engulfment of God's Blessing ("and overtake thee"). The English definition of the word for "overtake" is "to come up with in a course, pursuit, progress or motion; to catch."[2] Blessing will seek me out and find me! Let me remind you of Numbers 32:23b: "Be sure your sin will find you out." Just as my disobedience to God will overtake me, so will God's blessing if I follow Him! "Overtake" also brings with it the idea of surprise. This is better than finding money in the gutter! Let God's blessing overtake us so that we might glorify Him!

The Engagement of God's Blessing ("if thou shalt hearken unto the voice of the LORD thy God"). Here is the condition of this promise. It really is quite simple, isn't it? All we have to do to receive God's blessing is obey His Word. I enter into His blessing by submitting to the voice I love to hear! Jeremiah 15:16 says, "Thy words were found, and I did eat them; and thy word was unto me the joy and rejoicing of mine heart: for I am called by thy name, O LORD God of hosts." Instead of dreading the Word of God, hear it, and let it bring God's blessings upon you!

TOPICS: Blessing, Obedience, Word of God

---

2 *Noah Webster's First Edition of an American Dictionary of The English Language* (Chesapeake, VA: Foundation For American Christian Education, 1995)

DAILY BIBLE READING: Deuteronomy 29–31

TODAY'S VERSE: Deuteronomy 29:29: "The secret things belong unto the LORD our God: but those things which are revealed belong unto us and to our children for ever, that we may do all the words of this law."

WE HAVE A VERY INTERESTING verse to consider today. This verse confirms what we thought to be true: we are not as smart as we think we are! An old preacher once said, "It is not what I don't understand about this Book (the Bible) that bothers me, but what I do understand."

First, we are reminded of the **Magnified Mind of God** ("The secret things belong unto the LORD our God"). God is not stumped by truths that are hidden. Those things that are secret have been made so by the infinite wisdom of God Himself. There are some things that are reserved for the mind of God. With the Holy Spirit's leading, He can surely "guide us into all truth," but that is purely up to Him (John 16:13).

Second, we are reminded of the **Miniscule Mind of Man** ("but those things which are revealed belong unto us and to our children for ever"). The word for "revealed" means "to denude." Our ways and thoughts are so small compared to God's that truth of the Word of God has to be completely laid bare for us to grasp it. Hebrews 4:13 says, "Neither is there any creature that is not manifest in his sight: but all things are naked and opened unto the eyes of him with whom we have to do."

How small and pitiful we really are in the sight of God! We have such a hard time understanding what God has told us so plainly. Even the disciples had a hard time understanding the sayings of Christ. It is so sad that, according to this verse, our children have been cursed with the same limited understanding that we have. However, God has placed understanding in the hearts of those who love Him to reveal His thoughts to us. Proverbs 3:32 says, "For the froward is abomination to the LORD: but his secret is with the righteous." There are many teachings in this Book that I *do not* understand, but with the leading and guiding of the Holy Spirit, there is nothing that I *cannot* understand.

Third, we are reminded of the **Meaningful Mind of God** ("that we may do all the words of this law"). God's whole desire is that we might obey His Word! It is very easy to wring our hands and wonder about what God would have us do someday. All you need to know, my friend, is what God wants us to do *today!* Micah 6:8 says, "He hath shewed thee, O man, what is good; and what doth the LORD require of thee, but to do justly, and to love mercy, and to walk humbly with thy God?"

Before we close, know that Jesus came to make things plain and to reveal His truth to us. Mark 4:22 says, "For there is nothing hid, which shall not be manifested; neither was any thing kept secret, but that it should come abroad." Hallelujah!

TOPICS: Mind of God, God's Greatness, Obedience, Word of God

DAILY BIBLE READING: Deuteronomy 32–34

TODAY'S VERSE: Deuteronomy 33:27: "The eternal God is thy refuge, and underneath are the everlasting arms: and he shall thrust out the enemy from before thee; and shall say, Destroy them."

IF THE LORD IS our refuge or place, what kind of a place is He? Proverbs 18:10 says, "The name of the Lord is a strong tower: the righteous runneth into it, and is safe." What is this place of refuge like?

First, it is a **Place of Support** ("and underneath are the everlasting arms"). We never have to worry about falling! God has passed every inspection. There are no cracks in His foundation. "For other foundation can no man lay than that is laid, which is Jesus Christ" (1 Corinthians 3:11). I have never been stuck so badly that God could not rescue me! These are *strong* arms, *stalwart* arms, and *steadfast* arms. Don't stand upon sinking sand! Come to Him, and have a secure place to stay!

Second, it is a **Place of Safety** ("and he shall thrust out the enemy from before thee"). When God gets rid of all those who would do me hurt, then He is a place of safety for me. Psalm 23:5 says, "Thou preparest a table before me in the presence of mine enemies." There is nothing our enemies can do without the permission of God. Some would use Job to argue. You forget, my friend, that Job was allowed by God to endure such things. Those things that come to me are designed by God to draw me closer to Him and to show me His love and care in another way. But don't worry, He "will not suffer you to be tempted above that which ye are able; but will with the temptation also make a way to escape, that ye may be able to bear it" (1 Corinthians 10:13).

Third, it is a **Place of Success** ("and shall say, Destroy them"). What a place to be—one of *victory!* Romans 8:37 says, "Nay, in all these things we are more than conquerors through him that loved us." An old song says, "I am on the winning side/Yes, I am on the winning side/Out in sin no more will I abide/I've enlisted in the fight, for the cause of truth and right/Praise the Lord I'm on the winning side!"[3] Jesus did not come here to lose. When He said, "It is finished," it was not a statement of defeat, but one of victory! First Corinthians 15:57 says, "But thanks be to God, which giveth us the victory through our Lord Jesus Christ."

TOPICS: Safety, Success, Support, Victory

---

3 "I'm on the Winning Side" by Hale Reeves. © Copyright 1965. Renewed 1993, Stamps Quarter Music/BMI (admin. By EverGreen Copyrights). All rights reserved. Used by permission.

R. CHRIS HANKS

DAILY BIBLE READING: Joshua 1–3

TODAY'S VERSE: Joshua 1:8: "This book of the law shall not depart out of thy mouth; but thou shalt meditate therein day and night, that thou mayest observe to do according to all that is written therein: for then thou shalt make thy way prosperous, and then thou shalt have good success." This is one of my favorite verses in the Bible. Here, the Bible comments on itself.

FIRST, IT IS a **Particular Book** (*"This* book"). We are not talking about some proverbial writings from Confucius or Buddha, but the particular Word of God. We all need to understand that the critiques and criticisms against God's people are also against *this* Book! People do not want an absolute authority in their lives. Even today, they reject moral values founded upon the Word of God because of its scriptural basis. Evolution is an attack against this Book along with many other vices within our society, such as abortion, sodomy and same-sex marriage, and atheism.

Second, it is a **Precept Book** ("This book *of the law*"). This has nothing to do with the law of man, but with the law of God. These laws will convict the mind of man, confront his conscience, and demand his surrender.

Third, it is a **Proceeding Book** ("shall not depart"). Isaiah 40:8 says, "The grass withereth, the flower fadeth: but the word of our God shall stand for ever."

Fourth, it is a **Personal Book** ("out of *thy* mouth"). It deals personally with *your* desire, *your* love, and *your* heart for the Word of God. It should be in *your* mouth.

Fifth, it is a **Pondering Book** ("but thou shalt meditate therein"). This is one of the areas where we completely fail. Notice, I did not say that we *lack,* but that we *fail!* May we start pondering the many blessings and mighty workings of God and His grace in all that we do! Psalm 1:2 says, "But his delight is in the law of the LORD; and in his law doth he meditate day and night."

Sixth, it is a **Perpetual Book** ("meditate therein day and night"). This thought shows you the Book's refreshing depths. No matter how much you read the Bible, there will always be a profound new word which leads to awe of the holiness and character of God.

Seventh, it is a **Perceiving Book** ("that thou mayest observe to do according to all that is written therein"). God does demand our willful obedience to His Word. However, this goes further than just a mere mindless "doing" of His Word. He desires that we gain an understanding of doing His word. The word for "observe" means "to hedge about, to guard." We need to "observe" to do what is in the Scripture by taking great care concerning its truth and dedicating ourselves to its complete and thoughtful obedience.

Eighth, it is a **Prosperous Book** ("for then thou shalt make thy way prosperous"). The Bible has continual and effervescing properties of profit and prosperity for every life that it touches! Second Timothy 3:16 says, "All scripture is given by inspiration of God, and is *profitable* for doctrine, for reproof, for correction, for instruction in righteousness."

Ninth, it is a **Prevailing Book** ("and then thou shalt have good success"). Whatever issue might confront you, nothing can defeat you if this book is your prevailing power! What a blessing to hold the actual and literal Word of God!

TOPICS: Bible, Prosperity, Success, Word of God

DAILY BIBLE READING: Joshua 4–6

TODAY'S VERSE: Joshua 4:9: "And Joshua set up twelve stones in the midst of Jordan, in the place where the feet of the priests which bare the ark of the covenant stood: and they are there unto this day."

ISRAEL ACTUALLY SET UP two different memorials when they passed over Jordan. First, there was the memorial in this verse, which they set up in the midst of Jordan. Second, they set up a memorial in Gilgal from rocks collected from the midst of Jordan. I believe that we need to set up some memorials in our spiritual lives that will remind us of the great and mighty things God has done for us. Let us take a moment and look at this first memorial in the history of Israel.

First, it was a **Memorial of a Solid Foundation** ("And Joshua set up twelve stones in the *midst* of Jordan"). Earlier, in verse 3, the passage said, "out of the place *where the priests' feet stood firm.*" What a memorial for us to have! A fresh riverbed is not known for its solid foundation! Wherever God leads you is the place of a strong and mighty foundation. When we learn to live by the principles and precepts of the Word of God, we will find that it is a place of certainty and truth. As we build our lives on the solid foundation of Christ, we will be able to sing the old hymn, "On Christ the solid Rock I stand/All other ground is sinking sand!"[4]

Second, it was a **Memorial of a Saving Foundation** ("in the place where the feet of the priests which bare the *ark of the covenant stood*"). Did you build a memorial at the time and place of your salvation? What a great blessing it is to remember and rejoice over salvation! I go to that place often in my mind and remember what God did for me there. Psalm 78:7 says, "That they might set their hope in God, and not forget the works of God." I set up a memorial in my heart at the church on West 7th Street in St. Paul, Minnesota, as the place where the Lord saved my soul! I have taken my children to that place to show them and tell them of God's grace upon my life.

Third, it was a **Memorial of a Steady Foundation** ("and they are there unto this day"). This memorial is as steady and constant as Christ is in my life. The memorial is a picture of the steadiness that God gives to me. The memorial does not cease because God does not cease. They are there unto this day! No matter the deluge of water that washes over my soul, it cannot shake the work that God has done in me. What a blessing to know that no matter the trouble that might come in this life, there is an unbroken and unvarying work of God that will never change! In a society of constant change, make your memorial today of God's blessing and of the endless, relentless work of God in your life.

TOPICS: Memorials, Praise, Salvation

---

4 The words are from Edward Mote's hymn "My Hope Is Built," first published in 1836.

DAILY BIBLE READING: Joshua 7–9

TODAY'S VERSE: Joshua 9:14: "And the men took of their victuals, and asked not counsel at the mouth of the LORD."

THIS STORY IN OUR scheduled reading tells of the Gibeonites, inhabitants of the Promised Land. They deceived the princes of Israel to make a treaty with them so they would not die. Some look at Israel's conquering of the Promised Land as a barbaric invasion and merciless killing of innocent people. The truth, however, is that Israel was doing the will of God. All those nations had rejected God, rejected His law, and rejected His love. Because of their rejection of God and their disregard of His ways, God appointed them to destruction. Israel was never to make a league with the inhabitants of the land—but these Gibeonites, being subtle of heart, found a way to make the Israelites disobey the Lord and save their own necks at the same time. My question today is quite easy to answer: what was the sign of Israel's acceptance of the Gibeonites? They were accepted when "the men took of their victuals, and asked not counsel at the mouth of the LORD." Here are a few thoughts about our acceptance of the world though God has called us to something greater.

These Victuals Were Not Approved by God ("and asked not counsel at the mouth of the LORD"). The Lord would most assuredly have warned Israel against such an alliance. God desires you to be in the center of His will and obedient to His Word. He does not desire defilement, nor does He desire unfulfilled promises in your life. Proverbs 3:5–6 says, "Trust in the LORD with all thine heart; and lean not unto thine own understanding. In all thy ways acknowledge him, and he shall direct thy paths." Can you hear the Israelites' faulty thoughts in this story? The Israelites thought they had it right. Maybe God just wanted them to make the decision on their own and not bother Him with such trivial problems. I mean, how bad could the decision be? God knew that they wanted to do right—right? God is interested in every situation in your life and your following obedience. Learn to seek the Lord! James 1:5 says, "If any of you lack wisdom, let him ask of God, that giveth to all men liberally, and upbraideth not; and it shall be given him." Every decision must be brought before our Lord.

These Victuals Were Not Accepted by God. Disobedience is never acceptable. Even the Gibeonites knew this, for they made mention of it to Joshua and the people in verse 24: "Because it was certainly told thy servants, how that the LORD thy God commanded his servant Moses to give you all the land, and to destroy all the inhabitants of the land from before you." God desires full, complete, and immediate obedience. First Samuel 15:22 says, "Behold, to obey is better than sacrifice, and to hearken than the fat of rams."

These Victuals Were an Astonishment to God. What had God promised Israel? A land of milk and honey! Oh, they settled for so much less! God had spent forty years feeding them with manna in the wilderness, and look what they stooped to: bad bread, broken bottles, and battered britches and boots (see verses 4 and 5)! What did these inhabitants of the world know about good things? It is so amazing what our Lord gives us, and then how quickly we turn to "the weak and beggarly elements" of the world (Galatians 4:9). We willingly eat of the pigpen's pleasures when we could be fellowshipping with others of the Father's food and experiencing blessings from the very hand of God (Luke 15:11–32)! Once the Israelites entered the Promised Land, the manna stopped. Even then, they began to eat of the old corn of the land. Why do we stoop so low? There is nothing good that the world can give you when compared with the blessed hand of God! The prospect of God's future promises is much greater than what the world has to offer.

TOPICS: Deceit, Discernment, Promises, Temptation, Wisdom

DAILY BIBLE READING: Joshua 10–11

TODAY'S VERSE: Joshua 11:23: "So Joshua took the whole land, according to all that the Lord said unto Moses; and Joshua gave it for an inheritance unto Israel according to their divisions by their tribes. And the land rested from war."

THE STORIED WALLS of Jericho had fallen flat like the walls of a sand castle on the beach at high tide. Fear struck deeply into the hearts of all the inhabitants of the land. Joshua was on a mission from God, and nothing would stand in his way! One of the reasons that God blessed Israel as they entered the Promised Land was Joshua's obedience to God's Word. Joshua 11:15 says, "As the Lord commanded Moses his servant, so did Moses command Joshua, and so did Joshua; he left nothing undone of all that the Lord commanded Moses." God will bless us today if we obey Him with the same fervor and passion that Joshua had.

The Possession of the Land ("So Joshua took the whole land, according to all that the Lord said unto Moses"). Joshua finally realized his goal! I believe that Brother Joshua would agree with Proverbs 13:19a, which says, "The desire accomplished is sweet to the soul." We have too many people in the church today with temporal goals, worldly objectives, and fleshly ambitions. Thank God for a man who knew what God wanted him to do and who did it! Joshua did his job in taking the whole land, but we find that the tribes failed to drive out the inhabitants, for it was up to them to possess their land and destroy their enemies.

The Purpose of the Land ("and Joshua gave it for an inheritance unto Israel according to their divisions by their tribes"). The whole reason for fighting the battles was to receive the blessings that were promised to them. God had a purpose for the land that He had promised to His people. It was not just a collective purpose, but also an individual purpose. He had given it to them "according to their divisions by their tribes." Go out and fight for your providential destiny, and have victory today!

The Peace of the Land ("And the land rested from war"). There were still battles the tribes had to fight, but at this point there was finally a peace in which all knew it was the Israelites' land. You will never enjoy peace until you endure the war. Today, our nation of America has forgotten the privilege of peace and the responsibility of freedom because many have never experienced the conflict of liberty. It is an ongoing confrontation that requires more than we are sometimes willing to give. But it is a fight that must be fought and won if there will be a peace to enjoy one day. It sometimes becomes exhausting fighting battle after battle, but don't lose hope: there is a rest in sight!

TOPICS: Battle, Obedience, Victory, War

DAILY BIBLE READING: Joshua 12–14

TODAY'S VERSE: Joshua 14:12: "Now therefore give me this mountain, whereof the LORD spake in that day; for thou heardest in that day how the Anakims were there, and that the cities were great and fenced: if so be the LORD will be with me, then I shall be able to drive them out, as the LORD said."

THIS VERSE IS ABOUT a man named Caleb. Jones's *Dictionary of Old Testament Proper Names* says that his name means "dog" but also that his name is from an onomatopoetic root imitating the sound of striking or beating.[5] In other words, we can derive from the meaning of his name that this man was not afraid of a fight! We need Christian men and women who have a bulldog determination and are willing to stand toe-to-toe with evil and fight with the power of God.

He Looked for a Change ("Now therefore give me this mountain, whereof the LORD spake in that day"). Caleb remembered the failure of Israel when they rejected the Promised Land. The sentence of Israel from God rang in his ears every day they were in the wilderness. Though he had done righteously, the judgment of God upon unbelievers affected his life as well. Caleb walked through the wilderness for forty years because of someone else's sin. By the time they walked into the Promised Land, Caleb had a plan in mind. He was ready for a change! He had been marking the calendar for forty-five years.

He Looked for a Challenge ("for thou heardest in that day how the Anakims were there, and that the cities were great and fenced"). These people were the source of many stories and legends. The problem was these people *were* actually as tall as the tales said! Caleb was not looking for the easy way out. Neither the size of the people nor the strength of the cities would deter him from receiving God's promises. Let me remind you of what the Israelites said when they first saw the Anakims in Numbers 13:33: "And there we saw the giants, the sons of Anak, which come of the giants: and we were in our own sight as grasshoppers, and so we were in their sight." Alfred Jones quotes a Mr. Faber, who says it is more than probable that the sons of Anak were the same as the descendants of the Titans.[6] This challenge made Caleb's mouth water! When God has given a promise, there is nothing that can keep us from receiving it, unless we willfully reject it.

He Looked for a Champion ("if so be the LORD will be with me, then I shall be able to drive them out, as the LORD said"). Caleb always knew that his success was based upon God's presence and not upon his own performance. We must know the source of our strength! This was Caleb's admission of what David said when he fought Goliath many years later in 1 Samuel 17:47: "And all this assembly shall know that the LORD saveth not with sword and spear: *for the battle is the LORD's,* and he will give you into our hands." Let God fight the battle, and receive the victory!

TOPICS: Battle, Challenge, Faith, Promises, Victory, War

---

5   Alfred Jones, *Jones' Dictionary of Old Testament Proper Names* (Grand Rapids: Kregel, 1997), 81–81.

6   Alfred Jones, *Jones' Dictionary of Old Testament Proper Names* (Grand Rapids: Kregel, 1997), 31.

DAILY BIBLE READING: Joshua 15–17

TODAY'S VERSE: Joshua 17:18: "But the mountain shall be thine; for it is a wood, and thou shalt cut it down: and the outgoings of it shall be thine: for thou shalt drive out the Canaanites, though they have iron chariots, and though they be strong."

IN THIS PASSAGE, we see the Ephraimites talking with Joshua about increasing their land because they were too great (too big) for the land they had. Joshua told them that they were a great people and had great power, and they could go win more land if they wanted it. The Ephraimites decided they wanted Joshua to give it to them. They did not want to fight for it. We are living in a time in which many children are raised with a silver spoon in their mouths, but the truth is we are all that way at heart. I would like to encourage all who are reading this devotion: Let's go win it! God has called us to a town. We need to win it!

In today's story, Ephraim listed excuses as to why it was too hard to win new land. Here in verse 18, Joshua addresses all of their excuses.

Size Was Not an Excuse ("for thou shalt drive out the Canaanites"). These enemies were giants in the land, but the real question here is not, "How big is the enemy?" It's "How big is your God?" God told Caleb that He would give him Hebron where all the biggest giants lived. Caleb was excited, and in a fit of redneck righteousness he said, "Hey y'all, watch this!" and promptly destroyed the giants! Don't get discouraged by looking at the size of your enemy or the strength he possesses. Just remember, the bigger they are, the harder they fall!

Stories Were Not an Excuse ("for thou shalt drive out the Canaanites"). Not only had the Canaanites heard about the Israelites, but the Israelites had heard about them. Numbers 13:32 says, "The land, through which we have gone to search it, is a land that eateth up the inhabitants thereof; and all the people that we saw in it are men of a great stature." So many times, we run and hide in fear and reject the promise that God has given to us of complete and sincere victory. We need to tell ourselves a new story—one of faith and victory!

Supplies Were Not an Excuse ("though they have iron chariots"). We need to quit saying, "If only we had this, then we could do that." It is so easy to focus on the world's talents and possessions and begin excusing ourselves from fighting the battle. We are not to compare ourselves or our godly ministry with anything the world does. Their tools and resources are no match for the blessing of the Lord. Just ask Gideon, who won a great battle with a skeleton army of just three hundred men. Just ask David, who said to the giant Goliath, "Thou comest to me with a sword and with a spear and with a shield, but I come to thee in the name of the LORD of hosts" (1 Samuel 17:45). This list could go on and on.

Strength Was Not an Excuse ("and though they be strong"). It is easy to become discouraged and fearful of those who have flexed their muscles and hurt others. I believe that we need to be careful and use wisdom. If we humbly obey the Lord and follow Him, then He will give us victory over those who are much stronger than we. The Bible says in Psalm 98:1, "O sing unto the LORD a new song; for he hath done marvellous things: his right hand, and his holy arm, hath gotten him the victory." Thank God for His strength and His power in this fight!

TOPICS: Excuses, Faith, Intimidation, Strength, Victory

DAILY BIBLE READING: Joshua 18–19

TODAY'S VERSE: Joshua 18:8: "And the men arose, and went away: and Joshua charged them that went to describe the land, saying, Go and walk through the land, and describe it, and come again to me, that I may here cast lots for you before the LORD in Shiloh."

THIS VERSE IS RIGHT in the middle of two chapters which tell of splitting up the Promised Land for habitation. This task of dividing the land is applicable to our lives today.

First, the land would be divided **According to Their Sight** ("and Joshua charged them that went to describe the land"). Much depends on our view of the Christian life that God has given us to live. Our perception of godly things, of doctrinal things, and of holy things is one of the keys to God's blessing in this Promised Land. Haggai 2:3 asks, "And how do ye see it now?" I have to admit that my perception of the Christian life is much different now than it was when I got saved. It is even different than it was a couple of years ago! May we clear our vision in order to see the Lord at work in our hearts and lives.

Second, the land would be divided **According to Their Stride** ("Go and walk through the land"). By the way, this was not a race, but a walk. So is the Christian life! Some think our Christian life is a race, and only those who finish first win. Yet God has commanded us many times to "walk in the Spirit," "walk in my law," "walk in my statutes," "walk in all the ways," "walk in the fear of our God," "walk in newness of life," "walk in love," "walk in wisdom," "walk in light," and "walk in truth."[7] What a wonderful walk lies ahead of us *today!*

Third, the land would be divided **According to Their Surrender** ("and come again to me, that I may here cast lots for you before the LORD in Shiloh"). This verse has to do with Israel's return and submission to the will of God. When was the last time the will of God was just fine with you? Rather than casting lots, these men might have wanted to request for themselves a certain portion of land that they felt would fit their needs best. But if you look at verse 6, you will find that they were to divide the land into seven parts. Seven—the number of completion and perfection! No matter where you are or what you are doing when you find the will of God, it will be the perfect place for you! Just surrender to the place that God has you. There is no better land than the one He appoints you.

TOPICS: Christian Life, Surrender, Vision, Walk

---

7   Galatians 5:16; 2 Chronicles 6:16; Leviticus 26:3; Deuteronomy 5:33; Nehemiah 5:9; Romans 6:4; Ephesians 5:2; Colossians 4:5; Ephesians 5:8; 3 John 1:4.

DAILY BIBLE READING: Joshua 20-22

TODAY'S VERSE: Joshua 21:44: "And the LORD gave them rest round about, according to all that he sware unto their fathers: and there stood not a man of all their enemies before them; the LORD delivered all their enemies into their hand."

PRAISE THE LORD for the promises of God! To think that God has a promise of blessing for His people and that He is presently in the process of bringing those promises to pass! Hallelujah! Let's look for a moment at the phrase "According to all that he sware unto their fathers."

First, it was a **Continuing Promise** ("he sware unto their fathers"). The promise these Israelites were receiving and from which they were enjoying the benefits was not originally given to them, but to their forefathers. What a blessing to know that the promises of God continue! I am so glad that I am a beneficiary of the promise of the Messiah given in Genesis 3:15 to Adam and Eve. If that promise were just for them, we would be in a state of misery and debauchery today. This promise, however, is connected to the goodness of God and not the life of man, and so it continues while the goodness of God endures! All of us are reaping promises that were given to others.

Second, it was a **Confirming Promise** ("and there stood not a man of all their enemies before them"). This was a promise that could be manifested. Every time an enemy fell, it confirmed the promise and the truth of God Himself. From Sihon to Og, from Jericho to Hebron, and from the Euphrates to the Mediterranean, there was no king who could stand before the people with the precious promises of Almighty God. God's promises can still be confirmed today! Why don't you see for yourself? Psalm 34:8 says, *"O taste and see* that the LORD is good: blessed is the man that trusteth in him." He has promised never to leave—try it out! He has promised to walk with you along the way—try it out! He has promised to cut down every enemy whose wiles are bent toward violence or stealing your virtue—try it out!

Third, it was a **Conquering Promise** ("the LORD delivered all their enemies into their hand"). God's promise is also a present! God delivered the enemy into Israel's hand, and when He did so, Israel received all their land! For us, the promise of pardon comes with a gift of eternal life. We will not receive all of God's blessings until we enter into our final rest. Final blessings require a final victory. We will receive these final blessings as a result of the same promises in which we rejoice today! These are promises that keep on giving—not just for our time here on earth, but for the victory that awaits us in the Promised Land of our final rest.

TOPICS: Experience, God's Promises, Victory

DAILY BIBLE READING: Joshua 23–24

TODAY'S VERSE: Joshua 24:15: "And if it seem evil unto you to serve the LORD, choose you this day whom ye will serve; whether the gods which your fathers served that were on the other side of the flood, or the gods of the Amorites, in whose land ye dwell: but as for me and my house, we will serve the LORD."

THIS IS ONE of the most well-known verses in the Bible. As you visit people's homes, you will often find this verse displayed on their walls. This verse, however, was originally given to Joshua through the inspiration of the Holy Spirit. Let's ask God to help us understand it a little better.

First, we see that **Man's Wisdom Is Distorted** ("And if it seem evil unto you to serve the LORD"). Today this attitude seems to be the norm. We are constantly hit with a barrage of accusations and condemnations from political figures and the media machine that make going to church and serving God an evil thing. But how could serving our God seem to anyone to be an evil thing? Romans 8:7 says, "Because the carnal mind is enmity against God: for it is not subject to the law of God, neither indeed can be." Our belief system has even been reduced by doctors to being nothing more than a part in the brain that receives pleasure from religious experience—they have reduced our worship to a feeling that is fed from our brain. Don't worry; this kind of distortion didn't bother Brother Joshua very much—as we will see in just a moment.

Second, **Man's Worship Is Decided** ("choose you this day whom ye will serve"). This comes down to *choice*. Matthew 6:24 says, "No man can serve two masters: for either he will hate the one, and love the other; or else he will hold to the one, and despise the other. Ye cannot serve God and mammon." The understood thought is, "Every man will serve one master, but no man can serve two!" That is exactly what Joshua is saying here: Make your choice! Raise your banner! You will serve someone, but who will it be? Choosing *not* to decide is a decision of its own. Make the right choice.

Third, **Man's Will Must Be Determined** ("but as for me and my house, we will serve the LORD"). We need men and fathers who will stand and take the lead on this one! This will take nothing but sheer determination. One reason so many people leave their beliefs and churches today is because there is no determination to follow the Lord. They would rather follow themselves. What commitment is shown in this passage—"We *will* serve the LORD." Joshua did not care about any spin the world might put upon his determination to serve the Lord, for he was going to serve Him anyway! This was something that would not change. He would follow God to the end!

TOPICS: Choice, Commitment, Decision, Dedication, Worship

DAILY BIBLE READING: Judges 1–3

TODAY'S VERSE: Judges 3:22: "And the haft also went in after the blade; and the fat closed upon the blade, so that he could not draw the dagger out of his belly; and the dirt came out."

THIS WAS ONE of my favorite stories as I was growing up. Childish fascination with its humor drew me to the story, but the oddities of the story itself also caught my attention. Ehud was a left-handed judge sent by God to kill Eglon, king of Moab. King Eglon, however, was described as being "a very fat man." Today, let's look at this verse with the idea of defeating the flesh in our Christian life. Until some sins are destroyed, we may not understand how terrible they are. It is not until we defeat our sin that we see how bad it really is. As I look back on certain periods in my life I can say, "What took me so long to give that to the Lord?"

We Don't Realize How Consuming Our Sin Is ("And the haft also went in after the blade; and the fat closed upon the blade"). When we are in the midst of our sin, it is easy to dismiss it and claim, like all other addicts, "I am not addicted to it! I could give it up whenever I want!" But if that is true, and our behavior is wrong in God's sight, then why don't we just give it up? Because it has consumed us! You will not understand sin's grip upon your flesh or its control upon your heart until you destroy it.

We Don't Realize How Confusing Our Sin Is ("so that he could not draw the dagger out of his belly"). Ehud was doing the will of God and obeying Him, but he still lost something in this fight. I was brought up in a part of the country where it was a great loss and near tragedy if a man ever lost his pocket knife. There is a spiritual principle here: *When you fight with your flesh and win, it will* always *cost you something!* You must fill the void of something carnal with something that is spiritual. If you do not, the loss will confuse your spiritual heart. Our sin is very confusing in its nature. Psalm 44:15 reads, "My confusion is continually before me, and the shame of my face hath covered me." Though we are doing right in abandoning our sin, we can easily fall back into the same sin if it is not replaced with holiness. Even though Eglon was now dead, his death took away the very object that was used to destroy him.

We Don't Realize How Corrupt Our Sin Is ("and the dirt came out"). It was not until the deed was done that "the dirt came out." We never recognize the mess of our sin until after we have dealt with it and destroyed it. I have counseled men whose wicked and destructive behaviors have hurt their homes, their marriages, and their relationships with God. After they have dealt with the wickedness of their sin, they are able to look back and say, "I didn't know it was that bad." That is how mesmerizing carnal sin can be! I have seen many tearful eyes and sobbing hearts upon an altar. Afterward the person will often say, "I feel so clean!" It would sure help if we could see our sin through the eyes of God! Thank God for 1 John 1:9: "If we confess our sins, he is faithful and just to forgive us our sins, and to cleanse us from all unrighteousness."

TOPICS: Corruption, Deceit, Flesh, Sin, Victory

DAILY BIBLE READING: Judges 4–5

TODAY'S VERSE: Judges 4:21: "Then Jael Heber's wife took a nail of the tent, and took an hammer in her hand, and went softly unto him, and smote the nail into his temples, and fastened it into the ground: for he was fast asleep and weary. So he died."

WHAT A TREMENDOUSLY COURAGEOUS woman! This chapter tells us of two wonderful women whom God used in a great way to help bring about a great victory for His chosen people: Deborah the judge and Jael. Neither of these women were part of some feminist organization trying to set women free from their oppressors, nor were they trying to make a name for themselves. Deborah referred to herself as a "mother in Israel" in Judges 5:7, and Jael is called "Heber's wife" in our verse today. That's all! No hyphenations, no postscripts, no titles, and no educational honors. Is it possible that God has a purpose for each of us in the role where He has placed us, regardless of our earthly "qualifications"? Though it seems that Jael and her husband were riding the fence on their loyalties between Israel and Sisera (see verses 11–12), I believe there are some principles here for the godliest of ladies to consider. Let's take a moment to see why God used Jael to bring about a great victory, although she was not even an Israelite.

She Was a Resourceful Woman ("Then Jael Heber's wife took a nail of the tent, and took an hammer in her hand"). You would be surprised at what God could do with you if you would only offer Him what you already have. In Scripture, God almost always used what people already had. God used a lunch from a little boy to feed a multitude (John 6:5–9). God used the rod that Moses already had in his hand (Exodus 4:2). God used a boy and a sling to defeat a giant (1 Samuel 17). The Bible says of the virtuous woman in Proverbs 31:13, "She seeketh wool, and flax, and *worketh willingly with her hands.*"

She Was a Reserved Woman ("and went softly unto him"). There was no great attack, no battle plan, just a woman who was going to do a job. There was no time for hesitation, but neither was there time to sound a trumpet so others might notice. Literally, Jael walked softly and carried a big stick! Too many people want a fanfare for their service to the Lord and red-carpet treatment for coming to church. Matthew 23:5 makes known the problem of the Pharisees: "But all their works they do for to be seen of men." A soft and meek spirit was a character trait of Jael, for when Barak came looking for Sisera and tracked him to the home of Jael, she met him and said, "Come, and I will shew thee the man whom thou seekest. And when he came into her tent, behold, Sisera lay dead, and the nail was in his temples." Jael did not meet him with a dance. She did not proclaim her victory. But when Barak saw Sisera, the whole story was known. Again we see this principle in Proverbs 31:31: "Give her of the fruit of her hands; and let her own works praise her in the gates."

She Was a Resolved Woman ("and smote the nail into his temples, and fastened it into the ground: for he was fast asleep and weary. So he died"). If Jael started this work, she was going to finish it. And finish it she did! She did not do "just enough" to kill him—she drove the nail through his head and fastened it in the ground. The old boy would go no further! It would do us well to quit meddling around with sin and just nail it to the floor, never to be awakened again! You will never be able to control it. Sin cannot be tolerated; it must be destroyed.

TOPICS: Humility, Resolve, Resourcefulness, Sin, Victory, War

DAILY BIBLE READING: Judges 6–8

TODAY'S VERSE: Judges 7:2: "And the LORD said unto Gideon, The people that are with thee are too many for me to give the Midianites into their hands, lest Israel vaunt themselves against me, saying, Mine own hand hath saved me."

WHAT A TREAT Today we get to study the great and mighty Gideon. The story of Gideon's great victory over the Midianites with only three hundred men is told in even the youngest of Sunday school classes. There is hardly a Bible story in which God's power is more evident than this one. The Midianites had oppressed and abused God's people for seven years. When Israel cried to God for deliverance, God sought for a man He could use. Gideon would soon learn that God would not fight the battle as Gideon would have preferred. Instead, Gideon would have to trust in God and depend on Him for the victory.

The Verification of Israel ("And the LORD said unto Gideon, The people that are with thee are too many for me to give the Midianites into their hands"). This was the beginning of a process that would whittle the number of soldiers in Gideon's army from thirty-two thousand to three hundred. God will send us processes and tests in our Christian lives to expose us to ourselves and reduce us to a level where He can be glorified in us. God already knew what the people would do, but He also had to teach Gideon to accept His orders and trust in Him.

The Vaunting of Israel ("lest Israel vaunt themselves"). The word for "vaunt" means "to gleam, embellish; figuratively, to boast." How easy it is for us to embellish our boastings! We do our best to chrome our image so that others might not see what is really under the hood. Ask Elijah about this when he was discouraged and ran to Horeb for his life, and said "I, even I only, am left; and they seek my life, to take it away" (1 Kings 19:10b). Ask Ananias and Sapphira as they lied to the Holy Ghost and were killed in Acts 5. God even told Samuel not to be fooled by appearances in 1 Samuel 16:7: "But the LORD said unto Samuel, Look not on his countenance, or on the height of his stature; because I have refused him: for the LORD seeth not as man seeth; for man looketh on the outward appearance, but the LORD looketh on the heart." It is futile to attempt to hide what we really are from God.

The Vacillations of Israel ("against me"). How many times had the Israelites dedicated themselves to the Lord only to forget Him and His commandments shortly thereafter? How many times had they prayed for God's deliverance, received it, and then turned their backs on Him? Their existence could be summed up in three words: *rebellion, repentance, revival.* The rebellion lasted much longer than the other two. I have to say, under conviction by the Holy Spirit, that I have done the same thing. Their persecution and captivity were acts of God to draw Israel closer to Him! This should show us our constant need to depend upon Him every moment of every day. Second Timothy 2:13 is a blessing as we contemplate our failings: "If we believe not, yet he abideth faithful: he cannot deny himself."

The Vanity of Israel ("saying, Mine own hand hath saved me"). Such a claim comes from the greatest deceits of our own hearts. The fleshly desire for us to declare "Look at what I did!" is full of the deepest pride and selfish conceit. Our own hand has done nothing but plunge us into sin and cause us to defy the Lord and His way. Let us come humbly before Him and glorify His powerful hand. Psalm 98:1 says, "O sing unto the LORD a new song; for he hath done marvellous things: his right hand, and his holy arm, hath gotten him the victory."

TOPICS: Deliverance, Humility, Pride, Vanity

DAILY BIBLE READING: Judges 9–10

TODAY'S VERSE: Judges 9:38, "Then said Zebul unto him, Where is now thy mouth, wherewith thou saidst, Who is Abimelech, that we should serve him? is not this the people that thou hast despised? go out, I pray now, and fight with them."

THIS VERSE IS ABOUT a man named Gaal, who had been speaking evil of a man named Abimelech. When Abimelech finally came, the man who had been listening to Gaal run his mouth said, "Where is now thy mouth?" This is a good thought for us to consider today! Let me ask you, Christian, "Where is now your mouth?" We sure know how to talk a good game, don't we? But God has other things for us to consider.

We Run Our Mouths About Our Pride ("Where is now thy mouth, wherewith thou saidst, Who is Abimelech, that we should serve him?"). It is so easy to use our mouth in the character assassination of others in order to make ourselves look good. Some people do this to climb the ladder of success. It is much easier to talk about somebody who is not there. In verses 27 and 28, Gaal had gone into the house of the false god Baal-berith to eat and drink. While they were eating, they cursed Abimelech. They could not say enough bad things about him. They even used questions like, "Who does he think he is?" and "What gave him the right to be ruler over us?" This happens sometimes even in the church! Many homes like to "have the preacher for lunch." They get to talking and sharing prayer requests (which is nothing more than a mask for their cruelty and criticisms!) about the problems that are going on in the church and conclude, "Maybe our pastor just isn't the man for us today!" There are many verses in the Bible about our mouths and tongues and the vanities of our lips. The time will come when God will ask you, "Where is now thy mouth?"

We Run Our Mouths About Our Power ("is not this the people that thou hast despised?"). My, how Gaal had been talking about what he would do to Abimelech if he ever found him alone! He had been pointing out all of his weaknesses and flaws from a military standpoint. He had claimed that he should be leader rather than Abimelech. He even made a threat to Abimelech by telling him to get his army together so they could fight. Of course, Abimelech was not there when the threat was issued—Gaal knew he was safe in making these statements without Abimelech to hear! But Abimelech had a friend, Zebul, who shared this information eagerly. When Abimielech came, Zebul asked Gaal, "Where is now thy mouth?" My friend, don't boast of things that you cannot do, for *you* cannot do anything. Just remember what Zechariah 4:6 says: "Then he answered and spake unto me, saying, This is the word of the LORD unto Zerubbabel, saying, *Not by might, nor by power, but by my spirit,* saith the LORD of hosts."

We Should Just Prove It ("go out, I pray now, and fight with them"). Quit talking about how great a Christian you are—just prove it! Quit talking about how you love to share the gospel—just do it! Quit talking about the greatness of your spiritual conquests—just make them! Let's just be what we are supposed to be! Just remember that the last day will reveal all of our motivations and thoughts before God. I figured out as a teenager that most people who enjoy talking about themselves are not what they say they are. They are nothing more than a bag of hot air. God has given us a wonderful opportunity to prove our love, to prove our desire, to prove even our humility to Him by the way we live and worship Him! If we really mean what we say, we'll stop talking and live it.

TOPICS: Boasting, Criticism, Humility, Pride, Proof, Tongue

DAILY BIBLE READING: Judges 11-13

TODAY'S VERSE: Judges 13:25: "And the Spirit of the Lord began to move him at times in the camp of Dan between Zorah and Eshtaol."

THIS VERSE IS TALKING about Samson, the strongest man in the Bible. We will read about his exploits over the next two days and remember the great feats of strength and mighty works the Lord did through Samson for His honor and glory and to deliver His people from the hand of the Philistines. This chapter introduces Samson, his mother, and his father, Manoah. Samson is one of three Nazarites (not to be confused with *Nazarenes*) in the Bible. The Nazarite vow was a special vow before the Lord, lasting the Nazarite's whole life from birth. The first was the judge Samson, the second was the prophet Samuel, and the third was the preacher John the Baptist (who also came from a priestly line). All of these men were greatly used by God in powerful ways. This verse says that "the Lord began to move him at times." The word "move" here means "to tap, beat regularly, to impel or agitate, move, trouble." I would like to look at the way God wants to move us for a few moments today.

He Moved Samson to Do His Work. God has a work that He wants you to do. If you are tender toward Him, you will feel Him "move" you. I believe that God is tapping many people to do His work, but they are dismissing His call as some sort of nonsense or are being told by others that God would not really call anybody like that. *People are more "proud" today that God actually touched them than they are pushed to do what He wants them to do!* Churches today are looking and praying for "a move of God," but they are less concerned about what a "move of God" might require or accomplish in them. Don't misunderstand me: I am thankful every time I feel the move of God or see it happen in any service. However, we must accept the fact that a move of God requires a move of *us*.

He Moved Samson to Fight His War. We are in the middle of a war, my friend! This was a war that threatened Samson's *life*, killed his *wife*, and caused great *strife* (even with his own people, the men of Judah). There were times when Samson was *tired* in the battle. There were times when he was *tried* in the battle. There was a time when he was *taken* in the battle. But there were also times that he *triumphed* in the battle! God has promised us victory through Him if we will fight the battle He has chosen for us to fight. We are challenged in Jude 3 to *"earnestly contend for the faith."* Even Paul said at the end of his life, "I have fought a good fight, I have finished my course, I have kept the faith" (2 Timothy 4:7).

He Moved Samson to Stand as His Witness. One of the greatest things about the life of Samson was that he was a witness to a heathen nation of the power of Almighty God. At the end, when they took his eyes away, the Philistines brought Samson out to mock him and claim victory over him by their false god, Dagon. But in a time of great triumph, he showed them once again the power of Jehovah. His witness did not stop there, as we are exhorted to have the faith of Samson in Hebrews 11! What a witness! Just like Samson, allow yourself to be moved by God.

TOPICS: Battle, God's Will, Mission, Purpose, Service, War, Witness, Work

DAILY BIBLE READING: Judges 14–16

TODAY'S VERSE: Judges 16:20: "And she said, The Philistines be upon thee, Samson. And he awoke out of his sleep, and said, I will go out as at other times before, and shake myself. And he wist not that the LORD was departed from him."

WHAT A SAD STORY for one of the most colorful characters in the Bible! I don't know exactly what Samson was thinking. Delilah had done everything he told her to do to take away all of his strength. Why would telling her the real thing be any different? The truth is that we are very willing to do the same thing that Samson did. Let's catch a few warning signs from Samson's failures that might help keep us from certain destruction.

He Awakened Too Late ("And she said, The Philistines be upon thee, Samson. And he awoke out of his sleep"). The deed was already done! There was no going back to undo this. His hair was already cut, and it could not be undone. Many people desire good things, godly things, even holy things; but when they have allowed their lives to be destroyed, there is nothing left for them except the utter disappointment of knowing that they were too late.

He Assumed Too Much ("and said, I will go out as at other times before, and shake myself"). Samson thought that he might attain spiritual victory through physical resolve! Those two things will never work together. That is why Christians who think the blessing of the Lord depends on their desire will never understand true holiness or true victory. Instead, they are relegated to a miserable life of works and pride, as their righteousness is all about themselves. There is a movement today that teaches of "silent perfection," whereby we can by our own dedication, meditation, and works attain true spiritual perfection. That will never happen in this life! Isn't it amazing how quickly we can defile that which is holy? We can easily do the same thing Samson did! "I will go out and fight this battle for the Lord!" we say. "I will somehow *make* myself desire God more than ever, and then I shall be more spiritual than any others!" Such an argument is full of *self*, not of the *Spirit!*

I find it very interesting that Samson said he would "shake" himself. That word carries a fascinating connotation: it comes "through the idea of the rustling of mane, which usually accompanies the lion's roar." Old Samson had quite a high opinion of himself! This man, who one day had killed a lion with his bare hands, now thought of himself as a big daddy lion whom no one could defeat—even in his flesh! It would even be appropriate to say that nobody could mess with this lion's *pride!* Some of you may have seen tremendous victories that God has done in the past in your life: do not take them for granted, and do not think that those spiritual victories came because of your great and spiritual ability. Some say, "I trust in the *Lord*," yet some say, "*I* trust in the Lord." Even in spiritual things, they put the emphasis upon themselves, just like Samson!

He Acknowledged Too Little ("And he wist not that the LORD was departed from him"). Samson was so carnal that he didn't even know that God was not with him anymore! A spiritual man would know something as great as this. How could someone not even recognize whether the presence of God or the power of the Spirit was with him or not? The thing is, we do this all the time! That is why God has told us to walk in the Spirit. Galatians 5:16 says, "This I say then, Walk in the Spirit, and ye shall not fulfil the lust of the flesh." Samson had fed his flesh all the time, and he was not used to trusting or waiting on the Lord. When we are brought to our lowest point and we realize that God is not there and that our spiritual perception is completely wrong, we are suddenly put in a place of great uncertainty and vulnerability. What we thought was spiritual has turned out to be only religious at best. It is at this time that we must return to the basics of faith and learn to trust the Lord, seek His face, and worship Him for who He is.

TOPICS: Apathy, Flesh, Presence of God, Power, Pride,

DAILY BIBLE READING: Judges 17–19

TODAY'S VERSE: Judges 18:7: "Then the five men departed, and came to Laish, and saw the people that were therein, how they dwelt careless, after the manner of the Zidonians, quiet and secure; and there was no magistrate in the land, that might put them to shame in any thing; and they were far from the Zidonians, and had no business with any man."

THESE ARE VERY INTERESTING chapters for our reading, a little out of the norm for our usual Bible stories and sermons. These chapters do not give us information about a particular judge and how he delivered the people, but instead deal with a dark period of history in Israel's past. This verse tells us of the continuing mission of the tribe of Dan to possess the land. Here, they came upon a quaint little village that was alone.

They Had a False Sense of Security ("how they dwelt careless, after the manner of the Zidonians, quiet and secure"). Many people live with a false sense of security. Some people actually convince themselves that they are safe because they do not want to think the worst of anybody or any situation. You can see people on the news who say, "I can't believe this happened in our neighborhood." Many others will prey upon those who are secure, because they are the easiest targets. Is that not exactly what happened on September 11, 2001? Terrorists hijacked airplanes and rammed them into our buildings. A false sense of security will set us up for certain defeat. This is how the devil works as well. He wants you to feel comfortable and secure before he comes to destroy you. The Bible teaches in Ephesians 5:15, "See then that ye walk circumspectly, not as fools, but as wise."

They Had a False Sense of Subjection ("and there was no magistrate in the land, that might put them to shame in any thing"). The people of Dan had learned mutual submission; however, in their minds, this submission translated into self-righteousness. They began to say, "We don't need anyone to correct us. We can do it on our own." They thought they were better than everybody else. The verse said, "There was no magistrate in the land, that might put them to shame." How could a magistrate put them to shame? Only by exposing what was wrong! Nobody likes to be told that they are wrong. If a magistrate did this, it would mess up their record! It would hurt their image! They would rather "appear" to be right than to actually be right! Having a magistrate around is having the law around. Romans 3:20 says, "Therefore by the deeds of the law there shall no flesh be justified in his sight: for by the law is the knowledge of sin." The law exposes you and warns of other problems in your life. Galatians 3:24 says, "Wherefore the law was our schoolmaster to bring us unto Christ, that we might be justified by faith."

They Had a False Sense of Seclusion ("and they were far from the Zidonians, and had no business with any man"). Isolation never saved anybody. Some people believe that isolation will protect their homes and their children. We need to do what we can to protect our homes, but isolation is a drug that touches the hearts of many people and actually adds to their pride. It causes many Christians to act like they have arrived. It causes many preachers to become self-absorbed. They have forgotten the most important thing—God! Those who isolate themselves think it all depends upon them! Now they are their own authority. This is what the Amish and Mennonites have done: they are more concerned about isolation than they are about doctrine. Other men will not listen to the godly counsel of the authority that God has placed in their life, but refuse to be guided by the Word of God because they think *they* know what is best instead, for themselves and their families. They would deny all of these things with vehement indignation, but they have fallen into the trap and drugged stupor of isolationism.

TOPICS: Apathy, Isolation, Pride, Wisdom

DAILY BIBLE READING: Judges 20-21

TODAY'S VERSE: Judges 21:3: "And said, O Lord God of Israel, why is this come to pass in Israel, that there should be to day one tribe lacking in Israel?"

THIS VERSE FINDS the tribe of Benjamin after a great defeat in battle. All of the other tribes of Israel were trying to "restore their brother." Isn't that a novel thought for us today—to restore a wayward brother? Not to kick him after his fall. Not to sneer at him, thumb a nose, or raise an eyebrow and say, "You deserve what you got!" After the tribe's fall and judgment, the rest came together and began a restoration process. Romans 15:1 says, "We then that are strong ought to bear the infirmities of the weak, and not to please ourselves." It sounds to me like this needs to happen more in the Lord's house! We can learn about such restoration from Israel's example.

First, we see the **Prayer for a Fallen Brother** ("And said, O Lord God of Israel"). This is the first step to restoring a brother—praying for him! You will be surprised what prayer can do for one who has fallen. Luke 22:31–32 says, "And the Lord said, Simon, Simon, behold, Satan hath desired to have you, that he may sift you as wheat: but I have prayed for thee, that thy faith fail not: and when thou art converted, strengthen thy brethren." Jesus was praying for Simon Peter, knowing that he would one day fall and deny Him. I sure am glad Jesus did not kick Peter to the curb and tell him never to come back!

Second, we see the **Pain for a Fallen Brother** ("why is *this* come to pass in Israel"). Some people actually have no care about what others do. They are not burdened with someone else's struggles, and they do not care about anyone but themselves. By contrast, here we see the burden of family. Jude 22–23 says, "And of some have compassion, making a difference: and others save with fear, pulling them out of the fire; hating even the garment spotted by the flesh." The Bible says that we must help our brother and bear his burden: "Bear ye one another's burdens, and so fulfil the law of Christ" (Galatians 6:2). Can you feel another's inner struggle? Can you feel his or her pain? Remember, we are talking about someone who has acknowledged and been judged for sin. Don't lay sin upon such a person again! Now it's time to shoulder up and help pull the load.

Third, we see the **Poverty of the Fallen Brother** ("that there should be to day one tribe *lacking* in Israel"). A fallen brother has a need! One of the first things we must give to a brother or sister after their conviction is love! When God convicts our hearts, He also confirms His love to us. Praise the Lord! Galatians 6:1 says, "Brethren, if a man be overtaken in a fault, ye which are spiritual, restore such an one in the spirit of meekness; considering thyself, lest thou also be tempted."

James 5:20 tells us of the work of love and how it changes not only the outlook but the situation of those who are struggling with past sins and failures: "Let him know, that he which converteth the sinner from the error of his way shall save a soul from death, and shall hide a multitude of sins." Instead of bringing up the morally bankrupt past, start making deposits of God's love upon the repentant, and you will hide a multitude of sins! It was God's love that paid for my sin! This leads us to a final thought: if God has taken away our sin (Romans 11:27; 1 John 3:5), then why does it need to be hidden as James says? Because God took away my sin from *His* sight, but He hides my sin from *my* sight!

TOPICS: Restoration, Judgment, Love, Sin

DAILY BIBLE READING: Ruth 1-4

TODAY'S VERSE: Ruth 2:9: "Let thine eyes be on the field that they do reap, and go thou after them: have I not charged the young men that they shall not touch thee? and when thou art athirst, go unto the vessels, and drink of that which the young men have drawn."

RUTH IS ONE of my favorite books of the Bible. It is so full of rich pictures of God's love and redemption. There is no way to mistake its story for a picture of anything other than the work of our Kinsman Redeemer to purchase us, a Gentile bride, unto Himself. Our verse this morning quotes the first words that Boaz spoke to Ruth. These were words of great kindness and great care. The rest of their relationship began with these words. Think back on the story of Ruth that you read today in your devotion, and pay special attention to the gracious words of Boaz to bring blessings to the life of Ruth and Naomi. Let us consider the field that Boaz tells Ruth about in this verse.

It Was a Field of Passion ("Let thine eyes be on the field that they do reap"). Boaz wanted Ruth's desire to be upon his field. Do you look longingly upon the field that God has provided you? Do you have eyes only for that which your Beloved has given? Set your affection upon the wonderful field that lies before you! If you will quit setting your sights beyond the confines of the blessed field of God's will, you will find great pleasures, provisions, and possibilities to enjoy. Some desire to be free to forage for themselves in the world, but they will not find any more than what is provided for them in the center of the field of His will.

It Was a Field of Pursuit ("and go thou after them"). Ruth was told to go after the same servants that Boaz would later tell in verses 15 and 16, "Let her glean even among the sheaves, and reproach her not: and let fall also some of the handfuls of purpose for her, and leave them, that she may glean them, and rebuke her not." The whole time Boaz encouraged Ruth to pursue after his servants, he had a plan for her benefit! So it is with Christ and us. What if Ruth had decided to do something else and go to another place with another master? David said in Psalm 63:8, *"My soul followeth hard after thee: thy right hand upholdeth me."* Aren't you tired of chasing rainbows and looking for leprechauns? Let God satisfy your hopes and desires!

It Was a Field of Protection ("have I not charged the young men that they shall not touch thee?"). Since the master had already given Ruth the right to do as she pleased, there was nothing anybody else could do about it. He had given specific instructions to his workers to leave her alone. If the master protected her, then she was safe! Anyone who would challenge his order would face certain judgment. As God placed a hedge of protection about Job and his house, so God has placed us within the protection of His hand. Psalm 4:8 says, "I will both lay me down in peace, and sleep: for thou, LORD, only makest me dwell in safety." What a field of protection!

It Was a Field of Provision ("and when thou art athirst, go unto the vessels, and drink of that which the young men have drawn"). Boaz had thought of everything for this young lady and supplied her every need. The word for "vessels" means "something prepared." This takes forethought! Boaz had not met Ruth before, but her needs were already supplied before she ever came to his field! Psalm 36:8 says, "They shall be abundantly satisfied with the fatness of thy house; and thou shalt make them drink of the river of thy pleasures." Have you ever thought about the things God has prepared for His people? He has prepared a Book for our *sustenance*. He has prepared prayer for our *supplication*. He prepared Himself for our *salvation*. He prepared power for our *strength*. He prepared help for our *suffering*. And he prepared heaven for our *satisfaction*.

TOPICS: Desire, God's Will, Heaven, Protection, Provision,

R. CHRIS HANKS

DAILY BIBLE READING: 1 Samuel 1–3

TODAY'S VERSE: 1 Samuel 3:21: "And the Lord appeared again in Shiloh: for the Lord revealed himself to Samuel in Shiloh by the word of the Lord."

WHAT A STORY we read today about Hannah and her request to God for a son! Praise the Lord for a lady who could get her prayers answered! In today's verse, we now see Samuel serving in the house of the Lord and hearing the Word of God. Verse 20 says of Samuel, "And all Israel from Dan even to Beersheba knew that Samuel was established to be a prophet of the Lord." There was no doubt that God had chosen and prepared Samuel for a special work for His people. As part of the work of preparation, God appeared to Samuel. Nothing will prepare you to serve the Lord like a vision of God!

The Purpose of God's Appearance ("And the Lord appeared again in Shiloh: for the Lord revealed himself to Samuel"). The reason God appeared was because Samuel needed to see Him. I am not talking about seeing a vision of a ninety-foot Jesus. I am talking about God revealing Himself to His people. This was not to give Samuel some kind of "experience," but to prepare him for a spiritual work! The word for "revealed," as we have seen before, means "to denude." I believe that God is still revealing Himself to us today. How? Through His Word! Every time I pick up the Word of God, He "reveals" truth to me by the Holy Spirit. Have you ever exclaimed, "I never knew that was in the Bible"? If you have, you have also seen truth brought to light by the revelation of God. What a precious time for Samuel to see God as he had never seen Him before!

The Place of God's Appearance ("in Shiloh"). This was a place of God's choosing. God can reveal Himself anywhere, but God has a place where He has chosen to reveal Himself to His people. That place is Calvary. Have you met God at His place of peace? Don't think that you can meet Him upon your own altar or self-made place of false worship. All men must come by Calvary!

The Peace of God's Appearance ("in Shiloh"). The name "Shiloh" means "pacificator" or "tranquility" and comes from a root meaning "to be safe, secure"[8] There is a great, reverential fear when one stands in the presence of God, but there is also great peace. God is the very essence and supplier of true peace. Jesus Christ is even called the "Prince of Peace" (Isaiah 9:6). The only way for you to experience true peace in your life is for God to appear to you and to draw you to Himself.

The Precept of God's Appearance ("by the word of the Lord"). Anytime the Word of God is given, God is revealed. That shows us the importance of God's Word in church, of sharing it with others, and of reading and studying it day by day. God can appear in that place of quiet repose as you meet with Him in the Word. Second Timothy 2:9b says, "The word of God is not bound." That means the revelation of God is not bound!

TOPICS: Church, God's House, Peace, Revelation, Word of God

---

8   Alfred Jones, *Jones' Dictionary of Old Testament Proper Names* (Grand Rapids: Kregel, 1997), 334.

DAILY BIBLE READING: 1 Samuel 4–6

TODAY'S VERSE: 1 Samuel 4:3: "And when the people were come into the camp, the elders of Israel said, Wherefore hath the Lord smitten us to day before the Philistines? Let us fetch the ark of the covenant of the Lord out of Shiloh unto us, that, when it cometh among us, it may save us out of the hand of our enemies."

AFTER A BITTER DAY of defeat on the battlefield, Israel returned to camp and *reassessed* their stand. After this kind of defeat, losing four thousand men in one day, it was a time of *sorrow*. This was a time to *rethink* how they approached this battle: it was also a time of *strategy*. It was also a time of *submission*. They admitted that it was the Lord who had "smitten us today before the Philistines." What a great time to *repent!* But instead of repentance, they responded completely differently—and tragically. This is what happens when religion becomes ritualism.

They Set Their Attention Upon an Object ("Let us fetch the ark of the covenant of the Lord out of Shiloh unto us"). Ritualism sets its attention upon things. It loves idolatry. It enjoys the fantasy of "pretend," making grand statues of people as objects of worship. Exodus 20:4–5 says, "Thou shalt not make unto thee any graven image, or any likeness of any thing that is in heaven above, or that is in the earth beneath, or that is in the water under the earth: thou shalt not bow down thyself to them, nor serve them: for I the Lord thy God am a jealous God, visiting the iniquity of the fathers upon the children unto the third and fourth generation of them that hate me." In essence, the people had turned their attention from God toward the ark of the covenant. How could they sin in such a way? No matter what we do, whether in church attendance, Bible study, or prayer, our attention must be wholly upon God. Otherwise these acts in themselves can lead us into a ritualistic approach to God.

They Set the Attendance of God Upon an Object ("when it cometh among us"). They were more concerned about *the symbol* of the presence of God than *the actual* presence of God. It is easy to fall into this trap because the carnal mind does not want anybody *to think* we are without God, whether it is true or not! Our little maskings of the truth do not cover up the blatant lies that we live. Israel was not assured of God's power, but they could bring the ark of the covenant to themselves. *This is the true meaning of legalism, for they believed that they could bring the presence and the grace of God upon themselves by what they did.* Don't look for revival because of a favorite speaker who is coming, but because *God* is coming.

They Set Their Aspiration Upon an Object ("it may save us out of the hand of our enemies"). The people of Israel had heard of the many things that had happened with that old ark in the time of Moses and Joshua. They hoped these things would happen again! But they were wrong. The ark of the covenant was not going to do anything. That old crate they had built and covered with gold could not do anything! They needed God to save them! Church cannot save you or make you right with God. Israel wanted to win so badly, but only for themselves. They were not concerned about God getting the glory; they just wanted escape. That is what happens when ritualism occurs. If you follow this line of thought, you will find that ritualism destroyed these people! It gave them a false sense of *God's power* on their behalf. It gave them a false sense of *His presence* with them. It gave them a false sense of *His promises* and how He would keep them.

TOPICS: Idolatry, God's Presence, God's Power

DAILY BIBLE READING: 1 Samuel 7–10

TODAY'S VERSE: 1 Samuel 8:7: "And the Lord said unto Samuel, Hearken unto the voice of the people in all that they say unto thee: for they have not rejected thee, but they have rejected me, that I should not reign over them."

TODAY IS RECOGNIZED in our society as April Fool's Day—an appropriate day for this verse! Israel's desire for a king was not for the glory of God, but so they would feel better about themselves. The failure of Samuel's sons was not a real reason to seek a king, but an excuse. They were not going to miss this opportunity to get what they wanted from God so that they could be like everybody else. In two ways, we can see Israel's true foolishness in seeking a king.

Their Foolishness Was Expressed by Rejecting God ("for they have not rejected thee, but they have rejected me"). The word for "reject" in this passage means "to spurn, abhor, cast away." By rejecting God, Israel rejected and spurned His mercies. All that God had done for them did not matter any longer. They would rather live as they pleased. Rejecting God in your life is the epitome of foolishness. Proverbs 19:3 says, "The foolishness of man perverteth his way: and his heart fretteth against the Lord." It is easy for preachers to feel spurned when a church member rejects obedience and righteousness; however, it is a rejection and an abhorring of God, not of the preacher. When people reject the way of the Lord, they have followed foolishness to the very end, spurned the way of God, and embraced emptiness and destruction.

Their Foolishness Was Extended by Refusing God ("that I should not reign over them"). Only foolishness refuses to induct God as the King of the heart and allow Him to ascend the throne. *Israel chose to put their nation in the hands of a mere mortal so that they could be like all of the heathen nations that were around them!* What would you trade for God's watchful care over you and your family? Israel said, "God, instead of you, I think we would rather have a Saul!" Even though God ultimately chose the king, the Israelites had chosen anything but God! The greatest ruler upon earth would not be as good as God was. If their new king had the wisdom of Solomon, the philosophy of Socrates, the strength of Samson, the military might of Alexander the Great, the intelligence of Einstein, and the passion of Shakespeare, he would still not measure up in the smallest whit to the supreme qualities of Israel's Jehovah God!

TOPICS: Foolishness, Rebellion, Rejection, Stubbornness

DAILY BIBLE READING: 1 Samuel 11–13

TODAY'S VERSE: 1 Samuel 12:23: "Moreover as for me, God forbid that I should sin against the Lord in ceasing to pray for you: but I will teach you the good and the right way."

IN THIS VERSE, we see the mercies of a man of God. Though Israel rejected God from ruling over them, old Samuel still cared about them. Here are a few thoughts about this tender man and a hardened people.

His Responsibility Before God Was Still in Effect ("God forbid that I should sin against the Lord"). This is a good rule to live our lives by. We must recognize that our responsibility is before God and not man. Samuel could have "retired," gone home to Ramah, and picked up a fishing rod, never to think of those hardhearted people again. But he could not! He knew that would be a sin before the Lord whom he had served for so many years. Here is a little secret for all people, from preachers to parents to pew-sitters: it has always been about our *obedience to the Lord*, never about our results! Samuel said, "If I don't do this, then I will be sinning against God."

His Requests Before God Were Still Needed ("God forbid that I should sin against the Lord in *ceasing to pray for you*"). Samuel saw the empty void that would be left if he stopped praying for these people. Parents, don't stop praying for your children! They still need your prayers whether they are in *rebellion* or in *revival!* Friend, don't stop praying for your friends! They still need it whether they are in a *wrong prison* or the *right place!* Pastor, don't stop praying for your people! They still need it whether they are in *stubbornness* or *submission!* I thank God for parents and grandparents who prayed for me. Don't ever think that your prayer is in vain. Don't ever think that no one ever hears your message or cares about God. Don't ever think that it is a lost cause and that there is nothing you can do about it. Pray on!

His Rivers Before God Still Needed to Flow ("but I will *teach* you the good and the right way"). The word used here for "teach" means "to flow as water; to rain." Moses said, "My doctrine shall drop as the rain." Your scriptural ways and teachings still need to flow. This world does not need some old dried-up pond feeding it: learn to be a refreshing and a flowing stream. Neither our children nor the people in the pew need stagnant water. When they rejected him, Samuel had not stopped "running" in his spiritual growth. The spigot was still on! The water wheel was still turning! The glories of God still washed over his soul, and he was gushing with goodness and blessings from God! What a testimony to all of us today!

Samuel never did give the people a choice, but said, "But I *will* teach you the good and the right way." They still needed the truth whether or not they wanted it! The old preacher used to say, "Get under the spout where the glory comes out!" When you do that, you will be able to flow! Some of you need to go from being *cup* to being *faucet.* You must understand that others around you today are looking to you as the source of their spiritual growth. You can't help them grow if you give them a drink from your cup. You need to throw down a faucet that reaches down to the well of God's wisdom that will flow upon demand. I am not dismissing the goodness and grace of God. The point is that when you get full of God, His goodness will flow from you. That is why the Bible tells us to "be full of the Spirit."

TOPICS: Fullness, Holy Spirit, Pastor, Preacher, Responsibility, Study

R. CHRIS HANKS

DAILY BIBLE READING: 1 Samuel 14–15

TODAY'S VERSE: 1 Samuel 15:17: "And Samuel said, When thou wast little in thine own sight, wast thou not made the head of the tribes of Israel, and the LORD anointed thee king over Israel?"

THIS IS A GOOD THOUGHT for all of us to ponder today. As Samuel begins to speak, he says, "When thou was little." The word for "little" means "abbreviated." Usually when our pride is involved, we are not "abbreviated" but "exaggerated." Samuel reminds Saul of life before the anointing, how he was shy and timid and did not feel worthy of any honor. My, how things change—how easily we bloat with selfish arrogance! Here are a few thoughts for us from Samuel's warning.

True Humility Is an Expressed Humility ("When thou wast *little in thine own sight*"). This was not false humility expressed by Saul, but one that he genuinely felt and expressed in his life. When the time came to anoint Saul as king, he was nowhere to be found. God was the one who had to point out where he was. First Samuel 10:22 says, "Therefore they enquired of the LORD further, if the man should yet come thither. And the LORD answered, Behold, he hath hid himself among the stuff." Don't think for a minute that a hypocritical humility will fool God into blessing you.

True Humility Is an Exalting Humility ("wast thou not *made the head* of the tribes of Israel"). James 4:10 says, "Humble yourselves in the sight of the Lord, and he shall lift you up." God desires to lift up those who think little of themselves, but much about Him. Before you will ever experience the exalting hand of God, you must first be stripped of any and all pride that is being harbored within your heart. Humility is the first step toward *repentance*—think of David. It is the first step of *revival*—remember Nineveh. It is the first step toward *restoration*—the prodigal son. It is the first step toward the *revelation* from the Word of God—think of John on Patmos. It is the first step toward *reward*—all the saints will say, "Worthy is the Lamb." It is the first step toward the *resurrection*—for we must first die if we are to live.

True Humility Is an Empowering Humility ("and the LORD *anointed thee king* over Israel"). Of course, Jesus Christ is the greatest example of this humility. Philippians 2:8 says, "And being found in fashion as a man, *he humbled himself,* and became obedient unto death, even the death of the cross." Christ's humility did not end with just an expression or an exaltation, but with an empowering. Hebrews 10:12–13 reads, "But this man, after he had offered one sacrifice for sins for ever, sat down on the right hand of God; *from henceforth expecting till his enemies be made his footstool.*" The anointing and empowering that Saul received by direction from the Lord came as a result of his humility so that he could do the job that God wanted him to do. God wants to make His power known through your life. He can only do that if you are humble before Him.

TOPICS: Exaltation, Humility, Pride

DAILY BIBLE READING: 1 Samuel 16–17

TODAY'S VERSE: 1 Samuel 17:37: "David said moreover, The Lord that delivered me out of the paw of the lion, and out of the paw of the bear, he will deliver me out of the hand of this Philistine. And Saul said unto David, Go, and the Lord be with thee."

AS DAVID WAS CONVINCING King Saul to let him fight the Philistine, he remembered the battles on the Judean hillside with the enemies of the land that threatened his little flock. They were no different than this one who called himself Goliath. The proving fields of protecting sheep from the paw of the lion and the bear were now being understood as David faced the giant. We might call today's devotional "Lessons Learned in the Paw-Paw Patch."

The Lesson of Deliverance ("The Lord that delivered me out of the paw of the lion, and out of the paw of the bear"). David had to learn the lesson that only God could deliver him. David came to the utter realization of his own insufficiency while hearing the bleating of the sheep in trouble. When the wild beasts came, David knew that he needed someone bigger than he was to help him and deliver him from the lion and the bear. As a shepherd, David knew that a little lamb was in danger. What could he do but be faithful and deliver the helpless lamb? When the lamb was delivered, the lion and the bear set their attention, anger, and viciousness upon him. There was nowhere for him to run and hide. He needed help! He would have to learn the deliverance of the Lord. Many people, instead of fighting for the lamb, would be proud that they only lost one. It is only when standing for what is right that you will learn the Lesson of Deliverance in the Paw-Paw Patch.

The Lesson of Confidence ("he will deliver me out of the hand of this Philistine"). *If God delivered me before,* David thought, *He can deliver me now.* As you walk according to God's Word and His will, you will receive a great sense of confidence—for you will know He has done this before! This knowledge does not make every fight easy. You will not know *how* God will deliver: you will just know that He *will.* That will give you much confidence—not pride—in living your life for God and His glory. If you end up dying doing what He says, you will receive the Martyr's Crown. Many have chosen to be martyred because of the confidence they have in knowing and trusting God and His Word. Hebrews 11:35 says, "And others were tortured, not accepting deliverance; that they might obtain a better resurrection." It is this element of confidence that is missing in our lives today. People are unsure of their role in serving God and living this Christian life. Find your confidence in Him!

The Lesson of Commission ("And Saul said unto David, Go, and the Lord be with thee"). Once you have learned these lessons in the Paw-Paw Patch, there is something that God would have you to do. Once David convinced Saul of what was right and what David was willing to do, Saul sent him out. Do you realize that we have been sent out by the *King* to represent our land, our people, and our faith? We have been sent to fight the battle, but He has promised to win the victory! All we have to do is show up. When is the last time you showed up for the fight? You must understand that this is the way it will go down for the great battles that lie ahead as well. The Bible says that one day we will follow Christ on white horses, and He will defeat the nations with the sword of His mouth. All we have to do is go out for a Sunday afternoon horseback ride! It is His battle, and it will be His victory!

TOPICS: Confidence, Deliverance, Lessons, Submission, Witness

DAILY BIBLE READING: 1 Samuel 18–19

TODAY'S VERSE: 1 Samuel 18:15: "Wherefore when Saul saw that he behaved himself very wisely, he was afraid of him."

EVER SINCE DAVID'S VICTORY over the giant in the valley of Elah in chapter 17, Saul has been watching David with a jealous eye. Ever since he heard the young maidens' praise, "Saul hath slain his thousands, and David his ten thousands," in 1 Samuel 18:7, Saul had been wary of David. Jealousy will make a man do crazy things. However, the problem was not just that Saul was a jealous man, but that he was living the life of a fool in many other ways. Saul even recognized his own foolishness a few chapters later in 1 Samuel 26:21: "Then said Saul, I have sinned . . . *behold, I have played the fool,* and have erred exceedingly." Saul's foolishness began when he disobeyed God's command to utterly destroy the Amalekites. Sadly, his admission of foolishness was short-lived and insincere.

A Fool's Perception of Wisdom ("Wherefore when Saul saw"). Even a fool can recognize godly wisdom! Saul could not deny what he saw in David. Believe me when I say that the difference between foolishness and wisdom is quite noticeable. Though a fool would be hard-pressed to admit his folly, deep in his heart he knows there is a difference in the way he lives from the way he ought to live. Once a fool sees the difference, it is easy for him to become angry, for a fool is governed by his pride.

A Fool's Propaganda of Wisdom ("that he behaved himself very wisely"). Saul believed that he was wise and had convinced himself that such was the case. Proverbs 18:2 says, "A fool hath no delight in understanding, but that *his heart may discover itself.*" What a work of foolishness—Saul thought that he was the picture of true wisdom! Since God had chosen him to be king, wasn't that proof enough that he must be wise? Foolishness will deceive you and sell you a bill of goods about yourself to make you think more highly of yourself than you ought to think. Samuel warned Saul about this in 1 Samuel 15:17: "And Samuel said, *When thou wast little in thine own sight,* wast thou not made the head of the tribes of Israel, and the LORD anointed thee king over Israel?"

A Fool's Panic of Wisdom ("he was afraid of him"). The word here for "afraid" means "to shrink, fear (as in a strange place); also to gather for hostility (as afraid)." Saul was in a strange place that made him afraid. Since being set upon the throne, he had never played second fiddle to anyone. He felt that all the glory and honor should go to him! His fear also made him lash out against David and turned him into a physical threat. When Saul's fear settled in his heart, he became obsessed with the destruction of David to the point that he could not do anything but chase after him. The poison of Saul's fear contaminated his thought processes, and he ended his life seeking counsel from a witch. Don't allow the foolishness of your own fear to pull you down the vortex of spiritual destruction. It will dominate your mind and heart and will destroy all sensible reason that you may have left.

TOPICS: Deceit, Fear, Foolishness, Wisdom

DAILY BIBLE READING: 1 Samuel 20–22

TODAY'S VERSE: 1 Samuel 20:42: "And Jonathan said to David, Go in peace, forasmuch as we have sworn both of us in the name of the Lord, saying, The Lord be between me and thee, and between my seed and thy seed for ever. And he arose and departed: and Jonathan went into the city."

PERHAPS THE GREATEST friendship ever mentioned in the Bible is the friendship between Jonathan and David. If you have such a close companion as is modeled for us here, then you have been greatly blessed. Friendship is one of the most challenging areas of any life and one of the most problematic facing our youth. Few people can find a good friend, and even fewer know how to *be* a good friend. Friendship is one of life's most precious commodities and should never be taken for granted. Let us consider the principles given in this verse about the friendship of David and Jonathan and include them in all of our relationships as well.

The Blessing of a Godly Friendship ("And Jonathan said to David, Go in peace"). A godly friend desires peace for the other. The word for "peace" comes from a root meaning "to be safe." A good friend desires the well-being of his friend. I would like to remind you that Jesus has offered His peace as proof of His love toward us as a friend. John 14:27 says, "Peace I leave with you, my peace I give unto you: not as the world giveth, give I unto you. Let not your heart be troubled, neither let it be afraid."

The Binding of a Godly Friendship ("forasmuch as we have sworn both of us in the name of the Lord"). A godly friendship is voluntarily connected to God. This was no adolescent "cross your heart and hope to die" or "pinky swear" promise between these two men. The word used for "sworn" here means, "to seven oneself, i.e. swear (as if by repeating a declaration seven times)." That is a thoroughly thought-out promise! Of course, we acknowledge the fact that the number seven is the perfect number of completion. This was an oath of greatest truth and sincerity for both of them.

The Building of a Godly Friendship ("The Lord be between me and thee, and between my seed and thy seed for ever"). Every godly friendship must be built upon God. If it is built upon God, then it can touch others many years after we are gone, for Jonathan said, "And between my seed and thy seed for ever." This can be applied to the marriage relationship as well. Marriage vows must not be seen as making light promises to one another. The vows performed at a wedding are given before the Lord as an invitation for Him to be a part of your new home. Ecclesiastes 4:12b says, "And a threefold cord is not quickly broken." If you do not have God currently in your marriage or friendship, then you must change that!

The Burden of a Godly Friendship ("And he arose and departed: and Jonathan went into the city"). Especially when you are not together, your heart should be burdened for your friend. David and Jonathan had to say some sad good-byes to one another at this time. They knew they would face new trials without the encouragement of their friend, without the shoulder they had enjoyed leaning upon for so long. Yet, they would leave here encouraged because they said their good-byes in a loving and godly way and had a friendship that would endure any test that might come.

TOPICS: Friendship, Godliness, Love, Marriage

DAILY BIBLE READING: 1 Samuel 23–25

TODAY'S VERSE: 1 Samuel 25:16: "They were a wall unto us both by night and day, all the while we were with them keeping the sheep."

THE BIBLE CALLED NABAL a "churlish" man. The word for "churlish" means "cruel, grievous, and hard." Nabal was the opposite of what he should have been. Nabal was his *name,* and folly was his *game.* This verse comes from one of Nabal's servants as he described the kind and valiant acts of David and his men on the servants' behalf as they watched sheep in the mountain fields away from the master's house.

This verse also reminds me of our military. Thank God for the United States military! God has blessed America with great power, but He has also blessed her with good soldiers whose blood runs red, white, and blue! I send out my salute this day with a resounding "Hooah!", and I thank you for your sacrifice and defense of our country. What a blessing to have brothers and sisters whose motto truly is "God and Country!" Here are a few thoughts about David's men and also about our military.

They Were a Protective Wall ("They were a wall unto us"). Let's bring this verse home for a moment: just as we need military protection, we also need men and women who are willing to become walls in their own homes. The Bible says in Genesis 2:15, "And the LORD God took the man, and put him into the garden of Eden to dress it *and to keep it.*" One of Adam's jobs was to "keep" or "to guard and protect" the garden. If you don't protect your home from worldly influences and demonic attacks, nobody will. Spouses, if you don't protect your marriage from the heathen ways of our society, from the *immoral* advances of others to the *indecent* influences of the media, the *immodest* attacks of pornography, and the *improper* feelings of anger toward each other, your marriage will be doomed. Set up a protective wall around your home. And don't stop there. Set up a protective wall around your preacher, your church, your children, and your daily walk with God.

They Were a Perpetual Wall ("both by night and day"). We can sleep tonight because someone else is not. Have you ever been awakened by the terrorized cries of your child in the middle of the night? As you rushed to her side to pick her up, you felt her body tremble. As you grabbed him and pulled him close, he was immediately relieved by your presence. If you acted like you were going to leave, your child would grab you and squeeze tightly. Your children want to know that you will not leave them alone! What a comfort we have in knowing that our God "will never leave thee, nor forsake thee" (Hebrews 13:5). What a blessing in knowing that our military is perpetually vigilant for our well-being!

They Were a Peaceful Wall ("all the while we were with them keeping the sheep"). Sheep are easily spooked. Not only do they need a shepherd to reassure them, but they also need a peaceful place to refresh them. There is a great cry today for peace. It is important that the shepherd provide the sheep with peaceful places, or lack of peace will adversely affect their health. This is what our Lord has done for us! Psalm 23:1–2 says, "The LORD is my shepherd; I shall not want. He maketh me to lie down in green pastures: he leadeth me beside the still waters." As I continue to think about our military today, I am reminded of the threats and chaos they are enduring for us so that we can have peace here in our homeland. Very seldom do we even cast a thought about our safety throughout the day. That is only because someone has chosen to place him or herself in harm's way so that we can enjoy our freedoms and our peaceful land.

TOPICS: Faithfulness, Military, Peace, Protection

DAILY BIBLE READING: 1 Samuel 26–28

TODAY'S VERSE: 1 Samuel 27:10: "And Achish said, Whither have ye made a road to day? And David said, Against the south of Judah, and against the south of the Jerahmeelites, and against the south of the Kenites."

AS CHRISTIANS, we are part of God's construction crew! John the Baptist was sent as a mighty foreman to prepare a road for Christ. "Prepare ye the way of the LORD, make straight in the desert a highway for our God," Isaiah 40:3 says of John. Paul even characterizes himself as part of a first-century "chain-gang," as he was a bondservant for our Lord. Today, let's look at a few "roads" that we need to be working on.

Number one, the road to the Bible. **This Is the Road of His Precepts**. Psalm 25:12 says, "What man is he that feareth the LORD? *him shall he teach in the way* that he shall choose." The Word of God will show us the way that we should go.

Number two, the road to the throne. **This Is the Road of Prayer**. Hebrews 4:16 says, "Let us therefore come boldly unto the throne of grace, that we may obtain mercy, and find grace to help in time of need." Wear out a path to your prayer closet! Wear out the knees of your britches or your dress! Wear out the way to the place of intercession for your family and friends! Make a good road so that your children will see its message, its meaning, and its ministry.

Number three, the road to church. **This Is the Road to His Presence**. Hebrews 10:25 says, "Not forsaking the assembling of ourselves together, as the manner of some is; but exhorting one another: and so much the more, as ye see the day approaching." I remember as a child that there were times when we would all get in the car to go somewhere, and we would accidentally end up in the church parking lot! We were so used to going to church that we ended up there whether we meant to or not. I think if nobody had touched the wheel of the car, it would have brought us to church every time! Psalm 27:4 says, "One thing have I desired of the LORD, that will I seek after; that I may dwell in the house of the LORD all the days of my life, to behold the beauty of the LORD, and to enquire in his temple."

Number four, the road to the altar. **This Is the Road of His Purity**. Psalm 51:1 says, "Have mercy upon me, O God, according to thy lovingkindness: according unto the multitude of thy tender mercies blot out my transgressions." The altars in our churches need to be working at full capacity. Somebody needs to go down and take down the "out of order" sign that seems to be upon many of our church altars. I believe the altar should be our best friend—a place to make things right with God and one another. What a place of renewal, remembrance, and reverence!

Number five, the road to sharing the gospel. **This Is the Road to People**. Jesus said in John 14:6, "Jesus saith unto him, *I am the way*, the truth, and the life: no man cometh unto the Father, but by me." What a great road is given to a lost person! Some even use the "Romans Road" to show people the way to salvation. I heard an old-fashioned camp-meeting preacher say one time, "I don't care if you use the Romans Road, Galatians Gap, or Ephesians Boulevard, just get them to Christ!" Here in John 14, we find that Jesus is His own road! In essence, John the Baptist made a road for "the Road" to come in!

There are other roads we could talk about today, but here is your question: "Whither will *ye* make a road today?" You are building a road. What kind of road are you building?

TOPICS: Church, Prayer, Repentance, Witness, Word of God, Worship

DAILY BIBLE READING: 1 Samuel 29-31

TODAY'S VERSE: 1 Samuel 30:6: "And David was greatly distressed; for the people spake of stoning him, because the soul of all the people was grieved, every man for his sons and for his daughters: but David encouraged himself in the LORD his God."

WHAT A DEEP WELL was in the heart of David! After the city of his men was burned with fire, all of their families were taken, and they were spoiled, there was only One to whom he could turn for help. And today's verse says, "But David encouraged himself in the Lord his God." To whom do you turn when there is no one else? On whom do you lean when all you can do on your own is fall? David knew of One who would stand with him, and it was to Him that David made his plea. David said, "If I am going down, I am going down with God. I will not go down as a fool and an unbeliever!" What are some things that might drive you to your knees?

Distress ("And David was greatly distressed"). This word means "to be pressed; narrow." It reminds me of an hourglass. The grains of sand are "pressed" at the narrow part of the neck. It is a place of *pressure*. Many people will allow distress to turn them bitter, but David allowed it to turn him to the Lord. It is pressure that will turn a lump of coal into a sparkling diamond. Just wait! This is a *work of God!* It is a place of *patience*. All he could do was "wait on the Lord." There is nothing you can do in those places of distress. Just wait! This was a place to *wait for God*. It was also a place of *perfecting*. You see, there were very few choices for David. This would be a perfecting work in his heart that would show David more about himself than anything else. Just wait! This was the *will of God*.

Discouragement ("for the people spake of stoning him"). Death threats were nothing new to David. A lion and a bear wanted his life, Goliath wanted his life, King Saul wanted his life, his enemies wanted his life, and even later, his own familiar friend would want his life. Yet, how this must have hurt the heart of David! Men he had battled with side-by-side and shoulder-to-shoulder were now turning against him. These were men who had shared their thoughts and feelings with him, men who had pledged their allegiance to him. To be forsaken by an enemy is one thing, but to be forsaken by a friend is quite another. There are many who might read this devotion today who have experienced both distress and discouragement while being in the will of God. What do you do then? We will talk about that in a moment.

Despair ("because the soul of all the people was grieved, every man for his sons and for his daughters"). David's sorrow was much greater than anyone else's. Verse 5 says that David had lost his family too. But his sorrow and grief did not end there, for he felt the sorrow and grief of all his men! This is the curse of leadership! This is the curse of your pastor! To you it is a blessing because of his private prayers and the spiritual battles he fights for you because of his love and care for the flock. But to him, it is a great burden to bear. He does not bear it grudgingly, but it is a burden nonetheless. When you have a time of despair and grief, remember what David did.

What did David do in all of this? His was an act of **Devotion** ("but David encouraged himself in the LORD his God"). David was not going to quit on God! A preacher friend shared this thought with me a number of years ago. The word "encourage" has the root word "courage" in it. How could David have courage at a time like this? The only way David could take "courage" and be "encouraged" was to remember his *purpose* in the Lord! When we remember our purpose in God, there comes peace in our soul and encouragement to continue to trust in God. God had anointed David to do a work that he had not yet done. David knew that God had more for him to do for His glory! Find and remember your purpose in the Lord, and you will find the encouragement that comes with it.

TOPICS: Despair, Devotion, Discouragement, Distress, Purpose, Trouble

DAILY BIBLE READING: 2 Samuel 1–3

TODAY'S VERSE: 2 Samuel 1:21: "Ye mountains of Gilboa, let there be no dew, neither let there be rain, upon you, nor fields of offerings: for there the shield of the mighty is vilely cast away, the shield of Saul, as though he had not been anointed with oil."

WHAT A SAD and mournful chapter as we see David receiving the news of the death of his beloved friend Jonathan and of King Saul. To me, one of the saddest lines in the Bible is this one as it describes how Saul died: "As though he had not been anointed with oil." How could Saul have come to this point? Let me remind you that just before the battle in which Saul and Jonathan died, God would not speak to Saul; and because of that, Saul went to seek out a witch to conjure up the spirit of Samuel so that he could have spiritual counsel. Needless to say, he had come a long way from when he was first crowned king. As we apply this to our lives today, remember that oil in Scripture is a type of the Holy Spirit.

Saul lived a life that was **No Different from Living Without the Holy Spirit**. There was no **presence of God**. Many Christians live as though they are not saved (or, to use the biblical imagery, anointed with oil). This ought never to be said of a Christian! Saul did not seek the Lord's face in his daily walk. Saul did not respect the priests of God, for he had them killed. Saul did not respect the sacrifice of God, for he took it upon himself to offer it against God's clear command. Saul did not respect the will of God, for he sought to destroy David. He lived a life that, in essence, had no marks of the hand of Almighty God upon it.

Saul fought a battle in life and was **Defeated As If He Were Living Without the Holy Spirit**. There was no **power of God**. This battle was a useless and vain effort of human strength. Saul had seen many battles, but only in a few of them was the might of God displayed to bring a great victory. I have heard many Christians and preachers talk about the might of God in their lives in the "good ol' days." Oh, how they miss those days when God moved! For some reason, because they have not seen the hand of God moving in their life recently, they act like God is not moving at all anymore. *God is moving today!* God has a plan for our churches, our preachers, our children, and our communities, just as He did for the early church! Quit trying to save your pride by blaming an absence of God's power on the time in which we live! Find God! Find His Power! Let the Holy Spirit fill you, and you will find that old-fashioned, heaven-sent, glory-in-your-soul, hand-raising, face-crying, heart-bowing, mountain-moving, devil-defeating Christian worship is alive and well today and can be experienced in any life that bows, begs, and believes in God!

Saul ended his life and **Died As If He Lived Without the Holy Spirit**. There was no **praise of God**. There was no victory in this death. I have been to many a funeral and seen the grief of many people for the loss of a loved one. My heart, however, has been stirred at the funerals of old saints where the attendees still had the glory of God in their souls as they rejoiced over the life and death of their departed loved ones. Though there is sorrow in death, a Christian's death is different from an unsaved person's death, for his is a hope that lies ahead! Saul died, and that was it. This moved the heart of David so much that he said that Saul had died "as though he had not been anointed with oil." How you live this life can determine how your death will show forth the praises of God.

TOPICS: Holy Spirit, Shame, Testimony

DAILY BIBLE READING: 2 Samuel 4-6

TODAY'S VERSE: 2 Samuel 6:16: "And as the ark of the Lᴏʀᴅ came into the city of David, Michal Saul's daughter looked through a window, and saw king David leaping and dancing before the Lᴏʀᴅ; and she despised him in her heart."

WHAT A GLORIOUS DAY this was for David as well as for the nation of Israel. The ark was returning to Jerusalem! God had established the throne of David, and David was bringing the presence of the Lord into the capital of the kingdom. If only our leaders would humble themselves and bow their hearts before God once again so that God's peace and favor might rest upon this nation!

This should have been a day of rejoicing in every home. Yet David found that his joy in the streets of Jerusalem was nothing compared to the critiques and insinuations inside the walls of his own palace. What was it that turned Michal's heart from worshiping God? Here are a few thoughts about people's perceptions concerning our worship and adoration of the Lord.

She Was Concentrating on People Rather than God ("And as the ark of the Lᴏʀᴅ came into the city of David, Michal Saul's daughter looked through a window, and saw king David"). Whenever you look at people rather than God, something will displease you. Michal's heart should have skipped a beat as she saw the ark parade down Main Street. Instead, when she saw the ark, she looked for David. How easy it is for our hearts to be set upon men rather than God! David's heart was set upon God and upon His glory. That was demanding all of his effort, all of his thoughts, and all of his faculties.

She Was Concentrating on Perception Rather than God ("and saw king David leaping and dancing"). Our church worship has deteriorated as our concern for what others think has increased. It becomes a prideful matter and a source of embarrassment to raise a hand, to weep and testify, or to give a resounding "Hallelujah!" Forget what everyone else thinks, and concentrate on what God desires. If we would start glorifying God with all of our hearts and concentrate upon Him, we would begin to see the glory of God moving in our church services and ministries once again!

She Was Concentrating on Pride Rather than God ("and she despised him in her heart"). Somehow Michal turned this whole day into something about herself! One thing she never quite understood is that while she despised her husband, she was actually despising her God! She did not think *she* approved of David's worship. That is why people become so obsessed with the methods of people's worship! They feel that they are the Holy Ghost, and they want to determine what is right and appropriate in the house of God. I am not condoning a sensual, charismatic worship by any means. I still believe things ought to be done "decently and in order" (1 Corinthians 14:40). However, I believe that true heartfelt worship is more "in order" in God's house than a dead and dry religion! I know many people who would condemn the "leaping and dancing" of David and accuse him of many things, but before the Lord, it was accepted as a high form of worship. That is also why God has given us pastors. Worship for the pastor is twofold: he is to lead us in godly worship and to protect us from false forms of worship. I think sometimes it might surprise us how God would love for us to act in His presence.

Ephesians 2:22 will end our thought this morning: "In whom ye also are builded together for an *habitation* of God through the Spirit." This "habitation" has to do with preparing a "habitat" for God. If you have ever seen the effort, time, money, and research that goes into the construction of a zoo to determine the correct habitat for the animals in each and every sanctuary and exhibit, you understand a little more clearly what our "habitat" for God should be like. The makers of a zoo desire to make it as much like home as possible! Why don't we do that for God? What is going on in the presence of God right now? Why don't we make His house a natural habitat rather than putting Him wherever we want Him? Let us concentrate on Him and not on ourselves!

TOPICS: Impression, Manipulation, Pride

DAILY BIBLE READING: 2 Samuel 7–10

TODAY'S VERSE: 2 Samuel 9:3: "And the king said, Is there not yet any of the house of Saul, that I may shew the kindness of God unto him? And Ziba said unto the king, Jonathan hath yet a son, which is lame on his feet."

ONE OF MY FAVORITE stories in the Bible is this one about Mephibosheth. You can clearly hear the love and the mercy of the king for this man who was lame because of someone else's fall. Doesn't that remind you of what Christ has done for us? This verse shows us the thoughtful consideration of the king to exalt someone who had no right and no reason to be brought to the palace to enjoy the king's pleasures forevermore. Keep this picture plainly in view as you enter this verse study, and see your situation as that of Mephibosheth.

There Was No Greater King ("And the king said"). This was King David. When Christ comes to reign on this earth, He will sit upon the "throne of David." David is considered to be the best of the earthly kings of Israel. As he speaks, you can hear his mercy and his love, you can trust his judgment, and you can know his grace. Our Jesus is known as the King of Kings and Lord of Lords!

There Was No Greater Care ("Is there not yet any of the house of Saul"). I would understand if David just wanted to help any of the house of Jonathan, but he asks about the house of Saul. This is the greatest example of love and care for others! Matthew 5:44 says, "But I say unto you, Love your enemies, bless them that curse you, do good to them that hate you, and pray for them which despitefully use you, and persecute you." My friend, Jesus has done the same for us! We were enemies of God and the cross! The Bible says in Romans 10:5, "For if, when we were enemies, we were reconciled to God by the death of his Son, much more, being reconciled, we shall be saved by his life."

There Was No Greater Kindness ("that I may shew the kindness of God unto him"). What a powerful thought must have consumed David to be moved with such compassion to share the "kindness of God" with someone else! David did not want just to share the blessings of the king or the greatness of the throne, but the kindness of God! As David contemplated what God had done for him, he wanted to do that for someone else. What "kindness of God" was it that David wanted to share with others? It was *grace!* Hallelujah! "Amazing grace, how sweet the sound/That saved a wretch like me/I once was lost, but now am found/Was blind but now I see."

There Was No Greater Covenant ("And Ziba said unto the king, Jonathan hath yet a son"). This grace was connected to the covenant that David had with Prince Jonathan, the king's son! That covenant was the source of David's grace to Mephibosheth. Do you see the connection? Well, this might help: the name "Jonathan" means "Jehovah-given." Praise the Lord! John 3:16 says, "For God so loved the world, *that he gave his only begotten son.*" The reason we can enjoy the blessing of grace is because of the covenant made with the King's Son—the One who is "Jehovah-given"!

There Was No Greater Calamity ("which is lame on his feet"). David was not just kind to Mephibosheth, but was good to him. Mephibosheth was lame on both his feet because of someone else's fault. How sad! How cruel! There was nothing he or anybody else could do about it! He needed a king who would love and care about him enough to come to him. That is what Christ has done for all! He has come to invite us to a place that He has prepared for us. We cannot come on our own, so He has come to us! Praise the Lord! Accept His offer today!

TOPICS: Care, Covenant, Grace, Kindness, Love, Salvation

DAILY BIBLE READING: 2 Samuel 11–12

TODAY'S VERSE: 2 Samuel 11:11: "And Uriah said unto David, The ark, and Israel, and Judah, abide in tents; and my lord Joab, and the servants of my lord, are encamped in the open fields; shall I then go into mine house, to eat and to drink, and to lie with my wife? as thou livest, and as thy soul liveth, I will not do this thing."

BY THE TIME we read this verse, David has already committed adultery with Uriah's wife, Bathsheba. She has already determined that she is with child. David has hatched a plan to hide his sin by trying to get Uriah to go home and enjoy the pleasures of his home and wife for the evening. But Uriah, one of David's mighty men, summoned from the battlefield to obey his king's wishes, does not fulfill David's selfish plan because of his love of nation and call to duty. David ends up sending Uriah back to the front of the battle and murdering Uriah at the hand of the enemy. Uriah never even knows why. He dies because of a deceitful king and an unfaithful wife. We see the integrity of Uriah in this verse, integrity that must have preached many silent sermons against David's immorality.

Uriah Recognized the Covenant of Worship More Than David Did ("And Uriah said unto David, The ark . . ."). The very first thing out of Uriah's mouth was "the ark." His heart and mind were set upon the worship of God. His priorities were straight and right! Let me remind you that this was Uriah "the Hittite." This man had been saved from a heathen religion, a heathen people, and heathen ways. This man was changed! In everything he did, he put the Lord first. Even in fighting the battles for his country and his king, he fought for the Lord his God. Uriah would not be out of place, for his heart was set upon the ark of the covenant and worshiping God first.

He Remembered the Companies of War More Than David Did ("and Israel, and Judah, abide in tents"). He remembered that the country was at war. The battle was a collective effort. David was more concerned about treachery than he was about triumph. David had forgotten the war, but Uriah never forgot the nation of Israel that had gathered together to fight the enemy as a unified people.

He Respected the Code of the Warrior More Than David Did ("and my lord Joab, and the servants of my lord, are encamped in the open fields"). Uriah referred to the servants as individual men. To Uriah, there were names and faces on the numbers who had gone to war. David had failed to remember that Uriah was one of them! Uriah would never have participated in any comfort or pleasure that his comrades in arms could not, for he respected them more than that. They were his brothers. Some had probably saved his life at one time or another. They had watched each others' backs in the midst of battle. How could he forget them at a time like this? David did.

He Rejected the Comforts of His Wife More Than David Did ("shall I then go into mine house, to eat and to drink, and to lie with my wife?"). Uriah's answer was not because he did not love his wife, but because he was in the city on business. His priorities were in order. Uriah was serving the Lord, he was serving his king, he was serving his country, and he was serving his brethren. This was not the time to make sport or enjoy physical comforts that were perfectly lawful for him to engage in. This was a man in control of his desires. David had no control over his desires and was even willing to cross boundaries fulfill them with the wife of one of his faithful men behind his back.

He Responded with a Committed Will More Than David Did ("as thou livest, and as thy soul liveth, I will not do this thing"). These words must have rung in David's ears for many years. There was more character, integrity, and honor in the last couple of phrases of Uriah's statement than in anything that David had done for the whole season. Each word must have been a knife that struck fear and shame into the heart of David. Uriah said, "As thou livest . . . I will not do this thing." Uriah would not go home that night for David's sake. David, on the other hand, did live, and he did it for his own sake without regard for Uriah. Uriah was committed to his king and his God. David was just committed to himself!

TOPICS: Commitment, Control, Honor, Integrity, Shame, Sin, Temperance, Victory, War, Worship

April 14

DAILY BIBLE READING: 2 Samuel 13–14

TODAY'S VERSE: 2 Samuel 14:14: "For we must needs die, and are as water spilt on the ground, which cannot be gathered up again; neither doth God respect any person: yet doth he devise means, that his banished be not expelled from him."

IN THIS VERSE, a plea is made to King David to bring Absalom back to the kingdom and forgive him for killing one of the king's other sons. The thought of this verse touched the heart of David, for he had already felt this tenderness from God, who had received him back into fellowship after his sin with Bathsheba and the murder of Uriah. God's mercy was clear to him, and it's clear to us from this passage.

We See the Mind of God's Mercy ("yet doth he *devise* means"). The English definition for the word "devise" means to "form in the mind, invent, contrive, plan."[1] God *invented* a way to bring His people back to Himself. What a magnificent imagination our God has! God plotted the course of salvation and made a way for man to be reconciled to his Maker. We do not have a plan received by default, but one that was implemented by Almighty God! God's thought for salvation was hatched in His mind in eternity past and was put into motion by man's willful sin in the garden of Eden. It was the invention and wisdom of God that blessed us with gravity and the laws of thermodynamics. It was the invention of God that set the oceans in their bed and caused the wind to blow. But there is no thought or inventive action in creation that can show us the divine mercy of God more than the devised means of salvation.

We See the Means of God's Mercy ("yet doth he devise *means*"). God's was a plan that included the sacrifice of His own Son! It was a plan that included the salvation of man! This was a *beloved* means! It was a *bloody* means! It was a *bereaving* means!

We See the Ministry of God's Mercy ("that his banished be not expelled from him"). We serve a holy God. His holiness demands judgment for our sins. Every one of us deserves hell today! Yet, God has extended to us His infinite mercy that "his banished be not expelled from him." What a thought! God wants us back! Why? So we can bring dishonor to His name again? No! So that we can experience His mercies again! Lamentations 3:22–23 says, "It is of the Lord's mercies that we are not consumed, because his compassions fail not. They are new every morning: great is thy faithfulness." Rejoice in the blessed mercies of God today!

TOPICS: Forgiveness, Judgment, Mercy, Restoration

---

1 *Webster Comprehensive Dictionary: International Edition.* Vol. 1. Edited by Albert H. Marckwardt, Frederic G. Cassidy, and James B. McMillan. (Chicago: J.G. Ferguson, 1992)

R. CHRIS HANKS

DAILY BIBLE READING: 2 Samuel 15–17

TODAY'S VERSE: 2 Samuel 17:8: "For, said Hushai, thou knowest thy father and his men, that they be mighty men, and they be chafed in their minds, as a bear robbed of her whelps in the field: and thy father is a man of war, and will not lodge with the people."

TODAY'S READING COVERS the time when David ran for his life from his own son, Absalom. Here, God is bringing judgment upon David for his sin with Bathsheba so many years ago. May we all be reminded of the verse that says, "Be sure your sin will find you out" (Numbers 32:23). David found out that, as many old preachers say, "sin will always cost you more than you want to pay." However, God provided a way for David to come out of this judgment and defeat Absalom. One thing that jumps out at me in these few verses in chapter 17 is this: Hushai, David's friend, used David's might and his many stories of victory to put fear into the heart of Absalom. Absalom knew about David's war record: Hushai used an argument that began, "Thou knowest *thy father* and his men." We need fathers today who are still men! What did Absalom know about his father that changed his plan in this battle for the kingdom?

Absalom Knew that His Father Was a Man ("that they be mighty men"). It is sad to say that today we have a shortage of *men*. I did not say that we are short of male people. We are just short of real men. I would like to remind you that God is looking for men: "And *I sought for a man among them*, that should make up the hedge, and stand in the gap before me for the land, that I should not destroy it: but I found none" (Ezekiel 22:30). Where are the men who are willing to take a stand? Where are the men who are willing to lead their homes in spiritual things as well as in practical things? Even today, when I hear my dad call my name in a certain way, the hair on my neck will stand up like soldiers going to war! How can we learn godly fear when we do not respect or fear our fathers upon this earth? Let me remind you that I am talking about respect!

Absalom Knew What His Father Was Able to Do ("and they be chafed in their minds, as a bear robbed of her whelps in the field"). Hushai was telling Absalom, "You'd better be careful, because you just made him really mad." Don't think for a moment that Absalom did not know all of the mighty acts of his father and his men. I don't know that he lived a day without hearing about some old war or some old battle that spoke of the valiant efforts of these men! These acts were all written down, the minstrels sang of them, and the ladies talked of them constantly. When it came down to it, Absalom knew that David was able to do what was needed to win the battle.

Absalom Knew that His Father Was Not Afraid of the War ("and thy father is a man of war"). David believed that war was a part of life, and Absalom knew this. We are living in a time in which men are afraid of war and the battle. Even at home, men are afraid to fight the battle of enforcing the rules, keeping purity in the home, and submitting to authority. Men, every day we have to present ourselves for the battle. Even Paul said, "I have fought a good fight" (2 Timothy 4:7). It's still a good fight, Daddy! It's still a good fight, Mom! It is not a fight *with* your children; it is a fight *for* your children! We need to fight the battles that lie in front of us every day, trying to deceive us, defile us, and destroy us. If you will present yourself for the battle, the Lord will fight the battle for you.

I will give you one last thought: **Absalom Knew that David Trusted the Lord**. Somehow, though, Absalom dismissed this thought, banishing it to the back of his mind. Absalom knew that David was not perfect. He also knew that David's victories were a testimony of the Lord's blessings upon his life. If he was going to win the battle over his father, he would also have to beat God! What a sad thought! David had taught Absalom all about God. Absalom saw his father's love, worship, and devotion to God. Absalom, however, failed in his faith and did not have the same heart for God that David did. He wanted to rely on his personal charm, leadership ability, and military savvy to defeat his father. Absalom never counted on having to fight God to take the kingdom, and that was his biggest failure—rejecting the power that David had with God!

TOPICS: Authority, Fatherhood, Fear, Leadership, Trust

DAILY BIBLE READING: 2 Samuel 18-19

TODAY'S VERSE: 2 Samuel 19:10: "And Absalom, whom we anointed over us, is dead in battle. Now therefore why speak ye not a word of bringing the king back?"

WHAT A SENSITIVE and embarrassing time this must have been for the nation of Israel as Absalom was defeated and David was ready to take the throne yet again. This was a good reality check for them as they pondered their own works versus God's work. I believe that we need a reality check of our own as we contemplate what the Lord has done and what our mission upon this earth really is. This verse gives us something to consider down at the altar of our hearts as we lay prostrate before our wonderful Lord.

First, they had **Performed a False Promotion** ("And Absalom, *whom we anointed over us*"). In the beginning of Israel's history, the anointing of the king was something done by God. Somewhere along the line, the people determined that they were the ones who could call the shots and demand something for themselves. They even figured that whatever they decided, God would have to go along with it! God had anointed Saul over Israel: everybody knew that. God had anointed David over Israel: they also knew that! Now, Israel just wanted a change, and they felt they could do whatever they wanted to do. The point for us is that we have anointed and promoted many things in our lives, giving them a place to rule in our hearts that is not ours to give. God is the one who should determine who is king in our lives. It is very easy for us to put someone or something else in God's place of authority, but every time we do, there is much heartache and disappointment.

Second, they had **Persevered in Fervent Pride** ("Now therefore why speak ye not a word"). Their response sounds as if they were finally coming to their senses. They had lived long enough in their pride. It was time for a change! Likewise, we cannot get right until we are willing to repent of our sin. After going astray after Absalom, the people were finally asking themselves, "How long are we going to allow our pride to continue to lead us down this road of selfishness and destruction?" It is time for all of us to repent of our sinful habits, humble ourselves before the Lord, and do what God wants us to do! I must admit there have been times in my spiritual life when I went down to the altar in conviction and finally gave over to the Lord what He had long desired from me. When I got up, the question came, "What took me so long to do that?" It is our pride that keeps us from making things right with our God.

Third, they had **Promised Absalom First Place** ("of bringing the king back"). We must give God first place in our lives! It is His throne! It is His kingdom! Let God rule in your life once again. Today, you may need to let God have first place in your life. Perhaps you need to let God have first place—*again!* Bring Him back! Even in our churches, we have allowed God to take a back seat to our programs and our schedules, but we don't have His presence! We need to get God's presence back. Don't continue to live without putting God in His rightful place of honor and authority.

TOPICS: Pride, Priorities, Repentance, Revival, Surrender

DAILY BIBLE READING: 2 Samuel 20-22

TODAY'S VERSE: 2 Samuel 21:22: "These four were born to the giant in Gath, and fell by the hand of David, and by the hand of his servants."

THIS CHAPTER CONTAINS the accounts of the battles that David fought with Goliath's brothers. Today, we'll study the names of these giants and of the Israelites who defeated them. You will find here a pattern of great interest for any Christian. This verse makes sure to tell us that these enemies "fell by the hand of David and by the hand of his servants." Goliath means "exiled,"[2] but David means "beloved."[3] What a blessing it is to know that the beloved Son of God, our Great King, can defeat every foe that could cause us to be exiled from the presence of God.

Verse 16 speaks of one of Goliath's brothers named **Ishbi-benob. His Name Means, "His Seat Is in the High Place."**[4] Doesn't this remind you of what the devil said in Isaiah 14:13–14: "For thou hast said in thine heart, I will ascend into heaven, I will exalt my throne above the stars of God: I will sit also upon the mount of the congregation, in the sides of the north: I will ascend above the heights of the clouds; I will be like the most High"? That which goes against God desires to occupy the same place that God does! However, Ishi-benob was defeated by a faithful servant of David and one of his mighty men, Abishai. **Abishai Means, "Father of Gifts."**[5] What a great Father we have, and what wonderful gifts He has given us! James 1:17 says, "Every good gift and every perfect gift is from above, and cometh down from the Father of lights, with whom is no variableness, neither shadow of turning." Second Corinthians 9:15 echoes, "Thanks be unto God for his unspeakable gift."

Verse 18 speaks of another brother, named Saph. **"Saph" Means "Tall," but Its Root Means "To Stand at the Threshold."**[6] This sounds a lot like the warning God gave to Cain in Genesis 4:7: "If thou doest well, shalt thou not be accepted? and if thou doest not well, *sin lieth at the door.*" But we see it was the faithful servant Sibbechai who defeated him. **Sibbechai Means "Thicket of the Lord."**[7] What an exciting name! *Thicket* is defined as "a thick growth, as of underbrush through which a passage is not easily effected."[8] Often we say that something was caught in a thicket or even found refuge in a thicket. In other words, a thicket is "thick." So our lives should be a testimony of the growth of God in our lives. We have many people today who are thin and empty, but the Bible teaches that we are to be full of the Spirit.

Verse 19 just speaks of another giant. We have to go to 1 Chronicles 20:5 to find his name: "And there was war again with the Philistines; and Elhanan the son of Jair slew Lahmi the brother of Goliath the Gittite, whose spear staff was like a weaver's beam." Lahmi was his name. **Lahmi Means "A Warrior, an Eater."**[9] The root of his name means "to eat." Strong's gives another definition that says his name means "foodful." This has to do with our fleshly desires and appetites. First John 2:16 says, "For all that is in the world, the lust of the flesh, and the lust of the eyes, and the pride of life, is not of the Father, but is of the

2   Alfred Jones, *Jones' Dictionary of Old Testament Proper Names* (Grand Rapids: Kregel, 1997), 132.

3   Ibid., 93.

4   Ibid., 165.

5   Ibid., 8.

6   Ibid., 315.

7   Alfred Jones, *Jones' Dictionary of Old Testament Proper Names* (Grand Rapids: Kregel, 1997), 340.

8   *Webster Comprehensive Dictionary: International Edition.* Vol. 1. Edited by Albert H. Marckwardt, Frederic G. Cassidy, and James B. McMillan. (Chicago: J.G. Ferguson, 1992)

9   Jones, 222.

world." Lahmi was defeated by Elhanan, a servant of David ("the beloved," if you remember). **Elhanan Means, "Whom God Graciously Gave."**[10] What a gift from the grace of God!

Verses 20 and 21 speak of another brother. There is no name ever given for this one. The only thing we know are his physical attributes. He was a very unusual man: twenty-four fingers and toes in all! God describes this physical peculiarity for us with great detail. I believe this can be a warning to us about the deceitfulness of the strength of the flesh. This reminds me of 2 Chronicles 32:8: "With him is an arm of flesh; but with us is the LORD our God to help us, and to fight our battles." Do not trust in the arm of flesh, for it will fail you! This giant was defeated by one of David's own nephews, Jonathan. What a name! **Jonathan Means "The Lord Gave."**[11] God gave David a "Jonathan" when he needed him at different times in his life—first his friend, then his nephew. What "Jonathan" has God given you? It may be a friend that God has blessed you with upon this earth, or it could be the Friend found in Christ, who "sticketh closer than a brother." He has also given us His Holy Spirit who will never leave us or forsake us!

In every instance, God has blessed us with His love and His gift. Every one of these victors, including David himself, is a testimony of God's work in our lives and of his watch-care over us!

TOPICS: Appetites, Christ, Devil, Flesh, Holy Spirit, Lust, Satan, Self

---

10 Jones, 104

11 Ibid., 205–206.

DAILY BIBLE READING: 2 Samuel 23–24

TODAY'S VERSE: 2 Samuel 24:23: "All these things did Araunah, as a king, give unto the king. And Araunah said unto the king, The LORD thy God accept thee."

AFTER DAVID'S SIN in numbering the people, the judgment of God came upon the nation of Israel. When the death angel came to Jerusalem, the Lord stayed the hand of the angel for His love of the city. Immediately, Gad the prophet went to King David and told him to make an altar and a sacrifice to the Lord in the threshing floor of Araunah the Jebusite. There are some who believe that Araunah was the king of Jerusalem (or "Jebus") before David defeated it and claimed it for the Lord. It seems that Araunah had been there as proprietor of that piece of ground for a long time. Of course, this place was on the mountains of Moriah, where Abraham had been willing to sacrifice his only son to the Lord. We also know that in years to come, this would be the exact location of Solomon's Temple. Some scholars believe the garden of Eden was right in this place as well. These scholars also believe that Araunah's threshing floor could be the exact location where Adam and Eve ate the fruit of the Tree of the Knowledge of Good and Evil. While we can't know these things for sure, it wouldn't surprise me to learn that God had thought about all of these things in His great plan!

In the previous verses the Bible says that Araunah gave his threshing floor, the oxen, the threshing instruments, and other instruments of the oxen for wood. Araunah could have given these things without being a king at all, but he gave all with royal grandeur and dignity. This is what I would like to address this morning. How do you give unto the Lord?

His Manner of Giving Was One of Plenty. In verse 22 Araunah said, "Let my lord the king take and offer up what seemeth good unto him." What a witness this is to us today! When was the last time you offered your heart and life to God and said, "Just take it all!" The older I get, the more it seems that I cannot give enough to my Lord and Saviour. This goes far deeper than money. It goes to devotion and time. It goes all the way to my most private and spiritual worship. It goes to my service and my work. Thank God that when Jesus came, He gave as the King and gave it all!

His Manner of Giving Was One of Property ("All these *things* did Araunah . . ."). Araunah was willing to give all of his stuff. He was willing to give his threshing floor—*a place of his increase*. He was willing to give his oxen—*a prospect of his increase*. He was willing to give his instruments of threshing—*a performance of his increase*. Notice something: everything he was willing to give, he needed. He could even make the argument, "Lord, if I am going to be a good steward, then I need these things to honor you best." It amazes me how much people want to be good stewards when giving might cost them something! They sure don't mind spending their own money on what they want, but not on what would honor and glorify God! If we would obey and honor the Lord, we would never have a problem giving.

His Manner of Giving Was a Proselyte's Faith ("The LORD thy God accept thee"). Araunah knew what this was all about! He knew that this must be done. As an old inhabitant of Jebus before it was called Jerusalem, he remembered the old heathen ways of idolatry and worship. But from what he had seen under David's kingdom and example of worship, he knew that God was the only true God. He knew a sacrifice must be made before the Lord that would be acceptable in His sight. David is not the one who requested the oxen: Araunah did! He knew there must be a blood sacrifice from a pure offering. At this point, David's faith was also Araunah's faith!

Though David ended up buying these things from Araunah for the offering, we find in verse 24 that Araunah first gave these things freely. This sacrifice was actually given twice! Araunah gave it to the king, and then David gave it to the King! Keep giving your best to God each and every day.

TOPICS: Faith, Giving, Honor, Sacrifice

April 19

DAILY BIBLE READING: 1 Kings 1–2

TODAY'S VERSE: 1 Kings 1:29: "And the king sware, and said, As the Lord liveth, that hath redeemed my soul out of all distress."

IN TODAY'S VERSE, David is not far from death. Already, one of his sons, Adonijah, is jockeying for the throne. Since his father David was physically weak and almost dead, why not just claim the kingship as his own? But this was not a welcome prospect to everyone: if Adonijah was to take over, Solomon and Bathsheba most certainly would be killed. After talking with Nathan the prophet and Bathsheba, and being reminded of his oath to make Solomon king, David resolved to proclaim Solomon king of Israel. Though he was old and sick, David still had the ability to serve the Lord and make the right decisions for the kingdom. This verse tells us the authority that David claimed as giving him the right to make this decision. Consider the spiritual decision of David and the principles involved to help you make spiritual decisions in your life as well.

His Authority Was Based on the Existence of God ("And the king sware, and said, As the Lord liveth"). Every good decision should be based on God's existence. David gave assurance that Solomon would be king as certainly as God is still on the throne! We should choose to make the right choices according to our belief in God's reality. If God is not real, then our choices don't matter. If God is real, then our commitment to the Christian life and His Word must be connected to His existence, for only then can we have confidence in our Christian living. God has proven His existence in His Word, in His creation, at Calvary, and in the indwelling of the Holy Spirit in the life of every believer.

His Authority Was Based on the Expression of God ("that hath redeemed my soul"). David made his choice of king based on God's redemptive plan! The word for "redeemed" in this passage means "to sever, ransom, release." God had severed David from the hand of the enemy, released him from the bonds of the adversary, and ransomed him to Himself. There is nothing wrong with basing every spiritual decision on God's provision in salvation. After Calvary, how can we do anything *but* serve Him? After Calvary, how can we but give Him our hearts! He's our Saviour! I will therefore lay down my life and offer it to Him and sing His praises for evermore!

His Authority Was Based on the Exploits of God ("out of all distress"). The word for "distress" means "tightness, adversary, adversity, affliction, tribulation, trouble." This was David's testimony of God's faithfulness in his life. We all know that David had been in some tight spots! Here, at the end of his life, David was rejoicing that God had never failed him no matter what situation he faced! We all need to be reminded of Deuteronomy 31:6: "Be strong and of a good courage, fear not, nor be afraid of them: for the Lord thy God, he it is that doth go with thee; *he will not fail thee,* nor forsake thee." We often restrict what we allow God to do in our lives, thereby rejecting His provision and His deliverance. Remember what God has done in you and for you, and you will rejoice in God's wonderful faithfulness in every situation.

TOPICS: Deliverance, Faithfulness, God's Existence, Provision, Salvation

R. CHRIS HANKS

DAILY BIBLE READING: 1 Kings 3–5

TODAY'S VERSE: 1 Kings 4:29: "And God gave Solomon wisdom and understanding exceeding much, and largeness of heart, even as the sand that is on the sea shore."

THE GIFT OF WISDOM: What a testimony of God! What a blessing to Solomon! Proverbs 4:7 says, "Wisdom is the principal thing; therefore get wisdom: and with all thy getting get understanding." Wisdom is found in the *doctrines* of God, the *declarations* of God, the *descent* of God in Christ, the *desires* of God, and the very *depths* of God. God's greatest gift to man is wisdom. Even the redemptive plan fulfilled by Christ was the result of God's wisdom.

God blessed Solomon with His wisdom. Today, Solomon's wisdom is still talked about with great regard. God has even given us the Book of Proverbs, written by Solomon, to teach us about His wisdom. Let's consider what God has shared with us in this verse concerning His wonderful wisdom.

The Excellence of God's Wisdom ("And God gave Solomon wisdom and understanding"). Solomon did not gain this wisdom by meditation, by "finding himself," or even by education, but by seeking God. God is willing to give wisdom to you! James 1:5 says, "If any of you lack wisdom, let him ask of God, that giveth to all men liberally, and upbraideth not; and it shall be given him." This is much better than the worldly wisdom of this earth. The source of this wisdom is God! This wisdom has not been tainted by Socrates, Aristotle, Plato, Buddha, Gandhi, or Confucius. It has not been sullied by the vestiges of man's intellect or ability. Receive wisdom from the hand of God only or reject it with the greatest malice, for if it is not from God, then it is an imposter!

The Excess of God's Wisdom ("exceeding much"). God gave much because He has much! I need much wisdom. Man will never find what he needs in a book or an experience. He must go to the well of God's wisdom to draw it out. Romans 11:33 says, "O the depth of the riches both of the wisdom and knowledge of God! how unsearchable are his judgments, and his ways past finding out!" The word for "exceeding" means "vehemence," but when used with another word (in this case with the word "much"), it becomes an intensive or superlative. In other words, there is *so* much wisdom that God wants to give! God got sloppy in giving Solomon "exceeding much" wisdom! How much do you need? Know that God can meet and exceed your necessity.

The Expansion of God's Wisdom ("and largeness of heart"). God's wisdom will always change the one who receives it! What good would it have been if God gave Solomon the wisdom but not the ability to receive it? Or what if God gave Solomon "exceeding much" wisdom but not the means to use it? The word translated "largeness" has to do with width. God did not have to broaden Solomon's mind for this wisdom, but He had to broaden Solomon *himself* so that he might be able to use the wisdom as God had planned. Some people think that Christians are "narrow-minded" concerning things we believe. I remember an old preacher who held up his Bible, measured the binding on the back between his thumb and forefinger, and holding up his fingers said, "I'm about that narrow-minded right there!" The Word of God is as broad a thinking as we ever need to have! I believe that we just need to believe and obey what God says. I also believe that God will expand us to use the wisdom that He gives.

The Example of God's Wisdom ("even as the sand that is on the sea shore"). In order to help us understand how much wisdom He can give, God provided this visual picture of someone counting the grains of sand on a beach. Let me remind you, that is just one beach! No matter what God gives, He has so much more. Don't worry about asking for too much wisdom! You will never have to wait while it is on back order! There is an infinite supply because we have an infinite God.

TOPICS: Blessing, Understanding, Wisdom

DAILY BIBLE READING: 1 Kings 6–7

TODAY'S VERSE: 1 Kings 6:12: "Concerning this house which thou art in building, if thou wilt walk in my statutes, and execute my judgments, and keep all my commandments to walk in them; then will I perform my word with thee, which I spake unto David thy father."

WHEN SOLOMON FINISHED building the temple in all of its glory, God told him some important things about His presence and His pleasure that He felt Solomon should know. After Solomon worked so hard and did all that he could to make that place for the honor and glory of the Lord, God said, "Now, about that house!" Just because Israel had spent seven years in building it doesn't mean they were assured of God's blessing all the time. Just because they had used all the best materials doesn't mean they were insured against possible failure. Just because they had used all of their financial resources and given sacrificially doesn't mean they were assured of God's continual presence. In other words, God was confirming a conditional promise to them that He had made with David. Here are the three prerequisites of this promise.

The First Had to Do with a Godly Direction ("if thou wilt walk in my statutes"). Walking in God's statutes is a great decision that will direct our paths. Psalm 19:8 says, "The statutes of the LORD are right, rejoicing the heart: the commandment of the LORD is pure, enlightening the eyes." Is there any other place you would rather walk than in His statutes and His path? "Thy word is a lamp unto my feet and a light unto my path" (Psalm 119:105). Endless verses talk about the wonderful path that lies ahead of us in the protective shelter and sanctuary of the precious Word of God.

The Second Had to Do with a Godly Decree ("and execute my judgments"). Executing God's judgments actually has to do with pronouncing a verdict. What verdict have you given on the Word of God? What verdict have you given on the faithfulness of God? According to this verse, all we have to do is carry out and perform the verdict that *God has already made!* We know God's conclusions about *man's sin—this has to do with our witness.* We know God's conclusions about the *ministry's service—this has to do with our work.* We know God's conclusions about our *Mediator's sacrifice—this has to do with our worship.* We are to do the things that God has ruled and concluded already.

The Third Had to Do with a Godly Deference ("and keep all my commandments to walk in them"). If we do not hold the commandments of our God in high esteem, then we will have no desire to obey them. Today, we are lacking a respect for spiritual things concerning God and His Word. There is no longer an admiration for Calvary or a reverence for holy things. We have lost our awe of God. We do not tremble when we come into His presence any longer. We do not think of ourselves as beggars, but as blessings. Our entire view of ourselves is warped and distorted because of our selfishness and pride. Humility is a bygone thing, a relic in the history of the great revivals of the past, no longer on our list of spiritual needs today. Let us give God a godly deference of praise and glory by keeping His commandments. Jesus Himself said, "If ye love me, keep my commandments" (John 14:15).

What follows these thoughts in this verse is the completion of His promise: "Then will I perform my word with thee." There is so much that God has promised to those who love Him and serve Him with all their hearts. Galatians 6:9 says, "And let us not be weary in well doing: for in due season we shall reap, if we faint not."

TOPICS: Direction, Obedience, Submission, Word of God

April 22

DAILY BIBLE READING: 1 Kings 8

TODAY'S VERSE: 1 Kings 8:66: "On the eighth day he sent the people away: and they blessed the king, and went unto their tents joyful and glad of heart for all the goodness that the Lord had done for David his servant, and for Israel his people."

NEW BEGINNINGS. Don't you enjoy being given a fresh start? This verse tells us that it was on "the eighth day" that Solomon sent the people away from the celebration of the dedication of the temple. The number eight is the number of new beginnings.[12] Just for sake of example, the eighth day is the beginning of a new week. There were eight people on the ark who were brought to a new beginning. David, the son of Jesse and future king of Israel, was the youngest of eight sons—a new beginning for the nation and a new line of kings from the tribe of Judah. The list could go on. Here are some reasons why the people felt so blessed by their new beginning.

Blessed by the Example of Worship ("On the eighth day he sent the people away: and they blessed the king"). It was the king who had led them in worship. Wouldn't that be a great reason to rejoice? Would to God we had godly leaders who would not just lead the people of our nation politically, socially, or financially, but also spiritually! What a blessing to hear the voice of your own king invoke the blessing of Almighty God upon the people of his nation! If only our nation could see our leaders bow before God and humble themselves in His presence. Today, the world would say that such humility is a show of weakness. Biblically, however, we find it to be a testimony of great strength.

Blessed by the Extension of Worship ("and went unto their tents joyful and glad of heart"). Praise the Lord that they got something they could take home with them! That sounds like something for which you can give thanks! The word for "joyful" means "blithe or gleeful." When was the last time you were gleeful in other parts of your life because of how God spoke to you at church? That is exactly what our homes need today! Bring your worship home with you and enjoy the glee and gladness that results.

Blessed by the Experience of Worship ("for all the goodness that the Lord had done"). All of the blessings they had seen changed their church experience. This generation of Israelites had never seen God move and work as He did at the dedication service of the temple. There, they saw God do things, not just in number but in depth. Notice the verse says, "for all the goodness" and not just "all the good *things*." Once you find the "goodness of God," you can get lost in the immensity and glory of just *one* work that shows His love and His glory. Too many Christians today have "gotten over" their salvation! Revisit and remember what God has done for you, and stir up your love of God once again.

Blessed by the Expectation of Worship ("for David his servant, and for Israel his people"). This part of the verse creates much hope. David was dead, yet God still showed His love and goodness to His people for David's sake. What might God do next time! It also touched their hearts when God blessed them just because they were His people—"and for Israel his people." God did not only bless Israel because of David, but because of *whose* they were—God's! If God could bless them once, He could do it again! If He was willing once, He can be willing again! It dawned on these people that God was looking for an excuse to bless His people. Wouldn't that make you want to go back to God's house and seek Him again?

TOPICS: Church, Expectation, God's Goodness, Home, Hope, Leadership, Worship

---

12 E.W. Bullinger, *Numbers in Scripture* (Grand Rapids: Kregel, 1967), 200.

DAILY BIBLE READING: 1 Kings 9–10

TODAY'S VERSE: 1 Kings 10:13: "And king Solomon gave unto the queen of Sheba all her desire, whatsoever she asked, beside that which Solomon gave her of his royal bounty. So she turned and went to her own country, she and her servants."

WHAT POMP AND WHAT PRIDE must have presented themselves when the queen of Sheba visited Solomon! The whole city must have trembled at the earthly glory that was displayed upon her arrival. Yet, after her quest to search out Solomon's glory and wisdom, "there was no more spirit in her" (1 Kings 10:5). Solomon's wealth and wisdom far exceeded her expectations, for God's blessings go deep. In a further show of his greatness, Solomon endowed her with gifts upon her departure. Let us consider this verse in the spiritual light of our great King and the many blessings He bestows upon us.

It Was a Grand Fortune ("And king Solomon gave unto the queen of Sheba all her desire"). Isn't that the picture of our King? He has given us all our desire! The deeper I go as a Christian, the more I realize that Christ has given me things I didn't even know I wanted! This is not just talking about a man's desire for money and possessions. Psalm 37:4 says, "Delight thyself also in the LORD; and he shall give thee the desires of thine heart." This is speaking of more than just stuff! God has promised to give us the desires that we *should* have! Everything we could possibly want or need, He has already supplied. What a King we have!

It Was a Granted Fortune ("whatsoever she asked"). In other words, Solomon answered her requests. Our King will hear our prayers as well. This is not some prosperity gospel we are speaking of today, but a prayer according to the will of God. Remember, James 4:3 says, "Ye ask, and receive not, because ye ask amiss, that ye may consume it upon your lusts." God wants to answer our prayers, but our prayers must be according to His will. God has promised us answered prayer that shows forth His glory if it is asked in His name. John 14:14 says, "If ye shall ask any thing in my name, I will do it."

It Was a Grace Fortune ("beside that which Solomon gave her of his royal bounty"). All that the queen saw was *besides* what Solomon had given to her out of the treasures of the kingdom. This was all grace! My friend, there is so much more than forgiveness of sin and eternal life for you to enjoy as you follow your Lord! Psalm 68:19 says, "Blessed be the Lord, who daily loadeth us with benefits, even the God of our salvation. Selah." I have so much more than salvation! This Christian life holds more treasures than Fort Knox, the Louvre, the Crown Jewels, and every other precious thing upon this earth combined. Colossians 2:2–3 says, "That their hearts might be comforted, being knit together in love, and unto all riches of the full assurance of understanding, to the acknowledgement of the mystery of God, and of the Father, and of Christ; *in whom are hid all the treasures of wisdom and knowledge.*" What happens when we run out of this grace that God has so benevolently given? James 4:6 tells us, "But he giveth more grace." There is always more that He can give! How big is your imagination? God's grace exceeds it!

It Was a Going Fortune ("So she turned and went to her own country, she and her servants"). What was the queen of Sheba going to do? Go home to her country and share the wisdom of God with her people. God has never planned for us to horde what He has so graciously given. Others can benefit from the King's gift. Share the gospel and the gift of His grace with someone today!

TOPICS: God's Goodness, Grace, Prayer, Soul-Winning, Wisdom, Witness

R. CHRIS HANKS

DAILY BIBLE READING: 1 Kings 11–12

TODAY'S VERSE: 1 Kings 11:9: "And the LORD was angry with Solomon, because his heart was turned from the LORD God of Israel, which had appeared unto him twice."

WE NOW BEGIN to see the downfall of the wisest man in the Bible. In verse 1 of chapter 11, we find that Solomon's downfall began with his love for many strange women. We need to be careful of things or people who take away our love and devotion from our Lord. There is nothing in our lives that we should allow to turn our hearts from serving our Lord. Here are a few thoughts from this verse that will help keep us from the way of destruction.

What a Shame! ("And the LORD was angry with Solomon.") This is a testimony of Solomon's sin. God does not get angry with us for no reason. Every time the Bible states that the anger of the Lord was kindled, there were grievous sins associated with it. We are assured that God's heart toward His people is not set on anger, for the Bible says in Jeremiah 29:11, "For I know the thoughts that I think toward you, saith the LORD, thoughts of peace, and not of evil, to give you an expected end." God's anger is not something to trifle with. It is God's anger that will judge man for his sin. It is God's anger that will satisfy the fires of hell in eternal damnation. Hebrew 10:31 says it like this: "It is a fearful thing to fall into the hands of the living God."

What a Shock! ("Because his heart was turned from the LORD God of Israel.") How could this happen? How could anybody turn his heart from the Lord? As in Solomon's life, God has been so good to us every step of the way, and His faithfulness has been true. Yet, a proud and arrogant heart will lead to the sad conclusion of a man who rejects the way of the Lord. It is as if Solomon "repented" from loving God. The Bible teaches that we should turn away from the sin of the world, the flesh, and the devil. Instead, Solomon turned away from God! What a shock it is to me when people turn away from following the Lord. In Solomon's heart there was still the memory of the glory of the Lord that had filled the house when Solomon dedicated it to God. What a shock! There was the memory of the many thousands of sacrifices Solomon had given so freely from his devotion to the Lord. What a shock! There was the testimony that Solomon had shared with rulers all over the world of the love and faithfulness of Jehovah God to His people. What a shock! Now his heart was turned from the Lord!

What a Shun! ("Which had appeared unto him twice.") God had spoken and visited Solomon in His grace. Twice Solomon had heard the voice of the Lord. Twice he had heard the tenderness of God. What an encouragement to serve Him with all his heart! Yet he rejected these visitations and shunned the God of heaven. There are times when I think that if I saw Calvary, heard Christ speak, or had the Lord appear to me, I would never forsake Him. How proud and how boastful that thought really is! God indwells us with His Holy Spirit today. God speaks to us faithfully through His Word. Yet, we still struggle with our devotion and our commitment to Him. Though He has been faithful, though He has spoken to our hearts, it is so easy to shun God and follow our own carnal ways. This is something we must constantly guard against in our hearts.

TOPICS: Disobedience, Judgment, Rebellion, Shame

DAILY BIBLE READING: 1 Kings 13–14

TODAY'S VERSE: 1 Kings 14:27: "And king Rehoboam made in their stead brasen shields, and committed them unto the hands of the chief of the guard, which kept the door of the king's house."

TODAY'S STORY TELLS of the king of Egypt who came to fight with Jerusalem. After his victory and as he was taking all their treasures, he took with him the shields of gold that Solomon had made. Instead of fighting to get those shields back or even making more of the same kind, Rehoboam just made inferior replacements and forgot about it. I believe the shields represent doctrine that should never be changed. Today, the world and even churches are changing what the Bible says, and they are putting something in its place that looks similar but is not the same. Sometimes this replacement is done with the best of intentions, but we must not change those things that are of great worth to us in our faith.

A current example will help make this point: a movement called "Intelligent Design" is battling to enter our schools as an alternative to evolution. I believe it started with good intentions. However, we need to be careful that we do not put brazen shields for the shields of gold that we once had. The origin of our world is still called *creation!* That is a brazen shield. Some have changed their view of Scripture and its authority by saying that we do not have a perfect Word for us today. Nothing could be further from the truth! Let us not put a brazen shield for the doctrine of the infallibility of the Word of God. Here are a couple of thoughts about Rehoboam's shields.

First, they were **Hypocritical in Their Vision**. Polished brass can be made to look like gold. No matter how it looked, though, it would never be the same. We need a people of God today who are genuine in their beliefs, authentic in their character, and real in their worship. We sure don't need any more people saying of Christians, "They are just not real." There are many who can put on a good face when they come to church and carry their Bibles. They might fool the preacher. They might fool the people. They will never fool God. Ezekiel 30:27 says, "And I will cause you to pass under the rod, and I will bring you into the bond of the covenant." This is actually speaking of a shepherd who would make his sheep pass under the rod. The all-wise shepherd would take his rod and pull back the wool of each sheep as it passed into the fold. As he pulled the wool back, he would be able to see any lesions, parasites, and wounds that needed attention. This is where we get the phrase "to pull the wool over one's eyes." Let me tell you, my friend, you will not "pull the wool over the eyes" of God!

Second, they were **Hypocritical in Their Value**. Even if brass or bronze can be made somehow to look like gold, they will never be worth as much as gold! No matter how it is polished and shined, brass will never reach the value that this precious metal has. There are some things that are worth too much to give up! We cannot put brazen shields for the virgin birth, blood atonement, vicarious death and suffering of our Saviour, authority of the Word of God, or the deity of Jesus Christ.

Third, these shields were **Hypocritical in Their Vacancy**. What I mean is this: the properties and scarcity of gold give it its value. Brass is in abundance; gold must be labored over intensely, from mining it out of the earth to the melting process that gives it its purity. Rehoboam and those in his kingdom wanted people to think that it was just as hard to find that which was more abundant. In the time it took to make the brass look like gold, they could have found the real thing! Let me ask you this: where are you going to find the real thing today? There are not very many places to find "gold" left. The following verse of our main text also tells us that these shields were not on display all of the time, but had to be stored for safekeeping. It is a funny thing that imitations are never around when you need them! They fly away so quickly! The things that are real are with you constantly and make their presence known in your life. Proverbs 6 speaks of the value of wisdom and in verse 22 says, "When thou goest, it shall lead thee; when thou sleepest, it shall keep thee; and when thou awakest, it shall talk with thee." This is what we need today: something real and something present!

TOPICS: Deception, Hypocrisy, Lies, Virtue

R. CHRIS HANKS

DAILY BIBLE READING: 1 Kings 15–16

TODAY'S VERSE: 1 Kings 16:31: "And it came to pass, as if it had been a light thing for him to walk in the sins of Jeroboam the son of Nebat, that he took to wife Jezebel the daughter of Ethbaal king of the Zidonians, and went and served Baal, and worshipped him."

AHAB'S WICKEDNESS HAD BROUGHT the nation of Israel to a new low. Never before had they had someone as vile as Ahab on the throne of power. My, look at the "progress" that has been made since David last ruled! Israel's minds have really been expanded. Ahab and his depraved lifestyle fashioned a wicked "enlightenment" for many others in the nation. These were not good days in Israel. This verse tells us in one sentence many of the ways that Ahab worked his wickedness for his own personal pleasure.

He Had a Will to Wickedness ("And it came to pass, as if it had been a light thing for him to walk in the sins of Jeroboam the son of Nebat . . ."). Our will is the first problem we have concerning sin. This verse makes a comparison between Jeroboam's conduct and Ahab's. It is the Bible's equivalent to saying, "Do you remember how bad Jeroboam was? Well, with Ahab, that was nothing!" Our will to sin is ever so strong in the body of this flesh. Hear the Apostle Paul in Romans 7:25: "So then with the mind I myself serve the law of God; but with the flesh the law of sin." Only the Holy Spirit can give us victory over our flesh's will to sin.

He Took a Wife to Wickedness ("that he took to wife Jezebel the daughter of Ethbaal king of the Zidonians"). Ahab's marriage to Jezebel is referenced here as the greatest of the wicked things that Ahab ever did. This woman single-handedly made Baal worship the national official religion. You will not find anything in Scripture so treacherous as her false accusation and murder of Naboth, yet that was perhaps the simplest of her deeds. She worked her husband as if he were a marionette. For any yet-unmarried person who might be reading this devotion, may you be warned that your choice of spouse will affect your worship and dedication to the Lord. Choose wisely!

He Did a Work of Wickedness ("and went and served Baal"). We cannot blame all of Ahab's sin just on his sinful nature or on his wife. Ahab served Baal because he wanted to do it! The word for "serve" in this verse means "to work (in any sense); by implication, to serve, till, (causatively) enslave." Ahab worked, prepared, and "tilled" himself to be able to serve Baal. He literally signed himself up to be the slave of this false religion! Many times, such people don't even realize that their life is a dungeon and their worship a chain. They have fallen prey to the desire of Satan. Second Timothy 2:25–26 says, "In meekness instructing those that oppose themselves; if God peradventure will give them repentance to the acknowledging of the truth; and that they may recover themselves out of the snare of the devil, who are taken captive by him at his will."

He Continued in the Worship of Wickedness ("and worshipped him"). I have never understood idolatry. What was it about Baal worship that made it so appealing to people? Israel had problems with it for centuries. Baal worship, however, did not stop with idolatry. Baal worship included sexual immorality, sexual deviancy, and even human sacrifice. This was a worship that allowed you to do whatever your flesh wanted to do and encouraged you to fulfill your lusts and appetites. It was not just idolatry that enticed people, but fleshly gratification. If we are going to worship, let us worship God! The word for "worship" means "to depress, prostrate." Since these gods were not real, the people were bowing down and participating in self-worship. Instead of worshiping a false god that doesn't exist, may we prostrate ourselves before God Almighty, who deserves and desires our worship.

TOPICS: Carnality, Flesh, Idolatry, Marriage, Sexuality, Wickedness, Will, Worship

DAILY BIBLE READING: 1 Kings 17–18

TODAY'S VERSE: 1 Kings 18:21: "And Elijah came unto all the people, and said, How long halt ye between two opinions? if the LORD be God, follow him: but if Baal, then follow him. And the people answered him not a word."

ELIJAH! WHAT A MAN! What a colorful character and man of God we have to discuss today! John the Baptist, the forerunner of the Messiah, would come in the power and spirit of Elijah. Elijah would stand as a beacon of righteousness in one of the darkest times of Israel's history. I remember hearing this story multiple times in Sunday school as a child. My mind can still see the prophets of Baal cutting their bodies in an attempt to get fire to fall from heaven. I still watch Elijah build the altar of the Lord that had been broken, lay the sacrifice upon it, drench it with water, and kneel to pray. I can almost hear Elijah's prayer and feel the heat from the fire of heaven as it falls upon the altar, consumes the sacrifice and the altar, and licks up the water in the trench. There is no doubt that Elijah was God's man! Let's catch a glimpse of the boldness of Elijah and pray that we can have the same boldness to live our lives for the honor and glory of God.

The Boldness of Elijah's Manner ("And Elijah came unto all the people"). You will not find Elijah slinking around the corner and whispering to someone about God's will. He was sent to everyone whether they would hear or not. Elijah showed up and started making announcements. He had no fear because he knew his message was based on God's love for His people. Elijah also loved his country and wanted them to return to serving and worshiping God. First John 4:18 says, "There is no fear in love; but *perfect love casteth out fear: because fear hath torment.* He that feareth is not made perfect in love." If you love people and love God and His Word, you will have the boldness to share Jesus Christ with others, for that is the essence of true love.

The Boldness of Elijah's Message ("and said, How long halt ye between two opinions?"). Elijah got right down to business, didn't he? What a confrontation! This was a challenge to the reason and faith of the people. Elijah called it like it was. The word for "halt" has the implied meaning "to hesitate." Living two lives in two manners with two faiths will make anybody hesitate. James 1:8 says, "A double minded man is unstable in all his ways." Nobody likes someone who is two-faced. God has made this easy for us in telling us in Ephesians 4:5, "One Lord, one faith, one baptism." These last days are in need of Christians who will make clear decisions and not hesitate in the face of uncertain times.

The Boldness of Elijah's Mandates ("if the LORD be God, follow him: but if Baal, then follow him. And the people answered him not a word"). This sounds like good reasoning to me. Let's take the guesswork out of this thing. How have you seen the Lord work in your life? One of the reasons Israel struggled between Baal and God was that they had heard the stories about God but had never personally experienced anything of Him in their lives. When they went off the mountain on this day, they would say, "Let me tell you what I saw Jehovah do with my own eyes!" The clarity of Elijah's message made the people observe and discern between the actions of Baal and God. The Bible says, "The people answered him not a word." What the preacher said was right! Let's see who is real and deserving of all our worship, and then follow Him. No tricks, no gimmicks, and no deceptions. God has challenged us to do this in Psalm 34:8: "O taste and see that the LORD is good: blessed is the man that trusteth in him." Try Him yourself: you'll like Him!

TOPICS: Boldness, Decision, Double-mindedness, Love, Man of God, Witness

DAILY BIBLE READING: 1 Kings 19-20

TODAY'S VERSE: 1 Kings 19:5: "And as he lay and slept under a juniper tree, behold, then an angel touched him, and said unto him, Arise and eat."

IN THIS CHAPTER, Jezebel has sent Elijah a letter of certain death. The devil is always doing his best to intimidate and manipulate God's people and have them live in a spirit of fear and uncertainty. One of his greatest tactics is to keep God's people off balance. His desire is to keep you from living a life of joy, peace, and confidence in the Holy Ghost. So what did Elijah do? He ran. Discouragement and distress can do much damage to a person's emotional stability. You will find that many of your greatest battles will come after your greatest victories, just like Elijah after the victory on Mount Carmel. Yet, God did not leave his servant without hope but encouraged Elijah to cause him to trust in God once again. In this verse we see the Lord at work to encourage His man.

God Gave Him a Place of Rest ("And as he lay and slept under a juniper tree"). We do not need to become lazy people. The Bible says in Proverbs 20:13, "Love not sleep, lest thou come to poverty; open thine eyes, and thou shalt be satisfied with bread." But there are many times when we need sweet rest. Even Jesus knew when to pull away from the crowds and rest. After Elijah's epic battle with the prophets of Baal, he was spiritually, emotionally, and physically exhausted. He told Ahab to go eat, but he himself went into the mountain to pray for rain. Thank God for a man of God who can pray and shake heaven! God girded Elijah's loins, and he outran Ahab's chariot back to Jezreel. But there was no time for celebration, as Jezebel, upon Ahab's return, learned of her precious prophets of Baal and issued a death sentence upon the life of Elijah! Yet, in the midst of all this trouble, God gave him a place to sleep.

God Gave Him a Powerful Touch ("then an angel touched him"). Just when you think that God doesn't care anymore and that there is no way that you can go on, He will touch your heart and life and give you strength to continue to do His will. Sometimes He will use an angel to do His work, and sometimes He will touch you Himself! As an added note of encouragement, remember that God has never touched anything that He did not change! I remember the day that He touched me: my, what a change came into my life that day! I am still operating on the change that came upon me at the touch of God's hand.

God Gave Him a Precious Word ("and said unto him"). This was a word from the Lord sent through His angel. There is no greater blessing than a word from God! God has said, "The words that I speak unto you, they are spirit and they are life" (John 6:63). What a hope we have and a precious resource for any and every situation! If you need help, direction, or hope, go to the Word of God. Job said, "I have esteemed the words of his mouth more than my necessary food" (Job 23:13).

God Gave Him a Prepared Meal ("Arise and eat"). God had already fed Elijah's soul with a word; now He would feed his body with needed sustenance for the way. Think about it: a meal straight from the menu of heaven, prepared by an agent from God! So far, I have never heard either God or an angel rattling the pans in my kitchen early in the morning trying to whip up something for me to eat for the day! Yet, the same care that watched over Elijah watches over us. My friend, God knows exactly what you need! Let Him feed you! A few verses down you will find that Elijah went in the strength of that food forty days and forty nights to Horeb, the mount of God. Now *that* is a meal that will stick with you! Did you ever tell anybody that your grandma could cook a meal that would stick to your ribs? Wait till God gets ahold of the groceries! You will find that you have more strength and power with what God has prepared for you than in anything you could ever prepare for yourself.

TOPICS: Peace, Power, Rest, Strength, Supply, Word of God

DAILY BIBLE READING: 1 Kings 21–22

TODAY'S VERSE: 1 Kings 21:25: "But there was none like unto Ahab, which did sell himself to work wickedness in the sight of the Lord, whom Jezebel his wife stirred up."

OL' AHAB WAS QUITE a colorful figure in the Old Testament. He was the source of the drought in Israel as a judgment of God, he called the man of God his enemy, he was manipulated by one of the most wicked women ever to live, he was displeased if he didn't get his own way, and he was responsible for killing a righteous man to obtain possession of his field for selfish purposes. Yet through all of these things, he repented and God had mercy on him! This verse lays very serious charges against him.

First, we see that **Ahab Worked His Worth** ("But there was none like unto Ahab, which did sell himself"). Ahab was up for hire! There was nothing sacred in his value system. He was willing to do whatever was necessary to accomplish his goals, no matter how devilish it might be. This is not uncommon in our world today, whether in business, entertainment, news, or sports. People have sold themselves to the Almighty Dollar to get money, fame, friends, and prestige. If you think about it, Ahab was nothing but a peddler. He peddled his wares of vice and vanity to the highest bidder of whatever desire was pleading with him in his own soul. He prostituted himself for selfish gain and immediate gratification. Later in our reading you will meet a king, Manasseh, who was actually viler than Ahab, but you will not find anyone who *tried* to be viler than Ahab. What a reputation!

Second, we see that **Ahab Worked His Wickedness** ("which did sell himself to work wickedness in the sight of the Lord"). Whatever the Lord said to do, Ahab refused. Whatever the Lord forbade, Ahab embraced. The Bible says in Genesis 6:5, "And God saw that the wickedness of man was great in the earth, and that every imagination of the thoughts of his heart was only evil continually." We are bent toward wickedness in our hearts. Have you ever had a child who went through a phase in which he would do the opposite of what you told him to do? Stubbornness and rebellion are in our nature! I have seen my children hear my command, look at what they wanted to do, and look back at me as if they were contemplating whether disobedience was worth it. It is never worth it! Jeremiah 17:9 says, "The heart is deceitful above all things, and desperately wicked: who can know it?"

Third, we see that **Ahab Had a Wicked Wife** ("whom Jezebel his wife stirred up"). Some people should never be together. This was one of those couples! Even today, many thousands of years later, the accusations associated with the name Jezebel are enough to destroy the reputation of any well-meaning girl. It is extremely disturbing to me that our society has tried to turn the bad girl into one of honor. However, no one really wants to be associated with such a woman! No matter how cool it is, it is not right. R. G. Lee in his famous sermon "Payday Someday" told the story of Naboth, Ahab, Jezebel, and Elijah that we find in our reading. He said of Jezebel that she was the viper coiled beside the throne that the vile human toad Ahab squatted upon.[13] This lover of Baal and lover of herself was the one behind the spineless king, poking and prodding him into the wasteland of godlessness and wickedness. Don't be like either Ahab or Jezebel! Let God give you a new life, new hope, and new outlook on living for Him.

TOPICS: Choice, Decisions, Presumption, Sin, Wickedness

---

13 Robert Green Lee, *Payday Someday* (Nashville: Broadman & Holman, 1995), 18–19.

DAILY BIBLE READING: 2 Kings 1–3

TODAY'S VERSE: 2 Kings 2:13: "He took up also the mantle of Elijah that fell from him, and went back, and stood by the bank of Jordan."

I WOULD LIKE TO GIVE you a few thoughts today about Elijah's mantle. This was a mantle that was worn well upon the shoulders of a great man of God. It was a *surrendered mantle*. It was a *sanctified mantle*. It was a *storied mantle*. Thank God for a young preacher boy who saw the importance of a ministry with a mantle upon it! As Elisha went over to pick up the mantle after it had fallen from his master, he was not stooping down to pick up a relic and memorial of his mentor. *He was embracing the power of God.* I have been reminded of great men who have gone on to be with the Lord over the last few years: men like Tom Malone, Junior Bryson, and Lee Roberson. The list could be much longer. There is no doubt that these men had a mantle resting upon them! The question remains, who will think enough to take time to pick up the old mantle that these men left behind? We have a great work that lies ahead of us, but what kind of a work is it if we do not have a God-empowered mantle upon it? What will our children pick up after us when we are done: a ritualistic form of faith that is centered upon self and service, or a heart for the presence and power of God that is centered upon will and worship? Here are a few simple thoughts about this mantle for us to consider this morning.

It Was Surely an Old Mantle. Jeremiah tells us to "ask for the old paths" (Jeremiah 6:16). God has given us an entire Bible of witnesses that have gone on before, a "great cloud of witnesses" as Hebrews 12:1 puts it. These were men and women of faith, fervor, and favor. Today people are forsaking the old-time ways of doctrine in their preaching, the old-time ways of the Spirit in their power, and the old-time ways of surrender in their service. Where has revival gone? It has been ignored by the Baptists in the name of ritualism rather than repentance. It has been prostituted by the Charismatics in the name of sensualism instead of the true Spirit. It has been rejected by the world in the name of tolerance rather than truth. We need to go back and pick up the mantle that is waiting for someone to embrace it.

It Was Sometimes an Odd Mantle. The Bible says that John the Baptist came in the spirit of Elijah. John knew the importance of an old mantle. But John was a little different. Any man who dresses in camel's hair, eats locusts, and preaches repentance in the wilderness would seem to be a little different! There will be times when people will criticize your ways. There will be times when you are accused of being old-fashioned. Instead of being embarrassed, we should embrace such accusations! We still believe in fire-and-brimstone preaching! We still believe in calling sin *sin!* We still believe that God's way is the *only way!* Yes, we will stand out in these days in which we live. First John 3:1 says, "Behold, what manner of love the Father hath bestowed upon us, that we should be called the sons of God: *therefore the world knoweth us not, because it knew him not."* Some will think us odd. But they cannot deny the power of the gospel we preach!

It Was Certainly an Ordained Mantle. It sure is funny to me that no matter how much the people wanted to deny Elijah and John the Baptist, they could not deny the power of God in them. Even Ahab addressed Elijah as "thou man of God," though he hated him with every part of his heart. Here is a good question: where are the men of God today? It is sad to say that the number of true men of God is dwindling. We have plenty of vocational preachers. We need God-called men who have an unction on them as they stand before their people. We need laymen who will hold the banner high as did Philip and Stephen, the first deacons at the church at Jerusalem. People might deny us, but they should not be able to deny what God has done in us and is accomplishing through us! Anybody can have this old mantle upon his life. A willing heart, obedience to the Lord, and belief in His Word are all that are required to pick up the old mantle.

TOPICS: Calling, Man of God, Power, Unction

May 1

DAILY BIBLE READING: 2 Kings 4–5

TODAY'S VERSE: 2 Kings 5:3: "And she said unto her mistress, Would God my lord were with the prophet that is in Samaria! for he would recover him of his leprosy."

THIS STORY ABOUT NAAMAN is one of the most enjoyable Bible stories to tell. It has changed lives from children to adults and should hold a place of meaning in our hearts today. Chances are it's already familiar to you—but today's study might help you see a few things in a different light.

Thank God for a Little Maid and Her Testimony. Verse 2 called this girl a "little maid." We are not talking about a teenager, but a young child. Anyone of any age can be a witness for our Lord and Saviour! We need teens and adults with the same fervor this little maid had for her faith!

Thank God for a Loving Mother and Her Teaching. From whom do you think this little child learned what she knew about the Lord and His prophet? She did not learn it by her many personal life experiences. She learned from the knee of a godly mother! She learned in a home that feared God and believed in Jehovah. She learned about the man of God and his ministry by being where she was supposed to be and doing what she was supposed to do. So many times our children may miss a life-changing truth just because they are not where they should be. Sometimes a soccer game, an overnight stay, or even a party will keep them from the Lord's house and from hearing what God wants to tell them. We need mothers who will take their responsibility seriously and prepare their children to be a testimony of God to the world.

Thank God for a Learning Mistress and Her Tenderness. Had the mistress dismissed this little witness and held to her faith in her false god, Rimmon, all would have been in vain. But the mistress really loved her husband, Naaman, and every option had to be searched and every possibility tried. Very often it is the horrors of tragedy and trauma that can make someone sensitive to the need for God. Do you need a reason to come back to God today? The more tender your heart becomes, the easier it is to find a reason to come to the Lord and find help for your trouble.

Thank God for a Leprous Man and His Triumph. Praise the Lord for a man who followed God and received the blessing of God's hand at work in his life! Many people never would have made it to this point in their lives. Namaan was not healed through his faith, his culture, or his country. Yet, by the time he came up the seventh time from the muddy waters of the Jordan River, his faith in Jehovah God was born. What triumph did he have? It was a triumph over a certain death! It was a triumph to a new life! A question to ponder is this: what do we have to lose? There was nothing for Naaman to lose, especially considering that his life was at stake. Only God can give us the victory! Now that He has delivered me from my sin-sick disease, I owe my life to Him.

TOPICS: Faith, Parenting, Soul-Winning, Witness

R. CHRIS HANKS

DAILY BIBLE READING: 2 Kings 6-8

TODAY'S VERSE: 2 Kings 7:9: "Then they said one to another, We do not well: this day is a day of good tidings, and we hold our peace: if we tarry till the morning light, some mischief will come upon us: now therefore come, that we may go and tell the king's household."

SYRIA HAD LAID SIEGE against Israel, and Israel was starving in her own land. The Syrian army had come to destroy Israel, but this time God saved His people even though they did not know it! Four leprous men gathered the courage to walk into the host of the Syrians and ask for food. What did it matter to them? They were going to die anyway! If the Syrians had mercy on these lepers, they might get some food out of their apparently foolhardy action. As they walked into the camp, they found no one. God had chased away the entire army. Horses were still tied to the stakes. Donkeys had burdens full of goods. Tents were fully equipped and prepared for a lengthy stay. In the middle of their celebration, the goodness of God became apparent to these lepers. It was suddenly not about them any longer! There was much more that needed to happen. This sure sounds like living the Christian life. Here are some thoughts about these four lepers that can help us in our own lives and walks today.

First, we see their **Integrity** ("We do not well"). "This just is not right!" they stopped and exclaimed. "What are we doing here? There is more to this event than my hunger and appetite." God had given them more than they could ever eat. It had to be shared! Where has our conscience gone today? Do we not realize that God has given us more than enough? Why are we not moved about the needs of others? God has not given us this great gift of salvation to be hoarded and meted out in a miserly fashion. Someone once said that "A true soul-winner is nothing more than one beggar telling another beggar where he can go to find bread." A Christian of integrity will feel the need to share the good news with others.

Second, we see their **Responsibility** ("this day is a day of good tidings, and we hold our peace: if we tarry till the morning light, some mischief will come upon us"). How can we not share this gospel of God? A great responsibility lies ahead of us! God will hold us responsible for our care in giving the Word to the world. We have been called to do a job as a local church. Let us do it to the best of our ability.

Third, we see their **Opportunity** ("now therefore come, that we may go and tell the king's household"). This should have been a time of rejoicing for these leprous men. In a few more verses, we see that this sudden good news was at first accepted with great skepticism and sarcasm. When it was finally believed, it not only changed the way the leprous men had been living, but it affected all the people of Samaria. Everyone rejoiced! Every heart was glad! Every belly was full! And yet there was more that could be shared with others. We are not salesmen: we are giving free food! Let us share the true gift of God and His goodness with others, for there is no greater opportunity than this!

TOPICS: Integrity, Responsibility, Soul-Winning, Victory

DAILY BIBLE READING: 2 Kings 9–10

TODAY'S VERSE: 2 Kings 10:31: "But Jehu took no heed to walk in the law of the LORD God of Israel with all his heart: for he departed not from the sins of Jeroboam, which made Israel to sin."

JEHU WAS CAREFUL to obey the express commands of God at the beginning of his reign, but we see that he did not care to walk with God. How is it possible, after seeing the hand of God at work, knowing the blessings you have received are directly from His hand, and remembering that there are other promises to be had in the future, to dismiss and reject God's way? Yet it is common for us to do the same thing today! What has to take place for us to go from receiving God's blessing to rejecting God's presence so quickly? In this verse, we find three things that brought Jehu to refuse the presence of God.

Jehu Failed in His Hedge ("But Jehu took no heed to walk in the law of the LORD God of Israel"). The word for "heed" means "to hedge about (as with thorns), i.e. guard; generally, to protect." Jehu did not focus his heart, nor did he guard his relationship with God. We can all say with the old hymn "Come, Thou Fount," "Prone to wander, Lord, I feel it/Prone to leave the God I love." We must hedge our way about to stay on the path of God's blessing. Though our ministries need to expand, our paths need to contract! We must be reminded that the Christian life we live is a straight and narrow way. Jehu did not want any rules or boundaries; he wanted "Christian liberty." If only he'd known that Christian liberty is found within the confines of a hedged and guarded walk with God!

Jehu Failed in His Heart ("with all his heart"). We often fail in our hearts. Jeremiah 17:9 says, "The heart is deceitful above all things, and desperately wicked: who can know it?" We are not just talking here about blood pumping inside our chest, but about our *heart*. The definition of the word used for "heart" means "the heart (as the most interior organ)." The thought is simple: what is in you? The sports world has used the heart in many different ways to ask the same question. The NFL uses their logo with the sound of a heartbeat, and even Gatorade has an entire advertising campaign centered on the slogan, "Is *it* in you?" God told David in 1 Kings 8:18b, "Thou didst well that it was in thine heart." We must make sure that we take heed to the desires and direction of our hearts. Proverbs 4:23 says, "Keep thy heart with all diligence; for out of it are the issues of life."

Jehu Failed in His Heat ("for he departed not from the sins of Jeroboam, which made Israel to sin"). The word used for "depart" in this verse means "to turn off." The word "not" means that Jehu was not "turned off" by the sins of Jeroboam. We are often like him in this way—far too often "turned on" by some sin or thought that stands openly against God's Word. We will learn an interesting lesson if we take a moment to look at Job 1:1: "There was a man in the land of Uz, whose name was Job; and that man was perfect and upright, and one that feared God, and eschewed evil." The word that tells us that Job "eschewed" evil is the same word that tells us that Jehu "departed" not. In other words, what "turned on" Jehu, "turned off" Job. Don't allow your passions and desires to be turned on by things that displease a righteous, holy God!

TOPICS: Focus, Holiness, Passion, Purity, Sin, Walk

R. CHRIS HANKS

DAILY BIBLE READING: 2 Kings 11–13

TODAY'S VERSE: 2 Kings 13:4: "And Jehoahaz besought the Lord , and the Lord hearkened unto him: for he saw the oppression of Israel, because the king of Syria oppressed them."

JEHOAHAZ WAS THE SON of Jehu. Have you ever heard the phrase "Like father, like son"? That is what we have here. Jehoahaz enjoyed the sins of Jeroboam just like his daddy did. Yet in this verse, we see him ask God for help, and God hears him! What a testimony of God's mercy and love! This tells us that God's mercy is not earned, but is in itself grace (or "unmerited favor") from God! Romans 9:15 says, "For he saith to Moses, I will have mercy on whom I will have mercy, and I will have compassion on whom I will have compassion." God will give mercy to whomever He wants to give mercy! Praise the Lord! The line starts here! Even this old, wicked king who did not serve God, nor would he after God's blessing, still found mercy in the presence of Jehovah! How does this story apply to our lives today?

Jehoahaz Caressed God ("And Jehoahaz besought the Lord "). This is a lesson I learned from watching my sisters' treatment of my father, and it has been tried by my own daughters as well. The Hebrew word for "besought" is interesting to consider today: it means "properly, to be rubbed or worn," but if you look further in its definition, it has a good meaning as well: "also to stroke (in flattering), entreat." I cannot tell you how many times I saw one of my sisters climb up on my dad's lap, say all manner of sweet things to him (all lies, of course!), and stroke his face with their hands. My dad just ate it up! My sisters could get anything they wanted like that. It just wasn't fair to me! I loved him too, but I just showed it differently! When Jehoahaz "besought" the Lord, he really meant it. You would be surprised at how fast God moves in the life of someone who really loves Him and tells Him so! Why not stroke the face of God in your prayers? Not in flattery, but in entreaty!

Jehoahaz Was Connected to God ("and the Lord hearkened unto him"). The word for "hearkened" means "to hear intelligently, often with implication of attention." God's attention was completely focused on Jehoahaz. I want this connection! Psalm 4:3 says, "But know that the Lord hath set apart him that is godly for himself: *the Lord will hear when I call unto him.*" Do you realize that a godly prayer connects you to God and the throne room of heaven? Engage in this connection, and see what God will do!

God Cared for His People ("for he saw the oppression of Israel, because the king of Syria oppressed them"). When the verse says "The king of Syria *oppressed* them," the word used means, "to press, i.e. (figuratively) to distress." They were "put through the ringer." God cared about the troubles of His people. God cared about Israel while they were in Egypt. Exodus 3:7 says, "And the Lord said, I have surely seen the affliction of my people which are in Egypt, and have heard their cry by reason of their taskmasters; for I know their sorrows." Rest assured that God knows and cares about every "pressing" trial that you endure. It may seem that God has forgotten you, but He sees every test, and He knows every hardship. Only He can help you in your suffering!

TOPICS: God's Care, Love, Prayer

DAILY BIBLE READING: 2 Kings 14–16

TODAY'S VERSE: 2 Kings 14:27: "And the LORD said not that he would blot out the name of Israel from under heaven: but he saved them by the hand of Jeroboam the son of Joash."

THE WILL AND GRACE of God is unspeakably good! What a precious thought comes from this verse: that God would not blot out the name of Israel! This is something in which we can all rejoice. Reading a verse like this reminds me of the blessing of God in which I rejoice every day. Do you realize that God has made this promise to each of us as well? The Bible describes Christ's work in Colossians 2:14 as "blotting out the handwriting of ordinances that was against us, which was contrary to us, and took it out of the way, nailing it to his cross." Praise the Lord that instead of blotting out your name, He blots out the source of your condemnation! Here are a few thoughts from this verse.

First, God's decision not to blot us out is **Not About His Resources but His Resolve** ("And the LORD *said not that he would* blot out the name of Israel"). Only the pure goodness of God would keep Him from blotting out our names. There is no amount of good that we could do to merit this great work of grace! This was a conscious decision of God Himself on our behalf. What great mercy! What great love! What great hope we have for tomorrow!

Second, it was **Not About His Rejection but His Reception** ("the name of Israel from under heaven"). For what reason would God do such a work for undeserving men and women that He would not blot them out of His sight? The reason is that God wants to receive us as His own! God could reject us, but He has chosen to receive us! We still believe that "whosoever will" may come (Revelation 22:17). God sent His own Son to die for sinful man that He might make all acceptable in His sight! Rejoice today that He has made a way to receive us into His glory!

Third, it was **Not About His Respite but His Rescue** ("but he saved them by the hand of Jeroboam the son of Joash"). God did not just postpone Israel's judgment but *delivered* them from their trouble. His desire is to rescue His people! Though they deserved judgment, God was still merciful and did not blot them out. But He went further! He did not just leave them to figure it out on their own. He did not just leave them to their own devices. He gave them victory and deliverance! Praise God for what He has done for us today! He has rescued us from our sin and our trouble!

TOPICS: Deliverance, God's Goodness, Love, Salvation

R. CHRIS HANKS

DAILY BIBLE READING: 2 Kings 17–18

TODAY'S VERSE: 2 Kings 18:32: "Until I come and take you away to a land like your own land, a land of corn and wine, a land of bread and vineyards, a land of oil olive and of honey, that ye may live, and not die: and hearken not unto Hezekiah, when he persuadeth you, saying, The Lord will deliver us."

HERE CAME THE ENEMIES of the Lord to threaten and terrorize God's people. In doing so, they called God's man a deceiver and a liar. They did not stop there, however. They began to tell God's people how much like the world they were! It always amazes me that other religions want us to think that they are just like us. They have a different Jesus, a different gospel, a different Bible, and a different Spirit, but they will tell you that we believe the same thing. That is exactly what is happening in this verse, which says, "Until I come and take you away to *a land like your own land.*" This enemy of Israel was basically telling them, "What you got and what I got are the same." My, my, there is a vast difference between the two lands!

The world wants us to believe that we have the **Same Source of Supply** ("a land of corn and wine"). They think that their "land of plenty" is proof of their spiritual superiority. This is one of the mistakes of the prosperity gospel. Wealth does not prove the presence of God. Proverbs 15:16 says, "Better is little with the fear of the Lord than great treasure and trouble therewith." Having much has never proved anything! As a matter of fact, the less we have, the more dependent we are upon God to supply our need. The meekness of the Lord's Prayer is seen when Jesus said, "Give us this day our daily bread" (Matthew 6:11).

They want us to believe that we have the **Same Source of Sustenance** ("a land of bread and vineyards"). There has been a progression in this phrase: they went from a land of corn to a land of bread. All of the enemy's reasoning was centered on self-satisfaction. Even the work and labor of the world is set on their own needs and desires. Never in the Christian life are we to labor to supply our own needs. Jesus made this clear in Matthew 4:4: "But he answered and said, It is written, Man shall not live by bread alone, but by every word that proceedeth out of the mouth of God." We need a longing for spiritual things that will touch the heart of God. Matthew 5:6 says this: "Blessed are they which do *hunger and thirst* after righteousness: *for they shall be filled.*" And Ephesians 3:19 says, "And to know the love of Christ, which passeth knowledge, that ye *might be filled with all the fulness of God.*"

They want us to believe that we have the **Same Source of Spirit** ("a land of oil olive and of honey"). Remember, oil in Scripture is always a type of the Holy Spirit. We are living in a time today in which many have prostituted themselves, leaving the Holy Spirit for seducing spirits. This sensual religion is deceiving, for it is built upon feelings rather than truth. God has warned us of these hucksters that will come our way, "having a form of godliness but denying the power thereof" (2 Timothy 3:5). The Bible warns us again to be careful of these false spirits in 1 John 4:1: "Beloved, believe not every spirit, but try the spirits whether they are of God: because many false prophets are gone out into the world."

They want us to believe that it is a **Superior Source of Salvation** ("that ye may live, and not die"). This enemy was telling Israel, "If you continue in this way, you will die. Let me save you! You need to do this *my way!*" In essence, the enemy nation was denying the salvation of Jehovah God. They did not believe that God even cared. *This enemy leader was trying to prove that he cared more about Israel in defeating them than God cared about them to save them.* That is what the way of the world and the way of our flesh will tell us. However, if we give in to this way of thinking, we will meet with certain destruction. Our hope is in God! From the same story in a different book, we read, "With him is an arm of flesh; but with us is the Lord our God to help us, and to fight our battles. And the people rested themselves upon the words of Hezekiah king of Judah" (2 Chronicles 32:8). Hallelujah for the saving hand of the Lord our God!

TOPICS: Deception, Food, Holy Spirit, Salvation, Sustenance

DAILY BIBLE READING: 2 Kings 17–18

TODAY'S VERSE: 2 Kings 20:17-19: "Behold, the days come, that all that is in thine house, and that which thy fathers have laid up in store unto this day, shall be carried in Babylon: nothing shall be left, saith the LORD. And of thy sons that shall issue from thee, which thou shalt beget, shall they take away; and they shall be eunuchs in the palace of the king of Babylon. Then said Hezekiah unto Isaiah, Good is the word of the LORD which thou hast spoken. And he said, Is it not good, if peace and truth be in my days?"

I BELIEVE VERSE 19 to be one of the most selfish verses ever recorded in the Bible. After Isaiah told Hezekiah that God was going to judge him for bringing men from Babylon to see his treasures, Hezekiah was satisfied that the judgment would happen after his death. He had no burden and no vision for what lay ahead. This would have been the perfect time for Hezekiah to turn his face to the wall and pray, but even when he did that, it was for his personal health. We need people who would rather die with the power of God on them than live selfishly and bring God's judgment upon a future generation. Here are a few things for which Hezekiah lost his burden.

He Lost His Burden for the Future Kings ("Behold, the days come . . ."). All that had been passed down to him from the previous kings would be stripped and given to a heathen king and a heathen palace. The very things Hezekiah took pride in were now to be taken away. His inheritance suddenly did not matter anymore. He had lost the true value of those things that had been handed down to him from generation to generation, and somehow they had become nothing more than novelties in his own heart and mind. All that he would save for himself, he was not saving to give to the next king, but for an unbelieving king and kingdom.

He Lost His Burden for the Future Kingdom ("all that is in thine house, and that which thy fathers have laid up in store unto this day shall be carried into Babylon: nothing shall be left, saith the LORD"). This was a terrible promise: it meant no future kingdom for Judah. Hezekiah's disobedience before God was also a reflection of his true patriotism. Our nation has become mesmerized by the programs that are promised by our presidential candidates. We need a president who is concerned about our nation enough to fear the Lord and obey His Word. A true patriot is one who desires his fellow citizens to bow before a thrice-holy God and beg for His mercy. The Bible says, "Blessed is the nation whose God is the LORD" (Psalm 33:12). Hezekiah had lost his patriotism, for whatever happened to his people after he died was just fine by him!

He Lost His Burden for His Future Kids ("And of thy sons that shall issue from thee, which thou shalt beget, shall they take away; and they shall be eunuchs in the palace of the king of Babylon"). His future children had a promise of *pain* that awaited them. Their *pleasure* would be stripped away from them. And their *potential* would be nonexistent. It almost seems that this did not bother Hezekiah at all! Where is his sorrow and repentance? It was promised that his children and grandchildren would never have the opportunity to have their children sit on their knees. As a matter of fact, I believe this to prophesy directly about Daniel. Daniel's master was the master of the eunuchs. We have no record of Daniel ever marrying or having children. Daniel 1:3 tells us that the master of the eunuchs was to bring "certain of the children of Israel, *and of the king's seed,* and of the princes." It was also the prince of the eunuchs who changed Daniel's and the other Hebrew boys' names. Here in our text, we see Hezekiah easily dismiss this prophecy and not even think about it again. Daniel, Hananiah, Mishael, and Azariah should never have had to serve as eunuchs in the Babylonian palace, but because of the unrepentant heart of one of their grandfathers, they did. Let's care enough about those who are coming behind us to live humbly before God!

TOPICS: Discernment, Parenting, Patriotism, Preparation, Wisdom

R. CHRIS HANKS

DAILY BIBLE READING: 2 Kings 21–22

TODAY'S VERSE: 2 Kings 22:8: "And Hilkiah the high priest said unto Shaphan the scribe, I have found the book of the law in the house of the Lord. And Hilkiah gave the book to Shaphan, and he read it."

THIS VERSE IS BOTH exciting and disappointing. It was exciting for the people who found the book, but disappointing that nobody had previously found it. It tells us the view that some held toward the Word of God in the past. They looked at it as a *novelty* but not as a *necessity*. If the Word were the source of their living, they would have found it long ago. We don't even know how long they had been without the Word of God. The high priest found the book! Can you imagine the pastor of your church coming on Sunday morning and going through the motions of a church service all without the Word of God? That is what had been happening at the house of God!

This verse tells me that **Somebody Had Lost the Word of God** ("And Hilkiah the high priest said unto Shaphan the scribe, I have found the book of the law"). How could this happen? Doesn't it make you wonder who lost it to start with? If Israel lost the Word of God, it tells me that they had lost their *love* for the Word of God. They had lost their *longing* for the Word of God. Great was the wrath of the Lord against His people. Reading the book of the law brought forth the fruits of repentance and humbled them before God.

It also tells me that **Somebody Had Not Looked for the Word of God** ("I have found the book of the law in the house of the Lord"). If we lose something in our house that is needed, we will turn the house upside down looking for it. When are we going to get serious about looking for God? Everybody says they are looking for God, but few people find His presence and His power. The Bible, however, says that "he that seeketh findeth" (Matthew 7:8). Another reason I believe Israel had not looked for the book of the law is that they found it in the house of God. Where else would it be? They found it right where it should have been! When we start looking for God, we will find that He is in the place He's always been, and we should have started right there!

That tells me that **Somebody Had Not Looked *Into* the Word of God** ("I have found the book of the law in the house of the Lord. And Hilkiah gave the book to Shaphan, and he read it"). How long had the priests been laboring in the work of the Lord without having the book of the law to guide them, comfort them, and encourage them? It is easy for Christians to fall into the same trap. It is easy to get busy about the work of the Lord and bypass the Word of the Lord. We must remember that our reason for serving the Lord is found in His Word! Our service must be connected to our worship. As a pastor, there are many times when I walk through the auditorium and find Bibles in the pews. That tells me that someone is not able to look into the precious Word of God for those few days or the whole week. There have been other times when someone has left his Bible at church and called me the next day to ask if he could pick it up. Our precious and wonderful Bible has no ministry if we never crack it open to observe that which God has preserved for us.

TOPICS: Bible, Priorities, Word of God

DAILY BIBLE READING: 2 Kings 23–25

TODAY'S VERSE: 2 Kings 23:17: "Then he said, What title is that that I see? And the men of the city told him, It is the sepulchre of the man of God, which came from Judah, and proclaimed these things that thou hast done against the altar of Bethel."

WHAT A QUESTION is asked here! "What title is that that I see?" Josiah asked this as he did the very thing the man of God, who was now dead, had said he would do. What a great testimony! Josiah's question is a good one for us to contemplate for just a moment. What title is seen in your life?

Is It a Clear Title? This has to do with your **testimony**. In the day and time in which we live, our title needs to be clear. Proverbs 4:18 says, "But the path of the just is as the shining light, that shineth more and more unto the perfect day." Many today like to muddy the waters of doctrine, holiness, and virtue. It is very interesting to me how much people want to talk about "the gray areas" of Christian living. The Bible is very *clear* about God's way. But today, instead of having a clear testimony, many are trying to find loopholes that will permit their own selfish ways in Christian living.

If the Holy Ghost is in you and you allow Him to work in your life, your way will not be one that is opaque and vague in its nature, but one that will shine as a shining light. Do you remember what Jesus said about John the Baptist? "He was a burning and a shining light: and ye were willing for a season to rejoice in his light" (John 5:35). The world rejoices to see a clear testimony today! What has Jesus said to us? "Let your light so shine before men, that they may see your good works, and glorify your Father which is in heaven" (Matthew 5:16).

Is It a Correct Title? This has to do with **truth**. The headstone on this sepulcher said that this prophet was the man of God who had prophesied exactly what happened in Josiah's life. Thank God for a man who was willing to speak the truth! Oh to have truth back in our pulpits, back in our pews, and back in our prayers! Nothing will show the way of salvation better than the truth of the gospel. Nothing will convict the heart of a prodigal son more than the truth of his sin! Nothing will stir the hearts of God's people and bring about a revival more than the truth of the Word of God!

Is It a Careful Title? This has to do with **thought**. This headstone did not require much, but it did require thought. Have you ever known an elderly person, perhaps a grandparent, who did not talk much, but when he or she did talk, everybody shut up to hear what that person had to say? There was not much said upon that sepulcher, but what *was* said was enough! We need to take care that all we say is under the authority of the Word of God and the power of the Holy Spirit. I have had the privilege of being around some great men of God, and my, could they say something the exact way it needed to be said! I have been challenged by one sentence. I have been convicted with one question. I have been encouraged by a simple thought. The Word of God does the same thing. Should our title be any different?

TOPICS: Clarity, Testimony, Truth

DAILY BIBLE READING: 1 Chronicles 1–2

TODAY'S VERSE: 1 Chronicles 2:7: "And the sons of Carmi; Achar, the troubler of Israel, who transgressed in the thing accursed."

THE STORY OF ACHAN (called "Achar" in today's verse) is actually found in Joshua 7. Here we are many generations later, and we are yet again reminded of Achan's sin at the battle of Jericho. Instead of confessing and forsaking his sin, he hid it and tried to cover it up. We must be reminded of Proverbs 28:13: "He that covereth his sins shall not prosper: but whoso confesseth and forsaketh them shall have mercy." Our reading today included many generations and many names for us to remember. This name stood out to remind us of God's holiness, omniscience, and judgment. Let us consider Achan for a moment as he is listed in the midst of all these genealogies.

Achan the Disturbed One of Israel ("And the sons of Carmi; Achar, the troubler of Israel"). The word for "troubler" here means "to roil water, to disturb or afflict." Achan was a pot-stirrer. Joshua caught on to Achan's troubling ways when he said in Joshua 7:25, "Why hast thou *troubled* us? the LORD shall *trouble* thee this day. And all Israel stoned him with stones, and burned them with fire, after they had stoned them with stones." What a lesson for us to learn! Instead of letting our sin trouble us, why can't we give sin some trouble and run it right out of our lives? We see Paul using this thought in two different places. Pay attention to how he uses the word "malice." Colossians 3:8: "But now ye also put off all these; anger, wrath, *malice*, blasphemy, filthy communication out of your mouth." Ephesians 4:31 uses it like this: "Let all bitterness, and wrath, and anger, and clamour, and evil speaking, be put away from you, with all *malice.*" The first time, we are instructed not to have malice. The second time, we are instructed to get rid of sin with all our malice. It sounds like Paul was telling these early Christians to quit being victims of their sin and to start making trouble for sin in their lives!

Achan the Denying One of Israel ("who transgressed"). The word for "transgressed" means "to cover up, to act covertly, i.e. treacherously." There was treachery in the heart of Achan as he selfishly took that which was forbidden. Every transgression and act of sin is a denial of God. It is as if we are covertly working our own will in defiance of His will and work in our lives. Repentance would have been so much better than defiance! One of the things God has to save us from is ourselves. Second Timothy 2:25 says, "In meekness instructing those that oppose themselves; if God peradventure will give them repentance to the acknowledging of the truth."

Achan the Doomed One of Israel ("in the thing accursed"). The word for "accursed" means "a net (either literally or figuratively); usually a doomed object, things which should have been utterly destroyed." When Achan claimed those things from Jericho that God had said were to be dedicated to Him, he doomed himself with a curse. Not only did he curse himself, but he also cursed his family and everything in his house. Because of Achan's sin, many innocent people were doomed to God's judgment, especially those who were closest to him. May we not become a curse to those we care for most!

TOPICS: Conviction, Judgment, Sin

May 11

DAILY BIBLE READING: 1 Chronicles 3–5

TODAY'S VERSE: 1 Chronicles 4:9: "And Jabez was more honourable than his brethren: and his mother called his name Jabez, saying, Because I bare him with sorrow."

WHAT A DIFFERENCE a day makes! Yesterday we talked about Achan; today we will talk about Jabez. This little story is tucked away in the genealogies. If you are not careful, you might pass over it! It was placed here for a specific reason by the Holy Spirit. We do not have much information about this Bible character, but what giant things are said! Through Jabez's story we learn that no matter what problems we might face, God can deliver us and give us victory over any situation. Though today we will only look at the verse describing Jabez's troubles, I would encourage you to read his prayer to God and discover his triumphs.

He Had to Get Over His Family ("And Jabez was more honourable than his brethren"). I don't know what the actions were, but Jabez was identified by the actions of his brethren. Many have to deal with a family name or history that has no goodness or virtue whatsoever. From this story we learn that it does not matter if your family was known as horse thieves, slaves, drunkards, or cheats. God is bigger than either the Hatfield or McCoy name! He has even come to bring you into His own family! Don't feel that you are stuck because of your name: you *can* have victory over something that seems to be much bigger than you.

He Had to Get Over His Failings ("and his mother called his name Jabez"). Jabez's name means "he will cause pain," and it comes from a root meaning "to grieve, to hurt, to pain."[1] No doubt, every time Jabez failed, he was reminded of his name. He could easily have quit contributing anything to society. Much greater, he might never have had the blessing of God upon his life. The self-defeatist would say, "That's just what happens to me because I am always a failure." Paul referred to some of this attitude in 1 Corinthians 15:9–10a: "For I am the least of the apostles, that am not meet to be called an apostle, because I persecuted the church of God. But by the grace of God I am what I am." So what if you have failed in your past! Get over it! It does not have to be a part of your life any longer. Paul said again in Philippians 3:13, "Brethren, I count not myself to have apprehended: but this one thing I do, forgetting those things which are behind, and reaching forth unto those things which are before."

He Had to Get Over His Faults ("saying, Because I bare him with sorrow"). This was something that would hold on to Jabez for some time—the hurt and pain of his own mother! It was not his fault, yet he was the cause of someone else's pain and suffering. His own mother blamed him for the grief and anguish that came at his birth. There may be times, through no fault of your own, that you might be the cause of someone else's sorrow. Don't give up! The Lord can give victory, even over your faults or the hurts that come because of you even when you're *not* at fault. Trust in Him!

TOPICS: Failure, Family, Name, Reputation, Sin, Suffering, Trust, Victory

---

1   Alfred Jones, *Jones' Dictionary of Old Testament Proper Names* (Grand Rapids: Kregel, 1997), 172

DAILY BIBLE READING: 1 Chronicles 6-7

TODAY'S VERSE: 1 Chronicles 6:32: "And they ministered before the dwelling place of the tabernacle of the congregation with singing, until Solomon had built the house of the LORD in Jerusalem: and then they waited on their office according to their order."

OUR READING TODAY lists many names in the genealogies. Today's verse intrigued me with a couple of thoughts. These particular people had a particular ministry for which they were responsible.

These Men Were Selected for Ministry ("And these are they whom David set over the service of song"). God has chosen certain people to do certain things in the house of God. I also believe that the pastor can choose certain people to do certain things in the house of God (that is part of having "oversight," 1 Peter 5:2). In a few short years as a pastor, I figured out that not everybody should pick his own ministry! Not everybody has the gifts he thinks he has. There are certain things that people should be selected to do. The truth is that God has selected us for specific things in the church. Each one of us has a different ministry that he or she can do to meet needs that no one else can meet.

These Men Had a Singing Ministry ("And they ministered before the dwelling place of the tabernacle of the congregation with singing"). Music is a very important ministry: it's one of the most intensely spiritual, worshiping ministries in the church today. What a blessing it is to find godly musicians who have been with God and have a special touch upon them as they sing His praises and unite the hearts of the congregation together in music! In many churches, the music ministry has become more about personality and performance than about the measure of a worshiping heart. Music can be (and often is) one of the most self-centered areas of church work—but what a blessing it is to have people with musical talent *and* the ability and desire to glorify God with all their hearts! When such people are found, their impact is tremendous upon the hearts of the people who come to worship the Lord.

These Men Had a Serving Ministry ("and then they waited on their office according to their order"). Their ministry was not just one to be seen: it went far beyond that. The word used for "wait" here has different definitions. It can mean to be patient. It can also mean to serve. For instance, if you go to a restaurant and are seated, the hostess will tell you that your "waiter" or "waitress" will be with you in a moment. These are people who are there to serve you. We should be there to serve and to take every order, every desire, and every hope, so that we might please God and honor Him with our service. These men were willing to do whatever was necessary to serve their Lord. They were available to get their hands dirty and to do the real work of ministry if needed. There is no room for the diva-like attitudes that have pervaded our churches across the nation. There is nobody who should be above serving the Lord in whatever capacity he or she can.

TOPICS: Calling, Ministry, Praise, Service, Singing, Submission

DAILY BIBLE READING: 1 Chronicles 8–10

TODAY'S VERSE: 1 Chronicles 10:1: "Now the Philistines fought against Israel; and the men of Israel fled from before the Philistines, and fell down slain in mount Gilboa."

HERE WE FIND the Philistines and the Israelites doing what they would be doing for many years to come. This battle, though, would not be good for the Israelites: God had a plan to kill Saul and defeat the Israelites to bring David into the kingdom. It is never good to be on the opposite side from God, for all that such opposition promises is certain destruction! In this one little verse, we find the entire story of what happens when man stands against God. God was fighting against Saul because of his disobedience to the Word of God and as judgment upon him for seeking out a witch for spiritual guidance. Saul was responsible for many of the Israelites' deaths in this battle.

The Philistines Fought Against Israel ("Now the Philistines fought against Israel"). This was what they did—fought against God's people. One thing you can expect as a Christian is that the world will fight against you. The battle is on its way! Are you spiritually prepared? First John 3:1 says this: "Behold, what manner of love the Father hath bestowed upon us, that we should be called the sons of God: *therefore the world knoweth us not, because it knew him not.*" Israel was not so prepared, and their strength was gone. God had withdrawn His hand from them in judgment. How helpless it is to be powerless against your enemies. How hopeless it is when God actually fights against you!

The Israelites Fled From the Philistines ("and the men of Israel fled from before the Philistines"). It is always a sad day when Christians flee before their enemies. The word for "flee" means "to flit, to vanish away." The Bible says that the "righteous are bold as a lion" (Proverbs 28:1). How sad when God's people run and slink away in battle! We should not be "vanishing away" in the midst of battle. We ought to be presenting ourselves armed and ready! Let me remind you that in Ephesians 6, in which God shows the armor for the Christian, there is no armor for our backs! It is not time to flee. There may be times when we cannot advance and attack. There may be times when all we can do is stand, but what a sad thing to see the people of God running away from the battle!

The Israelites Fell Before the Philistines ("and fell down slain in mount Gilboa"). God has promised us complete and ultimate victory. I have known many people who are casualties of war. They no longer fight the battle. They have fallen prey to the evil one and sold their souls to the devil. They have taken their stand against God and have assured their ultimate defeat.

As a related thought, let me remind you that we should not be the ones to kill our wounded. The soldiers had heard about the death of their king and knew of the mocking of the enemy. They knew the enemy had taken the head of Saul and hung it in the temple of the false god Dagon. They knew the Philistines had taken Saul's and Jonathan's armor and sent it around to the false idols and the Philistine people in order to gloat in victory over Jehovah's people. The Israelite men in today's reading summoned all courage, found the bodies of their fallen leaders, and brought them back to give them a proper burial. You do not find the Israelites shaking their heads and agreeing to their sudden destruction. You find them mourning over their lost brothers and crying for their dead king. First Corinthians 10:12 says, "Wherefore let him that thinketh he standeth take heed lest he fall." One more Scripture to leave with you says, "Brethren, if a man be overtaken in a fault, ye which are spiritual, restore such an one in the spirit of meekness; considering thyself, lest thou also be tempted" (Galatians 6:1).

TOPICS: Battle, Defeat, Fear, Sorrow, Warfare

DAILY BIBLE READING: 1 Chronicles 11–13

TODAY'S VERSE: 1 Chronicles 11:18: "And the three brake through the host of the Philistines, and drew water out of the well of Bethlehem, that was by the gate, and took it, and brought it to David: but David would not drink of it, but poured it out to the Lord."

SINCE I WAS A LITTLE BOY, I have always enjoyed this passage. It was always interesting to hear about David's mighty men and their escapades on the Judean hillsides. The stories of the "three mighties" are even more powerful than the rest. This verse was not about a challenge on a battlefield, nor was it about winning a strategic position. It was purely about honoring their king! This verse goes far beyond loyalty in battle and speaks of the heart that these men had for the man of God who led them. Here are a few thoughts from this verse that might encourage us today to be mighty men of God.

These Were Men Who Knew How to Declare War ("And the three brake through the host of the Philistines"). This Delta Force, special ops soldiers of the Israeli army, broke through the host of their enemies to accomplish their objective. I can guarantee you that they played no games. There was too much at stake. They were willing to go to the ends of the earth. But it's their motivation that is most powerful: in their minds, they were not just there to win battles, *but to please their king!* When was the last time you did something just to please God? This service was over and above the regular call to arms. It demanded their hearts! Let us do something just for the honor and glory of our Supreme Commander! Let us declare war and break through the hosts of hell for the cause of Christ!

These Were Men Who Knew How to Draw Water ("and drew water out of the well of Bethlehem, that was by the gate"). Proverbs 20:5 says, "Counsel in the heart of man is like deep water; but a man of understanding will draw it out." We need men who know how to work a well. The first thing they must know is where the *source of the water* is. People are looking for everything without ever turning to God and His Word. James 1:5 says, "If any of you lack wisdom, let him ask of God." The second thing they need to know is the *sweetness of the water.* In the heart of David, this well was something special. This was a well he had grown up with. This was a well from which his father had given him drink. This was a well that had satisfied his great thirst in that dusty land after he played as a child or worked in the fields. David had never forgotten the sweetness of Bethlehem's well. There was no other taste like it. Third, they must know the *situation of the well.* These men did not bring a shovel with them. There were not going to make a well in Bethlehem: they were going to use what was already there! You don't need to dig a new one! Use the well of water that is already springing inside you to eternal life.

These Were Men Who Knew How to Dedicate Worship ("and brought it to David: but David would not drink of it, but poured it out to the Lord"). There was no great need for them to do this courageous deed other than to show their love for their king. David realized this and poured the water out as an offering to the Lord. Let me remind you that in the New Testament, Jesus received every precious act of worship that was done to Him. Why? *Because He was worthy!* The precious woman who brought her alabaster box of ointment and broke it on the feet of Jesus was precious in His sight (Mark 14:1–9)! If you do something for God in worship, He will accept it of you! I do not believe that these men were upset that David poured the water out before the Lord. They were honored! They had given something that their king had to give to the Great King! Give your worship to God, and let God do great things through you.

TOPICS: Battle, Dedication, Honor, Warfare, Worship

DAILY BIBLE READING: 1 Chronicles 14–16

TODAY'S VERSE: 1 Chronicles 16:8: "Give thanks unto the LORD, call upon his name, make known his deeds among the people."

VERSE 7 OF THIS chapter said, "Then on that day David delivered first this psalm." David was on a mission. With his morning coffee in his hand, David took this psalm to Asaph and his brothers to use on this glorious day—the day the ark of the covenant would come to him in Jerusalem! David was *focused* on what he would do that day. David was *fervent* about his love and worship to the Lord. David was *full* of God's glory and found a way to share it with others. With that in mind, let us look at our verse for today.

David Was Full of Praise ("Give thanks unto the LORD"). If there is anything we should be full of, it is praise. Is there ever a moment when we cannot be thankful for something? Psalm 68:19 says, "Blessed be the Lord, who daily loadeth us with benefits, even the God of our salvation. Selah." You don't have to look far to find something for which to be thankful! The Bible even gives us further instruction in 1 Thessalonians 5:18: "In every thing give thanks: for this is the will of God in Christ Jesus concerning you." Let me take a moment to explain this. The Bible says, *"In* every thing give thanks" not *"for* every thing give thanks." I do not thank God for allowing me to hit my thumb with a hammer. But while my thumb is throbbing, I can say, "Thank You, God, for saving my soul!" or "Thank You, God, for not letting me hit another finger too!" We could even thank God for the "hammer experience" because it caused us to look heavenward and give thanks to Him for His work in our lives.

David Was Full of Prayer ("call upon his name"). This sort of worship is dying in our churches today. When was the last time you were so moved that you had to pray? I am not talking about the prayer that is expected at the end of a service, but about a time when God touched you, and you had to go find a place to be alone with Him in prayer or you felt you might explode! You will find that when you start praising God, your prayers will usually follow close behind. True worship will drive you to your knees.

David Was Full of "Preach" ("make known his deeds among the people"). A little bit of a southern term for you today: I remember hearing an old preacher say about a young preacher, "That young man has some *preach* in him!" This is one area where we can all be preachers. Each and every one of us should "make known his deeds among the people." We can all testify of God's works in our lives. We can all point out the great works of creation and turn others to the grandest work of salvation for a lost and dying world. This world needs a voice to turn hearts toward heaven and help them realize the wonderful works of our Lord.

TOPICS: Praise, Prayer, Testimony, Witness

DAILY BIBLE READING: 1 Chronicles 17–20

TODAY'S VERSE: 1 Chronicles 17:9: "Also I will ordain a place for my people Israel, and will plant them, and they shall dwell in their place, and shall be moved no more; neither shall the children of wickedness waste them any more, as at the beginning."

GOD'S CARE FOR HIS PEOPLE is great! As God talks with David in this passage, you can hear the love, pleasure, and tenderness of God as His love for His people is on display. Today, let's look especially at the place about which God was speaking. Keep in mind that Israel was already in the Promised Land. God was now saying that there were places inside the Promised Land where He wanted to take them! Some people are in the Promised Land spiritually (that is, they've come to salvation), but they are still not in the land of blessing.

It Is a Provided Place ("Also I will ordain a place for my people Israel"). The word for "ordain" means to "invest officially." What a place to be: a place defined, developed, and delivered by God! Each one of us should desire to be in the place that God has provided and prepared for us. God had thought ahead and knew Israel's needs long before Israel knew them. Israel, and even David in this verse, had never thought about the prospect of going to a new place in the land where they were. That is the beauty of the immensity of God's place! God has provided places for me in my Christian life that I didn't even know were there. For example, many times I have read my Bible, come across a truth I have read before, and realized its existence for the first time! Ours is a provided place—ordained by God.

It Is a Planted Place ("and will plant them"). What a blessing this is! This reminds me of Psalm 1:3: "And he shall be like a tree planted by the rivers of water, that bringeth forth his fruit in his season; his leaf also shall not wither; and whatsoever he doeth shall prosper." This is a *promise of plenty* ("planted by the rivers of water"), it is a *promise of production* ("that bringeth forth his fruit in his season"), it is a *promise of perpetuity* ("his leaf also shall not wither"), and it is a *promise of prosperity* ("and whatsoever he doeth shall prosper"). To be planted shows the plan and intention of God.

It Is a Permanent Place ("and they shall dwell in their place"). What a blessed place this is! I don't know about you; but the older I get, the less I like moving. What a blessing to be in a place of permanence! That is where God has placed us spiritually. I am glad things do not always change in the spiritual realm. This permanent place gives confidence and peace in a changing world. What a blessing it is to quote Malachi 3:6: "For I am the Lord, I change not."

It Is a Peaceful Place ("and shall be moved no more"). The root for the word translated "moved" means "to quiver (with any violent emotion, especially anger or fear)." Second Timothy 1:7 says, "For God hath not given us the spirit of fear; but of power, and of love, and of a sound mind." Hallelujah for a peaceful place for God's people to dwell! Psalm 23:2 says that "he maketh me to lie down in green pastures: he leadeth me beside still waters." What a wonderfully peaceful place God has given to us!

Lastly, It Is a Protected Place ("neither shall the children of wickedness waste them any more, as at the beginning"). It might have been this verse and these promises of God in 1 Chronicles that made the Holy Spirit prompt David to write Psalm 23, for Psalm 23:5 says, "Thou preparest a table before me in the presence of mine enemies." These promises did not mean that past troubles, past pain, and past failures became nonexistent, but they did promise future victory! The root for the word "waste" here means "to fail, to wear out, to decay." God is promising a future land in the obedient, victorious Christian life that will be a place of protection. Let us be looking for this wonderful land. A wonderful land is promised us in eternity, but I believe that *this* land is one we can experience and possess today!

TOPICS: Peace, Protection, Provision, Satisfaction, Security

DAILY BIBLE READING: 1 Chronicles 21-24

TODAY'S VERSE: 1 Chronicles 22:11: "Now, my son, the LORD be with thee; and prosper thou, and build the house of the LORD thy God, as he hath said of thee."

IN THIS PASSAGE, David is preparing to die. He is giving final instructions to Solomon before he goes to be with the Lord. We can see in this verse that the building of the temple was heavy on the heart of David. How David longed to be the one to build the temple to honor God! But by God's decision, the builder would be Solomon. If you study all that David did for the temple, you will find that everything was already accomplished except for the actual erection of the structure. Every piece, part, tool, material, worker, and blueprint was supplied to Solomon: "All this, said David, the LORD made me understand in writing by his hand upon me, even all the works of this pattern" (1 Chronicles 28:19). David was consumed with Solomon doing what he had been called to do! Let's listen to this discussion between David, a man after God's own heart, and Solomon, the wisest man who would ever live.

We Hear a Father's Charge ("Now, my son, the LORD be with thee; and prosper thou"). Some would argue that there is nothing we can do to receive the presence of God in our lives. Truly, the presence of God is grace that cannot be earned: however, we do have a promise that tells us what to do to receive God's presence in James 4:8a: "Draw nigh to God, and he will draw nigh to you." David's charge was actually an instruction to Solomon. Why do we not seek the presence of the Lord anymore? We should say as Moses did in Exodus 33:15, "And he said unto him, If thy presence go not with me, carry us not up hence." Oh that God's people would desire His presence more than they do a form of religion or the schedule of a service! Let us be seeking the Lord and all of His goodness. Psalm 27:8 says, "When thou saidst, Seek ye my face; my heart said unto thee, Thy face, LORD, will I seek."

We Hear a Father's Challenge ("and build the house of the LORD thy God"). A good dad always has a challenge for his son—every young man needs a project upon which he can work. Building the temple would not be an easy task, but it would be possible. This was a project of worship! How have you been preparing your place of worship? Do you realize that we are to be preparing a habitation for God? Ephesians 2:21-22 says, "In whom all the building fitly framed together groweth unto an holy temple in the Lord: in whom ye also are builded together for an habitation of God through the Spirit." We must be preparing this place for our Lord. In Solomon's case, his tabernacle would affect others for generations to come! David's was a challenge that would strike awe in the hearts of others as they beheld its glory. There was no *obstacle, opponent,* or *objection* that could stand in Solomon's way.

We Hear a Father's Confidence ("as he hath said of thee"). In David's mind, this was all part of God's plan. Solomon might not have been quite convinced of it yet, but David knew! David knew that God had chosen his son for this particular task to honor Him. David also knew that if God had chosen Solomon for this task, then God would enable him to handle the task. By the end of David's life, he had learned to trust God without hesitation. You might learn such trust too after facing a lion and a bear in the field, a giant in the valley, a wicked king on the throne, and your own son who desired to kill you! David's confidence was not in Solomon's possibilities, but in God's promises! Maybe you are struggling with believing that God can do anything for you or through you. Don't lose faith in Him! Philippians 1:6 gives us this hope: "Being confident of this very thing, that he which hath begun a good work in you will perform it until the day of Jesus Christ." Again, 1 Thessalonians 5:24 tells us of God's promise to do the work through us: "Faithful is he that calleth you, who also will do it."

TOPICS: Building, Challenge, Commitment, Confidence, God's Presence, God's Promises, Work

R. CHRIS HANKS

DAILY BIBLE READING: 1 Chronicles 25–27

TODAY'S VERSE: 1 Chronicles 27:33: "And Ahithophel was the king's counsellor: and Hushai the Archite was the king's companion."

THIS PASSAGE SIGNALS the beginning of the end of God's judgment for David's sin with Bathsheba and murder of Uriah. Ahithophel was the grandfather of Bathsheba. (A man named Eliam was Ahithophel's son according to 2 Samuel 23:34, and Bathsheba was the daughter of Eliam according to 2 Samuel 11:3.) That makes everything he did make sense, doesn't it? Ahithophel finally had his chance to get back at David for defiling his grandbaby and killing her husband! His instruction to Absalom to spread a tent in the sight of all Israel with all of David's concubines is a testament to the venom of bitterness which ruled Ahithophel's heart. He also wanted to pursue David to kill him and to bring the people back to Absalom. Thank God for His everlasting mercy, for in all this He supplied David with a friend! Let's look at this verse and see some things God has for us.

The Brother of Folly ("And Ahithophel was the king's counselor"). The definition of the name *Ahithophel* is "the brother of folly."[2] As we already discussed in the introduction, Ahithophel was consumed by his bitterness. The folly of his bitterness is seen as his plan and desire was to destroy David, but he ended up taking his own life instead. Ahithophel was a great talent with great wisdom, but he ended his life dying like a fool.

The Blessing of a Friend ("and Hushai the Archite"). The name *Hushai* means "hasting of the Lord."[3] That sounds like a true friend—someone who will hasten to be at your side no matter what might be happening! Psalm 102:2 says, "Hide not thy face from me in the day when I am in trouble; incline thine ear unto me: in the day when I call answer me speedily." There are many times when it is good to know you have a Friend right there whenever He is needed. Psalm 46:1 says, "God is our refuge and strength, a *very present help* in trouble." Not only is our Friend close, but He is one upon whom we can rely. Proverbs 18:24 says, "A man that hath friends must shew himself friendly: and there is a friend that sticketh closer than a brother."

The Behavior of a Follower ("was the king's companion"). The offices of both these characters were much the same, but their actions were completely different. Ahithophel was the king's "counselor," which means "advisor," but Hushai was the king's "companion," which means "associate." Your behavior as a child of God will tell on you! Have you ever heard the saying, "Actions speak louder than words"? It was that way with Hushai and Ahithophel. One acted like he had the king's interest at heart until he betrayed him; the other proved that he would be faithful and true in the hardest of times. One tried to "advise" the king about his duty; the other "associated" with the king in his work. Which one are you? Why not be an associate with God in His work rather than trying to advise God on what He needs to do?

TOPICS: Bitterness, Foolishness, Friend, Humility, Pride, Sin

---

2   Alfred Jones, *Jones' Dictionary of Old Testament Proper Names* (Grand Rapids: Kregel, 1997), 20.

3   Ibid., 159.

DAILY BIBLE READING: 1 Chronicles 28-29

TODAY'S VERSE: 1 Chronicles 29:1: "Furthermore David the king said unto all the congregation, Solomon my son, whom alone God hath chosen, is yet young and tender, and the work is great: for the palace is not for man, but for the Lord God."

DAVID IS PREPARING everything for the house of God to be built. Here he is challenging the people and his son to do the work for the glory of God. In 1 Chronicles 28:19, we find that God had already given the blueprints of the building to David. David had done all that he could to get this building ready for construction, though he was not allowed to build it himself. Here are a few thoughts about Solomon and what lay ahead for him in this monumental task.

Solomon Was Chosen by a Divine Will ("Solomon my son, whom alone God hath chosen"). The purpose of this statement was twofold. First, it was a witness to all the people that their new king was chosen by God Himself. Second, it was an encouragement to Solomon. Now he could take the throne with confidence and power. He now knew that God was the one who had placed him there. How miserable it is to be somewhere you don't think you should be! If Solomon did not understand that he was chosen, his kingdom would have ended like Saul's in the center of his pride, or it would have been wrought with timidity and fear, with no power or certainty.

Solomon Was a Child with a Definite Weakness ("is yet young and tender"). This statement came from the heart of a daddy. It is as if David was saying, "Son, you've got a long way to go, and you ain't all that yet!" Every young man hates hearing this statement, but every young man needs to face his weaknesses. This was also a challenge to the people to rally behind their new and young king. The heart of this great king was in telling his faithful and loyal subjects to get behind their new king.

Solomon Was Charged with a Daring Work ("and the work is great"). Now Daddy gives his little boy and all the people a challenge: this was a great work! It was great in its *magnitude!* It was great in its *meaning!* It was great in its *ministry!* It was great in its *magnificence!* This is another thing a young man needs: he needs to latch on to something that is bigger than he is. How well I remember when the Lord started working in the hearts of the teens in our youth group in Columbus, Georgia. God really started moving when the teens realized that this was much bigger than they were, and they believed that God was the one to bring revival! God has never done much for those with unbelief. But when "Abraham believed God and it was counted unto him for righteousness" (Romans 4:3), God showed up, showed out, and showed off! God is waiting for an excuse just to show off, to glorify Himself, in the life of one who really believes Him!

Solomon Was Challenged by His Daddy's Worship ("for the palace is not for man, but for the Lord God"). This part of the verse blesses me tremendously. David did not set out to build a "house" for God. David did not even try to build a "temple." David was going to build a *palace!* How do you see your work for the Lord? David's resolve was connected to his worship and his perception of God. Whatever part he had in building this place for God, he would do his best to make it as grand a palace as possible. Wasn't his God worth it? Wasn't the temple a testimony of his love for God? Yes, David would do his best to honor the one he loved most!

TOPICS: Calling, Mentoring, Parenting, Preparation, Strength, Vision, Work, Worship

R. CHRIS HANKS

DAILY BIBLE READING: 2 Chronicles 1–4

TODAY'S VERSE: 2 Chronicles 2:6: "But who is able to build him an house, seeing the heaven and heaven of heavens cannot contain him? who am I then, that I should build him an house, save only to burn sacrifice before him?"

AS SOLOMON BEGAN to grow, he quickly became a spiritual giant. He desired wisdom above all things, and God blessed him. He also became a good witness to others. In chapter 2, verse 3, he testified of God's goodness to a heathen king and told of the great work of the house of God. In verse 6, we see some tremendous spiritual insights that Solomon possessed.

He Caught a Vision of Heaven ("But who is able to build him an house, seeing the heaven and heaven of heavens cannot contain him?"). What we find here is that Solomon understood the smallness of heaven when compared to God Himself. How, all of sudden, can heaven look so small? Because Solomon had caught a glimpse of God! The more you know God, the bigger He gets! How big is your God today? It is easy for us, though we know that He can do all things, to limit Him and His influence in our lives. And we end up just like so many cities in the gospels: "And he did not many mighty works there because of their unbelief" (Matthew 13:58). Instead, we need to catch a vision of God's greatness.

He Caught the Virtue of Humility ("who am I then, that I should build him an house"). This thought from Solomon holds much the same truth as his father, David, penned in Psalm 8:4: "What is man, that thou art mindful of him? and the son of man, that thou visitest him?" Once we see God, we get smaller. John the Baptist said much the same thing in John 3:30: "He must increase but I must decrease." Though Solomon was king over God's people and the whole realm, he found out as a young man that he was nothing! Today, we have many people trying to puff themselves up to be something, when in truth, we are all nothing before God.

He Caught the Value of Honor ("save only to burn sacrifice before him"). Solomon found his place before God: sacrificing before the throne of the King of Kings! This was not just a subservient role, but an honorable role. David, who before Solomon was the greatest king of Israel, said in Psalm 84:10, "For a day in thy courts is better than a thousand. I had rather be a doorkeeper in the house of my God, than to dwell in the tents of wickedness." This was not the last place Solomon wanted to be: it was the first place! Once we start realizing our worth, we will realize that God is so much more worthy of all our honor and praise.

TOPICS: Honor, Humility, Praise, Worship

DAILY BIBLE READING: 2 Chronicles 5-6

TODAY'S VERSE: 2 Chronicles 5:14: "So that the priests could not stand to minister by reason of the cloud: for the glory of the Lord had filled the house of God."

IF ONLY THIS WOULD happen more often in the house of God! So many times when we come to church, we come with a preconditioned idea of what will happen. I believe that many times we limit God's work because we think we know more than He does. What a blessing it is to see the Lord move in His own house! Let's look at the priests in this story and see how they apply to us.

They Couldn't Do What They Needed to Do ("So that the priests could not stand to minister"). It is so easy to become possessive of what happens in our churches. In some churches, preachers would be upset about a move of God because they did not get to preach their sermon! Some would get angry because they were not called upon to sing their song, and they had worked so hard to have it ready! When the glory of the Lord shows up in His house, man needs to take a step back and just take it in. There are many churches, even megachurches, that will never truly experience the presence and the glory of God.

They Couldn't See What They Needed to See ("by reason of the cloud"). This was no ordinary cloud: the root definition means, "a cloud (as covering the sky), i.e. the nimbus or thunder-cloud." The priests did not have to deal with a little fog; they had to deal with the makings of a storm! You will find an interesting description of God in Psalm 104:3: "Who layeth the beams of his chambers in the waters: *who maketh the clouds his chariot*: who walketh upon the wings of the wind." When the clouds start rolling, start looking for God to show up! Let us begin praying for the rains of God's presence to fall upon us once again! I had an old preacher tell me one time that he liked it when it got a little foggy in the services. He wasn't talking about the vagueness of the preaching, but about the presence of God! There were many times at the tabernacle when the cloudy pillar would meet the Israelites at the door, and when it moved, it led them to their next destination! Remember, 2 Corinthians 5:7 says, "For we walk by faith, not by sight." The day will come when every cloud will roll away at the presence of God and "every eye shall see him" (Revelation 1:7). At that day, we will know even as we are known. Until then, the Lord is covered by a cloudy veil; but He will one day be revealed.

What Really Needed to Happen Did Happen ("for the glory of the Lord had filled the house of God"). It is important to keep the main thing the main thing! Our hearts should desire that the glory of the Lord fill the house of God with His glory! The crowd around the temple might have said, "Well, we believe that things ought to be done decently and in order." I would argue that things *were* done decently and in order! Isn't it decent when God shows up? Isn't it decent when the Lord moves in His own house? Such a manifestation of God's presence, even when it messes up our programs, is more "in order" than our own formalistic approach to church. When God does show up, let Him do whatever He wants to do!

TOPICS: God's Glory, God's Presence, Worship

DAILY BIBLE READING: 2 Chronicles 7–9

TODAY'S VERSE: 2 Chronicles 7:1: "Now when Solomon had made an end of praying, the fire came down from heaven, and consumed the burnt offering and the sacrifices; and the glory of the Lord filled the house."

TODAY, LET'S CONCENTRATE on the prayer of Solomon. It was *a prayer of penitence,* it was *a prayer of pleading,* and it was *a prayer of passion.* Only a few people had their prayers answered by fire coming from heaven. Solomon was one of them. Here are a few thoughts about this prayer and how it ought to challenge us in our prayer lives.

It Was an Able Prayer. This is where many prayers fail. Not only do many prayers never get answered because they were never uttered, but many prayers never get answered because they were never right from the start. When I use the term "right from the start," here is what I mean. First of all, the prayers don't come right from the *heart.* When our prayers become just words, they lose all of their spiritual ability. If you do not believe me, let me remind you that the Spirit takes our prayer before God "with groanings which cannot be uttered" (Romans 8:26). Second, our prayers don't come right from the *need.* We do not ask God to meet our needs, but rather we "ask amiss" (James 4:3). We must pray according to the will of God and not according to our carnal way. Third, our prayers fail because they do not come right from the *spirit.* Many times our hearts are so full of sin that our prayers are stripped of any potential they might have. Psalm 66:18 says, "If I regard iniquity in my heart, the Lord will not hear me."

It Was an Approved Prayer. Something in this prayer touched the heart of God. We sure need more people who know how to speak with the Lord! Jesus gave us a model prayer to show us the way to the throne room of heaven in Matthew 6:9–15, a prayer that is simple and humble. Our prayers will not be heard because we have not first bowed in spirit before God in humility. Some people even misunderstand the verse in Hebrews 4:16: "Let us therefore come boldly unto the throne of grace, that we may obtain mercy, and find grace to help in time of need." This verse tells us to come boldly, but it does not tell us to come proudly! We must still come with humble hearts before a thrice-holy God!

It Was an Acceptable Prayer. We know this because God heard and God moved. The fire came down from heaven and accepted the offering that was connected to the prayer. You will find that most great prayers in the Bible had an offering that went with them, and when God did accept them, everybody knew it! You will also find that God was so moved by Solomon's prayer that the story ends up the same way as yesterday's story did—all clouded up in God's glory so that the priests could not perform their duties! When an *able prayer,* an *approved prayer,* and an *acceptable prayer* enters into God's presence, the fire of God will fall from heaven in a mighty display of God's power and pleasure!

TOPICS: God's Will, Prayer, Sin

DAILY BIBLE READING: 2 Chronicles 10–13

TODAY'S VERSE: 2 Chronicles 12:8: "And it came to pass, when Rehoboam had established the kingdom, and had strengthened himself, he forsook the law of the Lord, and all Israel with him."

I PITY REHOBOAM. How could anyone follow David, the man after God's own heart, and Solomon, the wisest man who ever lived? But Rehoboam had to do so. We see the reason for Rehoboam's failure in verse 14: "And he did evil, because he prepared not his heart to seek the LORD." If you are not looking for God, you will most definitely never find Him! Our main text does not show us the marks of a son of the wisest king who had ever lived, but the marks of a fool.

The Fragility of Parliamentary Security ("And it came to pass, when Rehoboam had established the kingdom"). Our hope is not in any government. Rehoboam thought that once he established the kingdom, he could do what he wanted. He quickly found out that his kingdom was very fragile. God soon stripped it away from his greedy and dominating hand. Our president will not save our country. Our military will not save our country. Our legislative process or grassroots movements will not save our country. Our security will be found in God and Him alone.

The Falseness of Physical Strength ("and had strengthened himself"). No matter how Rehoboam strengthened himself, it was not enough. He did what he thought he should do to make himself strong. He put people in the right positions. He fortified his cities. He prepared for war. All of those things are good, but without God, they are vanity! Psalm 20:7 says, "Some trust in chariots, and some in horses: but we will remember the name of the Lord our God." God is our strength! Our own might will most certainly deceive us, for it causes us to trust in an arm of flesh.

The Forsaking of Perfect Scripture ("he forsook the law of the Lord"). This was the real source of Rehoboam's failure. Yes, he trusted in himself, but even some Christians do that. When he forsook the law of God, it was a promise of utter destruction. This was not just failure; it was catastrophe. All we have is the Word of God. How can we forsake it? Job 23:12 says, "Neither have I gone back from the commandment of his lips; I have esteemed the words of his mouth more than my necessary food." We must say like the children's song, "I stand alone on the word of God, the B-I-B-L-E." If we would forsake anything, let it be our carnal living. May we forsake our faithlessness and the frivolity of fleshly living.

The Folly of Provoking Sedition ("and all Israel with him"). This sin of forsaking the law of God also affected a nation. It is amazing how many people will follow something that is completely wrong. Many people are looking for a reason or an excuse to live as they please without having to feel any remorse or responsibility for their wrongdoing. An entire nation was set up to do this, and they all broke fellowship with God. The Bible says in Hebrews 10:24, "And let us consider one another to *provoke unto love and to good works.*" Let us be the cause of bringing others to Christ, not the cause of leading them astray.

TOPICS: Deceit, Faith, Flesh, Word of God

R. CHRIS HANKS

DAILY BIBLE READING: 2 Chronicles 14–17

TODAY'S VERSE: 2 Chronicles 16:9: "For the eyes of the Lord run to and fro throughout the whole earth, to shew himself strong in the behalf of them whose heart is perfect toward him. Herein thou hast done foolishly: therefore from henceforth thou shalt have wars."

THESE WORDS WERE SAID to King Asa, who did not rely on God but bought the services of Syria to fight his battle. We must take heed to the last sentence in this verse: "Herein thou hast done foolishly: therefore from henceforth thou shalt have wars." Asa failed because his faith was not in God. In His rebuke of King Asa, God reveals to us His desire and lovingkindness toward His people who trust in Him. Some people struggle to believe that God actually loves them and desires to work in their lives. A verse that we should commit to memory is Psalm 40:5: "Many, O Lord my God, are thy wonderful works which thou hast done, and thy thoughts which are to us-ward: they cannot be reckoned up in order unto thee: if I would declare and speak of them, they are more than can be numbered." Our text today confirms yet again the desire of God to manifest His goodness to His people.

God Looks for an Excuse to Bless ("For the eyes of the Lord run to and fro throughout the whole earth"). God is searching. This particular verse does not, as other verses do, depict a search for a servant or a preacher. It is a search for someone to bless! Right now every hand should be up with voices shouting, "Pick me! Pick me!" I would like to remind you of Proverbs 15:3: "The eyes of the Lord are in every place, beholding the evil and the good." We know that God sees all and knows all. We accept the fact that God is omnipresent. Can you hear the difference between the two verses? Proverbs says that God's eyes are in "every place," but our verse says that His eyes "run to and fro throughout the whole earth." Proverbs says God's eyes are everywhere. Chronicles speaks of the exploration of God's eyes everywhere in seeking for someone to bless.

God Lives to Express Himself ("to shew himself strong"). The word used for this whole phrase means "to fasten upon; hence, to seize." God wants to show His strength by how He holds onto you! That reminds me of the old children's song which proclaims that the whole world is in God's hands. No matter what happens in my life, God will never let me go! There is neither mishap nor mistake when I am in His hand. Did you ever play a game with your father in which you tried to take something from his hand? I am amazed at the strength of my God and His power to keep me no matter what trials, troubles, or even sins I may face.

God Loves to Exalt his Servants ("in the behalf of them whose heart is perfect toward him"). Notice the phrase "in the behalf of them." It tells us of *God's concern*. He is making this promise for *us!* This is not for His benefit, but for ours! The rest of the phrase, "whose heart is perfect toward him," tells us of *God's condition*. In Scripture, the word "perfect" does not mean "sinless," but "complete." God wants you—all of you! Do you completely rest upon Him today? If you do, this has been promised to you! God loves to manifest Himself in the lives of those who put their trust in Him. James 4:10 says, "Humble yourselves in the sight of the Lord, and he shall lift you up."

TOPICS: Blessing, Humility, Promises, Security, Trust

DAILY BIBLE READING: 2 Chronicles 18–20

TODAY'S VERSE: 2 Chronicles 20:22: "And when they began to sing and to praise, the LORD set ambushments against the children of Ammon, Moab, and mount Seir, which were come against Judah; and they were smitten."

AS ONE OF THE righteous kings of Judah, Jehoshaphat began to praise the Lord before his army went to battle. That is foreign to many people who *might* praise the Lord *after* the battle if it goes according to plan. Jehoshaphat wanted to praise the Lord before he faced the enemy. Accepting God's will is the real meaning of meekness and trust. If you read the surrounding verses, you will find that Israel never planned on losing. They already knew their God was great, and they were getting ready to fight His battle under His orders. That is a recipe for certain victory! There are many times in the Bible in which God's people began to praise His name before they ever engaged enemy forces, and God wrought a great victory to bless them. Let's take a moment to see what happens when God's people sing.

God Wants to Hear You Sing ("And when they began to sing and to praise"). How God longs to hear you lift up your voice and sing His praises! If you ever want to have God's presence fill your heart, just sing! Psalm 22:3 says, "But thou art holy, O thou that inhabitest the praises of Israel." The word for "inhabitest" means "to sit down." When you begin to strike up the choir in your heart to sing a song of worship to the Lord, God immediately looks for a seat. He will stay as long as the concert lasts! When God hears you begin to hum to exalt His name in song, He turns the lights down and centers all of His attention upon you! You have the floor! It doesn't matter how well you sing. Your song will enter into His presence as the most wonderful of sounds that touches His heart!

God Works When You Sing ("the LORD set ambushments against the children of Ammon, Moab, and mount Seir, which were come against Judah"). The word translated "ambushments" means "to lay in wait." After God heard the song of His people, He went out to prepare for battle. The children of Ammon had no idea that God was already waiting for them! They didn't have a chance! Don't ever forget that the forces of heaven are moved when God's people begin to sing to glorify their Master. Though Judah did not know what God was going to do, there was nothing for them to worry about, for God was working for them.

God Wins When You Sing ("and they were smitten"). There is much we do not know about this battle. The verse just says, "They were smitten." In the following verse, we find that God turned the Ammonites upon each other so that when Judah finally showed up on the battlefield in verse 24, there was nobody there: "And when Judah came toward the watch tower in the wilderness, they looked unto the multitude, and, behold, they were dead bodies fallen to the earth, and none escaped." When God does the smiting, there is a real victory. This victory was so powerful and so magnificent that God's people reaped the blessing of their recital in a glorious way. Verse 25 says, "And when Jehoshaphat and his people came to take away the spoil of them, they found among them in abundance both riches with the dead bodies, and precious jewels, which they stripped off for themselves, more than they could carry away: and they were three days in gathering of the spoil, it was so much." All this came from a little praise performance from God's people!

TOPICS: Praise, Singing, Victory, Worship

DAILY BIBLE READING: 2 Chronicles 21–23

TODAY'S VERSE: 2 Chronicles 23:16: "And Jehoiada made a covenant between him, and between all the people, and between the king, that they should be the Lord's people."

JEHOIADA WAS A GODLY PRIEST who feared the Lord and taught Judah the way of God. After Athaliah's rampage in destroying all of her own children so she could rule the kingdom, Jehoiada stole Joash and hid him until the time was right for his coronation as king. For seven years, wicked Queen Athaliah ruled the land. Her murderous and wrathful spirit wreaked havoc among the people and affected their faith and worship. Baal worship was the rule, and the people lacked a godly man to bring them back to the Lord. Jehoiada was that man. However, he had to wait for the right time, and the right time would take seven more years. What great patience and planning it took to bring about a national change for the people of Judah! Thank God for a man of God, one who will show God's people His great love and mercy in preparing them a king to bring them back into the fellowship of God! Here are a few thoughts that might help us concerning our own dedication to the Lord.

It Was a Personal Covenant ("And Jehoiada made a covenant between him"). Jehoiada was not just trying to instruct others about their worship of the Lord, but he was willing to do it himself. This Christian life has got to take on a personal nature. If it never does, it will not mean much to us. Even his dedication to God was a testimony of what God had done for him. The name Jehoiada means "Jehovah-known." Does God know you? Matthew 7:23 says, "And then will I profess unto them, I never knew you: depart from me, ye that work iniquity." The question today is not whether you know God, but whether God knows you. This was a priestly covenant made by Jehoiada the high priest. If he was willing to make this covenant, why shouldn't everybody else follow?

It Was a Public Covenant ("and between all the people"). Some things need to be done together. Even in our churches, there are times when we come together and dedicate ourselves to the common proposition of serving God and following His commandments. The New Testament church was to be of one heart and one mind in the spirit of unity. At times, a rededication is needed that is both private and corporate in its function. Why is there hesitancy about rededicating ourselves and our churches to God? There should not be anything to hinder this covenant, and it ought to be facilitated in its mission.

It Was a Powerful Covenant ("and between the king"). If the king in his imperial power would follow this covenant, then it would carry a powerful message to all those in the kingdom. This did not diminish the responsibility of the people before God if the king did not commit himself to the Lord, but seeing their king serve and fear God would surely make their commitment much easier, and it would affect more people with the gospel. We can see this clearly illustrated for us in the kings of Israel and Judah. Every king who was wicked before God perpetuated a kingdom and a people who were wicked before God. Likewise, every king whose heart was tender toward God also had a call to revival among the people. Truly, Proverbs 29:2 should make us pray for godly leaders: "When the righteous are in authority, the people rejoice: but when the wicked beareth rule, the people mourn."

It Was a Purchased Covenant ("that they should be the Lord's people"). Does this statement not define what we should be—the Lord's people? First Corinthians 6:20 says, "For ye are bought with a price: therefore glorify God in your body, and in your spirit, which are God's." These were God's chosen people. If they left the way of the Lord, they would no longer be in His favor, though they would still be His people. But now, what a prospect! To be back in the favor of God and functioning exactly as God had planned! God's people will never be satisfied unless they are what God made them to be. God made them to be *His people!* I belong to the one who purchased me with His own blood! How can I do anything else but serve Him?

TOPICS: Commitment, Dedication, Promises, Worship

DAILY BIBLE READING: 2 Chronicles 24–26

TODAY'S VERSE: 2 Chronicles 26:5: "And he sought God in the days of Zechariah, who had understanding in the visions of God: and as long as he sought the Lord, God made him to prosper."

THIS PORTION OF OUR READING discusses King Uzziah of Judah. Uzziah was a good king, though he had his faults. What a great testimony of Uzziah is found in this verse: "He sought God." I hope that can be said of us as well. We should be seeking our God and His glory as our first order of business. Let's look at Uzziah's seeking and how it can help us to seek God more.

He Had an Inspiration to Serve God ("And he sought God in the days of Zechariah, who had understanding in the visions of God"). These words can be seen as good and bad. Uzziah "sought God in the days of Zechariah." Uzziah *should* have sought God all the time, not just in the days of Zechariah! However, this is a great testimony of Zechariah! It was his walk with God that stirred the heart of Uzziah to seek God for himself. We should be this kind of inspiration to others. Zechariah had "understanding in the visions of God." There was a *depth* to Zechariah that caused Uzziah to start seeking God. Shallow Christianity is no testimony. Paul had to declare in Romans 11:33, "O the depth of the riches, both of the wisdom and knowledge of God." There was a *delight* in devotion that caused another to take notice. If you like your Christian life, the world will notice! One reason that people don't want Christ or the Christian life today is because God's people don't even act like they enjoy it! Psalm 37:5 says, "Delight thyself also in the Lord; and he shall give thee the desires of thine heart." Uzziah was inspired because Zechariah also had a *dedication* about his love of God. He was committed to this thing!

He Had an Incentive to Serve God ("and as long as he sought the Lord"). Do you need a reason to serve God today? As long as Uzziah sought God, God blessed him! Is that a surprise? God has given us many promises and many reasons to serve Him till death or His return! First Corinthians 2:9–10 says, "But as it is written, Eye hath not seen, nor ear heard, neither have entered into the heart of man, the things which God hath prepared for them that love him. But God hath revealed them unto us by his Spirit: for the Spirit searcheth all things, yea, the deep things of God." There is so much that is coming, so much we have not seen, so much that is promised by God who has never broken a promise! There has not been one time in which God has failed me yet.

He Had in Increase in Serving God ("God made him to prosper"). It's a funny thing about serving God: you never stay at the status quo. Service to God always increases! God wants to build our faith. The Bible says that God "giveth *more* grace" (James 4:6). There is a great increase in store for those who seek God and His ways. Matthew 6:33 says, "But seek ye first the kingdom of God and his righteousness, and all these things shall be added unto you." Trying to fill ourselves with carnal and fleshly living always leaves people longing for more. Only God can satisfy the thirsty soul! The root meaning for the word "prosper" in this verse is "to push forward." In serving God, we prosper by advancing the gospel! We prosper by furthering the cause of Christ. Let's push on! Let's win more ground! Here, the Bible is telling us that God will give us *more* ground and increase us as we follow Him. The fact that we are losing ground today *is testimony of the fact that we are not following God;* for if we would follow Him, God would make us to prosper or "to push forward."

TOPICS: Blessing, Desire, Passion, Reward, Service

R. CHRIS HANKS

DAILY BIBLE READING: 2 Chronicles 27–29

TODAY'S VERSE: 2 Chronicles 29:7: "Also they have shut up the doors of the porch, and put out the lamps, and have not burned incense nor offered burnt offerings in the holy place unto the God of Israel."

VERSE 6 OF 2 CHRONICLES 29 lays a number of accusations against the fathers of the people of Israel. Hezekiah is forming his basis for serving the Lord and calling the people to worship God again. If anybody ought to be causing people to serve the Lord, it should be our fathers! Instead, we are living in a time in which fathers are causing their children to forsake the law of the Lord and turn their backs on God, on His house, and on His Word. Let us be in prayer for our fathers, that God may use them to bring the next generation back to the Lord through the ministry of their children. Here are some things that happened because of the failure of the fathers in Israel.

The Children Were Shut Out of the Way ("Also they have shut up the doors of the porch"). What a horrible thing to do—to shut your children out! This has to do with their **entrance to God**. The word for "porch" in this verse means "a vestibule, as bound to the building." Instead of making the way easy for the children to enter, the fathers shut the entrance to the presence of God. Some children today have fathers who have shut them out from the way of *salvation,* others from the way of *submission,* and still others from the way to *spiritual blessing.* Let us not be guilty of shutting anyone out of the way, especially our own children!

The Children Were Put Out of the Word ("and put out the lamps"). Psalm 119:105 says, "Thy word is a lamp unto my feet, and a light unto my path." What a horrible thing it is to put out someone's light. This has to do with their **enlightenment toward God.** I remember times when my father and I were in the woods at night. If he had the lantern or the flashlight, he would hold it in such a way that I could use the light he was shining. There were other times when he would let me hold it myself. Good fathers always have a care for the well-being of their sons. May we not put our children out of the light! If we put them out of the light, then we are putting them into darkness. That will lead them to the path of utter destruction. We need to give them a good light! There is a good light in the *ministry of gospel preaching.* There is a good light in teaching our children the *wisdom of God's precepts.* There is a good light in the *morality of godly purity.* The Bible says in John 3:19, "And this is the condemnation, that light is come into the world, *and men loved darkness rather than light, because their deeds were evil.*" Let us show the pitfalls of the world to keep our children out of the dangers of darkness.

The Children Were Kept Out of Worship ("and have not burned incense nor offered burnt offerings in the holy place unto the God of Israel"). This has to do with their **engagement with God**. How we need fathers who will lead their children to the holy place of the presence of God! There, they will see the *great price of the blood sacrifice of our Saviour.* They will see the *grand place of the throne of our Sovereign.* And they will see the *great power and glory of our Sanctuary,* Jesus Christ. May we be facilitators of our children's worship and enable them to enter into the presence of God! Worship should not be foreign to them. They should see its consistency, feel its reality, and engage its supernatural power by the life and testimony of their fathers!

TOPICS: Children, Parenting, Word of God, Worship

DAILY BIBLE READING: 2 Chronicles 30–31

TODAY'S VERSE: 2 Chronicles 30:27: "Then the priests the Levites arose and blessed the people: and their voice was heard, and their prayer came up to his holy dwelling place, even unto heaven."

THIS WAS A WONDERFUL TIME of repentance and returning to God by the people of Israel under the leadership of King Hezekiah. The king realized that the kingdom had not kept the Passover as was commanded by God, so he made a decree to proclaim its observance once again. The people obeyed willingly, and God gave them one heart to follow His commandments and to honor the Lord. We need to pray for leaders who will once again bring us back to God. Instead, today we have leaders who are trying to distance themselves from any form of religion and a media that is trying to demonize those churchgoing and moral people who live according to biblical principles. In this verse, we see three things about the Levites that are necessary for the people of God to recognize and appreciate.

They Encouraged the People ("Then the priests the Levites arose and blessed the people: and their voice was heard"). What a blessing it is to be encouraged! Often we do not encourage people enough when they do right. How well I remember when I was doing my best in school as a child, and I heard my teacher compliment me and praise my work. It made me work even harder! We do not serve God for accolades or to be noticed, but it sure is an encouragement to us when somebody gives a small "thanks"! God could use you to cheer the weary heart and to inspire someone in his faith. Try today to be an uplifter of those who are doing right. Even the most dedicated and committed Christians need a gladdening word every now and then. The last part of this first phrase says, "And their voice was heard." Don't mutter encouragement under your breath. Let everybody hear it!

They Entreated God ("and their prayer came up to his holy dwelling place"). Their word of encouragement turned into something greater—intercessory prayer! What a blessing it is to have someone praying for you! You may think of yourself as small and insignificant or even as limited in what you can do. But there is one thing for sure that you can do: you can pray! And when you pray, you are touching the heart of the God of the universe with your request. One of the greatest things you can do for another is to take his or her name before the throne of God in prayer.

They Entered Heaven ("came up to his holy dwelling place, even unto heaven"). The Levites did not enter heaven physically, but spiritually by prayer. This is where many prayers fail. They never seem to make it up the ventilation shaft! We need prayers that will actually make it into the presence of God. These, and only these, are powerful prayers! So many times our prayers are limited by our lifestyles and sins. Other times they are limited by their emptiness and selfish desires. James 5:16b says, "The effectual fervent prayer of a righteous man availeth much." Let us begin to have availing prayers for the glory of God.

TOPICS: Blessing, Encouragement, Leadership, Praise, Prayer

R. CHRIS HANKS

DAILY BIBLE READING: 2 Chronicles 32-34

TODAY'S VERSE: 2 Chronicles 32:7: "Be strong and courageous, be not afraid nor dismayed for the king of Assyria, nor for all the multitude that is with him: for there be more with us than with him."

THESE WORDS WERE SPOKEN by King Hezekiah to comfort the people of Judah after being besieged by Sennacherib, king of Assyria. The people needed this kind of comfort from their king at a time of distress. They needed to be reminded that trusting God is never out of style. Hezekiah's comfort in this verse covers three important areas that we can use today.

We Should Not Be Overthrown by Our Nature ("Be strong and courageous"). Being spiritually strong often goes against our grain. There are times when the old phrase "just suck it up and go on" doesn't seem to help. We are tired, weary, and worn. We want someone to look on our affliction and care about what we are going through, to offer pity, not encouragement. It is easy for us to try to rely upon our physical strength. *But this verse is not talking about our physical strength,* it is talking about our spiritual strength. Paul said in 1 Corinthians 16:13, "Watch ye, stand fast in the faith, quit you like men, be strong." Again, in Ephesians 6:10 he says, "Finally my brethren, be strong in the Lord and in the power of his might." In Nehemiah 8:10 we have this thought: "The joy of the Lord is your strength." Don't allow your old nature to dominate your spiritual courage. Be strong—in Christ! Be courageous—in Christ! In Joshua 1:6–9, God told Joshua three times to "be strong and very courageous." Find your strength in Him!

We Should Not Be Overthrown by Our Nerves ("be not afraid nor dismayed for the king of Assyria"). This is where many people fail. We are living in a time in which our nerves dictate what we do. People are having more psychological problems than ever before. Why? Because we have been overthrown by our nerves! Part of the plan of Sennacherib was to use mental torture to subdue little Judah. They laid siege for two years upon the city of Jerusalem. There was terror in seeing their enemy every day, ready for battle when they woke up. They saw them outside the walls at supper. When they laid down at night, they did not know if they would be greeted by an enemy's blade when they awoke. But God's people can have a special peace upon them! Psalm 23:5 says, "Thou preparest a table before me in the presence of mine enemies." We have become a people who are controlled by our circumstances. But God says in 2 Timothy 1:7, "For God hath not given us the spirit of fear; but of power, and of love, and of a sound mind." Remember that God is not worried about anything that might happen today. Or tomorrow. Or next year. That thought should comfort us as we trust in Him.

We Should Not Be Overthrown by Numbers ("nor for all the multitude that is with him: for there be more with us than with him"). I have heard many say, "God and I make a majority." No, my friend, God alone is the majority! Instead of trying to get God on our side, we need to make sure that we are on His side! What a promise we have in Psalm 91:7: "A thousand shall fall at thy side, and ten thousand at thy right hand; but it shall not come nigh thee." What an encouragement it is to know that being outnumbered is no problem whatsoever! This reminds me of Elisha when he was compassed about by the army of Syria in 2 Kings 6:15b–17: "And his servant said unto him, Alas, my master! how shall we do? And he answered, Fear not: for they that be with us are more than they that be with them. And Elisha prayed, and said, Lord, I pray thee, open his eyes, that he may see. And the Lord opened the eyes of the young man; and he saw: and, behold, the mountain was full of horses and chariots of fire round about Elisha." What a help this should be to us today!

TOPICS: Deliverance, Faith, Fear, Flesh, Power, Strength, Victory

DAILY BIBLE READING: 2 Chronicles 35–36

TODAY'S VERSE: 2 Chronicles 35:10: "So the service was prepared, and the priests stood in their place, and the Levites in their courses, according to the king's commandment."

THIS VERSE IS A LESSON on preparation. I firmly believe that one of the greatest sins in our generation is the sin of being ill-prepared. We will talk about our service further down in the devotion, but here I am talking about our will. We are not hearing God speak today, not because His Word is dead, but because we are not prepared to hear! We do not have revival, not because God is not willing, but because we are not prepared for it. The word used for "prepared" means "to be erect, i.e. to stand perpendicular." That sounds like somebody who is ready! The prepared person stands at undivided attention, with every muscle ready to do what needs to be done. The rest of our verse tells us three things that we need to be prepared to do.

They Were Prepared to Serve ("So the service was prepared"). Every bit, every action of the Levites' service to the Lord was completely prepared. There were no surprises. There were no last-minute changes. There were no regrets. The word for "service" means "work of any kind." What a blessing it is as a pastor to have people in their place and prepared in their service! You don't have to worry about springing something on such people, for they are prepared for everything. Whatever manner of work needed to be done, the priests and Levites were ready and prepared to do it fervently, to the fullest of their ability.

They Were Prepared to Stand ("and the priests stood in their place, and the Levites in their courses"). We need a people who are prepared to stand! God has instructed us in Ephesians 6:13, "Wherefore take unto you the whole armour of God, that ye may be able to withstand in the evil day, and having done all, to stand." We must stand accordingly! It does not matter if people do not like what the Bible says about an issue or a sin: we must do like the children's song which says, "I stand alone on the Word of God, the B-I-B-L-E!" This phrase says that the priests stood "in their place" and the Levites "in their courses." That tells us that there is organization and order to the way we should serve the Lord and one another. We must find our place, and when we are there, *stand!*

They Were Prepared to Submit ("according to the king's commandment"). These servants of God were obeying somebody else's will. Don't you know what 1 Corinthians 6:19 says? "What? know ye not that your body is the temple of the Holy Ghost which is in you, which ye have of God, and *ye are not your own?*" Again, we are told in 2 Corinthians 5:15, "And that he died for all, that they which live *should not henceforth live unto themselves,* but unto him which died for them, and rose again." We are here to obey and carry out the commandments of our King! Submission is greatly lacking in our churches today because many people want to be the big shot in their place of service. By contrast, we are to submit to all authority and engage in the service of the King. Are you prepared to do that today?

TOPICS: Preparation, Service, Stand, Submission, Word of God

DAILY BIBLE READING: Ezra 1–3

TODAY'S VERSE: Ezra 1:3: "Who is there among you of all his people? his God be with him, and let him go up to Jerusalem, which is in Judah, and build the house of the Lord God of Israel, (he is the God,) which is in Jerusalem."

LET'S BEGIN TODAY'S devotion with a reminder of who is speaking in Ezra 1. This was a proclamation by Cyrus, King of Persia! He was looking for those Jews who would return to their homeland and build the house of God. The world today is looking for people who really believe God like they say they believe God! We should not be waiting for the world to clamor for witnesses before we speak. Cyrus should have already had names and addresses of people who were unashamed of their faith and were faithful servants of God. The king was asking for help to build the house of God back in Jerusalem. Who else had more reason to help build God's house than God's people? Cyrus should have had to turn people away because of the sheer volume of volunteers. Psalm 107:2 says, "Let the redeemed of the LORD say so, whom he hath redeemed from the hand of the enemy." Your family, people in your factory, and even your friends should not have to ask for someone to point the way for them spiritually. They should know that they have someone in *you* who knows God and can share the gospel with them.

God Will Fill Your Need of Connection ("his God be with him"). This king requested God's blessing on these workers. Let me remind you that Cyrus was king of Persia, modern-day Iran. This area has always had problems and issues with the Jews. Iran's desire to destroy Israel, like that of many Arab nations today, was in force even back in biblical times. This request of Cyrus was a miracle from God! We see in this Scripture that as you surrender to the work of the Lord, there will be a connection that brings fulfillment to your life. Even an unbelieving king knew that if anyone engaged in the work of the Lord's house willingly, God's presence would be with him.

He Will Fill Your Need of Courage ("and let him go up to Jerusalem, which is in Judah"). "Going up" was not an easy task. Jerusalem was laid waste. There was no real law out there. Much of the land was controlled by tribal bands and warlords. But the Jews would find, as they submitted, that God would give them the courage to go. Some people have this backwards: they want the courage to go before they decide to go. We must first obey the Lord, and then He will provide the courage to do His will. These Jews had become satisfied with their captivity. They had forgotten the words of their own song in Psalm 137:5–6: "If I forget thee, O Jerusalem, let my right hand forget her cunning. If I do not remember thee, let my tongue cleave to the roof of my mouth; if I prefer not Jerusalem above my chief joy." They had forgotten the land of God and His house and were comfortable in their spiritual desert. Yes, this would take much courage.

He Will Fill Your Need of Construction ("and build the house of the LORD God of Israel"). The Jews needed to build something. This was a constant theme throughout their history. They were to build houses and cities when they took the Promised Land. Solomon built the temple. John the Baptist built a highway for the Messiah. Every person, priest, king, and prophet was to be a builder. Building the house of God will bless your heart, for you were meant to be a builder too!

He Will Fill Your Need of Confirmation ("he is the God, which is in Jerusalem"). Hearing a Persian king say "He is the God" would be confirmation that this was definitely God's will. We can use the same confirmation to be settled on the Lord in our love and service to Him. First Peter 5:10 says, "But the God of all grace, who hath called us unto his eternal glory by Christ Jesus, after that ye have suffered a while, make you perfect, stablish, strengthen, settle you." Settle down, Christian! Be assured of who God is! "He is the God"!

TOPICS: Building, Calling, Church, Courage, Commitment, Faith, Service, Work

June 2

TODAY'S VERSE: Ezra 4:19: "And I commanded, and search hath been made, and it is found that this city of old time hath made insurrection against kings, and that rebellion and sedition have been made therein."

BECAUSE OF HOW this verse reads, I must give you a little background for you to understand the thought I'd like to share with you today. The children of Israel had been in captivity for quite some time. Ezra had marshaled the people to begin to rebuild the house of the Lord. Of course, with every building project for the Lord, the devil and his imps like to cause trouble. The heathen wanted to be in on this little remodeling project, and they offered their help. Ezra quickly rejected their offer and told them that they had no part in building the house of Jehovah.

Desiring to halt all operations in the rebuilding of the temple and strike against the remnant in Jerusalem, these unfriendly neighbors did all they could to weaken the hands of the builders and hinder the people of God in their mission and resolve. Here, in chapter 4, they finally sent letters to the king and accused the fathers of the people of Israel of being a rebellious people, hurtful unto kings and provinces and moving sedition in the area. King Artaxerxes commanded for them to search out the accusation and found it to be true. Today, I'd like to address the testimony of the men and fathers who stood for things that made a difference many years later. It's a testimony I am thankful for!

I Am Thankful for a Heritage that Conquered the Land ("and it is found that this city of old time hath made insurrection against kings"). The word for "insurrection" in this passage means "to carry away, take." When King Artaxerxes read about these "insurrections," he was reading about the exploits of Saul, David, Solomon, Hezekiah, Jehoshaphat, and all the mighty men of Israel. These were men who were not afraid of war. We need people today who are willing to take land in the spiritual battlefield for their Lord. Romans 8:37 says, "Nay, in all these things we are more than conquerors through him that loved us." You will notice that these Israelite fathers "made insurrection against kings." In the spiritual realm, we need to find the seat of authority in every battle for the strongholds that rule over areas in our lives. Second Corinthians 10:5 says, "Casting down imaginations, *and every high thing* that exalteth itself against the knowledge of God, and bringing into captivity every thought to the obedience of Christ."

I Am Thankful for a Heritage that Carried the Load ("and that *rebellion* and sedition have been made therein"). This little idea of rebellion is a good thing! This was a heathen king and a heathen people that designated the people of God "rebellious." This was a daily rebellion. The Jews chose to walk with God every day. They denied the flesh every day. They fought the heathen system every day. They did not bow under the pressure of the mighty load that was laid upon them. It was said of Christ in Matthew 12:20, "A bruised reed shall he not break, and smoking flax shall he not quench, till he send forth judgment unto victory."

I Am Thankful for a Heritage that Cried for Liberty ("and that rebellion and *sedition* have been made therein"). The word translated "sedition" means "incitement of resistance to a lawful authority." What was lawful to these God-rejecting people was not lawful in the sight of God. The fathers of Israel stirred the people about the things of God. The prophets called for repentance in sackcloth and ashes. The Word of God was proclaimed in power for the return of the people to the house of God and His ministry. First Corinthians 6:12 says, "All things are lawful unto me, but all things are not expedient: all things are lawful for me, *but I will not be brought under the power of any.*" We need to get back to old-time preaching with the people of God stirred and revived by the things of God. We need to incite a resistance to the worldly system of denying the authority and perfection of the Word of God. We need to daily resist the spiritual oppression of God's people. We need to strengthen our thoughts concerning doctrine and the inspiration of God's Word. Let us incite a riot of revival!

TOPICS: Battle, Heritage, Old Paths, Preaching, War, Work

R. CHRIS HANKS

DAILY BIBLE READING: Ezra 7–8

TODAY'S VERSE: Ezra 8:23: "So we fasted and besought our God for this: and he was entreated of us."

WHAT A BLESSING when we can rejoice in the last part of this verse: "And he was entreated of us." I believe that God wants to answer the prayers you have been laying at His feet for so long concerning revival. It sure is good to know that God hears and answers His people! Here are a few thoughts about this verse that might help us to find God.

First, **There Was a Staying** ("So we fasted"). The word for "fasted" here actually means, "to cover over the mouth, to fast." We need to stay, or stop, the desires of our flesh. Actually, we might find that it would not hurt us to "cover over our mouths" for a number of reasons! Our mouths and lips and tongues cause so many problems that the Bible says the tongue is a "world of iniquity" and is "set on fire of hell." There needs to be a staying of our mouths when we come into the presence of the Lord. We need to cease from man's wisdom. We need to stop from the continual vanity of our lips. There is not enough fasting among the Lord's people today, and far too much feasting. Fasting is not a hunger strike against heaven. It is a dedicated time set apart to trust and rely upon God for our requests. As we fast and feel the pain of physical hunger, it is to drive us to our knees and beg for the mercy of God concerning our burden and request.

Second, **There Was a Searching** ("and besought our God for this"). The word used here for "besought" means "to search out, specifically in worship or prayer." The last part of 1 Chronicles 28:9 says, "If thou seek him, he will be found of thee; but if thou forsake him, he will cast thee off for ever." My mom's favorite verse was Matthew 6:33: "But seek ye first the kingdom of God, and his righteousness; and all these things shall be added unto you." Oh, that God's people would seek Him yet again! Oh, that we might look for Him as for hidden treasure! Psalm 27:8 says, "When thou saidst, Seek ye my face; my heart said unto thee, Thy face, Lord, will I seek." May we strive to see Him and His glory!

Third, **There Was a Satisfying** ("and he was entreated of us"). God was satisfied with His people's heart of worship. The word translated "entreat" means "to burn incense in prayer, and reciprocally, to listen to prayer." This is a two-way definition! *The people* burned incense in prayer, and *God* heard them! This is just the way it should be. We bow; God blesses! The only thing that moves the heart of God to be entreated of us is our heart of worship for Him. We need to burn spiritual incense in our prayers that it might be precious to Him and that He might smell a sweet-smelling savor. Let us pray that God might be entreated for us!

TOPICS: Blessing, Flesh, Revival, Prayer

June 4

DAILY BIBLE READING: Ezra 9–10

TODAY'S VERSE: Ezra 9:5: "And at the evening sacrifice I arose up from my heaviness; and having rent my garment and my mantle, I fell upon my knees, and spread out my hands unto the LORD my God."

WHERE HAS OUR HEAVINESS gone today? Here in our reading, Ezra has been stunned by the people's wickedness. He sat there to take in the plight of their standing before God. We find here that he did not do anything about it until the "time of the evening sacrifice." That is what Calvary will do for you! Beholding Calvary will expose the sin of your heart and lay a heaviness upon your spirit. We need this kind of repentance to return to the house of God and rest upon the hearts of His people. When the time came to act upon the sin in his life and the heaviness in his spirit, Ezra moved, repented, and prayed unto God. This verse is a lesson in brokenness that we will study for a moment.

There Was a Brokenness in His Covering ("and having rent my garment and my mantle"). We must realize that we are exposed and naked before God Almighty. Hebrews 4:13 says, "Neither is there any creature that is not manifest in his sight: but all things are naked and opened unto the eyes of him with whom we have to do." We must quit trying to hide behind the coverings of our flesh. There is nothing we can use to cover ourselves when it comes to the magnitude of our sin. We are in the open, with nowhere to go in the sight of God.

There Was a Brokenness in His Condition ("I fell upon my knees"). This affected Ezra's standing. He knew that he could not stand before God any longer! Would to God that His people would humble themselves before Him and cast themselves down in His presence! There is nothing prideful about repentance. A heart that is desperately seeking forgiveness does not care how it looks in the presence of others. Such a heart is pictured in the woman who entered into the presence of Jesus as He sat at meat with a Pharisee to break her alabaster box, anoint Him, and wash His feet with her tears (see Luke 7:36–50). The Jews who were gathered there mocked her for her shameless display of love and worship. The only two people who did not care what the others thought were Christ and the woman. Instead of such true brokenness, we have people today trying to build themselves up so that they will seem more important and spiritual than others. They are more concerned about their appearance than they are about their repentance.

Finally, **There Was a Brokenness in His Cravings** ("and spread out my hands unto the LORD my God"). The word here for "spread" means "to break apart, disperse." Instead of keeping his hands clenched in trying to protect himself from God, Ezra broke his hands apart and began to pray, beg, and crave some things from God instead. We often have a problem when we experience conviction: we bring our arms inward and defend ourselves. Defensiveness never works in the life of a Spirit-filled believer. Would you defend yourself against God's grace, mercy, and forgiveness? Open your arms to the Lord, and extend an invitation to allow God to touch and change you according to His divine will.

TOPICS: Brokenness, God's Forgiveness, Prayer, Repentance, Worship

R. CHRIS HANKS

DAILY BIBLE READING: Nehemiah 1–3

TODAY'S VERSE: Nehemiah 2:17: "Then said I unto them, Ye see the distress that we are in, how Jerusalem lieth waste, and the gates thereof are burned with fire: come, and let us build up the wall of Jerusalem, that we be no more a reproach."

WE ARE ALL in great distress today. Our nation is in great distress. Our homes are in great distress. Our children are in great distress. Our churches are in great distress. Some of this is because our forefathers have forsaken the way of the Lord and placed themselves above the Word of God. The place of God's promised presence and the "apple of his eye" is now laid waste. Some in Jerusalem had been living in these conditions for a long time. They had never seen the problem of having their land in waste and ruins. As a matter of fact, they had actually gotten used to it! My, how easy it is to get used to a place of destruction and accept it like it will never change! Here are a few thoughts about our walls and what we need to realize and do.

We Still Have a Responsibility ("come, and let *us* build up the wall of Jerusalem"). If we are not going to rebuild the wall, who will? There is nobody who will help us build up these walls again! Others do not understand why these walls were built in the first place. These were *strong* walls around the city of God. These were *storied* walls that helped God's people against the enemy. These were *stained* walls that could tell many stories. They were stained from the weather and the storms that had come in the past. They were stained from the battle that had ravaged their nation. But these are "our" walls, the people realized! Let us rise up and build! These walls had been beaten and broken down because the people had left the God of Israel. They needed to be built again so that the children of Israel might give themselves to the Lord.

We Still Need a Refuge ("build up the *wall of Jerusalem*"). Jerusalem's protection was gone, with nothing to keep her from the *enemies' wiles or from the enemies' will.* Our nation is hurting today, from our children to our churches, because the walls are broken down. We have got to start building these walls once again. These are walls that are prepared to help us against those who would do us harm. These are walls of *boundaries,* of *balance,* of *beauty.* These are walls from a wise master *builder!*

We Still Have a Reproach ("that we be no more a reproach"). If you still need a reason to build, how about the one given in this phrase? I sure don't want to be a disgrace to the cause of Christ! One reason it is so hard to reach people with the gospel today is that Christians are a joke and a disgrace to all that is identified with Christ. Instead of being a reproach *to* Christ, let us bear the reproach *of* Christ! That is what the Bible says Moses did in Hebrews 11:26: "Esteeming the reproach of Christ greater riches than the treasures in Egypt: for he had respect unto the recompence of the reward." Let us take Christ's reproach upon us rather than being a reproach to His name!

TOPICS: Battle, Build, Enemies, Protection, Refuge, Reproach, Responsibility, War

DAILY BIBLE READING: Nehemiah 4-6

TODAY'S VERSE: Nehemiah 4:2: "And he spake before his brethren and the army of Samaria, and said, What do these feeble Jews? will they fortify themselves? will they sacrifice? will they make an end in a day? will they revive the stones out of the heaps of the rubbish which are burned?"

SANBALLAT AND TOBIAH were great adversaries of Nehemiah and all the people of Israel who were rebuilding the wall of Jerusalem. At the end of verse 1, the Bible says that Sanballat "was wroth, and took great indignation, and mocked the Jews." It seems that when we finally start doing something for the Lord, the devil will do whatever is necessary to discourage us from serving God. The main question from our verse asks, "What do these feeble Jews?" When the enemy comes to mock you and your work for the Lord, you will find there is a pattern to the attack. The enemy will *disdain* you, *discourage* you, and so *defeat* you. These Jews never became defensive. They never became angry that someone would talk down to them like that. Actually, they agreed with the enemy! In such a disheartening situation, all they could do was pray. It would do us good to accept our feebleness and pray to God for help. I pray to God and receive help from Him, "for when I am weak, then am I strong" (2 Corinthians 12:10). In this verse alone, there are four things mocked by those who wanted to destroy the Jews.

First, They Mocked Their Strength ("will they fortify themselves?"). The truth is, we have no strength. In chapter 8, we find Nehemiah telling the people, "For the joy of the LORD is your strength." This question of fortification is a good one for us to ponder today. These people were defenseless. There was no wall, there were no gates, and there were no armies in Jerusalem. They were nothing but sitting ducks. They had nowhere to go, no one to help, and no place to hide. But Nehemiah rested himself upon the work that God had given him to do and trusted in the Lord to protect him and the people.

Second, They Mocked Their Sacrifice ("will they sacrifice?"). Sacrifice is something the world always mocks! Those who have been under the judging hand of God often struggle with such mockery, for the guilt of their past sin seems to make them unworthy of God's future work. Those who were mocking the Jews reminded them that the reason they were rebuilding the walls was because they had failed God before, and God had brought judgment upon them. These heathen adversaries also knew that there was no place for the Jews to sacrifice yet, because the place of their worship had been destroyed. In the Jews' minds, they were condemned if they did, and they were condemned if they didn't. But no matter how the world mocks the perfect sacrifice of God, we will rejoice boldly in the provision of God's pardon that He has graciously given.

Third, They Mocked Their Steadfastness ("will they make an end in a day?"). The adversaries did not believe the Jews had the fortitude to rebuild the wall. These accusations were against their resolve. Can you hear Sanballat and Tobiah now? "They tried to do this before and utterly failed. We'll give them a month, maybe two, and they'll give up again! Don't they know that this is bigger than they are?" We must rely upon our God to sustain us in our daily walk with Him. The Jews didn't have to finish the wall in a day! They just had to build *that* day. Sometimes it does seem long, and at other times it does not seem that we are making any headway on the project at hand. But little by little, the work is being accomplished. God will always bless faithfulness!

Fourth, They Mocked Their Supply ("will they revive the stones out of the heaps of the rubbish which are burned?"). The Jews did not even have the right materials to do what they wanted to do. What kind of a wall would this be if they could not get the needed materials? The materials they did have were no good! All they had was trash and rubbish. The only things that were left, they would have to pull out of the ashes! Yet there is a promise: "But my God shall supply all your need according to his riches in glory by Christ Jesus" (Philippians 4:19). Praise the Lord for a supply that God can give us from His own hand!

TOPICS: Mocking, Persecution, Provision, Ridicule, Sacrifice, Strength, Worship

DAILY BIBLE READING: Nehemiah 7–8

TODAY'S VERSE: Nehemiah 8:8: "So they read in the book in the law of God distinctly, and gave the sense, and caused them to understand the reading."

THIS CHAPTER CONTAINS many reasons why we do what we do in church today. From the introduction of a platform (verse 5, "For he was above all the people") to the use of a pulpit (verse 4, "And Ezra the scribe stood upon a pulpit of wood, which they had made for the purpose"); from the institution of a nursery (verse 3, "Before the men and the women, and those that could understand") to standing for the reading of God's Word (verse 5, "When he opened it, all the people stood up"); even to the lifting up of hands in worship (verse 6, "And all the people answered, Amen, Amen, with lifting up their hands: and they bowed their heads, and worshipped the LORD with their faces to the ground."). Today's verse focuses upon the preaching and teaching of the Word of God.

The Clarity of Godly Preaching ("So they read in the book in the law of God distinctly"). The word for "distinct" means "to separate." As a church member, you should desire that your preacher be one who brings clarity to the Word of God and to the Christian life. The vagueness of Christian Science, humanism, and any other self-centered religion has clouded our thinking by vain philosophy. We need a man who will give the Word of God and make the way clear and plain. First Corinthians 1:21 says, "For after that in the wisdom of God the world by wisdom knew not God, it pleased God by the foolishness of preaching to save them that believe."

The Connotation of Godly Preaching ("and gave the sense"). We need men today, preachers and pastors, who will not just hop on some hobbyhorse in their preaching but will methodically, proficiently, and purposefully "give the sense" of what the Word of God says. There are enough hobbyhorse preachers, just as there are enough Hollywood preachers. Where are the men of God who are not going to try to impress a crowd, but whose heart is to open the Word of God? Such men make a feast at which every person may dine on the best that heaven has to offer! There are reasons God has said what He has said. There are principles behind what He has said. There are pictures and themes in every story that exemplify the knowledge of God and will strengthen the heart of every believer, if we will find them. Oh, how we need men who will open these truths to others!

The Consequence of Godly Preaching ("and caused them to understand the reading"). This should be the end of every message: to cause the people to understand. That was the need of the Ethiopian eunuch before Philip, the preacher and deacon, came to help! I have been privileged to sit in the presence of some great preachers and feast on the finest of meats brought out of the depths of God's storehouse. They set an elegant table and offer the best food from faraway places to sharpen the taste of each listener to God's precious Word! Study is hard work for a man of God as he desires to have *the* message for his people that God lays upon his heart. Pray that God will bless your preacher as he studies God's Word and that God might use him to open your understanding as you hear that Word faithfully given.

TOPICS: Church, Clarity, Preaching, Study, Word of God

DAILY BIBLE READING: Nehemiah 9–11

TODAY'S VERSE: Nehemiah 9:29: "And testifiedst against them, that thou mightest bring them again unto thy law: yet they dealt proudly, and hearkened not unto thy commandments, but sinned against thy judgments, (which if a man do, he shall live in them;) and withdrew the shoulder, and hardened their neck, and would not hear."

THE REBELLION OF ISRAEL was on display for many years against a God who had been nothing but faithful and merciful to them. Sometimes we just don't see our own obstinacy until we have been punished for our sins. In the case of Israel, it took a man who left the comforts of service in a heathen palace, surrendered to the Lord's will, and began to build the walls of God's choice city to see the insurmountable pile of sin that had separated the people from God. None of us will ever see our need for mercy until we first recognize and admit our sin. Nehemiah recognized Israel's sin and the mercy of God's punishment to restore them to His blessing. I hope that you will hear Nehemiah's insights and his transparency in seeing the Lord's punishment for sin.

The Prosecution of Israel ("And testifiedst against them"). The word translated "testifiedst" means "to duplicate or repeat; testify (as by reiteration)." All God has to do to convict us is to go down the list of what we have already done. Our works, our thoughts, and our actions all speak loudly. The Bible tells us in John 2:25 that Jesus "needed not that any should testify of man: for he knew what was in man." God knows, good and well, man's capabilities. He knows that our works will manifest what we really are. Psalm 106:39 says, "Thus were they defiled with their own works, and went a whoring with their own inventions." Sin is not "everybody else's" fault, but our own. God will not have to drum up charges against us to convict us, but will only recount what we have already done. The Bible says in Deuteronomy 4:26 that God warned Israel about their willful sin against Him: "I call heaven and earth to witness against you this day, that ye shall soon utterly perish from off the land whereunto ye go over Jordan to possess it; ye shall not prolong your days upon it, but shall utterly be destroyed." My friend, be sure to know that God's Word will come to pass!

The Pleas to Israel ("that thou mightest bring them again unto thy law"). God's purpose in exposing our sin is to bring us back to the place of restoration! God wants to turn us back to the life that is found in His way, His favor, and His love. Every word of conviction that is spoken by God or found in His Word is a plea to His people to turn back to the good and the right way! In pleading with Israel, Jesus said in Matthew 23:37, "O Jerusalem, Jerusalem, thou that killest the prophets, and stonest them which are sent unto thee, how often would I have gathered thy children together, even as a hen gathereth her chickens under her wings, and ye would not!" How He desires for us to be restored in fellowship that He might give us blessing and goodness!

The Pride of Israel ("yet they dealt proudly, and hearkened not unto thy commandments"). It always comes down to something as simple as this—pride! The Hebrew word for "dealt proudly" means "to seethe, to be insolent." That explains so much about us! We are "boiling over" and seething in our own pride, self-sufficiency, and arrogance, so much so that we not only disobey God, but hardly even hear His Word at all!

The Purpose of Israel ("but sinned against thy judgments, which if a man do, he shall live in them"). Israel's pride caused them to sin against God presumptuously. They were bent on disobedience, and they thought nothing of it! What kindness is attributed to God's judgments in the phrase "Which if a man do, he shall live in them"! Yet, Israel purposed to reject the goodness of God so they could do things their own way. What heartache and trouble comes from doing things "our way"!

The Pulling of Israel ("and withdrew the shoulder, and hardened their neck, and would not hear"). God has laid His hand upon us in hope of revival and restoration, and we have pulled away and said, "Don't touch me!" Why would we rebel against the hand of God in our lives? In rejecting His mercy, we have claimed His judgment. Please don't pull away from God, but allow Him to draw you back into His fellowship and blessing!

TOPICS: Blessing, Pride, Rebellion, Repentance, Restoration, Sin

R. CHRIS HANKS

DAILY BIBLE READING: Nehemiah 12–13

TODAY'S VERSE: Nehemiah 13:2: "Because they met not the children of Israel with bread and with water, but hired Balaam against them, that he should curse them: howbeit our God turned the curse into a blessing."

THIS VERSE TELLS US why the Ammonite and the Moabite were not allowed into "the congregation of God for ever": because they had cursed and persecuted the people of God. Many would destroy God's people if they could. The devil would destroy you right now if he could. He has no use for God's people. Here are a few simple thoughts concerning the persecution of Israel by the Ammonite and the Moabite.

They Did Not Provide Pity for the People of Israel ("Because they met not the children of Israel with bread and with water"). Just recently, the news had a story about a man in Connecticut who was hit by an oncoming car. As he lay there in the street, the car turned down a side road to flee, bystanders just walked on by, and cars passed on the side. We are living in a time in which there is little pity shown for our fellowman. These people had no pity upon the people of God. Because of that, they were rejected by God and not allowed in the fellowship or worship of the congregation.

They Provided Perversion to the People of Israel ("but hired Balaam against them, that he should curse them"). God did not allow Balaam to curse the people of Israel, so this heathen prophet had to find another way to defeat them. Balaam's doctrine was all about fornication. His desire was to defile the people of Israel and make them stink in the sight of God. Like Balaam, the world today desires our defilement. Our homes, churches, and children are constantly being defiled by things that defy the way of the Lord. If we would fear our God and respect His commandments, we would reject those things that bring about great uncleanness in our lives.

God Provided Protection to the People of Israel ("howbeit our God turned the curse into a blessing"). No matter what these heathen nations desired to do, God was at work against their wicked ways. Every time they thought they had the children of Israel defeated, God would turn the curse into a blessing. Hallelujah for the protection of God! No matter how others intend to harm His people, they cannot do so unless it is permitted by God Himself. Satan himself could do absolutely nothing to Job without God's permission. We may wonder, then, why God would allow the suffering that came on Job, but the only answer I have is that it was the sovereign will of God. What happens is His decision. We do not have to agree with His decisions or even understand them! Isaiah 55:9 says, "For as the heavens are higher than the earth, so are my ways higher than your ways, and my thoughts than your thoughts." Even in the middle of Job's trials, he was experiencing the protection of God. First Corinthians 10:13 says it like this: "But God is faithful, who will not suffer you to be tempted above that ye are able; but will with the temptation also make a way to escape, that ye may be able to bear it." There is comfort in knowing that whatever God may allow us to endure, He will protect us from what we cannot handle!

TOPICS: Blessing, Judgment, Persecution, Protection, Sexual Sin

DAILY BIBLE READING: Esther 1–3

TODAY'S VERSE: Esther 2:17: "And the king loved Esther above all the women, and she obtained grace and favour in his sight more than all the virgins; so that he set the royal crown upon her head, and made her queen instead of Vashti."

THE KING ONLY HAD EYES for Esther! What mushy stuff we have to talk about today: it's like Valentine's Day all over again! You can almost hear the king singing a love song as he looks upon Esther. But there is truth for us here today. As I read this story, I am reminded of the great love our wonderful King has toward us! In this verse, we are introduced to a powerful love. It says, "And the king loved Esther *above all* the women." I can hear echoes of other verses here: "For God *so loved* the world" (John 3:16). "Behold, *what manner of love* the Father hath bestowed upon us" (1 John 3:1). "But God, who is rich in mercy, for his *great love* . . ." (Ephesians 2:4). Let us consider God's love for us as we see the king bring this lovely young lady to himself.

The Sight of Esther ("And the king loved Esther above all the women, and she obtained grace and favour in his sight"). Truly, for King Ahasuerus, "to see her was to love her." The Bible says in Lamentations 3:51, "Mine eye affecteth mine heart because of all the daughters of my city." To find grace in the sight of God—there is nothing so blessed! Five times in the New Testament—five is the number of grace—Scripture says that when Jesus saw the people, he was "moved with compassion" for them. Esther did nothing to demand the king's favor, and she did nothing to deserve it. It was a kindness and a grace that was freely given to her by the king.

The Spotlessness of Esther ("more than all the virgins"). Esther was pure. There is a lot to be said of purity, especially in the culture where we now live! In our Christian walks, God is continuing to make us pure in His sight. Ephesians 5:27 declares God's intent toward His church: "That he might present it to himself a glorious church, not having spot, or wrinkle, or any such thing; but that it should be holy and without blemish." No matter what kind of life you have lived previously, no matter in what defiling actions you have engaged, God desires to purify your heart and life and bring glory to His name!

The Selection of Esther ("so that he set the royal crown upon her head"). The king chose her! I am glad I was able to choose my own wife and she was able to choose me! I am thankful that ours was not some prearranged marriage accomplished by a transaction of our parents. My choice and selection of my wife was the essence of my love. Notice that the king chose Esther before she ever chose him. Doesn't that fit with 1 John 4:19? It says of Christ, "We love him, because he first loved us."

The Substitution of Esther ("and made her queen instead of Vashti"). Esther was given a place of exaltation that had already been another's! What a privilege! What an honor! She was placed in the midst of the king's blessing purely as a result of his favor and grace. Romans chapter 11 explains to us how the Gentiles were "graffed in" to the place of Israel. That is nothing but God's grace! We don't deserve to be here. We cannot boast about being here, for it was not wrought by our own power. We can only rejoice that we are here! Thank God for the wonderful work of His grace and for including us in His great plan!

TOPICS: Chosen, Grace, Love, Purity, Substitution

R. CHRIS HANKS

DAILY BIBLE READING: Esther 4–7

TODAY'S VERSE: Esther 5:2: "And it was so, when the king saw Esther the queen standing in the court, that she obtained favour in his sight: and the king held out to Esther the golden sceptre that was in his hand. So Esther drew near, and touched the top of the sceptre."

IN THE CONTINUING STORY of this book, Haman manipulated the king to destroy the Jews in the kingdom of Persia. His action had long, twisted roots. Haman was an Agagite, or a descendant of Agag. If you remember, Agag was the king of Amalek whom Samuel destroyed before the Lord. Amalek, which was an Edomite nation, came from Esau, Jacob's brother. Even now, many of the problems in the Middle East come from Edomite nations, not just Arab nations. This problem has been recurring for millennia. At this point in the story, Mordecai is now mourning in sorrow. Esther is uncertain of her future because she must hazard her life and go into the place of judgment to talk with her husband, whom she has not seen for a month. After having all the Jews fast and pray for the mercy of God, Esther boldly goes before the king to give her petition. Let's join the biblical account of the story already in action and see what happens to Esther.

The Ecstasy of Grace ("And it was so, when the king saw Esther the queen standing in the court, that she obtained favour in his sight"). What joy Esther must have felt, not from being in the court of the king, but in the extension of his grace! As she entered into the throne room of the king, she knew it was the place of his judgment. She stood alone, knowing that the king could decree death and be justified, yet she received grace and favor! What a relief to Esther! What a joy to the king! What a blessing to the Jewish captives!

The Extension of Grace ("and the king held out to Esther the golden sceptre that was in his hand"). There is no better picture of Christ than the extended scepter in the hand of the king to a subject who needs it! Even the gold is a picture of Christ's deity—and it was in the hand of the king! John 3:16 says, "For God so loved the world that he gave his only begotten Son." What love and hope is found in the extended scepter! In some places in Scripture, the English words "rod" and "scepter" have the same Hebrew root word found in Psalm 23:4c: "Thy rod and thy staff they comfort me." The scepter of the king was a comfort for Esther to see! I imagine that her eyes were upon the scepter as she entered the room, wondering, hoping, and praying that the king might hold it out for her salvation. And just as our King has done so for us, so Esther's king did so for her.

The Acceptance of Grace ("So Esther drew near, and touched the top of the sceptre"). The king's extension of the scepter was not enough. Esther had to accept it by touching it! God has extended His grace to man, but that is not enough. Man must accept it and receive it; otherwise the King has no other option but judgment for His rejected grace. Let's look at the very last phrase that says Esther "touched the top of the sceptre." She could have touched the scepter anywhere and received the same grace, but she chose the top! You see, it was closest to the king's hand! The Bible says in James 4:8a, "Draw nigh to God, and he will draw nigh to you." Get as close as you can to the hand of God, for you will most assuredly find His grace!

TOPICS: Faith, Grace, Love, Prayer, Salvation, Worship

DAILY BIBLE READING: Esther 8-10

TODAY'S VERSE: Esther 9:28: "And that these days should be remembered and kept throughout every generation, every family, every province, and every city; and that these days of Purim should not fail from among the Jews, nor the memorial of them perish from their seed."

WHAT A GLORIOUS ENDING to a struggle that seemed destined to doom God's people! Wouldn't this kind of deliverance cause you to set up some kind of memorial honoring God for His power and victory? The Jews were excited—even gleeful!—at seeing God deliver them from the hand of their enemies. To them, this deliverance was as big as the exodus from Egypt. It ranked with the crossing of the Red Sea and the Jordan River. Yes, the children of Israel would make a festival remembering God's watch care over His people! Today, Jews in synagogues the world over celebrate the Feast of Purim. During the feast, the congregation will read the entire book of Esther. Unger's Bible Dictionary says, "As often as the name of Haman is mentioned in the reading the congregation stamp on the floor, saying, 'Let his name be blotted out. The name of the wicked shall rot!' while the children spring rattles. After the reading the congregation exclaims, 'Cursed be Haman; blessed be Mordecai!'"[1] What a wonderful celebration!

The Remembrance of God's Deliverance Is to Be Purposed ("And that these days should be remembered and kept"). Remembrance of God's works will never be done by accident. The word for "remember" in this verse means "to mark, so as to be recognized." My wife likes to mark dates on the calendar to help us remember events. It might be for a family member's birthday, an anniversary, or some appointment. She knows she has to do this because I forget too easily! (I try to put my appointments and reminders in my PDA. If my PDA dies, I die with it!) We go to these lengths because some things are too important to forget. Make a purposeful mark upon the spiritual things God has done in your life. Highlight and underline a verse that God lays upon your heart. Put notes in your Bible from thoughts or sermons when God speaks to your heart. Remembering will not happen by accident!

The Remembrance of God's Deliverance Is to Be Popular ("throughout every generation, every family, every province, and every city"). This feast was to be the happening thing in Jewish society. How easily we are drawn to worldly fads and trends. Let's begin a craze that remembers a move of God! Let's put God in vogue in our churches! I am not being sacrilegious by demeaning God to the level of worldly fashions, but I am saying that we should make God popular in our homes and churches again. Truly, we have lost godliness by turning our churches into "praise centers" run by drama teams. Our youth groups have evolved into rock concerts and our children's ministries into amusement parks. Let's let God be the center of attention and popularize Him in the sight of our families, churches, and communities! In other words, He is the fashion; we must identify with Him.

The Remembrance of God's Deliverance Is to Be Perpetual ("these days of Purim should not fail from among the Jews, nor the memorial of them perish from their seed"). This event was just too good for them to forget! The word for "perish" means "to snatch away." How often after a work of God has that joy been snatched away! Luke 8:12 tells us that the devil would snatch away the Word of God from people's hearts: "'Those by the way side are they that hear; then cometh the devil, and taketh away the word out of their hearts, lest they should believe and be saved." Our remembrance of God and His work should never end!

TOPICS: Deliverance, Fashion, Memorials, Rejoicing, Remembrance, Victory

---

1   Merill F. Unger, *Unger's Bible Dictionary* (Chicago: Moody Press, 1985), 362.

R. CHRIS HANKS

DAILY BIBLE READING: Job 1-5

TODAY'S VERSE: Job 1:5: "And it was so, when the days of their feasting were gone about, that Job sent and sanctified them, and rose up early in the morning, and offered burnt offerings according to the number of them all: for Job said, It may be that my sons have sinned, and cursed God in their hearts. Thus did Job continually."

JOB IS TALKED ABOUT in both the Old and New Testaments. He is known for his patience and suffering. The Bible tells us much about his character, his purity, and his faith. One thing God told the devil about Job was that he "eschewed" evil (Job 1:8). The word for "eschew" means "turned off." Praise the Lord for a man who was not turned on but turned *off* by sin!

The book of Job is the first of the biblical books of poetry, works written in poetic meter. It contains many doctrinal teachings and insights that are helpful to us today. In our verse today, we see a godly man and how he directed and cared for the spiritual needs of his family. Observe this verse in the light of godly fatherhood and Job's righteousness.

The Purity of a Father's Heart ("And it was so, when the days of their feasting were gone about, that Job sent and sanctified them"). The word translated "sanctified" means "to be clean, ceremonially or morally." Job desired purity in his home and family. Usually, people in his day would sanctify themselves in preparation for an upcoming feast. Job did this *after* the feast was over as well! What a heart for righteousness and purity! God does care about what is inside you. Psalm 51:6 says, "Behold, thou desirest truth in the inward parts: and in the hidden part thou shalt make me to know wisdom." Job desired to teach his children about purity at all times, for the character of God demanded it.

The Prayers of a Father's Heart ("and rose up early in the morning, and offered burnt offerings according to the number of them all"). Thank God for a praying father! Each morning, Daddy Job rose up and prayed for his children. The verse says, "According to the number of them all." That means he sacrificed and called all ten children's names out in prayer to God every day! You can't tell me that his children did not notice their father's worship and prayer on their behalf! It meant more to them than we will ever know. You today may know of your parents' prayers for you and what that means. You may never have had a parent pray for you in your entire life. You have the chance to change that for your own children! There may be many things you cannot do, but you *can* pray! You may not know a lot about God or His Word, but you can pray! Offer your children's or grandchildren's names to God, and be a faithful prayer warrior for them today!

The Perceptions of a Father's Heart ("for Job said, It may be that my sons have sinned, and cursed God in their hearts"). There are some things that moms and dads just know. I often wondered how my parents knew everything I did! As a parent, you need to exercise your God-given ability to discern the motivations and intentions of your children. One way we sometimes know the temptations and sins of our children—as Job may have known them—is that we know our children are "a chip off the old block." Job knew his failures and that his children had the same struggles that he did as a man of flesh.

The Persistence of a Father's Heart ("Thus did Job continually"). Prayer and sanctification for his children was something Job would not quit doing! Thank God for a man who wouldn't quit praying, wouldn't quit teaching, and wouldn't quit observing! You may not know exactly what to do sometimes, but whatever you do, don't quit! The word for "continually" means "to be hot; a day (as the warm hours), from sunrise to sunset, or from one sunset to the next." In other words, Job did not just do this "the next day," but "the next day, all day long." It was not just something included in his day, but his very *lifestyle!*

TOPICS: Consistency, Discernment, Fatherhood, Teaching, Parenting, Prayer, Purity

June 14

DAILY BIBLE READING: Job 6-9

TODAY'S VERSE: Job 9:10: "Which doeth great things past finding out; yea, and wonders without number."

IN THIS CHAPTER, Job's discussion with his "friends" has already begun. I hope I never have friends like Job had! In this particular response, Job runs to what he knows about God. That sounds like a good place to run and hide to me! Even in the midst of your trouble and struggle, remember the power and goodness of an infinite God! In chapter 9, Job discusses God's wisdom, power, authority, and size. He even discusses God's works in the stars of the constellations. It is easy to think that we might get lost before God in the grandeur of His creation, but Jesus reminds us in Matthew 10:29–31, "Are not two sparrows sold for a farthing? and one of them shall not fall on the ground without your Father. But the very hairs of your head are all numbered. Fear ye not therefore, ye are of more value than many sparrows." Let it be known that we serve a great God!

The Magnitude of God's Works ("Which doeth great things"). The word for "great" has to do with age, distance, and height. Of God's age, we are told in Psalm 93:2, "Thy throne is established of old: thou art from everlasting." Of distance we are told in Psalm 139:7–8, "Whither shall I go from thy spirit? or whither shall I flee from thy presence? If I ascend up into heaven, thou art there: if I make my bed in hell, behold, thou art there." Of height we are told in Psalm 139:6, "Such knowledge is too wonderful for me; it is high, I cannot attain unto it." I believe we have to agree with Brother Job that our God doeth *great* things!

The Mystery of God's Works ("past finding out"). God calls many things "mysteries" in the Bible. It is helpful for us to know that there is no truth God cannot reveal to us; however, even when that truth is given, there are infinite depths where we still have not gone. Isaiah 40:28 tells us about the unsearchable depths of God: "Hast thou not known? hast thou not heard, that the everlasting God, the LORD, the Creator of the ends of the earth, fainteth not, neither is weary? *there is no searching of his understanding.*"

The Marvels of God's Works ("yea, and wonders"). Every sign and wonder God did was to show His chosen people His goodness and His love. My father explained the difference between "signs and wonders" to me like this in the feeding of the five thousand: The *wonder* was the miracle of taking the fish and bread and multiplying it for all to eat. The *sign* was the truth that Jesus is the "Bread of Life." Signs and wonders were intended to draw the people in their worship and woo them in their devotion. It had to be both signs *and* wonders because the wonder by itself was nothing! The wonder was only a tool to draw people to the sign. As I contemplate the signs of God's works in the heavens and all of creation, I stand in awe of His power and wisdom. Every wonder that God has done and continues to do today is to draw men to the truth of His love. The greatest wonder, however, is that God *is* love (1 John 4:8)! I am reminded of the hymn by George Beverly Shea: "Oh, the wonder of it all/The wonder of it all/Just to think *that God loves me!"*[2]

The Measures of God's Works ("without number"). There is no possible way that we could sit with pen and paper and enumerate the things that God has done. Even when we try to do as the song "Count Your Blessings" recommends, we forget so many blessings that we actually shortchange God in His "wonders without number." Psalm 71:15 says, "My mouth shall shew forth thy righteousness and thy salvation all the day; for I know not the numbers thereof." Remember, these are not just numbers of the signs of miracles, but the number of the *wonders of truths!*

TOPICS: Blessings, God's Power, Miracles, Mystery, Wonder

---

2 "The Wonder of It All" by George Beverly Shea. © 1956 Word Music, LLC. All rights reserved. Used By Permission.

DAILY BIBLE READING: Job 10–14

TODAY'S VERSE: Job 14:7: "For there is hope of a tree, if it be cut down, that it will sprout again, and that the tender branch thereof will not cease."

THIS IS A GREAT VERSE on the hope of revival: even after something has been destroyed, there is anticipation of a new beginning. This verse has powerful application to our spiritual lives. Keep in mind that we are talking about something that is already alive. If it is dead, then it would need a spiritual quickening, not just reviving. Many a person has been "cut down" by false accusations, worldly desires, personal failure, and sin. But no matter how far someone has gone down the road of disobedience, there is always the prospect of full and complete forgiveness and reinstatement in the favor of God!

The Ruin of a Tree ("For there is hope of a tree, if it be cut down"). I have been blessed lately by watching a man who has been coming to our church. He had fallen away from the Lord and decided to go down his own path. He had godly parents, and in particular a praying mother who never gave up on her son. One day the thought hit him: "What am I going to do when my mother passes away and she stops praying for me?" The first thing he did was get back in church and hear the Word of God! We were sharing verses one evening when this oil-field worker stepped up to the microphone and read the verse we are talking about today. In tears he said, "I'm glad that there is always hope even if the tree has been cut down!" He would tell you in no uncertain terms how his tree had been cut down, but now God has begun to work in his life even though he seemed to have no hope or life left!

The Rejuvenation of a Tree ("that it will sprout again"). New life! Is there anything better? Even though all of its maturity was gone, the tree had a new beginning, new color, new hope, new vibrancy, and new growth. The word for "sprout" means "to slide by." Isn't that the perfect picture of a sprout? I remember hearing farmers in Minnesota say that they would sit on their porches and listen to the corn grow. They told me that the growing season wasn't as long there as in some places, so corn would grow quickly in its beginning stages. A Christian's life is the same! Everything has changed when the sprout comes. It slides by, and sometimes you don't even notice until you look and see that it is different from what it once was! I must point out that verse 9 says, "Yet through the scent of water it will bud, and bring forth boughs like a plant." Water is often a picture of the Word of God in Scripture. Even when something for all practical purposes seems hopeless, a mist of the Word of God can bring new life into that which seems dead! The soul that has been destroyed by some sin or situation can smell the help of the Word of God within a hundred miles and begin to grow just from hope!

The Restoration of a Tree ("and that the tender branch thereof will not cease"). The restoration of the tree actually has a better prospect than its beginning. You might wonder how. Because tenderness has returned, and its growth "will not cease"! Many old trees have stopped growing. As a matter of fact, many trees started dying a long time ago. Some trees take hundreds of years to die. By contrast, this restoration promises that the tree's growth will continue in tenderness, and it will never stop! That sounds a lot like Psalm 1:3: "And he shall be like a tree planted by the rivers of water, that bringeth forth his fruit in his season; his leaf also shall not wither; *and whatsoever he doeth shall prosper.*"

TOPICS: Growth, Hope, Punishment, Restoration, Revival, Sin

DAILY BIBLE READING: Job 15-19

TODAY'S VERSE: Job 19:25: "For I know that my redeemer liveth, and that he shall stand at the latter day upon the earth."

JOB WAS RAKED OVER the coals by those who called themselves his friends. The older I get, the more I understand that self-righteousness is a spiritual narcotic for the carnal Christian. Job was feeling more than persecution: he was feeling betrayal. What should you do when you feel that nobody really cares? You do exactly what Job did, and start talking about God! Isaiah 41:10 gives us this hope: "Fear thou not; for I am with thee: be not dismayed; for I am thy God: I will strengthen thee; yea, I will help thee; yea, I will uphold thee with the right hand of my righteousness." If you have nowhere you can turn, remember God! Job knew that God would not only be faithful, but that He would one day rule this earth and stand here in victory.

The Persuasion of Job's Faith ("For I know"). Is there anything about which you are persuaded? Paul was persuaded in 2 Timothy 1:12: "For the which cause I also suffer these things: nevertheless I am not ashamed: for I know whom I have believed, and *I am persuaded* that he is able to keep that which I have committed unto him against that day." Though you may be uncertain about the economy, your job, or maybe even your family, there are some things you should know with absolute certainty because they are connected to the depths of your soul.

The Prospect of Job's Faith ("that my redeemer liveth"). This was the point of Job's faith! Though his Redeemer had not yet come to give His life as a sacrifice, Job knew that He lived! The Old Testament saints had to be saved the same way we are—by looking to the perfect sacrifice of Jesus Christ. Our hope is not found in some dogma or ritual, but in the person and work of the Son of God. If Jesus is alive today, then anything can happen! The potential is as infinite as He is! Jesus said in Mark 10:27, "And Jesus looking upon them saith, With men it is impossible, but not with God: for with God all things are possible." Our Redeemer came, died, and was buried, but He rose again and lives for evermore. We are all now able to say, "I know that my redeemer liveth."

The Prophecy of Job's Faith ("and that he shall stand at the latter day upon the earth"). What Job saw, he saw by faith. This was no little prophecy. He did not see something that would happen within the next year, nor something having to do with the life and ministry of Christ upon this earth, nor having to do with the Rapture. This prophecy saw all the way to the Second Coming of Christ! This was a prophecy of Christ's setting foot upon Mount Olivet and establishing His kingdom for the Millennial Reign. What a spiritual understanding Job had! It is seldom we find people who can see past the end of their noses in this old world in which we live. I am no exception! Let us set our eyes further into the work and Word of God that we might more fully understand His divine purpose.

TOPICS: Confidence, Faith, Persuasion, Possibilities, Prophecy

R. CHRIS HANKS

DAILY BIBLE READING: Job 20-23

TODAY'S VERSE: Job 23:13: "But he is in one mind, and who can turn him? and what his soul desireth, even that he doeth."

THE MORE I CONTEMPLATE this verse about God, the more it speaks to me. It is a great encouragement to me to know that I am involved in the thoughts of God Himself! Tremendous truths are a part of the thoughts of God.

His Thoughts Are Purposeful Thoughts ("But he is *in* one mind"). Let me quickly tell you what this verse does not say: it does not say, "But he is *of* one mind." That would have to do with God's nature. If it *did* say that, it would be good to know! But the fact that it says "But he is *in* one mind" tells me that this verse has to do with His choice! God is thinking of everything purposefully! What a tremendous blessing this is to all of us today! He has never been *double-minded*. The Bible says that "a double-minded man is unstable in all his ways" (James 1:8). God has never been *absentminded!* He has never forgotten me or His work in my life! He has never been *empty-minded*. From the beginning of creation, God has always had a reason and a purpose behind everything He has done! He has always been *single-minded*.

His Thoughts Are Proactive Thoughts ("But he is in one mind, and who can turn him?"). All good things that happen began in the mind of God. Jeremiah 29:11 says, "For I know the thoughts that I think toward you, saith the Lord, thoughts of peace, and not of evil, to give you an expected end." These were thoughts begun before time, when God knew the failings and sins of man to come and already had an eternal sacrifice planned, a Lamb slain before the foundations of the world who would be sacrificed upon Calvary! What a proactive thought!

His Thoughts Are Powerful Thoughts ("and who can turn him?"). God is in one mind, and who can turn Him? No one! There is nothing you can do about the thoughts of God! There is no point in fighting against the plan, provision, and perfection of God's grace. This is not about some Calvinist approach to salvation, but about God's bringing Calvary into existence for the sins of the world. People can reject God's plan of salvation for them, *but they cannot reject God's provision of salvation for them!* Those are powerful thoughts!

His Thoughts Are Pleasurable Thoughts ("and what his soul desireth, even that he doeth"). The word "desire" here means "to wish for." Psalm 135:6 says, "Whatsoever the Lord pleased, that did he in heaven, and in earth, in the seas, and all deep places." Earlier in this devotion, we saw the verse that said God's thoughts were "thoughts of peace and not of evil." Not only are they pleasing to Him, but they will be pleasing to us! Even if you do not like them, just wait, for they will turn out best! Romans 8:28 says, "And we know that all things work together for good to them that love God, to them who are the called according to his purpose." What should please us more than to receive the things that please God most?

TOPICS: Christ, Grace, Love, Sacrifice, Sovereignty

June 18

DAILY BIBLE READING: Job 24-29

TODAY'S VERSE: Job 28:28: "And unto man he said, Behold, the fear of the Lord, that is wisdom; and to depart from evil is understanding."

PROVERBS 4:7 TELLS US, "Wisdom is the principal thing; therefore get wisdom: and with all thy getting get understanding." If there is one thing we need each and every day, it is wisdom. Today's verse gives us great insight into the mind of God and His desire for man to seek wisdom. You cannot seek true wisdom without God, for anything you found would only be foolishness. Wisdom can only be imparted from God, as He is the only true source of its treasures.

The Qualified Subject of Wisdom ("And unto man he said"). This tells us who is eligible to receive wisdom—anybody! Man *can* have wisdom! One of the biggest problems we have concerning wisdom is that many people think they already have it, and few sense the need for it. James 1:5 says, "If any of you lack wisdom, let him ask of God, that giveth to all men liberally, and upbraideth not; and it shall be given him." Some today are seeking a worldly wisdom to be recognized and acknowledged, all for the sake of pride. Godly wisdom is never about self, but about God and His will upon this earth.

The Qualified Substance of Wisdom ("Behold, the fear of the Lord, that is wisdom"). This phrase sounds a lot like Proverbs 9:10: "The fear of the LORD is the beginning of wisdom: and the knowledge of the holy is understanding." Without fear, man does crazy things. He might challenge a truck on the highway or even try to drive a nail with his elbow. Pain is God's blessing to man, for it teaches him to respect things that could bring discomfort or harm. If we do not reverence or respect the Lord, we have lost our sense of "pain" and have placed ourselves in a danger zone that will bring pain and discomfort to our spiritual lives. The Bible describes such people in 1 Timothy 4:2 as "speaking lies in hypocrisy; *having their conscience seared with a hot iron.*" Our society today is seared by its lack of fear of the Lord. Our sin is witness of this spiritual lack of respect. We have spit in the face of God concerning His laws and commands and have relegated morality to what seems to best fit our situation. Romans 3:12-18 describes us well: "They are all gone out of the way, they are together become unprofitable; there is none that doeth good, no, not one. Their throat is an open sepulchre; with their tongues they have used deceit; the poison of asps is under their lips: whose mouth is full of cursing and bitterness: their feet are swift to shed blood: destruction and misery are in their ways: and the way of peace have they not known: there is no fear of God before their eyes."

The Qualified Step of Wisdom ("and to depart from evil is understanding"). Wisdom teaches us to leave those things that defy God. Proverbs 14:27 tells us about wisdom and the fear of the Lord: "The fear of the LORD is a fountain of life, to depart from the snares of death." It is the fear of God that will teach you how to depart from the snares of death and the evil way. Deliver yourself by departing from evil and embracing the wisdom of the fear of the Lord!

TOPICS: Evil, Fear of God, Understanding, Wisdom

R. CHRIS HANKS

June 19

DAILY BIBLE READING: Job 30–33

TODAY'S VERSE: Job 31:1: "I made a covenant with mine eyes; why then should I think upon a maid?"

IF THERE IS AN AREA that assaults more men today than any other, it is the lust of the eyes. We live in a sex-crazed and sex-driven society. Pornography and smut are around every corner and are easily accessible in the privacy of the home. Lust has claimed the best of preachers, the best of husbands, and the best of fathers. What is amazing is that even *women* today are becoming more involved in pornography than ever before. Some argue that "if it doesn't hurt anybody else, then it must be okay." Don't be deceived: God will not hold a man (or woman) guiltless for this sin. Matthew 5:28 says, "But I say unto you, That whosoever looketh on a woman to lust after her hath committed adultery with her already in his heart." Thousands of years ago before magazines, cable TV, and the Internet, Job recognized his inordinate desires and did something about them. How would it be possible for a man in a dry and dusty desert climate, totally without media or access to the wider world, to lust after a woman? That is easy—in his thoughts! Don't think there is nothing you can do about your lusts and appetites. The battleground is first in the mind. We are instructed in 2 Corinthians 10:5: "Casting down imaginations, and every high thing that exalteth itself against the knowledge of God, and bringing into captivity every thought to the obedience of Christ." This was quite a covenant in which Job voluntarily engaged before the Lord! Let us look a little deeper into this verse for truth about this covenant of character and purity that is needed in every home across our land.

It Was a Committed Covenant ("I made a covenant"). This was not a light decision that Job made on a whim. His decision was one of **purpose**. This kind of godliness and purity does not happen by accident. Some readers may put down this devotion and think, "Well, I've tried, and there is no way I can control my desires." That is not true! You *can* control what you do. You can decide as easily not to sin as you can to sin. Obedience is as easy as disobedience. The difference between the two is our will. The only way to control your will is to commit it to God. Psalm 37:5 says, "Commit thy way unto the LORD; trust also in him; and he shall bring it to pass." Notice that it says, *"He* shall bring it to pass." You might think that you cannot do this. You might be right. But God can! If you commit it to Him, He will do it in you. Too often, we don't completely commit our needs to Him, but hold on to them for security or pleasure. You cannot hold anything back in this kind of a covenant decision.

It Was a Connected Covenant ("with mine eyes"). This was not an esoteric promise that had no association to Job's body. He made this **personal**. If you embark upon a physical diet, you make a covenant with your mouth about what you put in it. The same is true with this covenant of purity. Any decision you make about your body must be connected to your body. Job said, "If my problem is lust, then I must decide what my eyes can and cannot see." Doesn't that sound logical? This was not a covenant with Hollywood or *Playboy,* for Job could not control them. It was not a promise to magazines at the checkout counter, for Job did not manage what was carried by the local merchants. It was a covenant with his eyes, and this was something that he *could* control.

It Was a Convicted Covenant ("why then should I think upon a maid?"). Job's reasoning was connected to his conviction. He desired to be **pure**. If his covenant was to remain intact, his devotion had to run deep. To be true to the covenant with his eyes, he could not tantalize his flesh by entertaining his mind. This is the very place where many covenants of this nature are broken. Job knew that the sincerity of his covenant could easily be destroyed just by his thoughts. Even to entertain such thoughts was ridiculous and silly to Job, for they would end with defilement.

TOPICS: Commitment, Conviction, Covenant, Manhood, Purity

DAILY BIBLE READING: Job 34–38

TODAY'S VERSE: Job 38:3: "Gird up now thy loins like a man; for I will demand of thee, and answer thou me."

DO YOU REMEMBER the old E.F. Hutton commercials? "When E.F. Hutton speaks, people listen!" This verse is God speaking to Job! The voice of God demands Job's complete attention, and it demands his total respect. I have to say, it demands *my* complete attention and *my* total respect! I am always amazed at how people reject the Word of the Lord. Jeremiah 32:33 says, "And they have turned unto me the back, and not the face: though I taught them, rising up early and teaching them, yet they have not hearkened to receive instruction." Not only is there disobedience rampant in our world today, but disrespect for the things of God. Let us hear what God demanded of Job when He spoke to him.

Strap Up ("Gird up now thy loins like a man"). I can only remember a few times when my dad challenged my manhood. It usually started like this: "All right, big boy, you think you're ready for this?" You can almost hear God telling Job, "All right, big boy, strap up and let's get to it! Cinch up your belt, tough man, and let's talk!" God's not playing any games here, my friend! This is not for the faint of heart! Things that are serious to God should be serious to us. Whatever God tells us to do, rest assured that accountability will follow!

Shut Up ("for I will demand of thee"). This is a simple "Don't speak until I am done!" God has laid all of His demands in His precious Word! What have you done with them? God is asking what you will do with His commands. Your duty right now is to surrender your will, submit to His Word, and hear it attentively. How can you give a good answer without first understanding the question? If you are not studying and listening to the Word, you are in a bad position.

Speak Up ("and answer thou me"). The time will come when you will have opportunity to speak and answer the Lord. When that time comes, you cannot dismiss the Lord as easily as Job tried to do. Job tried the silent treatment in Job 40:5: "Once have I spoken; but I will not answer: yea, twice; but I will proceed no further." God was beyond this point. Job should have been quiet much earlier! Now God demanded an answer! God said in Job 40:8, "Wilt thou also disannul my judgment? wilt thou condemn me, that thou mayest be righteous?" In essence, He said, "You think because you spoke too soon and now are quiet that I can't correct you?" Such behavior will not help your argument! Job finally did answer correctly in Job 42, and God vindicated him in the presence of his wicked friends. When it is time to speak, you had better make sure you have the right answer!

TOPICS: Attention, Manhood, Respect, Wisdom

DAILY BIBLE READING: Job 39–42

TODAY'S VERSE: Job 42:3: "Who is he that hideth counsel without knowledge? therefore have I uttered that I understood not; things too wonderful for me, which I knew not."

GOD HAS ALREADY COME into the conversation and asked Job some very pointed and personal questions. In this chapter, we see Job in abject humility before God of a kind that we have not seen in the entire book. Verse 6 says, "Wherefore I abhor myself, and repent in dust and ashes." We all need to experience the same response that Job did. Job's statements here give us a clear view of the power of God's Word in his life. God's Word is not only a support to a weak soul, but also be a confrontation to a proud heart. God asks eighty-three questions to Job in chapters 38–41. Let us consider Job's response to the Word of God.

The Piercing of God's Word ("Who is he that hideth counsel without knowledge?"). This was a direct reference to God's very first question to Job in Job 38:2: "Who is this that darkeneth counsel by words without knowledge?" Job could not get beyond the very first question God asked him! Isn't that just like the Word of God? When it is given, it will pierce to the center of your soul! This was Job taking responsibility for his silly and selfish words. Far too often, we wax verbose when we should wax silent. How sad when people hear the Word of God but are not pierced by its message! Think about God's Word as you hear it, and let it do what it does, for it is a sword!

The Penitence of God's Word ("therefore have I uttered that I understood not"). Job, in response to his friends, had chattered away about his feelings and defended himself, thinking it was up to him to set things right. When God spoke, Job admitted the failures of his own thoughts and perceptions. He was convicted of speaking what he really did not know. Job was confronted and shamed by his own words and understood that the only thing that could set things straight was the Word of God. God equates this problem with wickedness in 2 Peter 2:12: "But these, as natural brute beasts, made to be taken and destroyed, *speak evil of the things that they understand not; and shall utterly perish in their own corruption.*" There is so much to say concerning God's salvation, goodness, and glory—why should we speak words of disdain when we do not fully understand God's motives or plan? Job realized this too late and said in Job 40:4, "Behold, I am vile; what shall I answer thee? I will lay mine hand upon my mouth." Oh, that we would learn to lay our hands upon our mouths before we speak in ignorance and pride!

The Preeminence of God's Word ("things too wonderful for me, which I knew not"). The more you get into the Word of God, the more you will know that Scripture is bigger than you ever imagined! In God's Word, we are exposed to the thoughts of a merciful God and His infinite love for fallen man. Too wonderful for us! We are taught of God's holiness and shown the way of righteousness. Too wonderful for us! We are shown that Christ is the centerpiece of every precept and that His Spirit indwells the believer to change us into His image. This is too wonderful for us! God's Word is a powerful and a wonderful Word. Enjoy it today!

TOPICS: Bible, Conviction, Repentance, Word of God

June 22

DAILY BIBLE READING: Psalm 1-9

TODAY'S VERSE: Psalm 1:1: "Blessed is the man that walketh not in the counsel of the ungodly, nor standeth in the way of sinners, nor sitteth in the seat of the scornful."

WHAT A WAY TO START this songbook for the Jews: "Blessed is the man"! The word "blessed" means "happiness." I have heard many preachers discuss how our joy is not necessarily about happiness. They say happiness has to do with "happenings," while our joy flows from God. While there is some merit to those thoughts, the truth is that we can also have happiness in our Christian lives! As we follow the thoughts of Psalm 1 about happiness, we are warned of three different places not to go in order to maintain a blessed life.

The Recommendation of the Ungodly ("Blessed is the man that walketh not in the counsel of the ungodly"). Why would you put yourself under the advisement and counsel of an ungodly person? That will not lead you in the path of true happiness. The word for "ungodly" means "morally wrong, bad person." Proverbs 19:21 says, "There are many devices in a man's heart; nevertheless the counsel of the LORD, that shall stand." It amazes me that in the time in which we live, people all over the world, including those who profess Christ as Saviour, are seeking Dr. Spock, Dr. Ruth, and Dr. Phil for life answers. Even if some of their counsel is right, why not go to the source of divine wisdom and find out truth from God's Word? Psalm 119:105 says, "Thy word is a lamp unto my feet, and a light unto my path."

The Route of Sinners ("nor standeth in the way of sinners"). Hanging around the path of sinners is never good. Even our own modern laws allow "guilt by association." The word for "way" is defined as "a road (as trodden); figuratively, a course of life or mode of action." The Bible tells us clearly in Matthew 7:13, "Enter ye in at the strait gate: *for wide is the gate, and broad is the way, that leadeth to destruction,* and many there be which go in thereat." I do not need to stand in the broad paths of sin to receive true happiness. The word for "sinner" means "criminal or one accounted guilty." I can remember both my parents and grandparents quoting 1 Corinthians 15:33 to me often: "Be not deceived: evil communications corrupt good manners." If you want true happiness, you'd better have the right friends!

The Residence of Scorners ("nor sitteth in the seat of the scornful"). The word "sitteth" means "to sit down, to dwell, to remain." Have you ever heard the phrase, "They made their own bed, now they have to lie in it"? These sinners have made a home somewhere they never should have been. The word for "scornful" comes from a root meaning "to make mouths at, to scoff." I sat right by such people in my junior-high-school English class. Every time the teacher would say something or correct them in class, they would make a face and mock the teacher. That is the true definition of a scorner! The way of happiness will never be found making a home with the scornful.

TOPICS: Blessing, Counsel, Happiness, Joy, Scorners, Sin, Ungodly, Wisdom

R. CHRIS HANKS

DAILY BIBLE READING: Psalm 10–18

TODAY'S VERSE: Psalm 18:3: "I will call upon the Lord, who is worthy to be praised: so shall I be saved from mine enemies."

THIS PSALM WAS David's prayer of thanksgiving to God for delivering him from all of his enemies. Why not take a moment this morning to thank God for delivering you? Don't ask Him for anything—just give thanks! As I look back upon what God has done for me, I am humbled at God's goodness! I feel that I can agree with Jeremiah in Lamentations 3:22–23: "*It is of the Lord's mercies that we are not consumed, because his compassions fail not. They are new every morning: great is thy faithfulness.*" David said much the same thing in Psalm 139:5–6 when he was contemplating the goodness of God and could not understand it: "Thou hast beset me behind and before, and laid thine hand upon me. Such knowledge is too wonderful for me; it is high, I cannot attain unto it." Three things from our verse tell us why David felt he was blessed.

He Has Waited on My Prayers ("I will call upon the Lord"). David had called upon the Lord countless times and laid his petitions at the feet of God, yet he knew he could pray once again! Psalm 145:18–19 says, "The Lord is nigh unto all them that call upon him, to all that call upon him in truth. He will fulfil the desire of them that fear him: he also will hear their cry, and will save them." The fact that God wants to hear our prayers and will do so again causes thanksgiving to flow from the depths of my heart! He has heard my prayers and has promised to continue to do so!

He Is Worthy of My Praise ("who is worthy to be praised"). Is there any doubt about this? Revelation 5:12 says, "Saying with a loud voice, Worthy is the Lamb that was slain to receive power, and riches, and wisdom, and strength, and honour, and glory, and blessing." There is no other person or being that is deserving of all our praise. The word for "praise" here means "to be clear (orig. of sound, but usually of color); to shine; hence, to make a show." Here is a question: In what kind of light have you put God before others? How do you "color" Him? How clear have you made Him in the sight of others? He is deserving of the best we have to offer!

He Has Won My Pardon ("so shall I be saved from mine enemies"). What hope and security David shows in this statement! God's failure is never even an option. Complete trust and faith are placed upon God in this prayer of deliverance. The word used for "saved" means "to be open, wide, or free." What a thought! We can be freed from our enemies! John 8:36 tells us, "If the Son therefore shall make you free, ye shall be free indeed." That is exactly what Jesus did for us on Calvary! Now we have the great opportunity to live our lives for God. Romans 6:22 says, "But now being made free from sin, and become servants to God, ye have your fruit unto holiness, and the end everlasting life."

TOPICS: Assurance, Mercy, Praise, Prayer, Thanksgiving, Worthy

June 24

DAILY BIBLE READING: Psalm 19–22

TODAY'S VERSE: Psalm 19:1: "The heavens declare the glory of God; and the firmament sheweth his handywork."

IT AMAZES ME the number of people who have swallowed the myth of evolution hook, line, and sinker. They just dismiss the notion that a Creator could have had a hand in everything that we see. We have literally seen Romans 1:22 come to pass in our time: "Professing themselves to be wise, they became fools." As many have indicated in the past, it takes more faith to believe what evolutionists say than it does to believe that an Almighty God not only created the universe, but is interested and involved in its daily function and work. We see this even more plainly a few verses later in Romans 1:25: "Who changed the truth of God into a lie, and worshipped and served the creature more than the Creator, who is blessed for ever. Amen." Let us take a moment to shut our mouths, cast our eyes to the heavens, and hear what they might be saying about God.

The Shoutings of the Heavens ("The heavens declare"). The word for "declare" means "to score with a mark as a tally or record, to inscribe, and also to enumerate, to recount, celebrate." The heavens, or the skies, have been following a list since the day they were created in the wisdom and power of God. I don't believe they've had to start over, since they have not yet reached the end of the list! Every moment they are faithful to give their witness of the wonders of God's creation. I have always been astounded at the vastness of our sky and outer space. Whether it is the images of the Hubble Telescope, the discovery of a new planet, emissions of radio frequencies from some distant star, or a new discovery in our own solar system, we are reminded by the heavens of our own influence in the universe and of the magnitude of an omnipotent God.

The Shinings of the Heavens ("the glory of God"). The word for "glory" means "weight, splendor." It is as if the heavens are saying, "As you behold these things with your eyes, imagine what the glory of God must be!" This glory reminds me of the *shekinah* glory of God. First Timothy 6:15–16 says, "Which in his times he shall shew, who is the blessed and only Potentate, the King of kings, and Lord of lords; who only hath immortality, *dwelling in the light which no man can approach unto;* whom no man hath seen, nor can see: to whom be honour and power everlasting. Amen." Jesus has now received His glory and has ascended to the right hand of the Father. Hebrews 1:3 tells us that Jesus is the "brightness of his glory." And Revelation 1:16 says, "And he had in his right hand seven stars: and out of his mouth went a sharp twoedged sword: and *his countenance was as the sun shineth in his strength.*" This is what the heavens are trying to tell us! Only the wise will receive it. They are enumerating and celebrating the weight and splendor of God!

The Showings of the Heavens ("and the firmament sheweth his handywork"). The word for "sheweth" means "to front, i.e. stand boldly out opposite." This is no secret! God's power is apparent to all who see! Romans 1:20 says, *"For the invisible things of him from the creation of the world are clearly seen,* being understood by the things that are made, even his eternal power and Godhead; so that they are without excuse." The grammar of this expression tells us that the firmament is "continuing" to show us God's handiwork. From the mighty mountains and oceans to the colors of a butterfly or coral reef, the handiwork of God is on constant exhibit and display. In an even greater capacity are His wonders shown in the great expanse of the skies: from the clouds that carry water from heaven to the endless theatrical productions we see in the clear night sky, God's glory is shown!

TOPICS: Creation, Faith, God's Glory, Wisdom

R. CHRIS HANKS

DAILY BIBLE READING: Psalm 23–31

TODAY'S VERSE: Psalm 27:2: "When the wicked, even mine enemies and my foes, came upon me to eat up my flesh, they stumbled and fell."

WE FIND IN THE BEGINNING of this psalm that David said, "The Lord is my light." He knew that there would come *dark times, discouraging times,* and *distressing times.* He continues in this psalm to tell us about those who are trying to destroy him and how the Lord will deliver him and exalt him above his enemies. Our main verse today gives us some insights into the warfare that a believer faces. Have you ever felt that it was you against the world? In verse 2, we find that there were times that David would be *outmaneuvered* ("came upon me to eat up my flesh"). In verse 3, we find that there were times he would be *outnumbered* ("though an host should encamp against me.") Later in verse 3, we find that there were times he would be *outfought* ("though war should rise against me"). But verse 4 tells us that he would never be *outdone* ("One thing have I desired of the LORD, that will I seek after; that I may dwell in the house of the LORD all the days of my life, to behold the beauty of the LORD, and to enquire in his temple"). Today, let's take a closer look at verse 2.

The **Adversaries of the Christian** ("When the wicked, even mine enemies and my foes"). David places his adversaries in three categories: the wicked, his enemies, and his foes. The root of "the wicked" means "to spoil, to make good for nothing." These are people who are spiritually depleted of anything good or virtuous. They desire to defeat you by *defilement.* Truly, they are "rotten to the core." The second group is found in the word "enemies," the root of which means "an opponent." This is the person who competes with you every step of the way. This enemy opposes every "good" way. Enemies oppose you in every part of your life and will do their best to defeat you. They desire to defeat you by *domination.* The last group is called "foes," from a root meaning "to hate." Hatred is a bitter enemy and will target your spirit by continual competition with no relief. The desire of your foes is to defeat you by *deceit.*

The **Assault on the Christian** ("came upon me to eat up my flesh"). Notice that every one of these groups had the exact same goal in mind: "To eat up my flesh." Let us be careful to note that our enemies do not want to corrupt us, but to consume us! All of these adversaries trying to eat us up remind me of the warning given concerning the devil in 1 Peter 5:8: "Be sober, be vigilant; because your adversary the devil, as a roaring lion, walketh about, seeking whom he may devour." Every assault that you endure, dear Christian, is with the intent to devour you. It is not just about harm or hurt, but about dining upon your spiritual being until you are completely destroyed.

The **Assurance of the Christian** ("they stumbled and fell"). Before we get to thinking that David was worried until he saw his enemies stumble and fall, we must remember what he said in verse 1: "The LORD is my light and my salvation; *whom shall I fear?* the LORD is the strength of my life; *of whom shall I be afraid?*" David never was afraid of them—not for a moment! He was perfectly happy with the Lord's watch care over him and had learned to trust in God. First John 4:4 persuades us to the same courage: "Ye are of God, little children, and have overcome them: because *greater is he that is in you, than he that is in the world.*" We can rest in great confidence knowing that our Saviour will confound the wicked in their own devices!

TOPICS: Adversaries, Assurance, Deliverance, Enemies, Foes, Trust

DAILY BIBLE READING: Psalm 32-36

TODAY'S VERSE: Psalm 34:8: "O taste and see that the Lord is good: blessed is the man that trusteth in him."

IN THE FOUR VERSES prior to this one, David gives us reasons that bring us to his spiritual explosion in verse 8. God had answered the prayers of David and delivered him from wicked men who hated him and did not fear God. Verse 6 tells us that God hears a poor man! Can someone give me a witness and say "Amen!" Verse 7 tells us that the "angel of the Lord," a type of Christ, gives us His wonderful protection and encircles us with His power. The heading of this psalm reads, "A Psalm of David, when he changed his behaviour before Abimelech; who drove him away, and he departed." Let me remind you that the headings of these psalms are not notes by other authors, but are actually part of the original psalm. The whole reason David wrote this song was to give praise to the Lord for His wonderful works on his behalf. Let's hear what David says about the Lord in this verse!

The **Flavor of God** ("O taste and see"). This is more an instruction to experience God than it is about your actual taste. Many parents have a rule in their house at suppertime: You have to taste everything. You cannot just dismiss something because you think you don't like it. It was mandatory in our home that we experience everything placed before us at a meal. The same is true of God and His Word. You need to jump in it and ingest it all! You cannot pick and choose what you want to believe about God, nor will skepticism or a hesitant unbelief qualify as experiencing God in His fullness. It is all or nothing!

The **Favor of God** ("that the Lord is good: blessed is the man"). Notice that this invitation to experience or "taste" God does not even entertain the possibility that you might not like Him. This is not about whether religion "will work for you." The invitation is this—"Try Him; you'll like Him!" Why not find out for yourself? The verse goes on to say, "Blessed is the man." I want to be included in that blessing! Many people do not really believe that God has their best interests at heart, or even worse, they think that God's blessing is only upon the "really good ones" and that they do not measure up. Embrace the fact that God wants to bless you!

The **Flight to God** ("that trusteth in him"). The word here for "trusteth" means "to flee for protection, to confide in." That is something I can enjoy experiencing! How many times do I need a place where I can run? How often do I need a fortress where I can hide? While I am found under God's shadow, I experience His love and His power in ways I have never experienced it before!

TOPICS: Blessing, Experience, Favor, Grace, Protection

R. CHRIS HANKS

DAILY BIBLE READING: Psalm 37–41

TODAY'S VERSE: Psalm 39:4: "Lord, make me to know mine end, and the measure of my days, what it is; that I may know how frail I am."

WHAT WAS IT THAT MADE the psalmist pray this prayer? It was his decision in verse 1 to "sin not with my tongue." Sounds like a great desire, but oh, how difficult to do! James 3:5 tells us, "Even so the tongue is a little member, and boasteth great things. Behold, how great a matter a little fire kindleth!" The only way for our tongue to be brought back to reality is to be confronted with its mortality. The verse in James says that the tongue "boasteth great things." What pride and arrogance is found in this little member of our mouths! The only thing to bring it to our level is the understanding that we are nothing. Let us consider today's verse in light of the inadequacy and uncertainty of our flesh.

The Fickleness of Man ("Lord, make me to know mine end"). The writer already understands that he knows nothing about his limitations. The word used for "mine end" means "extremity, border." How often man lives beyond himself! It is a blessing from the Lord to reveal the borders of our finite being. Man's fickleness is exposed by the instability of his faith and convictions. James 1:8 says, "A double minded man is unstable in all his ways." Clearly, this is a man that has no depth perception in his own life or in his service to the Lord. Second Corinthians 4:18 says, "While we look not at the things which are seen, but at the things which are not seen: for the things which are seen are temporal; but the things which are not seen are eternal."

The Finality of Man ("and the measure of my days, what it is"). The "measure" of something has a beginning and an end; otherwise, it could never be measured. Every time we visit the casket or graveside of a family member or friend, we are reminded of the measure of our days. I have heard some preachers talk about the "dash" of life. Every tombstone has a beginning date and an ending date, but it is the dash that represents the entire life. Most people are concerned only about their mad dash through life! The three words "what it is" should be considered with sincerity. Exactly what "is" our life? James 4:14 tells us plainly: "Whereas ye know not what shall be on the morrow. *For what is your life? It is even a vapour, that appeareth for a little time, and then vanisheth away.*" There are very interesting words to consider from this verse. The word "vapour" means "mist." That mist appears for "a little time." The word "little" means "puny." What a puny existence we lead here upon this earth! How can we boast of anything? We are a puny people with puny desires who lead puny lives. Finality strikes fear into the heart of man. A saved person can rejoice, for there is no fear of death. We look beyond to eternal life with God!

The Frailty of Man ("that I may know how frail I am"). The word here for "frail" means "destitute." The English definition of "frail" is "weak." Jesus knew this, for He said in Matthew 26:41, "Watch and pray, that ye enter not into temptation: the spirit indeed is willing, but the *flesh is weak.*" Again, Jesus said in John 15:5, "I am the vine, ye are the branches: he that abideth in me, and I in him, the same bringeth forth much fruit: for without me ye can do nothing." Put your faith in Him today, and be strengthened in your spirit!

TOPICS: Death, Double-mindedness, Faith, Trust, Weakness

DAILY BIBLE READING: Psalm 42-49

TODAY'S VERSE: Psalm 45:1: "My heart is inditing a good matter: I speak of the things which I have made touching the king: my tongue is the pen of a ready writer."

HAVE YOU EVER BEEN overwhelmed by the goodness of God? That is how the psalmist felt when he wrote this song for the glory of God. The word translated "inditing" means "to gush" or even "to boil or bubble up." Would it be all right for us to gush together about things we love about God? If you have never felt this inward gush, you need to set your heart upon Him and what He has done for you. Perhaps you have been cast under the cares of this world by enduring persecution, grieving and sorrowing through betrayal or loss, or even carrying burdens of financial distress or family struggles. Make a point today to begin "inditing" some things about God! Paul and Silas did that very thing in the midst of the Philippian jail when they were in bonds and began singing in the middle of the night. You can gush anywhere! Do it right now, wherever you are! If you are not saved, this devotion will not make any sense to your spirit, for there is no real reason for an unsaved person to enjoy God. Come to the Lord today, and learn what it means to be so full of His goodness that it gushes out of you!

Thrilled with the Thoughts of God ("My heart is inditing a good matter"). Notice that David began to "gush" in a "good matter." The word for "good" means "good *in the widest sense.*" Hallelujah! This matter is as wide as God's love is! As wide as the east is from the west, for that is how far He has cast your sin from you! Think about all the good things that He does for you. Psalm 68:19 says, "Blessed be the Lord, who daily loadeth us with benefits, even the God of our salvation. Selah." These truths that we contemplate now about God have their basis in Jeremiah 29:11: "For I know the thoughts that I think toward you, saith the Lord, thoughts of peace, and not of evil, to give you an expected end." God has included me in His plan! He has called me into His work! He has given me His Word! What wonderful thoughts!

Thrilled with the Throne of God ("I speak of the things which I have made touching the king"). The psalmist is talking of things he has done in honor of his king. What have you done to honor the Lord? If you would serve God out of a heart of worship, your heart would begin gushing with good things too! Do you realize today that you are to be serving God Almighty? Do you realize that this is the same God Isaiah described in Isaiah 40:22, "It is he that sitteth upon the circle of the earth"? This is the same God whose throne we will see with the rainbow about it. It is the source of the crystal sea, and we will cast our crowns before Him in honor and reverence of His glory! (See Revelation 22.)

Thrilled with a Thesaurus for God ("my tongue is the pen of a ready writer"). With this little phrase, I am reminded of the sermon by the late Dr. S. M. Lockridge. Dr. Lockridge was the pastor of Calvary Baptist Church for just over forty years. In his sermon "The Lordship of Jesus Christ," he preached a part that many people know as "That's My King." One sentence he said was this: "[God] is the superlative of anything good that you choose to call Him." How ready is your tongue to describe God? Let your thoughts and words glorify Him! Psalm 35:28 says, "And my tongue shall speak of thy righteousness and of thy praise all the day long." There are new words added each year to our dictionary. Let's make a new word and begin to use it to the point that it must be included in our regular vocabulary. He is the Calva-redeemer of eter-nipotent regener-sal-justification! Praisalujah!

TOPICS: Meditation, Praise, Word of God, Worship

R. CHRIS HANKS

DAILY BIBLE READING: Psalm 50–56

TODAY'S VERSE: Psalm 51:8: "Make me to hear joy and gladness; that the bones which thou hast broken may rejoice."

THIS PSALM IS A HUMBLE PRAYER of confession from David for his sin of adultery with Bathsheba and his murder of Uriah. I love this psalm. Even with David's horrible sin, he was still able to come before God and ask forgiveness! This was not presumptuous on the part of David, but reasonable, for he knew that God's "mercy endureth for ever" (Psalm 107:1). Hebrews 4:16 gives us the same hope today: "Let us therefore come boldly unto the throne of grace, *that we may obtain mercy,* and find grace to help in time of need." Not only is this a testimony of God's mercy, but also of God's judgment of sin. Never think, my friend, that you are getting away with your sin. There will be a reckoning day! My grandmother would remind me of this by quoting the last part of Numbers 32:23: "And be sure your sin will find you out." I hope that our spirit will be like David's in this time of shame and sorrow: submitted and surrendered.

The Rejoicing of God ("Make me to hear joy and gladness"). One of the first things David desired was to hear something happy. There was no joy in his pride and selfishness in taking Bathsheba unto himself. The murder of Uriah began a downward spiral that snatched away every bit of joy David had ever had. Often, when a sin such as this comes out in the open, many people have to deal with the hurt, but the offender is finally glad it has come out. It is a relief to him, and he is finally able to begin the healing process. For months, all the way to the birth of his baby, David had a miserable feeling in the middle of his gut that sat upon his soul. What he missed most was the sweet fellowship and joy he had once had with his loving God. After the discipline of God, there is nothing so blessed as hearing the songs of Zion and the sounds of the gospel!

The Restraints of God ("that the bones which thou hast broken"). This speaks of the punishment that comes with our sin. The whole reason for punishment is to draw us closer to the Lord. God gives us restraints that should keep our hearts and minds focused upon Him. Have you ever seen a child after hearing his father or mother say "no"? It seems as if he is weighing his options. Is continuing in disobedience really worth it or not? These restraints are not about control, but about keeping us in the place of joy. Learn to enjoy the punishments of God, for they are meant to keep you close to His heart!

The Restoration of God ("may rejoice"). This phrase is not about David rejoicing, but about the "broken bones" rejoicing. That is a restoration! How is it possible that the very things used in defilement and sin could bring forth praise unto the Lord? Isn't that the question for each and every one of us? We were all the enemies of God, yet by His grace, we have been brought into fellowship! Paul said in Galatians 1:23, "But they had heard only, That he which persecuted us in times past now *preacheth the faith which once he destroyed.*" Paul was nothing but a bag of "broken bones" that was now giving praise unto the Lord! Don't fear the pain of the healing process. Cast your eyes further down the road and see the very bones that have been broken by the mercy of God begin to rejoice and point others to the mercy of God!

TOPICS: Discipline, Forgiveness, Joy, Mercy, Punishment, Restoration

DAILY BIBLE READING: Psalm 57–64

TODAY'S VERSE: Psalm 60:4: "Thou hast given a banner to them that fear thee, that it may be displayed because of the truth. Selah."

GOD HAS GIVEN US a great banner in which to rejoice, and it is Christ. Isaiah 11:10 says, "And in that day there shall be a root of Jesse, which shall stand for an ensign of the people." That ensign, or banner, is our Messiah!

Every time I think of a banner or a flag, I am reminded of Old Glory. How majestic she is as she waves in the breeze! She is recognized around the world and strikes fear into the hearts of her enemies. In this verse, God brings hope to our hearts and help to our spirits by the delivery of a great banner to His people.

It Is an Excellent Banner ("Thou hast given a banner to them that fear thee"). This is a banner from heaven and of God's design. It is a banner of *identity*. It clearly tells all the identity of our *Master (Christ)*, our *mission (commission)*, our *motherland (country)*, and our *might (courage)*. It is also a banner of *unity*. It draws us together and gives us a common cause. This banner stands for the spiritual freedom that was bought with the blood of our precious Saviour. It gives joy and hope to those who stand under it.

It Is an Exposed Banner ("that it may be displayed"). The reason for having a banner is so it can fly! We are living in a time in which many people are ashamed of their Christianity. People are ashamed of their faith and their testimony. Some do not want to share the gospel with others because they are afraid of what others might think. God has given us a banner to unfurl, raise to the highest height, and fly to the glory of God! This banner must be exposed to the world. The banner God has given us to fly is a lighthouse to a ship in a storm, a fort in the midst of a battle, and a hospital in time of pain. Let that banner fly!

It Is an Expounded Banner ("because of the truth"). No matter how people try to malign the banner, they still cannot deny its truth! It is because of the truth that it must fly! It must stand in the war and proclaim its message with power and glory. There are those who fight against it and try to soil its image, but that blood-soaked banner must continue to fly for truth's sake. John 14:6 says, "Jesus saith unto him, I am the way, *the truth,* and the life." Many have tried to defile the character of our Saviour. They have tried everything to defile His name, humanize His spirit, and deny His deity. Yet the flag still flies! There is no reason for Christ to continue to hold out His hand to man, but He still flies the banner of salvation and forgiveness to all who will accept Him. Thank God for His expounded truth!

TOPICS: Blood, Christ, Deity, Identity, Testimony, Word of God

R. CHRIS HANKS

DAILY BIBLE READING: Psalm 65–69

TODAY'S VERSE: Psalm 69:4: "They that hate me without a cause are more than the hairs of mine head: they that would destroy me, being mine enemies wrongfully, are mighty: then I restored that which I took not away."

THIS VERSE SHOWS the hurt of a child of God, a man of God, who was hated "without a cause." Such hatred is always a disturbing and a hurtful thing. We understand it when we are punished for our sin. But to be hurt without a cause goes against our grain—it's something we will never understand. That thought alone should make us appreciate our Saviour so much the more! No one ever suffered more in complete innocence than He did.

When hate takes over a person's heart, he becomes set upon the destruction of the person he hates. In this psalm, David knew that God would deliver him. We can find some help in this verse, knowing that David's hope can be our hope.

Their Multitude Cannot Destroy You ("They that hate me without a cause are more than the hairs of mine head"). It is easy to look at the odds and become discouraged. The Hebrew word for "more" means "to cast together, to multiply by the myriad." My, how easy it is for the wicked to multiply themselves! But no matter how many there are, God has given us hope of His protection and strength. Psalm 60:12 says, "Through God we shall do valiantly: for he it is that shall tread down our enemies." In God Almighty is a number much greater than the world. Though at times your battle will seem to be you against the world, rest and trust in Him, for He is greater than the world. I know that many have gone before us who were not delivered from their troubles. Thank God for the many martyrs who gave their lives for the sake of the gospel of Christ so willingly! Some would look at them and say, "See, the multitude destroyed them!" I would argue that the multitude did *not* destroy them! The multitude had no power over their souls. No matter what, there is no reason to fear the multitude.

Their Motives Cannot Destroy You ("being mine enemies wrongfully"). The word used for "wrongfully" means "an untruth, a sham." People do not often need a good reason to get mad, make a false accusation, or fight against God's children. As a matter of fact, they are more than willing to make up a reason if need be! Their motto is, "Never let the facts stand in the way of a good story." Most problems in church are really no problems at all once they have been investigated and searched out. We can better bear the burden of suffering if our hands are clean. First Peter 2:19–20 says, "For this is thankworthy, if a man for conscience toward God endure grief, suffering wrongfully. For what glory is it, if, when ye be buffeted for your faults, ye shall take it patiently? but if, when ye do well, and suffer for it, ye take it patiently, this is acceptable with God."

Their Might Cannot Destroy You ("are mighty"). We are so easily swayed by anything we think is stronger than we are. David knew this better than anyone as he stood in the valley with a sling in his hand to fight the mighty giant Goliath for the glory of the Lord. Saul had already said Goliath was a "man of war from his youth," but that did not hinder David from fighting for the Lord. David said in 1 Samuel 17:45, "Then said David to the Philistine, Thou comest to me with a sword, and with a spear, and with a shield: but I come to thee in the name of the Lord of hosts, the God of the armies of Israel, whom thou hast defied." We will trust in the Lord for His great strength!

Before we close, I would like to share from a different angle the thought of the last part of the verse: "Then I restored that which I took not away." Is this not what Christ has done for us? He did not take away our good standing with God: our sin did! He restored us to the place of perfection in spite of our failure and our sin. Praise God for His restoring ministry, given to us though it was our own sin that separated us from God!

TOPICS: Lies, Outnumbered, Persecution, Restoration, Sin

July 2

DAILY BIBLE READING: Palm 70–75

TODAY'S VERSE: Psalm 71:3: "Be thou my strong habitation, whereunto I may continually resort: thou hast given commandment to save me; for thou art my rock and my fortress."

THANK GOD for a strong habitation! The meaning of the Hebrew for "strong habitation" is "a cliff, a rock or boulder, a refuge, an edge (as precipitous)." This is a habitation that will not easily be attacked. These walls will never be breached, these buildings will never be stormed, and this foundation will never be shaken! What a strong habitation we have today! Here are a few thoughts about the "habitation" we have in our God.

He Is to Us a Resort ("whereunto I may continually resort"). I am using this word in the sense that we use it today. God is a place of **peace**. Resorts today are used as places of refreshment and rejuvenation. A resort is not just a place to stay, like a motel, but a place to get away from the troubles of the world to rest. This concept is much like the garden of Gethsemane to which Jesus "resorted" often (John 18:2)! There are many times when I need to be refreshed in my spirit. According to this verse, I can find that place of refreshment in God. Because this *principle* of refreshment is found in Scripture, I can find this *place* of refreshment in the Word of God. Because the Holy Ghost is in me, I can take that place with me wherever I may go. We have a portable resort that goes everywhere we go!

He Is to Us a Redeemer ("thou hast given commandment to save me"). God is a place of **pardon**. I have often wondered why God would want to save me. To think that He gave commandment to do so shows His forethought and love for me and my sin-sick soul. The word for "save" carries a few meanings: "to be open, wide, or free." Jesus did not just save me from my enemies or from my troubles, but also brought me into a wide place to enjoy spiritual freedom! John 10:9 says, "I am the door: by me if any man enter in, he shall be saved, and shall go in and out, and find pasture." What freedom we have that can only be found in Christ! Psalm 18:19 says, "He brought me forth also into *a large place;* he delivered me, because he delighted in me."

He Is to Us a Rock ("for thou art my rock and my fortress"). God is a place of **protection**. Many times we feel that we are completely exposed to the world and all its weapons of mass destruction. But we have a rock! Proverbs 18:10 says, "The name of the LORD is a strong tower: the righteous runneth into it, and is safe." What a place of safety! Nothing can ever reach us here! Isaiah 33:16 says it like this: "He shall dwell on high: *his place of defence shall be the munitions of rocks:* bread shall be given him; his waters shall be sure." Let us find solace and protection in our blessed Rock of Ages.

TOPICS: Peace, Pardon, Protection, Redemption, Safety

R. CHRIS HANKS

DAILY BIBLE READING: Psalm 76–79

TODAY'S VERSE: Psalm 78:41: "Yea, they turned back and tempted God, and limited the Holy One of Israel."

WHAT A SAD VERSE in the Bible! How pitiful! How silly! How short-sighted! Did the people not realize they were hurting themselves? It is easy to dismiss their sinful and selfish ways with a "tsk! tsk!" knowing that we would never be so flagrantly foolish in our own spiritual lives. The problem is that we do the very same thing all the time. As a matter of fact, we are often much worse, for we would disguise our actions much better! It is important to us to at least *act* like we are spiritual! This hypocrisy is actually much worse than outright rebellion, because it denies the care and love of God who can see through our pious actions feigned from a false heart. It even denies the omniscience of God, for we are acting like He does not know our motives and intentions. We care more about what the people on this earth think about our relationship with God than we care about what God knows. Let's look at three points to keep us from the same fate as the unfaithful Israelites.

Their Turning ("Yea, they turned back"). How brash and bold! How much more disrespectful can you be to God than to turn back from Him? I have no desire to go back to where I was before God saved me! What a blessing when He saved me and gave me new hope and new joy! To what would you return today? Just because the way gets hard is no reason to quit on Him! So many people turn at just the time God would bring deliverance. Remember that God "will not suffer you to be tempted above that ye are able" (1 Corinthians 10:13). There is no time for retreat; we must continue!

Their Tempting ("and tempted God"). It is fine to "try God out," but it is not fine to "tempt God out." Psalm 34:8 says, "O taste and see that the Lord is good: blessed is the man that trusteth in him." Go ahead, try Him: you will find that you will like Him. But whatever you do, do not *tempt* Him in your little test. Matthew 4:7 says, "Jesus said unto him, It is written again, Thou shalt not tempt the Lord thy God." It is easy for us to tempt God when we do not get our way. We tempt Him in our defiance, our fear, and even our pain. Instead of pointing a finger in God's face, may we come humbly beseeching Him and His mercy! Those hearts that are willing to tempt God belong to bitter souls that have rejected the way of the Lord in their lives.

Their Tying ("and limited the Holy One of Israel"). The Israelites tied God's hands and put Him in a box. They only wanted God working in the things and the ways they wanted Him to work. They would not have believed Romans 8:28, which says, "And we know that all things work together for good, to them that love God, to them who are the called according to His purpose." Why would someone limit God? Some limit God out of ignorance. They do not even realize what they are doing. Others, however, limit God because of a lack of trust. They want to be in control and do not trust God to do a good job. They do not believe that He has their best interest at heart. They do not care for the spiritual things of God's character or His purpose. The root for the word "limited" in this verse comes from the idea of "scraping to pieces, to grieve." To limit God is to scrape His heart and make Him grieve for all the things He could do in your life, and for all the things that you could be with His blessing. Don't limit Him; let Him be free!

TOPICS: Limiting God, Perseverance, Rejection, Tempting God, Unbelief

July 4

TODAY'S VERSE: Psalm 86:10: "For thou art great, and doest wondrous things: thou art God alone."

AS WE CELEBRATE the Fourth of July across America, we should spend some time dwelling on the greatness of God. When was the last time you turned your head heavenward and thanked God for being great? Has there been a time recently when you stopped a conversation to share a testimony about the greatness of God? Psalm 86 is one of my favorite psalms as we hear David ask God for help, mercy, and deliverance. His prayer here in this psalm is full of the praises of God as David begins to think of how wonderful and great his Lord is. I would challenge you today to dwell on the greatness of God for a moment.

As David begins to celebrate God in his heart, he first makes mention of **God's Position** ("For thou art great"). Have you ever thought about what makes God great? At once, our minds are flooded by many different attributes. There are almost one thousand times in Scripture that the Bible uses the word "great." This verse is a progressive sentence on God's greatness. Every phrase goes to the next level. The beginning statement is that God is great. As a matter of fact, He is great in all good things! He is great in His foreknowledge, His character, and His love. Our list could continue forever.

Next, David refers to **God's Power** ("and doest wondrous things"). In other words, though God is great because of who He is, He is not limited just to the greatness of His nature. What He can *do* makes Him great as well. The underlying Hebrew for "wondrous things" means "to separate, to distinguish." Many things distinguish our God from all others. Our God has redeemed those who have trusted Him to Himself. Our God is the God of *Creation!* Our God is the God of *Calvary!* Our God is the Great *Comforter!* Those *are* great things!

The last thing to which David refers is **God's Preeminence** ("thou art God alone"). Where all others fail, God stands alone! Some claim themselves to be greater than all men, and they may be right. Who is to say that one is better or worse than another? But when it comes to being God, one stands alone! In this progressive verse on the greatness of God, this is the pinnacle of David's praises of God's greatness! The last part of Isaiah 44:8 says, "Is there a God beside me? yea, there is no God; I know not any." What a blessing to know that our God is the *only* God! To Him we bow! To Him we ascribe all greatness!

TOPICS: God's Position, God's Power, God's Preeminence

R. CHRIS HANKS

DAILY BIBLE READING: Psalm 88–92

TODAY'S VERSE: Psalm 89:1: "I will sing of the mercies of the Lord for ever: with my mouth will I make known thy faithfulness to all generations."

THERE IS SOMETHING SPECIAL about the singing of God's people. The Bible teaches that singing should be a part of our lives every day. Ephesians 5:19 says, "Speaking to yourselves in psalms and hymns and spiritual songs, singing and making melody in your heart to the Lord." Can you think of anything better than to sing about our Lord and His everlasting mercy? That is how the psalmist begins this song—in the mercy of God! Have you every begun meditating on the mercy and goodness of God only to let yourself be borne up by its strength and power and carried away by the vastness of its truth? We are so confined by quips and definitions that we have denied the full spectrum of mercy's essence. The mercy of God is as infinite as God is! Immerse yourself in its depths!

The Intonation of My Praise ("I will sing of the mercies of the Lord for ever"). This has to do with my **song**. This is not a song that is required, but one that is offered from a heart of love. This is an *excited* song about the power of God's works! This heart is so spontaneously enraptured by the mercy of God that it must break out in spiritual song. It is also an *expounded* song. This is not some meaningless folk song or senseless drivel by an ungodly artist, but is based upon the mercy of God. This is a song that has a core, substance, and body. We see that it is also an *everlasting* song, for it will be sung "for ever." It will last as long as God's mercy lasts. This does not mean that the song will be repeated many times, but that it will be sung as it is written—unendingly. We might as well begin singing it now if we will sing it for eternity!

The Implement of My Praise ("with my mouth will I make known"). This has to do with my **system**. We are warned about the mouth and its great failings throughout all of Scripture. James 3 discusses the mouth and tongue in great detail and warns us of its wickedness. James 3:11 poses a question for us to consider: "Doth a fountain send forth at the same place sweet water and bitter?" This truth demands not only our consideration, but our response. What will you do with your mouth? Instead of letting it run wild at your house, broker some major deal for your company, tell some pointless joke, or even defend yourself (though you may be falsely accused), why not make it an instrument of righteousness by using it to tell of God's wonderful mercy?

The Issue of My Praise ("thy faithfulness to all generations"). This has to do with my **subject**. God's mercy is all about God's faithfulness. Is there a better biblical illustration of this than Lamentations 3:22–23? "It is of the Lord's mercies that we are not consumed, because his compassions fail not. They are new every morning: great is thy faithfulness." The question then follows, how might I tell this to all generations? By teaching the truth diligently to my children! The future generations must know about God's mercy; it is up to us to share it with them, though we may never know them. Enjoy God's faithfulness by recognizing His mercy in your life.

TOPICS: Faithfulness, Mercy, Mouth, Praise, Song

July 6

DAILY BIBLE READING: Psalm 93–101

TODAY'S VERSE: Psalm 102:2: "Hide not thy face from me in the day when I am in trouble; incline thine ear unto me: in the day when I call answer me speedily."

THE HEADING OF THIS PSALM says, "A Prayer of the afflicted, when he is overwhelmed, and poureth out his complaint before the LORD." I have to say, there are times when I fall into the category of afflicted, overwhelmed, and pouring out my complaint to God! I praise God for putting these verses here so that we may know what to do when trouble comes our way. Praise the Lord that we have a personal Book to help with personal problems so we can have personal victory! This psalm is a prayer coming from a burdened heart that needs divine help. Thank God that He has prepared a way for us to come into His presence and lay our petitions at His feet—it is called prayer! Don't ever feel badly about taking your requests to the Lord and praying to Him to supply your need.

He Was Asking for a Divine Readiness ("Hide not thy face from me in the day when I am in trouble"). If Israel had disobeyed His commands and served other gods, God had promised to "hide His face" from them. This was a plea for God not to find them at fault, but to stand ready to hear their prayer and help them in their need. What good would it be to have a god who is not available when you need him most? That was Elijah's accusation against the worshipers of Baal in 1 Kings 18:27: "And it came to pass at noon, that Elijah mocked them, and said, Cry aloud: for he is a god; either he is talking, or he is pursuing, or he is in a journey, or peradventure he sleepeth, and must be awaked." We need, and indeed we have, a God who is ready to hear us when we call. God has already promised this to us in Psalm 50:15: "And call upon me in the day of trouble: I will deliver thee, and thou shalt glorify me."

He Was Asking for a Divine Response ("incline thine ear unto me"). The word for "incline" means "to stretch or spread out, to bend away." Literally, this prayer asks for God to be "bent" toward hearing it. I have never understood those who will not pray because they do not want to bother God with their troubles. If we believe God to be both omnipotent and omnipresent, can we not believe that He can answer our prayers and needs? I love it when my three-year-old little boy starts calling to me, "Daddy, Daddy!" Sometimes I will continue to work but halfheartedly say, "What?" He will say to me without apology, "Daddy, look at me!" He still isn't sure if he will get his request; but if I look at him, he will at least know that I've heard him ask! It is the same principle here when the psalmist says, "Incline thine ear unto me."

He Was Asking for a Divine Rush ("in the day when I call answer me speedily"). The word translated "speedily" means "hurrying, hastily." Luke 18:7–8a says, "And shall not God avenge his own elect, which cry day and night unto him, though he bear long with them? I tell you that he will avenge them *speedily*." Let it be said that God will answer our prayers according to His time, but there is nothing wrong with asking for an answer with urgency. Psalm 46:5 tells us the following: "God is in the midst of her; she shall not be moved: God shall help her, *and that right early*." God can answer my prayer at the very moment I need it! God is moved by the urgency of our necessity, but our timing must coincide with God's timing.

TOPICS: Burden, Fatherhood, Need, Prayer

R. CHRIS HANKS

DAILY BIBLE READING: Psalm 102–105

TODAY'S VERSE: Psalm 103:1: "Bless the Lord, O my soul: and all that is within me, bless his holy name."

THIS HAS ALWAYS BEEN one of my favorite verses in the Bible: one that shows *passion, power,* and *praise!* We need to return to blessing God in our lives. I have heard preachers say that it is presumptuous for us to do this because it is impossible for us to "bless the Lord." They are so afraid of some "charismatic experience" that they have failed to accept the Word of God.

The Celebration of Our Blessing ("Bless the Lord, O my soul"). Strong's defines the word for "bless" as "to kneel, to bless God as an act of adoration." Of course, we are centering our praise and blessing upon "the LORD"! This means Jehovah God! What a celebration this must be! There is no creature upon earth more deserving than He to receive our blessing! There is no substance or force in the heavens more worthy of our blessing than the great God, Jehovah! With what should we bless Him? With our souls! The word translated "soul" means "a breathing creature, vitality." Is there a better way to bless God than with our breath? Was it not He who "breathed into man the breath of life and man became a living soul" (Genesis 2:7)? There is also urgency in this, for one day our breath will become short and eventually stop. There is a limited amount of time for us to breathe upon this earth. Let us bless His name as we breathe! Psalm 150:6 says, "Let everything that hath breath praise the LORD. Praise ye the LORD."

The Consuming of Our Blessing ("and all that is within me"). This is the place where we must not fail: in an all-consuming passion for blessing our Lord! At best, we usually worship God with "part that is within me." Many try to worship and bless God with "nothing that is within them." Our hearts today are so pulled by our *surroundings,* our *situations,* and even our *substance* that we seldom think about God and blessing Him with the same passion David had—with "all that is within me."

The Cause of Our Blessing ("bless his holy name"). We are serving a thrice-holy God! We must bow before Him in humble adoration. The word translated "name" means "through the idea of definite and conspicuous position, an appellation as a mark or memorial of individuality." If there is something "conspicuous" about God, it is His holiness! The Bible says in 1 Peter 1:16, "Because it is written, Be ye holy; for I am holy." What a reason today to serve our Lord and bless His name—for His holiness!

TOPICS: Blessing, God's Name, Praise, Song, Worship

July 8

DAILY BIBLE READING: Psalm 106–109

TODAY'S VERSE: Psalm 107:4: "They wandered in the wilderness in a solitary way; they found no city to dwell in."

THIS VERSE IS CLOSELY CONNECTED to verse 2, which says, "Let the redeemed of the Lord say so, whom he hath redeemed from the hand of the enemy." Verse 4 tells us from what God had redeemed the people. As we read the surrounding verses, we can see many other things from which God redeemed them. Do you remember what it was like before you got saved? This verse will remind you of life before Christ.

They Wandered Around ("They wandered in the wilderness"). It is terrible just to wander around aimlessly for any amount of time, much less for forty years! What an empty life! Israel actually wandered in the wilderness waiting for the generation that had disobeyed God to die. They went from place to place with no particular plan. Their job was to learn to follow the pillar of smoke by day and the pillar of fire by night—wherever it might go. In our own lives, after we have been in the wilderness for a week or so, it is time to go home and get back to work and the regular grind of living. What a pointless and frustrating place to be—in the wilderness, going around and around in circles because of our own sin!

They Wandered Alone ("in a solitary way"). Yes, the Lord was with them, and that was enough. But even God makes mention of His people being alone. Multitudes of people today would give anything to have a real friend. The worst feeling is to be in a crowd and be alone! That was what it was like before we were redeemed. How can you experience true love without Christ? How can you have a real friend without the one who "sticketh closer than a brother" (Proverbs 18:24)? Those arrogant souls who defy God's gift of salvation and proudly declare that they would rather go to hell with their friends have no idea of the loneliness that awaits them in the torments of hell!

They Wandered Apart ("they found no city to dwell in"). In the wilderness, Israel had no identity. They were a people without a country. They had no *protection,* no *possession,* and no *profession* to claim. Though God's promise to the Jews was about a promised land, they needed to set their eyes upon a heavenly land that awaited them on the other side. Even Abraham had to learn this by faith. Hebrews 11:10 says, "For he looked for a city which hath foundations, whose builder and maker is God." God gave the promise of a land to Abraham, but Abraham set his eyes on heaven and looked to the presence and abode of God! A heavenly city awaits the Christians who are yet upon this earth! As strangers and pilgrims on this earth, we must learn to sing, "This world is not my home, I'm just a-passing through."[1] We must have eyes that will look beyond this place and set our hearts upon that which we can see only by faith!

Thank God for His redemption that has saved us from all these wanderings.

TOPICS: Barrenness, Faith, God's Will, Identity, Loneliness, Lost, Wilderness

---

R. CHRIS HANKS

DAILY BIBLE READING: Psalm 110–118

TODAY'S VERSE: Psalm 118:6: "The Lord is on my side; I will not fear: what can man do unto me?"

WHAT A GREAT THOUGHT to contemplate this morning: the confidence of the Christian life! This kind of confidence is sought by the entire world. People today are looking for something that is sure, stable, and sound, but it will never be found apart from Jesus Christ. Hebrews 10:35 says, "Cast not away therefore your confidence, which hath great recompence of reward." Let us rejoice in God's care, which blesses us with this great confidence.

The Position of Our Confidence ("The Lord is on my side"). Our confidence is found in the presence of God! It would do us well to know that God is not on "our side" because of us, but because of Himself! As a matter of fact, the only reason He is on our side in this verse is because we are found "in Him." Verses 2, 3, and 4 all say, "Let _____ now say, that his mercy endureth for ever." God is on our side because of His own mercy that was bestowed upon us in the gift of salvation!

The Poise of Our Confidence ("I will not fear"). What assurance and conviction is found in this little phrase! Once you have seen Calvary and the great sacrifice of our Lord and Saviour Jesus Christ, once you have perceived the great pain and suffering of God's Son, once you understand that it was He who stared into the eyes of Satan and willingly walked into the gauntlet of God's judgment, what do you have to fear? With a mighty statement upon the cross, Jesus said, "It is finished"! Judgment was done! Sin was defeated! A way was made! You can say, just as the psalmist said, that "I will not fear."

The Power of Our Confidence ("what can man do unto me?"). Before I finish this thought, I would like to point out that many have lost their lives for their faith. Many have given their lives as martyrs. I believe that every Christian should read *Foxe's Book of Martyrs* to remember what many have endured for their faith in Christ. But the truth of this verse still endures! "What can man do unto me?" Nothing! Knowing that my soul is forever saved gives me great confidence! They may destroy our bodies, but they cannot touch our spirits! There is absolutely nothing men can do when it comes to our hope of salvation and security in Christ. Man did not give us this confidence in Christ, and man cannot take it away!

TOPICS: Confidence, Faith, Power, Presence of God, Protection, Trust

July 10

DAILY BIBLE READING: Psalm 119

TODAY'S VERSE: Psalm 119:11: "Thy word have I hid in mine heart, that I might not sin against thee."

THIS VERSE IS ONE of the most well-known in the Bible and has been memorized by many as children. Some even learn it as a song. Almost every verse in Psalm 119 refers to the Word of God in some way, and this verse is no different. If only we had more Christians who would take this verse seriously and commit it to their hearts, I believe our churches would experience revival in ways we only read about today, and Christians would be mighty in faith and power! Here are a few thoughts about this Word that should challenge us in our Christian life.

It Is a Proactive Word Against Sin ("Thy word have I hid"). The first salvo in our spiritual warfare must be fired by the Christian. As we continue to watch the mighty arms race across the globe, we are reminded that our spiritual warfare must be prepared for contact with the enemy. One of America's greatest deterrents to her enemies has been her military might. The definition for the word translated "hid" in this verse means "to hide, to hoard or reserve." We need to start hoarding and reserving Scriptures for the battle that is coming our way! Our great defense as Christians is the Word of God: the most powerful of all weapons upon this earth! Second Corinthians 10:4 says, "For the weapons of our warfare are not carnal, but mighty through God to the pulling down of strong holds."

Not only is the Word a great defense, but it is also a great *offense* against those things that would defy the way of God. Hebrew 4:12 says, "For the word of God is quick, and powerful, and sharper than any twoedged sword, piercing even to the dividing asunder of soul and spirit, and of the joints and marrow, and is a discerner of the thoughts and intents of the heart." We can make a preemptive strike against any sin and temptation with the Word of God.

It Is a Personal Word Against Sin ("I hid in mine heart"). I am not the source of this wonderful Word of which we speak, yet it is "my Word." If we never make God's Word personal and commit it to our hearts, it will never become personal in its fellowship with us or in its application to our lives. The devil is waging a personal war against you! He is aiming for your worship—is that personal? He desires to have you that he may "sift you as wheat"—is that personal? He desires the hearts of your children—is that personal? He desires to destroy your spousal relationship—is that personal? He desires to defile your mind and body—is that personal? Until we start taking these things personally, we will never make His Word personal in our lives either!

It Is a Protective Word Against Sin ("that I might not sin against thee"). God's Word is to protect us from those things that demand God's judgment. The meaning for the word translated "sin" is "to miss, to sin, to forfeit." Have you ever thought about what you are "missing" or "forfeiting" when you sin? God's Word is there to make sure you don't miss out on the blessings of living right. Some would say, "I never get anything when I do right!" I believe this verse might help. Galatians 6:9 says, "And let us not be weary in well doing: for in due season we shall reap, if we faint not." You may not see the reward this side of heaven, but there is a reward that will last for eternity. God's Word is there to protect you from the guilt and shame of sin before God. No matter how you feel, you don't have to sin! We have the help of God's perfect Word to keep us from sin.

TOPICS: Bible, Heart, Memorization, Sin, Word of God

DAILY BIBLE READING: Psalm 120-130

TODAY'S VERSE: Psalm 124:7: "Our soul is escaped as a bird out of the snare of the fowlers: the snare is broken, and we are escaped."

I AM SO GLAD God has given us a Bible that is perfect, with every word inspired by God's own breath! This verse should make every person who has been cleansed by the blood of the Lamb to rejoice in the redemptive act of God. This psalm begins in verses 1 and 2 by saying, "If it had not been the LORD who was on our side." Where would you be today in your Christian life without Christ? Of course, the answer is "Without hope!" He has not given us temporary relief from our sin, but full and complete forgiveness that is evidenced by this verse! Let us take a moment to look at this verse a little more closely.

First, we see the **Certainty of a Sinner's Destruction** ("Our soul is escaped as a bird out of the snare of the fowlers"). We see a most important principle in this verse. The bird is already in the snare! This is not a case of whether or not the bird *might* be caught. When we first see the bird, he is already ensnared. That is how Christ found me and you: already ensnared in sin! All people begin life ensnared by Adam's sin. Romans 5:12 says, "Wherefore as by one man sin entered into the world, and death by sin, and so death passed upon all men, for that all have sinned." The nature of sin was passed to each and every person born on this earth. Don't worry, though. Lest we blame Adam unnecessarily, we have also committed sin ourselves. Romans 3:23 says, "For all have sinned and come short of the glory of God." Every sinner is in the snare of the fowler with no hope to free himself.

Second, we see the **Certainty of the Snare's Defeat** ("the snare is broken"). This is an action verb, and it is in the present tense! The snare *is* broken! It is not that the snare *was* broken, but the snare that *is* as broken now as when it was first broken by the death, burial, and resurrection of the Lord Jesus Christ. When Jesus cried, "It is finished," the snare was broken. We see this evidenced in Revelation 1:18: "I am he that liveth, and was dead; and, behold, I am alive for evermore, Amen; and have the keys of hell and of death." The word for "broken" means "to burst" and implies an outside force. The verb is passive. "The snare is broken" means that the action was done unto it! Hallelujah for the wonderful victory of Christ! Rest assured that a burst snare will never work again.

Third, we see the **Certainty of the Saint's Deliverance** ("and we are escaped"). Freedom! The word translated "escaped" here means "to be smooth, to escape as if by slipperiness, to bring forth young." That is what the blood did for me! When I was plunged in the blood of Christ, *sin* could not hold me, *Satan* could not hold me, and *self* could not hold me. I am free! We are free from certain destruction. We are escaped, with no possibility of ever being caught again! We are free forever!

How is that possible, you ask? Did you see the last part of that definition? It is "to bring forth young." This all happens with a new birth! Praise the Lord! If you are not saved, trust in Jesus Christ as your personal Saviour, and let Him free you today!

TOPICS: Deliverance, Judgment, Punishment, Sin, Victory

DAILY BIBLE READING: Psalm 131–140

TODAY'S VERSE: Psalm 137:2: "For there they that carried us away captive required of us a song; and they that wasted us required of us mirth, saying, Sing us one of the songs of Zion."

THIS IS A SAD PSALM as it brings us to the land of Babylon, where God's people are captives. The subjects of Nebuchadnezzar have laid their requests upon the newly assimilated Israelites. Many of them may have been trophies of conquest. Perhaps the rivers of Babylon talked about in verse 1 were more beautiful and clean than those in Israel. Leprous Naaman made that claim in 2 Kings 5:12a: "Are not Abana and Pharpar, rivers of Damascus, better than all the waters of Israel?" To God's people, however, the muddy waters of Jordan were far better than the clearest waters in a heathen land! The heathen victors probably thought they were doing the people of Israel a favor by delivering them from their desert land. Even today, the world does not understand our interest in the things of God. Hear the callings of the world upon God's people as they are led away in captivity.

The World Cannot Require a Spiritual Song ("For there they that carried us away captive required of us a song"). The world wants to act like they enjoy the Christian life. They enjoy using our terminology. They know songs like "Amazing Grace." But there is a difference: they desire to prove their spirituality, not to engage in worship. They think they can identify with what you sing. They really want to prove that they are just as spiritual as you are. The Hebrew for "they that carried us away captive" means "to transport into captivity." As the Babylonians led Israel away from their homeland, they wanted to hear the songs they had heard concerning God's people. With every step away from the Promised Land, tears were shed as the people of Judah were transported to a godless nation and a wicked people. The people of the world cannot require this spiritual song, for they do not understand the source of its splendor.

The World Cannot Rejoice in a Spiritual Song ("and they that wasted us required of us mirth"). Not only did the Babylonians want their captives to sing, but they wanted them to rejoice just as if nothing had ever happened. The word for "wasted" means "causing to howl." The one who had caused the greatest pain and suffering in their lives now demanded their spiritual joy. The word for "mirth" means "blithesomeness or glee, religious or festival." How could they be happy when they had been taken from the place of their religious happiness and victory? The world cannot identify with our happiness. Such joy cannot be understood; it must be experienced. Literally, the Babylonians were saying, "Show us how you do that." That kind of joy is not brought by action, but by adoration.

The World Cannot Respect a Spiritual Song ("saying, Sing us one of the songs of Zion"). To the world, this song is nothing but a novelty. You can hear them saying amongst themselves, "Isn't that quaint?" "Their melodies are lovely!" Yet they will hear and will turn again to live as they please and do as they will. They are more interested in the performance of the song than they are in the substance. No matter what they say, do not be deceived by their inviting tones and interested questions, for they do not respect the song of the redeemed. Remember what we are told in 1 John 3:1: "Behold, what manner of love the Father hath bestowed upon us, that we should be called the sons of God: *therefore the world knoweth us not, because it knew him not.*" They think our songs are a cultural issue; but to us, they are a spiritual issue.

TOPICS: Deception, Faith, Singing, Truth, Worship

DAILY BIBLE READING: Psalm 141–150

TODAY'S VERSE: Psalm 144:1: "Blessed be the Lord my strength, which teacheth my hands to war, and my fingers to fight."

IF DAVID LEARNED anything throughout his life, it was to trust in the Lord in the midst of battle. David clearly knew that his success on the battlefield had nothing to do with his ability or knowledge. Enemies feared David because they knew that God fought his battles. As this psalm is written, we hear David's acknowledgment of God as the Great Warrior who brought about every success and victory in his life. Perhaps the insights from this verse might help us to rely upon God in our daily spiritual battles.

He Is the Source of My Strength for the Battle ("Blessed be the Lord my strength"). David made sure there were no mistakes made here. He knew he had no strength—he did not say that the Lord would *add* strength. He did not say that the Lord *helped* his strength. All he said was "the Lord my strength." We must come to the end of ourselves and realize that no strength comes from our own being. The word translated "strength" means "a cliff, a sharp rock, as compressed." Even today, cliffs and rocks are used as a defense against enemies. God alone is the one to whom I run for defense against those who would do me harm. Our enemies do not have the same strength as we do, for Deuteronomy 32:31a says, "For their rock is not as our Rock." We have a great Rock who is our strength!

He Is the Source of My School for the Battle ("which teacheth"). This psalm was written by David, the same David who defeated Goliath with a sling and a stone. He was still submissive to the teaching ministry of God. Just because he could not wear Saul's armor when he fought Goliath didn't mean that he could not learn how to wear it later, and it didn't mean he couldn't learn how to use a sword or spear in the midst of battle. Somewhere along the line, he did learn the art of war. When the time came, he was ready to be taught by God. The word for "teacheth" means "to goad, to teach (the rod being an Oriental incentive)." Sometimes God will "goad" you in order to teach you something. Pain will sometimes be involved in your spiritual lessons. This is not God being mean, but God being merciful. We must submit to His teaching, for He knows the battles that lie ahead.

He Is the Source of My Skill for the Battle ("my hands to war, and my fingers to fight"). Both of these thoughts teach us about skill. The hand was used to hold a sword, but the fingers were used to pull a bow. They both were greatly used upon the battlefield. The more we submit to God's teaching, the more He will be able to use us in the battle! We need Christians who will learn the art of war and use every possible means to fight the battle for the glory of God. If we would allow God to teach and use us, then we will be able to say, like Paul in 2 Timothy 4:7, "I have fought a good fight, I have finished my course, I have kept the faith." Let's fight a *good* fight!

TOPICS: Battle, Skill, Strength, Training, War

July 14

TODAY'S VERSE: Proverbs 4:7: "Wisdom is the principal thing; therefore get wisdom: and with all thy getting get understanding."

THE BOOK OF PROVERBS is one of the most wonderful Bible books to read as it carries great application for Christian living and focuses the reader on the value and necessity of godly wisdom. We are living in a time when self is exalted and wisdom is shamefully neglected. As this book was written to the "young man" to keep him from evil and to train him in the way of the Lord, so too we all must seek God by seeking wisdom.

This verse first tells us to **Keep the Main Thing the Main Thing** ("Wisdom is the principal thing; therefore get wisdom"). The meaning of the word translated "principle" is "the first, in place, time, order or rank." The book of Proverbs tells us a number of times that wisdom is the "main thing." *Its virtue is enduring. Its value is eternal. Its vision is earnest.* Just a couple of verses earlier, in chapter 5 verse 5, Proverbs says, "Get wisdom, get understanding: forget it not; neither decline from the words of my mouth." We need a return to this all-consuming passion of seeking God's wisdom. What a promise we have in James 1:5 concerning our seeking of the divine wisdom of God! "If any of you lack wisdom, let him ask of God, that giveth to all men liberally, and upbraideth not; and it shall be given him."

The verse also tells us to to **Keep the Main Thing the Meaningful Thing** ("Wisdom is the principal thing; therefore *get* wisdom"). The word used for "get" means "to procure, to own, attain, buy." If you have any means to acquire wisdom, do it! This reminds me of the parable in Matthew 13:45–46: "Again, the kingdom of heaven is like unto a merchant man, seeking goodly pearls: who, when he had found one pearl of great price, went and sold all that he had, and bought it." Any comfort of this life should not be so tempting that it would hinder us from seeking and receiving the wisdom of God!

The verse also tells us to **Keep the Main Thing the Motivational Thing** ("and with all thy getting get understanding"). The quest for wisdom and understanding should be the driving force behind our lives. This is the thing that should make us tick. John Phillips says that many people's lives are summed up in this little phrase: "With all thy getting."[2] With that in mind, with *all* your getting, "get understanding." We should be provoked and determined to focus every force behind the ambition to seek out God and His wisdom. This single-minded passion should grip our souls with a fury as we frantically forsake all and seek God—the embodiment of wisdom itself. Proverbs 8:11 says, "For wisdom is better than rubies; and all the things that may be desired are not to be compared to it." Wisdom must be our motivation!

TOPICS: Desire, Priorities, Understanding, Wisdom

---

2   John Phillips, *Exploring Proverbs*, Vol. 1 (Neptune, NJ: Loizeaux Brothers, 1995), 111.

R. CHRIS HANKS

DAILY BIBLE READING: Proverbs 5–9

TODAY'S VERSE: Proverbs 7:10: "And, behold, there met him a woman with the attire of an harlot, and subtil of heart."

SINCE PROVERBS WAS WRITTEN to the young man, there is much in the book concerning the "strange woman": passages written to warn him of her, her ways, and her appeal to the flesh. It is a foolish man who says he is not "bothered" by the wiles of a temptress and her will to entice and seduce him to immoral behavior. This is one lesson that our entire society needs to hear and to heed. The saddest thing today is that our boys are not the only ones being destroyed by this way of living: but our young ladies are being taught step-by-step how to *become* the very monster God warns young men to avoid. We need a cleansing and a rededicating of our hearts, minds, and bodies to the Lord, that He might have a pure vessel to glorify Him.

This Woman Was a Wise Huntress ("And, behold, there met him a woman"). I am not speaking here of a godly wisdom, but a fleshly wisdom. She knew what she wanted, and she knew how to get it no matter who else her actions affected. The end result is **death!** She was a good hunter! She says in verse 15, "Therefore came I forth to meet thee." She had every intention to meet this young man to tempt him and draw him away. Just a few verses later, in verses 22–23, the Bible says, "He goeth after her straightway, as an ox goeth to the slaughter, or as a fool to the correction of the stocks; till a *dart strike through his liver;* as a *bird hasteth to the snare, and knoweth not that it is for his life.*" Such a woman knows exactly what she needs to do to catch her prey. In Proverbs 6:26, we see the same thing mentioned: "For by means of a whorish woman a man is brought to a piece of bread: and the *adulteress will hunt for the precious life.*" She is not trying to defile those who are defiled already, but those who are clean and pure in the sight of God. I believe that God actually looks at this much like rape, for verse 21 says, "With her much fair speech she caused him to yield, with the flattering of her lips *she forced him.*"

This Woman Was a Wretched Harlot ("a woman with the attire of an harlot"). The result is **defilement**. There is an important principle here: the Bible says she had the attire of a harlot. It *is* possible to look like one even if you are not one! Christian young ladies definitely have a responsibility in the way they dress. Godliness, modesty, and difference are all marks of a virtuous woman. In today's society, it has become acceptable to accentuate and advertise a woman's body in such a way that it is a temptation to the godliest of men! But no matter what society has accepted, we must obey and honor the Lord, lest we defraud an unsuspecting person or even be unfaithful to our spouses by provoking sexual thoughts and feelings in others. But we know by the rest of this chapter that this woman did not *just* dress like a harlot; she really was one. The very first step of her hunting expedition was the lure of a seductive and revealing outfit.

This Woman Had a Wicked Heart ("and subtil of heart"). The result is **deceit**. The word translated "subtil" means, in the bad sense, "beseiged, hidden things." She had declared war upon this young man, yet he did not even know it. He was duped by her speech. Verse 21 says, "With her much fair speech she caused him to yield." Proverbs 5:3 says the same thing: "For the lips of a strange woman drop as an honeycomb, and her mouth is smoother than oil." It would be easy just to blame her for this sin. It would even be easy to mock him who was so easily taken. What was he thinking? Couldn't he just see through it all? But the Bible is careful to tell us that our hearts are as deceitful as this harlot was. Jeremiah 17:9 says, "The heart is deceitful above all things, and desperately wicked: who can know it?" This woman preyed upon the weakness of all men—a deceitful heart! Be careful of this woman and her ways!

TOPICS: Death, Deceit, Defilement, Prostitution, Purity, Strange Women, Wickedness

DAILY BIBLE READING: Proverbs 10–14

TODAY'S VERSE: Proverbs 14:12: "There is a way which seemeth right unto a man, but the end thereof are the ways of death."

THIS VERSE IS A GREAT WARNING against our natural way, our fleshly mind, and our carnal heart. A great war is being waged on the mind each and every day. Our minds can be clouded by *natural reason,* which has no spiritual faith in God. Our minds can be conquered by *natural rebellion,* which has no spiritual fruit to God. Our minds can be corrupted by *natural reveling,* which has no spiritual favor from God. When our minds are clouded, the way which we should go is not so easily seen. We must be careful to go the right way, for it could mean our lives!

This Way Is a False Way ("There is a way which *seemeth* right unto a man"). This is a very arrogant place to be! The Bible says in Galatians 6:3, "For if a man think himself to be something, when he is nothing, he deceiveth himself." I will never forget the very first time I went into a house of mirrors as a child. What seemed to be the right way never was. What was most deceiving about that house was that I saw myself everywhere I turned, but all it showed was where I had been and not where I needed to go! Because of that, I had to feel my way around to find the exit. When we have been defeated to the point where we must follow our "feelings" to find the way out, we are in a great distress.

This Way Is a Fractured Way ("but the end thereof are the ways . . ."). What in the beginning of this verse was called "a way" has now been multiplied in the latter part of the verse: "but the end thereof are the *ways.*" I cannot tell you how many times I have been asked, "Preacher, how did I ever end up here?" The answer is simple: there was a time when a way seemed right, but it was not the way of God and could not be found in His Word. That way will split and fracture into a million pieces, all of which will take you to a place of sudden destruction. One thing we can count on as Christians is that God's way will never break or fracture, for Jesus said, "I am the way." He is a foundation no other man can lay, and it is not cracked. It is a way that is *clear.* It is a way that is *constant.* It is a way that is *confident.*

This Way Is a Failed Way ("but the end thereof are the ways of *death*"). This sounds like a way that needs to be avoided! Jesus said in John 10:10, "I am come that they might have life, and that they might have it more abundantly." When I got saved, I received eternal *life!* Those who reject the way of salvation have chosen eternal death. Why would I choose a way that is doomed by the dread of death? A Christian should desire to *live* for God and enjoy His fellowship! Don't go the failed way of selfish and sensual living, for it will lead you down the path of death. The Bible has already declared for the Christian that "Death is swallowed up in victory" (1 Corinthians 15:54)! If death has no more power, why should I follow its failed objective and forfeit the greatest blessing of letting my Lord lead me into His place of peace and life?

TOPICS: Death, Deceit, Failure, Man's Wisdom, Sin

DAILY BIBLE READING: Proverbs 15–18

TODAY'S VERSE: Proverbs 18:24: "A man that hath friends must shew himself friendly: and there is a friend that sticketh closer than a brother."

THE TOPIC OF FRIENDSHIP reaches every age and affects every member of society. Our children are affected tremendously by it, and they easily give in to the pressure of a friend's desires. The ideal of having and making a friend is very intoxicating, and many a Christian young person has forsaken the way of the Lord in order to please someone else. The book of Proverbs discusses this topic many different times and gives good wisdom concerning being a good friend as well as making and keeping one.

First, we see the **Cultivation of Friendship** ("A man that hath friends *must shew himself friendly*"). In order for friendship to succeed, there must be hard work. This is true of any relationship. It is tragic when a couple gets married and then quits working at the relationship. If anything is going to be done right, it will require an investment. We must be careful to invest ourselves in the right relationships. Because of the importance of godly friends, every friendship must be brought before the Lord in extensive prayer. Every relationship must meet the requirements found in Scripture to ensure its proper perspective and to protect our hearts from falling away from the way of the Lord.

Second, we see the **Commitment of Friendship** ("and there is a friend that sticketh closer"). I believe this verse is speaking of our great Friend and Saviour, Jesus Christ! He was committed to us no matter the cost. He gave Himself as a sacrifice for man's sin and laid down His life of His own will to redeem us unto Himself. What a committed Friend we have! In turn, we need to be committed to our friends as well. We commit ourselves to them only in such a way that we might be a godly influence to draw them closer to the Lord. What a wonderful and coveted friendship there would be if each friend committed himself to being a godly friend and encouraged the other to do the same.

Third, we see the **Connection of Friendship** ("than a brother"). Thank God for a connection! Jesus connected Himself to us by becoming flesh that He might be our Saviour! The connection we have is based on the cross. But that connection can grow to be so much more! The word for "sticketh" means "to adhere." We must adhere our hearts to the Word of God, our souls in prayer, and our wills in service. How sad it is to hear when a husband and wife have a problem connecting. They would even say that they have "drifted apart." When God made man and woman, Adam said in Genesis 2:24, "Therefore shall a man leave his father and his mother, *and shall cleave unto his wife*: and they shall be one flesh." The perfect picture of God's connection to man is the picture of the connection that a husband and a wife should have as they adhere together!

TOPICS: Commitment, Companionship, Friendship, Marriage

DAILY BIBLE READING: Proverbs 19–24

TODAY'S VERSE: Proverbs 20:11: "Even a child is known by his doings, whether his work be pure, and whether it be right."

I REMEMBER BOTH my mom and grandma quoting this verse to me at different times when I was a youth. Thank God for godly parents and grandparents who try to instill God's Word into the hearts of the next generation! Usually, this verse was quoted in response to something I had done that needed to be corrected. As this verse begins with "Even a child," we should be reminded that so much the more will an adult be known! We live in a time in which the accepted thinking is that it really does not matter what we do as long as our hearts are right. I have even heard some say, "Well, God knows my heart." God does know our hearts, and yet He holds us responsible for our actions and our deeds. In other words, the end does *not* justify the means!

Our Work Will Be Scrutinized ("Even a child is known by his doings"). The word "known" in this verse means "to scrutinize, to look intently at." Every work that is done will be scrutinized and discerned. We need to mind the fact that it is not our grade-school teacher or even our local government who will inspect, examine, and analyze our every work, but God Himself. God has told us that others will scrutinize our work as well, for in Matthew 7:20 Jesus says, "Wherefore by their fruits ye shall know them." We must exercise the godly wisdom that God has given to us to discern the fruits of our children. Just as a parent needs to discern the "doings" of a child, children of God must discern the "doings" of the world that we might keep from the evil way.

Our Work Should Be Sanitized ("whether his work be pure"). The word for "pure" means "clear." We need to be clear in the way we live. There should never be ulterior motives driving our manner of living. We need to be cleansed from the roots of our fleshly nature and let the purity of the Holy Spirit's fruit be clearly seen. First Timothy 4:12 says, "Let no man despise thy youth; but be thou an example of the believers, in word, in conversation, in charity, in spirit, in faith, in *purity*." There is a great ministry to be done in the cleansing of our hearts and lives for the glory of the Lord. James 4:8 says it like this: "Draw nigh to God, and he will draw nigh to you. Cleanse your hands, ye sinners; and purify your hearts, ye double minded."

Our Work Will Be Spiritualized ("and whether it be right"). The earlier phrase "whether his work be pure" carries with it the idea of appearance. "Whether it be right," on the other hand, carries with it the idea of reality, of the work's properties all the way through. Is our work right indeed? Not that it just seems to be right, but that it really is? Time will tell, my friend! Right doings are the basis of *right*eousness. The term "whether it be" should mean to us "it had better be"! We must make sure that our work is right, that is, based upon God and His Word and coming from a pure heart.

TOPICS: Clarity, Holiness, Purity, Spiritual, Testimony, Work

DAILY BIBLE READING: Proverbs 25–27

TODAY'S VERSE: Proverbs 27:17: "Iron sharpeneth iron; so a man sharpeneth the countenance of his friend."

TODAY, WE HAVE A GREAT NEED for truly good, godly friends. Everybody wants a good friend, but few are willing to *be* one. That, however, is the basis for having friends. Proverbs 18:24a says, "A man that hath friends must shew himself friendly."

Much is said in the Bible about both good and bad friends. God has given us the good fortune of having friends upon this earth. One of the greatest blessings of being a Christian is that Jesus has called us His friends. John 15:15 says, "Henceforth I call you not servants; for the servant knoweth not what his lord doeth: *but I have called you friends;* for all things that I have heard of my Father I have made known unto you." I hope that our appreciation for real friendship will be strengthened by the thoughts in this verse.

The Form of a Godly Friendship ("Iron sharpeneth iron"). Iron is one of the top five most plenteous elements upon the earth. Iron is used in forging steel for structures, tools, and the finest instruments for precise workmanship. Hardly any part of our lives is free of iron's influence in some way, shape, or fashion. The strength and use of iron depend upon what you do to it. What purpose does your friendship have in your life? It will all depend on what you do with it!

The Friction of a Godly Friendship ("so a man sharpeneth"). I will never forget watching my father take out a long, round piece of steel and a knife and begin to scrape them together when I was a child. When I asked, he told me that he was sharpening the knife. That was hard for me to understand. Yet, with every pass of the blade, it was sharpened. Gouges in the knife blade would begin to be smoothed out, and the knife would regain its edge so it could do the job it was created to do. That is the purpose of a godly friend—to help you do what you were created to do! Sometimes there is scraping, scratching, and scuffing, but it is all meant to make you better. That reminds me of Proverbs 27:6: *"Faithful are the wounds of a friend;* but the kisses of an enemy are deceitful." A good friend will direct you in godliness and push you in the way of holiness. Hebrews 10:24 says, "And let us consider one another to provoke unto love and to good works."

The Face of a Godly Friendship ("the countenance of his friend"). The word "countenance" literally means "the face." Our face is one of the most important features we have. Four out of our five senses can only be found on our faces. It is easy to forget a name, but much harder to forget a face. The face introduces us to a stranger and excites the heart of a friend. I remember reading a story about Abraham Lincoln when he was looking for someone to fill a position. One of the aides mentioned the name of a man of whom Lincoln said, "I do not like his face." His aides were taken aback by his response and said that no man can help what his face looks like. Lincoln replied, "Every man over forty is responsible for his face."[3] You, my friend, can have an impact upon the face of your friend. Be careful, for this is a great power not to be taken lightly!

TOPICS: Encouragement, Faithfulness, Friendship, Godliness

---

3   The story is told at http://www.sermonillustrations.com/a-z/l/lincoln.htm.

July 20

DAILY BIBLE READING: Proverbs 28–31

TODAY'S VERSE: Proverbs 31:2: "What, my son? and what, the son of my womb? and what, the son of my vows?"

I AM THANKFUL that the Bible gives a healthy dose of instruction on being a virtuous lady. This chapter teaches ladies about being good homemakers—the greatest and most powerful job on the face of the earth! However, I would like to look at a verse in the beginning of this chapter in which a virtuous mother instructs her son, Lemuel. The book of Proverbs begins with a father talking to his son. Almost all of the first seven chapters begin with the phrase "My son." This last chapter, however, begins with a mother talking to her son. In verse 4, she warns her son about *strange women*. In verses 5–7, she warns him against *strong wine*. In verses 8–9, she discusses *simple wisdom*, defending the weak and judging righteously. And in verses 10–31, she talks, ever so lovingly, to her son about the *spiritual woman*. In our verse today, we will look at the basis of her entire motherly speech and hear her proposition.

    The Authority of Her Teaching ("What, my son?"). Here, this mother lets her son know that she was a God-ordained authority in his life. God chose her to be over him, and God chose him to be under her. I guess this is where the argument "Because I'm the mom!" got started! Though a wife is to be submitted to her husband's leadership, parenting is a partnership. There are many great things a godly mother can and should teach her children. Mothers, don't take this responsibility too lightly! I am always touched by Deborah, a judge of Israel, who said in Judges 5:7, "The inhabitants of the villages ceased, they ceased in Israel, until that I Deborah arose, that I arose a mother in Israel." *Rise up, Mother!* Rise up and teach your sons and daughters the way of the Lord!

    The Affinity of Her Teaching ("and what, the son of my womb?"). There is an attachment between mother and son that a father will never have. She is telling him, "You were part of me. You drew your life from me. You shared my blood, my food, and my body." That is an intimate thought. She bore her son in pain and sorrow that no father will ever know or experience. I have heard some mothers say, "I brought you into this world, and I can take you out!" If you have trained and taught your children properly, they will respect the fact that you were the one who loved them, nurtured them, and helped them in their time of helplessness. There is nothing more loving and precious than a mother with a newborn babe.

    The Authenticity of Her Teaching ("and what, the son of my vows?"). Here, this mother tells her son that he is a legitimate child. She was true to her promise to her husband and her God. This child was no "mistake," but a blessing from a righteous and holy union that God had blessed. This godly woman waited for marriage to have *him*. If she had not waited in the will of God, she would not have had him, but a different babe with different DNA and a different outlook on life. This mother was real and genuine from the beginning. Would to God we had more mothers like this today! Your children will respect you more if you will live by a holy and godly conviction.

TOPICS: Authority, Godliness, Holiness, Love, Motherhood, Parenting

R. CHRIS HANKS

DAILY BIBLE READING: Ecclesiastes 1–3

TODAY'S VERSE: Ecclesiastes 1:9: "The thing that hath been, it is that which shall be; and that which is done is that which shall be done: and there is no new thing under the sun."

ECCLESIASTES WAS A WRITTEN SERMON by the "preacher," Solomon. It is a sermon of sorrow and regret, most likely written at the end of his life to look back over the vanity of a life that is lived completely for self and fleshly desires. Solomon withheld nothing from his own heart, only to realize that he wanted more. At times we all go down this road in our lives, and like Solomon, we end up with an empty feeling. A testimony of Solomon's selfish ways can be seen in Ecclesiastes 2:10: "And whatsoever mine eyes desired I kept not from them, I withheld not my heart from any joy." To Solomon, *possessions* and *prosperity* were no object. *Permission* was no object. *Popularity* was no object. Even his *perceptions* were no object. Yet, in the next verse he says, "And, behold, all was vanity and vexation of spirit, and there was no profit under the sun." It is not until chapter 12 in the conclusion of this message that the preacher tells us what to do about the emptiness of life: "Remember now thy Creator in the days of thy youth." That is the only thing that is not vanity and vexation of spirit! In today's verse, we will keep that conclusion in mind as we listen to Solomon's natural reasoning.

The Fleshly Life Is a Purposeless Life ("The thing that hath been, it is that which shall be"). In the flesh, what can we do to change this world? Nothing! It will continue in a purposeless mess. That is the way our society and our nation have gone, and they will continue to do so. Living our lives without God gives the most unsatisfying and helpless feeling. The only one who can change anything is God!

The Fleshly Life Is a Self-Perpetuating Life ("and that which is done is that which shall be done"). What an outlook! Even if my personal situation changes, the way of life will not change. That is the way our flesh is. My flesh never changes. It is a voracious beast that only thinks of itself. It will put me in the same place each and every day. Whether people are around me or not, my flesh has its own desires. Whether money is available or not, my flesh still wants to fulfill its lusts. Whether I want to change my situation with a positive mental attitude or not, my flesh still craves its own exaltation. The longer it goes, the more self-perpetuating it becomes. My flesh has no imagination, no creativity, and no originality, but is consumed with passion for itself. Because of that, I know that it will do tomorrow what it does today.

The Fleshly Life Is a Pointless Life ("and there is no new thing under the sun"). If we cannot change, what reason do we have to continue in life? Some might hold to making money as their reason for living. Some might hope that witty inventions and clever discoveries will change our outlook. The problem is, none of those things change *us!* Millionaires, scientists, and inventors have taken their own lives out of despair because of the pointlessness of the natural life. The only way to have a fulfilling life with true hope and joy is with Christ and the Holy Spirit living within us!

TOPICS: Carnality, Emptiness, Flesh, Hopelessness, Purpose, Vanity

July 22

DAILY BIBLE READING: Ecclesiastes 4–7

TODAY'S VERSE: Ecclesiastes 4:13: "Better is a poor and a wise child than an old and foolish king, who will no more be admonished."

THIS VERSE CARRIES the same truth and wisdom we have recently read all through the book of Proverbs. What I would like to point out to you today is that Solomon is speaking of himself! This book of regrets has stirred his remembrance of his life in the beginning of his reign. He remembers the *purity* of his heart. He remembers the *passion* of his heart. He even remembers the *perceptions* of his heart. There was no doubt that Solomon was wise as a young man. I would remind you of the beginning of his reign, when God appeared to him and was pleased to hear this young man ask for wisdom. God gave him more wisdom than anyone who had lived before or would live after him. Now Solomon is at the end of his life and realizes that he is nothing but an "old and foolish king." Three things of significance are discussed here.

The Celebration of Simple Living ("Better is a poor and a wise child"). True wisdom is simple to get—so much so that even a child can have it! Children were often used by Christ to illustrate simple but profound faith and trust. We find in Matthew 18:3 that Christ uses this illustration to show the simple faith of salvation: "And said, Verily I say unto you, Except ye be converted, and become as little children, ye shall not enter into the kingdom of heaven." After salvation, however, we often struggle in our maturing in the Christian life. How sad that our deceitful sin strips us of the innocent faith we had in our Lord and Saviour! How quickly we leave the place of blessed and simple faith to have our hearts and minds spoiled by the enemy in a faithless fit of sinful living! Second Corinthians 11:3 says, "But I fear, lest by any means, as the serpent beguiled Eve through his subtilty, so your minds should be corrupted from the *simplicity* that is in Christ."

The Condemnation of Silly Living ("than an old and foolish king"). The word used for "foolish" means "fat, stupid, or silly." A foolish life has control of nothing. As we follow Solomon's life, we can see that he lived completely for selfish pleasure and ended up being the silliest wise man in history. Solomon is testifying here of the foolishness of his heart in his old age. While he was living foolishly, he was blinded by his own desires. Though he could still return to God, the scars of foolish living would always torment his spirit in the remembrance of wasted years.

The Characterization of Stubborn Living ("who will no more be admonished"). It is one thing to be unaware of correction. It is another to be unwilling to be corrected. This blatant display of stubbornness is not uncommon in our churches today. Solomon here remembers the same folly that was the downfall of King Saul. Samuel warned Saul about this in 1 Samuel 15:23: "For rebellion is as the sin of witchcraft, and *stubbornness* is as iniquity and idolatry. Because thou hast rejected the word of the Lord, he hath also rejected thee from being king." Solomon's whole reason for living a silly life was because he had first lived a stubborn life. To reject the Word of the Lord is certain destruction. John 12:48 says, "He that rejecteth me, and receiveth not my words, hath one that judgeth him: the word that I have spoken, the same shall judge him in the last day." It was because of stubbornness and a hard heart that the people of Israel did not receive the promises of God. The other way is much easier and more blessed to experience.

TOPICS: Foolishness, Simplicity, Submission, Tenderness, Wisdom

DAILY BIBLE READING: Ecclesiastes 8–12

TODAY'S VERSE: Ecclesiastes 11:5: "As thou knowest not what is the way of the spirit, nor how the bones do grow in the womb of her that is with child: even so thou knowest not the works of God who maketh all."

THE CONTEXT OF THIS VERSE speaks of sowing seed. Verse 4 tells us not to worry about the wind or the weather when it is time to sow, or we will never have a time of reaping. The verse after our key verse, verse 6, tells us to sow in the morning and in the evening, for we do not know which of these will bring forth fruit. With that context in mind, we return to our main text. This verse tells us three things we do not understand, and all three have to do with new life.

We do not understand the **Way of an Expressed Spirit** ("As thou knowest not what is the way of the spirit"). The Hebrew meaning of "spirit" is "wind, the resemblance of breath." It speaks of our life—our **existence**. Life is a puzzling thing of which we know little. Not even scientists in their multimillion-dollar labs and great journals of medical science and history can create life. It must be given by the Life-giver. Even a test-tube baby is brought together through means devised by God and not by science. James 4:14 says, "Whereas ye know not what shall be on the morrow. For what is your life? It is even a vapour, that appeareth for a little time, and then vanisheth away." Life expresses to us its characteristics by showing us that it is both fragile and fleeting.

We do not understand the **Womb of an Expectant Mother** ("nor how the bones do grow in the womb of her that is with child"). Particularly, this is speaking of the manner in which the bones grow in the womb. This speaks of growth—or **expansion**. The bones are very important to each and every one of us. Not only do they support our bodies and give them structure, but they carry the ingredients of our lifeblood in the marrow. Though doctors understand some basics of bone health and how bones heal and re-form, they have never figured out how the bones of a baby begin to grow in the womb of its mother!

We do not understand the **Works of an Excellent Creator** ("even so thou knowest not the works of God who maketh all"). The Bible says in Isaiah 55:9, "For as the heavens are higher than the earth, so are my ways higher than your ways, and my thoughts than your thoughts." This speaks of purpose—or **exaltation**. God wants us to glorify Him for His wonderful works. My friend, God does know what He is doing! Our flesh wants to condemn God for things we don't understand. Romans 9:20 says, "Nay but, O man, who art thou that repliest against God? Shall the thing formed say to him that formed it, Why hast thou made me thus?" Here we are trying to defy God in things we cannot even comprehend! All that the Bible says about God when He completed the creation of the world is in Genesis 1:31: "And God saw every thing that he had made, and, behold, it was very good." Not only did God make all things physical, but all things spiritual! He made a way of glorification!

Some would say, "But what does all this mean, and what is its impact on me today?" The answer is simple! It is in the context in verse 4—we are to *sow!* For existence, expansion, and exaltation to happen, we must sow the seed! Sow the seed for the salvation of souls. Sow the seed of faith in acceptance of God's will. Whatever you do, just sow the seed.

TOPICS: Discernment, Faith, Growth, Holy Spirit, Soul-Winning, Sowing, Word of God

DAILY BIBLE READING: Song of Solomon 1-8

TODAY'S VERSE: Song of Solomon 5:16: "His mouth is most sweet: yea, he is altogether lovely. This is my beloved, and this is my friend, O daughters of Jerusalem."

WITHOUT A DOUBT, the Song of Solomon, also referred to as Canticles, is the most beautiful book in the Bible. Such great care is taken to show us the wonders and beauties of the special relationship between a man and his wife. This in turn shows the love of Christ and His bride, the church. No matter what interpretations some hold about certain parts of this book, or how many characters are involved, one cannot deny the love that man and wife have for one another and its implications in our spiritual lives. As we look at today's verse, we will think of our Beloved and rejoice in Him.

I Cannot Deny the Appeal ("His mouth is most sweet"). The word rightly translated as "sweet" has a root that means "to suck, to relish." It brings to mind Psalm 34:8, which says, "O taste and see that the LORD is good: blessed is the man that trusteth in him." His mouth, His words, His communications all have me enraptured by their beauty and are sweet to my taste. In speaking of God's Word and His judgments, Psalm 19:10 says, "More to be desired are they than gold, yea, than much fine gold: sweeter also than honey and the honeycomb." Their sweetness makes me want to return for more and enjoy the sweet fellowship, the sweet thoughts, and the sweet hope we have in God's Word! Psalm 119:103 says, "How sweet are thy words unto my taste! yea, sweeter than honey to my mouth." Our wonderful Saviour and King possesses a great appeal.

I Cannot Deny the Attraction ("yea, he is altogether lovely"). In speaking of the fleshly view of Christ, Isaiah 53:2b says, "He hath no form nor comeliness; and when we shall see him, there is no beauty that we should desire him." However, for the Christian who has already believed, there is great beauty and attraction in Him! Those things that repulse the world are the very things that draw us to Him! Isaiah 33:17 says, "Thine eyes shall see the king in his beauty." The apostle Paul said in Galatians 6:14, "But God forbid that I should glory, save in the cross of our Lord Jesus Christ, by whom the world is crucified unto me, and I unto the world." George Bennard in the hymn "The Old Rugged Cross" wrote, "In the old rugged cross/Stained with blood so divine/A wondrous beauty I see/For 'twas on that old cross/Jesus suffered and died/To pardon and sanctify me." The words "whom my soul loveth" can be found in the Bible only five times (five is the number of grace), and each of these occurrences is found in the Song of Solomon. Even more interesting, each time it is the young bride speaking of her bridegroom! What a picture for us today! Do you love Him? Are you attracted to Him? We should be able to say as the bride did, "Yea, he is altogether lovely."

I Cannot Deny the Adoration ("This is my beloved, and this is my friend, O daughters of Jerusalem"). The root of the word for "beloved" means "to boil." There is a bubbling and a boiling in my soul every time I think about Jesus! There is a fervent heat that touches my heart with every thought of Christ! Not only do I love Him passionately, but He is my friend. Many married people make the mistake of not treating their spouses as friends. What greater friend can I have than the One who loves me most? Proverbs 18:24 says, "A man that hath friends must shew himself friendly: *and there is a friend that sticketh closer than a brother.*" Not only do I love Him no matter what, but there is not a time when I do not enjoy His presence and His fellowship! The bride's testimony of her love for her husband ends with a witness to others: "O daughters of Jerusalem." We should tell someone today of the greatness of our Beloved. Share the appeal, attraction, and adoration of Christ with someone else today!

TOPICS: Attraction, Friendship, Love, Marriage, Taste, Worship

R. CHRIS HANKS

DAILY BIBLE READING: Isaiah 1–3

TODAY'S VERSE: Isaiah 3:8: "For Jerusalem is ruined, and Judah is fallen: because their tongue and their doings are against the Lord, to provoke the eyes of his glory."

WHAT A TRAGEDY is recorded for us here! This was the place that had been the apple of God's eye. Psalm 48:2 says, "Beautiful for situation, the joy of the whole earth, is mount Zion, on the sides of the north, the city of the great King." Jerusalem, a testimony of God's love, and Judah, a testimony of God's faithfulness, were now gone. What is it that would bring about such a terrible judgment? The verse lists the three reasons why God brought His judgment and wrath upon the people of Judah and brought them into captivity.

First, God judged Israel **Because of Their Announcements** ("because their tongue . . ."). They had allowed their wickedness to affect their speech. James 3:1–12 warns us of the dangers of our tongues, calling them "a world of iniquity." Psalm 73:8–9 says, "They are corrupt, and speak wickedly concerning oppression: they speak loftily. They set their mouth against the heavens, and their tongue walketh through the earth." When our tongues are against the Lord, we assert ourselves as an authority over Him and claim His holiness to be a lie. We must be careful that we do not allow our tongues to run away with us! Matthew 12:36–37 addresses this topic by saying, "But I say unto you, That every idle word that men shall speak, they shall give account thereof in the day of judgment. For by thy words thou shalt be justified, and by thy words thou shalt be condemned." Our mouths have a particular problem, and that is our hearts! Our lips will only speak what we have allowed to develop within our hearts. Matthew 12:34b says, "For out of the abundance of the heart the mouth speaketh."

Second, God's judgment came **Because of Their Actions** ("and their doings are against the Lord"). This is a progressive problem. Our announcements are followed by our actions. If we talk about an action, we will eventually do it. Hosea 7:2 says, "And they consider not in their hearts that I remember all their wickedness: *now their own doings have beset them about*; they are before my face." Those actions that defy the Word of God and His ways are called *sin, iniquity, transgression, error, trespass, lawlessness,* and *unbelief.* Man acts like he does not understand why God has a problem with our sinful actions. Yet God is not playing around with the sin of man. Isaiah 59:2 says, "But your iniquities have separated between you and your God, and your sins have hid his face from you, that he will not hear."

Third, God brought judgment and wrath **Because of Their Audacity** ("to provoke the eyes of his glory"). The spirit behind this sin is presumptuous in nature and actually tempts the glory of God. The word for "provoke" means "cause to make bitter." How could someone actually think to do that to God? In the time in which we live, such a spirit is much more prevalent than we might think! We provoke God to jealousy by our disloyal and unfaithful hearts. We allow our desires to govern our worship, and so we start worshiping ourselves and serving our flesh instead of loving God. This is no different than when the devil tempted Christ in the desert and demanded that Christ bow and worship him (Matthew 4:8–10). Some would look at that instance in amazement at the audacity of Satan. Yet, his attitude was no different than ours when we desire God to do things our way. We have tried to turn God into our little slave or servant boy. This kind of audacity will lead us to a place of utter destruction. Let us take note of the failings of Jerusalem and Judah in this verse and keep ourselves from the place of God's judgment.

TOPICS: Actions, Mouth, Rebellion, Sin, Tongue, Worship

July 26

DAILY BIBLE READING: Isaiah 4–7

TODAY'S VERSE: Isaiah 5:2: "And he fenced it, and gathered out the stones thereof, and planted it with the choicest vine, and built a tower in the midst of it, and also made a winepress therein: and he looked that it should bring forth grapes, and it brought forth wild grapes."

WE ARE GIVEN a similar account of a vine that God brought out of Egypt in Psalm 80:8–16. Though this story was given with a different meaning, there is no doubt that references to God's "vine" are talking about God's people. You can hear God's love and disappointment for this vine as He mournfully asks in verse 4a, "What could have been done more to my vineyard, that I have not done in it?" As Isaiah paints us a picture of God's anger and judgment upon His people, we must be reminded that God is giving us the same opportunity to honor Him with our lives and our substance.

The Protection of His Vineyard ("And he fenced it"). Every garden needs protection. The Song of Solomon 4:12 says, "A garden inclosed is my sister, my spouse; a spring shut up, a fountain sealed." It is fenced to protect it from predators and those who would trample its tender plants. The boundaries that have been set by the great Gardener are a mercy extended to the inhabitants of the garden.

The Preparation of His Vineyard ("and gathered out the stones thereof"). Pulling out stones is hard work, especially in stony ground. I live in the Rocky Mountain region in the high desert. There is a reason they call them the "Rocky" Mountains! It seems that our soil grows rocks: even if you get rid of them one year, you have to do it again the next, and the year after that, and so on. It takes time, effort, exertion, and attention to prepare the field to receive the planting of the Lord.

The Planting of His Vineyard ("planted it with the choicest vine"). The word translated "planted" means "to strike." Have you ever thought about how God started our vine? He started by being "stricken"! Isaiah 53:4 says, "Surely he hath borne our griefs, and carried our sorrows: yet we did esteem him stricken, smitten of God, and afflicted." This vine is "the choicest vine"! Adam Clarke says in his commentary on this verse that many believe it refers to the Valley of Sorek, which was famous for its wine. The upper Valley of Sorek was the same place as Eschol, where the Israelites found clusters of grapes so big that they would put them on a staff and bear them between each other.[4] Literally, the word translated "choicest vine" means "in the sense of redness; a vine stock (properly, one yielding purple grapes, the richest variety)." We are blood-thought, blood-bought, and blood-wrought! And we are of the "richest variety" according to the will of God!

The Power of His Vineyard ("and built a tower in the midst of it"). We could call this the "Tower of Power." The word translated "midst" means "to sever, a bisection, the center." What tower has God built in the midst? We have a great tower here in our garden. It is a tower that the world despises, for it is connected to shame! Paul said in Galatians 6:14, "But God forbid that I should glory, save in *the cross* of our Lord Jesus Christ, by whom the world is crucified unto me, and I unto the world."

The Production of His Vineyard ("and also made a winepress therein"). God has an expectancy of harvest, for He has made a wine press. You don't plant a vineyard for its looks, but for its fruit! Jesus said in John 15:5, "I am the vine, ye are the branches: he that abideth in me, and I in him, the same bringeth forth much fruit."

The Problem of His Vineyard ("and he looked that it should bring forth grapes, and it brought forth wild grapes"). Though we have a great Gardener who expects a harvest from His vineyard, He has not violated our free will. The Hebrew definition for "wild grapes" means "poison-berries; wild grapes." If we would obey the Word of the Lord, we would not bear wild grapes, but fruit in which He can be pleased.

TOPICS: Calvary, Christ, Cross, Fruit, Gardening, Power, Preparation, Protection, Sin

---

4   Adam Clarke, *Holy Bible with Commentary and Critical Notes*, Vol 3. (New York: B. Waugh and T. Mason for the Methodist Episcopal Church, 1846), 694.

R. CHRIS HANKS

DAILY BIBLE READING: Isaiah 8-10

TODAY'S VERSE: Isaiah 9:6: "For unto us a child is born, unto us a son is given: and the government shall be upon his shoulder: and his name shall be called Wonderful, Counsellor, The mighty God, The everlasting Father, The Prince of Peace."

THOUGH THIS VERSE FALLS in our reading in the midst of summer, it brings forth thoughts of Christmas! This is one of scores of prophecies concerning the coming of the Messiah. Many Jews today are still waiting for the Messiah to come. They have completely missed the reality of His birth, His miracles and works upon the earth, His sacrifice for fallen man, His ascension to the Father, and His indwelling of every believer by His Spirit. If there is a reason to rejoice today, it is that this verse has already come to pass. We rejoice in this child! Let every carol flood your heart with joy as you think on this verse today.

The Wonder about Him ("For unto us a child is born, unto us a son is given"). The incarnation is a wonder that man will never understand. It shows us the love of God, from His *inventions* to His *intentions*. We hear this same thought in John 1:14: "And the Word was made flesh, and dwelt among us, (and we beheld his glory, the glory as of the only begotten of the Father,) full of grace and truth." God came not as the Almighty, though He was almighty. It is often said at funerals what Paul said in 1 Timothy 6:7: "For we brought nothing into this world, and it is certain we can carry nothing out." Yet, Christ came into this world so that one day He could take us all out with Him! What a wonder was wrapped in the form of a little child!

The Weight upon Him ("and the government shall be upon his shoulder"). The responsibility of God's laws all rest upon Christ. That is why He fulfilled all the law when He was upon this earth. Abraham asked the question in Genesis 18:25b, "Shall not the Judge of all the earth do right?" That was the burden Christ carried upon this earth. Everything in the Christian life is centered around His righteousness. Romans 10:4 tells us about His righteousness and what it means to us: "For Christ is the end of the law for righteousness to every one that believeth." There is no other who can bear up the weight of God's eternal and perfect government and satisfy the demands of divine judgment.

The Worship Due Him ("and his name shall be called Wonderful, Counsellor, The mighty God, The everlasting Father, The Prince of Peace"). Five names are listed here (five, as we've seen, is the number of grace). One has to do with His *personality,* one His *psychology,* another His *power,* yet another His *paternity,* and yet another His *position,* but all have to do with His *preeminence.* Hearing these names should make you desire to bow your head in reverence and adoration of the divinity and holiness of Jesus Christ, our Saviour and Redeemer.

TOPICS: Christ, Christ's Birth, Incarnation, Righteousness, Salvation, Worship

July 28

DAILY BIBLE READING: Isaiah 11–15

TODAY'S VERSE: Isaiah 14:9: "Hell from beneath is moved for thee to meet thee at thy coming: it stirreth up the dead for thee, even all the chief ones of the earth; it hath raised up from their thrones all the kings of the nations."

TODAY'S SCHEDULED CHAPTERS run the gamut of God's dealings with man, from His mercy and love to the horrors of hell and the defeat of Satan. Hell is a topic that is often ignored in Christianity today. It is almost as if people believe that if we don't talk about it, it will just go away. What a sad day when we find a way around a topic that is spoken of more in the Bible than heaven itself! This verse is primarily speaking of Nebuchadnezzar, the king of Babylon. This was a great warning from God to Nebuchadnezzar to change his ways, for judgment was nigh. But the warning is not for him only. The truth is that if the warning was true for Nebuchadnezzar, then it is true for everyone else who has not put his or her faith in Christ, for "God is no respecter of persons" (Acts 10:34). Here are a few thoughts about the reality and character of hell that we should contemplate.

The **Excitability of Hell** ("Hell from beneath is moved for thee"). Hell is a voracious monster that will never be satisfied. It is excited by every unbelieving soul that is brought under the power of death and sent there for eternity to suffer the torments of denying Christ. Isaiah 5:14 says, "Therefore hell hath enlarged herself, and opened her mouth without measure." Hell grows and grows with the excited hope of receiving more and more to fulfill its insatiable appetite. It displays unequaled enthusiasm for those who are evil and have rejected the way and the Word of God.

The **Inevitability of Hell** ("Hell from beneath is moved for thee *to meet thee at thy coming*"). For every evil heart that has denied, rejected, and spit in the face of Calvary's cross and the perfect sacrifice of Jesus Christ, there is but one fate that lies ahead. It is not a possibility; it is a fact! Hell is happy to come and meet you. It is more excited about your arrival than the dog that greets you at the door with a wagging tail.

The **Brutality of Hell** ("it stirreth up the dead for thee, even all the chief ones of the earth; it hath raised up from their thrones all the kings of the nations"). Let there be no misunderstanding about what is happening in this verse. There will be no great meetings and parties in hell that people will enjoy. No sinner will ever enjoy the company of another in this place of eternal anguish. All you will hear will be the endless cries of ultimate suffering. This part of the verse, however, tells of others that hell "stirreth up" for us, including "all the chief ones" and "all the kings of the nations." Here, we understand the sadistic glee of those in great agony and distress. You will not find greater brutality than in those who rejoice in the pain and suffering of another. Those men who have sold their souls and used their positions on the earth to dominate, destroy, and strike dread into the hearts of people will rejoice when one from their own ranks comes to join them in their demise.

The truth of this verse should encourage our hearts to share the gospel with the lost so that they do not go to this place of eternal damnation. If there should be a lost soul reading this devotion today, know that your hope of escape from this horrible place can only be found in trusting Jesus Christ as your personal Saviour. Trust in Him today, and place your reservation in an eternal home in heaven!

TOPICS: Hell, Judgment, Pride, Punishment, Torment

R. CHRIS HANKS

DAILY BIBLE READING: Isaiah 16–20

TODAY'S VERSE: Isaiah 17:7: "At that day shall a man look to his Maker, and his eyes shall have respect to the Holy One of Israel."

MUCH OF THE BOOK of Isaiah is about different facets of the judgment and chastisement of God. It would do us good to know that the judgment of God is not just meant to be punitive, although that is what we acknowledge most, but to be restorative. In other words, God's judgment is meant to draw us back into His loving, merciful favor and restore our fellowship with Him once again.

We find here that God's correction is to **Bring Us Back to Reality** ("At that day shall a man look to his Maker"). It is almost as if we can hear this man saying, "What have I been doing?" We need the "smelling salts" of the judgment of God to bring us right back to the reality of life's meaning and ministry! Too many Christians want to live the Christian life, but they want to live it without restrictions, and they resent the principles and precepts of the Word of God. They fight to "regain their Christian liberty." What a false line of reasoning! Christian liberty has never negated the holiness of God! As a matter of fact, we have all the liberty in heaven and on earth to live our lives for God under the authority found in His Word. Some would say there is a contradiction here. There is no contradiction to the person who has learned to walk in the Spirit! It is the judgment of God that will bring us back to the reality of who He is.

God's correction is to **Bring Us Back to Repentance** ("At that day shall a man *look to his Maker*"). This implies a difference from the way he had been looking. "Repentance" actually means "to change the mind." After the judgment of God, an immediate change caused this man to cast his eyes heavenward and look to the Source of all life. We need to be refocused upon God and set our eyes upon Him in love and tenderness. The hymn writer Helen Howarth Lemmel wrote, "Turn your eyes upon Jesus/Look full in His wonderful face/And the things of earth will grow strangely dim/In the light of His glory and grace." Look to Him and live!

God's correction will **Bring Us Back to Respect** ("and his eyes shall have respect"). Isn't disrespect often the real reason for our sin and the basis of our pride? The nation of Israel, much like people today, had lost their awe of God. It is the ultimate disrespect to be like the Laodicean church in Revelation 3. Just like them, we are lukewarm and increased with goods. We think we have need of nothing. Revelation 3:17b says of them that they "knowest not that thou art wretched, and miserable, and poor, and blind, and naked." We need God more now than ever before! Don't dismiss the chastisement and punishment of God, for it can be your greatest blessing, taking you by the hand to show you the place of respect that you once had.

And finally, God's correction will **Bring Us Back to Remembrance** ("and his eyes shall have respect to the Holy One of Israel"). How easily we forget who our God is! But now we see Him again as the the Holy One of Israel and are reminded of His great redemptive work, of His plan that included "the Lamb slain from the foundation of the world" (Revelation 13:8). Praise the Lord for everything that reminds us of Him!

TOPICS: Forgiveness, Remembrance, Repentance, Respect, Revival, Trust

DAILY BIBLE READING: Isaiah 21–24

TODAY'S VERSE: Isaiah 23:9: "The LORD of hosts hath purposed it, to stain the pride of all the glory, and to bring into contempt all the honourable of the earth."

MANY OF THESE VERSES are talking about Tyre, a great but very wicked city. One thing we must remember concerning cities, kings, countries, and governments is that it is God who raises them up and brings them down. They are not great because of what they are, for in a moment, God can turn them into nothing. This verse will help us see the danger of our personal pride so that we might humble ourselves before the Lord.

We see **God's Enticement Against Man's Arrogance** ("The LORD of hosts hath purposed it"). As we read about the exaltation of Tyre, we find, beginning in this verse, that the Lord purposed to bring it down. God will actually entice proud souls to lift themselves up before God so that He might bring upon them swift destruction. This is exactly what happened when God hardened the heart of Pharaoh. Pharaoh's first response to Moses is found in Exodus 5:2: "And Pharaoh said, Who is the LORD, that I should obey his voice to let Israel go? I know not the LORD, neither will I let Israel go." For ten times after that, Pharaoh's heart was hardened, to the end that he might be destroyed. There is nothing so easily enticed as man's pride. Once man thinks "more highly [of himself] than he ought to think" (Romans 12:3), it is an easy road to lifting himself up before God. Let us remember Lucifer, the son of the morning, who once sat in the presence of God and saw His majesty and glory. Yet, after seeing God's glory, instead of humbling himself, he lifted himself up and declared that he would depose God and take His throne to rule all creation, leading to his becoming Satan (see Isaiah 14:12–14). Once pride *sets in,* God begins to *set up* for the certain downfall of the proud.

Next, we see **God's Endeavor Against Man's Arrogance** ("to stain the pride of all the glory"). The word translated "stain" means "to bore, to wound, to begin as if by an opening wedge." God's purpose is to destroy man's pride. He must destroy man's pride if He is ever to be glorified. He begins to bore through the hardened substance of man's conceit with the sole purpose of destruction. This is the first little hole in the great dam of man's pride. Once that first hole is made, it is just a matter of time before the whole dam comes crashing down. This work of God will "stain the pride of *all* the glory." There will not be any glory upon the earth that will be able to stand against the work of God.

Last, we see **God's Effortlessness Against Man's Arrogance** ("and to bring into contempt all the honourable of the earth"). The word for "contempt" means "to be light, literally swift, small, sharp, easy." It is no contest for the Lord to stand against man's small being and false sense of invincibility. The English definition of "contempt" is "the act of despising."[5] This little nugget from Noah Webster's 1828 American Dictionary of the English Language is even more revealing: "This word is one of the strongest expressions of a mean opinion which the language affords." God is bringing into contempt "all the honorable of the earth" because of their pride, and He is doing it with the greatest of ease! First Peter 5:5–6 tells us, "Likewise, ye younger, submit yourselves unto the elder. Yea, all of you be subject one to another, and be clothed with humility: *for God resisteth the proud, and giveth grace to the humble. Humble yourselves therefore under the mighty hand of God,* that he may exalt you in due time."

TOPICS: Arrogance, Foolishness, Pride

---

5   *Noah Webster's First Edition of an American Dictionary of The English Language* (Chesapeake, VA: Foundation For American Christian Education, 1995)

DAILY BIBLE READING: Isaiah 25-28

TODAY'S VERSE: Isaiah 26:3: "Thou wilt keep him in perfect peace, whose mind is stayed on thee: because he trusteth in thee."

WHAT A BLESSED VERSE for us to study today! In chapters 25 and 26, Isaiah is moved to openly offer his praise to the Lord and claim God as his salvation. The world is clamoring today to know true peace. This is a time of terrorism and uncertainty in the money market, and fear grips every page of the newspaper. In the day in which we live, it is good to know that there is "perfect peace" to be had! Much is said about peace in the Bible. God wants us to have real and true peace. Jesus said in John 14:27, "Peace I leave with you, my peace I give unto you: not as the world giveth, give I unto you. Let not your heart be troubled, neither let it be afraid." Not only is this peace real, but it is offered by our Lord and accessible by His Spirit. Here are a few thoughts about this special peace.

It Is a Protected Peace ("Thou wilt keep him in perfect peace"). The word for "keep" means "guarded." God is guarding us in the provision and maintenance of His peace! What kind of peace is it? Perfect peace! The Hebrew word for "peace" here is *shalom*. The verse actually says, "Thou wilt keep him in *shalom shalom*"—"peace peace." Can you think of anything more perfect than that? To have peace given upon peace truly is *perfect* peace! The New Testament speaks of this perfect peace in Philippians 4:7: "And the peace of God, which passeth all understanding, shall keep your hearts and minds through Christ Jesus." This is expressed beautifully in the old hymn, "Peace, peace, wonderful peace/Coming down from the Father above/Sweep over my spirit forever, I pray/In fathomless billows of love."[6]

It Is a Propped Peace ("whose mind is stayed on thee"). Yes, the word translated "stayed" here means "to prop, to lean upon or to take hold of." So many people have their peace "propped up" by their money, the current status of a relationship, or a happiness that is based upon "good happenings" and not upon Christ. All of these things will one day fall down. The stock market will turn, there will be an unexpected bill or illness, but God's peace will still be there. The status of a relationship can change in a moment when blame is passed around, expectations are not met, or immoral behaviors are exposed, but God's peace will still be there. If your happiness is based upon good happenings and not God-given joy, just wait, those happenings will change and so will your happiness—but God's peace will still be there for the one who has wholly leaned upon it! Make sure that your mind is propped up by God, for He will never leave nor forsake you!

It Is a Persuaded Peace ("because he trusteth in thee"). This verse carries the meaning of a place to go "for refuge, to trust, be confident, sure." That sounds like God and my precious Jesus to me! Because I am fully confident in Him, my mind is "stayed" upon Him. All of these things are dependent one upon the other. It is my trust in God that develops my dependence upon God, and it is my dependence upon God that moves God to protect me in His perfect peace! If this is my promised end, then, O my soul, trust thou in God and Him alone! What a great promise of peace lays ahead for the soul that has learned to trust in Him with conviction! The well-known words of Proverbs 3:5-6 help us with this: "Trust in the LORD with all thine heart; and lean not unto thine own understanding. In all thy ways acknowledge him, and he shall direct thy paths." Once your trust is completely placed in God, you will find that this perfect peace in your life is a persuaded peace in your heart!

TOPICS: Confidence, Faith, Joy, Peace, Protection, Trust

---

6   The hymn quoted is "Wonderful Peace" by W.D. Cornell.

DAILY BIBLE READING: Isaiah 29–32

TODAY'S VERSE: Isaiah 30:21: "And thine ears shall hear a word behind thee, saying, This is the way, walk ye in it, when ye turn to the right hand, and when ye turn to the left."

WHAT A BLESSING to study this verse today! There is never a time in which we do not need the Word of God, but sometimes God will bless us with a special word to help us along the way. Here are a few simple thoughts from this verse to encourage us for the road that lies ahead.

The Caring Ministry of the Word of God ("And thine ears shall hear a word behind thee, saying . . ."). This verse pictures the sound of the shepherd's voice calling from behind to his sheep as they travel. The importance of this word is that it is not based upon the intelligence or even the awareness of the sheep, but upon the grace of God. There will be dark times when we need such a word. There will be uncertain times when we need such a word. There will be unknown times when we need such a word. Thank God for the unfailing presence of the Word of God in our lives!

The Clarifying Ministry of the Word of God ("This is the way"). If there is anything we need today, clarity is it! A clear path, a definite path, an illumined path: these are all things our hearts should desire the Lord to reveal to us as we follow Him. Yogi Berra, the renowned New York Yankee baseball catcher known for his wit and "Yogi-isms," is credited with saying, "When you come to a fork in the road, take it." That sounds good, but it is not possible in the Christian life. A choice must be made, and we must make the right choice. How are we to know which way to go in this crazy, upside-down, topsy-turvy world where evil is good and good is evil? There is only one way—the Word of God! The Word of God will make clear every step we need to take. Psalm 37:23 says, "The steps of a good man are ordered by the LORD: and he delighteth in his way."

The Commanding Ministry of the Word of God ("walk ye in it"). God's direction is not up to a vote. Once we hear the Word of God, we must obey! The command in this verse is progressive, for we are to "walk" in it. The commands of God give us something to do, but they also give us something to *continue doing*. This idea is found in Ephesians 2:10: "For we are his workmanship, created in Christ Jesus unto good works, which God hath before ordained that *we should walk in them.*"

The Convincing Ministry of the Word of God ("when ye turn to the right hand, and when ye turn to the left"). Wherever the will of God will take us, the Word of God will help us! If this is not convincing enough of a promise for you, then nothing will be! Stateside or on the foreign field, the Word of God will work. In places we often go or have never been before, the Word of God will work. If we are carrying out our regular plans or something we have never tried before, the Word of God will work! What a blessing and a promise we have concerning the inerrant and infallible Word of God!

TOPICS: Bible, Care, Direction, Word of God

R. CHRIS HANKS

DAILY BIBLE READING: Isaiah 33–36

TODAY'S VERSE: Isaiah 33:16: "He shall dwell on high: his place of defence shall be the munitions of rocks: bread shall be given him; his waters shall be sure."

TODAY'S VERSE IS CONNECTED to verse 15, which describes a righteous man: "He that walketh righteously, and speaketh uprightly; he that despiseth the gain of oppressions, that shaketh his hands from holding of bribes, that stoppeth his ears from hearing of blood, and shutteth his eyes from seeing evil." The blessing of our verse is dependent upon the righteous life lived in verse 15. God is still looking to bless those who walk uprightly and obey His laws. I love to read about God's blessings. We can rejoice in them, for they promise that our work is *not in vain!* We are told in Galatians 6:9, "And let us not be weary in well doing: for in due season we shall reap, if we faint not."

The **Dwelling of a Righteous Man's Home** ("He shall dwell on high"). The word translated "dwelling" comes from "the idea of lodging, to reside, permanently stay." This is a place we will enjoy forever. Psalm 16:8 says, "I have set the LORD always before me: because he is at my right hand, I shall not be moved." Not only is it a *permanent* place, but it is a *prominent* place, for the verse says, "He shall dwell *on high*." We have been told the same thing in Ephesians 2:6: "And hath raised us up together, and *made us sit together in heavenly places in Christ Jesus.*" Some argue that they are not worthy of such an honor. I have to agree! None of us are worthy. That is what makes God's grace so amazing! James 4:10 says, "Humble yourselves in the sight of the Lord, and *he shall lift you up.*"

The **Defense of a Righteous Man's Life** ("his place of defence shall be the munitions of rocks"). The word for "defence" means "a cliff (or other lofty or inaccessible place)." This has to do with exaltation to a *summit.* That sounds like a good place to be! The word for "munitions" means "a fastness (as a covert of ambush):—castle, fort, (strong) hold." This has to do with *strength.* The word for "rocks" means "a craggy rock, a fortress." This has to do with *security.* Praise the Lord for a sanctuary from trouble! Remember that this place is supplied by God for His people.

The **Delivery of a Righteous Man's Bread** ("bread shall be given him"). This sounds like an early-morning delivery of fresh-baked bread for God's people! Jesus mentioned this in His model prayer for His disciples in Matthew 6:11 when He said, "Give us this day our daily bread." God wants to supply our every need. He will not leave us destitute and forsaken. I am always blessed by Matthew 15:32: "Then Jesus called his disciples unto him, and said, I have compassion on the multitude, because they continue with me now three days, and have nothing to eat: and *I will not send them away fasting,* lest they faint in the way." God will supply every spiritual and physical need so that we may glorify Him!

The **Dependability of a Righteous Man's Water** ("his waters shall be sure"). Man can live longer without food than he can without water. The word translated "sure" means "to build up or support; to foster as a parent or nurse; to render (or be) firm or faithful." What sure and secure waters He has promised to the righteous man! In that desert climate in the Middle East, the supply of water was paramount. Jesus said to the woman at Jacob's well in Samaria in John 4:14, "But whosoever drinketh of the water that I shall give him shall never thirst; but the water that I shall give him shall be in him a well of water springing up into everlasting life." Those, my friend, are *sure* waters!

TOPICS: Exaltation, Godliness, Holiness, Protection, Righteousness, Salvation, Supply

DAILY BIBLE READING: Isaiah 37–39

TODAY'S VERSE: Isaiah 38:18: "For the grave cannot praise thee, death can not celebrate thee: they that go down into the pit cannot hope for thy truth."

THE WORDS "LAST CHANCE" are powerful in both good and bad ways. A run on a bank is the last chance to withdraw your money before you lose it. A "going out of business" sign usually means a last chance to get what you want at a really good price. I will never forget almost making a deal on a car I wanted. The car dealer called with his final offer, my last chance to take it. I rejected it. It was hard hanging up the phone and knowing that I had just lost my last chance. We all need to know that life on this earth is our last chance to serve God, praise Him, and make things right with Him before we move into eternity. Let us make the most of this last chance!

We Have One Chance to Expound ("For the grave cannot praise thee"). The word translated "praise" comes from a root meaning "the hand, to throw." This reminds me of a performer being honored by flowers thrown upon the stage. Literally, *this life is our last chance to use our fleshly lips to throw our praises toward God* for His wonderful works and His infinite love. What a wasted life it truly would be if we never recognized His hand and thanked Him for His work. Don't wait, for one day it will be too late!

We Have One Chance to Express ("death can not celebrate thee"). The word for "celebrate" means "to be clear (orig. of sound, but usually of color); to shine." It is actually the root *halal,* used at the beginning of *hallelujah.* I love the idea of "color" and "shining" in our thoughts of God! That sounds like a celebration, doesn't it? We are all artists making pieces of work to honor and glorify God in our lives. How do you color God? How do you express your thoughts and make God clear and shining in the eyes of others? Don't wait, for one day it will be too late!

We Have One Chance to Expect ("they that go down into the pit cannot hope for thy truth"). The word translated "hope" means "to expect." What a blessing it is to know that we can have eternal life! That is not a hope in the sense of possibility, but in the sense of expectation! The fate of those who have died is already sealed; their last chance to change it is gone. Those who accept Christ are assured of heaven, but those who reject Him have condemned themselves to eternal damnation. But eternal destination is not the only issue at hand. In his letters, Paul not only discussed the security of his salvation, but also his commitment to living the Christian life with every fiber of his physical body. He knew that this was his last chance! Philippians 1:20 says, "According to my earnest expectation and my hope, that in nothing I shall be ashamed, but that with all boldness, as always, so now also Christ shall be magnified in my body, whether it be by life, or by death." I remember my soccer coach yelling on the sidelines just before timeout, "This is your last chance! Do your best! Leave it all on the soccer field!" So I say to you! Give it all, my friend, for there will be no new opportunities to serve the Lord or make an impact for Christ! Give all of yourself in your worship and your service!

TOPICS: Dedication, Praise, Service, Worship

DAILY BIBLE READING: Isaiah 40–42

TODAY'S VERSE: Isaiah 40:31: "But they that wait upon the Lord shall renew their strength; they shall mount up with wings as eagles; they shall run, and not be weary; and they shall walk, and not faint."

THIS IS ONE of the most well-known verses in the Bible and in the book of Isaiah in particular. Should you go to any Christian bookstore at any given time, you will find a picture, book, or card with a soaring eagle upon it and this verse underneath. This verse has helped many people at different times to draw strength from God and caused them to continue in the face of adversity.

The proposition of this verse is found in its very first phrase: "But they that wait upon the Lord." The rest of the verse is dependent upon this thought. The interesting root behind the word "wait" means "to bind together, perhaps by twisting." Picture a hay field. When the hay is cut, it is left to dry for a few days. There is not much strength in hay. It does not have the ability to bear up any weight or to be used to add strength to a structure. But then the baler comes, gathers it, binds it with twine, and leaves it to be retrieved later. When it is "bound together" as a bale, hay has much strength! If we take things that seem simple, weak, and worthless and bind them together in faith, we will have something strong that can bear up against any weight or force.

Waiting upon God Has a Molting Ministry ("shall renew their strength"). Many connect this phrase directly to the eagle in the next phrase. Psalm 103:5 says, "Who satisfieth thy mouth with good things; so that thy youth is renewed like the eagle's." How are an eagle's youth and strength renewed? It is known that eagles live to a very old age. Yet, I have heard it said that in his old age, the eagle will go through a molting process that brings renewed vigor to his strength. It doesn't matter what your problem and dilemma might be, nor does your age matter; you can have renewed strength by waiting upon the Lord. This molting has to do with a *change!*

Waiting upon God Has a Mounting Ministry ("they shall mount up with wings as eagles"). The word translated "mount" literally means "to ascend." Very few people today are mounting in their Christian lives. Most are just trying to stay steady. They are not pushing themselves to greater heights in their faith, nor are they attempting more in their service; they have accepted the status quo. Where are those Christians who are "always abounding in the work of the Lord" (1 Corinthians 15:58)? This mounting has to do with a *challenge.*

Waiting upon God Has a Moving Ministry ("they shall run, and not be weary"). The Bible makes it very clear that we are in a great race, though "the race is not to the swift" (Ecclesiastes 9:11). First Corinthians 9:24 confirms this by saying, "Know ye not that they which run in a race run all, but one receiveth the prize? So run, that ye may obtain." The key here is not to finish first. We are commanded in this verse just to "run, that ye may obtain." The word for "weary" means "to gasp, to be exhausted." Many have become tired in their Christian lives and don't think they can go on one more step. If that is you, you need to learn to "wait upon the Lord." This moving ministry has to do with a *charge.*

Waiting upon God Has a Marching Ministry ("and they shall walk, and not faint"). Though we are in a race, the Bible refers to the Christian life as a *walk.* Many times in Scripture we are commanded to "walk in the Spirit," "walk in love," and "walk in faith." Adam and Eve knew this in the garden, for God came walking to them in the cool of the day to spend time with His creation. God still desires for us to walk with Him. This marching ministry has to do with *cheer.* There is nothing like walking with the Lord every day in this life!

In this verse, we have gone through a slow progression downward. We have gone from mounting to running and now to walking. No matter what attitude or challenge we face, we must be strong in the Lord!

TOPICS: Ministry, Perseverance, Revival, Strength, Waiting

August 5

DAILY BIBLE READING: Isaiah 43–45

TODAY'S VERSE: Isaiah 43:19: "Behold, I will do a new thing; now it shall spring forth; shall ye not know it? I will even make a way in the wilderness, and rivers in the desert."

IN THIS CHAPTER, the Lord speaks to the nation of Israel and gives them a great blessing in telling them of His love and reassuring them that He has not forgotten them. In fact, He tells them that their deliverance from Babylon will be greater than their deliverance from Egypt when they walked through the Red Sea. There are three main thoughts in this verse that may help us understand God's work in our lives as well.

First is the **Promise of a New Thing** ("Behold, I will do a new thing"). This has to do with God's **freshness.** He is telling His people about a new creation. The word for "new thing" literally means "fresh." We are drawn to things that are new. Modern marketers even package and sell that "new car" smell! Second Corinthians 5:17 says, "Therefore if any man be in Christ, he is a new creature: old things are passed away; behold, all things are become new." I have news for you, my friend: God is constantly doing new things in the life of a believer to keep the freshness of salvation real! Lamentations 3:22–23 speaks about "new mercies": "It is of the LORD's mercies that we are not consumed, because his compassions fail not. They are new every morning: great is thy faithfulness." There are many other things God can and will make new in a Christian's life: He gives new hope, new joy, new life, new beginnings, and a new outlook.

Second is the **Promise of New Springs** ("now it shall spring forth"). The word for "spring" does not have anything to do with water: it actually means "to sprout, bear, or bring forth." This has to do with God's **fruit.** This is a promise we can all anticipate in our Christian lives. Fruit-bearing is God's great desire for us as we live for Him! John 15:8 says, "Herein is my Father glorified, *that ye bear much fruit; so shall ye be my disciples.*" God wants us to bear fruit with such great desire that He is willing to do it for us. Galatians 5:22–23 tells us of *the fruit of the Spirit:* "But the fruit of the Spirit is love, joy, peace, longsuffering, gentleness, goodness, faith, meekness, temperance: against such there is no law." What a promise this is to us as we contemplate its immediate work, for "now it shall spring forth"!

Third is the **Promise of New Streams** ("I will even make a way in the wilderness, and rivers in the desert"). This has to do with God's **feeding.** New water always brings new life. When water comes in the desert, it is not just fruit that comes in response: *everything* comes back to life. A couple of years ago, Death Valley received an incredible amount of rain. Because of that rain and the abundance of water that ran for a short time in the valley, the entire valley bloomed with flowers from seeds that had been there for years upon years.[1] There are seeds in your life that have been deposited by ravaging winds in seeming places of desolation, but when the water of God's Word or the river of a revival begins to flow, you will find that those places of desolation begin to bloom with the blessing and life of Almighty God! Remember, no matter how dead and desolate that place in your heart seems to be, Jesus said, "I am the way, the truth, and the life" (John 14:6). He is *all* life! He can bring life in places which seem to have no hope. A few days ago, we read Isaiah 32:15, which says, "Until the spirit be poured upon us from on high, and the wilderness be a fruitful field, and the fruitful field be counted for a forest." Thank God for the beautiful rain of the Holy Ghost that will make new streams and new rivers in our lives!

TOPICS: Fruit, New Life, Promises, Supply, Sustenance

---

1   J. Michael Lester, *Streams in the Desert* (Lancaster, CA: Striving Together Publications, 2005), 103.

R. CHRIS HANKS

DAILY BIBLE READING: Isaiah 46–49

TODAY'S VERSE: Isaiah 49:10: "They shall not hunger nor thirst; neither shall the heat nor sun smite them: for he that hath mercy on them shall lead them, even by the springs of water shall he guide them."

WE HAVE COME to the part of Isaiah in which Jehovah reassures Israel of His love for them by the promise of the Messiah, the Holy One. He confirms His faithfulness to them, though they had forsaken Him. This verse gives many great and tremendous promises for the nation of Israel which are also applicable to us today. According to Romans 11:17, we have been grafted in the place of Israel and now receive the promises of God's love and care for His people: "And if some of the branches be broken off, and thou, being a wild olive tree, wert graffed in among them, and with them partakest of the root and fatness of the olive tree." Let us remember, though, that Israel will receive all their promises one day and that we should be humbled because of our position in Christ, for God is able to graft them again! Let's look more closely at the promises today.

There is a **Promise of His Provision** ("They shall not hunger nor thirst"). There are many verses in the Bible concerning God's provision for His people, none of which are more well-known than Philippians 4:19: "But my God shall supply all your need according to his riches in glory by Christ Jesus." We can see God's heart to provide even when the disciples were trying to send the multitudes away, and Jesus told them, "I will not send them away fasting" (Matthew 15:32). Hallelujah for a God who knows and supplies every one of our needs!

There Is a **Promise of His Protection** ("neither shall the heat nor sun smite them"). At times, we need protection from the elements which are beyond our control. To have the God of the universe protect us from those things we cannot control gives us faith and trust in Him and His ability. Psalm 121:5–6 says, "The Lord is thy keeper: the Lord is thy shade upon thy right hand. The sun shall not smite thee by day, nor the moon by night." What a promise—not just of protection, but of comfortable protection!

There Is a **Promise of His Presence** ("for he that hath mercy on them shall lead them"). If someone is going to lead me, I want it to be someone who already has mercy upon me! Notice what the verse says: "For he that *hath* mercy." It does not say "For he that *had* mercy." This is not a past mercy, but a present and continuing mercy that we enjoy every day! Whenever God speaks of His people, He always speaks of leading them, not of driving them. A good shepherd will lead his flock, but a bad one will drive it and destroy it! Whenever God uses the word "drive," He is always talking about His enemies. William Bradbury wrote in the hymn "He Leadeth Me," "He leadeth me, O blessed thought!/O words with heav'nly comfort fraught!/Whate'er I do, where'er I be/Still 'tis God's hand that leadeth me!"

There Is a **Promise of His Pleasantness** ("even by the springs of water shall he guide them"). Did you catch that? *"Even* by the springs of water." He will *even* take us there! He will show us many places and testify of many good things, and He will *even* take us to the place that is tender to His heart! He will lead us not only to those things that please us, but to those that please Him most. Why do we fight the places where God is trying to lead us? Do we not know that He knows the way much better than we do? Job 28:23 says, "God understandeth the way thereof, and he knoweth the place thereof." Let us wait and trust in Him, for He doeth all things well!

TOPICS: Mercy, God's Presence, Promises, Protection, Provision

DAILY BIBLE READING: Isaiah 50–53

TODAY'S VERSE: Isaiah 53:6: "All we like sheep have gone astray; we have turned every one to his own way; and the Lord hath laid on him the iniquity of us all."

WHAT A TREMENDOUS VERSE we have to meditate upon this morning! This whole chapter is full of gospel glory as it prophesies of our precious Lord and Saviour Jesus Christ and His great work on the cross. There are only a few chapters in the Old Testament that carry the gospel so clearly and explain the crucifixion as this chapter does. As we look at this verse, may we think of our failures in sin and of God's faithfulness in salvation.

First, we see **Our Inclusion in Failure** ("All we like sheep"). Notice that this verse begins with "All we." This truth, however hard it is to hear, must be accepted in order for us to receive the free gift of salvation. Romans 3:23 says, "For *all* have sinned and come short of the glory of God." Not one person reading this devotion is able to exempt him or herself from this horrible inclusion in man's sin. The next part of the verse says we are "like sheep." There is no animal so dumb, so trusting, so stubborn, or so disobedient as a sheep. First Peter 2:25 says, "For ye were as sheep going astray."

Second, we see **Our Indifference in Failure** ("have gone astray"). Human beings have become indifferent to the way of our Lord! We don't really care if we commit some sin. Everybody is doing it! Not only have we come to the point where we do not feel any conviction against sin, but we explain it away and somehow accept that the "end justifies the means." This attitude of indifference is actually a doctrine of demons. First Timothy 4:1–2 says, "Now the Spirit speaketh expressly, that in the latter times some shall depart from the faith, giving heed to seducing spirits, and doctrines of devils; speaking lies in hypocrisy; *having their conscience seared with a hot iron.*" God help us to see our straying from the Word as God sees it!

Third, we see **Our Insolence in Failure** ("we have turned every one to his own way"). It is in our insolent pride and haughty spirit that we have left the way of our Great Shepherd to seek our own way. Isaiah 55:7 says, "Let the wicked forsake his way, and the unrighteous man his thoughts: and let him return unto the Lord, and he will have mercy upon him; and to our God, for he will abundantly pardon." This is closely related to Proverbs 14:12: "There is a way which seemeth right unto a man, but the end thereof are the ways of death." Pride will drive us to seek out our own way as nothing else will do. The word for "sheep" used in this verse comes from a root meaning "to migrate; a collective name for a flock." How many times during our "migration," as our Great Shepherd has led us to the wonderful and grassy fields of His Word, have our eyes desired the grass that seems to be greener on the other side of the fence? We desire to fill our bellies with those things that are away from His presence.

Fourth, we see **Our Iniquity in Failure** ("and the Lord hath laid on him the iniquity of us all"). What a blessed Lord we have! Romans 5:8 says, "But God commendeth his love toward us, in that, *while we were yet sinners, Christ died for us.*" Let's review our main verse for today: "*All we* like sheep *have gone astray;* we have *turned every one to his own way;* and the Lord hath laid on him *the iniquity of us all.*" My, how wicked we are! We sure don't have much to add to this salvation equation, do we? All we have is our sin and "the iniquity of us all" that was laid upon Him! Praise the Lord for His wonderful goodness and His salvation that is nothing less than a miraculous work of grace!

TOPICS: Calvary, Christ, Failure, Pride, Sin, Will

DAILY BIBLE READING: Isaiah 54–58

TODAY'S VERSE: Isaiah 54:1: "Sing, O barren, thou that didst not bear; break forth into singing, and cry aloud, thou that didst not travail with child: for more are the children of the desolate than the children of the married wife, saith the LORD."

THIS FASCINATING VERSE, given to the nation of Israel, is a great encouragement to all who are struggling with their "lot in life." Many Christians are so dissatisfied with what God has allowed to happen to them that they are on the verge of quitting on God and throwing in the towel in their spiritual lives. Some have been let down by family, friends, or even a pastor. But as real as such letdowns may be, no one has ever been let down by God! Today's verse can encourage us in living the Christian life.

We Must Sing Past Our Plight ("Sing, O barren, thou that didst not bear"). The instruction to sing is given to her who is barren. Not only has she not had children, but she will not and cannot have children. Yet God tells her to begin singing by faith! No matter how a situation seems to our understanding, we must ever hold to our hope in Christ and Him alone! The barren woman is commanded to sing by God, who already knows what the end will be! Psalm 42:5 says, "Why art thou cast down, O my soul? and why art thou disquieted in me? hope thou in God: for I shall yet praise him for the help of his countenance." No matter how bad our circumstances might be, and no matter if it seems we have no prospects, we can trust in the Lord and His power.

We Must Shout Past Our Problems ("and cry aloud, thou that didst not travail with child"). The word for "cry" does not mean to shed tears, but "to gleam, be cheerful, to sound clear, bellow." Look more closely at the phrase "Thou that didst not travail with child." You can almost hear people pointing her out and saying, "Look what she didn't do! She didn't have a child! She can't have a child! Ha! She is not as good a Christian as we are, because we have God's blessing!" Can't you hear the taunting of those around her? Yet God's instruction to her is "to gleam, be cheerful, bellow." In the midst of the persecution and jeering of those who look with glee upon your problems, start shouting the victory! Who cares if they call you crazy; they are already calling you barren! I would rather be in love with my Jesus and believe in His Word than have the ease of life but no proof of God's presence. We must realize that God's greatest blessings are often found in places of greatest turmoil and persecution.

We Must See the Potential of His Promises ("for more are the children of the desolate than the children of the married wife, saith the LORD"). The Israelites' joy, though they were in captivity, could not be based on a whim, but on the promises of God! God gave this promise though there seemed to be no reason to believe it would ever happen. We do not even have a timetable of when God's promise would come true. There is no telling how long this poor lady had to endure the taunting of neighbors and the ostracizing of society. But now it did not matter, because she had a promise! God's promises will never fail! Second Corinthians 1:20 says, "For all the promises of God in him are yea, and in him Amen, unto the glory of God by us." Praise God for promises in which we can trust!

TOPICS: Hope, Praise, Promises, Rejoicing, Singing

DAILY BIBLE READING: Isaiah 59–62

TODAY'S VERSE: Isaiah 59:1: "Behold, the Lord's hand is not shortened, that it cannot save; neither his ear heavy, that it cannot hear."

I CANNOT THINK of a more empowering or encouraging verse than this. There may be times when you'll wonder if God is still there or if He is interested in you. This verse expels each of those fears! The word Lord is in all capital letters, telling us that it is the name of Jehovah that is used in the Hebrew. God is as strong as He ever has been, and He can hear and answer your prayer today just as He did in days of old! We can be sure that God is still working His will as He did in the beginning of time. God said in Malachi 3:6, "For I am the Lord, I change not."

The Extension of God's Hand ("Behold, the Lord's hand is not shortened"). This tells us that God is **not little**. The word for "shortened" means "to dock off." There is no place God's loving arm cannot go to reach the vilest of people, and there is no pit so deep that He cannot pull the wickedest of sinners to safety! You do not face any problem that God cannot solve. Take your petitions to Him, for we have a God who *can!*

The Expectation of God's Work ("that it cannot save"). This tells us that God is **not limited**. God is still saving people today! I have heard some say that God cannot save them because of what they have done. My friend, salvation is not based on what you have done as a sinner, but on what He did as a Saviour! Hebrews 7:25 says, "Wherefore *he is able also to save them to the uttermost* that come unto God by him, seeing he ever liveth to make intercession for them." Praise the Lord that He not only is able to save my soul, but He is able to *keep* me saved as well!

The Exercise of God's Will ("neither his ear heavy, that it cannot hear"). This tells us that God is **not lacking**. The word translated "heavy" means "to be heavy, i.e. in a bad sense (burdensome, severe, dull)." What if we had a God too burdened to hear or even care about our prayers? There is no burden He cannot bear. First Peter 5:7 says, "Casting all your care upon him; for he careth for you."

TOPICS: God's Will, God's Work, Hope, Possibilities, Power, Salvation, Trust

R. CHRIS HANKS

DAILY BIBLE READING: Isaiah 63–66

TODAY'S VERSE: Isaiah 66:2: "For all those things hath mine hand made, and all those things have been, saith the LORD: but to this man will I look, even to him that is poor and of a contrite spirit, and trembleth at my word."

GOD BEGINS THIS DISCUSSION by magnifying Himself in the sight of man. In verse 1, He talks about His throne in heaven and declares that the earth is nothing but a footstool. Then He asks the questions, "Where is the house that ye build unto me? and where is the place of my rest?" Sometimes we think too highly of what we have done for God. After all, where would God be without us? Such pride and arrogance deserves a divine rebuke. Listen to God's speech to man, meant to draw our adoration and place it upon Himself.

The Center of God's Authority ("For all those things hath mine hand made, and all those things have been, saith the LORD"). Everything that *is* has been made by the hand of God. God is not impressed by the works of our hands. What we do on our own, we do because God has given us the mind, heart, understanding, and materials! Psalm 24:1 says, "The earth is the LORD's, and the fulness thereof; the world, and they that dwell therein." Solomon says eloquently in 1 Chronicles 29:14, "But who am I, and what is my people, that we should be able to offer so willingly after this sort? for all things come of thee, and *of thine own have we given thee.*"

The Center of God's Affection ("but to this man will I look"). The word for "look" means "to scan, i.e. look intently at; by implication, to regard with pleasure, favor or care." That is how I want God to look at me! If we are talking about God's love, count me in! When I started dating the lady who would one day become my wife, one of the most enjoyable things about her was how she looked at me. Believe me, it was much different from how my own family looked at me! It was even much different from how the rest of *her* family looked at me! Listen carefully, for God is getting ready to tell us about this person to whom He will look with love and grace.

The Center of God's Attention ("even to him that is poor and of a contrite spirit, and trembleth at my word"). The word "poor" here does not have anything to do with financial need; it means "depressed in mind or circumstances." This principle does not bode well for today's self-esteem movement. Our problem is not that we don't think enough about ourselves, but that we think *too much* about ourselves! The Bible teaches us here that we need to "depress" ourselves in the presence of God. The word for "contrite" means "maimed, dejected." Isaiah 57:15 says, "For thus saith the high and lofty One that inhabiteth eternity, whose name is Holy; I dwell in the high and holy place, with him also that is of a contrite and humble spirit, to revive the spirit of the humble, and to revive the heart of the *contrite* ones." Again, Psalm 51:17 says of contrition, "The sacrifices of God are a broken spirit: a broken and a contrite heart, O God, thou wilt not despise." You might ask, "Contrition about what?" That is answered in the last part: "And trembleth at my word." It is all about our respect and reverence for the Word of God. There is no doubt that God will love the man who loves His Word!

TOPICS: Attention, Authority, Bible, Love, Word of God

DAILY BIBLE READING: Jeremiah 1–3

TODAY'S VERSE: Jeremiah 3:15: "And I will give you pastors according to mine heart, which shall feed you with knowledge and understanding."

AMIDST ALL OF THE VERSES talking about "backsliding Israel" and "treacherous Judah," we find this verse assuring Israel of God's continued work to bring them back to Him. God's promise of a pastor was a great mercy to a backsliding people! Though it is generally accepted that God is here speaking of civil rulers who would finally help Israel find God, there is no doubt that God was not mistaken in using a New Testament term and office with which we can identify today. Let's look at the principles in this verse about a good pastor for God's people.

He Is a Present from God ("And I will *give* you"). There is no doubt that a good pastor is a gift from God. Ephesians 4:11–12 tells us plainly that pastors are a gift of God to the people of God: "And *he gave* some, apostles; and some, prophets; and some, evangelists; *and some, pastors and teachers;* for the perfecting of the saints, for the work of the ministry, for the edifying of the body of Christ." We live in a time when God's people do not appreciate the gift God has given them in their pastors. I do not believe you should glorify the man God has given you, for we must only glorify Christ—but you must respect, love, take care of, and be thankful for your pastor. I have been in churches where the people did not think there was any difference in church function between them and their pastor. No such idea is ever found in Scripture. Paul himself told the people in Corinth, "I ought to have been commended of you." Whoever you might be, take a moment and thank God for the pastor that *He* has given you!

He Is a Pastor from God ("pastors according to mine heart"). The word for "pastor" means "to tend a flock." This pastor would be according to the heart of God. Yes, there are preachers who have entered into churches and done nothing but tear down the people and destroy the church, but God does not call these men "pastors." He calls them "hirelings." Some, He even says, "come to you in sheep's clothing, but inwardly they are ravening wolves" (Matthew 7:15). Let me take a moment to talk to any pastor reading this devotional: Be a man after God's own heart! If you catch God's heart for your people, they will love you! We must live by good principles: integrity, honesty, character, and vision are all good things. However, these things alone do not make a man after God's heart. You cannot be a good man of God without those things, but there is still a work that needs to be done to give you a heart for God.

He Leads in Pastures from God ("which shall feed you with knowledge and understanding"). The word for "which shall feed" is the same word for "pastor" that we just discussed. Here is the rest of the definition: "to tend a flock; to pasture it; to graze." Too many preachers today have found no new pastures since Bible college or the last conference they attended in which to feed their people. Acts 20:28 says, "Take heed therefore unto yourselves, and to all the flock, over the which the Holy Ghost hath made you overseers, *to feed the church of God,* which he hath purchased with his own blood." As the man of God opens his Bible, the people are not amazed at his vocabulary, homiletical savvy, or persona, but they are touched at the richness of the handfuls of spiritual food that have been carefully prepared, labored and prayed over, and studied to feed God's people. Dr. John R. Rice said of the preaching of the late Dr. R. G. Lee, "The scholarly gleaning of incident and illustration from the treasures of scholarly memory and library make a rich feast for the hearer. The banquet table is spread with bread from many a grain field, honey distilled from the nectar of far-off exotic blossoms, sweetmeats from many a bake shop, strong meat from divers markets, and the whole board is garnished by posies from a thousand gardens."[2] Thus should be any message from a God-sent pastor in the pasture!

TOPICS: Church, Feeding, Leadership, Pastors, Provision

---

2   Curtis Hutson, *Great Preaching on The Holy Spirit* (Murfreesboro, TN: Sword of the Lord Publishers, 1988), 234.

R. CHRIS HANKS

DAILY BIBLE READING: Jeremiah 4–5

TODAY'S VERSE: Jeremiah 4:3: "For thus saith the LORD to the men of Judah and Jerusalem, Break up your fallow ground, and sow not among thorns."

JEHOVAH GOD SHARES a fascinating thought with the men of Judah and Jerusalem in this verse. Because it is preserved for us in the Bible, we know this thought is also for us today! Let's strive to understand God's purpose in speaking these words to His people.

These Are Words of Brokenness ("For thus saith the LORD to the men of Judah and Jerusalem, *Break up* your fallow ground"). If there is a gaping hole in our Christian lives today, it is in the area of brokenness. We do not have brokenness over our sin, nor do we feel sadness over our failings. Psalm 51 is the prayer of guilty David after his adultery with Bathsheba was exposed. Verse 17 says, "The sacrifices of God are a broken spirit: a broken and a contrite heart, O God, thou wilt not despise." If there is a reason we do not see a need for the power of God, it is because we are not broken. The word for "break" literally means "the gleam of a fresh furrow." We need the gospel plow to set its sharp edge upon our hearts and run deep into the soil to prepare it for whatever the Master desires. Every time you feel the plow of God upon you, let the plow do what it does, for it is the Lord who is trying to break up things that have become hardened to His will.

These Are Words of Barrenness ("Break up your *fallow ground*"). Fallow ground is ground that was plowed but left unseeded. It lay dormant with no fruit and no prospect for growth other than weeds or a few scraggly plants missed in the harvest time the year before. Some people become satisfied with this kind of a life. They are proud of their "clean land" and do not mind that they have no fruit. God did not create us to be a barren field, but a fruitful field. As a matter of fact, a barren field is the very thing from which God is working to keep us. Isaiah 32:15 says, "Until the spirit be poured upon us from on high, and the wilderness be a fruitful field, and the fruitful field be counted for a forest." Let us get rid of our fallow ground and pray for a fruitful ground.

These Are Words of Blessedness ("and sow not among thorns"). It's very interesting that God speaks of thorns here, in the midst of teaching us to be fruitful. After we have broken our fallow ground, it is important that we sow the good seed in the right places. Recall the Parable of the Sower in Matthew 13. Verse 7 says, "And some [seed] fell among thorns; and the thorns sprung up, and choked them." Jesus applies this to our lives in verse 22: "He also that received seed among the thorns is he that heareth the word; and *the care of this world, and the deceitfulness of riches,* choke the word, and he becometh unfruitful." That explains everything, doesn't it? This is one reason our hearts need to be "broken"—so that the thorns of our lusts and the desires of fleshly living will be destroyed! Some ponder only the vanity of material possessions and the cares of this world, and in their lives the seed is choked out. Let us look for the blessedness of a fruitful field apart from the choking deceitfulness of the world.

TOPICS: Barrenness, Blessing, Brokenness, Preparation, Repentance, Tenderness

DAILY BIBLE READING: Jeremiah 6–8

TODAY'S VERSE: Jeremiah 6:16: "Thus saith the Lord, Stand ye in the ways, and see, and ask for the old paths, where is the good way, and walk therein, and ye shall find rest for your souls. But they said, We will not walk therein."

WE LIVE IN A TIME when there is a great forsaking of the old paths in favor of a more "tolerant" way of religion. People, even Christians, have left the great doctrines of the Bible so that they might be more "inclusive" of others. I believe that we are to reach people and be like Paul when he said in 1 Corinthians 9:22, "To the weak became I as weak, that I might gain the weak: I am made all things to all men, that I might by all means save some." However, *we are not to reach people at the expense of the truth.* In no way and at no time are we to compromise our doctrine. Jesus never changed the message or the doctrine that He preached and taught, and He gave His life for this faithfulness. This verse tells us to do three things concerning the old paths. First, the old paths should be our *dwelling* ("stand ye in the ways"). This has to do with where we should abide. Next, the old paths should be *distinguished* ("and see"). We should know what the old path is in contrast to some new path. And third, the old paths should be *desired* ("and ask for the old paths"). We should yearn to be on the old paths for the glory of the Lord. Let us start asking for these old-time ways concerning God's Word, way, and will.

These Old Paths Are Proper Paths ("and ask for the old paths, *where is the good way*"). The word for "good" here is the same word used to describe Moses as a baby in Exodus 2:2 ("a goodly child"). Yet, in speaking about Moses, Hebrews 11:23 says, "Because they saw he was a *proper* child." The old-time way is a right and a proper way! Without question, there is a proper way in which we are to serve, obey, and worship our Lord and Saviour. We must make sure that "our" way is the right way! How do we know the proper way to give glory, honor, and worship to the Lord? It must be in the Word of God! First Timothy 3:14–15 says, "*These things write I unto thee,* hoping to come unto thee shortly: but if I tarry long, *that thou mayest know how thou oughtest to behave thyself in the house of God,* which is the church of the living God, the pillar and ground of the truth." Second Timothy 3:16–17 gives this instruction to believers: "All scripture is given by inspiration of God, and is profitable for doctrine, for reproof, for correction, for instruction in righteousness: that the man of God may be perfect, throughly furnished unto all *good* works."

These Old Paths Are Persistent Paths ("and walk therein"). The word translated "old paths" means "to tramp; a beaten track:—path." It is a place where somebody has been time and again. Second Timothy 3:14 says, "But *continue thou in the things which thou hast learned* and hast been assured of, knowing of whom thou hast learned them." We need to keep walking in the paths of old every day. The old paths of the virgin birth, blood atonement, deity of Christ, bodily resurrection of Christ, inerrancy of Scripture, salvation by grace (plus nothing and minus nothing), the imminent return of Christ, hell and a place of eternal damnation, future fellowship in heaven with God and believers, the indwelling and empowering of the Holy Ghost, the eternal security of the believer—to list these doctrines is to name just a few. We need to make paths for our children so they may know where to go and what to do when they get older. Let us walk in the paths that have been trodden before us. God wants us to continue to walk in the same paths to the church, to the altar, and to a witness in our community.

These Old Paths Are Peaceful Paths ("and ye shall find rest for your souls"). Many people are trying to find a way that works for them, but without ever trying God's way. When we do things God's way, we will find that we finally have the peace that was promised to those who follow Him. Walking in the old paths will give us peace of mind and heart, along with confidence in Christian living! Hebrews 10:35 says, "Cast not away therefore your confidence, which hath great recompence of reward." There seems to be a great lack of rest in the hearts of Christians today. One of the main reasons is that they are not following the old paths! In the old paths are satisfaction, surrender, and serenity.

TOPICS: Paths, Peace, Perseverance, Preaching, Worship

R. CHRIS HANKS

DAILY BIBLE READING: Jeremiah 9–11

TODAY'S VERSE: Jeremiah 9:24: "But let him that glorieth glory in this, that he understandeth and knoweth me, that I am the LORD which exercise lovingkindness, judgment, and righteousness, in the earth: for in these things I delight, saith the LORD."

THE WORD FOR "GLORY" and "glorieth" in the beginning of this verse is the Hebrew word *halal*, which begins the familiar word *hallelujah!* This verse is saying that if you have any reason to praise, to shout, or to be happy, then you need to get happy about this! Do you need a reason to start praising today? Then the rest of this devotion is just for you!

We Must Glory in God's Disposition ("But let him that glorieth glory in this, that he understandeth and knoweth me, that I am the LORD"). As we have seen before, "LORD" in all capital letters refers to Jehovah God! This is a God of loving nature, longsuffering temperance, and impeccable character. We should glory that we understand and know Him. This has not only to do with what we believe ("understandeth") but also with what we experience ("knoweth")! The Jamieson-Faussett-Brown commentary says that we should know God theoretically and also practically.[3] I couldn't agree more! Let us glory in Him!

We Must Glory in God's Doings ("that I am the LORD which exercise lovingkindness, judgment, and righteousness, in the earth"). I am very glad today about what God has *done,* but I also rejoice in what He is *continuing* to do! Every day is an exercise of God in mercy and lovingkindness. Every day He is giving a perfect verdict in judgment! Every day He is defending those who trust in Him with His righteousness! First Kings 8:56 says, "Blessed be the LORD, that hath given rest unto his people Israel, according to all that he promised: *there hath not failed one word of all his good promise,* which he promised by the hand of Moses his servant." Thank God for His faithfulness to His promises!

We Must Glory in God's Delights ("for in these things I delight, saith the LORD"). When was the last time you got happy about what God enjoys and loves? God does not just "exercise lovingkindness, judgment, and righteousness, in the earth" out of duty, obligation, or even responsibility. He does these things because He enjoys them! The word translated "delighteth" means "to incline to." How precious it is to know that Jesus is "inclined to" these wonderful things! A number of things "delight" and "please" the Lord. He delights to hear the prayer of the upright (Proverbs 15:8). He delights to hear my praise (Psalm 69:30–31). He delights to see my ways please Him (Proverbs 16:7). He delights to accomplish His Word (Isaiah 55:11). He delights to fill me and work in the Spirit (Romans 8:8). He delights to see my faith (Hebrews 11:6). May we begin to take great joy in the delights of our Lord!

TOPICS: Delight, Glory, Praise, Righteousness, Seeking God

---

3   Robert Jamieson, A.R. Fausset, David Brown, A Commentary, Critical and Explanatory, of the Old and New Testaments. Vol. 1. (New York: Fleming H. Revell, 1917), 516

DAILY BIBLE READING: Jeremiah 12–14

TODAY'S VERSE: Jeremiah 12:9: "Mine heritage is unto me as a speckled bird, the birds round about are against her; come ye, assemble all the beasts of the field, come to devour."

TODAY, I WANT TO get personal and look at this verse with my past in mind. When I refer to "my past," I am referring to life before salvation. No matter how old each of us was at the time of salvation, we can all identify on a spiritual level with the failure of a carnal past. Let us remember what our past was like that we might rejoice in the goodness and grace of God!

The Hopelessness of My Heritage ("Mine heritage is unto me as a speckled bird"). This hopelessness has to do with **defilement.** The word for "speckled" here means "dyed (in stripes), i.e. the hyena." We can do nothing about our sinful heritage. Our Adamic nature and deceitful hearts are "dyed in the wool" sinful. The very next chapter of our reading uses the same thought in verse 23: "Can the Ethiopian change his skin, or the leopard his spots?" There are some things over which we have no control! What a blessing to know that God can do anything with our situation, for He is not limited by our failures! Isaiah 1:18 says, "Come now, and let us reason together, saith the LORD: though your sins be as scarlet, they shall be as white as snow; though they be red like crimson, they shall be as wool."

The Helplessness of My Heritage ("the birds round about are against her"). This helplessness has to do with **difference.** Have you ever been around birds for any length of time? I vividly remember going inside a chicken house with thousands upon thousands of chickens. I will never forget walking with the farmer down the middle of that big house and seeing a group of chickens gathered around one poor little creature, pecking it furiously. He reached down, picked it up, and said, "Let me show you something." He looked for a minute on that little chicken and finally said, "There it is," and then showed it to me: a speck of color. He said, "That little speck is what makes this one different from all the other chickens; and because of that difference, they will kill it. This chicken will die." That is the way the world works. The world is great even at destroying those it calls its friends. If you wait long enough, it will destroy you and your love for God.

The Harmfulness of My Heritage ("come ye, assemble all the beasts of the field, come to devour"). This harmfulness has to do with **destruction.** It's not just about being rejected by those who are like you, but being devoured by everything around you. You become the world's prey. Deliverance is going to take something much bigger and greater than you! In this verse, there is a call to "assemble . . . come to devour." This reminds me of what people did to our Saviour as He hung on the cross: "And sitting down they watched him there" (Matthew 27:36). They gathered to sit there, drink in the scene, and feed upon the hatefulness of Calvary. They wanted to "consume" Jesus in their wrath! Little did they know that they were being consumed by their own anger and bitterness as they centered all of their wickedness upon Him who was pure! We see this discussed in the prophecy of the cross in Psalm 22:20: "Deliver my soul from the sword; *my darling from the power of the dog.*" We find that God can give us such deliverance in Hebrews 7:25: "Wherefore *he is able also to save them to the uttermost* that come unto God by him, seeing he ever liveth to make intercession for them." Hallelujah for a deliverance from certain destruction by our wonderful Saviour!

TOPICS: Failure, Guilt, Hope, Persecution, Sin

DAILY BIBLE READING: Jeremiah 15–18

TODAY'S VERSE: Jeremiah 15:16: "Thy words were found, and I did eat them; and thy word was unto me the joy and rejoicing of mine heart: for I am called by thy name, O Lord God of hosts."

THE WORD OF GOD is most precious to His children. I pray that you will be encouraged to study your Bible more even today! Jesus said in John 6:63, "It is the spirit that quickeneth; the flesh profiteth nothing: *the words that I speak unto you, they are spirit, and they are life.*" The Bible even calls Jesus the Word of God in John 1:1–3. If we love Jesus, then we will love His Word, dedicate ourselves to its study, and heed its every command. Hear this verse from the depths of the heart of Jeremiah as he expresses his joy to the Lord concerning His Word.

The Consumption of the Word of God ("Thy words were found, and I did eat them"). The Word of God is without doubt the spiritual sustenance of the believer. The Bible says in Job 23:12, "Neither have I gone back from the commandment of his lips; I have esteemed the words of his mouth more than my necessary food." We cannot live without hearing, tasting, and ingesting the Word of God. To do so is not just an obligation, but an honor! Psalm 19:9–10 says, "The fear of the Lord is clean, enduring for ever: the judgments of the Lord are true and righteous altogether. More to be desired are they than gold, yea, than much fine gold: sweeter also than honey and the honeycomb."

The Contentment of the Word of God ("and thy word was unto me the joy and rejoicing of mine heart"). The word translated "joy" means "cheerfulness," and the word for "rejoicing" means "blithesomeness or glee." Nothing else can content my soul and bring joy to my heart like the Word of God! If the Word of God angers you or challenges your spirit, then you need to make your heart right with God. Psalm 119:165 says, "Great peace have they which love thy law: and nothing shall offend them." In this verse, the word "peace" means "safe." Is there anything to make you feel more content than joy and safety? What great peace comes from loving God's Word!

The Connection of the Word of God ("for I am called by thy name, O Lord God of hosts"). The whole reason Jeremiah loved the Word of God was because of his connection to Jehovah! If we are called by God's name, shouldn't we love His Word? If I happen to be traveling, I love to hear the voice of my wife. We are connected! There is nothing I would rather hear than the voice of the one I love. So it is with Christ! Doesn't it stand to reason that if we love Him, we will love to hear His Word? Being a Christian means that we are called by His name. It's not that we call *ourselves* by His name, but that others have attributed His name to us! Does your life exemplify the character, holiness, and grace that God does? Some may call us "Christians" as a criticism, thinking it a derogatory term. I accept it as an honor!

TOPICS: Bible, Contentment, Joy, Obedience, Testimony, Word of God

DAILY BIBLE READING: Jeremiah 19-21

TODAY'S VERSE: Jeremiah 20:11: "But the Lord is with me as a mighty terrible one: therefore my persecutors shall stumble, and they shall not prevail: they shall be greatly ashamed; for they shall not prosper: their everlasting confusion shall never be forgotten."

JEREMIAH MAKES A BOLD CLAIM in the phrase, "But the Lord is with me." What an honor it is to make that claim! How thankful I am to know that God is with me every step of the way, and that He will never leave nor forsake me (Hebrews 13:5)! Assurance of the presence of God is worth far more than money. The phrase goes on to describe God "as a mighty terrible one." The words translated "terrible one" mean "fearful, powerful or tyrannical." This does not mean that God is a tyrant to me, but to my enemies. It is God's power that makes my persecutors stumble! The word for "persecutors" means "to run after usually with hostile intent." These persecutors may be flesh and blood, or they may be your failures, your past, and your troubles. Have you ever been chased by something that scared you to death? That is the sense of this term. What does this verse say will happen to our persecutors while we are in the presence of God? Let's look at the next three phrases.

My Enemies' Stumbling ("therefore my persecutors shall stumble"). The word for "stumble" means "to totter or waver (through weakness of the legs, especially the ankle)." They literally have no leg to stand on! It is certain that if our persecutors stumble, they cannot run after and pursue us! What made them so weak all of a sudden? They saw that the Lord was with us and that He is a "terrible one"! Their fear rendered them powerless! They had no more strength to come after us.

My Enemies' Shame ("they shall be greatly ashamed; for they shall not prosper"). The word for "ashamed" literally means "to pale." Our persecutors have not turned red in embarrassment, but white in disgrace! David said in Psalm 35:4, "Let them be confounded and put to shame that seek after my soul: let them be turned back and brought to confusion that devise my hurt." Those who seek your spiritual life will one day be made ashamed before God.

My Enemies' Suffering ("their everlasting confusion shall never be forgotten"). This goes far beyond shame—this is utter humiliation. This is what Christ has done to the enemies of the believer! Colossians 2:15 says, "And having spoiled principalities and powers, *he made a shew of them openly, triumphing over them in it.*" The word for "openly" means "all outspokenness, frankness, bluntness, publicity." Jesus will be proclaimed victor every moment for eternity. All those people, troubles, and devils that have tried to defeat you will be immortalized as those who failed to claim you as their own!

TOPICS: Battle, Enemies, God's Presence, Persecution, Protection, Victory, War

DAILY BIBLE READING: Jeremiah 22–24

TODAY'S VERSE: Jeremiah 23:29: "Is not my word like as a fire? saith the Lord; and like a hammer that breaketh the rock in pieces."

THIS TESTIMONY ABOUT GOD'S WORD does not just come from a prophet, though that would be good enough—it comes from Jehovah God! What a blessing it is to hear how God speaks of His own Word! If God believes in the Bible, we should too! Let your mind and heart be completely set upon the blessed Word of God as we look at three main thoughts from this verse.

It Is a Purifying Book ("Is not my word like as a fire?"). No other agent can purify as well as fire. It consumes impurities and purifies the most precious of metals that their worth might increase. Many things need to be purified by the fire of God's Word. Our *pleasure in God* needs to be purified. Jeremiah 20:9 says, "Then I said, I will not make mention of him, nor speak any more in his name. But his word was in mine heart as a burning fire shut up in my bones, and I was weary with forbearing, and I could not stay." Our *prayers to God* need to be purified. James 5:16b says, "The effectual fervent prayer of a righteous man availeth much." The English definition for "fervent" means "to be hot, to boil , to glow."[4] We need our prayers to be purified by the heat of God's promises and precepts in His Word. Our *passion for God* needs to be purified. Luke 24:32 says, "And they said one to another, *Did not our heart burn within us, while he talked with us by the way, and while he opened to us the scriptures?*"

It Is a Pounding Book ("and like a hammer"). The word used for "hammer" actually means "to pound." This has to do with two things: *power* and *persistence*. There is no force on earth like the Word of God! Its power only begins to be measured in Genesis 1:3, where we read, "And God said, Let there be light: and there was light." This power is the Word of God's *endowment*. The hammer pounds; it is a continuing work. This is the Word of God's *endurance*. Isaiah 55:11 says, "So shall my word be that goeth forth out of my mouth: it shall not return unto me void, but it shall accomplish that which I please, and it shall prosper in the thing whereto I sent it." The Word of God will not return until it has done what it has been sent to do, and it will not fail! Many times I have heard the Word of God preached and done nothing to respond to the invitation. The next day, that same Word will enter into my heart and preach the message all over again! It pounds away at my *denial!* It pounds at my *defiance!* And it pounds at my *disobedience!* It will never go away, but keep pounding at every heart that will hear its sound.

It Is a Pulverizing Book ("that breaketh the rock in pieces"). The Word will break that which needs to be broken! Thank God for a tool that can break *the hardest heart, the hardest neck,* **and** *the hardest will.* The Word also brings judgment upon those who would destroy it! Jesus said in Matthew 21:44, "And whosoever shall fall on this stone shall be broken: but on whomsoever it shall fall, it will grind him to powder." This was a testimony about Himself as the Chief Cornerstone. And exactly who is He? He is the Word! What a pulverizing Word we have that continues to speak to us in power and glory!

TOPICS: Bible, Power, Prayer, Rebellion, Tenderness, Word of God

---

4 *Noah Webster's First Edition of an American Dictionary of The English Language* (Chesapeake, VA: Foundation For American Christian Education, 1995)

DAILY BIBLE READING: Jeremiah 25–27

TODAY'S VERSE: Jeremiah 26:16: "Then said the princes and all the people unto the priests and to the prophets; This man is not worthy to die: for he hath spoken to us in the name of the LORD our God."

JEREMIAH, THE WEEPING PROPHET, did not have it easy upon this earth. He spoke the Word of the LORD to the people without compromise and without hesitation. In this chapter, they were ready to kill him, not because he spoke badly of the city (although that was how they accused him) but because they did not like what he had to say. It is so easy to get mad at the messenger rather than the message, for if we reject the message, we've rejected God. We just don't want it to look that way! In this verse, some people came to Jeremiah's rescue and saved him from the wicked hands of men who wanted to destroy him. They came to save him for one reason only: "For he hath spoken to us in the name of the LORD our God."

They Recognized his Responsibility ("for *he* hath spoken to us in the name of the LORD our God"). They realized that Jeremiah was not there speaking on his own behalf, but had been sent by God. Just the fact that he came to them in the name of the LORD was enough to send shivers up and down their spines. They did not take it lightly. If Jeremiah had come in the name of the LORD without God's backing, God would deal with him. Their view was that they did not have to defend God, for God was more than able to take care of Himself. But if Jeremiah came in the name of the LORD and God *had* sent him, then his message must be important enough to demand their undivided attention. They knew that if God had sent Jeremiah to them, then a great burden and responsibility lay upon his heart. He did not come lightly.

They Responded in Readiness ("for he hath *spoken to us* **in the name** of the LORD our God"). Did this not at least demand their attention, which should be followed by their action? These men were glad that somebody was finally willing to give it to them straight! No more piddling around with some preacher with a personal agenda. They finally had someone with a message on his heart, and they were ready to hear it! Whenever we hear a word from the Lord, we must be ready to immediately act upon it. In my years in the ministry I've learned that God's people *want* to hear from God's Word. They may not always agree with it; they may not always obey it; but they sure do want to hear it! What a relief it is to hear from the Lord when you read His Word or go to church! My father-in-law, Dr. Clay McNeese, gave me some advice before I went to preach at a preacher's fellowship. He said, "Well, sheep like sheep food." That is some good country wisdom for you today! God's people like God's Word. If we are really God's people, we will desire to hear His thoughts, no matter what they are. If they are thoughts of blessing, a child of God will want to hear them. If they are warnings, a child of God will still desire to hear them, for they are *God's* words!

They Respected God's Righteousness ("for he hath spoken to us in the *name of the LORD OUR GOD*"). Jeremiah gave these men many judgments, but each one was based on "the name of the LORD our God." These people knew that Jeremiah was sent by a righteous and a holy God. They had never forgotten the power and glory of Jehovah. If this man of God had come in God's holy, righteous, and self-existent name, then they had to hear the words that had been given to this preacher! If we would respect God more, we would hear His man and His Word more!

TOPICS: God's Name, Pastor, Respect, Responsibility, Word of God

DAILY BIBLE READING: Jeremiah 28–30

TODAY'S VERSE: Jeremiah 29:11: "For I know the thoughts that I think toward you, saith the LORD, thoughts of peace, and not of evil, to give you an expected end."

FEW VERSES IN THE BIBLE surpass this one in encouragement and hope. In the midst of the Major Prophets, in which there is condemnation and judgment given, this verse stands as a shining beacon of hope for God's people! As I read it, my heart wants to sigh in relief. Sometimes our hearts condemn every action we take, no matter how good or noble, because we know that whatever we do, it is not good enough. But what an encouragement is left for us in 1 John 3:20: "For if our heart condemn us, *God is greater than our heart,* and knoweth all things"! Again, some Christians live their lives in fear, wondering if the Lord really cares about them. It is as if they are constantly looking for the judgment of God rather than living in the joy of the Holy Ghost. Psalm 56:9 says, "When I cry unto thee, then shall mine enemies turn back: *this I know; for God is for me.*"

First, we see the **Purpose of God** ("For I know the thoughts that I think toward you, saith the LORD"). The words "thought" and "think" have interesting meaning behind them. Their Hebrew root has to do with "contrivance, machine, or intention, plan" and even "to weave or to fabricate." In other words, God has contrived and woven a plan just for us! He forged the steel and cast the mold so that He could prepare the way that would bring us into His blessing! What wonderful intentions our God has for us! He made a way for us; and in the same manner, He is making a path for us to follow that is completely in His will.

Second, we see the **Peace of God** ("thoughts of peace, and not of evil"). Is there anything better than God's peace? What great plans He has for us! The future will be a place of safety. It will be a place of security. It will be a place of simplicity. That sounds like a good place to be! Jesus said in John 14:27, "Peace I leave with you, my peace I give unto you: not as the world giveth, give I unto you. Let not your heart be troubled, neither let it be afraid." Many desire to have this peace with all their heart and can never find it because it must come from God. This peace is not obtained; it is imparted! You will only find it when you seek Him.

Third, we see the **Posterity of God** ("to give you an expected end"). The only way to have an "expected end" is to have God's end. The future is uncertain. Nobody knows what the stock market will do today. Nobody knows what the government will do today. Even the weatherman does not surely know what the weather will be today. The only expected end is found in the plan of God. The word for "expected" means "cord, hope." So many people are looking for something to hold on to! Why not hold on to the scarlet cord of God's grace, the hope that can help us in every problem? Hebrews 6:18 says, "That . . . we might have a strong consolation, who have fled for refuge to *lay hold upon the hope* set before us." What little string are you holding on to today? A string of your own works? Are you holding on to the cord of your religious views? The frayed rope of deceitful and lustful living? Are you holding on to satisfying your fleshly desires? The only hope we have is to lay hold of Christ!

TOPICS: Blessing, Hope, Peace, Promises, Purpose

DAILY BIBLE READING: Jeremiah 31–32

TODAY'S VERSE: Jeremiah 32:39: "And I will give them one heart, and one way, that they may fear me for ever, for the good of them, and of their children after them."

THIS VERSE HAS SUCH an extraordinary flavor to it as we see the Lord giving something special to His people. This is a reference to the work of God among them, but it is also a promise of God to them. Don't you like it when God begins to give out promises? He has not failed on one yet! What a thrilling time it is to see the Lord get excited about giving His people something that is special to His heart!

The Result of God's Work ("And I will give them one heart, and one way"). Anytime God's people are unified and working together in solidarity, it must be a work of God! Much can be done with a church that is single-minded in the work of the Lord. In Philippians 1:27, Paul desires to "hear of your affairs, that ye *stand fast in one spirit, with one mind striving together* for the faith of the gospel." What a blessing it is to be in a place where personal glory and acknowledgment do not matter. Truly, one of the greatest blessings man can experience is that described in Psalm 133:1: "Behold, how good and how pleasant it is for brethren to dwell together in unity!"

The Reason of God's Work ("that they may fear me for ever"). All our love, respect, worship, and service are based on the "fear of the Lord." Romans 3 tells us of the characteristics of the wicked when it says in verse 18, "There is no fear of God before their eyes." All is vanity under such an attitude. How can we learn of God's splendor, strength, or even salvation without the fear of the Lord in our lives? Proverbs 9:10 says, "The fear of the LORD is the beginning of wisdom: and the knowledge of the holy is understanding." When we are walking in the way that God has given, we will continually set our hearts and affections upon Him.

The Reward of God's Work ("for the good of them, and of their children after them"). God always gives a reward to those who do His will and sets His favor upon those who seek Him. God's will is for our own good! Notice the reward that comes with seeking God in Jeremiah 29:13: "And ye shall seek me, *and find me,* when ye shall search for me with all your heart." Let me tell you something, child of God: God does have your best interest at heart. His reward will not just affect you for a week, but for your life. Keep your eyes focused on that which lies ahead, for that is the true reward.

TOPICS: Fear of God, God's Work, Promises, Trust, Unity

R. CHRIS HANKS

DAILY BIBLE READING: Jeremiah 33-34

TODAY'S VERSE: Jeremiah 33:3: "Call unto me, and I will answer thee, and shew thee great and mighty things, which thou knowest not."

THIS IS PERHAPS ONE of the most well-known verses on prayer in all of Scripture. It comes from the mouth of Jeremiah while he is being held in prison. What a hope Jeremiah had! Even in prison, he was faithful to give the Word of the LORD to the people of God. I wonder how many of us would have preferred to give warning of God's judgment to those who had turned their backs on God, rather than the hope of answered prayer! Is there a better picture of the longsuffering of God than this constant call to His people, begging them to return and offer their prayers to Him? He will surely answer them in "great and mighty things."

Prayer's Plea ("Call unto me"). This has to do with our **request**. The word for "call" means "the idea of accosting a person met." What a powerful word describing how we can pray! It almost scares me to think that God is telling us to "accost" Him in prayer. Hebrews 4:16 says, "Let us therefore come boldly unto the throne of grace, that we may obtain mercy, and find grace to help in time of need." God is not telling us to come *proudly,* but to come *boldly!* We have no right to demand things from God in prayer, but God is moved by our bold requests, for they show our full and complete trust in Him to meet our needs. If we really believed that God would give us what we ask, would that not change the way in which we ask? Mark 11:24 says, "Therefore I say unto you, What things soever ye desire, when ye pray, believe that ye receive them, and ye shall have them." What confidence we can have as we come to the Lord to "cry" for our request! Still struggling with the idea of crying out to God in prayer? Try this New Testament verse in Luke 18:7-8a: "And shall not God avenge his own elect, which cry day and night unto him, though he bear long with them? I tell you that he will avenge them speedily."

Prayer's Persuasion ("and I will answer thee"). This has to do with God's **response**. What a promise is given here: He *will* answer! John 14:14 tells us the same thing: "If ye shall ask any thing in my name, *I will do it.*" God is looking for someone to believe Him and put Him to the test. Second Chronicles 16:9 says, "For the eyes of the LORD run to and fro throughout the whole earth, to shew himself strong in the behalf of them whose heart is perfect toward him."

Prayer's Performance ("and shew thee great and mighty things, which thou knowest not"). This has to do with God's **recital**. God is looking to perform on the stage of your life. Very interesting words here describe what He is going to "shew" us. First, "great things." The word translated "great" means "great (in any sense); hence, older"—it carries the idea of time. God has done things in the past that you have not experienced yet. He has answered prayers you have not yet prayed—the answers have been waiting for you for years! Next is "mighty things." The word for "mighty" means "to gather grapes; i.e. inaccessible by height or fortification." When things are too high for us, praise the Lord, He can lift us! Has He not caused us to sit together with Him in heavenly places (Ephesians 2:6)? This has to do with height. David said in Psalm 139:6, "Such knowledge is too wonderful for me; it is high, I cannot attain unto it." Though I cannot attain to something, yet God can take me to it! Last is knowledge. The word translated "know" means "to know (properly, to ascertain by seeing)." This has to do with experience. How much I want to experience the things I have never seen! How much I want to see the Red Sea part in my own life situations! What a blessing it would be to see Jericho's walls fall in places that need conquering today! God can do it, and He has promised to do it for the person who will call unto Him!

TOPICS: Blessing, Possibilities, Prayer, Promises

DAILY BIBLE READING: Jeremiah 35–37

TODAY'S VERSE: Jeremiah 36:28: "Take thee again another roll, and write in it all the former words that were in the first roll, which Jehoiakim the king of Judah hath burned."

EVER SINCE THE BEGINNING of time, both the devil and people have tried to do away with the Word of God. What a futile work! In today's passage, we read that God had His Word written and delivered to King Jehoiakim, but he chose to deny it and dispose of it. The truth is that many are trying to do the same thing with the Word of God today. They don't like being confronted with their sin, so they try to dispose of the Word that reveals that sin. God is not threatened by our unbelief. Romans 3:3 says, "For what if some did not believe? shall their unbelief make the faith of God without effect?" Let us hear and submit to God's Word, for it teaches us of His mercy and grace.

Denying the Word of God Does Not Destroy It ("Take thee again another roll, and write in it"). God's Word keeps coming back. The Word of God still existed though its pages had been burned. Jesus said in Mark 13:31, "Heaven and earth shall pass away: but my words shall not pass away." The lion cannot shred it, the tyrant cannot overrule it, the king cannot burn it, the chain cannot bind it, the government cannot regulate it, and the bomb cannot break it. No matter what they try to do to it, it will return, for it cannot be destroyed. John 10:35 says, "And the scripture cannot be broken." Hallelujah for an indestructible Word in which we can hope!

Denying the Word of God Does Not Dismiss It ("all the former words that were in the first roll"). No matter what the king did to get rid of the Word, he was still responsible for all of it. Try as he might, he could not dismiss the Word of God. This generation needs to know that as well! John 12:48 says, "He that rejecteth me, and receiveth not my words, hath one that judgeth him: the word that I have spoken, the same shall judge him in the last day." Just as King Jehoiakim could not dismiss the Word of God, you will not be able to easily dismiss the Word of God in your life either!

Denying the Word of God Does Not Defeat It ("which Jehoiakim the king of Judah hath burned"). King Jehoiakim, though regal and respected in the kingdom, was not strong enough to defeat the Word of God. Isaiah 40:8 says, "The grass withereth, the flower fadeth: but the word of our God shall stand for ever." It is the Word of God that will prevail! Hebrews 1:3 tells us the victory that the Word of God demands: "Who being the brightness of his glory, and the express image of his person, and upholding all things by the word of his power, when he had by himself purged our sins, sat down on the right hand of the Majesty on high." Nothing will ever fall as long as it is *His* Word!

TOPICS: Bible, Indestructible, Power, Truth, Victory, Word of God

DAILY BIBLE READING: Jeremiah 38-40

TODAY'S VERSE: Jeremiah 38:6: "Then took they Jeremiah, and cast him into the dungeon of Malchiah the son of Hammelech, that was in the court of the prison: and they let down Jeremiah with cords. And in the dungeon there was no water, but mire: so Jeremiah sunk in the mire."

EVEN WHEN YOU ARE DOING the will of God, you can face persecution and trials. Sometimes it is *because* you are doing the will of God that you will face persecution and trials! In this passage, Jeremiah had been nothing but faithful to give the Word of God to Israel. They should have been thankful. They should have bowed their heads in reverence and repented in sackcloth and ashes. Instead, they took the man of God and tried to dispatch him by throwing him into a wretched pit. Were it not for the mercy of a spineless king who sent servants to rescue him covertly, Jeremiah would surely have died in that dark and dank hole in the ground.

He Was Cast Out for His Faith ("Then took they Jeremiah, and cast him into the dungeon of Malchiah the son of Hammelech, that was in the court of the prison"). The word translated "cast" means "to throw out, down or away." These wicked men thought no more of Jeremiah and his little prophecies from God than to throw him out with the trash. They had no respect for this man of God or for the God who had sent him. Jesus remembers this in Luke 13:28 when he says, "There shall be weeping and gnashing of teeth, when ye shall see Abraham, and Isaac, and Jacob, and all the prophets, in the kingdom of God, *and you yourselves thrust out.*" Someday you may be persecuted and cast out for your faith, but the Bible tells us in Matthew 5:12 to "rejoice, and be exceeding glad for great is your reward in heaven: for so persecuted they the prophets which were before you."

He Was Let Down for His Faithfulness ("and they let down Jeremiah with cords"). They should have embraced the man of God for his faithful witness, but instead they let him down. I have known preachers who have been "let down" by their congregations after they were faithful to preach the Word. We need men like Aaron and Hur who supported the man of God as he obeyed the Lord. Praise the Lord they did not let Moses down! If they had done so, it would have affected the entire nation. The Bible tells us of the godly people of faith in Hebrews 11:13: "These all died in faith, not having received the promises, but having seen them afar off, and were persuaded of them, *and embraced them,* and confessed that they were strangers and pilgrims on the earth." We should not let the next generation down because of our lack of faith. Let's embrace the faith and encourage others in the work of the ministry.

He Was Sunk Down for His Fervency ("And in the dungeon there was no water, but mire: so Jeremiah sunk in the mire"). Jeremiah sank from the sheer weight of his body, not because he desired to sink in the mire. Despondency and discouragement can affect any servant of God! And all this happened to Jeremiah because he didn't water down the Word of God to His people! The list of those who have sunk in deep depression while they still served God is long. Paul deals with this reality in 2 Corinthians 4:16-18: "For which cause we faint not; but though our outward man perish, yet the inward man is renewed day by day. For our light affliction, which is but for a moment, worketh for us a far more exceeding and eternal weight of glory; while we look not at the things which are seen, but at the things which are not seen: for the things which are seen are temporal; but the things which are not seen are eternal." Instead of sinking down under the circumstances, lift up your heart unto God and rejoice in His goodness.

TOPICS: Faith, Faithfulness, Discouragement, Depression, Persecution, Promises, Trials

 *August 25*

DAILY BIBLE READING: Jeremiah 41–43

TODAY'S VERSE: Jeremiah 42:6: "Whether it be good, or whether it be evil, we will obey the voice of the LORD our God, to whom we send thee; that it may be well with us, when we obey the voice of the LORD our God."

IN TODAY'S READING, the people finally come to Jeremiah to ask him to intercede for them and get direction from the Lord in what they should do. The Lord was waiting for His people to come back to Him. Have you ever realized that the Lord is just waiting for you to give up so that He can show forth His glory and His grace in your life? If only we would pray this prayer and mean it from our hearts, then we would see the Lord do great things in us and around us. The people's response so moved God that He demonstrated His tenderness in verse 10: "If ye will still abide in this land, then will I build you, and not pull you down, and I will plant you, and not pluck you up: for I repent me of the evil that I have done unto you." Verse 12 says, "And I will shew mercies unto you, that he may have mercy upon you, and cause you to return to your own land." The Lord is waiting on a submissive and surrendered spirit. James 4:6 says, "But he giveth more grace. Wherefore he saith, God resisteth the proud, but giveth grace unto the humble."

They Made a Commitment (*"Whether it be good, or whether it be evil,* we will obey the voice of the LORD our God"). This was a commitment to obey even if God's command went against their desires or their reason. So many people want to serve the Lord only if it makes sense, fits their schedule, or accomplishes their will. They betray a lack of trust that God knows what is best and is able to do it. Romans 8:28 says, "And we know that all things work together for good to them that love God, to them who are the called according to his purpose." We should desire to do the Lord's will because we love Him and believe that His will is best—no matter the cost!

They Made a Contract (*"we will obey the voice of the LORD OUR GOD, to whom we send thee"*). They finally came out with their promise! It was an unconditional promise of obedience. God wants people who are obedient to Him. Samuel told Saul of God's great desire for obedience in 1 Samuel 15:22: "And Samuel said, Hath the LORD as great delight in burnt offerings and sacrifices, as in obeying the voice of the LORD? Behold, to obey is better than sacrifice, and to hearken than the fat of rams." Have we forgotten that our obedience is proof to the world of our love for God? John 14:15 says, "If ye love me, keep my commandments." The worst testimony of a Christian is a disobedient spirit and lifestyle.

They Had a Cause (*"that it may be well with us,* when we obey the voice of the LORD our God"). Do you need a good reason to obey the Lord? How about this: "That it may be well with us"! This promise should set us on a mission to conform our lives to His Word. All of our efforts should be focused on obeying His commands so that it might be well with us. We set ourselves up for complete failure when God has given us the recipe and the promise of complete goodness and victory! Find yourself a cause in the promise of the good that awaits those that obey His Word and seek His face!

Before we close, it must be noted that despite their positive words, these people failed miserably in the end, for they did not obey God. As a matter of fact, they did the opposite of His command and received the judgment of God for their actions. Jeremiah 43:7 says, "So they came into the land of Egypt: for they obeyed not the voice of the LORD." Do not let this happen to you! When you make a promise to God, keep it.

TOPICS: Blessing, Commitment, Obedience, Promises, Trust

R. CHRIS HANKS

DAILY BIBLE READING: Jeremiah 44–47

TODAY'S VERSE: Jeremiah 44:10: "They are not humbled even unto this day, neither have they feared, nor walked in my law, nor in my statutes, that I set before you and before your fathers."

IN THE MIDST OF JUDGMENTS and prophecies of chastisement, we have this verse that tells us the reason for God's judgment. Every punishment we receive has been earned many times. It is only by the mercy of God that He is longsuffering to give us these judgments, for they are meant to draw us back into His love. So many people hate the judgments of God, for they seem to them like an end—but they are anything but that! During our time upon this earth, God's judgments are a means to a new beginning in our fellowship with Him.

The Pride of Man ("They are not humbled even unto this day"). If there is one thing God hates, it is pride. Of what does man have to boast? Nothing! He cannot save himself. He cannot exalt himself. He cannot even take care of himself! Psalm 138:6 says, "Though the Lord be high, yet hath he respect unto the lowly: but the proud he knoweth afar off." The meaning for the word translated "humble" is "to crumble." When is the last time you "crumbled" before the Lord? Perhaps we have become too familiar with the word "humble." We should start "crumbling" before our Lord because of His holiness. First Peter 5:6 encourages us in this very thing: "Humble yourselves therefore under the mighty hand of God, that he may exalt you in due time."

The Presumption of Man ("neither have they feared"). The only reason man would not fear an Almighty God is because he has presumed things he ought not to presume. The Bible teaches in Numbers 15:28–30 that a sacrifice could be offered for ignorant sin, but the soul that sinned presumptuously would be cut off from his people. Psalm 19:13 prays, "Keep back thy servant also from presumptuous sins; let them not have dominion over me: then shall I be upright, and I shall be innocent from the great transgression." The only reason we would dare sin presumptuously is because we do not fear God. Oh, for a renewed fear of God and His Word in our lives! Such fear would send revival back into our homes and churches with a vigor that has never been matched in all of history!

The Posture of Man ("nor walked in my law, nor in my statutes"). Let us think this through: If man is not walking in God's law or in His statutes, in what then is he walking? In his own way! Proverbs 14:12 says, "There is a way which seemeth right unto a man, but the end thereof are the ways of death."

The Plainness of God ("that I set before you and before your fathers"). It is amazing how man wants to blame God for his own failures! In this part of the verse God is telling them, "I put my commands in the plainest way and in the plainest place for you and your fathers to see and obey, but ye would not." We cannot blame God for our failure to obey His Word! The book of Proverbs, the book of wisdom, tells us plainly that *"Wisdom crieth without; she uttereth her voice in the streets: she crieth in the chief place of concourse,* in the *openings of the gates: in the city she uttereth* her words" (Proverbs 1:20–21). Again, Proverbs 8:1–3 says, "Doth not wisdom *cry?* and understanding *put forth her voice? She standeth in the top of high places,* by the way *in the places of the paths. She crieth at the gates,* at the *entry of the city,* at the *coming in at the doors."* God has placed His will and His Word in front of each and every one of us. If we start looking for His will and spiritual things, we will see that they are here in plain view!

TOPICS: Humility, Obedience, Pride, Respect, Wisdom

August 27

DAILY BIBLE READING: Jeremiah 48–49

TODAY'S VERSE: Jeremiah 48:10: "Cursed be he that doeth the work of the LORD deceitfully, and cursed be he that keepeth back his sword from blood."

THIS IS NOT THE KIND of sweet little verse with which we like to start our days, but it's well worth reading and meditating upon. It ought to drive all of us to spiritual decisions and create some substance in our beliefs. Do you remember when you used to play marbles as a child and you would "play for keeps"? We are not involved in some little game. This is a war for souls and a war for our surrender, and rest assured, it is still for keeps! God is very serious about the way we live our Christian lives and the manner in which we serve Him. Here are a few simple thoughts about our service to God.

The Denouncing of a False Work ("Cursed be he"). I don't want to be cursed by the Lord! The word translated "cursed" actually means "execrate, denounce, damn, or curse." That is pretty strong language! God wholeheartedly rejects every false work. If we would have a heart for God, we would hate and curse every false work as well. Psalm 119:104 says, "Through thy precepts I get understanding: *therefore I hate every false way.*" Perhaps you can hear the anger of God a little more clearly in Matthew 23:14 as Christ condemns the Pharisees, scribes, and lawyers for their false ways: "Woe unto you, scribes and Pharisees, hypocrites! for ye devour widows' houses, and *for a pretence* make long prayer: therefore ye shall receive the greater damnation." The word for "pretence" literally means "outward showing." There is a curse to those who reject the true and right way in favour of falseness and show.

The Deceitfulness of a False Work ("that doeth the work of the LORD deceitfully"). God does not see deceitfulness as any different from treachery. If we choose to live a deceitful life so others will accept us, are we not being treacherous to their souls—either in giving them a false hope or by affirming something other than the truth in their lives? God is not interested in the deceitful living of Christians nowadays. He is looking for someone *genuine* and *authentic* in his living. Even though the people of Israel hated many of the Old Testament prophets because of their messages from the Lord, they still respected them and wanted to hear their messages, for they were "real." We don't need a doctored-up Christianity; we need the real thing in all its unadulterated purity. Enough with fraudulently appearing to be something we are not! Aren't we accused enough of being hypocrites? Let's make our way the true way!

The Denial of a False Work ("cursed be he that keepeth back his sword from blood"). This last part of the verse carries the same curse for anyone who is not engaged in the holy fight. That is what the deceitfulness of a false work will do. Our living a lie takes the sword from our hand! A real Christian will fight in this spiritual war. Contrary to what some might say, we *are* in the midst of a battle. If you just stand your ground as a Christian, your gospel sword will get some bloodstains upon it. Paul encouraged us in 1 Timothy 6:12 to "Fight the good fight of faith." Sometimes it is all we can do to fight in this epic battle, but fight we must! Ephesians 6:13 says, "Wherefore take unto you the whole armour of God, that ye may be able to withstand in the evil day, and having done all, to stand." We cannot lose ground on the blood atonement, the virgin birth, the deity of Christ, His bodily resurrection, the truth and veracity of the Word of God, holy Christian living, or condemnation of sin. Don't deny the right way, but keep fighting the fight!

TOPICS: Battle, Deceitfulness, Denial, War

DAILY BIBLE READING: Jeremiah 50

TODAY'S VERSE: Jeremiah 50:34: "Their Redeemer is strong; the LORD of hosts is his name: he shall throughly plead their cause, that he may give rest to the land, and disquiet the inhabitants of Babylon."

THIS VERSE IS SIMPLE, yet powerful in its message. Why would God think twice about us? That He does so makes my heart melt in utter humility! "LORD, what is man, that thou takest knowledge of him! or the son of man, that thou makest account of him!" (Psalm 144:3). What a blessing to know that God not only knows about us, but is interested in our lives and is willing to defend us for His glory!

For His Own Sake ("Their Redeemer is strong"). As you read, remember that this Jewish Redeemer has come to fight on our behalf. This verse is a direct reference to the kinsman redeemer law of the Old Testament (see the book of Ruth for a clear depiction of this law). There is no other reason for God to redeem us except that He wants to do this for Himself, and He will do it because He can! Second Chronicles 16:9a says, "For the eyes of the LORD run to and fro throughout the whole earth, *to shew himself strong* in the behalf of them whose heart is perfect toward him." In this verse, the word for "strong" means "hard, bold, and violent." This world will see God come with a violence that will strike fear in the hearts of unbelievers as He comes to take vengeance for His children.

For His Name's Sake ("The LORD of hosts is his name"). God *will not* let His name fall to the ground! Praise the Lord for the great name of our God! Psalm 23:3 says, "He leadeth me in the paths of righteousness for his name's sake." We are pardoned and saved, can experience revival, can have our sins purged, can have the works of God in our lives, can be quickened, and can have His mercy, all for "his name's sake"! This phrase says, *"The Lord of hosts* is His name." That tells of His military might! We have a God of military hosts who has never lost a battle! Learn His name and know it. Rejoice in the name of our God, for it is a powerful name! Psalm 148:13 says, "Let them praise the name of the LORD: for his name alone is excellent; his glory is above the earth and heaven." One day, the Bible says, all people will bow at the name of Jesus! Philippians 2:10 says, "That at the name of Jesus every knee should bow, of things in heaven, and things in earth, and things under the earth." What a name—Jesus!

For His People's Sake ("he shall throughly plead their cause"). Just like a legal advocate pleads for his client, God will plead for those He redeems. First John 2:1 says, "My little children, these things write I unto you, that ye sin not. And if any man sin, we have an advocate with the Father, Jesus Christ the righteous." Our Advocate will thoroughly plead our cause. Isn't it special that we can find such New Testament theology in an Old Testament book? The word translated "plead" is a very interesting word meaning "to toss, grapple; mostly figuratively, to wrangle, hold a controversy." This proves what a great God we have! He is willing to do anything for us and for our welfare.

For His Enemies' Sake ("and disquiet the inhabitants of Babylon"). In English we can see a play on words, for God will always "disquiet" those who were "quiet" before. The Hebrew word translated "disquiet" means "to quiver, with any violent emotion, especially anger or fear." Those who feel they have the power to hurt God's people will one day be hurt themselves. We have a great God; He is strong; He is the great general of a great army and will triumph over man's selfish ways to give peace to His people!

TOPICS: Deliverance, God's Power, Promises, Victory

August 29

DAILY BIBLE READING: Jeremiah 51-52

TODAY'S VERSE: Jeremiah 51:16: "When he uttereth his voice, there is a multitude of waters in the heavens; and he causeth the vapours to ascend from the ends of the earth: he maketh lightnings with rain, and bringeth forth the wind out of his treasures."

I LOVE VERSES that show the power and authority of our God over all of creation! All creation bows before Him! The wonders of our universe originated in the mind of God and were placed by His hand and His Word. Is it a wonder that His voice thunders like the sound of many waters, or that His greatness exceeds our own, overwhelming our puny existence on this earth? This verse is actually telling us of the power and authority of the Word of God. Everything that happens in it is dependent upon the very first phrase, "When he uttereth his voice." This should not be hard to us to believe, for Hebrews 11:3a tells us, "Through faith we understand that the worlds were framed by the *word* of God."

First, we see the **Reaction of Creation** ("When he uttereth his voice, there is a multitude of waters in the heavens"). The word translated "multitude" means "a noise, tumult, a crowd." All creation is moved at the voice of God! Creation always responds to the Creator. Psalm 104:32 says, "He looketh on the earth, and it trembleth: he toucheth the hills, and they smoke." The winds and sea obeyed Christ when He spoke. The fig tree withered when He spoke. Jesus even told the Pharisees that if the people would hold their peace from praising Him, the rocks would cry out! What a mighty God!

Second, we see the **Response of Creation** ("and he causeth the vapours to ascend from the ends of the earth"). The word for "ascend" means "to ascend, be high or *actively mount*." The air is constantly moving, turning, twisting, and rising, all because of the Word of God! If only Christians would be moved and "actively rise" when they hear the Word of God! Isaiah heard an angel and saw the "posts of the door moved at the voice of him that cried"—we have the privilege of hearing the Word of God Himself! If our praise would begin to "ascend" to heaven, we would see the voice and the presence of God move on our behalf. Paul and Silas one night were praising God for their persecution, and Acts 16:26 says, "And suddenly there was a great earthquake, so that the foundations of the prison were shaken."

Third, we see the **Revelation of Creation** ("he maketh lightnings with rain"). We can learn so much about the Creator by studying creation. How can God make lightning with rain? I was always taught that water and electricity don't mix! Adam Clarke in his commentary says, "For the electric spark, by decomposing atmospheric air, converts the hydrogen and oxygen gases, of which it is composed, into water; which falls down in the form of rain."[5] Isn't God's word magnificent?

Fourth, we see the **Release of Creation** ("and bringeth forth the wind out of his treasures"). Have you ever felt the wind blow? What a refreshing blessing from the Lord! Did you know that we can feel the wind blow in a spiritual way as well? Acts 2:2 says, "And suddenly there came a sound from heaven as of a rushing mighty wind, and it filled all the house where they were sitting." You should be able to hear a wind begin to blow when you open the Word of God this morning! Can you feel it begin to blow as we are speaking now? Are we praying for God to release the wind from His treasures so that we can experience His wonderful blessings? Remember what Jesus told Nicodemus in John 3:8: "The wind bloweth where it listeth, and thou hearest the sound thereof, but canst not tell whence it cometh, and whither it goeth: so is every one that is born of the Spirit." When you sense the wind out of God's treasures, thank Him for sharing His wealth with you!

TOPICS: Bible, Creation, Nature, Revelation, Wonder, Word of God, Worship

---

5   Adam Clarke, *Holy Bible with Commentary and Critical Notes*, Vol 4. (New York: B. Waugh and T. Mason for the Methodist Episcopal Church, 1846), 390.

DAILY BIBLE READING: Lamentations 1–2

TODAY'S VERSE: Lamentations 1:1: "How doth the city sit solitary, that was full of people! how is she become as a widow! she that was great among the nations, and princess among the provinces, how is she become tributary!"

EVEN THE NAME of this book tells us the great grief and sorrow in which Jeremiah wrote. The Hebrew word for "lamentations," used in several forms in Scripture, means "to bewail, to groan, to mourn . . . a dirge accompanied by beating upon the breasts or instruments." We are talking about the deep anguish, misery, and woe of someone's heart. Jeremiah's sorrow came as a result of Israel's rejection of God's Word and their deliverance into the hands of their enemies. Even in this first verse of the book, we catch a glimpse of Jeremiah's heartache as he remembers Jerusalem.

Israel Had Experienced Great Desolation ("How doth the city sit solitary, that was full of people!"). The city that was once called the apple of God's eye was now empty and bare. It had teemed with activity, from commerce to religious festivals, but that was past. Loneliness is a terrible companion. This solitary city was empty only because of God's judgment. It was what the Old West would call a "ghost town." There was more life in the city when enemies were plundering the palace than there was now! But even if we are spiritually desolate today, we have this promise in Galatians 4:27: "For it is written, Rejoice, thou barren that bearest not; break forth and cry, thou that travailest not: for the desolate hath many more children than she which hath an husband." There is always hope where God is concerned!

Israel Had Experienced Great Death ("how is she become as a widow!"). It was as if no one cared for Israel anymore. Poor and forlorn this lady now was! No glory. No compassion. No friend. This was clearly a cause for serious bereavement and mourning. Praise the Lord that God can bring new life!

Israel Had Experienced Great Disgrace ("she that was great among the nations, and princess among the provinces"). Gone were the days of grandeur in the reigns of David and Solomon. Forgotten were the sacrifices at the Temple. Most nations, at one time, had been forced to check with Jerusalem before going forward with their plans. That was no longer necessary. Yet even now, Israel still had hope if the people would repent. We have that same hope today. James 4:10 says, "Humble yourselves in the sight of the Lord, and he shall lift you up."

Israel Had Experienced Great Defeat ("how is she become tributary!"). This was a great shame for Israel. They had once been the authority receiving the tributary money from all those they had conquered, but now they were in captivity. Yet, God still had—and has!—a plan for His people Israel. In Jeremiah 29:14 we hear the words, "And I will be found of you, saith the LORD: and I will turn away your captivity, and I will gather you from all the nations, and from all the places whither I have driven you, saith the LORD; and I will bring you again into the place whence I caused you to be carried away captive." This is a promise of future victory and exaltation! We can hope in God no matter how bad our situation may be.

TOPICS: Death, Defeat, Desolation, Judgment, Hope, Loneliness, Punishment, Restoration, Victory

DAILY BIBLE READING: Lamentations 3-5

TODAY'S VERSE: Lamentations 3:26: "It is good that a man should both hope and quietly wait for the salvation of the LORD."

THIS CHAPTER IS VERY DIFFERENT from most other chapters in Scripture. Jamieson-Fausset-Brown's commentary tells us that "The stanzas consist of three lines, each of which begins with the same Hebrew letter."[6] Twenty-two Hebrew letters, multiplied by three lines in each stanza, gives us sixty-six verses, corresponding to the number of books in the Bible. Three, the multiplier, is also the number of divinity. Our text is found in the ninth stanza under the heading of the Hebrew letter *Teth*. It is interesting that all three of these verses, verses 25 through 27, begin with the word "good." Let's hear what our verse is telling us is so good.

There Is Sweetness in Waiting on God ("It is good"). There is nothing as sweet and peaceful as a man waiting on God. Waiting is a *good* thing. It is not disappointing, nor is it angering. The Bible just calls it "good." What a pleasant word! God thinks so much of this word that it is used seven hundred and twenty times in Scripture. God used it in the beginning to describe His creation; now He turns and says that it is *good* for you to wait upon Him.

There Is Satisfaction in Waiting on God ("that a man should both hope . . . "). This whole phrase comes from a word meaning "to twist or whirl (in a circular or spiral manner), i.e. (specifically) to dance." I have a daughter, our middle child, who is a twirler. If she has a minute to wait, she twirls. There have been times when we were getting ready to load up in the van and leave, and she would just be twirling in the living room or kitchen. I would stop her and ask, "Bethany, what are you doing?" She would just say, "Spinning—just waiting till we go!" She wasn't worried or concerned. She was satisfied with waiting on her father and his timing for taking her away! Hallelujah! Let's start spinning and waiting upon God!

There Is Silence in Waiting on God ("and quietly wait"). Have you ever been around someone who didn't have much to say? My wife's grandfather, an old Baptist preacher, didn't have much to say; but if and when he did speak, you had better listen! Far too often, our mouths are running and our minds have stopped. We need to learn to wait in silence, listening for the Word of God to lighten our path in daily life and also for the Trumpet of God that will call us away!

There Is Salvation in Waiting on God ("for the salvation of the LORD"). The word translated "salvation" carries "the sense of rescue." Though God has already saved my soul from eternal punishment, many other times He saves and rescues me from troubles, trials, and even enemies. Proverbs 20:22 even tells us not to fight our own battles: "Say not thou, I will recompense evil; but wait on the LORD, and he shall save thee."

TOPICS: Deliverance, Patience, Salvation, Satisfaction, Trust

---

6   Robert Jamieson, A.R. Fausset, David Brown, A Commentary, Critical and Explanatory, of the Old and New Testaments. Vol. 1. (New York: Fleming H. Revell, 1917), 562

DAILY BIBLE READING: Ezekiel 1–3

TODAY'S VERSE: Ezekiel 1:1: "Now it came to pass in the thirtieth year, in the fourth month, in the fifth day of the month, as I was among the captives by the river of Chebar, that the heavens were opened, and I saw visions of God."

TODAY'S VERSE IS THE VERY FIRST in a new book. I love how it ends: "That the heavens were opened, and I saw visions of God." We should desire this each and every day of our lives! However, the only way we can see "visions of God" today is by faith. All visions are now subjected to the Word of God. God will no longer give new revelation apart from His Word to man. All revelation is in the Scriptures and must therewith be confirmed. The truth of God's Word can be taught to us by the Holy Spirit, but Scripture will never contradict itself! In this verse, we see three things that could not limit God in giving to His servant, the son of man, an open heaven and a vision of Himself. (Ezekiel is referred to as "the son of man" well over eighty times in this book. That gives us a true type and picture of Jesus Christ!)

God Is Not Bound by a Period of Time ("Now it came to pass in the thirtieth year, in the fourth month, in the fifth day of the month"). Thirty years it had been! How many people would have given up on God by then? Thirty years *in captivity,* no less! Had God forgotten His people and His promises? The easiest thing for Ezekiel and the other captives to do would be to give up on their hope of freedom and following God. Thank God for faithful people who were still waiting and trusting in God to reveal Himself and His work! If it has been a long time since you heard from God, every time in the past that God moved and spoke to you should be a reminder to seek Him again!

God Is Not Bound by a Prison of Trial ("as I was among the captives"). The people of Israel were in captivity because of their disobedience. Even in the midst of punishment, God can change your life! Some people mistakenly believe that God will only give revival to those who deserve it. Let's be honest with ourselves: who among us deserves it? For God to show up, ever, is grace! It is true that God wants to send revival to those who seek Him, trust Him, and have given their hearts to follow Him, but if God gives such people revival, they must receive it as a gift and blessing and not as their right. Whether you are in a "prison" because of your own doing or because of some situation beyond your control, remember that God spoke to captives in the land of Babylon so many years ago and gave them His Word as a point of strength!

God Is Not Bound by a Place of Trouble ("by the river of Chebar"). Where was this river of Chebar? It was not in the promised land of God's blessing to His people. Aren't you glad today that God is not bound by location? God can speak to your heart right here, right now! God can hear you in the prayer closet as He can hear you utter a prayer in the emergency room. It does not matter where you are right now! God can bless you with His presence at this very moment. Psalm 69:17 says, "And hide not thy face from thy servant; *for I am in trouble:* hear me speedily." God is more concerned about your *problem* than He is about your *place.* Whether or not you have *failed your Lord, fallen in your loyalty, or fainted in your life,* God can be right where you are with you! Be looking for Him constantly, for He knows what you need and when.

TOPICS: God's Faithfulness, Trials, Prayer

DAILY BIBLE READING: Ezekiel 4–7

TODAY'S VERSE: Ezekiel 4:1: "Thou also, son of man, take thee a tile, and lay it before thee, and pourtray upon it the city, even Jerusalem."

THIS PROPHECY OF EZEKIEL is of utmost importance.

The diorama Ezekiel made was planned by God so that His people might receive a warning. Ezekiel made a model of the city being besieged by the enemy as a prophecy of what God was going to do because of their disobedience and attempts to change the Word of God. More often than not, God prepares pictorial illustrations for our learning, yet we seldom see their importance or their significance. As a young boy, I loved audio and visual lessons. Whether it was flannelgraph, an object lesson, or even flashcards, I loved to *see* something while the teacher taught. As an adult, I've heard preachers describe someone in their congregation as "a living message." Through the living message of Ezekiel, God gave Israel a model and an object lesson.

It Was a Prepared Lesson ("Thou also, son of man, take thee a tile, and lay it before thee"). It's a funny thing about object lessons—they must be prepared. God is easily able to prepare a lesson for us to see or to prepare *in* us a lesson for others. Sometimes we wonder why God would have us go through some trial that brings great pain and struggle. I know of a preacher who went through a difficult time as a young man. He told his story as an illustration one night and was approached by twin teenage brothers immediately following the service who were going through the very same thing. When they asked the preacher why God would allow something like that to happen, the preacher looked at those young men and said, "Maybe just because God knew that one day I would stand before two young men going through the same thing who need to know that God loves them and is with them through this time of trial." God will go a long way to prepare a lesson! Don't become angry at what the Lord is doing in your life, for He may use you and your story to save a soul from hell or to give encouragement to another Christian to follow Him.

It Was a Pictorial Lesson ("and pourtray upon it the city"). The lesson on the tile was something the people could actually see. As a man, I share the characteristic of not being very good at following enclosed instructions! However, when I do use instructions, it is of necessity, and I need pictures to show me what the words are telling me. Jesus gave us the picture of washing the disciples' feet in John 13:15: "For I have given you an example, that ye should do as I have done to you." The prophets give us pictures of how we are to act in trouble and affliction: "Take, my brethren, the prophets, who have spoken in the name of the Lord, for an example of suffering affliction, and of patience" (James 5:10). Even Christ, the very Son of God, lived upon the earth in part to give us the perfect picture of how to live the Christian life in the power of the Holy Ghost: "For even hereunto were ye called: because Christ also suffered for us, leaving us an example, that ye should follow his steps" (1 Peter 2:21). What a picture has been left here!

It Was a Pertinent Lesson ("even Jerusalem"). You could say that this illustration hit home. Have you ever left a service thinking that the preacher was talking to you? I know of a couple that visited a church service. As soon as they picked up their children, left the church, and closed the car door, they said to one another, "That was weird! He answered every question we have asked each other this week!" How is that possible? Is there really a little bird that tells the preacher everything that is going on in your life? No, that pertinent lesson you hear is the work of the Holy Ghost! God knows what is going on in your heart and life, and He makes His message pertinent to you!

TOPICS: Lessons, Preachers, Word of God

R. CHRIS HANKS

DAILY BIBLE READING: Ezekiel 8–11

TODAY'S VERSE: Ezekiel 8:8: "Then said he unto me, Son of man, dig now in the wall: and when I had digged in the wall, behold a door."

IN THE PREVIOUS VERSES, God took Ezekiel by his hair in the Spirit and showed him the abominable works the people had been doing. When God brought him to the door of the court, it was to show him a hole in the wall. By doing this, God showed Ezekiel a people who were *busy in their sin* **and** *broken in their substance,* and who had a *breach in their security.* They were hiding behind a wall that was broken and open to the eyes of all. Even in its perfect state, this wall could not have kept them from the sight of God. Proverbs 15:3 says, "The eyes of the LORD are in every place, beholding the evil and the good." When Ezekiel began this God-ordained inspection, he was appalled at the wickedness of all that was happening. Many times in this chapter God says, "Turn thee yet again and thou shalt see greater abominations that these." If we could see through the eyes of a holy God, we would be convinced of man's utter corruption and of God's mercy.

We see an **Expressed Inspection** ("Then said he unto me, Son of man, dig *now*"). Our making things right with God must be done immediately! Salvation cannot wait! Second Corinthians 6:2 says, "Behold, now is the accepted time; behold, *now is the day of salvation.*" Repentance cannot wait! Isaiah 55:6 says, "Seek ye the LORD *while he may be found,* call ye upon him while he is near." Revival cannot wait! Hebrews 3:13 says, "But exhort one another daily, *while it is called To day;* lest any of you be hardened through the deceitfulness of sin." Many people have missed salvation, revival, and the presence of God because of five little words: "I will do it later." If the Holy Spirit is convicting you, deal with it now! Don't delay!

We see an **Expanded Inspection** ("dig now in the wall"). Ezekiel's discovery began as a little hole in the wall. It was much bigger by the time he was done! As a matter of fact, the next verse says, "And he said unto me, *Go in.*" If Ezekiel could walk into the hole, we know it was quite a bit bigger than it was in the beginning! There has been many a time when I was listening to the preacher clothed in my own righteousness and covered up with some sack I had thrown on to disguise my pet sin. As the man of God began to open the Word of God, the Holy Spirit began to find the holes in the loose clothes I wore as a pretense. By the end of the sermon, I sat in tattered rags, knowing that there is nothing hidden from God's sight. He had digged in my wall and found so much more! Hebrews 4:12 says, "For the word of God is quick, and powerful, and sharper than any twoedged sword, piercing even to the dividing asunder of soul and spirit, and of the joints and marrow, and is a discerner of the thoughts and intents of the heart."

We see an **Exposed Inspection** ("and when I had digged in the wall, behold a door"). Now we need to hear the next verse in Hebrews: "Neither is there any creature that is not manifest in his sight: but all things are naked and opened unto the eyes of him with whom we have to do" (Hebrews 4:13). When God expanded His convicting work, He exposed more things than Ezekiel knew existed! When Ezekiel began to dig in this wall, he found a door. Have you ever come to a place you knew well, only to say later, "I never even knew that was there!" As we walk with Him, God will show us many things about ourselves, the Word of God, and the Christian life that we don't even know are there!

TOPICS: Conviction, Holy Spirit, Preaching, Revival

DAILY BIBLE READING: Ezekiel 12–15

TODAY'S VERSE: Ezekiel 14:14: "Though these three men, Noah, Daniel, and Job, were in it, they should deliver but their own souls by their righteousness, saith the Lord GOD."

WE HAVE HERE A SPARK of spiritual glory in the midst of chapters of impending doom. Some would argue that this verse isn't very encouraging because it says that even these three great men of God would be unable to save the nation. It is very sobering when someone has gone past the help of intercessory prayer. The nation of Israel was so far gone that not even the righteous prayers of these three godly men could keep the judgment of God from coming upon them. So what is it that makes this verse so encouraging to me? It is this phrase: "They should deliver but their own souls by their righteousness." Let it be said very clearly here that we are not talking about eternal life and delivering ourselves from hell, but rather about doing right and delivering ourselves from the punishment of God in our earthly lives. Yes, our works upon this earth do matter! "He that covereth his sins shall not prosper: but whoso confesseth *and forsaketh them* shall have mercy" (Proverbs 28:13). What a testimony Noah, Daniel, and Job had that even Jehovah God would refer to their works as righteous! Let's look at the characteristics of these men that can help us do right in the sight of God.

A Prepared Noah. We are told of the thing that marked Noah's faith in Hebrews 11:7: "By faith Noah, being warned of God of things not seen as yet, moved with fear, *prepared* an ark to the saving of his house; by the which he condemned the world, and became heir of the righteousness which is by faith." Noah was *prepared in the work*. He prepared the ark as God directed, with the greatest detail in *materials* (gopher wood and pitch), *measurements* (cubit measurements), *modifications* (window, door, and cubit above), and *mission* (to get the animals). Second, he was *prepared in the Word*. Second Peter 2:5 says that God "spared not the old world, but saved Noah the eighth person, a preacher of righteousness." Third, he was *prepared in his witness*. Noah tried for over one hundred years to tell others of God's judgment, but they would not hear. His family heard and believed for themselves, and Noah was able to save his own house!

A Pure Daniel. Daniel was a contemporary of Ezekiel. Scholars believe that Daniel was already in his fourteenth year of captivity as he served a heathen king in a heathen land. Daniel, however, had achieved celebrity status as his initial pilgrimage to Babylon, and his commitment to obeying the law of God had already been reported. Daniel 1:8 tells us, "But Daniel purposed in his heart that he would not defile himself with the portion of the king's meat, nor with the wine which he drank: therefore he requested of the prince of the eunuchs that he might not defile himself." What an encouragement this must have been to the remnant living in broken walls and burned gates in Jerusalem! Thank God for those who will not compromise but hold to the precepts and righteousness of the Word of God!

A Patient Job. James 5:11 tells us of the most gleaming of Job's characteristics: "Behold, we count them happy which endure. Ye have heard of the *patience of Job, and have seen the end of the Lord;* that the Lord is very pitiful, and of tender mercy." Job was willing to endure affliction and trust in the Lord to make things right. Job saw the death of his children, the loss of all his possessions, the corruption of his body, and even the scorn of his wife, yet "in all this Job sinned not, nor charged God foolishly" (Job 1:22). Though you may go through circumstances and situations that seem unfair, be patient and trust in the Lord, for He will make all things right!

TOPICS: Patience, Perseverance, Preparation, Purity

R. CHRIS HANKS

DAILY BIBLE READING: Ezekiel 16–17

TODAY'S VERSE: Ezekiel 16:4: "And as for thy nativity, in the day thou wast born thy navel was not cut, neither wast thou washed in water to supple thee; thou wast not salted at all, nor swaddled at all."

THE BEGINNING VERSES of chapter 16 are a history lesson to the nation of Israel from God Himself, like a father telling his children stories of when they were babies. First, we see their *reputation at birth* (verse 3—their father was an Amorite; their mother a Hittite). Second, we see the *review of their birth* in verse 4. Third, we see the *rejection of their birth* (verse 9—they were cast out into the open field. Fourth is their *rescue at birth* (verse 6, God said unto them, "Live"). Fifth is the *reinforcement of God's blessing* in verses 7–14. Sixth, we see the *reproach of their betrayal,* **verses 15–43**. Seventh is the *rebuke of God's burden* in verses 44–59. Finally, we see the *restoration of God's blessing* in verses 60–63. With that overview in mind, let us look a little more carefully at verse 4 as God reviews Israel's birth.

Their Life Began with an Act of Abortion ("And as for thy nativity, in the day thou wast born thy navel was not cut"). This was an unwanted pregnancy. Because of that, the parents did not cut the umbilical cord. If an infant's umbilical cord is not cut, the child, still connected to the placenta, will bleed to death. From the beginning, nobody wanted Israel. In our global society, we can see how often this is still true today. Maybe you can identify with Israel's story as a person who was seen as unnecessary and unwelcome. The good news is that, as in the case of Israel, God wants you!

Their Life Began with Abandoned Attention ("neither wast thou washed in water to supple thee"). As a father of five, I participated in the first bath each of my children received. One of the first things the doctor or nurse does after primary care has been given is to give the newborn a bath. No matter what is going on, the new baby will receive a bath within the first hours of its birth. Thank God for the water of the Word of God that immediately begins to wash every new believer! How sad it is when a baby does not receive the attention it needs. Without the attention of a caregiver, it is certain that an infant's life will end in shame, pain, and rejection. God saw us all in such a condition: in the shame of our sin, the pain of our suffering, and the rejection of relations and religion that could not help us in our problem. Praise the Lord for His wonderful attention to us!

Their Life Began with Abnormal Affection ("thou wast not salted at all, nor swaddled at all"). A moment ago, we learned about the washing in "water to supple thee." That has to do with lack of tenderness. Here we read that Israel was "not salted at all." This has to do with lack of toughness, or firming of the skin. A baby would be salted in a solution to firm its skin, then swaddled—just as Mary wrapped the baby Jesus in swaddling clothes to protect Him and to keep Him warm. For a mother to reject her baby and not desire to nurse it, take care of it, and meet its every need shows a total lack of natural affection. Care and affection go into the effort of a mother to take a vulnerable, misunderstood child and with the most cautious and meticulous manner, begin to wrap him up in a motherly love. Israel had never experienced that with anybody until God took them and wrapped them in His love and tender care.

Many scholars attest that this Scripture refers to the Egyptians' treatment of Israel and God's care for them as they left their captors and began their life as a nation. God is reminding Israel of how He found them—destitute and left for dead! We should all be able to thank God and praise Him for His wonderful love.

TOPICS: Care, Love, Neglect, Rejection, Word of God

DAILY BIBLE READING: Ezekiel 18-20

TODAY'S VERSE: Ezekiel 18:23: "Have I any pleasure at all that the wicked should die? saith the Lord God: and not that he should return from his ways, and live?"

THE WORLD HAS A DISTORTED VIEW of God. They don't really believe that God loves them, because natural thought cannot understand why a God who is omnipotent would not give us everything we want. It has never dawned on the world that God wants what is good for them and has already provided what is best in the sacrifice of His only Son. Contrary to what the world will tell you, God does not want to destroy anybody! Psalm 78:38 says, "But he, being full of compassion, forgave their iniquity, and destroyed them not: yea, many a time turned he his anger away, and did not stir up all his wrath." Some would ask why the Lord created hell. I would ask why anyone would reject Christ! This verse tells us of the wondrous love of God and His desire that man come unto Him for forgiveness to begin a new relationship with Him.

God Desires Rejoicing Rather than Retribution ("Have I any pleasure at all that the wicked should die? saith the Lord God"). The word translated "pleasure" means "to incline to, to bend." God is not bent toward judgment! Though He will be glorified by the destruction of the wicked, He takes no joy from their hardened hearts and future judgment. The Bible tells us very clearly in Luke 15:7, "I say unto you, that likewise joy shall be in heaven over one sinner that repenteth, more than over ninety and nine just persons, which need no repentance." God would much rather rejoice in the salvation of a sinner than give him what he deserves!

God Desires Repentance Rather than Reprimand ("and not that he should return from his ways"). God desires that we change our hearts and minds toward sin and see it through His eyes. We are often so clouded by our own desires and fleshly appetites that we cannot even see the sin that God sees. Luke 13:5 says, "I tell you, Nay: but, except ye repent, ye shall all likewise perish." The word "repent" in this New Testament verse means "to think differently." Many have done away with the term "repent" so as not to be offensive: this is a deadly mistake. *Repentance* is a Bible word, has a Bible function, and will produce a Bible result.

God Desires Revival Rather than Reckoning ("and live"). I did not really start to live until I was right with God! True revival comes after true repentance. Some people are trying to find this kind of life and peace by doing penance or even by trying to forgive themselves. What emptiness this leaves! It is only after the sorrow of repentance that God can bring new life, hope, and joy back into our lives to give us purpose and passion once again.

TOPICS: Mercy, Repentance, Revival, Sorrow

DAILY BIBLE READING: Ezekiel 21–22

TODAY'S VERSE: Ezekiel 22:30: "And I sought for a man among them, that should make up the hedge, and stand in the gap before me for the land, that I should not destroy it: but I found none."

THE SPOTLIGHT OF THIS VERSE is not on the man or the gap that needs to be filled. Its focal point is that which is not even mentioned—what is inside the hedge! If there was nothing important in the hedge, it would not need protection. Take it all away, and you would have nothing but a plain field. But that's not the case; rather, it's what is within the hedge that gives this verse impact. It's what is within our homes, our churches, and our hearts that makes the hedge so important. If that wasn't true, we'd all be competing for the best and most beautiful hedge to please God most. Instead, God draws our attention to the necessity of protecting what matters most. Hear the heart of our God as He alerts us to the value of what is inside our hedge.

God Was Looking for a Building Man ("I sought for a man among them, that should make up the hedge"). God found a man in Noah, Abraham, Moses, and Joshua. He found a man after His own heart in David. God is not just looking for a robot or some mindless imp to do His bidding, but for a man! I believe that God is still looking for a man today. The word for "make up" means "to wall in or around:—close up, fence up, hedge, inclose." God said that Abraham was a builder in Genesis 18:19: "For I know him, that he will command his children and his household after him, and they shall keep the way of the LORD, to do justice and judgment." We are to be built up in our Christian lives for the honor and glory of the Lord: "Rooted and built up in him, and stablished in the faith, as ye have been taught, abounding therein with thanksgiving" (Colossians 2:7).

God Was Looking for a Blocking Man ("and stand in the gap before me for the land"). God's command to the fathers in Israel was to teach the law of God to their children in order to block access to the evil way. We need men and fathers who will stand and be willing to lay down their lives for the sake of their children's innocence. They should block the evil influences upon their families, whether those influences come through media, friends and relationships, or even worldly amusements. We need blocking men who will protect their relationships with their wives from anything that would destroy them. We must block a hindering spirit in our churches and worship the Lord in spirit and in truth.

God Was Looking for a Burdened Man ("before me for the land, that I should not destroy it: but I found none"). This verse reminds me of Job as he made sacrifices for his children, thinking that they might have committed sin in their hearts against God. God was looking for someone who cared about the land and the people in it, but He found none. Is that what has happened today in Christians and in churches? Are we so apathetic that we really do not care for our community or for the souls represented therein? As Jesus looked out over Jerusalem, He wept. Let us get our burden back!

TOPICS: Building, Burden, Fathers, Prayer, Stand, Soul-Winning

DAILY BIBLE READING: Ezekiel 23–24

TODAY'S VERSE: Ezekiel 24:19: "And the people said unto me, Wilt thou not tell us what these things are to us, that thou doest so?"

UP TO THIS POINT, God has used Ezekiel to show forth God's message, whether by a diorama, a verbal message, or an object lesson as we see in this chapter. Yet, never had anything penetrated the heart of Israel as much as God's order in this chapter. God told Ezekiel that He would take away the love of the prophet's life at a stroke, bringing great grief to Ezekiel's heart. But what was the command of God to Ezekiel to show the people? Verses 16 and 17 give the order: "Yet neither shalt thou mourn nor weep, neither shall thy tears run down. Forebear to cry, make no mourning for the dead." Ezekiel was not allowed to mourn for the wife that he loved so much! This was finally something that would touch the hearts of the people of Israel—a death with no mourning! At last, the people demanded a response from Ezekiel as to what God was doing in his life.

A Personal Employment ("And the people said unto me, Wilt thou not tell us"). The people recognized that it was Ezekiel's duty and obligation to tell them what was going on. Finally, they wanted spiritual understanding about what the Lord was trying to show them. They began to ask him some pointed questions. So often, people do not want to hear what the preacher has to say—but when they *do* want to hear the Word of the Lord, they want it straight! Do you realize that we have a responsibility to tell others the straight truth of the gospel? It is our duty and obligation to share the Word of God with the lost! I don't want someone looking at me someday and asking, "Why didn't you tell me?" Ezekiel 33:8 says, "If thou dost not speak to warn the wicked from his way, that wicked man shall die in his iniquity; but his blood will I require at thine hand."

A Personal Explanation ("what these things are to us"). The people knew they needed someone to interpret what God was trying to tell them. Thank God for a man who knew what the Lord was telling his people! We need to hear the Word of God and learn "what these things are to us." How does the Word of God concern you and your life? What a great question to ask! For Israel to ask this question shows that a work of God had tenderized their hardened hearts. It took grief and sorrow for them to turn to the Lord and say, "How does this affect me?"

A Personal Experience ("that thou doest so?"). The last question in this verse is about the work of God in the preacher's life. They knew God was doing something in Ezekiel before they ever received it. Their question to him was much like the question, "How did you ever do it?" They also knew that Ezekiel's life was a warning to them as God kept reaching out to His people to return from the land of His judgment into the realm of His love. The whole reason God does what He does is to bring people unto Himself! What we find in this story is that God will do anything to bring His people back. He will even take the wife of someone who is obedient to show those who are disobedient how serious their offenses have been. That, my friend, is God's mercy! What a merciful God we serve!

TOPICS: Conviction, Duty, Preachers

DAILY BIBLE READING: Ezekiel 25–27

TODAY'S VERSE: Ezekiel 26:3: "Therefore thus saith the Lord God; Behold, I am against thee, O Tyrus, and will cause many nations to come up against thee, as the sea causeth his waves to come up."

TODAY'S READING DISCUSSES those who have gone against God's will and stood against God's people, trying to destroy them. God here levels this condemnation against them in order to make their ears tingle and give them proper warning. What a threat this was against the enemies, but what a thrill to the people of Israel! This is a principle we must learn: If you are on the receiving end of God's anger, take heed, for destruction is coming! If you are on the defending end of God's anger, what peace and comfort you can know! On what side are you this morning? For the child of God who is right with Him, this is a call to arms in the morning and a lullaby to sleep at night!

It Was a Condemnation of Terror ("Therefore thus saith the Lord God; Behold, I am against thee"). There are no more sobering and fearful words in the Bible than these: "I am against thee." They should bring every soul on earth to its knees! God is against our corrupt human nature. This prophecy against Tyrus was because of his pride, arrogance, and conceit. Romans 8:7 tells us, "The carnal mind is enmity against God: for it is not subject to the law of God, neither indeed can be." Don't be caught in that place of terror. Acts 5:30 warns us, "But if it be of God, ye cannot overthrow it; lest haply ye be found even to fight against God." That, my friend, will be a battle no person wins!

It Was a Condemnation of Tribulation ("and will cause many nations to come up against thee"). Tribulation will not necessarily come from one place—it will often come from an alliance of those who are against God. God would break every treaty and form of peace Israel thought they had to bring swift and sudden destruction upon them. Even those who were Israel's greatest companions would turn their backs and become their enemies.

It Was a Condemnation of a Tide ("as the sea causeth his waves to come up"). This warns us of the relentlessness of God's judgment. Whether high tide or low tide, the tide still comes in. This verse warns of God's anger as a state of prolonged high tide against His enemies, for it says, "As the sea causeth his waves *to come up.*" God's anger will rise and swell until it has completely consumed that which stands so rebelliously in its way. I heard the late Dr. Adrian Rogers say on the radio, "Even now the raging waves of God's wrath are furiously pounding against the dam of His mercy."[1] What a thought to consider today! What would happen if God's mercy were removed? Man would be overcome by the force and the flood of God's relentless judgment. Don't be on the side against God. If you cross to His side, you will enjoy the fellowship of His love instead!

TOPICS: Judgment, Punishment, Terror

---

1 Permission to use this quote was obtained from Love Worth Finding Ministries; visit www.lwf.org.

DAILY BIBLE READING: Ezekiel 28-30

TODAY'S VERSE: Ezekiel 28:14: "Thou hast been in Eden the garden of God; every precious stone was thy covering, the sardius, topaz, and the diamond, the beryl, the onyx, and the jasper, the sapphire, the emerald, and the carbuncle, and gold: the workmanship of thy tabrets and of thy pipes was prepared in thee in the day that thou wast created."

EZEKIEL TAKES UP his lamentation in verse 12 about the king of Tyre. This king was so evil that he allowed himself to be controlled by the devil. In today's verse, God refers to the king of Tyre as if he were the devil himself. Oh, how sad it is when one of God's creations has defied Him to the point of joining with the one who has sold himself to resist God and His plan for the rest of his time! One question that comes up often is, "Why did God make the devil?" The answer is that God did not make the devil. He made Lucifer. Lucifer became the devil by his own free will. God's creation was one of glory and greatness. The same can be said of man, but once again, man used his free will in a way that was not consistent with its Creator, and so has separated himself from his God. This verse gives us insight into God's creation of Lucifer before he became Satan.

A Creation of Magnificence ("Thou hast been in Eden the garden of God; every precious stone was thy covering, the sardius, topaz, and the diamond, the beryl, the onyx, and the jasper, the sapphire, the emerald, and the carbuncle, and gold"). How beautiful Lucifer must have been! The next verse says that he was "the anointed cherub that covereth." Different angels have different duties. The cherub's job was to guard the holiness of God, and Lucifer was the anointed cherub. Many believe that he was the only one able to be at the throne of God by himself. Use your imagination for one moment: think of how Lucifer looked as the *shekinah* glory of God radiated from the throne and cascaded off this beautiful, multicolored covering in a kaleidoscope of brilliant tints and hues into the vastness of heaven and even into universal space! But for some reason, Lucifer thought that some of this glory belonged to him, and he began to exalt himself and desire to sit in the throne that was reserved for God alone!

A Creation of Music ("the workmanship of thy tabrets and of thy pipes"). Some say that not only did Lucifer have musical ability, but that he was music itself. With every move and every thought, his was music meant to glorify God. Today, we can see the result of Satan's defiling music, perverting what is meant to be one of God's holiest gifts. Satan's music today is nothing more than a compilation of corrupt compositions, defiled dancing, and licentious lyrics bent around rebellion and self-pleasure. His music has even crept into churches today. Those ignorant souls who declare that "only the lyrics matter" have been duped by the simplest of Satan's attacks. It was music that warned Moses and Joshua of spiritual trouble in the camp when they came down from the mountain. Exodus 32:17-18 says, "And when Joshua heard the noise of the people as they shouted, he said unto Moses, There is a noise of war in the camp. And he said, It is not the voice of them that shout for mastery . . . but the *noise of them that sing do I hear.*" Only the devil's music sounds like "noise" and "war." Let our music glorify God as it issues from our hearts in spiritual worship.

A Creation of Ministry ("was *prepared* in thee in the day that thou wast created"). The only reason God created anything was to prepare it to glorify and serve Him! God had a job for Lucifer to do, but he rejected the way of the Lord. When Lucifer was thrown out of heaven, he took one third of the angels with him. Have you ever thought about how many other people are affected by your lack of service and obedience to the Lord? Our mission upon this earth to glorify God was what pleased Him when He created us! Let us fulfill that mission faithfully.

TOPICS: Devil, God's Purpose, Satan

DAILY BIBLE READING: Ezekiel 31–33

TODAY'S VERSE: Ezekiel 33:11: "Say unto them, As I live, saith the Lord God, I have no pleasure in the death of the wicked; but that the wicked turn from his way and live: turn ye, turn ye from your evil ways; for why will ye die, O house of Israel?"

EVEN IN THE OLD TESTAMENT, we can see the loving-kindness and longsuffering of our Lord. It is sad that so many people view God as a clouded fist waiting to drop out of the sky upon every worker of iniquity. That has never been the way our Lord has worked, and He defends His name and honor against such a picture vigorously in this verse. It was a message to be *carried* to them ("Say unto them"), a message given to the man of God to give to the people. It was also a message to *convince* them ("As I live"). It was something they could count on, for there would never be a time when God would not live! It was also a message that would *convict* them ("saith the Lord God"). God did not have to give the people this message, but He chose to give it because He loved them!

First, we see the **Message of Remorse** ("I have no pleasure in the death of the wicked"). God does not desire to destroy anybody. Can you hear the love of God calling out in its fair tones of hope and expectation? God did not make hell for man, but man will go there if he rejects God's great gift of salvation. Matthew 25:41 says, "Then shall he say also unto them on the left hand, Depart from me, ye cursed, into everlasting fire, *prepared for the devil and his angels.*" Nothing hurts God more than bringing judgment upon someone who will not respond to His love.

Second, we see the **Message of Repentance** ("but that the wicked turn from his way and live"). God's greatest desire for those who have gone in their own way is that they repent and turn themselves to the Lord. Cain, Esau, Baalam, Ahab, Manasseh, Pharaoh, Nebuchadnezzar—God wanted them all to turn to Him and repent of their sin. If we do not respond to God while He is near, we will end up in the helpless and hopeless place of never finding peace with God. Hebrews 12:16–17 tells us of the vain and fleshly attempt of Esau when it was too late to repent, "He was rejected: *for he found no place of repentance, though he sought it carefully with tears.*" The problem at this point was not that Esau would not repent, but that he could not! Don't end up in the forlorn place of God's judgment.

Third, we see the **Message of Request** ("turn ye, turn ye from your evil ways; for why will ye die, O house of Israel?"). Here, God Almighty is pleading with Israel. Ezekiel 18:23 says, "Have I any pleasure at all that the wicked should die? saith the Lord God: and not that he should return from his ways, and live?" We hear this same thought again in the New Testament in 2 Peter 3:9: "The Lord is . . . *not willing that any should perish,* but that all should come to repentance." His opportunity is still open to "whosoever will."

TOPICS: Conviction, Preachers, Repentance, Responsibility

DAILY BIBLE READING: Ezekiel 34–35

TODAY'S VERSE: Ezekiel 34:14: "I will feed them in a good pasture, and upon the high mountains of Israel shall their fold be: there shall they lie in a good fold, and in a fat pasture shall they feed upon the mountains of Israel."

WHAT A BLESSING it is to hear the Good Shepherd speak about taking care of His sheep. What a promise! What a pleasure! What a prospect!

Several things are "good" in this verse. The first is a **Good Pasture.** As we leave our protective fold and enter into a new field prepared by our Shepherd today, we are amazed at its verdant splendor and flourishing hills. As we open the precious Book, we are met by the sweetest fragrance of a thousand blooming fields! There is nothing as fertile and thriving as this precious pasture in God's Word! Do you not think that He will give us good things to eat? Luke 11:13 says, "If ye then, being evil, know how to give good gifts unto your children: how much more shall your heavenly Father give the Holy Spirit to them that ask him?" God wants to give good things to His sheep and His children. He even says, "Man shall not live by bread alone but by every word that proceedeth out of the mouth of God." The word of God is our meat, our milk, our honey, our water, and every good and nourishing thing there is for us! Savor its taste, ruminate and meditate over its thoughts, and let it strengthen and sustain you.

The next thing we see is **Good Peace** ("they shall lie in a good fold"). The word translated "lie" means "to crouch, on all four legs folded, like a recumbent animal." Whenever you are around a skittish animal, you will find that it is hard to make it lie down in peace. This reminds me of Psalm 23:2: "He maketh me to lie down in green pastures." What a place of peace God has prepared for us, even in the midst of our enemies! Oh child of God, sheep of faith in Christ, learn how to rest and lie down in His peace! John 14:27 says, "Peace I leave with you, my peace I give unto you." Accept and love His peace today!

The third thing we see is the fold, or **Good Place.** God tells us that His is a "good fold," and for that we are thankful. But He also tells us that it is "upon the high mountains of Israel" and upon the "mountains of Israel." We live in Colorado, and I have been on some of the highest peaks in the lower forty-eight states. When you are upon the mountains, you cannot help but look in awe upon the wonderful creation of God! These are mountains of *vision.* They are clean. They rise far above the dirt and smog of busy cities. They are pristine. These are mountains of *virtue.* The air is clean, the streams pure, and the vegetation fresh. Biblically, the mountains are symbolic of war and challenge. The mountains that God will lead us to are mountains of *victory!* Every foe we meet is a future victory that awaits us! Look around and enjoy the view of this great spiritual land! Enjoy the "good" life in God's presence!

TOPICS: God's Blessing, Peace, Provision, Shepherd

R. CHRIS HANKS

DAILY BIBLE READING: Ezekiel 36–38

TODAY'S VERSE: Ezekiel 37:1: "The hand of the Lord was upon me, and carried me out in the spirit of the Lord, and set me down in the midst of the valley which was full of bones."

THE STORY OF THE VALLEY of dry bones carries with it a great hope for revival. The real cause of revival in this passage is found a little later in verse 4: "O ye dry bones, hear the word of the Lord." There will never be a revival apart from the preaching and hearing of the Word of God! If we are going to have revival again in America, we must recognize that it will not happen apart from God's miraculous power and grace. Today, we will look at this verse through the eyes of one with a spiritual hunger for revival.

The Presence of God ("The hand of the Lord was upon me"). Many today have never felt the hand of God upon them in their worship, their witness, or their work for the Lord. Oh, for God to manifest Himself to us today! We have the promise of God in Matthew 18:20: "For where two or three are gathered together in my name, there am I in the midst of them." We know that God is here, but how we long for God to "prove" that He is here by laying His hand upon us as we worship Him! Sometimes He will fill a place with His glory, and other times He will speak in a still small voice. How I long for Him to have the preeminence! It is easy to have church, do what we do, and go home. But it was God's hand on Ezekiel that "carried him out in the spirit of the Lord and set him down in the midst of the valley." When God's presence is with us, things happen! My friend, when God shows up, you don't have to convince anybody of anything, for it is evident!

The Power of God ("and carried me out in the spirit of the Lord"). We are so easily carried about by our own desires and philosophies of Christian living that we have forgotten what it is like to be carried by the Spirit of God. If we do not pray in the Spirit, worship in the Spirit, or walk in the Spirit, how can we have revival? Zechariah 4:6 says, "Then he answered and spake unto me, saying, This is the word of the Lord unto Zerubbabel, saying, Not by might, nor by power, but by my spirit, saith the Lord of hosts." The true power of God is in the Spirit of God. We easily take up a pragmatic way about church work and worship that defies the Spirit of God. This is why we are commanded to turn away from anything that looks spiritual but has no Spirit of God in it: 2 Timothy 3:5 says, "Having a form of godliness, but denying the power thereof: *from such turn away.*"

The Passion of God ("and set me down in the midst of the valley which was full of bones"). God had something He wanted to show Ezekiel, and He was burdened about it! The word translated "set me down" is the same word that is first used in Genesis 8:4, which says, "And the ark *rested.*" Sometimes God will "settle you down" to show you an important truth or teach you a spiritual lesson about His love and His passion. Verse 2 tells us that God went further than just setting Ezekiel down to see: He "caused me to pass by them round about." That phrase means that God caused Ezekiel to "cross over and circle" what God wanted him to see. There was no doubt a lesson that God did not want Ezekiel to miss! Just because things seem hopeless doesn't mean they are! These were *dead* bones, and only God could bring life (John 14:6, "Jesus saith unto him, I am the way, the truth, and the life: no man cometh unto the Father, but by me"). These were *dry* bones, and only God could bring moisture (Job 21:24, "His breasts are full of milk, and his bones are moistened with marrow"). And these were *dislocated* bones (they had to come together "bone to his bone" in verse 7), and only God could bring them together again. Let us be looking for a resurrection and revival as God continues to move in our midst!

TOPICS: Burden, Holy Spirit, Power, Presence of God, Resurrection, Revival

DAILY BIBLE READING: Ezekiel 39–40

TODAY'S VERSE: Ezekiel 39:28: "Then shall they know that I am the LORD their God, which caused them to be led into captivity among the heathen: but I have gathered them unto their own land, and have left none of them any more there."

THIS VERSE PROPHESIES the end of God's restoration of Israel. I am glad we can say with David in Psalm 23:3, "He restoreth my soul"! What a great blessing to know that the end of God's judgment is coming! God's judgment, however, is not complete until His work of restoration has begun in fellowship, in fervency, and in faith. This verse shows us three major points that lead to God's restoration. During this restoration process, it is important that our spirits and attitudes toward the way of the Lord are tender and receptive to the correction we receive.

The Mind of God ("Then shall they know that I am the LORD their God, which caused them to be led into captivity among the heathen"). Notice that this verse tells us that God "caused [Israel] to be led into captivity." Why would God do such a thing? Let me remind you that with the exception of hell and the lake of fire, all of God's disciplines, chastisements, and judgments are issued with the intent to bring the guilty back to Himself. The phrase "which caused them to be led into captivity" comes from a root meaning "to denude (especially in a disgraceful sense); by implication, to exile (captives being usually stripped)." Every bit of shame, discomfort, and pain was exercised so that God's people would return to Him. In His judgment, God is using the shame of our sin as the catalyst for repentance.

The Mercy of God ("but I have gathered them unto their own land"). It is only by God's mercy that we can experience the wonders of His restoration. God is not obligated to give us mercy, for we deserve His full and complete judgment. What a blessing that there are forty-one verses in the Bible telling us that His "mercy endureth for ever"! No wonder the psalmist said in Psalm 89:1, "I will sing of the mercies of the LORD for ever: with my mouth will I make known thy faithfulness to all generations."

The Mastery of God ("and have left none of them any more there"). God is not bringing His people back most of the way, nor is He bringing most of them back. He is bringing them *all* back *all* the way! This shows His omnipotence in power and glory! Hallelujah for the full and complete work of God to extend His restoring hope to our hearts by bringing us back *all the way!* His work of salvation was complete in bringing us out of the pit and dungeon of sin; why would His restoring work be any different?

TOPICS: Conviction, Forgiveness, Mercy, Renewal, Shame

R. CHRIS HANKS

DAILY BIBLE READING: Ezekiel 41–43

TODAY'S VERSE: Ezekiel 43:2: "And, behold, the glory of the God of Israel came from the way of the east: and his voice was like a noise of many waters: and the earth shined with his glory."

THIS VERSE IS NOT SPEAKING about the rapture, but about the return of Christ. Verse 1 says, "Afterward he brought me to the gate, even *the gate that looketh toward the east.*" What a wonderful time when He will come triumphantly through the Eastern Gate! There will be no hindrance to His entrance. No Muslim graveyard will impede that glorious parade when Jesus Christ comes back to rule and reign in His Millennial Kingdom. That Eastern Gate, though it has been sealed, will open as a curtain to receive the Majesty of Heaven and Earth.

A Glorious Vista ("And, behold, the glory of the God of Israel came from the way of the east"). The word for *behold* is a prolonged word of interjection. In other words, it is trying to get your undivided attention! This will be something to behold! The Bible tells us that nobody will miss this awesome sight. I believe that as all saw Christ in Revelation 1:7, so all people will see Him upon His return. Oh, what glory He will have at His return! Those who fight against God and against His people will be overtaken by the glory that He possesses. It will come from the way of the east. That is exactly how God has done all these things from the beginning. Things always began in the east and worked their way westward. All knowledge has come from the east to the west. All science has come from the east to the west. So now, our Lord will come from the east to the west to set up His kingdom and show His glory.

A Glorious Voice ("and his voice was like a noise of many waters"). This was the voice that said, "Let there be light." This voice is talked about many times in Scripture. Psalm 46:6b says, "He uttered his voice, the earth melted"; and Psalm 68:33b says, "Lo, he doth send out his voice, and that a mighty voice." Yet it is also His voice that tenderly calls every sinner unto Himself. His voice is still actively calling people every moment of every day. Hebrews 4:7b says, "To day if ye will hear his voice, harden not your hearts."

A Glorious Vision ("and the earth shined with his glory"). What a time this will be when we see the earth shine with His glory! The earth today is groaning in its fallen state, as is said in Romans 8:22: "For we know that the whole creation groaneth and travaileth in pain together until now." How much the earth is longing for the glory of God to be in it again! There will come a time in which God will purge this old earth with fire and make it new, but even now it is longing for the glory of God to reign upon it under the authority of Jesus Christ. Can you imagine what it will be like when this earth shines with His glory? The word for "shine" means "to be luminous." The earth will not shine because of the sun, but because the Son gives it His glory!

TOPICS: God's Glory, God's Voice, Second Coming

DAILY BIBLE READING: Ezekiel 44–45

TODAY'S VERSE: Ezekiel 44:23: "And they shall teach my people the difference between the holy and profane, and cause them to discern between the unclean and the clean."

IN TODAY'S VERSE we read about the mission that God gave the priests to accomplish with His people. God wants His people to know about His moral character as well as about their depravity. If we are to follow Him and desire to live a holy life, we must be confronted by our own utter collapse and complete failure concerning our sinful nature. It is the Word of God and the conviction of the Holy Spirit that will expose our inadequacies and our faults.

The Delivery of the Preacher ("And they shall teach my people"). This word for "teach" has a multifaceted definition that is applicable to us in every dimension: "to flow as water (i.e. to rain); to lay or throw (especially an arrow, i.e. to shoot); figuratively, to point out (as if by aiming the finger)." This teaching first of all is not to be *stagnant*. The definition begins, "to flow as water." This is a constant *pouring*. It will consistently teach its truth in new ways of power and principle. It was also not to be *senseless*. The next part of the definition says, "to lay or throw (especially an arrow, i.e. to shoot)." This is a constant *purpose*. The arrow was a very defined weapon. It was not boiling oil to be poured upon a multitude. It was not some kind of weapon of mass destruction. It was meant for one particular enemy: it was very focused in its purpose. The message was very sensible and plain. This teaching was not *subtle*. The last part of the definition is "to point out (as if by aiming the finger)." This is a constant *pointing*. Thank God for preachers who are "pointed" in their preaching, although many times it will not be the message that cuts into your heart and points out your sin, but the Holy Spirit. When Stephen preached his message, the Bible says that the listeners "were cut to the heart." Sometimes the message of God will point it out and expose the very thing you are trying to hide.

The Difference of Policy ("the difference between the holy and profane"). God has very definite views concerning holy things and profane things. The word "difference" was rightly supplied in the King James, because the next Hebrew word, for "between," means "distinction." There is something distinctly different between holy and profane. The Bible says we need to beware of those who try to obscure the lines between right and wrong: "Woe unto them that call evil good, and good evil; that put darkness for light, and light for darkness; that put bitter for sweet, and sweet for bitter!" (Isaiah 5:20). This, my friend, is a description of the very time in which we are living! Many Scriptures tell us to differentiate between right and wrong, holy and profane. God has said that there is a difference. We must submit to His wisdom and truth and learn what those differences are.

The Discernment of Purity ("and cause them to discern between the unclean and the clean"). This is an area in which many of us have failed in our Christian lives—developing spiritual discernment. Hebrews 5:12–14 says this to us very plainly: "For when for the time ye ought to be teachers, ye have need that one teach you again which be the first principles of the oracles of God; and are become such as have need of milk, and not of strong meat . . . But strong meat belongeth to them that are of full age, even *those who by reason of use have their senses exercised to discern both good and evil*." We can easily take a glass out of the dishwasher and wash it by hand because it didn't get completely clean, yet we cannot seem to spiritually discern between clean and unclean things. Where has our spiritual discernment gone? Let us learn and discern the things that God has prepared for us today!

TOPICS: Discernment, Holiness, Preachers, Purity

DAILY BIBLE READING: Ezekiel 46–48

TODAY'S VERSE: Ezekiel 47:15: "Afterward he measured a thousand; and it was a river that I could not pass over: for the waters were risen, waters to swim in, a river that could not be passed over."

I ENJOY READING in this chapter of the waters that came out of the right side of the altar. It reminds me of when our "altar," Jesus Christ, was crucified and had His side pierced, and "forthwith came there out blood and water" (John 19:34). These waters continued flowing and became so great they could not be passed over, for they were "waters to swim in."

Many Christians are living in shallow water, with shallow faith, shallow understanding, shallow expectancy, and shallow commitment. This translates in our churches to muted mouths in our witness, feeble feet in our walk, and hesitating hearts in our desire and decision to serve the Lord. What a testimony it would be if we would wade out into deep waters of faith! Jesus wanted Simon (the fleshly name of Peter) to go out into deep water in Luke 5:4: "Launch out into the deep, and let down your nets for a draught." In deep water, one cannot stir up dust, jump ship, or throw mud at others. In deep water, one is subject to tides and currents. When a hurricane approaches land, big ships are turned loose to go out to sea into deep water. If they are tethered to the shore, they will be destroyed. Deep water can be your protection as well. Get your sea legs going, and go out by faith into the deep waters of God where you can experience a maritime miracle! Let's take a moment to look at this verse in light of the depths Jesus plunged to bring salvation to mankind.

These Were Unfeasible Depths ("Afterward he measured a thousand; and it was a river that *I could not pass over*"). It was beyond Ezekiel's ability to cross to the other side of these waters. There are some things we should not be able to "get over"! Don't ever get over what Jesus did for you on Calvary! Don't ever get over the tremendous waters that have come out of the side of the altar for the salvation of our souls. The degree of divine judgment that was against us created a pit and chasm that desired our complete destruction, but thank God for the waters that covered that judgment and lifted us above the chasm of our sin! Let me say it like this: "I cannot just pass over my Passover!" God may have passed over our judgment, but we should never pass over His mercy and grace!

These Were Unfathomable Depths ("for the waters were risen, waters to swim in"). The Bible never tells us how deep these waters got. We will never know the depths of sorrow, pain, and agony our Lord went through to purchase salvation for us. So too, we will never know the depths of His love, His power, and His care to make that same salvation available to mankind. No place God has determined for us to go upon this earth will ever go as deep as our Saviour has gone. This water has borne us up by its own strength and has literally lifted us up to the heavenlies.

These Were Unfordable Depths ("a river that could not be passed over"). The beginning of the verse says, *"I could not pass over."* Here it is saying, *"No one can pass over."* The point is not to get to the other side, but to go where the blood atonement will bear you up by its own power and carry you on its currents and tides to the glory of God. This is something that even the angels in heaven cannot get over! Why do you think there is "joy in the presence of the angels of God over one sinner that repenteth" (Luke 15:10)? Because the idea of salvation is amazing to them! No finite being will ever be able to absorb in truth or in deed the wonders of love and salvation from Almighty God to fallen man!

TOPICS: Blood, God's Depths

DAILY BIBLE READING: Daniel 1–2

TODAY'S VERSE: Daniel 1:8: "But Daniel purposed in his heart that he would not defile himself with the portion of the king's meat, nor with the wine which he drank: therefore he requested of the prince of the eunuchs that he might not defile himself."

I REMEMBER BEING TAUGHT this verse as a little child. Many sermons have been preached from this passage, and many books have been written on it. Philip P. Bliss, one of the great hymn writers, wrote a hymn called "Dare to be a Daniel," and the phrase has been used by many others as well. What do you dare to be today? Why not be a Daniel? In this verse, we find that Daniel was committed to obeying the Lord in all that he did. If only we had people with the same fervor and passion as Daniel did about godliness! Here are three principles of Daniel's life that might help us in our Christian lives.

He Was a Purposed Man ("purposed in his heart"). The word translated "purposed" means "to put." We need to put things in our hearts that will give us a cause. Too many people today live in a nomadic, transient manner without purpose, direction, or bearing. We must have some kind of purpose in order to live a life that is right before God. David knew this, for he asked his brother, "Is there not a cause?" (1 Samuel 17:29). When you have a cause, every decision and situation will take on a different meaning and govern your life accordingly. Find a purpose in God today.

He Was a Pure Man ("he would not defile himself"). What a testimony! This would be the beginning of a pattern for the rest of Daniel's life. If your life is lived according to the precepts of the Word and for the glory of God, it will be full of God's blessing and a witness of God's presence. A great description of Daniel's life is found in Proverbs 20:11: "Even a child is known by his doings, whether his work be pure, and whether it be right." Again, we see God's concern for youth and their purity in 2 Timothy 2:22: "Flee also youthful lusts: but follow righteousness, faith, charity, peace, with them that call on the Lord out of a pure heart." Purity is dismissed in our wicked society today, but do not think for a minute that God does not care about it!

He Was a Praying Man ("he requested of the prince of the eunuchs"). Daniel was looking for a way to do right. The meaning for the word translated "request" is "to search out (by any method, specifically in worship or prayer); to strive after." What a blessing it is to see someone seeking out a way to do right by prayer. First Corinthians 10:13 encourages us to do this very thing: "There hath no temptation taken you but such as is common to man: but God is faithful, who will not suffer you to be tempted above that ye are able; but will with the temptation also make a way to escape, that ye may be able to bear it." If a man is looking for the escape from evil, he can always find it.

Each one of these qualities in Daniel's life was connected to the others. His purpose was connected to his purity; his purity was connected to his prayer; his prayer was connected back to his purpose. This is how he lived his life—all the time, every day, in a heathen land—for the glory of God. Daniel's purpose changed his lifestyle and affected the lives of unbelievers in the process. We ought to desire to live an undefiled life so that Christ will be exalted. Titus 2:12 says, "Teaching us that, denying ungodliness and worldly lusts, we should live soberly, righteously, and godly, in this present world." Truly, let's dare to be a Daniel!

TOPICS: Prayer, Purity, Purpose

DAILY BIBLE READING: Daniel 3-4

TODAY'S VERSE: Daniel 3:25: "He answered and said, Lo, I see four men loose, walking in the midst of the fire, and they have no hurt; and the form of the fourth is like the Son of God."

THERE ARE PERHAPS FEWER than five stories in the Bible as well-known as this one. Shadrach, Meshach, and Abednego were sure of their resolve to obey the Lord and stand for what was right, no matter the cost. We will look at this verse today from the aspect of God's deliverance and His freedom!

They Experienced God's Deliverance ("He answered and said, Lo, I see four men loose"). Let me tell you this: these three Hebrew boys were already free when they were being bound up to be thrown into the furnace. Once they had made their decision, they threw themselves completely upon the altar of sacrifice and offered themselves to God. They were free from selfishness: what great strength there is in giving yourself to God! They were free from sorrow: what great joy there is in obeying God and His Word! They were free from shame: what great confidence there is in doing right! Galatians 5:1 says, "Stand fast therefore in the liberty wherewith Christ hath made us free, and be not entangled again with the yoke of bondage." Again, John 8:36 says, "If the Son therefore shall make you free, ye shall be free indeed." When Jesus raised Lazarus from the dead, He said, "Loose him, and let him go" (John 11:44). Our Saviour has come to "proclaim liberty to the captives and the opening of the prison to them that are bound" (Isaiah 61:1). Many people think that the Christian life is about rules and restrictions, but it is about *freedom!* Just like Shadrach, Meshach, and Abednego, I would rather be free in the fire of persecution than bound to the blessings of the world!

They Enjoyed God's Deliverance ("walking in the midst of the fire, and they have no hurt"). This little experience did not stop these young men from serving God. It did not ruin their spirit, restrict their service, or reject their sincerity! Instead, it confirmed each one of these things! Isaiah 43:2 says, "When thou passest through the waters, I will be with thee; and through the rivers, they shall not overflow thee: when thou walkest through the fire, thou shalt not be burned; neither shall the flame kindle upon thee."

They Expected God's Deliverance ("and the form of the fourth is like the Son of God"). Even Nebuchadnezzar knew anything was possible with God! To the king, this startling event answered *every* question. When he finally recognized that there was Someone Else at work in this situation, he bowed before God and acknowledged His power. The last part of verse 29 says, "Because there is no other God that can deliver after this sort." We need to set our hearts upon the presence of God; for when God comes, He will do greater things than we have ever known!

TOPICS: Deliverance, Persecution, Perseverance

DAILY BIBLE READING: Daniel 5-7

TODAY'S VERSE: Daniel 6:5: "Then said these men, We shall not find any occasion against this Daniel, except we find it against him concerning the law of his God."

I CANNOT TELL YOU how many times I heard the story of Daniel and the lion's den while a youth in Sunday school, and I never got tired of hearing it! What faith Daniel had! What victory! The Bible clearly says that his enemies could not "find any occasion against this Daniel." What a testimony! In order for his enemies to destroy Daniel, they would have to legislate against his religion. Sounds familiar, doesn't it? There will be times when your enemies will come against you to destroy you. This verse shows us the intentions and strategies of the enemies of God in their desire to destroy God's people.

The Snares of the Wicked ("Then said these men, We shall not find any occasion"). The word for "find" means "disclosure of a covered or forgotten thing." What a search must have been going on behind the scenes against Daniel! You talk about conspiracies! This rivals Watergate in notoriety. They left no stone unturned, no file untouched, and no acquaintance unaffected. The Bible describes this in Proverbs 16:27: "An ungodly man *diggeth up evil:* and in his lips there is as a burning fire." The word for "occasion" means "a pretext (as arising artificially)." These people did not mind laying down false accusations! There was no depth to which they would not stoop to get what they wanted. Politics was alive and well even back in a heathen monarchy thousands of years ago. Daniel practiced the truth of Psalm 119:110: "The wicked have laid a snare for me: yet I erred not from thy precepts."

The Snarls of the Wicked ("against this Daniel"). Daniel's enemies didn't even refer to him as a real person, but instead referred to him as *"this* Daniel." Oh, how they hated him! Every time they thought about him, their lips would curl and their teeth would show. Stephen heard the same snarls when he was stoned. The Bible says in Acts 7:54 that Stephen's persecutors "gnashed on him with their teeth." What do you do when your enemies are seething with bitterness that is centered upon you and your ultimate destruction? There is nothing you can do but wait. David said in Psalm 23:5, "Thou preparest a table before me in the presence of mine enemies." We must wait on the promises of God, the Word of God, and the power of God!

The Sneers of the Wicked ("except we find it against him concerning the law of his God"). To the politicians of Babylon, Daniel's faith was a joke! Their anger was actually centered upon their unbelief concerning God. They were willing to take on Daniel's God and hoped to show Him to be a farce! You see, they thought that if they could destroy Daniel, it would stand to reason that his faith was in vain. My, how they hated his "religion"! Daniel's dedication and faithfulness to worship his God was convicting, and they wanted no part of it. The word used for "find" is the same word used earlier in the verse that means "disclosure of a covered or forgotten thing." These men kept going over Daniel's faith, and they knew they were missing something. There had to be something connected to his faith in God that would bring certain death! Yet, remember the end of the story. If you find yourself in the same situation, don't allow the sneers and mocking of your enemies to discourage you from continually serving God with all your heart!

TOPICS: Faithfulness, Hatred, Mocking, Scorn, Snares

DAILY BIBLE READING: Daniel 8-9

TODAY'S VERSE: Daniel 9:21: "Yea, whiles I was speaking in prayer, even the man Gabriel, whom I had seen in the vision at the beginning, being caused to fly swiftly, touched me about the time of the evening oblation."

DANIEL'S PRAYER LIFE was one of the reasons he was such a great man. Not only did he spend time in prayer, but he received answers to his prayers! Oh, that God would give us men and women who know how to shake heaven with their prayers! The Bible very clearly states why our prayers are not answered in James 4:2–3: "Ye lust, and have not: ye kill, and desire to have, and cannot obtain: ye fight and war, yet ye have not, because ye ask not. Ye ask, and receive not, because ye ask amiss, that ye may consume it upon your lusts." God is more than willing to hear those who will believe in Him through their prayers. Let's look more closely at the answer to Daniel's prayer in today's verse.

It Was an Immediate Answer ("Yea, whiles I was speaking in prayer"). Many people think that if they start praying now, God will not answer them for weeks or even months down the road. Because they need an immediate answer, they will not even kneel down to pray. It's almost as if they expect God to have to think about their problem before giving them an answer. Matthew 6:8 says, "Be not ye therefore like unto [the heathen]: for your Father knoweth what things ye have need of, before ye ask him." If God knows what we need before we ask Him, He can answer our requests immediately! Remember that our sense of time is warped. God dwells in eternity. Even when Lazarus had been dead for four days, God resurrected him from the dead—right on time!

It Was an Impressive Answer ("even the man Gabriel, whom I had seen in the vision at the beginning"). This was God's messenger angel! This was this same Gabriel who would appear to Mary to tell her of the glad tidings of carrying the Christ child! God does not always send an angel in answer to prayer, but I suspect He sends them more than we realize. Hebrews 13:2 says, "Be not forgetful to entertain strangers: for thereby some have entertained angels unawares." Today's verse also tells us that Daniel had spoken with Gabriel before. Daniel just didn't stop bugging God with his requests, did he? What a blessing that we are not on a ration of prayers! God can hear all our prayers simultaneously.

(Before we move on, a note is needed: though God may send angels to minister to us, we do not pray to angels, nor do we worship them! Judges 13:16 says, "And the angel of the LORD said unto Manoah, Though thou detain me, I will not eat of thy bread: and if thou wilt offer a burnt offering, *thou must offer it unto the LORD*." Colossians 2:18 says, "Let no man beguile you of your reward in a voluntary humility and worshipping of angels, intruding into those things which he hath not seen, vainly puffed up by his fleshly mind.")

It Was an Imperative Answer ("being caused to fly swiftly"). This message was urgent! The word used for "being caused to fly" means "to tire (as if from wearisome flight)." This was a message that had to get here quickly! God does care about us and our burdens, and He knows the necessary timing. Luke 18:7–8a says, "And shall not God avenge his own elect, *which cry day and night unto him*, though he bear long with them? I tell you that *he will avenge them speedily*."

It Was an Illustrated Answer ("touched me about the time of the evening oblation"). God answered Daniel and touched him "at the time of the evening oblation," or the ninth hour. Let me remind you that the ninth hour was the time of the final evening oblation: the sacrifice of Christ Himself. Matthew 27:46 says, "And about the ninth hour Jesus cried with a loud voice, saying, Eli, Eli, lama sabachthani? that is to say, My God, my God, why hast thou forsaken me?" No prayers could ever be answered were it not for the "evening oblation" of Calvary!

TOPICS: Angels, Calvary, God's Care, Prayer

DAILY BIBLE READING: Daniel 10–12

TODAY'S VERSE: Daniel 10:19: "And said, O man greatly beloved, fear not: peace be unto thee, be strong, yea, be strong. And when he had spoken unto me, I was strengthened, and said, Let my lord speak; for thou hast strengthened me."

HAVE YOU EVER FELT that you had no strength left? You did not quit because you lacked a reason to keep going, but because you had no strength. Even for a godly man like Daniel, our spiritual battle can lead to utter exhaustion. It stands to reason that weariness can smother your effectiveness. Some are exhausted because of *self*. This is a *personal problem*. They have allowed their own minds to make them weary. They are worn out just by thinking about the Lord and His work. Others are exhausted because of *schedule*. This is a *priority problem*. They cannot seem to find the time to serve God or to spend with Him. Still others are exhausted because of *Satan*. This is a *power problem*. Though Satan is capable of throwing a powerful punch, perpetual pecking can bring down the strongest of warriors! As you contemplate this verse, let your mind be thoughtful about Brother Daniel and his need for divine strength to continue serving the Lord.

He Was Strengthened by a Word from Heaven ("And said"). This angel from heaven had a word on his heart. Truly, these were "good tidings"! If you are discouraged, down, and depleted, run to the Word of God for strength! God has likened His Word to milk, water, honey, and meat. Why? To tell us of its strength-giving qualities! Job said in Job 23:12, "Neither have I gone back from the commandment of his lips; I have esteemed the words of his mouth more than my necessary food."

He Was Strengthened by a Wonder from Heaven ("O man greatly beloved"). Perhaps the greatest wonder upon this earth is how an infinite and eternal God could love finite and sinful man! I have never ceased to be amazed at John 3:16: "For God so loved the world." The greatest miracle Jesus did upon this earth had nothing to do with feeding the multitudes or healing a disease. It was His love for people! Many times, the Bible speaks of Jesus being "moved with compassion" for people. This phrase can also be applied to you. You are a person "greatly beloved"! No matter what you have done or where you have been, you are loved dearly by God Himself.

He Was Strengthened by a Welfare from Heaven ("fear not: peace be unto thee, be strong, yea, be strong"). What a blessing to know that God has thoughts of peace towards us! Jeremiah 29:11 says, "For I know the thoughts that I think toward you, saith the LORD, thoughts of peace, and not of evil, to give you an expected end." Now I can be strong in my *problems,* for He said, "Peace be still" (Mark 4:39). I can be strong in my *path,* for He gave His Word "to guide our feet into the way of peace" (Luke 1:79). And I can be strong in my *purpose,* for He said, "Peace I leave with you, my peace I give unto you" (John 14:27). His peace upon our lives should strengthen us in our faith, our fervor, and our fight.

TOPICS: Bible, Love, Peace, Purpose, Strength, Word of God

DAILY BIBLE READING: Hosea 1–7

TODAY'S VERSE: Hosea 6:1: "Come, and let us return unto the Lord: for he hath torn, and he will heal us; he hath smitten, and he will bind us up."

THE STORY OF HOSEA is one of great emotion. It is hard for me to read this book without weeping as I think of God's love and my failures. There is more passion in this book than Shakespeare ever dreamed of! Hosea is a living narrative to the nation of Israel of the love of God for His people. God's people had adulterated themselves and prostituted their worship in idolatry, yet God would take them back! Hosea lived this picture in front of the nation of Israel and experienced great betrayal through the whoredoms of his wife. Yet, as a picture of God's love, Hosea brought her back to himself time and again. Praise the Lord for His constant drawing of His people to Himself no matter their lack of faithfulness to Him!

There Is Always a Hope for Revival ("Come, and let us return unto the Lord"). There is always room for repentance. No matter how far you are from God, there is always a place to turn around and come home! Luke 15:17–18 tells us of the Prodigal Son's repentance: "And when he came to himself, he said, How many hired servants of my father's have bread enough and to spare, and I perish with hunger! I will arise and go to my father, and will say unto him, Father, I have sinned against heaven, and before thee." A stigma is attached to repentance that should not be there. Repentance is connected to revival, not retribution! How much our heavenly Father longs to see us repent and return to Him in renewed and restored fellowship!

There Is Always a Healing in Revival ("for he hath torn, and he will heal us"). Notice that this verse does not just talk about the damage of our sin, but about God's chastisement. The word for "heal" is the Hebrew word *rapha,* which means "Giant, to heal, to mend, to cure." When you read about the "Rephaims" in Genesis 14 and 15, you are reading about giants who were also known as "quick healers." *Rapha* is a reminder of the name of God, *Jehovah Rophe,* which is defined for us in Exodus 15:26: "I am the Lord that *healeth* thee." With God's chastisement comes healing. Instead of becoming bitter against God for the judgment of your sin, wait; for God will surely bring healing where He brought judgment. David said after his sin with Bathsheba, "Make me to hear joy and gladness; *that the bones which thou hast broken may rejoice*" (Psalm 51:8).

There Is Always a Help in Revival ("he hath smitten, and he will bind us up"). The word for "smitten" means "to strike, beat." After God has smitten, there is not much strength left; however, God will strengthen that which has been bruised. The whole reason for His judgment is to bring us back into fellowship and love! Once God's punishment has been given, He begins to strengthen those things that hurt most.

TOPICS: Healing, Repentance, Restoration, Revival

DAILY BIBLE READING: Hosea 8–14

TODAY'S VERSE: Hosea 13:14: "I will ransom them from the power of the grave; I will redeem them from death: O death, I will be thy plagues; O grave, I will be thy destruction: repentance shall be hid from mine eyes."

BY THE TIME GOD SPOKE these words, Israel had done everything they could to destroy themselves. Have you ever looked back over your life and recognized that you should not even be here today? God said in Hosea 13:9, "O Israel, thou hast destroyed thyself; but in me is thine help." I sure am glad that God can help us even when we ruin everything! What mercy He shows to us every day! Today's verse goes into detail as to how exactly God will "help" Israel.

First, we see the **Commitment of God** ("I will ransom them from the power of the grave; I will redeem them from death"). Seven times in this chapter, God says "I will." Seven indicates that these promises are truly perfect and complete! God first gave them the promise of the resurrection. The word translated "power" means "the hand, (the open one indicating power, means, direction, as in distinction from the closed one)." The word for "ransom" holds a different meaning than I anticipated when I first studied this verse: it means "to sever." What meaning can these words have for us today? When God shed His blood to ransom us, it severed us from the hand of death!

Second, we see the **Chastisement of God** ("O death, I will be thy plagues; O grave, I will be thy destruction"). The day is coming in which God will conquer death once and for all. The fear of death has a hold on our flesh. Jesus came to deliver us from the clutches of the fear of death and its power. Hebrews 2:14–15 says, "Forasmuch then as the children are partakers of flesh and blood, he also himself likewise took part of the same; that through death he might destroy him that had the power of death, that is, the devil; and deliver them who through fear of death were all their lifetime subject to bondage." When would this happen? At Jesus' resurrection! He became the firstfruits of the resurrection of all men (1 Corinthians 15:20). Revelation tells us that Jesus has the keys of hell and of death! As a matter of fact, it wasn't much of a fight. You can hear the taunting of Christ in 1 Corinthians 15:55: "O death, where is thy sting? O grave, where is thy victory?" What a day when death will finally get what is coming to it!

Third, we see the **Consuming of God** ("repentance shall be hid from mine eyes"). God will not stop until death is completely consumed! We hear this same thought in 1 Corinthians 15:54b: "Death is swallowed up in victory." That word "swallowed" means "to drink down, i.e. gulp entirely." God's mercy is extended only to man. He will not have mercy upon His enemies of death, hell, and Satan! When God said that "repentance shall be hid from my eyes," it was a promise of annihilation. God is not going into this fight with His eyes shut, but He promises to shut His eyes against the enemies we see in this verse.

TOPICS: Death, Judgment, Resurrection, Victory

DAILY BIBLE READING: Joel 1–3

TODAY'S VERSE: Joel 2:14: "Who knoweth if he will return and repent, and leave a blessing behind him; even a meat offering and a drink offering unto the Lord your God?"

IF THERE IS HOPE for revival given in Scripture, this is the verse! If there is hope for America, this is the verse where we will find it. God's people had walked away from Him and received severe judgment because of their doings. God never casts away His children! Every discipline is to bring His child back to Himself and renew relationship in the full fellowship of the Spirit. Today's, let's examine three points in this verse.

The Appeal for God's Mercy ("Who knoweth if he will return and repent"). This verse closely resembles what the king of Nineveh said in Jonah 3:9: "Who can tell if God will turn and repent, and turn away from his fierce anger, that we perish not?" Some might say it is not right to ask a holy and just God for help because we deserve judgment. I say, cast yourself at the ever-merciful feet of God and see if He will not show you grace! First John 1:9 shares with us the willingness of our Lord to forgive our sin: "If we confess our sins, he is faithful and just to forgive us our sins, and to cleanse us from all unrighteousness."

The Application of God's Mercy ("and leave a blessing behind him"). This is what God does! The word translated "leave" means "to swell up, be redundant." Doesn't what Jesus did on Calvary get bigger to you as you live your Christian life? Don't you realize that He keeps on giving and forgiving? He is predictable when He forgives our sin, because He's done it all before! Thank God for His "redundant" mercy and ministry!

The Appeasement of God's Mercy ("even a meat offering and a drink offering unto the Lord your God"). What blessing would God leave behind Him? *Why* would God leave a blessing behind Him? A couple of things strike me about this part of the verse. Many people think that they must make appeasement to God and leave *their own blessing* behind themselves. Wasn't this the problem in the beginning with Cain and Abel? Instead of leaving our offering, we need *His* offering. The second thing is that God is going to perform and leave this blessing Himself. God has never offered a sacrifice to Himself that wasn't acceptable! When God performs the sacrifice, you can know that it was done properly! Is that not what Jesus has done with the sacrifice of Himself to God? Hebrews 9:14 says, "How much more shall the blood of Christ, *who through the eternal Spirit offered himself without spot to God . . .*" Was Jesus' sacrifice acceptable to God? Yes!

What a beautiful picture this passage gives of someone far from God who repents and returns to the Lord, and then God with great care, preparation, and precision makes a sacrifice for the sinner that is pleasing to Himself! Hallelujah! You may think that you are too far away from God to be brought into close fellowship with Him again. You are denying His infinite mercy! You are unbelieving of Christ's priestly ministry! Why don't you let Him make that offering and sacrifice to God on your behalf? It will be accepted!

TOPICS: Mercy, Offering, Sacrifice

DAILY BIBLE READING: Amos 1–5

TODAY'S VERSE: Amos 5:9: "That strengtheneth the spoiled against the strong, so that the spoiled shall come against the fortress."

THE LAST PART of Amos 5:8 says, "The Lord is his name." We are definitely talking about Jehovah, strengthening the spoiled! Are we not overcomers? Doesn't the Bible say "Greater is he that is in you, than he that is in the world" (1 John 4:4)? No matter what has happened in your life that may remind you of some failure or defeat, God can strengthen you again and change you into a victor for His glory.

A Message of Escape ("That strengtheneth the spoiled"). This word for "strengthened" means "to break off or loose." The very first part of strengthening someone is to loose him from bondage. What a strengthening time in my life when Jesus came, cut the bands of my sin, and loosed me from my great yoke of bondage! Some of my readers may have been spoiled by an enemy in the sin of a selfish life, a sensual life, or a secret life. The word translated "spoiled" means "violence, ravage, desolation." Many today have been spoiled from moral purity, spiritual victory and blessing, peace in living, and fellowship with God. Yet God is able to deliver you today from the ravages of sin and wickedness!

A Message of Enablement ("That strengtheneth the spoiled against the strong"). How can one who has been beaten down by continual defeat and relentless pounding rise again to live a life of hope and fulfillment? It will take a work of God! It's very interesting that the preposition "against," when used this way, means "always in this last relation with a downward aspect." How much I anticipate "looking down upon" my enemies! Isaiah gives us this hope that one day we will look down upon the devil: "They that see thee shall narrowly look upon thee, and consider thee, saying, Is this the man that made the earth to tremble, that did shake kingdoms" (Isaiah 14:16). God can enable us to fight against the strong ones that have dominated us for so long.

A Message of Exultation ("that the spoiled shall come against the fortress"). The Bible teaches that our Saviour has bound up the strong man (the devil) to deliver us from his grasp (Mark 3:25–27). There are Christians today who have no joy in their Christian lives, no substance from their Bible reading, no pleasure in the house of God, and no desire to serve the Lord. If that is you, *please read today's verse again!* God will strengthen you, though you were spoiled, to come against the enemy's fortress—not just to meet him in the open field for another battle, but at his back door! You can defeat any foe even at the place where it is *entrenched!* Victory is in your grasp! God told Joshua before he went into the Promised Land and faced Jericho's mighty walls that "there shall not any man be able to stand before thee all the days of thy life: as I was with Moses, so I will be with thee: I will not fail thee, nor forsake thee" (Joshua 1:5). Walk right up, go right in, and take back what the enemy has stolen from you today! Do you remember that joy you once had? Do you remember your sincere, heartfelt, fervent worship? Walk right in and take it back for the glory of God! Let God fight this battle for you today.

TOPICS: Battle, Deliverance, Victory

DAILY BIBLE READING: Amos 6–9

TODAY'S VERSE: Amos 7:15: "And the LORD took me as I followed the flock, and the LORD said unto me, Go, prophesy unto my people Israel."

AMOS, A FARMER PROPHET, had a ministry both to the northern kingdom of Israel and the southern kingdom of Judah. His name means "burdened." Today's verse is Amos's defense of his calling as a prophet, for some did not accept him. Even people back in Bible days had a hard time accepting God's man!

How well Amos remembered the time when God laid His calling and His claim upon his life! God's calling is no trivial matter, and it is nothing with which we should trifle.

God's Entitlement ("And the LORD took me"). To take a man is God's prerogative. Amos thought he was going to be farming for a long time in the fields of Israel, but God had different plans. Don't ever think that God cannot use you in full-time ministry or even as a layperson in your church in a powerful way. One thing you must accept is that God can do whatever He wants with your life! First Corinthians 6:20 says, "For ye are bought with a price: therefore glorify God in your body, and in your spirit, which are God's." God does not have to ask permission! You have no right and no claim upon "your" life.

God's Essay ("as I followed the flock"). God is trying to teach us all a couple of very important lessons here. The first is on *leadership*. You cannot be a good leader until you are first a good follower! Amos had to learn how to be a follower of the flock before he could lead the flock in God's laws. The second lesson was on *labor*. Amos had followed the flock and done every duty he was called to do faithfully. God does not use lazy people. As a matter of fact, you will find that God often uses those who are busiest. God doesn't have a habit of calling people who are drinking lemonade in the shade while others are doing the work. God spoke to Moses out of a burning bush while he was tending the flock in the desert. When Samuel anointed David to be king, they had to fetch him from watching the flock. When Elijah threw his mantle upon Elisha, Elisha was plowing with twelve yoke of oxen.

God's Employment ("and the LORD said unto me, Go, prophesy unto my people Israel"). God reassigned Amos to a new and different duty. This was not what Amos had planned, nor was he prepared for it. God, however, knew that he was ready for the job that lay ahead. Are you a discouraged preacher, worker in ministry, or Christian helper in the work of the Lord? Don't worry: God did not make a mistake in calling you to your place of service! God knew your limitations and was counting on that fact that you would rely on Him when the work was too big for you! We have this encouraging verse in 1 John 2:27: "But the anointing which ye have received of him abideth in you, and *ye need not that any man teach you: but as the same anointing teacheth you of all things, and is truth, and is no lie, and even as it hath taught you, ye shall abide in him.*" What God said to Amos, He is saying to you: "Go to my people."

TOPICS: God's Calling, Leadership, Ministry, Preaching, Work

DAILY BIBLE READING: Obadiah and Jonah 1–4

TODAY'S VERSE: Jonah 1:17: "Now the LORD had prepared a great fish to swallow up Jonah. And Jonah was in the belly of the fish three days and three nights."

THE STORY OF JONAH is one of the most well-known in the Bible. Most people hear it before the age of six. How much more exciting can a story be than to hear of a man swallowed whole by a whale and living to tell about it? Of course, there is more to the story than that. The man of God, Jonah, did not want to go to Nineveh, but desired their destruction. Yet, when he *did* go, the wicked people of Nineveh heard the Word of God and repented for their sins. Hallelujah for the mercy of the Lord! Even though Jonah was not right with God throughout, this story is a picture of Christ and His suffering for our sin. Let's consider this story and how it relates to our Saviour in His salvation work.

There Was a Prepared Punishment ("Now the LORD had prepared a great fish to swallow up Jonah"). God has always had a punishment in mind for sin. God prepared this whale, and Jonah figuratively became his own sin as he was consumed by God's judgment. This picture is given in 2 Corinthians 5:21: "For he hath made him to be sin for us, who knew no sin; that we might be made the righteousness of God in him." God has chosen to punish sin in one way, and that punishment came on Jesus as He hung upon the cross on Calvary. Those who reject Jesus Christ and the punishment He endured will be cast into the lake of fire.

There Was a Prepared Place ("And Jonah was in the belly of the fish"). Matthew 12:40 declares, "For as Jonas was . . . in the whale's belly; so shall the Son of man be . . . in the *heart of the earth*." Christ went to a place that was prepared for Him by His Father for the punishment of man's sin so that He could go to "prepare a place for you" (John. 14:2). In another type of this preparation, God told Abraham, "Take now thy son, thine only son Isaac, whom thou lovest, and get thee into the land of Moriah; and offer him there for a burnt offering upon one of the mountains *which I will tell thee of*" (Genesis 22:2). God already had a place in mind!

There Was a Prepared Period ("three days and three nights"). The picture of Christ is clear here. Again, we see it in Matthew 12:40: "For as Jonas was three days and three nights . . . so shall the Son of man be three days and three nights." In Jonah 2, a powerful picture of Christ is given to us in the person of Jonah. He gives us the picture of a death, a burial, and a resurrection. Thank God for His perfect timing: Christ was not a day late! He rose again after His prepared period was accomplished!

TOPICS: Christ, Judgment, Salvation, Sin

DAILY BIBLE READING: Micah 1–7

TODAY'S VERSE: Micah 6:8: "He hath shewed thee, O man, what is good; and what doth the Lord require of thee, but to do justly, and to love mercy, and to walk humbly with thy God?"

THIS VERSE IS OFTEN VIEWED as "the Golden Rule" of the Old Testament. It covers both our relationship to God and our relationship with man. Many are trying to live their Christian lives while only guessing what is right and wrong. This is extremely dangerous, because guessing can cause us to live as Israel did in the book of Judges when "every man did that which was right in his own eyes" (Judges 17:6). God does not want any guesswork to be involved! It is a great blessing to know exactly what God wants us to do and how He wants us to act.

A **Revelation from God** ("He hath shewed thee, O man"). God is not leaving anything to chance! The word translated "shewed" here means "to front, i.e. stand boldly out opposite." God has set the truth right in front of you. He has done this in many different ways. First, He has showed us righteousness in the New Testament through the *example of His Incarnate Son*. First Peter 2:21 says, "For even hereunto were ye called: because Christ also suffered for us, leaving us an example, that ye should follow his steps." He has also showed us through the *exposure of His Inspired Scriptures*. Second Timothy 3:16–17 says, "All scripture is given by inspiration of God, and is profitable for doctrine, for reproof, for correction, for instruction in righteousness: that the man of God may be perfect, throughly furnished unto all good works." Lastly, He has showed us His will in the *examination of His Indwelling Spirit*. John 14:26 says, "But the Comforter, which is the Holy Ghost, whom the Father will send in my name, he shall teach you all things, and bring all things to your remembrance, whatsoever I have said unto you."

A **Righteousness from God** ("He hath shewed thee, O man, *what is good*"). This is not based upon anyone's personal criteria. God is showing us exactly what is good in His sight: good in character, good in virtue, good in hope, good in principle, good in worship, and good in godliness. He has showed us what is good in His Word and commandments, but He has not stopped there! Hasn't He showed us good things by what He does for us? Hasn't He given us good blood in His sacrifice, a good hope of His second coming, and a good reason to serve Him? The Bible tells us that God will still give us good things if we ask Him. Matthew 7:11 says, "If ye then, being evil, know how to give good gifts unto your children, how much more shall your Father which is in heaven give good things to them that ask him?"

A **Requirement from God** ("and what doth the Lord require of thee, but to do justly, and to love mercy, and to walk humbly with thy God"). The word for "require" means "to tread or frequent." God wants us to "frequent" some places in our Christian lives. He calls us "to do justly." This has to do with our *works*. Don't you know that what we do is important to the Lord? The word translated "justly" means "verdict." It is not just what we *want* to do, but what He has declared right for us to do. He calls us "to love mercy." This has to do with our *walk*. Our conversation, or manner of living, is high on the priority list of God! A clean, clear testimony before men is essential and vital if they are to be saved. We are bearing the name of Christ! And we are called "to walk humbly with thy God." This has to do with our *worship*. Your worship of God is directly connected to your view of yourself and your view of God. We must enter into His presence in humiliation and meekness of soul. The gospel shows us infinite love and mercy that goes beyond our wildest dreams. That should make us walk humbly with Him!

TOPICS: Christian Living, Duty, Revelation, Righteousness, Word of God

DAILY BIBLE READING: Nahum 1–3

TODAY'S VERSE: Nahum 1:15: "Behold upon the mountains the feet of him that bringeth good tidings, that publisheth peace! O Judah, keep thy solemn feasts, perform thy vows: for the wicked shall no more pass through thee; he is utterly cut off."

NAHUM'S NAME MEANS "consolation." His prophecy is of the destruction of Nineveh, a prophecy meant to warn that city and also to be an encouragement to the people of Israel. Jonah did not want revival in Nineveh, yet they humbled themselves and repented before God. By contrast, Nahum prayed and preached to Nineveh for repentance and never saw it. Nahum here directly references Isaiah 52:7, which is also quoted in Romans 10:15 in reference to the good news of the gospel of Christ and worldwide missions. In this case, the words refer to the news of Israel's deliverance from their oppressors. Wouldn't those be good tidings to hear if you were in bondage? What a welcome voice this was to the people of God in captivity! Today, let's study the three sections of this verse.

The first is a **Positive Outlook** ("Behold upon the mountains the feet of him that bringeth good tidings, that publisheth peace!"). This was a promise of peace in a message from God. This was a message that required *exertion* ("upon the mountains the feet of him"). Somebody was using great effort to bring this message of hope and expectation. This was a message that revealed *elation* ("that bringeth good tidings"). The word here literally means, "to be fresh, full (rosy, and figuratively, cheerful)." There is nothing more exciting than hearing a message from the Lord! This was a message that rejoiced in *exclamation* ("that publisheth peace!"). Is there a better message than that of perfect peace? Nahum didn't think so! He ended this in an exclamation: "Peace!" Jesus said in John 14:27, "Peace I leave with you, my peace I give unto you: not as the world giveth, give I unto you. Let not your heart be troubled, neither let it be afraid."

The second is a **Performing Outwork** ("O Judah, keep thy solemn feasts, perform thy vows"). This tells us to be passionate about serving the Lord and staying true to His commands. We must get excited about serving God and doing His work! The word for "keep" means "to move in a circle, to march in a sacred procession, to observe a festival; by implication, to be giddy." Out of sheer excitement, we should celebrate the goodness of our God over and over again. When you get done circling God in your service and your worship, it will bring great joy and excitement in your spiritual life. When was the last time you "got giddy" over your work and worship of the Lord?

And the third is a **Promising Outcast** ("for the wicked shall no more pass through thee; he is utterly cut off"). What a promise this was to the people of Israel! God was finally promising them that their enemies would not come through anymore, but would be cut off. We have a promise of a future outcasting in which to rejoice. The day will come when the devil will be cast into the lake of fire. He will be utterly cut off. What an exciting promise this is to God's people—but what a horrifying promise to the devil and all those who work wickedness! Their only hope is utter destruction. People of God, keep your eyes on the great and final promise: God will cast out our enemies to give us a full and lasting peace.

TOPICS: Duty, Excitement, Joy, Pastor, Preaching, Promise, Service

R. CHRIS HANKS

DAILY BIBLE READING: Habakkuk 1-3

TODAY'S VERSE: Habakkuk 2:2, "And the Lord answered me, and said, Write the vision, and make it plain upon tables, that he may run that readeth it."

WITHOUT STUDYING THIS VERSE, it can be challenging to get the right idea of its message. Habakkuk is waiting on the word of the Lord, as we can see in verse 1. He is using whatever means necessary ("set me upon the tower") to hear and understand what God will say concerning his arguments ("what I shall answer when I am reproved"). In any situation in life, it will help you a great deal to get the right perspective from the Word of God.

The Pictures of the Word of God ("write the vision"). Have you noticed that most of Scripture is a picture? From Moses' writing about creation, we can picture what it must have looked like. Similar pictures are found in every major story in the Bible: the Passover, the Exodus, the great battles upon the Judean hillside. Even all that the prophets did were pictures that God was sending His people. How about the picture of a little stall in Bethlehem? How about the revelation that John wrote about his vision? It is said that "A picture is worth a thousand words." Have you ever gone through a box of old pictures that were never put in a photo album? There have been a number of times when I've looked at one of those pictures to say, "What is this? I don't remember anything about this!" It is almost as if God is telling Habakkuk to turn a nearly forgotten picture over and write on the back exactly what it is.

The Plainness of the Word of God ("make it plain upon the tables"). We need preachers today who will make the message plain! Some scholars believe that Habakkuk was actually instructed to use large letters so that everybody could understand. It is sad to me when a preacher gets up and muddies the waters of salvation. Where are the preachers who desire power in plainness? We all need to be plain in our witness and in our testimony.

The Pressing of the Word of God ("that he may run that readeth it"). The Word of God *demands immediate action*. Some would say that this Scripture is saying "that whoever runs can read it." What it is actually saying is "that whoever reads it can run." Has the Word of God changed your life? We should have urgency in these last days in how we live. When God speaks to your heart in church, you need to make a decision immediately. The Word of God, responded to immediately, will change the direction you go, the speed you go, and the reason you go.

TOPICS: Christian Race, Obedience, Plainness, Word of God

DAILY BIBLE READING: Zephaniah 1–3

TODAY'S VERSE: Zephaniah 1:7: "Hold thy peace at the presence of the Lord God: for the day of the Lord is at hand: for the Lord hath prepared a sacrifice, he hath bid his guests."

THERE ARE POWERFUL THOUGHTS in every phrase of this verse, but today, we will just look at the first: "Hold thy peace at the presence of the Lord God." In Christianity today, we need a respect for the presence of God once again. We are living in a time in which there is no respect, no awe, and no care for the presence of God. In essence, man is more concerned about man's presence than he is about God's presence! The word translated "hold thy peace" means "hush." It would do us good to keep our mouths shut in the presence of the Lord! An old saying goes, "It is better to be thought a fool and be silent than to open your mouth and remove all doubt." This is good counsel to all of us. "Hold thy peace at the presence of the Lord God." *What could we say when God appears?* Here are three thoughts about what God's presence offers us.

What Could We Say about His Attendance? Here we see God's **grace!** We do not deserve God's attention or attendance to us. There is nothing we can say to show God's people that He is present in a special way; His entrance speaks for itself! If a preacher has to convince people that God was in a place in a special way, then God wasn't there! When God does come, there is tenderness, respect, and awe in the hearts of the people. There is no need to persuade men of His presence: they will automatically acknowledge it. We are also looking forward to His return at the rapture, and believe me, everyone will know!

What Could We Say about His Appearance? Here we see God's **glory!** Peter tried to say something when he saw Christ on the Mount of Transfiguration. What he did say got him into trouble (Matthew 17:4–6). The best thing he could have done was to keep his mouth shut! When Daniel saw God, he held his peace. When John saw Christ on Patmos, he held his peace. Psalm 46:10a says, "Be still, and know that I am God."

What Could We Say about His Acquaintance? Here we see God's **gift!** What a gift to man that God offers him friendship! What mercy is shown in the fact that God will come in His manifest presence to acquaint Himself with man. God interests Himself in man's love, man's trials, man's joys, and man's troubles. Psalm 8:4a says, "What is man, that thou art mindful of him?" What a testimony of God's love as He outstretches His hand toward man! Psalm 139:3 says, "Thou compassest my path and my lying down, *and art acquainted with all my ways.*" In order to familiarize Himself with us, God familiarized Himself with sorrow and persecution. Isaiah 53:3 says, "He is despised and rejected of men; a man of sorrows, and *acquainted with grief.*" How humbling it is to know that God has brought His presence to be our friend and walk in relationship with man! And of course, look at the wonderful relationship that we have with our Saviour! John 15:15a says, "Henceforth I call you not servants; for the servant knoweth not what his lord doeth: but I have called you friends." What a friend we have in Jesus! What words can we use to describe this friendship? What can we say to explain it? Have you ever been at a loss for words when describing to someone what God means to you? The blessing of God's presence cannot be explained; it must be experienced!

TOPICS: God's Glory, God's Presence, Grace

DAILY BIBLE READING: Haggai 1–2

TODAY'S VERSE: Haggai 1:14: "And the LORD stirred up the spirit of Zerubbabel the son of Shealtiel, governor of Judah, and the spirit of Joshua the son of Josedech, the high priest, and the spirit of all the remnant of the people; and they came and did work in the house of the LORD of hosts, their God."

IT SURE IS GOOD TO KNOW that everything we need in our Christian lives is found and provided for in the Word of God. In verse 12, we find that once the people heard the Word of the Lord, they responded. We will never have revival until we start responding to the Word of God. What a blessing it was for Israel to know that though they were yet in captivity, God was still at work speaking to His people and stirring them to do a work for Him!

The first thing the people needed was a **Spiritual Awakening** ("And the LORD stirred up"). The Hebrew word for "stirred" means "to open the eyes, to wake." Without a doubt, Christians are asleep today. Romans 13:11 says, "And that, knowing the time, that now it is high time to awake out of sleep: for now is our salvation nearer than when we believed." Our American churches have been lulled to sleep by their apathy, their material possessions, and the satisfaction of their own feelings concerning religion. Some churches are not merely asleep, they are dead! What is sad is that today we need a resurrection more than a revival.

Second, they needed a **Spiritual Announcing** ("the spirit of Zerubbabel the son of Shealtiel, governor of Judah, and the spirit of Joshua the son of Josedech, the high priest, and the spirit of all the remnant of the people."). In this part of the verse, we see the names and positions of the people who were stirred. We need revival today from the presidency to the peasants; from the pulpit to the pew. When is the last time you were able to say that you were stirred in the things of God? Would your name be listed with those who have been changed by the spirit of revival? God is still calling men to do His work! God will call them by name and distinguish them for the great work that He is doing.

Third, they needed a **Spiritual Answering**. What did these men do when they heard the word of the Lord from Haggai? "They *came and did work* in the house of the Lord." The word for "work" is very interesting: it means "deputyship, i.e. ministry; generally, employment (never servile)." These men were willing to fall in line with the authority God had given. Never did they feel that they were "enslaved" to their duties in the house of God! They found their place of service, heard the leader tell them what needed to be done, and put their hand to the plow. The verse does not say, "They did *the* work in the house," but that "They *did work* in the house." This work stretched from maintenance to ministry. The last part of 1 Corinthians 16:15 describes Christians who "have addicted themselves to the ministry of the saints." God has called, but we are still waiting for people to serve in the house of the Lord. Christ told us to pray for workers: "Pray ye therefore the Lord of the harvest, that he will send forth labourers into his harvest." Let us answer the call to work in the house of the Lord.

TOPICS: Commitment, God's House, Revival, Servanthood

DAILY BIBLE READING: Zechariah 1–5

TODAY'S VERSE: Zechariah 3:1: "And he shewed me Joshua the high priest standing before the angel of the Lord, and Satan standing at his right hand to resist him."

PRAISE THE LORD for a man of God who was willing to stand in any day and any hour! Joshua the high priest (the name *Joshua* in the Old Testament is the same name as *Jesus* in the New Testament!) was willing to stand between God and man as a go-between and willing to stand before Satan as a God-between! By giving Zechariah this vision, God showed him that He had a purpose, a proof, and a principle to teach us for His glory. What has God shown you lately? Let us take a moment to consider the picture that God is showing us today.

An Acknowledgment of Grace ("And he shewed me Joshua the high priest standing"). Joshua did not stand there on his own merit, for the priesthood had been handed down to him by lineage. He was there because of something given to him, *not* because of something he earned. It is generally accepted that this Joshua in verse 1 is actually a type of Israel as she stands before God. It would do us all a lot of good to acknowledge and accept our place before God *as a work of grace and not of merit*. Isn't that what Israel was supposed to learn? Because she never learned this lesson of grace, God grafted the Gentiles into the place of the nation of Israel (Romans 11:13–32).

An Advocate of Grace ("standing before the angel of the Lord"). This Joshua stands before the angel of the Lord. There are times in the Old Testament when the term "the angel of the Lord" is referring to the Messiah, or Christ Himself. This verse is one of those times. I don't know of a better place to stand! We will look at who else is standing there in a moment, but if Christ is there, it is the best place to be! Joshua was standing before Christ. Christ would be his Defender just like He would be yours. First John 2:1 says, "My little children, these things write I unto you, that ye sin not. And if any man sin, we have an *advocate with the Father, Jesus Christ the righteous.*" What are you standing before right now? Some may be standing at a crossroads. Don't stand before your decisions, stand before God! Go to the throne of heaven, and stand in the presence of God today. As you do, He will stand in your stead to plead your cause and defend you for His name's sake!

An Adversary of Grace ("and Satan standing at his right hand to resist him"). Satan surely wasn't invited to this place, but here he is! Isn't it amazing the times and places he appears? This Adversary stood before Joshua to "resist him." We all know that the devil does not have to lie about our sin before God. All he has to do is tell the truth! What are we to do in such a situation? Keep our mouths shut, and let God take over! Verse 2 says, "And the Lord said unto Satan." What could we say to justify ourselves anyway? Let God justify you in the presence of the enemy! Every time the guilt of your past comes knocking at your heart's door and you feel the shame of unworthiness set upon your soul, remember Calvary!

TOPICS: Christ, Grace, Satan, Uncertainty

DAILY BIBLE READING: Zechariah 6–10

TODAY'S VERSE: Zechariah 9:16: "And the LORD their God shall save them in that day as the flock of his people: for they shall be as the stones of a crown, lifted up as an ensign upon his land."

IF YOU ARE OF THE FAITH of Abraham and have trusted in Christ for salvation, you are an ornament of God's grace. Paul spoke of this in 1 Thessalonians 2:19: "For what is our hope, or joy, or *crown of rejoicing? Are not even ye in the presence of our Lord Jesus Christ* at his coming?" Did not God speak the same thing in Malachi 3:17? "And they shall be mine, saith the LORD of hosts, in that day *when I make up my jewels;* and I will spare them, as a man spareth his own son that serveth him."

These Jewels Are Valuable ("for they shall be as the stones of a crown"). You may not think you are valuable to God, but listen to His Word about you. Matthew 10:31 says, "Fear ye not therefore, ye are of more value than many sparrows." Romans 8:32 says, "He that spared not his own Son, but delivered him up for us all, how shall he not with him also freely give us all things?" God cares about you! David said in Psalm 139:17, "How precious also are thy thoughts unto me, O God! how great is the sum of them!" Never think that you are not valued by God!

These Jewels Are Honorable ("stones of a crown"). What a place of honor for these jewels—they sit upon the divine head of our Sacred King! Even the crown jewels of England in their splendor have no meaning and no majesty without a brow on which to set! We have no glory of ourselves, but desire only to adorn the head of Him who is worthy. Ephesians 2:6 says, "And hath raised us up together, and made us sit together in heavenly places in Christ Jesus." Just like a crown, we have been raised together with Him in His place of authority!

These Jewels Are Noticeable ("lifted up as an ensign upon his land"). There was a time when these jewels were rough and uncut, but now they have a place where others cannot help but notice their place of prominence. Adam Clarke says in his commentary that these stones are "offering themselves to the attention of every passenger."[1] What a noticeable difference Christ makes in our lives! Don't think for a minute that your family, your friends, and your neighbors don't notice the difference in what you are now compared to what you were before you were saved. One day, when you are exalted with Christ, they will notice even more!

TOPICS: Exaltation, Honor, Glorification

---

1   Adam Clarke, *Holy Bible with Commentary and Critical Notes*, Vol 4. (New York: B. Waugh and T. Mason for the Methodist Episcopal Church, 1846), 788.

DAILY BIBLE READING: Zechariah 11–14

TODAY'S VERSE: Zechariah 13:6: "And one shall say unto him, What are these wounds in thine hands? Then he shall answer, Those with which I was wounded in the house of my friends."

THESE LAST FEW CHAPTERS of Zechariah are full of detailed prophecies of the coming Messiah. They discuss everything from the price for which He would be sold to the miseries of the Tribulation and the circumstances of Christ's second coming. There are over one thousand passages in the Bible that were prophetic when they were first penned by the inspiration of the Holy Spirit. Many of those prophecies have already been fulfilled, and the rest will be fulfilled in the not-too-distant future. This verse has a great impact upon me as I can see my Saviour in each and every horrifying word. I hear the tenderness of the one who asks the question, "What are these wounds in thine hands?" as if I can hear a little child asking his father or grandfather, "What happened to you here?"

   These Are Wounds of Blessing ("And one shall say unto him, What are these wounds in thine hands?"). These wounds were obtained because of God's love for the one who is asking! The implied meaning of this verse is simple: Jesus is saying, "I did this for you!" In John 3:16 we learn of Jesus Christ and His love, and we hear it again in 1 John 3:16a: "Hereby perceive we the love of God, because he laid down his life for us." He did so freely, not begrudgingly, that He might redeem us to Himself and share His eternal glory with all those who are saved by His grace.

   These Are Wounds of Beating ("What are these wounds in thine hands?"). The word for "wounds" means "a blow." It is the same word used for wheat that is "beaten" in 2 Chronicles 2:10; it literally means "to flail." Our Lord suffered a tremendous beating at the hands of Pilate, the chief priests, the Roman soldiers, and *our sins!* Great blows were laid upon His hands as the soldiers drove nails into the hands of the one who formed man from the dust of the ground and flung the stars into existence. Isaiah 53:5 says, "But he was wounded for our transgressions, he was bruised for our iniquities: the chastisement of our peace was upon him; and with his stripes we are healed." May we never forget the merciless beating and physical suffering our Lord endured!

   These Are Wounds of Betrayal ("Then he shall answer, Those with which I was wounded in the house of my friends"). There is nothing so hurtful as to be hurt by a friend. Many who read this today have been betrayed by someone they supposed to be closest to their hearts. Trust and confidence turned to horror and pain as you saw your friend give you over to the enemy with utter disregard. Jesus felt this also. The cat-o'-nine-tails did not hurt nearly as much as the embrace of betrayal! The plucking and pulling of Christ's beard did not compare to the pain felt in the brush of Judas's beard. The piercing of the nails in His hands was nothing compared to the traitor's lips upon His cheek. Luke 22:48 says, "But Jesus said unto him, Judas, betrayest thou the Son of man with a kiss?" There is nothing as disgusting as using the trust of friendship to mark a man and then to sentence him to a miserable crucifixion!

   The implication of this verse in our lives goes much further. Is it possible that we have wounded Jesus and betrayed Him today? Even as Christians, do we sell Him out and turn our backs on His calling upon our lives for some sinful pleasure or selfish desire? The longer I think about Calvary, the more precious those wounds are to me!

TOPICS: Calvary, Salvation, Suffering

DAILY BIBLE READING: Malachi 1–4

TODAY'S VERSE: Malachi 3:6: "For I am the LORD, I change not; therefore ye sons of Jacob are not consumed."

THIS SHORT SENTENCE carries powerful thoughts as our Lord speaks of who He is. In very few words, He gives us infinite truths about Himself that are essential to our love, honor, and respect for Him. This confirms to us that He is worthy of all our praise. Let us take a moment to consider three things about our God.

Our God Is Unchallengeable ("For I am the LORD"). Remember, when "LORD" is set in all capitals, it is God's name "Jehovah" that is used in the Hebrew. Isaiah 45:6 says, "That they may know from the rising of the sun, and from the west, that there is none beside me. *I am the LORD, and there is none else.*" *Jehovah* means "Self-Existent One." There is no one to challenge God in His wisdom, His throne, or His purpose. None can counsel Him in the ways of man, for "he knew what was in man" (John 2:25). God has looked for a competitor or an equal, and He has found none. Isaiah 44:8 says, "Fear ye not, neither be afraid: have not I told thee from that time, and have declared it? ye are even my witnesses. *Is there a God beside me? yea, there is no God; I know not any.*"

Our God Is Unchangeable ("I change not"). Isn't it good to know that, with many things changing in our world every moment, there is still Someone who doesn't change? What confidence this gives to the Christian! What consolation this gives to the sinner! What courage this gives to the soldier! Our world is full of uncertainty, from the daily price of gas to the ever-changing stock market. Here is a question to ponder: why would God need to change? He is perfect, He knows all, He has a plan that is working (and will work forever), and He has all power. He not only doesn't *want* or *need* to change, but He cannot be *made* to change! Our security in having an unchangeable God is not in any danger of being threatened!

Our God Is Unspeakable ("therefore ye sons of Jacob are not consumed"). It is only because our God cannot be challenged and cannot be changed that His mercy is still in full working order! What a blessing to have a God whose "mercy endureth for ever"! God is saying in this verse, "It is not because of your works that you are not consumed, but because of Me and My everlasting mercy that is extended to you today." What unspeakable mercy! The word for "consumed" means, "to end, to cease, be finished, perish." I thank God that He has not consumed us for our failings. I have to say with David in Psalm 139:6, "Such knowledge is too wonderful for me; it is high, I cannot attain unto it."

TOPICS: Immutability, Mercy, Omnipotence

October 8

DAILY BIBLE READING: Matthew 1–4

TODAY'S VERSE: Matthew 3:17: "And lo a voice from heaven, saying, This is my beloved Son, in whom I am well pleased."

WE HAVE NOW BEEN a week and nine months in the Old Testament. Now we turn our hearts and ears to the New Testament. Thank God for the New Testament, the New Covenant, and the New Agreement of God with man! I am always excited when Jesus comes on the scene!

This verse follows the obedience of Christ in baptism and the descent of the Holy Spirit upon Him like a dove. Now, we hear the voice of the Father. Some context is needed here: by the time God speaks in the Gospel of Matthew, He has been silent for over four hundred years—since the end of the Old Testament. All of a sudden, we hear the rumblings of the intonation of Almighty God as He speaks with great feeling about His Son and lays His stamp of approval upon the person and work of Christ.

We hear the **Announcement of His Presentation** ("This is"). This was the time! God was now introducing His Son to the world. Yes, the angels had announced His birth to the shepherds, and the wise men had followed a star, but it was here that God spoke and said, "This is." He was saying, "Let Me introduce My Son to you." This was the time that contained all hope for the future of eternity. This was the moment that would begin the last leg of God's redemptive plan as He prepared for Calvary.

We see the **Acknowledgment of His Person** ("my beloved Son"). At this moment, God bowed to God. God the Father did not pull rank over God the Son. He was not speaking down to Him; He was exalting Him. He accepted Jesus Christ as an equal. It was not Christ who first claimed to be God's Son, but the Father who proclaimed it! It was not the Son who wanted to be equal to the Father, but the Father who claimed to be equal with the Son! So many people think there is a hierarchy in the Godhead. That is not so. God is God. The Father is just as much God as the Son. The Son is just as much God as the Spirit. The Spirit is just as much God as the Father. At this moment, the Father acknowledged the Son's rightful place in the Godhead as well as His perfect work and rightful name as redeemer of mankind, for that was the eternal work of the Son.

We see the **Approval of His Pleasure** ("in whom I am well pleased"). The word for "pleased" here means "approved." Yet, even this does not make the Father more important than the Son. Actually, you will find that God is always pleased with Himself. The word for "well-pleased" means that nothing else could bring joy and blessing to the heart of God like the Son's obedience in following through with the plan of salvation. This is exciting to me as I am now approved by God by the same plan: because God was pleased with the Son, by my faith in Him, He is now pleased with me!

TOPICS: God's Pleasure, Jesus Christ, Trinity

R. CHRIS HANKS

DAILY BIBLE READING: Matthew 5-6

TODAY'S VERSE: Matthew 6:13: "And lead us not into temptation, but deliver us from evil: for thine is the kingdom, and the power, and the glory, for ever. Amen."

I AM DRAWN to the last part of this verse because of its humility, awe, recognition, and praise. Shouldn't this be our response and respect toward God every moment of every day? If we will let this verse consume us with passion and fervency in every task, we will end each day refreshed, knowing that our hearts have been blessed by a day of worship. Let us observe three powerful thoughts.

His Majesty ("For thine is the kingdom"). Do you believe that Christ is king? You will one day behold Him in His majesty! He is not only *a* king, He is *the* king! Revelation 19:16 says, "And he hath on his vesture and on his thigh a name written, KING OF KINGS, AND LORD OF LORDS." The late Dr. S. M. Lockridge, in his sermon "The Lordship of Christ," said, "He didn't carve His initials into the mountains, but He owns it! He didn't copyright the songs that the birds do sing, but He owns it!" Should we not come boldly yet humbly before God's throne in prayer? Hebrews 4:16 says, *"Let us therefore come boldly unto the throne of grace,* that we may obtain mercy, and find grace to help in time of need."

His Might ("and the power"). Genesis 17:1 says, "And when Abram was ninety years old and nine, the LORD appeared to Abram, and said unto him, *I am the Almighty God.*" The Greek word translated "power" means "force, specially miraculous power." It is the same root from which we get "dynamite." What great force and power resides with our God! He is known as Almighty God! His might is seen in His creation of man in the past, His salvation for man in the present, and His exaltation of man in the future.

His Magnificence ("and the glory"). Make sure today of your salvation! If you are saved and have accepted Christ's wonderful gift and trusted in His blood, then you will one day see Him in His glory. The word for "glory" is defined as "glory, as very apparent." God's glory is most assuredly not a secret! Isaiah saw Him high and lifted up. John saw Him on Patmos and fell down as dead! Peter, James, and John saw Christ transfigured before them and worshiped. When we see Him, we will bow before Him and lay our crowns at His feet with great trembling and many tears! Jesus' prayer to His Father in John 17:5 says, "And now, O Father, glorify thou me with thine own self with the glory which I had with thee before the world was." Christ desired the Father's glory above all things! It is our sin that has separated us from His glory. Romans 3:23 says, "For all have sinned, and come short of the glory of God." Yes, His glory will be something to behold!

TOPICS: Glory, Power, Prayer

DAILY BIBLE READING: Matthew 7–9

TODAY'S VERSE: Matthew 9:24: "He said unto them, Give place: for the maid is not dead, but sleepeth. And they laughed him to scorn."

THE RULER IN THIS STORY came to Jesus to ask Him to heal his daughter. As Jesus was coming, a diseased woman came and was healed of her issue of blood. When Jesus finally made it to this ruler's house, the little girl had already died. (As a side note, thank God for a father who was more concerned about finding Christ than he was about spending the last few moments with his dying daughter! *Once you get God in the picture, anything can happen!)*

When Jesus approached this man's home, He was greeted by the problem of a dead maid, by dead music, by dead men of unbelief, and by dead mourning. I am glad Jesus is bigger than His surroundings! Let me tell you that when God comes, He can do anything, anytime, anywhere!

In today's verse, we see Jesus asking for space. Please don't be guilty of not having space for God in your life!

These mourners **Allowed Death to Push God Out of Their Lives.** Maybe you have gone through the tremendous heartache of the loss of a loved one. I cannot tell you that God will raise your loved one from the dead today, but I can tell you that if that person was saved, you can anticipate a coming resurrection! First Thessalonians 4:13–14 says, "But I would not have you to be ignorant, brethren, concerning them which are asleep, that ye sorrow not, even as others which have no hope. For if we believe that Jesus died and rose again, even so them also which sleep in Jesus will God bring with him."

They also **Allowed Disbelief to Push God Out of Their Lives.** Pain and sorrow was the instrument that brought out their disbelief. When hard times come in your life, *believe on!* When there is no hope, *hope on!* When you want to quit, *keep on!* Of Abraham, Romans 4:18a says, "Who against hope, believed in hope." What a sad commentary on the faith of this day when the mourners would not believe in the Son of God! It is the same commentary our society is frantically writing every day. Matthew 13:58 says, "And [Jesus] did not many mighty works there because of their unbelief." God can still choose to do these works, but He is not required to do so. Second Chronicles 16:9a says, "For the eyes of the LORD run to and fro throughout the whole earth, to shew himself strong in the behalf of them whose heart is perfect toward him."

They also **Allowed Derision to Push God Out of Their Lives** ("they laughed him to scorn"). What does it take to make someone mock God? We are living in a time in which governments, lifestyles, the entertainment industry, and our social lives all defy God and His Word. Romans 3:12 and 18 say, "They are all gone out of the way, they are together become unprofitable; there is none that doeth good, no, not one . . . There is no fear of God before their eyes." In today's story, all of this happened because they did not have any space for Christ. I remember as a little boy hearing the story of Bethlehem and feeling anger against the innkeeper because he did not have any room for Jesus. Will you make room for Jesus in your sorrow, anger, and pain? Though your marriage is hurting and your child is straying? Give place to God, let Him bring resurrection to these "dead" problems, and watch Him do a divine work in your life!

TOPICS: Death, Faith, Hope, Power of God, Unbelief

DAILY BIBLE READING: Matthew 10–12

TODAY'S VERSE: Matthew 11:6: "And blessed is he, whosoever shall not be offended in me."

THIS BLESSING WAS GIVEN to John the Baptist, who was in prison. John had sent some of his disciples to Christ to confirm that He was the Messiah they were waiting for. In response to John's question, Jesus showed these disciples His works and told them to tell John not to be offended in Him. If there was anyone Jesus wanted to tell about His being the Christ, I believe it was John. But John would have to trust Him all the way to being beheaded by a heathen king

Jesus' answer may have surprised these disciples. I have heard of a lot of things, but being offended in Christ? The Greek word for "offended" is *skandalizo*. It means "to entrap, i.e. trip up (figuratively, stumble (transitively) or entice to sin)." It is the root of our English word *scandal*. How could anyone ever become offended in Christ? Let me give you a few thoughts and verses that can help clarify this for all of us.

Some Are Offended by His Work. The cross has always been a point of contention. Matthew 26:31 says, "Then saith Jesus unto them, All ye shall be offended because of me this night: for it is written, I will smite the shepherd, and the sheep of the flock shall be scattered abroad." Jesus was prophesying that the disciples would forsake Him. They wanted a symbol that would make them feel good, not a bloody, rugged cross, "an emblem of suffering and shame."[2] Crucifixion was not what they had in mind. This wasn't how it was supposed to be. Today, people still stumble at the cross.

Some Are Offended by His Witness. Contrary to some people's claims, Jesus always gave everyone a clear presentation of the gospel. He bore witness to man's utter failure and sin and His own sacrifice and pardon. Luke 4:26–28 says, "But unto none of them was Elias sent, save unto Sarepta, a city of Sidon, unto a woman that was a widow. And many lepers were in Israel in the time of Eliseus the prophet; and none of them was cleansed, saving Naaman the Syrian. And all they in the synagogue, when they heard these things, were filled with wrath." These people didn't like to hear about how others were saved *if they hadn't been saved in the way they had always believed about salvation.* Jesus talked about Gentiles and how God had mercy on them. The Jews didn't like a witness that did not include their *ritual,* their *religion,* their *righteousness,* or their *respect.*

Some Are Offended by His Word. Matthew 15:12 says, "Then came his disciples, and said unto him, Knowest thou that the Pharisees were offended, *after they heard this saying?*" People are offended at the Word of God because of their *sin.* Some are offended because of their *suffering.* They do not think they should have pain in their lives. People are offended at the Word of God because of their *stumbling.* First Peter 2:8 says, "And a stone of stumbling, and a rock of offence, even to them which *stumble at the word,* being disobedient." John says the same thing in John 6:60–61: "Many therefore of his disciples, when they had heard this, said, This is an hard saying; who can hear it? When Jesus knew in himself that his disciples murmured at it, he said unto them, Doth this offend you?"

Some Are Offended by His Worship. Matthew 13:55–57a says, "Is not this the carpenter's son? is not his mother called Mary? and his brethren, James, and Joses, and Simon, and Judas? And his sisters, are they not all with us? Whence then hath this man all these things? And they were offended in him." These Pharisees and scribes did not like the fact that others were worshiping Christ. They were always trying to bring Christ down to their level instead of exalting Him. Don't be offended in Christ! Today's verse says, "And blessed is he, whosoever shall not be offended in me." We will receive the blessing of the Lord if we are not offended in Him in any of these areas!

TOPICS: Bible, Calvary, Gospel, Witness, Worship

---

2   As George Bennard's classic hymn "The Old Rugged Cross" so memorably reminds us.

DAILY BIBLE READING: Matthew 13–14

TODAY'S VERSE: Matthew 14:23: "And when he had sent the multitudes away, he went up into a mountain apart to pray: and when the evening was come, he was there alone."

THIS VERSE DETAILS Jesus' preparation for meeting with His Lord. Every man should meditate upon the principles of this verse. Problems in our churches today are not because we don't schedule enough special meetings. They're not because we do not have enough ministries. No, the cause of many of our problems today is that God's people are not prepared to meet with God. Many times at the invitation at the end of a service, our hearts are just softened enough to hear what the Lord is trying to tell us. We should be starting our services sometimes when they are ending! What could God do in our churches and in our lives if we were tender to His Word before the service ever began? Let's look at Jesus' preparation.

He Desire and Purposed to Be with God ("he sent the multitudes *away*"). If you are going to spend quality time with God, at times you will have to dismiss others to make it happen—you'll have to go **away.** Allow yourself to be driven by the need to spend time with God, and do not let anybody stand in the way! It is essential that you have private time with God. Schedules, appointments, and duties can cloud our spiritual desires and cause us to miss what God is trying to tell us.

He Designed and Planned to Be with God (and went up into the mountain *apart*"). It took time, dedication, commitment, preparation, and effort to go up the mountain. What are you willing to do to spend time with your God? We need to separate ourselves from the cares of this life—we need to be **apart.** That is the whole definition and meaning of *sanctified*—set apart from the world and unto God. Second Timothy 2:4 says, "No man that warreth entangleth himself with the affairs of this life; that he may please him who hath chosen him to be a soldier."

He Embraced the Desolation of Privacy to Be with God ("he was there *alone*"). There can be a great difference between "being alone" and "loneliness"—sometimes, we need to be **alone** with God. This would not be the last time that Christ would be alone. There would come a time when He would be alone after being forsaken by those He had called friends. He would be alone in Pilate's hall. He would be alone walking up Calvary's hill. Even His Father would leave Him and make Him bear the sin of the world— *alone!* Because of Christ's work, we will never know that loneliness. You will find there are things that you can only say to God when you are all alone with Him. You will also find there are things that God can say to you! Let me tell you the greatest thing about this: when you are alone with God, *you are not alone.*

TOPICS: Devotions, Sanctification, Separation, Walking with God

DAILY BIBLE READING: Matthew 15–17

TODAY'S VERSE: Matthew 15:27: "And she said, Truth, Lord: yet the dogs eat of the crumbs which fall from their master's table."

THANK GOD FOR A MOTHER who was concerned about the spiritual life of her daughter! We find in verse 22 that this woman's daughter was "grievously vexed with a devil." If only we had more parents like this lady, parents who are concerned about their children. Instead, we have parents today who don't want to be "inconvenienced" by their children's silly problems or personal issues. What a sad comment on our society! Many of our adults are so self-centered that they could not teach or train their children if they had to. They do not understand that they are rearing a generation that is spiritually depleted of any love or respect for God. This passage is testimony of a mother who knew that only God could help with the spiritual battle for her daughter.

She Acknowledged God's Mind ("And she said, Truth, Lord"). The first order of business, if we want to see our prayers answered and God working in our homes, is recognition of the truth of God's Word. The woman did not have to consider His Word or take it under advisement; she immediately confessed that His Word was right. I would like to point out that God's word in verse 24 was to her wounding: "I am not sent but unto the lost sheep of the house of Israel." She could have taken that statement as a message of *religion*, *rejection*, or even *racism*. Many would have turned around right there and given up on God. But she accepted the wounding and won healing because of it. The pain of the truth of God's Word does not render impotent the promises of God's Word! She had to see herself as an undeserving sinner, and she did. Her request, however, was not about her, but about God—and so she continued to request it.

She Appealed to God's Mercy ("yet the dogs eat of the crumbs"). This woman was saying, "I will continue to contend with the Almighty based on the hope of His mercy." If God would strike her dead, it would be no more than what she was already suffering. There was no greater pain or discomfort than seeing her precious little daughter in the clutches of Satan. No matter what Christ called her, she had to find the way to His mercy! She appealed to His power by just asking for crumbs. She knew that He could do all things; and because of that, she asked for a crumb.

She Accepted God as Master ("which fall from their master's table"). Her response was this: "Even if You are not my Father as of the children gathered at Your table, You are still my Master!" She accepted her place as the dog of the house that would receive God's food while scrabbling under the table! She knew it would not be too long before she received a blessing from her Master's hand. She was ready to admit that it was all about Jesus, and upon Jesus she waited. Let us wait for our Master to move, for He will quickly supply our need and bless us with His goodness. Malachi 3:10 says, "And prove me now herewith, saith the LORD of hosts, if I will not open you the windows of heaven, and pour you out a blessing, that there shall not be room enough to receive it."

TOPICS: God's Promises, God's Word, Persistence, Prayer

DAILY BIBLE READING: Matthew 18–20

TODAY'S VERSE: Matthew 18:20: "For where two or three are gathered together in my name, there am I in the midst of them."

IN THIS PASSAGE, Christ tells us that we need to make sure our hearts are right with one another in church. If a matter cannot be resolved, it is to be taken before the church to determine what action needs to be taken. But here, in verses 19 and 20, we hear Him talk about two or three people who have gathered to pray and worship God. What a blessing and an encouragement it is to man to have this spirit of love and unity in God's house! It is also a blessing to God when man loves and helps his brother. Psalm 133:1–2 says, "Behold, how good and how pleasant it is for brethren to dwell together in unity! It is like the precious ointment upon the head, that ran down upon the beard, even Aaron's beard: that went down to the skirts of his garments." God wants His people to love each other and come together in His name.

We Have a Fellowshipping Worship ("For where two or three are gathered together"). Thank God for the fellowship we can have with one another as we come together to worship God! Just the fact that we *can* come together is a miracle! How is it possible that people from so many different backgrounds, environments, and social standings can come together, get along, and join forces for the common cause of the gospel of Christ? This must be a work of God! There is a tremendous truth included in the grammar of the words "are gathered together." This participle is given to us in the perfect tense. That means "it describes an action or a process that took place in the past, the result of which have continued to the present."[3] Jesus is telling His disciples that when they come together in His name, it will set a spiritual prospect for the future. Every time we come together in fellowship to worship our Lord and Saviour, it makes a difference in the future! We are here as a result of the faithfulness of someone who came before us. Thank God for the continual work that is done through the fellowship of His people!

We Have a Focused Worship ("in my name"). The whole reason we should come together is Christ. The Bible tells us in Acts 4:12, "Neither is there salvation in any other: for there is none other name under heaven given among men, whereby we must be saved." If we are not saved by any other name, then there is no other name that deserves our worship. If it is not Christ who *brings* us together, then there is nothing to *keep* us together. If Christ brings us together, nothing can tear us apart! We should not come together because of a coffee shop in our church, or because of its bookstore, or even because of its programs, but because of Christ!

We Have a Favorable Worship ("there am I in the midst of them"). What a blessing when God comes into our midst. *Midst* means "middle." Not only should Jesus be our focus, but He should be the center on which everything revolves. That is the definition of *preeminent*. Colossians 1:18 tells us that Jesus desires to be "preeminent," or the center of everything. "And he is the head of the body, the church: who is the beginning, the firstborn from the dead; *that in all things he might have the preeminence.*" The only way we can ever stay on center is that He must first be the central part of our lives!

TOPICS: Church, Fellowship, Worship

---

3   Spiros Zodhiates, *The Complete Word Study New Testament with Parallel Greek* (Chattanooga: AMG, 1992), 866.

DAILY BIBLE READING: Matthew 21–22

TODAY'S VERSE: Matthew 22:46: "And no man was able to answer him a word, neither durst any man from that day forth ask him any more questions."

THE CRITICAL AND HYPOCRITICAL MINDS of the Pharisees gathered together for the sole purpose of stumping Christ with questions and entangling Him in His own answers. Adam Clarke in his New Testament commentary[4] says that in one day and in one chapter, Jesus defeated the four main sects of Jewish religion in such a way that they would not challenge Him ever again. Instead, they began making their plans to destroy Him. The Herodians were defeated by His answer to their question about taxes. The Sadducees were defeated by His explanation of the resurrection. The lawyers and scribes were defeated by His answer about the greatest commandment. And the Pharisees were defeated by Jesus' answer about the humanity and deity of the Messiah. Here are three things to see about the Pharisees after their conversation with Christ.

They Could Not Do ("and *no man was able*"). This speaks of their flesh. The Word of God always renders the flesh powerless. Jesus said in John 15:5, "Without me ye can do nothing." The religious leaders could not even answer Him a word. Their arguments seemed so good in their practice sessions! They thought they would be able to make a fool of the Creator. What do you think you might do today? You cannot do anything without Him!

They Would Not Dare ("neither durst any man"). The word for "durst" means "boldness." Along with "neither," this means they had no boldness and no courage left. After you had been stripped mentally naked and exposed in your silly thoughts, would you have any boldness? Their cocky spirit and bold ways were completely destroyed in the presence of God, who will expose the wickedness of man and the pride of his heart. Hebrews 4:13 says, "Neither is there any creature that is not manifest in his sight: but all things are naked and opened unto the eyes of him with whom we have to do." Even Job, when he was ashamed of himself before the Lord, said "Behold, I am vile; what shall I answer thee? I will lay mine hand upon my mouth" (Job 40:4). Let us remember humility when we come into His presence.

They Should Not Demand ("from that day forth ask him any more questions"). These religious leaders felt they had every right to demand an answer from God. The problem was they were not seeking an answer, but an assassination. If they could prove that Jesus had no idea what He was doing, they would be vindicated in the eyes of the people and have grounds to dismiss Him as a kook or kill Him as a blasphemer. Their pride was at the center of this whole foolish display of man's wisdom. After the smoke cleared from this gunfight on the streets of Jerusalem, only Christ was left standing. They would never again try to take Him in this fashion. Their shamelessness was evident and their hatred of God revealed. Instead of coming humbly into His presence and bowing before Him, they continued on their prideful way of justifying themselves in the sight of the people. Their pride now turned to perversion and their bravado to bitterness. Let us not be like the Pharisees, lest we meet their fate!

TOPICS: Bible, Christ, Omniscience, Pride

---

4   Adam Clarke, *The New Testament* with Commentary and Critical Notes, Vol. 1 (New York: G. Lane & C. B. Tippett Theological Seminary for the Methodist Episcopal Church, 1846), 217.

October 16

DAILY BIBLE READING: Matthew 23-24

TODAY'S VERSE: Matthew 24:25: "Behold, I have told you before."

WE HAVE HERE a very little verse with very big implications. Matthew 24–25 speaks of the last times. If there is anything to which we should be paying close attention, it is to the signs of the times. This verse is in the context of God speaking to His disciples about the last times and what He has already told them concerning their future.

It Is a Verse of Respecting. Do you respect the Word of the Lord? God has spoken! Listen, O ye earth! Listen, ye world leaders and governments of man! Listen, ye fathers and mothers! Listen, ye children! Listen, ye preachers and men of God! Just the fact that the verse says "I have told you before" confirms to us that God knows all things! I would rather trust the Lord who knows all than follow my own understanding and live in fear or ignorance. Today, when people hear the words "Thus saith the Lord," they go about their business and are not changed. There was a time when men would stop in their tracks and humble their hearts at the Word of the Lord! Let us respect Him once again and hear His Word.

It Is a Verse of Warning. There will be no excuse! As a boy growing up, I was always fearful of hearing my father say, "Now son, I *told* you . . . " This statement was usually followed by a trip to the woodshed. That is exactly what this verse is saying—"I told you!" Ecclesiastes 1:18 says, "For in much wisdom is much grief: and he that increaseth knowledge increaseth sorrow." Great responsibility comes with hearing and knowing what God has said. Don't think that holy living is not important—He told you it was. Don't think that being in church faithfully is not important—He told you it is. Don't think He doesn't love you—He told you He does. Don't think that He does not care about your worship—He told you the truth about that too!

It Is a Verse of Remembering. If God has told us something, let us remember what He has said! Second Peter 1:12 says,"Wherefore I will not be negligent to put you always in remembrance of these things, though ye know them, and be established in the present truth." What a step of growth and maturity for the disciples when they came and saw an empty tomb! What did they do? Luke 24:8 says, "And they remembered his words." Now it all made sense! The Word of God will change your outlook as well as your understanding of God's will. When He reminds us that He has told us a truth, He is also telling us to remember what He said.

TOPICS: Bible, Encouragement, Obedience

DAILY BIBLE READING: Matthew 25–26

TODAY'S VERSE: Matthew 26:8: "But when his disciples saw it, they had indignation, saying, To what purpose is this waste?"

THIS IS ONE of the most *beautiful stories in Scripture*. It is one of the most *blessed stories by our Saviour*. And it is one of the most *berating stories to the saints*. I love to read this story over and over, and it is a favorite of preachers. When they asked for what purpose the ointment was wasted, these hypocritical disciples completely misunderstood what wasting was. *Waste* means "ruin, or loss." When was the last time you wasted something on God? That's right—you can't! These disciples missed that because they were more concerned about their actions than about who Jesus was.

Let's Waste Our Worship upon Him. This woman came to worship Christ and brought her best spice in an alabaster box. Many Christians think that their work for God is more important than their worship of God. *It never is!* Your worship of God is always first. Jesus always allowed the people to worship Him. If God was here with us today, this lady's "gaudy" method of worship would still be the right thing to do! The only time Jesus stopped people's worship of Him is when they were ready to make Him king when He had not yet completed His eternal work of salvation. Let's just waste all of our worship on Him!

Let's Waste Our Wealth upon Him. Much has been said about this "precious ointment" and how it was worth almost a year's wages. Once your heart is set upon worshiping God, your money will follow, and no amount will seem to be "too much." Have you been able to out-give God yet? Let me remind you of Matthew 6:21: "For where your treasure is, there will your heart be also." Let's just "ruin" our wealth upon Him!

Let's Waste Our Work upon Him. Jesus said, "She hath wrought a good work upon me." This woman's work was not about herself, but about Him! How I wish that every Christian would learn this simple lesson! The word translated "wrought" means "toil." So many people spend themselves on their job or their schedule, but will not do the same in their work for the Lord. What a shame that we are worn out by the stuff we do for ourselves but are never worn out for the Lord and His work! Let's give all that we have to the point where we are completely exhausted by our efforts. If that happens, you will find that God will give you more strength and grace to continue in service for Him. Let's waste our work upon Him!

Let's Waste Our Witness Upon Him. Verse 13 says that this woman's work would be "told for a memorial of her." The word for "memorial" means "memorandum." Because she was willing to witness and testify of the Lord, He would testify of her! There is a continual witness of what she did many centuries later—even for us today! You may think that nobody notices or cares about your worship, but they are paying attention! Hebrews 6:10 encourages us to keep serving Him: "For God is not unrighteous to forget your work and labour of love, which ye have shewed toward his name, in that ye have ministered to the saints, and do minister." Go ahead and "ruin" your witness upon Him!

TOPICS: Giving, Wealth, Witness, Work, Worship

DAILY BIBLE READING: Matthew 27–28

TODAY'S VERSE: Matthew 27:32: "And as they came out, they found a man of Cyrene, Simon by name: him they compelled to bear his cross."

HERE WE ARE at Calvary's lonely hill to look at an ugly scene, with an ugly mob, to do an ugly deed. The Bible never says that Christ fell under the load of the cross. It has been surmised that He did because Simon was asked to bear the cross for Him. The word "compelled" means that they asked Simon to be a courier. Isn't that exactly what we have all been asked to do? Be couriers of the cross? There is much at stake if we do not bear Christ's cross! Luke 14:27 says that we need more people like Simon of Cyrene: "And whosoever doth not bear his cross, and come after me, cannot be my disciple." May we faithfully bear the cross upon which Christ hung as a curse to redeem man unto Himself.

The Cross Confronts Our Pride. If Simon was to bear this cross, he first had to pick it up. This has to do with our *will*. There are people who are not ashamed about anything in their spiritual lives, but who will never bow to pick up this cross. Picking up this cross will not help your self-esteem. As a matter of fact, it will expose it! The Bible speaks of Moses in Hebrews 11:26 that he esteemed "the reproach of Christ greater riches." There is an accusation and a criticism that comes with picking up this old rugged cross.

The Cross Consumes Our Praise. The definition of the word translated "bear" is "to lift up." This has to do with our *worship*. The higher you lift the cross, the less you are seen. Lift it so sinners might see. Lift it so the saints might see. Lift it so the Saviour will see! Why are we ashamed of the cross that testifies of the unconditional love of God? Paul said in Galatians 6:14, "But God forbid that I should glory, save in the cross of our Lord Jesus Christ." We need to lift up this cross as high as possible so that others will see it, rather than dragging it so that others only see us.

The Cross Confirms Our Place. To "bear" the cross necessitates taking it up. This has to do with our *walk*. There was a *destination* for Simon of Cyrene and this old rugged cross. It had to be taken up the "Way of Suffering." So there is for you, O Christian, a place that will lead to rest, exaltation, and victory. What a place to anticipate! Don't give up now, for "your redemption draweth nigh" (Luke 21:28). What a time it will be when our faith becomes sight! "It will be worth it all, when we see Jesus!"[5]

TOPICS: Faithfulness, Suffering, Will, Worship

---

5 "When We See Christ" by Esther Kerr Rusthoi. © 1941 New Spring, Inc (ASCAP) (Administered by Brentwood-Benson Music Publishing, Inc.) All rights reserved. Used by permission.

DAILY BIBLE READING: Mark 1–3

TODAY'S VERSE: Mark 2:12: "And immediately he arose, took up the bed, and went forth before them all; insomuch that they were all amazed, and glorified God, saying, We never saw it on this fashion."

THE MIRACULOUS HEALING of the palsied man is a great testimony to four men who had faith that Jesus could heal their friend. These men were so determined to bring him to Christ that they opened the roof to let him down into the midst. Much work, much effort, and even much damage was done to get their friend the help he needed. The story is also a testimony of the healed man himself. He had a great impact for Christ from the moment he was healed.

He Had an Obedient Testimony ("And immediately he arose, took up the bed . . . "). In verse 11, Jesus commanded the palsied man, "Arise, and take up thy bed, and go thy way into thine house." Praise the Lord for a man who immediately did what the Lord told him to do! First, *Jesus told him to do something he had not been able to do.* But when Jesus arrived, his possibilities changed! Next, *Jesus gave him victory over his past.* All this man did every day was lay on that bed. If anybody wanted victory over that bed, it was him! He had become a slave to his disease. Then, *Jesus told him to go somewhere he had not been able to go.* For the first time, this man was able to go in *his* way, not in the way someone else took him. I am not talking about his *house,* but I am talking about his *way!* Wherever somebody wanted to take him was where he went. Even if people took him "where" he wanted to go, they could not take him "how" he wanted to go. Maybe he would have jumped over the curb and walked on the other side of the street, or perhaps he would have skipped—now he could do it all. What a blessing to hear Christ say "Go thy way"!

He Had an Open Testimony ("and went forth before them all"). Our faith in Christ demands an open testimony to the world! That is why baptism is so important. Baptism does not save us, but it does openly show the world that we are identifying with Christ in His death, burial, and resurrection.

They Had an Overwhelming Testimony ("insomuch that they were all amazed, and glorified God"). When the Bible says that the man "went forth before them all," it means that he did it and was gone. In other words, it happened once and it was over. But the phrase "they were all amazed" is different: it is a continual action. Don't ever give up, my friend, for a single thing you do may have lasting effects upon someone else! Didn't the action of the four friends have a lasting and continuing effect upon this man? Now his action made continuing effects upon others! When he did this, all the observers glorified God.

They Had an Observant Testimony ("We never saw it on this fashion"). "Never" means "not even at any time." There had never been a point in the past when the people had seen something like this. The word for "fashion" is often translated as "likewise," "on this wise," or "so." The Lord's words are a fashion show that will never be duplicated or go out of style!

TOPICS: Glorifying God, Miracles, Obedience, Praise, Testimony

DAILY BIBLE READING: Mark 4–5

TODAY'S VERSE: Mark 5:19: "Howbeit Jesus suffered him not, but saith unto him, Go home to thy friends, and tell them how great things the Lord hath done for thee, and hath had compassion on thee."

THIS CHAPTER TELLS US the story of Legion. A man was possessed with devils and living among tombs. Jesus Christ gave him tremendous spiritual deliverance. After living in tombs and cutting himself with stones, this man eagerly wanted to stay with Christ and follow Him. If Christ had done that for you, wouldn't you just want to give your life back to Him? I am amazed at the willing heart of an old demoniac to serve his Lord and appalled at the apathy and selfishness of many today who will not even share the gospel of Christ with others. How often we exemplify Luke 7:47: "Wherefore I say unto thee, Her sins, which are many, are forgiven; for she loved much: but to whom little is forgiven, the same loveth little." Until you realize the insurmountable amount of your debt and the matchless grace of God in forgiveness, you will never appreciate the work of Christ.

The Mission from Christ ("Howbeit Jesus suffered him not, but saith unto him, Go home to thy friends"). The personalized gospel is the greatest thing a Christian can share with others! There is nothing so powerful as the Word of God and a personal testimony confirming one's faith. This man didn't need any training to share his experience: he was immediately ready after his conversion! Jesus sent him to those over whom he had the most influence. If anybody knew of this man's past problems and past failures, it was his friends! What a testimony as he returned whole with nothing but the glory of God flowing from his lips! Often, Christians bypass sharing the gospel with family or friends because of embarrassment. Don't allow familiarity to shut your mouth from sharing the good news with those who are closest to you.

The Magnification of Christ ("and tell them how great things the Lord hath done for thee"). We must realize that the real testimony is about Christ and not about us! If you will notice, we are not to share just the greatness of the things that He has done, for that would be merely fact. We are to share "how" great things He has done. This has to do with magnitude. God shook heaven and earth to save our souls! He stood eye to eye with all the wickedness and vileness of this earth, became sin for us, and defeated death, hell, and the grave! He did this *all for us!*

The Ministry of Christ ("and hath had compassion on thee"). If Christ can have compassion on a demoniac, then He can have compassion on you! He can give us nothing better than His compassion and mercy! The definition of the word for "compassion" is "to compassionate, by word or deed, specially, by divine grace." Hallelujah for the love of God that shed His grace on me!

TOPICS: Christ's Love, Compassion, Missions, Testimony, Witness

DAILY BIBLE READING: Mark 6-7

TODAY'S VERSE: Mark 7:24: "And from thence he arose, and went into the borders of Tyre and Sidon, and entered into an house, and would have no man know it: but he could not be hid."

THE LAST SIX WORDS of this verse carry great impact: "But he could not be hid." Some today are trying to hide their relationship with God. How is it that we are trying to hide the One who loved us so and gave His life on Calvary? Something happens in the heart of a believer at the moment of salvation, and that new relationship will come out! It is the natural progression for Christ to be shown in the life of His children. As we look at a verse, it is important to note what it does *not* say.

It Does Not Say "He Would Not Be Hid." That would have to do with **permission**. One thing I have found to be true is that God loves to play hide and seek. Psalm 27:8 says, "When thou saidst, Seek ye my face; my heart said unto thee, Thy face, LORD, will I seek." Not only has He given us permission to seek Him and find Him, but it is His greatest desire that we do so! The glorification, exaltation, and magnification of Christ in the life of every believer is the pinnacle of our works as Christians.

It Does Not Say "He Should Not Be Hid." That would have to do with **prerogative**. What right do we have to determine who should or should not hear about Christ? What a privilege we have to show forth the blessing of the Saviour in our lives! He is not picking and choosing who is allowed to show forth His praise and His mighty acts. He does not deny us joy in the Christian life by not allowing us to show forth His mighty works through our *salvation, sanctification, separation,* and *supplication.* The word for "hid" means "to lie hid, unwittingly, be ignorant of, unawares." God will make Himself known to every heart and mind. There is no possible way for anyone to be ignorant or unaware of who God is and what He can do. Colossians 1:27 says, "To whom *God would make known* what is the riches of the glory of this mystery among the Gentiles; *which is Christ in you,* the hope of glory."

It *Does* Say "He Could Not Be Hid." This has to do with **possibility**! What possibilities await the Christian! What blessedness comes with Christ showing Himself in you! Galatians 1:15–16 says, "But when it pleased God, who separated me from my mother's womb, and called me by his grace, *to reveal his Son in me,* that I might preach him among the heathen." God desires to do this, not just *for* you, but *to* you! With God's presence, great and tremendous possibilities come our way. Kings, tyrants, and rulers have all tried to hide Him from view, but He cannot be hid. If you are truly living your life for the honor and glory of Christ, then He will shine out of you!

TOPICS: God's Will, Testimony, Witness

DAILY BIBLE READING: Mark 8–9

TODAY'S VERSE: Mark 9:2: "And after six days Jesus taketh with him Peter, and James, and John, and leadeth them up into an high mountain apart by themselves: and he was transfigured before them."

CHRIST'S TRANSFIGURATION was an event that changed the lives of Peter, James, and John. Peter talked about its impact on his life in 2 Peter 1:17–18. Among other things, it was a lesson on leadership. Countless books have been written on leadership and how to reach your goals. You can read principles of developing your leadership from A–Z, from Adams to Ziglar. However, as Christians, we should take our lessons from the greatest Leader who ever walked the planet and find the principles that He used while upon this earth. How did He develop His disciples into leaders?

Select the Servants of Your Vocation ("And after six days Jesus taketh with him Peter, and James, and John"). *Determine* who you will work with as a leader. Jesus called many by name and picked them by hand. He called them unto Him as they were cleaning their nets by the sea or walking on the road to Damascus to persecute Christians. We need to be careful about those we allow to be close to our plan of action. Once they have been chosen, they must be discipled and developed. Training is important in the *development* of new leaders. Once they are developed, we must teach them *delegation*. The closer we get to Calvary, the more we see Christ delegating projects to His disciples. At the end, He sent them to go to the city to prepare for the Passover, and He did not even show up until it was time. As He gave His life as a sacrifice, He showed them His *desire* and His passion for God's will. Then they were instructed to *deliver* the gospel to others.

Share the Secrets of Your Vision ("and leadeth them up into an high mountain apart by themselves"). You will not find a greater leader than the Great Shepherd! In this phrase, we see that Jesus *led* His disciples to a place of greater vision—the high mountain! There they were, separated from the world and all of its influences so that He might share a greater vision with them. This private setting would change their perception of Christ as well as their ministry for the future.

Show the Splendor of His Veneration ("and he was transfigured before them"). The Greek word for "transfigured" here is the same word that gives us "metamorphosis." Literally, Christ was changed before them! Oh for preachers, teachers, and leaders who will show the glory of God to the people! His *garments changed,* His *glory shone,* His *guests appeared.* The emphasis, however, came when *God spoke* and plainly glorified the Son in the midst of them all! If you would be a good mentor, you will realize that nothing short of God's glory will cause your disciples to be good leaders with the power and presence of God upon their lives!

TOPICS: God's Glory, Leadership, Training, Vision

DAILY BIBLE READING: Mark 10–12

TODAY'S VERSE: Mark 10:43: "But so shall it not be among you: but whosoever will be great among you, shall be your minister."

IN THIS VERSE, God is going to tell us what is great! The word translated "great" is the Greek word *megas*. It simply means "big." I have met many people in church who thought they were the "big one." In this verse, however, we hear what Christ thought it meant to be "big" in our service and worship. Do you want to be great in the right way? Listen up as our Lord tells us the only spiritual way we can achieve greatness!

Greatness Comes from Service. This has to do with being an **attendant**. The word for "minister" is the same root as in the word "deacon." The deacons of the local church were to be "attendants" and "servants" of the church. Jesus was telling His people that they could not be great until they learned how to serve others. Our wonderful Saviour showed us this greatness in John 13 when He girded Himself with a towel and bowed before each of His disciples to wash their feet. When He was done, He said, "If I then, your Lord and Master, have washed your feet; ye also ought to wash one another's feet. For I have given you an example, that ye should do as I have done to you" (John 13:14–15). As the humble servant of God, Jesus put His Father's will above His own and became a servant to man.

Greatness Comes from Submission. This has to do with **authority**. The picture given here is of a master and servant. If it is in your job description to help or assist another person, then that other person sits in a position of authority over you. The Bible commands us in Ephesians 5:21: "Submitting yourselves one to another in the fear of God." It is never hard to serve self, but to serve others is truly a sign of greatness!

Greatness Comes from Surrender. This has to do with **autonomy**. Many struggle with this in their spiritual lives. They come to a point where they do not mind submitting to God, for they know that He is worthy. But they struggle with surrendering themselves to the will of God, for then they cannot control their lives or their futures. Today's verse teaches us plainly that our will must be completely released. First Corinthians 6:19 says, "What? know ye not that your body is the temple of the Holy Ghost which is in you, which ye have of God, and *ye are not your own?*" This is not your life: it is His. It is not your church: it is His. It is not your body: it is His. This wonderful lesson on surrender will teach us many things about true greatness!

TOPICS: Service, Submission, Surrender

October 24

DAILY BIBLE READING: Mark 13–14

TODAY'S VERSE: Mark 14:62: "And Jesus said, I am: and ye shall see the Son of man sitting on the right hand of power, and coming in the clouds of heaven."

AFTER THE JEWS' KANGAROO COURT of false accusations and disagreeable testimony, Jesus admitted His deity, setting in motion the events of His death. Finally, the venom of the high priest and rulers of the Jews would be released upon this Nazarene! This was the moment for which they had all been waiting. But Jesus had been waiting for this time as well. Many times, the Bible talks about "his hour" as Jesus' hour of suffering, humiliation, and the work of salvation. In this verse we find Christ not only claiming His Godhood, but giving the questioners so much more than what they asked.

His Reality ("And Jesus said, I am: and ye shall see"). Jesus started His answer by saying, "I am." This is a direct reference to Exodus 3:14: "And God said unto Moses, I AM THAT I AM." Jesus first shows His *preeminence!* The next part of His answer, "and ye shall see," offers them a *promise.* Not one of His promises has ever fallen to the ground! They would be able to see Him on the right hand of power, not just hear about it from some other source. They would either be exonerated in His death, or they would be exposed in their unbelief. He then offers to them a *proof* ("ye shall see the Son of man"). No one can accuse God of doing His work in the dark. Even as the apostle Paul said before King Agrippa in Acts 26:26, "For the king knoweth of these things, before whom also I speak freely: for I am persuaded that none of these things are hidden from him; *for this thing was not done in a corner.*" God's work of redemption has always been open.

His Royalty ("the Son of man sitting on the right hand of power"). When the accusers see Christ on the right hand of the throne of God, they will not be able to deny His kingdom or His glory! They will acknowledge that His sitting upon the throne did not require a heavenly coup: it is His throne by right! No one can deny that sitting next to God on the throne is sitting next to power. What these men rejected in their spirit was the fact that Jesus has as much power as God does, for He is God!

His Return ("and coming in the clouds of heaven"). Before Jesus died on the cross, He prophesied of His return. He will return first of all in *vindication of His person.* Revelation 1:7 says, "Behold, he cometh with clouds; and every eye shall see him, and they also which pierced him." He will return in *victory of His pardon.* First Corinthians 15:57 says, "But thanks be to God, which giveth us the victory through our Lord Jesus Christ." And He will return in *vengeance of His people.* Second Thessalonians 1:7–8 says, "And to you who are troubled rest with us, when the Lord Jesus shall be revealed from heaven with his mighty angels, in flaming fire taking vengeance on them that know not God, and that obey not the gospel of our Lord Jesus Christ."

TOPICS: Christ's Majesty, Christ's Return, Preeminence, Vengeance, Victory

DAILY BIBLE READING: Mark 15–16

TODAY'S VERSE: Mark 16:6: "And he saith unto them, Be not affrighted: ye seek Jesus of Nazareth, which was crucified: he is risen; he is not here: behold the place where they laid him."

THIS WAS THE THIRD MORNING after Jesus' death, and three ladies came to His tomb to anoint His body and remember His work. As they approached the tomb at daybreak, they were concerned with one issue—rolling away the stone that covered the entrance to the sepulcher. As they drew closer, they noticed that the stone was gone! They must have wondered what had happened. Upon their entrance, they saw a man sitting in the tomb in a long white garment. Our verse today records the angel's words, spoken to these ladies following the resurrection of Christ.

Comfort to a Dreading Heart ("And he saith unto them, Be not affrighted"). No matter what situation we face, Christ does not want His children to fear. Not only were the disciples saddened by Christ's death, but they were fearful for their own lives as a result of the threatenings of the Jewish leaders. The word translated "affrighted" means "to astonish utterly." After the shock of the crucifixion and finding something unexpected in the tomb, this was a comforting and welcoming word.

Connection to a Dismayed Heart ("Ye seek Jesus of Nazareth, which was crucified"). Immediately, the angel connected to their hearts by telling them what their innermost desire was—to see Jesus! When the ladies heard this word, they felt connected to someone who was sympathetic toward them. This was not an accusation the angel made, but an association. The angel identified with the pain of their loss by saying, "Which was crucified." In God's work of comfort, He will connect with that genuine spirit of love and worship that resides in your heart.

Conquest to a Defeated Heart ("he is risen; he is not here"). What a victorious statement is given here! The angel did not say that Jesus was moved or relocated, but that "He is risen!" What greater victory is possible than power over death? Not only was Jesus not there to greet them upon His victory, but He was already working! God has not given us the victory just so we can gloat, but so we can "go."

Confirmation to a Doubting Heart ("behold the place where they laid him"). The angel gave these women an opportunity to inspect the tomb themselves, both physically and mentally. The word of faith was reason enough to believe in His resurrection, but God offered them so much more to confirm both its work and its truth. They were to "believe" already; now they were instructed to "see" for themselves. The word for "behold" is an "interjection that was used to denote surprise." Jesus had risen! Just as He said!

TOPICS: Comfort, Crucifixion, Fear, Proof, Resurrection, Victory

October 26

DAILY BIBLE READING: Luke 1

TODAY'S VERSE: Luke 1:53: "He hath filled the hungry with good things; and the rich he hath sent empty away."

THIS VERSE COMES right in the middle of Mary's praise to God and magnification of His work—that He would send His Son as a Saviour to man! From verses 46–55, we have her entire song of praise. She begins it by saying, "My soul doth magnify the Lord." If only we had more people who would make magnification of the Lord the most important part of their lives!

In today's verse, let's focus on the beginning, which reminds me of one of the Beatitudes from Matthew 5:6: "Blessed are they which do hunger and thirst after righteousness: *for they shall be filled.*"

God's Answer to Emptiness ("He hath filled"). What a "filling" God can give! When I think of *filling*, I am usually thinking about a pie or the sweet white stuff in the middle of a Twinkie, but this is so much more filling! We can be "filled with thy praise" (Psalm 71:8). "Let the whole earth be filled with his glory" (Psalm 72:19). And of course, as Christians we are "filled with the Spirit" (Ephesians 5:18). The Bible speaks of many, many more fillings. This chapter alone speaks three times of different people who were filled with the Holy Ghost. The word for "filled" also has the meaning of "satisfied." Of one thing you can be sure: when God does the filling, you will be both filled and satisfied!

God's Acknowledgment of Hunger ("the hungry"). The word for "hunger" means "through the idea of pinching toil; to crave." The Bible says in Mark 15:3 that Joseph of Arimathea "craved" the body of Jesus. Do you "crave" the Lord? Do you crave His Word? It is said that true hunger is the greatest force upon the body of man and that under certain conditions he will kill others to fill his belly. David "craved" God as we read in Psalm 63:1: "O God, thou art my God; early will I seek thee: my soul thirsteth for thee, my flesh longeth for thee in a dry and thirsty land, where no water is."

God's Abundance of Blessing ("with good things"). The word for "good things" also means "benefits." The Bible says, "Bless the LORD, O my soul, and forget not all his benefits" (Psalm 103:2). And Psalm 116:12 asks the question, "What shall I render unto the LORD for all his benefits toward me?" Thank God that the Lord will fill us with good things! God wants to give His people and His children the best! We hear this truth loud and clear in Luke 11:13: "If ye then, being evil, know how to give good gifts unto your children: how much more shall your heavenly Father give the Holy Spirit to them that ask him?" Doesn't it make good sense that God wants to give us the best? A note of caution, however: we often think that "good things" have to do with our ease, comfort, and desires, but the good things God wants to give us have to do with our faith. He has promised in Psalm 84:11 to give us good things as we glorify Him in our lives: "For the LORD God is a sun and shield: the LORD will give grace and glory: no good thing will he withhold from them that walk uprightly." Your praise ought to be connected to these "good things!"

TOPICS: Blessing, Faith, Spiritual Hunger

R. CHRIS HANKS

DAILY BIBLE READING: Luke 2–3

TODAY'S VERSE: Luke 2:14: "Glory to God in the highest, and on earth peace, good will toward men."

I AM INTRIGUED by the message of the angels, for 1 Peter 1:12b says, "Which are now reported unto you by them that have preached the gospel unto you with the Holy Ghost sent down from heaven; *which things the angels desire to look into.*" The angels are not allowed to share the gospel of Christ upon this earth. That privilege has been given to us! This was a lone announcement given to the public concerning the Messiah. For many of the angels, this was the only opportunity they would have to talk about God the Son. This was something they rehearsed with great care. This multitude of angelic beings had one sentence to preach. Let us consider this sentence as they meant for us to receive it.

They Spoke of God's Praise ("Glory to God in the highest"). What would make the angels say this phrase? This was not a praise of personal thanksgiving, for Jesus did not come to redeem the angels. This was a praise of His worth! The angels had seen God in heaven. They had seen Him as we never have! If you had been in the presence of God, beholding His glory and singing His praise, and then you came to man on earth, would you not want to give praise to God and tell man of the glory he had never seen? This was a testimony of the angels to man, saying, "You have no idea what you are getting in the person of Christ!"

They Spoke of God's Peace ("and on earth peace"). There is no peace on earth. As the days approach of the return of our Lord, the Bible teaches in Jeremiah 6:14b that man will be endlessly seeking and asking for peace, but he will find none: they cry "peace, peace; when there is no peace." The only peace man can have was made possible when the Prince of Peace came to this earth. That was literally "peace on earth"! Jesus has extended His peace to whosoever will accept His gift of salvation.

They Spoke of God's Pleasantness ("good will toward men"). In Greek, the word for "good will" means "satisfaction, delight, kindness, wish, purpose." Note that this was not good will "amongst" men, but "toward" men. Only God could extend this kind salutation from heaven. There is tremendous truth in the word "toward." Strong's Concordance says of the Greek for this word that it is "a primary preposition denoting (fixed) position (in place, time or state), i.e. a relation of rest." Our relation of rest is completely dependent upon the "fixed" position of the birth of Christ in Bethlehem so long ago! What a truth is taught in a seemingly insignificant preposition! We can now rest, satisfied, in the work of God.

TOPICS: Christ's Birth, Peace, Praise

October 28

DAILY BIBLE READING: Luke 4-6

TODAY'S VERSE: Luke 5:4: "Now when he had left speaking, he said unto Simon, Launch out into the deep, and let down your nets for a draught."

JESUS USED SIMON'S BOAT to address the crowd that had gathered to hear Him speak, but He was not done speaking when He ceased to preach. He had something He needed to share with Simon. We need to listen to the Lord speak even after the service is done! Jesus was using Simon's stuff, but He did not yet have Simon. It is easy for us to think that once we give God one of our possessions and see Him use it for His honor and glory, then we are completely submitted to Him. Nothing could be further from the truth. God is not just looking for your stuff: He wants you!

The **Driving Force of God's Will** ("Launch out"). Before we can obey the Lord and follow His will, we will have to leave the land. We must let go of our security. What is tying you to the shore today? Why not loose the line from the dock and head out to sea? Grammatically, this word "launch" requires an immediate action from the subject, or Simon. We need to accept the understood "you" of any command God gives us and immediately obey it.

The **Deep Foundations of God's Will** ("into the deep"). The word for "deep" means "profundity, mystery, deep": it is the Greek word *bathos,* from which we get our word *bathysphere.* A bathysphere will take you to the greatest of ocean depths. How deep have you gone in the depths of God's love, scriptural truth, and Christian living? Romans 11:33 says, "O the depth of the riches both of the wisdom and of knowledge of God! how unsearchable are his judgments, and his ways past finding out!" Far too often, we live our lives around the shore in the shallows. Oh for Christian people who will thrust out from shore and enter into deep waters concerning their faith and their fervor for God! You can't stir up dust in deep water! You can't throw mud in deep water! You can't jump ship in deep water! In the deep water, we are fully committed and able to follow God.

The **Descending Fathoms of God's Will** ("and let down your nets"). This has to do with our submission. How willing are we to let our nets, our possessions, our guards down? This instruction of God deals with the failures and painful past of Simon's life. In Luke 5:5, Simon told Christ, "Master, we have toiled all the night, and have taken nothing: nevertheless at thy word I will let down the net." Simon had to be confronted with all the times he had tried to serve God in his flesh and failed. He was exhausted, but he had to do it again! When we serve God in obedience and in the power of His Spirit, the results will change!

The **Draught of Fishes of God's Will** ("for a draught"). This shows us the expectancy that comes with obeying God and trusting in His power. Even though Simon didn't expect anything, Jesus did! Some reading this today might say, "I've already tried serving God, and it doesn't work!" I would have to agree with you—*if* you did it in your own power and strength. If you will try serving God in God's power, you will find that it is much different than you could ever dream! A draught of blessings awaits the Christian who will follow the Lord's will, commit his life in service, and dedicate his heart in worship!

TOPICS: Faith, God's Will, Obedience, Submission, Surrender

DAILY BIBLE READING: Luke 7

TODAY'S VERSE: Luke 7:39: "Now when the Pharisee which had bidden him saw it, he spake within himself, saying, This man, if he were a prophet, would have known who and what manner of woman this is that toucheth him: for she is a sinner."

THIS WOMAN, IN GREATEST HUMILITY, fell at the feet of our Lord in the most abject manner. She began to worship Him in the only way she knew how. We see showers of sorrows as she washed His feet with her tears. The Pharisee, in his self-righteousness, could not even bear to see what was taking place before him. This religious crowd never saw the light, never saw their sin, and never responded to the gospel. If anything, he should have been the one to help this wayward woman come to the Lord in her sorrow and guilt and trust in Him. We see this pharisaical response in three ways.

First was the **Denial of His Deity** ("if he were a prophet"). Simon did not even believe Jesus was a prophet, much less God. This event actually brought relief to Simon's proud mind, for now he perceived Jesus to be below him, for at least he himself was a Pharisee! His own fleshly ways got the best of him as he said of Christ, "If He were a prophet, He would have known better." Simon knew the Messiah would have a spirit of discernment associated with His office. Clearly, he did not believe that Jesus had that discernment, for why would He allow an impure woman to tamper with Him if He was God? Although God warned His people in Isaiah 65:5 not to be "holier than thou," the Pharisees, it has been said, would not allow a woman to stand closer to them than four cubits.[6] Simon would never have allowed this woman in such close proximity, much less allowed her to defile him with her touch!

Second was the **Derision of Her Desire** ("would have known who and what manner of woman"). According to the Pharisee, there were two reasons for this woman *not* to worship Jesus if He was God. This verse says, *"Who* and *what manner."* In Simon's mind, she had no right to come to God because of her *people.* Her heathen traditions were proof to Simon that she was not Jewish. She was a Gentile. No doubt this woman's heathen ways were despicable in his sight. It was a heathen practice to kiss the feet of an idol or a statue, not a Jewish tradition! How could she bring her idolatrous ways into a religious atmosphere? She and Jesus must both be fakes! The truth is, the heathen of Jesus' day understood more about worship than the religious crowd of the Jews! As a matter of fact, this woman got it just right! This Pharisee also did not believe that she could come to God because of her *problem.* She was a horrible sort of woman by that day's standards. Yet the Bible says that she "toucheth him." The word for "touch" means, "to touch, to attach oneself to." She would not let Him go! Hebrews 4:15 says, *"For we have not an high priest which cannot be touched* with the feeling of our infirmities; but was in all points tempted like as we are, yet without sin." Praise the Lord that He is not bound by our Gentile nature and is willing for us to touch Him by faith!

Third was the **Determination of Her Depravity** ("for she is a sinner"). Isn't this the epitome of the pharisaical way? Nothing but condemnation! This is a condemnation against both the woman's character and her nature. Religious people have always prided themselves on being better than others. Simon did not even care that *she agreed* with his deduction. Yes, our sin has separated us from God, but it is by the acknowledgment of our sin that we are offered forgiveness, mercy, and grace. Yes, we need God's amazing grace!

TOPICS: Criticism, Self-Righteousness, Sin

---

6   J.W. McGarvey, *The Four-Fold Gospel* (Cincinnati: Standard Publishing Co., 1914), 292.

DAILY BIBLE READING: Luke 8–9

TODAY'S VERSE: Luke 8:39: "Return to thine own house, and shew how great things God hath done unto thee. And he went his way, and published throughout the whole city how great things Jesus had done unto him."

AFTER THIS DEVIL-POSSESSED MAN was delivered and set free by Christ, his life changed. He had no desire but to be with his Saviour and do His work. Christ responded with the words in today's verse that others might know of His power, His love, and the hope of deliverance. Let's look at the significance of this man's returning "to thine own house."

It Was a Return to a Specific Family. Do you care for the salvation of your family? If you do not pray for your family, no one will. What about your children? Brothers and sisters? Mother and father? Grandparents and aunts and uncles? We *must* care for the spiritual well-being of our homes and our families. Even though it was too late, the rich man wanted to pray and send someone back to tell his family about the terrors of hell. Don't wait until it is too late! Tell them now!

It Was a Return to a Specific Fellowship. A home ought to be a place of fellowship. If we are comfortable anywhere, it should be in our own homes with our own families. How sad it is when families only speak of worldly things each day. A tremendous blessing comes with speaking of spiritual things in the place where you live. Turn this place of fellowship around, and let your house ring with the praises of God in worshipful music and words of spiritual encouragement that will bring every mind to the place of acknowledging God's love.

It Was a Return to a Specific Form. Two interesting words are used in this verse: "shew" and "published." God had a specific job for this man to accomplish and a specific way to do it. The word for "shew" means "to relate fully." Zodhiates defines it as, "To conduct a narration through to the end."[7] Don't stop short of sharing your faith! Continue to the end! People need to hear the end of the gospel and of faith in Christ! The word for "published" is the same word translated "preach" and means "to herald (as a public crier); especially divine truth." There needs to be fervency in our pulpits again! There was a time when men would come to church to watch the preacher burn in the passion of a holy flame from the Word of God upon his heart! First Corinthians 1:21 says, "It pleased God by the foolishness of preaching to save them that believe." Let us return to the old-time way and the old-time form of preaching and relating the meaning of the gospel in its fullness!

It Was a Return to a Specific Faith ("Shew how great things God hath done unto thee"). The man's was a testimony of *description*—"how great things." Can you testify of great things God has done? Tell someone! His was a testimony of *prescription*—"how great things *God hath done*." These things were thought and wrought in the mind of God. God prescribed His works for you just like a doctor prescribes medicine for your health. God knew what you needed and accomplished it so that you could glorify Him. This goes beyond salvation and covers everything He has ever done in your life. The man's was also a testimony of *inscription*—"how great things God hath done *unto thee*." The work is "dedicated" to one person—it has not been done upon anyone else! Your testimony is a testimony of what God has inscribed upon you, and it is your job to share and testify of those things.

TOPICS: Praise, Soul-Winning, Testimony, Witness

---

7   Spiros Zodhiates, *The Complete Word Study New Testament with Parallel Greek* (Chattanooga: AMG, 1992), 896.

TODAY'S BIBLE READING: Luke 10–11

TODAY'S VERSE: Luke 10:20: "Notwithstanding in this rejoice not, that the spirits are subject unto you; but rather rejoice, because your names are written in heaven."

WHEN JESUS SPOKE these words to His disciples, they had just returned after experiencing great power over demonic spirits. Christ had also given them power over serpents and scorpions and over all the power of Satan. Here, He was careful to share with His disciples that their joy should not come from *victory over Satan* but from the *value of salvation*. In other words, our achievements over Satan are not nearly as important as our association with our Saviour!

Do you need a reason to rejoice today? Let me quickly tell you what Jesus did *not* say. He did *not* say, "Rejoice in your good works and holiness." He did *not* say, "Rejoice in your spiritual understanding." He did *not* say, "Rejoice in your spiritual desires." Instead of rejoicing in *us* today, let's rejoice in Christ, our *true source of joy*.

It Is a Personal Salvation ("because *your names*"). Hallelujah! Jesus called my name! John 10:3 says, "To him the porter openeth; and the sheep hear his voice: *and he calleth his own sheep by name,* and leadeth them out." I love to look at all the people He called by name: "Zaccheus, make haste, and come down." "Lazarus, come forth." "Jesus saith unto her, Mary." What a special thing to have your name called! Do you remember when Jesus called your name in salvation? It's nice that your father's or mother's name is written in heaven, but is *yours?* If your name is there, you have cause to rejoice!

It Is a Proof Salvation ("because your names *are written*"). Adam Clark says in his commentary that "this form of speech was taken from the ancient custom of writing names of all the citizens in a public register."[8] If you are saved, the records are set, and your name has been documented as receiving the priceless gift of salvation! This record is proof that Jesus has known you! He will say to others, "I never knew you: depart from me." The mind of God, the heart of God, and the hand of God came together to pen your name upon the heavenly records of divine salvation. God will not forget what He has written. Once it is written, it is done! These names are not written upon some heavenly Post-It note somewhere around the great office of heaven. Revelation 21:27 says they are *"written in the Lamb's book of life."* What a book in which to be recorded!

It Is a Princely Salvation ("because your names are written *in heaven*"). Some look for their names to be printed upon a door; others want theirs to be carved into the side of a building, but we just want our names in a book in heaven. If our names were written anywhere else, it would not be real or lasting. Because our names are written in heaven, the record is real and we are royalty! Our Elder Brother is the Prince of Princes—we are royalty!

TOPICS: Eternal Security, Exaltation, Joy, Salvation

8   Adam Clarke, *Holy Bible with Commentary and Critical Notes*, Vol 4. (New York: B. Waugh and T. Mason for the Methodist Episcopal Church, 1846), 431.

DAILY BIBLE READING: Luke 12–13

TODAY'S VERSE: Luke 12:34: "For where your treasure is, there will your heart be also."

OUR THOUGHT THIS MORNING concerns the heart. You might think that nobody notices what's in you, but your heart is the greatest tattletale of your life! Don't think for a moment that your heart is on your side. Jeremiah 17:9 says, "The heart is deceitful above all things, and desperately wicked: who can know it?" Since this is true, we must carefully consider how the Bible teaches us to deal with our hearts, lest we end up in destruction. Proverbs 4:23 says, "Keep thy heart with all diligence; for out of it are the issues of life." We must each take great pains to make sure that our heart is in tune with God and not with itself. Your heart will tell all about you.

It will tell the **Way Your Life Is Facing** ("For *where* your treasure"). This has to do with your **direction**. Which direction is your heart facing right now? Here is a little wisdom from my old basketball coach: As you defend someone playing basketball, your coach will tell you to focus on your opponent's hips. Arms, eyes, legs, and shoulders can fake out the best of defenders, but people are always facing the same direction as their hips. The same thing is true with our spiritual hearts. Your heart will tip off the direction your life faces.

It will tell on **What Your Heart Is Fixed** ("your treasure"). This has to do with your **desires**. You might try to tell others that your heart is fixed upon spiritual things, but the things you think about constantly tell on you. You might wish your heart was centered upon God, but every moment, it is consumed with *selfish desires, simple deceits,* and *spiritual deadness.* The Bible says in Luke 6:45, "A good man out of the good treasure of his heart bringeth forth that which is good; and an evil man out of the evil treasure of his heart bringeth forth that which is evil: for of the abundance of the heart his mouth speaketh." Yes, my friend, your heart will tell all about your treasures and desires!

It will also tell the **Places Your Heart Frequents** ("where your treasure *is,* there will your heart *be*"). This has to do with your **dwelling**. If you treasure your children or grandchildren, you will visit them. If you treasure clothing, you will shop. If your treasure is in the Word of God, you will frequent its wonderful pages. If a Christian loves God, he will dwell in His house, His Word, and His Spirit. What is your heart saying about you by the treasures that are exposed in your life?

TOPICS: Deceitfulness, Heart

DAILY BIBLE READING: Luke 14–15

TODAY'S VERSE: Luke 14:34: "Salt is good: but if the salt have lost his savour, wherewith shall it be seasoned?"

I GREW UP HEARING about this salt in Sunday school. I have heard messages on its meaning many times. There is no doubt that "salt is good." Salt is good for many things: it is an *additive for preservation,* it is an *aggravation to perversion,* and it is an *appreciation to pleasure.* Salt will cause a soul to desire water or bring out the sweetness of a fruit. But if we are not careful, it's easy to get sidetracked by these things and miss the main thought of the verse. Let's look today at the admonition to save our savor: "but if the salt have lost his savor."

Salt May Lose Its Savor Over Time. Maybe nothing has happened to the salt. Maybe it has been in the same place, with the same owner, for years. Time, though, has caused it to lose its savor. Perhaps you are in the same place you have always been, but you know that over time you have lost your savor. Your passion, your pungency, and your purpose have been lost. We must make sure that our savor is still strong. Many will tell you all they used to do in the service of the Lord, when in truth, they are doing nothing for Him now. Time has slowly taken away the potency of their love and service to the Lord.

Salt May Lose Its Savor Over Trouble. Maybe the elements have caused the salt to lose its savor. Even humidity can affect its taste. Maybe something was dropped into it that has taken away its power and meaning. Perhaps some trial beyond your power has mixed itself into the granules of your life and changed your consistency. Don't allow trouble to take away your savor! Psalm 32:7 says, "Thou art my hiding place; *thou shalt preserve me from trouble;* thou shalt compass me about with songs of deliverance. Selah."

Salt May Lose Its Savor Over Taste. Sometimes a change of taste changes the impact of salt upon food. Maybe your salt has lost its savor because you have lost your taste for spiritual things. The problem in this case is not the salt, but you. I have heard some say they don't serve the Lord today because it's just not the same as it used to be. Their tastes have changed. They don't like the old-time ways any longer. Now they would rather experience God through a new medium. Don't let your taste take away from who God is!

TOPICS: Apathy, Tenderness, Testimony, Trouble, Witness

November 3

DAILY BIBLE READING: Luke 16–18

TODAY'S VERSE: Luke 18:8: "I tell you that he will avenge them speedily. Nevertheless when the Son of man cometh, shall he find faith on the earth?

TODAY'S VERSE IS CONNECTED to a parable Christ told concerning a begging widow and an unjust judge that can be found in the first seven verses of our chapter. His point was to show the mercy of an unjust judge in contrast to our heavenly Father, who knows our needs and loves us with an infinite love. If an unjust judge will hear the request of someone who does not deserve it, do we not think our heavenly Father will hear His children and help them in their quandaries? Many times children think they need something, but parents know their children's needs better than the children do. This verse is meant to lift our faith in God and help us to trust in His protective and providing hand.

The Quarrel of God's Retribution ("I tell you that he will avenge them"). The day is coming when God will set all things straight. God does not like His enemies to mishandle and persecute His people. Don't take it upon yourself to fight your own battles, for the Lord will fight for you. Romans 12:19 says, "Dearly beloved, avenge not yourselves, but rather give place unto wrath: for it is written, Vengeance is mine; I will repay, saith the Lord." God has a quarrel with those who reject His Word and His holiness. All His enemies will understand the terror of Hebrews 10:31: "It is a fearful thing to fall into the hands of the living God."

The Quickness of God's Response ("he will avenge them speedily"). The meaning here is of a "short, brief period of time." This reminds me of the return of Christ at the rapture, described in 1 Corinthians 15:52: "In a moment, in the twinkling of an eye, at the last trump: for the trumpet shall sound, and the dead shall be raised incorruptible, and we shall be changed." All troubles, all pain, all struggles, and all uncertainty will fade in the glorious beauty of Jesus' wonderful face upon His return! Oh, that will be glory for me! To think that we are just a moment away from His return! What peace! What hope! What joy! What strength!

The Question Upon Christ's Return ("Nevertheless when the Son of man cometh, shall he find faith on the earth?"). This is one of the most thought-provoking and soul-searching questions in the Bible. When Jesus comes, will those who call themselves Christians be faithful to Him and to His cause? The word translated "faith" means "persuasion, credence, moral conviction." Will we continue in this faith or quit in our flesh? There may be times when you wonder if it is worth it. Hold on my friend, for "it will be worth it all, when we see Christ"![1]

TOPICS: Faith, Prayer, Rapture, Vengeance

---

1 "When We See Christ" by Esther Kerr Rusthoi. © 1941 New Spring, Inc (ASCAP) (Administered by Brentwood-Benson Music Publishing, Inc.) All rights reserved. Used by permission.

R. CHRIS HANKS

DAILY BIBLE READING: Luke 19–20

TODAY'S VERSE: Luke 19:46: "Saying unto them, It is written, My house is the house of prayer: but ye have made it a den of thieves."

WE WILL NEVER CONVINCE GOD that the busyness of our churches is equal to worship. How many times must the leaders at the temple have said that all of those vendors in the house of God were a good thing because "at least the people would come by the house of God." I believe that God is more interested in having true worship in His house than He is in getting people there. Though promotion can be a great tool, our hearts must be centered upon worshiping God and giving the gospel of Christ—and *nothing else*. Here are a few thoughts from this verse concerning God's house.

The Prophecies of God's House ("Saying unto them, It is written"). God has always had something special in mind for the place where His people meet with Him. If we believe that the Bible is God's Word, we should see what God's Word has to say about His house. First Timothy 3:15 says, "That thou mayest know how thou oughtest to behave thyself in the house of God." Scripture gives us a way we are to "behave" in God's house.

The Possession of God's House (*"My* house"). If we would accept that the church is *God's* house, many problems in church would never even come up. Too many people think the church is their personal possession. Too many deacons think the budget is their bank account. Too many children think the building is their personal playground. Too many preachers think the pulpit is their place of personal glory. Too many singers think the platform is their stage. Too many members think that the property and the materials and equipment are for their personal use. It is *God's* house!

The Personality of God's House ("is the house of prayer"). There is a proper demeanor to God's house. Jesus did not say it was a house of singing, although that is important. He did not say that it was a house of preaching, though that is blessed and necessary. He said it was "the house of prayer." Whatever happens in the house of God should humble our hearts and make us pray in His presence. It was and still should be a house of prayer!

The Persecution of God's House ("but ye have made it"). The pronoun translated "ye" is an emphatic personal pronoun. Jesus is emphatically using it here in this verse, emphasizing *who* did *what*. This bold accusation tells us what man does. The word for "made" means "to qualify." Jesus is saying, *"You* have qualified the house of God as a den of thieves." The greatest of preachers here points the finger and accuses man of destroying what is His. How often we "make" the house of God something that it should not be! It is not to be a place of wrong doctrine, entertainment, merchandising, or self-promotion! If we would let it be what Christ determined it to be in the beginning, we would find that it would also meet the needs of people today.

The Perversion of God's House ("a den of thieves"). The word for "den" means "grotto, a cavern, a cave." Instead of being a place hidden out of shame and disgrace, the house of God should be a lighthouse proclaiming the goodness of God to mankind. The world is doing all it can to turn the church into a den of thieves. Malachi 3:8 says that we can rob God in our *giving*. First Chronicles 16:29 says, "Give unto the LORD the glory due unto his name," so we see that we can rob Him of His *glory*. The Bible says in Ephesians 4:8–16 that God has given us gifts to serve and glorify Him, so we can rob Him in our *gifts*. We are to go and give the gospel to the lost, so we can rob Him in our *goings*. Let us not pervert God's house by bringing shame upon it in robbing Him of that which is rightfully His!

TOPICS: God's House, Prayer, Reverence, Worship

DAILY BIBLE READING: Luke 21–22

TODAY'S VERSE: Luke 21:4: "For all these have of their abundance cast in unto the offerings of God: but she of her penury hath cast in all the living that she had."

THE BIBLE TALKS of several times when Jesus was actually in the temple. And exactly where was He? Around the offering plates every time! Mark 12:41 says that Jesus "beheld *how* the people cast money into the treasury." God is interested in *how* you give! It is not only the *measure* that interests Him, but the *manner* in which we give. Let me give you a couple of thoughts about this poor widow and how we are to give.

First, you cannot give **According to What Is Left Over** ("all these have of their abundance cast"). Jesus recognized their **pride.** The word for "abundance" means "to superabound, in excess, exceed, be left." Just because the rich had a lot left over, they would go ahead and give much. That never does touch the heart of God. God has never been impressed with second place, no matter how much you give. He is to be preeminent in every part of our worship of Him, including our giving. Should we do anything less for God who gave it *all* to us willingly?

Second, you cannot give **According to What Is Going Out** ("she of her penury hath cast in"). Jesus recognized her **poverty.** The word for "penury" means "deficit, poverty, want." In other words, this woman did not let her debt or her lack keep her from obeying and worshiping her Lord. She did not sit down and figure out what she could *not* give. It was not a question as to whether or not she could afford to give. In her mind, she could not afford *not* to give!

Third, we must give **According to Sacrifice** ("all the living that she had"). Jesus recognized her **present.** Giving all was not a difficult decision for her, since she was not just trying to have a living here on earth. Her "living" was found in God! She had already recognized her life as being in her love for her God and not associated with this earth. She had laid hold of the truth found in 2 Samuel 24:24 concerning the empty giving of an offering without sacrifice: "Neither will I offer burnt offerings unto the LORD my God of that which doth cost me nothing." God has always been touched by sacrifice, even to the point of satisfying Himself for the payment of man's sin. This is greatly illustrated by Cain and Abel. Cain made a donation, but Abel gave a sacrifice! Someone once said that Cain was the first to figure out that you can't get blood out of a turnip. When Abel gave his offering, he not only gave the immediate prosperity of what the lamb was to him, but he gave the future prosperity of what the little lamb could bring.

We must remember that God is not trying to get all our money. He is interested in blessing you, but He also deserves to be worshiped with that which He supplies. What a liberating moment when you realize it is all His anyway!

TOPICS: Giving, Sacrifice, Tithing

DAILY BIBLE READING: Luke 23–24

TODAY'S VERSE: Luke 24:45: "Then opened he their understanding, that they might understand the scriptures."

MY FATHER-IN-LAW ONCE PREACHED, "Whatever you know about the Bible, you know only because God has revealed it to you." Today, there is a tremendous lack of understanding of God's Word. There is much knowledge, but very little understanding or discernment. How sad it is to think that many people base their spirituality on little more than their knowledge of Bible trivia! The fact that you know a reference, a name, or a story is not necessarily proof of your spiritual condition. Let us develop a hunger and thirst for God's Word and be like the Bereans in Acts 17:11: "These were more noble than those in Thessalonica, in that they received the word with all readiness of mind, and searched the scriptures daily, whether those things were so."

Studying God's Word Was the Will of God ("then opened he"). Doesn't it mean something to you that God wants you to understand His thoughts? If you are struggling with finding the will of God for your life and wondering what you should do, wait. He *will* tell you. You forget that He wants you to know His will more than you do! Sometimes we act like it is up to us to find God's will. What a shame! Let's wait on Him to "open" things for us. Let's allow Him to lead.

Studying God's Word Was a Work of God ("then opened he their understanding"). The word for "opened" means "to open thoroughly, as with a first born." It took a divine work for this to happen. When Jesus "opened their understanding," He did not merely crack the door, He flung it wide open! He *thoroughly* opened their understanding! There are many things in the Bible I *do not* understand, but by the guiding and teaching of the Holy Spirit, there is nothing in the Bible that I *cannot* understand! Part of the definition of "opened" means "that of a first born." There is no doubt that the womb is completely and thoroughly opened with the coming of the firstborn! Only God can bring such life! He can do it in your understanding as well.

Studying God's Word Was about the Word of God ("that they might understand the scriptures"). Jesus did not open their understanding of quantum physics, but of something with greater truth, greater possibilities, and greater depth—His Word! The word for "understand" means "to put together." God will give us the ability to put together the truths of God's Word with the ministry of God's Word. There is no greater work God could have done for the believer than to enable him to grasp the truths of His Word. People get sidetracked searching for obscure teachings that may exist in a verse instead of seeing that there is more than we can ever comprehend exploding off every page. Let the Word of God be something to you today!

TOPICS: Discernment, Understanding, Word of God

November 7

DAILY BIBLE READING: John 1-3

TODAY'S VERSE: John 1:38-39: "Then Jesus turned, and saw them following, and saith unto them, What seek ye? They said unto him, Rabbi, (which is to say, being interpreted, Master,) where dwellest thou? He saith unto them, Come and see. They came and saw where he dwelt, and abode with him that day: for it was about the tenth hour."

BEFORE TODAY'S VERSES, the disciples of John heard him declare that Jesus was the "Lamb of God, which taketh away the sin of the world," and they left all and followed Him. God is still looking for disciples like that today!

The conversation between Christ and these disciples is precious. Jesus even asked them an intimate question in verse 38: "What seek ye?" That is a very searching question for us today. Let me ask you the same thing: "For what are you searching?" People are looking for peace, satisfaction, truth, hope, and even love. Some are looking for answers, while others are just looking for a friend. These disciples went to the right place to find what they were searching for—to our Blessed Lord! It would do us well to begin our search with Him. If we do, we will most definitely find our answer!

The disciples answered with the question, "Where dwelleth thou?" This is one of the most spiritual answers you will find in the Bible. They were looking for where God lived. If only we would seek the same thing! I would like to share a few places *where He is right now.*

He Is at the Right Hand of the Father! This is a place of **exaltation.** Hebrews 12:2 says that we are "looking unto Jesus the author and finisher of our faith." Romans 8:34 tells us that Jesus is interceding for us at the right hand of God at this very moment. And to think that He has gone to prepare a place for us that *we might be where He is* (John 14:2)—at God's right hand! What a prospect lies ahead for us!

He Is at the Right House of Worship. This is a place of **exhortation.** That is why God gave you your church—for your exhortation. Ephesians 2:22 says, "Ye also are builded together for *an habitation of God* through the Spirit." You should go to church looking for God, for it is His house. Even if your church is small, He is there. Matthew 18:20 says, "For where two or three are gathered together in my name, *there am I in the midst of them.*" If you allow Him to be the Good Shepherd in your church, He will continue to dwell there.

If you are saved, **He Is Right Here with You.** This is a place of **exultation.** The English definition of the word "exult" is "to leap for joy; hence to rejoice in triumph, to rejoice exceedingly, at success or victory."[2] Hallelujah! Just the fact that Jesus is with us guarantees that He has given us the victory! It is a great blessing, as we read this devotion, to know that Jesus is here—right now! First Corinthians 3:16 says, "Know ye not that *ye are the temple of God,* and that the Spirit of God dwelleth in you?" Walk today in His presence. If you are not saved and do not have His presence in your life, ask Him for it right now, and He will dwell in you!

TOPICS: Exaltation, God's House, Holy Spirit, Victory

---

2   *Noah Webster's First Edition of an American Dictionary of The English Language* (Chesapeake, VA: Foundation For American Christian Education, 1995)

R. CHRIS HANKS

DAILY BIBLE READING: John 4–5

TODAY'S VERSE: John 4:11: "The woman saith unto him, Sir, thou hast nothing to draw with, and the well is deep: from whence then hast thou that living water?"

THIS STORY IS ONE of the most beloved in all of Scripture. This is one of the first places in the New Testament where we see the love that God has for the Gentiles, and especially for this unnamed Gentile woman to whom He extends salvation. This woman came for a drink, but Jesus wanted to give her a well! In this verse, she gives three reasons for her inner struggle to accept this free gift.

First, there was a **Problem with Drawing Water** ("thou hast nothing to draw with"). In her mind, Jesus did not have the means nor the tools to draw water for her! She even thought she was more qualified to draw this living water because she had a vessel! In a word, she did not deem Him capable because of His **looks.** She did not think she should trust Him with her salvation. Isaiah 53:2 says of Jesus, "There is no beauty that we should desire him." This woman wanted to see a physical reason to trust in Jesus, but there was none. The Jews wanted to see a kingly Messiah in whom they could rejoice with pride. Instead, they received one in utter humility whom they rejected with the greatest malice. Yet, even when you can't see it, you can rest assured that Jesus is more than capable of saving the worst sinner! Acts 4:12 says, "Neither is there salvation in any other: for there is none other name under heaven given among men, whereby we must be saved."

Second, there was a **Problem with a Deep Well** ("the well is deep"). This woman basically accused Jesus of being too shallow! She said, "You have no idea what you're in for when you go down that well." She thought this little job was literally over His head! She did not deem Him capable because of His **littleness.** Instead, it is we who know nothing of the fathoms of His depths. Romans 11:33 says, "O the depth of the riches both of the wisdom and knowledge of God! how unsearchable are his judgments, and his ways past finding out!" I am glad Jesus went down to the depths of sin and the grave for me!

Third, there was a **Problem with Denied Worth** ("whence then hast thou that living water?"). She just did not believe Him. She looked at Jesus and said, "You don't have what it takes." She did not deem Him capable because of His **limits.** Interestingly, this argument of hers rested on two earlier arguments which were already faulty. Her reasoning was confused! Her conclusion that He did not have living water was wrong because she could not see beyond her first two conclusions about Him. This is how dangerous natural thought from a carnal viewpoint can be. It can affect eternity! I have known Christians who will not experience God's goodness because they have limited His abilities. He is so much more than they—and this woman—ever dreamed!

TOPICS: Belief, Christ's Work, Faith

DAILY BIBLE READING: John 6

TODAY'S VERSE: John 6:19-21: "So when they had rowed about five and twenty or thirty furlongs, they see Jesus walking on the sea, and drawing nigh unto the ship: and they were afraid. But he saith unto them, It is I; be not afraid. Then they willingly received him into the ship: and immediately the ship was at the land whither they went."

IF THERE IS ANYTHING with which we can all identify, it is being in the midst of a storm. What a blessing it is to know that Christ cares about every storm and heartache we experience! How many of us would have been so blinded by this storm that we would fail to see Christ walking on the sea? Not only did the disciples see Him, but they invited Him into their boat. We need more people who are willing to get Christ into their boat! I have always been fascinated by the last phrase: "And immediately the ship was at the land whither they went." I would like to share a thought about how to get where you've been trying to go.

First, you must Hear the Word of God ("he saith unto them, It is I; be not afraid"). You will never get where you are going without hearing the Word of the Lord. No matter how hard you try, no matter how detailed your plans, no matter how strong your friends, you must hear the Word of God. We are living in a time when people will not hear. There is never a better time to hear the Word of the Lord than in the midst of a howling wind and thunderous storm.

Second, when you hear the Word of God, you will Not **Fear the Wild Gale** ("they were afraid"). When Jesus appeared, the disciples had just been operating in utmost fear. They had fear in darkness. In the midst of this storm, they could not tell anything about their welfare. They were full of uncertainty. The darkness clouded their minds with doubts about the Lord's will, for it was Christ who had sent them away in the boat. They had been with Him all day and were completely exhausted. Now they had to deal with the storm. For all practical purposes, they thought they would die. When they brought Jesus into the boat, there was hope, there was power, and there was love. First John 4:18 says, "But perfect love casteth out fear."

Third, He will bring you **Near the Will of God** ("they were at the land whither they went"). This account never mentions that Jesus stopped the storm. John was more interested in where Jesus was trying to take the disciples than in what Jesus was going to do for them! If He takes us where we've been trying to go, what difference does it make if the storm continues? Instead of trying to get Jesus to stop your storm, look for where He is trying to take you as a result of having you in the storm! God was trying to take them to another destination in their faith. Wait for the Lord, and let Him bring you to the other side.

The ultimate meaning of this passage is simple—bring Christ into your boat!

TOPICS: Fear, Trust, Word of God

DAILY BIBLE READING: John 7–8

TODAY'S VERSE: John 8:42: "Jesus said unto them, If God were your Father, ye would love me: for I proceeded forth and came from God; neither came I of myself, but he sent me."

OUR READING TODAY is one of great conflict between Christ and the Jewish rulers. Their passion to destroy and murder Christ has greatly grown, and they have even stooped to a level where their fervency for spiritual purity becomes their shame as they bring a woman taken in the act of adultery. They wanted to catch Christ in some inconsistency in the Jewish law and were willing to lay this woman's life on the line to do it. In our verse for today, we hear Christ detail His obedience to God and His purpose upon the earth.

Jesus first talked about the **Proof of Their Relationship** ("Jesus said unto them, If God were your Father, ye would love me"). A simple "If . . . then" statement is given to the Pharisees. The conclusion is the end result of a relationship with God: "Ye would love me." If we were God's children, it would be natural for us to love Christ. God has told us in His Word that no man can love God and reject His Son. It is impossible to love God and not love the One He loved and sent to pay for man's sin. The ultimate form of disrespect and contempt toward God is to rebuff the greatest of gifts ever offered to mortal man in the sacrifice of God's Precious Lamb.

Jesus then talked about the **Position of the Redeemer** ("for I proceeded forth and came from God"). This is referring to Christ's source. I believe in the eternal Sonship of Jesus Christ! John 1:1–2 says, "In the beginning was the Word, and the Word was with God, and the Word was God. The same was in the beginning with God." Jesus Christ was in heaven and participated in the glory of God in eternity past. When "the fullness of the time was come" (Galatians 4:4), He came forth from the realms of glory and left His place of wonder and His position of grandeur to take on the likeness of man and become his Saviour. Jesus' words here describe not only His origin, but also His meekness and humility in His love toward man.

And Jesus talked about the **Purpose of the Redeemer** ("neither came I of myself, but he sent me"). Jesus refers to Himself as completely submitted to the will of the Father. The word for "sent" is *apostello*, the same Greek word we translate "apostle." Hebrews 3:1b speaks of Christ being that apostle for us: "consider the Apostle and High Priest of our profession, Christ Jesus." The fact that God would "send" Jesus to us proclaims a divine purpose in His life! There was a mission, a job, a goal that had to be accomplished. Jesus shared all of these thoughts with the wicked Pharisees to tell them of His wonderful work of redemption.

TOPICS: God's Glory, God's Will, Loving God

DAILY BIBLE READING: John 9–10

TODAY'S VERSE: John 10:18: "No man taketh it from me, but I lay it down of myself. I have power to lay it down, and I have power to take it again. This commandment have I received of my Father."

THIS CHAPTER SHOULD BE of great interest to every Christian as we hear the Good Shepherd talk about His love and care for His sheep. There are three complete sentences in this one verse. The number three is the number of divine completeness and perfection.[3] What a picture we have here, without even discussing a word contained in the verse! God places everything exactly where He wants it for a reason. His future trip up Calvary's lonely and agonizing road, His will to give up His life, and His glorious resurrection are discussed in this one little verse.

He first speaks of an **Offering of Sacrifice** ("No man taketh it from me, but I lay it down of myself"). For all those who have trusted in Christ as their Saviour, this verse should hold special meaning. No force could pry His life from Jesus' hand! He willingly gave His body, His blood, and His life for the redemption of sinful man. An interesting truth comes from the grammar of the words in this sentence. The words for "taketh" and "lay it down" are present indicative in their use and conjugation. All that means is that "something is occurring while the speaker is making the statement."[4] While Jesus was speaking, He was laying down His life! Here is another thought: while He was speaking and laying down His life, nobody was able to take it from Him! This tells us that His voluntary offering of Himself was done before He ever made it to Calvary.

Second, He speaks of the **Omnipotence of the Saviour** ("I have power to lay it down, and I have power to take it again"). Jesus was not fearful of death, nor was He hesitant about the resurrection. It was all the same to Him! That is the very essence of Matthew 28:18 after His resurrection when He revealed Himself to His disciples: "And Jesus came and spake unto them, saying, *All power is given unto me* in heaven and in earth." If you cannot recognize God's omnipotence at creation, you must acknowledge it at the empty tomb! One of these acts did not require any more power or drain Him of divine glory any more than the other.

Third, He speaks of the **Obedience of the Son** ("This commandment have I received of my Father"). Jesus' life and death were done in subjection and submission to the will of His Father. The Bible talks extensively about the obedience of Christ. It is of utmost importance to the teaching of salvation, for if Jesus had been disobedient, His sacrifice would have been rendered useless! Philippians 2:8 says, "And being found in fashion as a man, he humbled himself, and *became obedient unto death, even the death of the cross.*" Don't discount the importance or the meaning of the obedience of Christ to the commandment of His Father—an obedience which was not without pain and suffering. Isaiah 53:4 says that Jesus was "smitten of God, and afflicted," and again, in Isaiah 53:10 we read, "Yet it pleased the LORD to bruise him; he hath put him to grief." Praise the Lord for Jesus' full and complete obedience to His Father!

TOPICS: Calvary, Christ's Submission, Gospel, Omnipotence

---

3   E.W. Bullinger, *Numbers in Scripture* (Grand Rapids: Kregel, 1967), 108.

4   Spiros Zodhiates, *The Complete Word Study New Testament with Parallel Greek* (Chattanooga: AMG, 1992), 867.

DAILY BIBLE READING: John 11–13

TODAY'S VERSE: John 13:12: "So after he had washed their feet, and had taken his garments, and was set down again, he said unto them, Know ye what I have done to you?"

THIS STORY SHARES a very tender time between Christ and His disciples before their final Passover and the path to Calvary. Jesus asks a question for the ages when He says, "Know ye what I have done to you?" In order to understand that question, we need to see the types, or pictures, in the story.

The Picture of His Humility ("So after he had washed their feet") Our Saviour knelt down to wash the feet of His own disciples. This was not His first, or His last, act of humility. The greatest way in which Christ humbled Himself was to become a curse for us: "Christ hath redeemed us from the curse of the law, being made a curse for us: for it is written, Cursed is every one that hangeth on a tree" (Galatians 3:13).

The Picture of His Honor ("and had taken his garments"). Our Saviour took the garments of His glory back to Himself after His death and resurrection, after laying them aside, and He robed Himself in flesh. That is the picture of the Incarnation. "And the Word was made flesh, and dwelt among us" (John 1:14). Peter, James, and John received just a glimpse of Jesus' glory on the Mount of Transfiguration. As a matter of fact, to receive His glory again was one of Jesus' great requests in the prayer of John 17:5: "And now, O Father, glorify thou me with thine own self with the glory which I had with thee before the world was." After His resurrection, He received His glorified body and took His garments back.

The Picture of His Habitation ("and was set down again"). The Holy Spirit was careful to give us this account and say that Jesus was "set down *again*." After His resurrection, our Saviour took His rightful place at the right hand of the Father. The High Priest never sat down in the temple. There were no chairs, for his work was never done. When Jesus said on Calvary, "It is finished," He was at last able to take His rightful place and be seated beside the Father. While Stephen was being stoned, he saw Christ at the right hand of the Father. Hebrews 8:1 says, "We have such an high priest, who is set on the right hand of the throne of the Majesty in the heavens."

After this act of humility, honor, and habitation, Jesus asks the question, "Know ye what I have done to you?" Let's contemplate this question throughout the day: it is meant for us. Do you know what Jesus has done to you? Let the question search your heart. Just remember that His question says, "Know ye what I have done *to* you," not *for* you! God has done a work *to* us! There was actually a work of God done *to* me! Rejoice in this personal work that can change your life for eternity.

TOPICS: Christ's Humility, God's Glory, Incarnation, Salvation

DAILY BIBLE READING: John 14–16

TODAY'S VERSE: John 16:33: "These things I have spoken unto you, that in me ye might have peace. In the world ye shall have tribulation: but be of good cheer; I have overcome the world."

THE LAST FEW CHAPTERS record a sweet time between Jesus and His disciples as He prepared for Calvary. You can hear the disciples asking questions as they never have before. The manner of their questions and Jesus' gentle answers sounds like a junior Sunday school class and its teacher. This really was a precious time for all of them.

A number of times in John's Gospel and also in his epistles, he writes the phrase, "These things have I spoken unto you" or "These things have I written unto you." Here are three thoughts from this verse.

First, Jesus talks about **Peace from the Written Word** ("that in me ye might have peace"). He has spoken these things that we might have peace. There is no peace without the Word of God! The words translated "ye might have" is in the grammatical subjunctive mood, meaning that it was to be a continuous repeated action regardless of when it took place.[5] However, it is subject to a condition. What is that condition? He already told us: *"That in me* ye might have peace." We cannot have peace without being in Christ! Of course, the Bible tells us that Jesus is the Word of God. There is a quietness that comes directly from the inspired Word of God. People are looking for peace as they never have before. What greater peace can you have than walking in the holiness found in the Word of God? What greater peace can you have than what is found in the promises of God's Word? Psalm 119:165 says, *"Great peace have they which love thy law: and nothing shall offend them."*

Second, we are told about the **Persecution from the Wicked World** ("in the world ye shall have tribulation"). The word for "tribulation" means "pressure, affliction, persecution." Do you feel the pressures of the world? The news shows the wickedness of man's sin and the slant of the world's eyes against the Word of God and believers. Yet these things do not bring fear, because we already have peace! They just declare that, as Abraham, Isaac, and Jacob, we are strangers and pilgrims upon this earth. "This world is not my home, I'm just a passing through/My treasures are laid up somewhere beyond the blue."[6]

Third, we are told about the **Prevailing of the Worshipful Word** ("I have overcome the world"). Jesus is telling His disciples that His seeming defeat will be His greatest joy! As He seems to lose, He will conquer! He tells us to "be of good cheer." The Greek grammar commands us to do something in the future that involves continuous or repeated action.[7] In other words, when the tribulation does come, we will need to be continually and repeatedly in "good cheer." How can we have "good cheer" while we are going through trials? Because we already know the outcome—Jesus has already won! Is that not something in which we should rejoice? There is an old song that says, "Well I am on the winning side, I am on the winning side/ Out in sin no more will I abide/I've enlisted in the fight for the cause of truth and right/Praise the Lord! I now am on the winning side!"[8] On which side are you today?

TOPICS: Peace, Persecution, Tribulation, Word of God

---

5   Spiros Zodhiates, *The Complete Word Study New Testament with Parallel Greek* (Chattanooga: AMG, 1992), 868

6   "This World Is Not My Home (I'm Just Passing Thru)" by Albert E. Brumley. © Arr. Copyright 1936. Renewed 1964 by Albert E. Brumley & Sons/SESAC (admin. By EverGreen Copyrights). All rights reserved. Used by permission.

7   Spiros Zodhiates, *The Complete Word Study New Testament with Parallel Greek* (Chattanooga: AMG, 1992), 867

8   "I'm on the Winning Side" by Hale Reeves. © Copyright 1965. Renewed 1993, Stamps Quarter Music/BMI (admin. By EverGreen Copyrights). All rights reserved. Used by permission.

DAILY BIBLE READING: John 17–18

TODAY'S VERSE: John 18:29: "Pilate then went out unto them, and said, What accusation bring ye against this man?"

WHAT A QUESTION for all of us today! The Greek word for "accusation" is *katagoria,* the root word for our *category,* and it means "complaint, criminal charge." Pilate was asking for specifics: "What are the categorical charges of criminal intent against this man?" Of course, there were none. But neither the Jews nor the Romans would let the facts stand in the way of a good trial and subsequent crucifixion. Let's look today at a few accusations against Jesus which rejected His deity.

He Was Accused of Illegitimacy. The Jews never did accept the virgin birth. They said, "We know not from whence he is" (John 9:29). They tried to rub Jesus' origin in His face again when they responded, "We be Abraham's seed" (John 8:33). Each time they brought His birth up, it was with a disparaging remark as to legitimacy. Even today, many reject Christ because they believe He was the result of some relationship between a Roman soldier and Mary. Yet, we know the promise was made to Mary that, "The Holy Ghost shall come upon thee, and the power of the Highest shall overshadow thee: therefore also that holy thing which shall be born of thee shall be called the Son of God" (Luke 1:35).

He Was Accused of Iniquity. John 10:33 says, "The Jews answered him, saying, For a good work we stone thee not; but for blasphemy; and because that thou, being a man, makest thyself God." Jesus' words would have been blasphemy if He were not who He said He was. He gave them proof after proof of His deity and His perfection. Even the heathen Pilate had to admit, "I find no fault in this man" (Luke 23:4). The religious leaders hated Jesus so much that they even tried to get Pilate to change the inscription that hung over His head accusing Him of His "crime." Hebrews 4:15 speaks of the perfection of Jesus Christ in this manner: "For we have not an high priest which cannot be touched with the feeling of our infirmities; but was in all points tempted like as we are, yet without sin."

He Was Accused of Immorality. Even today, there are many who believe that our blessed Christ was not pure but had an indecent relationship with Mary Magdalene. The world is always looking for a way to bring God down to the baseness of man's sinful and vile nature. If the godless can do that in their own minds, it will allow them to live as they please, for then there are no absolutes.

The question is now for you. "What accusation bring ye against this man?" I have known many people to give up on God because of dashed hopes or changed plans. Unexpected troubles, unanswered prayers, and unfruitful living make them think that God does not exist. That kind of selfish and prideful response against God is never justified. Isaiah 45:9c says, "Shall the clay say to him that fashioneth it, What makest thou? or thy work, He hath no hands?"

I have a few accusations of my own today. I accuse Christ of being faithful every day in every situation! Of showing mercy no matter what I do! Of leading me in the way that I should go! Of never leaving or forsaking me! Of standing true to His Word! And of wrapping His divine arms around me and loving me though I am unlovely! To all these accusations, the verdict stands: they are true!

TOPICS: Christ's Perfection, Faithfulness, False Accusations

November 15

DAILY BIBLE READING: John 19–21

TODAY'S VERSE: John 19:39: "And there came also Nicodemus, which at the first came to Jesus by night, and brought a mixture of myrrh and aloes, about an hundred pound weight."

THE CRUCIFIXION OF CHRIST puzzled the disciples and made them fearful for their own lives. What would you have done at this time? Many of the disciples would never have been caught near the tomb of Christ because of *panic*—**fear**. Many would not have come because of *pain*—**mourning**. Many would not have come because of *pouting*—**misunderstanding**. They were still putting the pieces together to figure out if Jesus was the Messiah or not. But Nicodemus never did forget who Christ was, and he was not ashamed to be known as one of Jesus' followers any longer. His gift is mentioned here by the Holy Spirit for us to know and understand.

It Was a Gift of Earnestness. This gift came from the depths of Nicodemus's heart. He had been living his life of discipleship in the greatest secrecy. Up until now, we have seen him struggle with his personal belief. The first time he appears in Scripture, we see him come under the cloak of darkness to ask questions he did not have the fortitude to ask during the daytime. The second time, we hear him ask a question in defense of Christ against those who maligned His character. He has been intrigued by Christ, but not committed. Here at the burial, he is committed. He is not worried if a Roman soldier, a Jewish leader, or a disciple will see him worship Jesus Christ, or the manner in which he worships. He has become an earnest disciple at last.

It Was a Gift of Expression. Scripture tells exactly what he brought. This is the third time myrrh is mentioned, brought, and presented to Christ. The first was at His birth ("They presented unto him gifts; gold, and frankincense, and myrrh," Matthew 2:11). The gift of the wise men was accepted because they worshiped Him. The second was on the cross ("Gave him to drink wine mingled with myrrh," Mark 15:23). This gift was not accepted because the soldiers and crowd did not worship Him, but mocked Him. The third is right here. This myrrh was accepted because it was given with a sincere spirit of worship.

It Was a Gift of Enough. Some have mentioned that there was "too much" given here. They believe that possibly over two hundred bodies could have been anointed with what Nicodemus brought.[9] The word I have chosen to exemplify Nicodemus's gift is *enough*. I do not believe the gift was in excess. When you are honoring your Lord, how much is too much? It is beautiful when God's people start to worship the Lord and just want to keep testifying more, giving more, and serving more! When it comes to love—pour it on! When it comes to worship—slather it on! When it comes to honoring Him—dump it on! When Nicodemus was done, the fragrance probably filled the room, just like it did when the little sinner woman broke her alabaster box full of ointment and *poured* it on the feet of Jesus. Had Nicodemus had brought even *more*, it would have been acceptable in the sight of God!

TOPICS: Boldness, Dedication, Giving, Worship

---

9   Adam Clarke, *Holy Bible with Commentary and Critical Notes*, Vol 4. (New York: B. Waugh and T. Mason for the Methodist Episcopal Church, 1846), 654.

DAILY BIBLE READING: Acts 1–3

TODAY'S VERSE: Acts 1:8: "But ye shall receive power, after that the Holy Ghost is come upon you: and ye shall be witnesses unto me both in Jerusalem, and in all Judaea, and in Samaria, and unto the uttermost part of the earth."

THIS VERSE HAS BEEN much discussed concerning witnessing and soul-winning for the Christian, and rightfully so. It ranks right up there with the Great Commission verses in Matthew 28:19–20, Mark 16:15, and Luke 24:47. But today, let's leave the topic of missions for a moment and see if there might be something else for us in this verse.

First, we see a **Holy Ghost Power** ("But ye shall receive power"). Many know that the Greek word for "power" is *dunamis,* from which we get our English word "dynamite." What great power this truly is! It does not come from within us, but "with Him." When we get the Holy Ghost, we get power! If this is not something you need, stop reading now, and you can go on to the next devotion. When the verse says "ye shall receive power," the word for "receive" means "to take, or to get hold of." This power has been given to all who are saved, but you may need to get ahold of it, or better yet, let it get ahold of you!

Second, we see a **Holy Ghost Presence** ("the Holy Ghost is come upon you"). The word for "upon" means "superimposition." Have you ever seen something superimposed or placed over top of something else? There is a board game entitled *Outburst.* The answers are hidden by different colored inks on a card. To find the answer, the judge has to put the card in a little holder with a red film. Literally, the player "superimposes" the red film on top in order to reveal the answer underneath! You can also use superimposition to hide things underneath that don't need to be seen—this works both ways! What a picture, and what a ministry the Holy Spirit and His presence have in our lives today!

Third, we see a **Holy Ghost Production** ("Ye shall be witnesses unto me"). God wants all His children to be a witness and will do a work in them to make them so! The word for "witness" is the same Greek word from which we get our English word *martyr.* This is a *surrendered witness.* What we need today is Christians who will be witnesses to the end. It is also a *simultaneous witness*—they were to be "witnesses *both* in" various places. The wording actually means that we are to be in all places at once! How is this possible? By sending missionaries all over the world to share the gospel of Jesus Christ! It is also a *subservient witness.* To go to "the uttermost parts of the earth" means to go to the farthest, most final, and lowest places. We need people who will humble themselves to fulfill this role and go anywhere to give the gospel to lost and dying souls.

TOPICS: Holy Spirit, Missions, Power, Witness

DAILY BIBLE READING: Acts 4–6

TODAY'S VERSE: Acts 5:41: "And they departed from the presence of the council, rejoicing that they were counted worthy to suffer shame for his name."

THE LEADERS HAD ALREADY THROWN Peter in prison, but God sent an angel to free him and told him to go back to the temple to teach the people along with John. After the authorities found them and brought them to the high priest, they demanded of Peter why he spoke in the name of Jesus. Peter stood with great boldness and power and confessed that Jesus was the only Saviour who could forgive sins. (What a blessing it must have been to Peter to have another opportunity to confess Christ—this time he would not deny Him!) After much discussion and listening to Gamaliel, the leaders decided to beat the apostles, let them go, and command them not to speak in the name of Jesus anymore. If there is anyone who wanted to help people who were suffering for their faith, it was Peter. He used the word "suffer" fifteen times in the book of 1 Peter. Let us see how Peter and the apostles responded to suffering for Christ.

The **Pleasantness of Suffering** ("And they departed from the presence of the council, rejoicing"). The word for "rejoice" means "to be cheerful, i.e. calmly happy or well-off." There is a peace that comes with suffering for the One who saved you! The word is a present participle, meaning that it was a continuous action contemporaneous with the leading verb.[10] As they departed, they were continually rejoicing! They took no space to lick their wounds. How can we have cheer in tribulation? Jesus told His disciples in John 16:33b, "In the world ye shall have *tribulation:* but be of good *cheer;* I have overcome the world." This thought must have flooded the minds of the apostles as they departed "rejoicing."

The **Privilege of Suffering** ("that they were counted worthy"). What an honor it was to these disciples to suffer! They viewed themselves as unworthy of being identified with Christ. Had you asked any of them how they compared with Him, they would have shaken their heads, fallen down on the ground, and asked for forgiveness for any thought of their own that would liken them to Christ. But these were accusations from others, and so they would wear them as the most honorable of all medals! It was a privilege to identify with Him. Philippians 3:10 says, "That I may know him, and the power of his resurrection, and the fellowship of his sufferings, being made conformable unto his death."

The **Pain of Suffering** ("to suffer shame"). This is a fascinating word that is given to us. The Greek translated "to suffer shame" means "to render infamous, i.e. (by implication) condemn or maltreat." I have never desired to become infamous! Here is the difference: Pat Garrett was famous, but Billy the Kid was infamous. Elliott Ness was famous, but Al Capone was infamous. We see here that the high priest and council counted and treated the disciples as if they were infamous. That, my friend, is suffering shame! What a privilege to be counted a criminal for Christ's sake!

The **Purpose of Suffering** ("for his name"). Is there anything better than to suffer for the blessed name of Christ? We have always been identified with His name. Acts 11:26c says, "And the disciples were called Christians first in Antioch." The world may say His name in anger; but to us, it is sweeter than the sound of angels singing! We must learn to love His name.

TOPICS: Cheer, Honor, Identification, Suffering, Tribulation

---

10 Spiros Zodhiates, *The Complete Word Study New Testament with Parallel Greek* (Chattanooga: AMG, 1992), 867

DAILY BIBLE READING: Acts 7–8

TODAY'S VERSE: Acts 8:35: "Then Philip opened his mouth, and began at the same scripture, and preached unto him Jesus."

THE ACCOUNT OF THE CONVERSION of the Ethiopian eunuch has great importance in Scripture, for it shows us how much God cares for one soul. Philip was commissioned to leave the revival that was taking place at the church in Jerusalem to go into the desert. There, he found a man described in verse 27: a *powerful man* ("an eunuch of great authority"), a *prominent man* ("under Candace queen of the Ethiopians"), and a *prosperous man* ("who had the charge of all her treasure"). This man was trying to muddle his way through the Scriptures while reading the book of Isaiah. What a blessing it was to the heart of Philip as the Ethiopian eunuch opened his heart to receive the Word of God! We will look at three principles of Philip's witness that will be helpful to us in sharing the gospel of Christ with others.

There Was a Readiness to Speak ("Then Philip opened his mouth"). How many times do we fail to "open our mouths" and speak? We don't have much trouble turning our mouths loose to talk about many other things, but they suddenly go quiet when we speak about Christ and spiritual things. Is there a more important or weighty matter than that of eternal life? We must open our mouths to speak of things that are eternal in nature, spiritual in worship, and gracious in mercy.

There Was a Relevance of Scripture ("and began at the same scripture"). To Philip, it did not matter where the Ethiopian was reading in the Scripture, for it is all connected. He knew the Word of God. He used the passage the Ethiopian was reading to spontaneously preach to a one-man congregation in the middle of the desert! I'll tell you what we can learn from this—we need to study the Scriptures! First Peter 3:15 says, "But sanctify the Lord God in your hearts: *and be ready always to give an answer to every man that asketh you a reason* of the hope that is in you with meekness and fear." If someone mentioned a verse to you today, would you be able to begin at that verse and tell them of the gift of God?

There Was a Reverence of the Saviour ("and preached unto him Jesus"). We can learn a good principle of Bible study right here. How does the verse we are reading, or any verse, pertain to Christ? The message is not just *about* Him, but it *is* Him! Wherever you are in Scripture, find the cross and run to it! It is there you will find Him. Seek Him in the Scriptures, and show Him to those who cannot see.

TOPICS: Bible Study, Christ, Witness

November 19

DAILY BIBLE READING: Acts 9–10

TODAY'S VERSE: Acts 9:15: "But the Lord said unto him, Go thy way: for he is a chosen vessel unto me, to bear my name before the Gentiles, and kings, and the children of Israel."

WHEN OUR LORD APPEARED to Saul as he traveled to Damascus, he became blind and had to wait for Ananias to pray for him before he could see again. Ananias began to reason with the Lord because he knew that Saul had come to persecute believers. This verse is God's response to Ananias concerning the discipleship of Saul, who would later become Paul.

First, we see that the future **Paul Was a Chosen Vessel** ("But the Lord said unto him, Go thy way: for he is a chosen vessel unto me"). Paul was a vessel handpicked by the Lord for a specific purpose. The word "vessel" brings with it the idea of a potter's house with all the vessels he has made on stands and shelves around the entire shop. The potter can even make a vessel for a specific need. Like any artist, the potter probably has a piece or two that stands out as his best work. If you ask the artist which piece *he* likes most, he will likely pick a different piece than you would, because there are things about that pot that you do not know. Paul was not a vessel that a customer picked, but that the potter picked! This one was special! It truly is special when God handpicks a preacher, a missionary, or any servant to do His will. We are chosen vessels of our Master's hand!

Second, we see that **Paul Was a Carved Vessel** ("to bear my name"). I have had the opportunity to hear Dr. Mike Bagwell preach from this portion of Scripture about "bearing God's name." A potter felt that some special vessels needed to be inscribed. This is much like a painter who puts his name upon the canvas. The potter would take the vessel, turn the piece upside down, take an engraving tool, and carve or etch his own name upon the bottom of the vessel, that others might know who was responsible for making such a piece. Nobody could claim that masterpiece but the one whose name was placed upon it! Do we not carry Jesus' name upon us? Is this not so that others might know it was He who did this work in our lives?

Third, we see that **Paul Was a Commissioned Vessel** ("before the Gentiles, and kings, and the children of Israel"). God had a purpose and a place where He wanted this vessel to go. The first was to the "Gentiles"—this had to do with *races*. These were all non-Jews. The second was to "kings"—this had to do with *rulers*. Why did God choose to send His gospel to rulers? So that many might be saved as the result of a ruler hearing the gospel! God blessed our nation by allowing our founding fathers to hear the gospel. The third was to the "children of Israel"—this had to do with *relations*. I am glad that God cares about family! God's desire was that men from strangers to brothers might hear and know the promise of the gospel of Christ and trust in the Lord as their Saviour.

TOPICS: Servant, Testimony, Witness

R. CHRIS HANKS

DAILY BIBLE READING: Acts 11–12

TODAY'S VERSE: Acts 11:24: "For he was a good man, and full of the Holy Ghost and of faith: and much people was added unto the Lord."

THIS VERSE SPEAKS of Barnabas, a wonderful man whom God used greatly in the foundation of the church at Jerusalem. It was Barnabas who brought Paul to the disciples after his Damascus-road conversion. It was Barnabas who restored John Mark to the ministry and made him useful again in the service of the Lord. Barnabas did many things that nobody else would do, and God blessed them greatly. A few things about Barnabas give us a window into what made him a great and usable vessel to God.

First, we see that **He Was a Fine Man** ("For he was a good man"). This kind of man is hard to find today. "Good" is not talking about his nature, but about his character. We must notice that this was not said of Barnabas by a person, but was narrated by the Holy Ghost. It is an honor when others speak well of you and think you to be good. How much better is it when the Holy Spirit calls you good?

Second, we see that **He Was a Full Man** ("full of the Holy Ghost"). The word for "full" means "replete, covered over." Many men are full of themselves, full of the world, and full of knowledge, but few are full of the Holy Ghost. This is the secret power of Christian living! Ephesians 5:18 says, "And be not drunk with wine, wherein is excess; but be *filled* with the Spirit." This filling didn't just have an influence in Barnabas's life, but it *controlled* his life.

Third, we see that **He Was a Faithful Man** ("full of the Holy Ghost and of faith"). To be "faithful" is to be "full of faith." First John 5:4 says, "For whatsoever is born of God overcometh the world: *and this is the victory that overcometh the world, even our faith.*" If we would have a good testimony in heaven and upon earth, we can only receive it by our faith. Hebrews 11:2 tells us, "For by [faith] the elders obtained a good report." The best way to have a good testimony is to be full of faith.

Fourth, we see that **He Was a Fruitful Man** ("and much people was added unto the Lord"). Fruitfulness in the church is what naturally happens when all other things are in order. Fruitfulness is also what God desires for all of us. John 15:8 says, "Herein is my Father glorified, that ye bear much fruit; so shall ye be my disciples." The Spirit's work in you will always affect others around you! Jesus prophesied that His disciples should not witness until they had received the power of the Holy Ghost: "But ye shall receive power, after that the Holy Ghost is come upon you: and ye shall be witnesses unto me" (Acts 1:8). Fruit follows fullness! Notice that the verse does not speak of "some" fruit, but of "much" fruit being added. Hallelujah!

TOPICS: Faith, Fruit, Fullness, Holy Spirit

DAILY BIBLE READING: Acts 13–15

TODAY'S VERSE: Acts 15:18: "Known unto God are all his works from the beginning of the world."

AFTER QUOTING FROM THE BOOK of Amos, James, our Lord's half-brother, uses verse 18 in a very unique way to calm the nerves of the apostles and people who had gathered together about questions concerning circumcision. This little verse answers the entire problem. In today's Christianity, many people look for obscure beliefs and find a certain joy if they think they can locate a gray area. Instead, we should be studying for more clarity! If God is operating in clarity, we need to find the mind of God in order to add confidence to our Christian walk. Let's take a moment to see how this short, powerful verse was used for the glory of God.

First, it reminded the Christians that all this had happened by **Divine Appointment.** James was reminding them that though this problem had crept up on the church, nothing had crept up on God. God has known all of His own works from the beginning of the world and what would happen as a result of them. This whole issue had been planned and appointed by God. I like what the old preacher once said: "Has it dawned on you that nothing dawns on God?" We need to stop operating in crisis mode! God hasn't developed a nervous tic about our situations. He has appointed them in our lives to show us His wisdom, power, understanding, and strength.

Second, it reminded them to trust in **Divine Advisement.** This is often a place where we fail. We look at a situation and say, "What am I supposed to do?" Let me say this: *you*, YOU, cannot do anything!" What is a preacher to do with a situation in which he fears that something could hurt his flock? James went to Scripture and let the Holy Ghost guide him in its truth. As a matter of fact, he found his answer in one of those "obscure minor prophets." If you are looking for God's will, *let God show you His will.* If you are trying to find an answer, look to the Word of God. God will not fail you there!

Third, it reminded them of God's **Divine Accomplishment.** Maybe you are facing turbulence or turmoil and don't know what to do. God knows all about it. Better yet, *God already knows what He will do about it.* And even better, God has given you His Word so you may seek and find out what He will do about it! If a situation in your life was brought about by divine appointment, you can trust that there is a design for divine accomplishment. Isaiah 55:11 tells us the accomplishing power of God's Word: "So shall my word be that goeth forth out of my mouth: it shall not return unto me void, but it shall accomplish that which I please, and it shall prosper in the thing whereto I sent it."

As you go today, remember the feeding of the five thousand. Jesus put the challenge to the disciples to feed them. Why would He send the disciples scrambling to meet a need that was impossible for them to meet? Because He already had a plan of divine accomplishment to feed all five thousand people and have twelve baskets left over! You can trust the same power and the same Jesus to work in your own life.

TOPICS: God's Purpose, God's Word, Trust

DAILY BIBLE READING: Acts 16–18

TODAY'S VERSE: Acts 16:9: "And a vision appeared to Paul in the night; There stood a man of Macedonia, and prayed him, saying, Come over into Macedonia, and help us."

WE WILL UNDERTAKE the topic of worldwide missions as we consider this great Macedonian call. It is the task of the New Testament church to reach the world with the gospel of Jesus Christ. If you love Christ, you will have a burden for your fellow man to know the love of God regardless of race or culture. We are losing the fight of worldwide missions because we have more missionaries coming home than we are sending. The missionaries who are willing to go cannot go because they must wait upon God's people to support them. Until churches get a global burden and a vision for souls, we will utterly fail to give toward the propagation of the gospel. Today, let us catch the vision that God has for missions.

The Phenomenon of Missions ("And a vision appeared"). When Paul had this vision, it impressed upon him the love of God for all men. Notice this was not Paul's vision: rather, "A vision appeared." This was God's vision! Never before had Paul known that God wanted the world to be saved. The word for "vision" means "something gazed at, a spectacle." Missions is a spectacle in the sight of God, and it has His undivided attention! What was Paul's reaction to the vision? The word translated "appeared" is much deeper in its meaning than just "voluntary observation": it means "with wide-open eyes, as at something remarkable." The vision of missions is a remarkable vision! It demands our complete attention!

The People of Missions ("There stood a man of Macedonia"). The reality of missions is people! We have such a twisted idea of what scriptural missions is all about that we forget that it involves people. There are real people in foreign lands who are dying without Christ! There are real Muslims who need the gospel of Christ! There are real natives who need Jesus! There are real neighbors in *your neighborhood* who must hear of God's love!

The Plea of Missions ("and prayed him"). Not only is there a call of God to worldwide missions, but there is a call from the people. Charles H. Gabriel wrote these words in his song "Send the Light": "There's a call comes ringing o'er the restless wave/'Send the Light! Send the Light!'/There are souls to rescue, there are souls to save,/Send the Light! Send the Light!" Can you hear the plea? Send someone over there to tell them of the gift of Christ!

The Price of Missions ("saying, Come over into Macedonia"). Notice that the man in the vision did not say, "Come over here, and we will reimburse you for your trip." It is God's people who are to support missionaries in sending the gospel wherever it needs to go! Some it will cost in money. Others it will cost in time. Still others it will cost in their lives! The price is too high *not* to send the gospel to the lost.

The Privilege of Missions ("and help us"). What a tremendous blessing it is to help someone find Christ! We cannot save others. All we can do is bring them to Him! Is there anything better we can do with our lives than to show others the Way, the Truth, and the Life? Our message will help them beyond measure! Be a part of missions in your local church and send the gospel to the "uttermost parts of the earth" (Acts 1:8).

TOPICS: Giving, Missions, Obedience, Sacrifice, Vision, Witness

DAILY BIBLE READING: Acts 19–20

TODAY'S VERSE: Acts 20:24: "But none of these things move me, neither count I my life dear unto myself, so that I might finish my course with joy, and the ministry, which I have received of the Lord Jesus, to testify the gospel of the grace of God."

PAUL SAID THAT NOTHING moved him in his faith. Praise the Lord for people who are not easily moved when Satan tries to shake their faith and service. What moves you? The Bible says in 1 Corinthians 15:58 that we should be "stedfast, unmoveable." Paul had security and confidence in living.

The Fragility of Life Did Not Bother Him ("neither count I my life dear unto myself"). Paul knew his life was not his own. He had been bought with a price! He had settled this argument a long time ago. There is great freedom and liberty that comes with living your life completely for God.

Finishing the Race Is What Pressed Him ("that I might finish my course with joy"). Don't just be content to finish the course: finish it with joy! How do you do that? According to the *place He has laid* for you! According to the *plan in which He has led* you! According to the *purpose He has listed* for you! You can hear the wonderful joy of the apostle Paul at the very end of his life in 2 Timothy 4:7–8: "I have fought a good fight, I have finished my course, I have kept the faith: henceforth there is laid up for me a crown of righteousness, which the Lord, the righteous judge, shall give me at that day: and not to me only, but unto all them also that love his appearing." You can finish your course the same way!

The Fulfillment of Helping Others Is What Blessed Him ("and the ministry, which I have received of the Lord Jesus"). How fulfilling it is to serve the Lord by helping others! It will change both your outlook and your output when you begin to put others ahead of yourself. When is the last time you put someone else's desires ahead of your own or were moved to minister to another's spiritual need? God laid this ministry upon Paul's heart. When God lays it on you, peace and joy will fills your heart as you obey the Lord's will.

The Fruit of the Gospel Is What Encouraged Him ("to testify the gospel of the grace of God"). Paul knew that his testimony of loving those he had once persecuted and destroyed was a great and powerful message for others to hear. Paul's thought was this: "If God will save me, God will save anybody!"

All of these perspectives will help you be sure and secure in your service and love to God.

TOPICS: Commitment, Grace, Ministry, Surrender, Witness

R. CHRIS HANKS

DAILY BIBLE READING: Acts 21-23

TODAY'S VERSE: Acts 21:13: "Then Paul answered, What mean ye to weep and to break mine heart? for I am ready not to be bound only, but also to die at Jerusalem for the name of the Lord Jesus."

THIS WAS THE BEGINNING of the end for Paul. Soon after his departure, he would be detained and subsequently sent to Rome to appeal to Caesar. Oh, the heaviness that entered into the heart of these people who loved him! How they begged him not to go to Jerusalem! Paul would have none of it, for the Lord had made clear what needed to happen. Would to God we had men and ladies today with this kind of resolve and commitment to God in their hearts! Let us learn from Brother Paul and have the same determination to serve our Lord through the midst of trial and tribulation.

There Are to Be No Regrets in Serving God ("Then Paul answered, What mean ye to weep and to break mine heart?"). There should be **no horror** in serving the Lord. Many Christians have been discouraged in their faith because of the sorrows of their families and pleas from their friends. We must be willing to part with everything on this earth. There is no doubt that Paul was a man on a mission. Philippians 3:8 says, "Yea doubtless, and *I count all things but loss* for the excellency of the knowledge of Christ Jesus my Lord: for whom I have suffered the loss of all things, and *do count them but dung,* that I may win Christ." How did Paul ever get to a point where he could operate with such resolve? A few verses later, in Philippians 3:13, he tells us, "Brethren, I count not myself to have apprehended: but this one thing I do, *forgetting those things which are behind, and reaching forth unto those things which are before.*" Regret begins with a backward glance. This was not a time to be thinking about what might have been. We need to operate with forward vision. Jesus Himself said in Luke 9:62, "No man, having put his hand to the plough, and looking back, is fit for the kingdom of God."

There Is to Be No Reserve in Serving God ("for I am ready not to be bound only"). There should be **no hesitation** in serving the Lord. You cannot blink when trouble comes your way. The issue and influences of fear in your life need to be handled once and for all! How many times have I seen people struggle because of the difficulty that arrived when they started serving the Lord? God never promised that we would lead trouble-free lives! We have a twisted view of gumdrop fields, peanut-brittle roads, and whipped-cream-clouded skies in our service to God. This is a battlefield! There can be no wavering and no second-guessing in the service of the Lord. James 1:8 says, "A double minded man is unstable in all his ways."

There Is to Be No Resistance in Serving God ("but also to die at Jerusalem for the name of the Lord Jesus"). There should be **no holdings** in serving God. Paul would not even fight to keep his own life. It was the Lord's to do with as He pleased. If God required his life, then so be it. The time would come when God *would* require the life of Paul at the hand of Nero's executioner. What Paul was trying to say was that as far as he was concerned, he had already died! There would be no resistance to God's will in his life! The Bible is careful to share with us how Jesus approached the end of His life in Isaiah 53:7: "He was oppressed, and he was afflicted, yet he opened not his mouth: he is brought as a lamb to the slaughter, and as a sheep before her shearers is dumb, so he openeth not his mouth." There was no resistance from Jesus to God's sacrifice for mankind; should there be any resistance from those who are serving Him? Let us be tender and submitted to the hand of the Lord, and let His will become our will.

TOPICS: Commitment, Dedication, Service

DAILY BIBLE READING: Acts 24–26

TODAY'S VERSE: Acts 24:25: "And as he reasoned of righteousness, temperance, and judgment to come, Felix trembled, and answered, Go thy way for this time; when I have a convenient season, I will call for thee."

OUR THOUGHT TODAY COMES from the word Felix used here for his excuse—"convenient." Many things in this life are not convenient. I have never had a flat tire that was convenient. I have never had a sickness that was convenient. You could add to the list with many other scenarios that you would not consider convenient. Here's a big one: to the natural man, there is never a convenient season to deal with his spiritual condition. God, however, has said in 2 Corinthians 6:2 that there is no more convenient time than now to take care of your spiritual need: "Behold, now is the accepted time; behold, now is the day of salvation." Let's take a closer look at three reasons Felix thought it inconvenient to deal with his spiritual condition.

The Simplicity of the Scriptures Makes Spiritual Decisions Inconvenient ("And as he reasoned of righteousness, temperance, and judgment to come"). There can be no reasoning of any of these things without the Word of God. Felix had trouble accepting the truth of God's Word. We must be careful to accept the Word of God: it should be our only rule of faith and practice. Jesus said in John 12:48, "He that rejecteth me, and receiveth not my words, hath one that judgeth him: the word that I have spoken, the same shall judge him in the last day." Don't allow your future judge to be viewed as an inconvenience in your Christian life!

The Shame of Sin Makes Spiritual Decisions Inconvenient ("Felix trembled"). This is old-time Holy Ghost conviction. It's a funny thing about conviction: carnally speaking, there is never a good time for it. The word translated "trembled" means "to cause to fear, alarmed, affrighted." Many things about our sin should cause alarm. Man no longer fears his own sin, but accepts it and embraces it. Oh, that man would have sorrow for his sin! Psalm 38:18 says, "For I will declare mine iniquity; I will be sorry for my sin."

The Schedule of Self Makes Spiritual Decisions Inconvenient ("and answered, Go thy way for this time; when I have a convenient season, I will call for thee"). Felix just didn't have time in his schedule to deal with his spiritual condition when Paul was before him. This is perhaps the worst of all of his excuses! Some interesting Greek words are used for the phrase "When I have a convenient season." It is as if he is saying, "When I can participate in an opportunity to do this, I will." Was there really a better time than right then? God's man was there! God's Word was spoken! God's Spirit had moved! Following this excuse, we hear the most arrogant of all phrases: "I will call for thee." The Greek word used here means "to call elsewhere." Isn't it interesting that our flesh doesn't want to go back to the place where it fell under conviction? It is very presumptuous for any man to think he has God at his beck and call for whenever he thinks he might be ready to receive the gift of salvation. Instead, we must be ready when God offers the gift to us! Let us not be governed by the inconvenience of our flesh, but by the opportunity of the Spirit.

TOPICS: Conviction, Opportunity, Word of God

R. CHRIS HANKS

DAILY BIBLE READING: Acts 27–28

TODAY'S VERSE: Acts 27:25: "Wherefore, sirs, be of good cheer: for I believe God, that it shall be even as it was told me."

THIS FASCINATING VERSE gives us great insight into the apostle Paul's faith. Verse 20 tells us exactly what happened in this storm: "And when neither sun nor stars in many days appeared, and no small tempest lay on us, all hope that we should be saved was then taken away." The sailors had no hope for reprieve from the storm and no reason to rejoice in the ship. How could a man be a help to people in such a situation? Paul was going through the same thing they were! He saw the storm, he felt the gales, and he heard the thunder! Doing the only thing a man of God could possibly do, Paul stood forth in the middle of them all and brightened their day with the Word of God. Where the Word is concerned, nothing is ever found to be hopeless! Proverbs 29:25 says, "The fear of man bringeth a snare: but whoso putteth his trust in the LORD shall be safe."

Paul Was Unashamed of His Belief in God ("for I believe God"). Paul was so unashamed that he just told everybody on the ship to be happy because he believed in God ("Wherefore, sirs, *be of good cheer: for I believe God*"). That is something they should all have been blessed by hearing! You would be surprised at how others can draw strength from your faith! And don't you know that Paul felt better after telling them that he believed in God! Everybody should know that we believe in God and are unashamed to admit it.

Paul Was Unchanging in His Faith ("that it shall be"). The only things on which you can count in this life are God and His Word. Paul had been in this predicament previously, and he knew there was only one Person on whom he could rely—God. Paul affirms here his belief in the precepts of God's Word. He believed in every truth taught in the Word that was given to him. He believed in every *promise* and every *prophecy* of God's Word. Paul's statement itself was based upon a promise. God had promised and prophesied of the shipwreck *and* the safety of Paul and the sailors. Verse 22 says, "And now I exhort you to be of good cheer: for there shall be no loss of any man's life among you, but of the ship." Today, we still live under promises and prophecies: God's promises are for us, and every prophecy of the end times found in the Word of God will come to pass.

Paul Was Unwavering in His Trust in the Word of God ("even as it was told me"). In this time of trouble, Paul ran to the Word of God and sank all of his faith in it. If you have to believe in something today, why not make it the Scriptures? You will find that they are true in every situation. James 1:6 exhorts us to "Ask in faith, *nothing wavering.* For he that wavereth is like a wave of the sea driven with the wind and tossed." We can hear the apostle Paul's unwavering belief and trust in God in 2 Timothy 1:12: "For I know whom I have believed, and am persuaded that he is able to keep that which I have committed unto him against that day." Increase your faith and accept the truth of God's Word, for your faith may be the catalyst to draw others to Christ!

TOPICS: Belief, Faith, Testimony, Word of God

DAILY BIBLE READING: Romans 1–4

TODAY'S VERSE: Romans 3:27: "Where is boasting then? It is excluded. By what law? of works? Nay: but by the law of faith."

THE APOSTLE PAUL is wonderful to read, and the Epistle to the Romans, sent through Paul's pen by the Holy Spirit, is perhaps the crowning jewel of doctrine for the believer. Some of the greatest blessings of reading Paul are his questions, which he follows with powerful answers. Today's question is a great one, a problem for many and a praise to God: "Where is boasting then?" Before you go into the schedule and activities of your day, answer this question about your salvation. What pride do you have today in the fact that Jesus saved you? The answer is simple: we can have no pride in the grace of God, for it is a gift!

I believe this to be a **Problem for Calvinism.** Without going through all of the details of Calvinistic thought and belief, I would like to make a simple pertinent observation: If we have been chosen above others for salvation while other souls are damned to hell, we can feel the urge to boast. The ideas of Calvinism, for some, can be arrogant and prideful. If we subscribe to them, it would be very easy to say, "The Lord saw something in me that He did not see in others to call me to salvation and reject them from eternal life." Is that not a boast, putting the emphasis upon ourselves rather than upon Christ? The next part of the verse says, "It is excluded." The word for "excluded" means "to shut out." There is *no* reason for boasting; it has been banished!

I believe this to be a **Problem for Christians.** It is common for Christians to boast in their response to the gospel. Here again, we have put the emphasis upon ourselves rather than God. It saddens my heart to hear a Christian say, "Yes, God saved me, but I had to believe." We always like to put in our little two cents about "our" faith: "God saved me, but it was my faith." This is wrong. No matter how we manipulate grace, we cannot include our works in salvation! How do we fail to see that God had to give us the faith to believe in Him?

I believe this to be a **Praise for Christ.** Every part of salvation is a remembrance of God's mercy! No part of salvation is a result of my doing. Faith? He gave it to me! Belief? He did it through me! Change of heart? He convicted me! Verses 23–26 trumpet the praise of *God,* not of the Christian: let us look at them, and perhaps you will see my point: "For *all have sinned,* and come short of the glory of God; being *justified freely by his grace* through the *redemption that is in Christ Jesus:* whom *God hath set forth* to be a propitiation through *faith in his blood,* to *declare* his *righteousness* for the remission of sins that are past, through the *forbearance of God;* to declare, I say, at this time *his righteousness:* that *he might be just,* and the *justifier of him which believeth* in Jesus." The only thing *we* did in the whole equation of salvation is found in verse 23: we "sinned." As you read these verses, you will find that God is the One who emphasizes the work of Christ in salvation. You will find that there is *no boasting* in your salvation! Hallelujah to the Lamb of God, who taketh away the sins of the world!

TOPICS: Forgiveness, Grace, Praise, Pride, Salvation, Sin

DAILY BIBLE READING: Romans 5–8

TODAY'S VERSE: Romans 8:37: "Nay, in all these things we are more than conquerors through him that loved us."

INCLUDED IN OUR READING today are three of the most powerful chapters in the entire Bible—Romans 6, 7, and 8. You will not find more spiritual truth or depth in the Bible than you will find in these chapters. I only wish my mind could take in the vastness and scope of their spiritual truths! Take a moment to sit and soak in the depths of God's wisdom and work today.

Our verse today is a tremendous one to claim and enjoy. Are you down today? You can have victory! Are you facing troubles and trials? Look at this verse!

First, we see the **Scope of Our Victory** ("in all these things"). Every obstacle the inspired writer discussed, every argument he mentioned, every thought that stood in the way of our complete victory has been conquered! "In all these things" includes *"All* these things." Exactly what are "all these things" that oppose us? Scripture clearly includes anybody who hates us in verse 33: "Who shall lay any thing to the charge of God's elect?" It also includes everything that is trying to separate us from the love of God in verses 35–39. We can have complete victory in "all these things" that rise up against God and His way.

Second, we see the **Success of Our Victory** ("we are more than conquerors"). The word that is used for "more than conquerors" literally means "to vanquish beyond." What else is there to do after you conquer something? Make it your own, rule over it, dominate it, and make it home! Have you thought about what Jesus went beyond to do? He went beyond our faults and our failures! He has "vanquished beyond" every situation we can imagine!

Third, we see the **Source of Our Victory** ("through him that loved us"). Yes, this victory is only through our Lord and Saviour Jesus Christ. It would do us all good to come to the quick understanding that we cannot win any victory in ourselves. In Romans 7:18, Paul says, "For I know that in me (that is, in my flesh,) dwelleth no good thing." Our victory can come only through the finished work of Christ. First Corinthians 15:57 says, "But thanks be to God, which giveth us the victory *through our Lord Jesus Christ."* Hallelujah! He won the victory and has given it to us to enjoy!

TOPICS: Christ, Victory, Warfare

DAILY BIBLE READING: Romans 9–11

TODAY'S VERSE: Romans 11:11: "I say then, Have they stumbled that they should fall? God forbid: but rather through their fall salvation is come unto the Gentiles, for to provoke them to jealousy."

IN THESE CHAPTERS we are not wading in shallow waters, but are borne by the power and the weight of a great tide and carried out to the unfathomable depths of God's love and scriptural truth. These are, as Ezekiel says in Ezekiel 47:5, "Waters to swim in." Our devotion today may even be hard to understand. You may not even *want* to understand it. I just ask that you listen to the Word of God and let the Spirit guide you into all truth. For a greater grasp of the truth supporting our thought for today, take in the surrounding chapters and context. You may want to make this a matter of further study.

In today's verse, God is speaking of His unfailing love for Israel, His chosen people. It sure is comforting to know that God's love never fails! Here are a few thoughts from this verse that might help us see God's love in a greater light.

First, we see the **Mercy of God's Stumblingblock** ("Have they stumbled that they should fall?"). We know from the Scripture that the nation of Israel has stumbled at the law and fallen at the cross of Christ. Here, God lets us know that this stumbling fall is not a fall unto death. They may be down, but they are not out! God answers this possibility with an emphatic "God forbid." William Plumer says of the phrase *God forbid,* "The original of this phrase occurs ten times in this epistle. It is a very strong form of denial."[11] The phrase carries the idea of the apostle showing great hatred for what is said. He is saying, "What a detestable thought! That thought should not even enter your mind! Don't ever think it again!" He is trying to help these Roman Gentiles, some who were still unsaved and some who had for many years been wicked heathen whose mindsets were not yet fully changed, to understand exactly where the Jews are standing today. This stumbling was not to hurt the nation of Israel, but to bring them back. We will understand this even better in a moment.

Second, we see the **Ministry of God's Stumblingblock**. This is where all Gentiles ought to bow their heads and thank God for the stumblingblock of Israel! "Through their fall salvation is come unto the Gentiles." This is how God included us in the plan of salvation! This may sound second-class to you, but I'm just thankful that I was *allowed* to enter. I have never seen someone get upset about being upgraded to first class on a flight. They are always very thankful for the opportunity.

Third, we see the **Meaning of God's Stumblingblock** ("for to provoke them to jealousy"). This is the part that might be hard for some to take. Gentile, God is using you for one reason—to make Israel jealous so they might come back to God! Nobody likes to feel used, especially in the realm of love. Personally, I am still glad that I was *allowed* to enter! This doesn't mean that God does not love you or me. In fact, He has directed events in such a way as to allow us entrance into His kingdom—and He didn't have to do that! Why not look at it like this: God is using *you* to bring back His chosen people to Himself! What a privilege!

Moreover, God is using us to bless Israel so that Israel will turn around and bless us. Verse 12 says, "Now if the fall of them be the riches of the world, and the diminishing of them the riches of the Gentiles; how much more their fulness?" Look at all the ways God has blessed us today as a result of the "stumbling" of Israel. If you think God's grace and blessings are good now, with Israel diminishing in prominence in the divine plan, *just wait till they come back and receive God's blessings!* In this passage God is saying, "Gentile, you ain't seen nothing yet! It's going to get better for you too!"

TOPICS: Gentiles, God's Knowledge, Jews, Mercy

---

11 William S. Plumer, *Commentary on Romans* (Grand Rapids: Kregel, 1993), 112.

R. CHRIS HANKS

DAILY BIBLE READING: Romans 12–16

TODAY'S VERSE: Romans 15:3: "For even Christ pleased not himself; but, as it is written, The reproaches of them that reproached thee fell on me."

WE ARE LIVING in a time when people only want to please themselves. They live their lives to satisfy every desire they might have and drink up the pleasures they can find upon this earth. The thought of Christ not pleasing Himself has been a recurring theme over the last few chapters. God is concerned about our Christian lives, our testimony, and holy living. This little phrase tells us a lot about how to live in accordance with the will of God. What would have happened if Christ had come just to please Himself?

There Would Have Been No Suffering. Don't ever forget the amount of suffering that Christ endured to satisfy the judgment of God upon sin. Had He come only to please Himself, He would never have fulfilled Scripture by saying, "I thirst." He would have never have submitted to being forsaken by God. He would never have drunk from that bitter cup of suffering to pay for man's sins. Without suffering, Christ would have had no glory. First Peter 1:11 says, "Searching what, or what manner of time the Spirit of Christ which was in them did signify, when it testified beforehand *the sufferings of Christ, and the glory that should follow.*" There will be suffering in our lives and in the lives of others as well: it is a ministry to make us tender and change us into the image of Christ.

There Would Have Been No Submission. John 6:38 says, "For I came down from heaven, not to do mine own will, but the will of him that sent me." You cannot please yourself and do the will of God at the same time. I am glad Jesus came to submit to the will of God and not to please Himself. We are living in a time in which even advertisements are encouraging people to "Have it your way." Indulge yourself," they say, because "you deserve it." Scripture tells us in no uncertain terms in Matthew 16:24, "Then said Jesus unto his disciples, If any man will come after me, *let him deny himself,* and take up his cross, and follow me." If you are going to be Christ-like, you too must deny yourself and submit to the will of God in your life.

There Would Have Been No Salvation. If Christ's suffering and submission had not happened, salvation could not have happened. Philippians 2:8 says, "And being found in fashion as a man, he humbled himself, *and became obedient unto death, even the death of the cross.*" I am both glad and thankful that Jesus did not come to please Himself. He came to please His Father. And boy, did He do a good job of pleasing His Father! Matthew 3:17 says, "And lo a voice from heaven, saying, This is my beloved Son, *in whom I am well pleased.*" Even now, God has exalted Christ and given Him a seat at His right hand. And what is the best news in our lives—by pleasing His Father, He pleased *us!*

TOPICS: Christ's Salvation, Christ's Submission, Christ's Work

December 1

DAILY BIBLE READING: 1 Corinthians 1–5

TODAY'S VERSE: 1 Corinthians 3:13: "Every man's work shall be made manifest: for the day shall declare it, because it shall be revealed by fire; and the fire shall try every man's work of what sort it is."

THIS PASSAGE GIVES us a little glimpse of the judgment seat of Christ, or as some would call it, the *Bema* seat. For the Christian, there will be no judgment of sin before God, for that was done on Calvary. Every unbelieving person who has ever lived will stand at the Great White Throne and give account of every sin and action they ever committed. However, you *will* be at one of the judgments. One is a judgment of condemnation ("the Great White Throne") while the other is a judgment of commendation ("the Bema seat"). The believer's judgment at the judgment seat of Christ will determine his rewards. Some will receive their reward purified, and some will not receive anything, for their works will be consumed. The judgment seat of Christ will sift through the actions of our lives and search out our thoughts, motivations, and passions in our service to the Lord.

It Will Be a Day of Explicitness ("Every man's work shall be made manifest"). The word for "manifest" means "shining, apparent." When God shines the light upon your life, nothing will escape His view. This is a promise. First Corinthians 4:5 says that God will both *bring to light the hidden things of darkness, and . . . make manifest the counsels of the hearts:* and then shall every man have praise of God." The work of this judgment will be to bring praise to God!

It Will Be a Day of Exclamation ("for the day shall declare it"). There will be no whispers, no secret meetings, and no negotiations behind closed doors. The word translated "declare" means "to make plain." We have a great need today for plainness in Christian living. Every cloak that is used to mask who we are and every ulterior motive will be taken away so that our hearts will be plain, not only to God, but to us as well. That is why God has given us His Word. James 1:23 says, "For if any be a hearer of the word, and not a doer, he is like unto a man beholding his natural face in a glass." God has taken great pains to make our sin plain to us here through the reading of His Word. If we will not see ourselves through the Bible, then He will make our natures plain at the judgment seat of Christ.

It Will Be a Day of Exposure ("because it shall be revealed by fire"). The Greek word for "revealed" means "to take off the cover." It would do us well to acknowledge that our sin will not just be uncovered, but that it will be consumed and violently exposed by fire. Every secret thought will be searched out and exposed. God and His heavenly flamethrower will walk through every room of your heart and expose it for exactly what it is.

It Will Be a Day of Examination ("and the fire shall try every man's work of what sort it is"). The word for "try" means "to test." Some good things can come from this examination, but that depends upon your preparation! God will seek out which parts of your work pass His test and which parts fail. May we carefully and thoughtfully prepare for the test that is approaching at Christ's judgment seat.

If you are unsaved, you will not have such an examination. The Book of Life will be opened, your name will not be found, and you will be cast out of God's presence for all eternity. If you are found at the Great White Throne, your end will be the lake of fire and the second death. Trust in Christ today, and make sure you attend the other judgment so that He may search your works and reward you instead.

TOPICS: Judgment Seat, Motives, Rewards

R. CHRIS HANKS

DAILY BIBLE READING: 1 Corinthians 6–8

TODAY'S VERSE: 1 Corinthians 6:20: "For ye are bought with a price: therefore glorify God in your body, and in your spirit, which are God's."

IN PAUL'S EPISTLE to the Corinthians, he shows the church of Corinth, under divine inspiration, the spiritual way of Christian living. The apostle begins verse 19 with a question: "What?" It is a question of disbelief on his part. It is like him saying, "Are you kidding me?" The church was asking questions that showed ignorance of who they were—that they were the temple of God. The Spirit of God will teach His children and show them how to live for His glory. Verse 19 is almost as if Paul was saying, "God should not have to waste divine breath on this, because you already know it in your heart!" Today, let us move into verse 20, considering it in light of our life for God.

There Is a Remembrance of the Blood of Our Saviour ("For ye are bought with a price"). Paul reminds us here of the great sacrifice of Jesus Christ upon the altar of the old rugged cross. He reminds us of the wet, red payment of the blood of Christ that was given so willingly. Acts 20:28 tells us, "Take heed therefore unto yourselves, and to all the flock, over the which the Holy Ghost hath made you overseers, to feed the church of God, *which he hath purchased with his own blood.*" We must always remember the blood of Christ, the price that was paid for our redemption. Everything else in this verse rests upon this phrase. The word for "bought" literally means "to go to market." Jesus went to the "market" of man's soul and paid the valued price in the full weight and glory of His own blood!

There Is a Rejoicing in Body and Spirit ("therefore glorify God in your body, and in your spirit"). Most people recognize that we should at least glorify God in our spirits. This verse also tells us that we should honor Him with our bodies. This goes directly against our flesh. We must glorify God in how we treat our bodies. In verse 19, we read that our bodies are the temple of the Holy Ghost. What we do to our bodies, put in them, and subject them to is of great concern to God, for how we treat our bodies is a testimony of the glory that we give Him. The psalms teach us how to glorify God with our bodies in song, with instruments, and with our witness. They command us to lift our voices, clap our hands, and rejoice in His work. The book of Psalms ends with this command in Psalm 150:6: "Let every thing that hath breath praise the LORD. Praise ye the LORD."

There Is a Responsibility of the Bonds of the Sovereign ("which are God's"). Verse 19 ends by saying, "Ye are not your own." This last phrase in verse 20 is the same thought: "Which are God's." The greatest truth we could learn is that every part of our lives belongs to God. From our time to our substance to our members, all is God's. Paul said in Romans 1:1, "Paul, a servant of Jesus Christ, called to be an apostle, separated unto the gospel of God." The word for "servant" here means "slave, bond-servant." We are the Lord's bondmen! Let us glorify Him by serving Him with all our hearts!

TOPICS: Blood, Glorifying God, Servanthood

DAILY BIBLE READING: 1 Corinthians 10–13

TODAY'S VERSE: 1 Corinthians 13:11: "When I was a child, I spake as a child, I understood as a child, I thought as a child: but when I became a man, I put away childish things."

THIS LITTLE VERSE SPEAKS of spiritual maturity. We are in a time of "vertically challenged" or small Christians. Our growth has been stunted by the immaturity of selfish living and carnal lusts. In many ways, we live, experience, and learn spiritual things as if we were little children. Hebrews 5:12–14 challenges us to grow up and mature in our Christian lives in several areas.

The Immaturity of Our Spiritual Speech. The word for "child" in this verse is not describing an older child, but an infant. I never had the gift of tongues when my children were born: I never could understand the goo-goos and ga-gas of babies. There were many times I had a hard time understanding my children even when they got older. I would look at them, listen intently to what they were trying to say, and then tell them in the greatest sincerity of heart, "Son, I don't understand a word you're saying!" We need to progress from the onomatopoetic sounds of childish talk and learn the truth and meaning of spiritual communication.

The Immaturity of Our Spiritual Opinions. The word for "understood" means "to exercise the mind, to entertain or have a sentiment or opinion." Exactly how does a baby "understand"? His opinions are limited to himself. It did not take me long to figure out that our precious new baby only thought of himself. A baby does not care about the parents' sleep at night, their schedule, their plans, or their feelings. The baby is the most selfish of all people in the home! (Some parents may still harbor a little bitterness over that!) Now that our oldest has grown up some, we do not allow him to dominate or dictate our lives any longer. Why? Because *he had to change his opinion of himself* as he continued to grow!

The Immaturity of Our Spiritual Reason. The word for "thought" is the same word from which we get our term *logic*, and it literally means "to take an inventory." What kind of logic does a baby have? How can he take inventory of anything? There is no reason in what babies do. Likewise, many Christians simply have no reason for how they live their lives. Our thinking must be drawn from the reason that is found in Scripture.

The next part of the verse says, "but when I became a man, I put away childish things." It is time for us to *grow up!* There are many things I enjoyed as a child that just don't excite me anymore. I'm sure this happened to you too! What happened? We all grew up! How about spiritual growth? How about your attitude and relationship with your church? Have you grown? It is odd to me to see a grown man sitting down reading a comic book or trying to dress and act like a kid again. It is sad because such people are looking for acceptance and acknowledgment. I have seen Christians do the same thing in spiritual situations. The problem? They never did mature. Let us grow spiritually and progress in our spiritual lives. And how do we grow? Read the rest of our chapter today—1 Corinthians 13, "The Love Chapter." The first thing essential to spiritual growth is . . . charity!

TOPICS: Spiritual Growth, Thoughtfulness, Understanding

DAILY BIBLE READING: 1 Corinthians 14–16

TODAY'S VERSE: 1 Corinthians 16:9: "For a great door and effectual is opened unto me, and there are many adversaries."

THERE ARE SEVERAL BIBLICAL REFERENCES to doors. God shut the door of the ark upon Noah and his family (a *door of protection*). God warned Cain that if he did not do well, "sin lieth at the door" (a *door of partition*, **Genesis 4:7**). The Israelites struck the posts of the door with blood at the Passover (a *door of propitiation*). Jesus Himself is the door of salvation (a *door of pardon*). Isaiah said that the "posts of the door moved at the voice of him that cried" (a *door of power*, **Isaiah 6:4**). The angels rolled back the stone from door of the sepulchre and sat upon it (a *door of promise*). Jesus is standing and knocking at our heart's door (a *door of partnership*). Today's door is equally important.

We see first that it is a **Door of Opportunity** ("a great door and effectual"). In your life, you will find that God's will is always full of opportunity. We are not talking about small opportunity: this verse calls it both "a great door and effectual." The word for "great" here means "big." Not all opportunity is God's will, but God's will always offers great opportunity. When Philip was told by the Spirit to go to the desert, he had a great opportunity. Not only was it "great," but it was also "effectual," or "active and operative." In other words, it was *possible*. No matter how impossible your situation may seem, no matter how dead your town may be, no matter how forlorn your family may be, God can make opportunity "operative" in your life.

It is also a **Door of Opening** ("opened unto me"). God opens the doors of His will. Many preachers can testify of the opening work of the Holy Ghost in their lives and ministries. When it seems that there is no way, God makes a way. God is never shut in. I have known many elderly Christians who were considered to be "shut-ins," but that had no bearing on their witness. God can open a door of opportunity to witness when it seems there is none available.

It is a **Door of Opposition** ("and there are many adversaries"). When you are in the middle of the Lord's will, you will find many adversaries. The word translated "adversaries" means "to lie opposite." God's will is seldom, if ever, without adversaries. Many times, we are one of our own biggest enemies! The Bible says in 2 Timothy 2:25, "In meekness instructing *those that oppose themselves;* if God peradventure will give them repentance to the acknowledging of the truth." We should not be opposing ourselves in our service to the Lord. We know that battles will come. Let the battles present themselves on their own. These adversaries will bring trouble, but it is a trouble that will glorify the omnipotence of God. With great joy comes great sorrow. With great victories come great battles. So too, with great potential come great problems. Don't be fearful of what lies ahead or what kind of opposition awaits you, for God will make it possible for you to do His will!

TOPICS: Opportunity, Opposition, Victory

DAILY BIBLE READING: 2 Corinthians 1–5

TODAY'S VERSE: 2 Corinthians 4:1: "Therefore seeing we have this ministry, as we have received mercy, we faint not."

I DON'T KNOW about you, but there are times when I need encouragement not to quit. There is nothing more aggravating than someone who quits, yet we have all done so at different times in our lives. Proverbs 24:10 says, "If thou faint in the day of adversity, thy strength is small." We need to increase our strength if we are going to continue in the face of hardship. Do you need a reason to keep going this morning? Here are a few reasons why we can't quit.

Because of God's Word ("Therefore"). We cannot quit because of a **message** that we have been given. I was always taught that if there was a "therefore" in a passage of Scripture, I had to find out what it was there for. This one is there to continue a thought begun earlier in 2 Corinthians. There have been many times I was discouraged and did not want to continue, but then God gave me something from His Word to strengthen my heart and my life. I have found that all of Scripture has that same power. I can't quit because of what has been written. What a Book we have! Not just a book that contains His thoughts, but a Book that is empowered with His very breath!

Because of God's Work ("seeing we have this ministry"). We cannot quit because of a **ministry** we have been given. This is not just talking about preachers! Each one of us has a ministry. We can't quit because of our *families*. Dad, you have a ministry to your wife and children. Mom, you have a ministry to your husband and home. Church member, you have a ministry to your pastor and your church. We can't quit because of our *friends*. We have a ministry to our neighbors, our coworkers, and our acquaintances. And we can't quit because of our *foes*. Saved person, you have a ministry to all the lost. Whether they like you or not, you have a ministry to them. Even if they are enemies of the cross, it would be a sad day if they entered the torments of hell because you never shared the gospel.

Because of God's Welcome ("as we have received mercy"). We cannot quit because of the **mercy** we have been given. God has received you and welcomed you into His presence! I can't quit because God has never quit on me! The verb here is in the passive voice, meaning that the subject is receiving the action of the verb. God is the One who did the action, not me! I have been given the mercy of Almighty God! *I can't quit now!*

TOPICS: Mercy, Ministry, Word of God

DAILY BIBLE READING: 2 Corinthians 6–9

TODAY'S VERSE: 2 Corinthians 6:14: "Be ye not unequally yoked together with unbelievers: for what fellowship hath righteousness with unrighteousness? and what communion hath light with darkness?"

THIS VERSE IS A POWERFUL SCRIPTURE on biblical separation. Every time you find the word *separation* in Scripture, it is not talking about standards—it is talking about people. Standards have to do with growth. Separation has to do with people. Whenever we are told to be separated, it is always for us to be separated from someone. Why do you suppose this is? Does it mean some are better than others? Of course, the answer is an emphatic "No!" We are all sinners. However, there are some good reasons for us to live separated lives.

There Is a Real Yoke ("Be ye not unequally yoked together with unbelievers"). Many people look at this verse and dismiss it as some silly and intolerant dogma. That's a dangerous thing to do. Whether in business, marriage, or worship, we need to be careful not to be yoked with unbelievers. This does not mean that we do not have contact with unbelievers, but we should not be *yoked* with them. God is not saying that we should not work with unbelievers, but even while at work, we will be separated from them by our belief. We should not enter into a partnership with them that cannot be wholly dedicated to God and His ways. Have you ever thought about why this is? A Christian has spiritual desires and boundaries that are placed upon him by the Word of God. Those limits are for a reason. *This is a yoke of importance. This is where we live.*

It Is a Righteous Yoke ("for what fellowship hath righteousness with unrighteousness?"). The word for "fellowship" means "participation." Our participation in unrighteousness through our fellowship with others is of great concern to our Lord. Lest someone misunderstand, this is not to remove spiritual liberty, but to create it. If our unequal yoke bonds us to unrighteousness, we have limited liberty to serve the Lord. You can't do anything for God if those in the yoke are pulling in different directions. Christian liberty is not just about what we can do, but about what we can do for the Lord. *This is a yoke of imbalance. This is how we lift.*

It Is a Relationship Yoke ("and what communion hath light with darkness?"). The word *communion* is important here. How can we be separate from others if we are bound to them in a contract or vow? This verse goes from our professional relationships all the way to our personal relationships. We can love the souls and love them as people, but we cannot love them as brothers because there is no spiritual relationship with unbelievers. Every relationship that is "unequally yoked" is lifeless because the love of God does not have free course to lead and work in that relationship. *This is a yoke of impotence. This is how we love.*

Jesus said in Matthew 11:28–30, "Come unto me, all ye that labour and are heavy laden, and I will give you rest. Take my yoke upon you, and learn of me; for I am meek and lowly in heart: *and ye shall find rest unto your souls*. For my yoke is easy, and my burden is light." Now here is a yoke that fits right, feels right, and pulls right!

TOPICS: Relationships, Separation, Testimony

December 7

DAILY BIBLE READING: 2 Corinthians 10–13

TODAY'S VERSE: 2 Corinthians 11:3: "But I fear, lest by any means, as the serpent beguiled Eve through his subtilty, so your minds should be corrupted from the simplicity that is in Christ."

TODAY'S VERSE IS BOTH a warning and an encouragement to Christians everywhere. It speaks of something that is under attack by the flesh, the devil, and the world—our minds. A recent anti-drug slogan proclaims, "A mind is a terrible thing to waste." Nothing truer could be said! But while the slogan addresses only drugs, the truth is that many have fallen prey to the subtlety of the devil through philosophy and vain deceit as well as through the carnality and lustful desires of the flesh.

The Serpent's Mind ("as the serpent beguiled Eve"). This is a **seductive mind.** The word for "beguiled" means "to seduce wholly." This verse takes us all the way back to Genesis 3 and reminds us of the ambush of Satan upon Eve. The temptation was sensuous in its character and devilish in its destruction. The serpent's mind is presumptive in its nature, defying the way of God and searching out its own fleshly way. By doing so, the serpent seduces all who are close to his hypnotic stare.

The Subtle Mind ("through his subtilty, so your minds should be corrupted"). This is a **spoiled mind.** The definition of the word for "subtilty" is "adroitness, (i.e. in a bad sense) trickery or sophistry:—(cunning) craftiness." Subtlety will rot out any good mind and defile it with that which is against the way of the Lord. There is nothing to be said for the subtle mind that is full of trickery and deceit. It is full of the devil, for it was Satan who deceived Eve through subtlety. Those minds that like to throw bricks and hide their hands are full of devilish thoughts and influences. They are full of criminal intent and corrupted integrity. The verse tells us that our minds can "be corrupted" by the devil's subtlety. The word for "corrupted" means "to shrivel, to wither, to spoil, to ruin." Eating the fruit brought about banishment from God's precious garden and separation from God by sin.

The Simple Mind ("from the simplicity that is in Christ"). This is the **spiritual mind.** The word translated "simple" does not mean "stupid," but rather, "singleness, (i.e. subjectively), sincerity (without dissimulation or self-seeking)." You do not have to know all about evil to know it is wrong! The Bible says in Romans 16:19, "For your obedience is come abroad unto all men. I am glad therefore on your behalf: but yet I would have you wise unto that which is good, and simple concerning evil." God has made the Christian life easy to live. It is not hard to know or to do the will of God.

Let us have the mind of Christ. Philippians 2:5 says, "Let this mind be in you, which was also in Christ Jesus." Don't look for worldly wisdom, but for the mind of Christ!

TOPICS: Deceit, Mind, Subtlety, Wisdom

R. CHRIS HANKS

DAILY BIBLE READING: Galatians 1–3

TODAY'S VERSE: Galatians 3:22: "But the scripture hath concluded all under sin, that the promise by faith of Jesus Christ might be given to them that believe."

PAUL AND TIMOTHY both preached the gospel in Galatia (see Acts 16:1–6). Paul visited this church on all three of his missionary journeys. The Galatians' big problem was their desire to mix the law and grace. We hear this in Paul's question in Galatians 3:2–3: "This only would I learn of you, Received ye the Spirit by the works of the law, or by the hearing of faith? Are ye so foolish? having begun in the Spirit, are ye now made perfect by the flesh?" Let us observe the Holy Spirit's thoughts on this topic that we might understand the work of God.

The Scripture's Conclusion ("But the scripture hath concluded all under sin"). The Word of God has already concluded that everybody is a sinner! The word for "concluded" literally means "to shut together." It's a done deal! No amount of good works will ever get you out of being a sinner. Once a sinner, always a sinner!

The Saviour's Contract ("that the promise by faith of Jesus Christ"). The word for "promise" means "an announcement (for information, assent or pledge; *especially a divine assurance of good).*" Doesn't God's promise of eternal life to those who believe in Him qualify as "a divine assurance of good"? God has made us a promise that will never be broken! Second Corinthians 1:20 says, "For all the promises of God in him are yea, and in him Amen, unto the glory of God by us." This is a contract or covenant based upon the blood atonement of Jesus Christ.

Our Salvation's Contact ("might be given to them that believe"). This phrase is given in what is grammatically called the subjunctive mood. This means that it is "connected with some supposed or desired action"[1] If God has already given us "a divine assurance of good," doesn't it follow that this is something that is desired? The passive voice in the phrase "To them that believe" is again telling us that the action of the promise is *happening to those that believe.* In other words, the believers are not getting the promise (that would require action on their part); rather, the promise is being given to them! It is God who sought us and has given us everything that is good and right according to His wisdom. He will do this for all those who believe and accept His free gift of salvation, wrapped in the Person and work of His blessed Son, Jesus Christ.

TOPICS: God's Promises, Jesus Christ, Salvation, Word of God

---

1 Spiros Zodhiates, *The Complete Word Study New Testament with Parallel Greek* (Chattanooga: AMG, 1992), 868.

DAILY BIBLE READING: Galatians 4–6

TODAY'S VERSE: Galatians 6:9: "And let us not be weary in well doing: for in due season we shall reap, if we faint not."

WE HAVE ALL FELT exhausted at one time or another. There are even times when we just get tired of doing right. My flesh never gets tired of doing wrong, but it sure does of doing right! This verse to the church at Galatia is a great encouragement to keep on keeping on. It is a charge to Christians to keep doing right no matter what we feel like. We shouldn't mind our feelings, because they will deceive us every time. Here are a few thoughts from this verse to persuade you to continue in well doing.

Strength to Continue ("And let us not be weary in well doing"). The idea here is not that you need to get strength to continue, but that there *is* strength to continue! You may not understand how to just "continue" doing right. Isaiah 40:30–31 says, "Even the youths shall faint and be weary, and the young men shall utterly fall: *but they that wait upon the* LORD *shall renew their strength;* they shall mount up with wings as eagles; they shall run, and not be weary; and they shall walk, and not faint." Far too often, we hurry down the road of temptation, frustration, and turmoil, and we miss the peace and strength that comes from waiting on God. Today's verse actually gives strength to those who are waiting upon God. With promised strength from God, how can we allow our flesh to tell us we are tired of doing right?

Season to Continue ("for in due season we shall reap"). A time of reaping is coming! Yes, sometimes you might wonder if it is worth it all. Rest assured, a reckoning day is coming! This time is nothing but a season, and our lives are nothing but a vapor. Our years are nothing but a wisp of time that will show forth an eternal harvest and confirm the promise of God's faithfulness and goodness. If we are faithful, we will recognize the truth that Esther Rusthoi wrote in her song: "It will be worth it all, when we see Jesus/Life's trials will seem so small when we see Christ/One glimpse of His dear face all sorrow will erase/So bravely run the race till we see Christ."[2] Nothing will compare to what awaits us on the other side.

Settled to Continue ("if we faint not"). We must be settled in our hearts that God is true, otherwise we will have reason to faint. Fear is a cause of fainting. Many Christians today pale at the sight of some trouble that lies ahead. They become dizzy in their Christian lives because they keep their eyes on themselves and their spiritual duties rather than on Christ. If we keep our eyes focused on the Lord, we will have the strength to continue in well-doing.

TOPICS: Commitment, Confidence, Strength

---

2 "When We See Christ" by Esther Kerr Rusthoi. © 1941 New Spring, Inc (ASCAP) (Administered by Brentwood-Benson Music Publishing, Inc.) All rights reserved. Used by permission.

DAILY BIBLE READING: Ephesians 1–3

TODAY'S VERSE: Ephesians 2:6-7: "And hath raised us up together, and made us sit together in heavenly places in Christ Jesus: that in the ages to come he might shew the exceeding riches of his grace in his kindness toward us through Christ Jesus."

I LOVE TO THINK about heaven, but I like even more to read that *God* is thinking about heaven! In today's verse, God gives us information about heaven and how it affects our future place with Him. I hope you will take a moment to think about heaven today as we all look forward to being raptured to meet the Lord in the air.

The Thoughts of Heaven ("And hath raised us up together"). The words for "raised us up together" mean "to rouse (from death) in company with, to revivify." God had to raise me up! He had to raise us and pull us out of the pit (Psalm 40:2)—this was a *rescue!* He had to raise us from the dead (Ephesians 2:10)—this was a *resurrection!* He *will* raise us up to catch us away (1 Thessalonians 4:16–17)—this is a *rapture!* A blessing is found in this phrase in the word "together." In the mind of God, all this was done at the same time! What fellowship that we can rejoice and experience the salvation and forgiveness of our Lord "together"!

The Thrones of Heaven ("and made us sit together in heavenly places in Christ Jesus"). The Greek translated "made us sit together" is much like the last phrase. It means "to give (or take) a seat in company with." This is a great exaltation, for I know where Jesus is seated! Hebrews 1:3 tells us that Jesus "sat down on the right hand of the Majesty on high." That is where you and I will be! During the Millennial Reign, what will those who are saved be doing? Reigning with Him! Revelation 20:6 says, "Blessed and holy is he that hath part in the first resurrection: on such the second death hath no power, but they shall be priests of God and of Christ, *and shall reign with him a thousand years.*"

The Thrill of Heaven ("That in the ages to come he might shew the exceeding riches of his grace in his kindness toward us through Christ Jesus"). What pleasure awaits us in the ages to come! Christ raised us up together, He made us sit together, and now He will show us the riches of His grace together! I believe it will take every second of eternity to show us all the riches of His grace! Some would say this verse only covers the age of Tribulation while we are at the judgment seat of Christ, the Marriage Supper of the Lamb, and the age of the Millennial Reign of Christ. I would argue that it covers the ages of eternity that will follow! Ephesians 3:21 says it like this: "Unto him be glory in the church by Christ Jesus throughout all ages, world without end. Amen." God will never run out of ways to show us something new about His grace and His kindness through His only beloved Son, Jesus Christ!

TOPICS: Exaltation, Glory, Resurrection

DAILY BIBLE READING: Ephesians 4–6

TODAY'S VERSE: Ephesians 4:12: "For the perfecting of the saints, for the work of the ministry, for the edifying of the body of Christ."

THIS VERSE TELLS US just how much God loves the church. We read in verse 11 of several gifts God has given to the church; in verse 12, we see why He has given them. I am sure glad that God did not leave us without what we need! Every gift mentioned is a person called of God to do the work of God. Down through the ages, God has had a special ministry for His men to work with His people. I thank God for willing and able ministers who are faithful in His work. Let us look at the threefold reason for these gifts to our churches.

First, They Are Completing Gifts ("the perfecting of the saints"). The word *perfect* here does not mean sinless perfection, but "complete furnishing." The work of the preacher is to help you be complete in your Christian life. The preacher is to teach and preach the Word of God, and we know that the Word of God is given to us "that the man of God may be perfect, throughly furnished unto all good works" (2 Timothy 3:17). Have you ever walked into a beautiful house only to find it void of furniture, curtains, homely accents, and ornaments of decoration? With every house that we have moved into over the years, cold buildings were never home until my wife began to furnish them with what they needed so that we might live according to our needs, our identity, and our comforts. The preacher is to help complete and furnish your life in every spiritual application. It is in your best interest to listen to the man of God so that you might grow to be complete and mature in your Christian life.

Second, They Are Competent Gifts ("for the work of the ministry"). As the pastor leads the flock, it is to do the work of the ministry. The Holy Spirit will work through the preacher to teach you and focus you in the work of the ministry. If you are in a church but not in the ministry, you are rejecting God's gift in your life—your pastor. Many people today just want to attend church without lifting a finger in this work of the ministry. God has never saved anyone to be a pew-sitter. There may be things you cannot do, but you *can* do the work of the ministry in some fashion until you reach the other side. Your preacher is God's gift to you to help you do that.

Third, They Are Construction Gifts ("for the edifying of the body of Christ"). The word for "edifying" literally means "architecture, a structure." We need to be brought together joint-to-joint and edge-to-edge as a sanctuary of the glory of God. We must come together and unite behind a common cause—the glory of Jesus Christ! On every job, there is a foreman who is the final authority to instruct the workers on the blueprints and construction of the building. This is not about everybody "doing their thing." It is about doing things the right way, in the right order, for the right result. God planned it like this!

TOPICS: Growth, Pastor, Maturing, Submission

DAILY BIBLE READING: Philippians 1-4

TODAY'S VERSE: Philippians 3:17: "Brethren, be followers together of me, and mark them which walk so as ye have us for an ensample."

PHILIPPIANS IS KNOWN as the "Joy Book." In every instance, the Apostle Paul is trying to show the Philippians the joy of the Christian life. In chapter 3, he has just talked with them about "counting all things but loss," "knowing [Christ] and the power of his resurrection," and "pressing toward the mark." Though Paul was not a pastor, you can hear his pastoral heart in his letters and in his preaching with passion and fervency. Let's listen to what he says to the church at Philippi—and to us.

First, he tells us to hear the **Shepherd's Voice** ("Brethren, be followers together of me"). Can you hear Jesus' shepherdly voice calling out to these precious sheep? "Come on, follow me, you can do it!" The word for "followers together" means "co-imitator." This reminds me of the game we used to play as children called "Follow the Leader." It was simple: do what the leader does! The leader would do all kinds of odd things, and everybody behind him had to do the same thing. We were never embarrassed to do those things because everybody was doing them—together. This is exactly what Jesus, the Great Shepherd, has asked us to do. John 10:27 says, "My sheep hear my voice, and I know them, *and they follow me.*" Let us be imitators of Christ!

Second, he instructs us of the **Sheep's Vision** ("mark them which walk so as ye have us for an ensample"). The word for "mark" is the same word from which we get our English "scope." It means "to take aim at, spy." Here is a good question for you today: "At what are you aiming?" There are traits in certain Christians that we should mimic in our lives. Of course, there was no greater example than Christ Himself. The Air Force has as their motto, "Aim High." Our motto should be "Aiming Higher." Hebrews 12:2 says, "Looking unto Jesus the author and finisher of our faith; who for the joy that was set before him endured the cross, despising the shame, and is set down at the right hand of the throne of God."

Third, he speaks of the **Shepherd's Variety** ("so as ye have us for an ensample"). The word used for "ensample" means "a die [or dice](as struck)." This has to do with a mold. There is no doubt that we are to be of a specific sort, kind, and variety. Didn't Paul say that he bore the marks of Christ? Galatians 6:17 says, "From henceforth let no man trouble me: *for I bear in my body the marks of the Lord Jesus.*" So many people today want to make their own image and be their own person, yet the Bible is very clear that we should be *like Christ*. Romans 8:29 says, "For whom he did foreknow, he also did predestinate *to be conformed to the image of his Son,* that he might be the firstborn among many brethren." God desires us to fit a very specific mold.

TOPICS: Following, Identification, Leadership

DAILY BIBLE READING: Colossians 1-4

TODAY'S VERSE: Colossians 2:3: "In whom are hid all the treasures of wisdom and knowledge."

TODAY, LET'S GO on a little expedition to look for some of these "hidden treasures." One thing we know about hidden treasure is that it comes with a map. If there was no map, it would not be a *hidden* treasure, it would be a *lost* treasure! I am glad to know that God's treasure is not lost, just hidden! Even if something has been hidden on purpose, you can rest assured that everything hidden is hidden with the intent that someone find it. Let us not just go out looking for a nugget here and there. Let's grab our picks and shovels and look for the mother lode! We are not archeologists, but miners!

The Purpose of a Hidden Treasure ("*In* whom are hid"). There is a reason for hiding a treasure. We hide things today for protection and safekeeping. There are times when I will hide things from my children to see if they can find them as a game. Whoever finds the "treasure" gets to keep it! A favorite game growing up was always Hide and Seek. The real fun of the game was not in hiding, but in seeking! That is the way it is with the things of God. The fun in this game is found in seeking. Proverbs 2:3–5 says, "Yea, if thou criest after knowledge, and liftest up thy voice for understanding; if thou seekest her as silver, and searchest for her as for hid treasures; then shalt thou understand the fear of the Lord, and find the knowledge of God."

The Person of the Hidden Treasure ("In *whom* are hid"). God did not want to keep this treasure for Himself, for if He did, He would not have told us that it is found in Christ. That is quite a place to look! There is no greater place, no bigger place, and no more blessed place to look than in Christ. We can walk around in Him for the rest of our lives and continually find new blessings, new hopes, and new fortunes. How excited we would be to be hunting for gems in a place we were should to find them! So much more can we find treasure in Christ! Unlike mines that eventually become exhausted, we will never find the end of His goodness no matter how much we mine in His Word, His will, and His worship.

The Pleasure of the Hidden Treasure ("hid all the treasures of wisdom and knowledge"). There must be something special hidden if it is worth finding. You will never look for anything in Christ that is not worth being found! He has hidden these things for us with great anticipation of our finding each spiritual blessing and truth that He has placed within His Word. When we find one treasure, there will be another on which we can set our sights!

TOPICS: Christ's Fullness, God's Word, Seeking

DAILY BIBLE READING: 1 Thessalonians 1–5

TODAY'S VERSE: 1 Thessalonians 2:4: "But as we were allowed of God to be put in trust with the gospel, even so we speak; not as pleasing men, but God, which trieth our hearts."

WHAT A BLESSED VERSE to consider today as we look at the blessings of the gospel of our God! In just talking about the gospel, the apostle Paul gets excited and explains why our gospel—our "good news"—is far above any other gospel. He is talking about the gospel of Jesus Christ—there is no other gospel! Confucius has a religion, but no gospel! Buddha has a religion, but no gospel! Islam has a religion, but no gospel! What is it that makes our religion a gospel? It is the death, burial, and resurrection of Jesus Christ (see 1 Corinthians 15:1–4). No other religion has these, because *they have no gospel.* The same author and apostle goes further in Galatians 1:8: *"But though we, or an angel from heaven, preach any other gospel unto you than that which we have preached unto you, let him be accursed."* These verses wreak havoc on the doctrines of Mormonism, Christian Science, and Russellism (Jehovah's Witnesses). This gospel of Jesus Christ stands alone!

The **Greatness of Our Opportunity** ("as we were allowed of God"). We have been chosen! What an honor! We have been allowed of God. This goes far deeper than an obligation ever will, for it is an opportunity! This is not an aggravation, but an advantage. What a privilege we have today to serve our Lord by carrying this gospel across the globe for His honor and glory so that others might be saved!

The **Guardianship of Our Gospel** ("to be put in trust with the gospel"). We have a great responsibility along with this precious gospel. All great privileges come with great responsibilities. Paul said in Romans 1:14, *"I am debtor* both to the Greeks, and to the Barbarians; both to the wise, and to the unwise." Paul recognized his responsibility to give the gospel of Christ to all people. This was the only way God intended it to be used. Since we have a responsibility, we will also be held accountable for what we do with it.

The **Glory of Our Mission** ("not as pleasing men, but God"). We can actually *please God* with the way we use this gospel. That means that sharing the gospel is a work of faith, for Hebrews 11:6 says, "But without faith it is impossible to please him." Faith always pleases God, and we are guaranteed that sharing our faith pleases Him as well! The problem many have with their work for the Lord is that they are pleasing men! John 12:43 says, "For they loved the praise of men more than the praise of God." If you love to please God, you will love to share the gospel!

TOPICS: Gospel, Responsibility, Testimony, Witness

DAILY BIBLE READING: 2 Thessalonians 1–3

TODAY'S VERSE: 2 Thessalonians 3:5: "And the Lord direct your hearts into the love of God, and into the patient waiting for Christ."

GOD HAS ALWAYS BEEN interested in our hearts. Romans 8:27 tells us, "And he that searcheth the hearts knoweth what is the mind of the Spirit." God has a vested interest in what is happening in our hearts! He has warned us in Proverbs 4:23 to "keep thy heart with all diligence; for out of it are the issues of life." Why do you suppose God is so interested in our hearts? Because He has commanded us in Mark 12:30, "And thou shalt love the Lord thy God with all thy heart." If our hearts entertain any other desire or motivation, the supremacy and preeminence of God in our hearts is greatly threatened. Our hearts are to be completely occupied with love and adoration of God.

The **Direction of Our Hearts** ("And the Lord direct your hearts"). The word for "direct" can be used two different ways: it is used as a guide or direction in location, but it also means "to straighten fully." We sometimes use this terminology in giving directions— "As the crow flies, it is about three miles to your destination." This direction is a "more direct" route. Our Lord knows that our hearts need both guiding and straightening. I have found that as God leads me, He has to "unbend" my thoughts, ideals, and reasoning. We are so often twisted by our desires and hopes that we cannot see the way of the Lord. God knew that man was like this, and that is why He sent John the Baptist as a forerunner of the Messiah. Matthew 3:3b says of John, "Prepare ye the way of the Lord, make his paths straight." God wants our hearts to be straight according to His ways.

The **Destination of Our Hearts** ("into the love of God"). Is there a better place to go than into the love of God? If I were in an Uncle Remus story and the devil were after me, I would have to cry out right here just like Br'er Rabbit: "Just don't fling me in that brier patch, Brer Fox!" Throw me into the love of God where there are pleasures forevermore, hope without end, mercy that is everlasting, and courage for what lies ahead! Every morning, we should wake up and make the love of God our goal and destination for the day!

The **Development of Our Hearts** ("and into the patient waiting for Christ"). The word used for "patient waiting" means "cheerful endurance, constancy." This is a developing and maturing work of God. Paul had to learn this before he could write about it. Philippians 4:11 says, "For I have learned, in whatsoever state I am, therewith to be content." Can you be cheerful and content in what the Lord is doing in your life? Again we see this same principle in 1 Timothy 6:6: "But godliness with contentment is great gain."

TOPICS: Direction, Growth, Maturing, Patience

DAILY BIBLE READING: 1 Timothy 1–6

TODAY'S VERSE: 1 Timothy 4:16: "Take heed unto thyself, and unto the doctrine; continue in them: for in doing this thou shalt both save thyself, and them that hear thee."

PAUL WROTE THESE WORDS to Timothy to give his young preacher boy some advice in the ministry. I am thankful for older men who took time to mentor me and teach me in the way that I needed to go. Old men of God have an essential ministry, not just to other preachers, but to young men. The home is one piece of our society that has experienced catastrophic failure. The church is not far behind. We need to start teaching the younger generation how to live their lives for the glory of the Lord. Let's look at the ways Paul directed Timothy.

Personal Consideration ("Take heed unto thyself"). The words translated "take heed" mean "pay attention to." It is easy for us to compare ourselves with others. This is very dangerous, for our prideful hearts will give us a bloated sense of self-worth and will not even consider how we compare to Christ, the true measurement. Second Corinthians 10:12 says, "For we dare not make ourselves of the number, or compare ourselves with some that commend themselves: but they measuring themselves by themselves, and comparing themselves among themselves, are not wise." What a great instruction from an old preacher! No matter how godly we think we might be, we must recognize that the need for revival first begins with us.

Personal Creed ("and unto the doctrine"). Notice that Paul did not say "his doctrine," but "the doctrine." There is only one doctrine, and it is God's! The word for "doctrine" means "instruction (the function or the information)." All doctrine is twofold in its work. There is the teaching of it as information, and there is the understanding of it in function. Paul's instruction to Timothy was that biblical teaching needed to become *his own* doctrine. In other words, Timothy needed to know what he believed and why. There are many who know the right words of belief, but they have not yet taken ownership of them in their life application. There is a rhyme and reason in what we believe. May we learn it and then live it.

Personal Continuation ("continue in them"). The word for "continue" means "to stay over." Many today are jumping ship concerning what they believe. There is little loyalty to church in their hearts, let alone doctrine. When someone asked you to stay over at their house as a child, it usually meant overnight. There is great application concerning "staying over" in the truth and presence of the Word of God. Make it your dwelling place. Make yourself at home with the Word of God and its doctrine.

Personal Compensation ("for in doing this thou shalt both save thyself, and them that hear thee"). This phrase starts with "for in doing," which is a present active participle. That tells us that this is a continuous or repeated action. The word for "this" is a demonstrative pronoun that tells us there is a particular thing we should be doing. We must "keep on continuing" in the doctrine of God! This phrase is followed by a blessing of protection: "Thou shalt both save thyself, and them that hear thee." Paul is not suggesting that Timothy will do the work of salvation, but that his study and commitment to the Word will save him and those he teaches from the destruction that comes from wrong doctrine.

TOPICS: Doctrine, Preaching, Word of God

DAILY BIBLE READING: 2 Timothy 1–4

TODAY'S VERSE: 2 Timothy 3:5: "Having a form of godliness, but denying the power thereof: from such turn away."

SECOND TIMOTHY 3 BEGINS by speaking about the perilous times of the last days. The word for "perilous" in verse 1 means "to reduce the strength." There is no doubt we are living in a time when the church is *sapped*. All its vigor and all its potency are gone. The church seems to have had all of its strength taken away and is relegated to a lifeless existence. That is why many churches seem to have no flavor. That is why the whole world continues its slide into wickedness exponentially. We know that the world will continue to get worse, but it is not pleasant to watch, as it seems to have completely lost its moral compass and is gaining momentum as it slides past the morals of God's Word. Things older saints greet by saying, "I never thought I would see the day when . . ." are becoming commonplace and alarm us no more. Here are a few thoughts about today's verse and the last times.

These Are Deceitful Times ("having a form of godliness"). This is a very deceitful time as people are deceived by the "appearance" of true religion, sucked in by the trappings of religious words, and fleeced by televangelists who hold no doctrine and are not governed by the pattern of the Word of God. The most dangerous thing today is that there are some who seem to have something spiritual about them, but who lack what matters most—God! When law officers are taught how to recognize counterfeit money, they are not shown the counterfeit, but the real thing. They are instructed about genuine money's ink, its security features, its fine micro-print, and even its feel. We need to get to the point where we recognize the real thing! Paul told us in Romans 8:16 that the Spirit would "bear witness with our spirit." First John 4:1 says, "Beloved, believe not every spirit, *but try the spirits whether they are of God:* because many false prophets are gone out into the world." We are losing many people from our churches because they are being deceived and have not been grounded in the faith.

These Are Dangerous Times ("denying the power thereof"). To deny the power of godliness is to deny the Spirit! Zechariah 4:6 says, "Then he answered and spake unto me, saying, This is the word of the LORD unto Zerubbabel, saying, Not by might, nor by power, *but by my spirit,* saith the LORD of hosts." There is a temptation for pastors and preachers today to change what they believe in order to "be more inclusive," "be more tolerant," or "reach more people." When they make such changes, they are not governed by the Spirit of the Lord, but by the will of the people. The word for "denying" means "to contradict, to disavow." What can we do without God's power? What impact can we make on this world that is "going to hell in a handbasket"? Give me the Ol' Time Power! Give me good, sound doctrine that is not merely a form, but that possesses the strength and power of God Himself!

These Are Demanding Times ("from such turn away"). These deceitful and dangerous times demand our attention and our action. What are we to do? *Turn away!* The word used for "turn away" literally means "to deflect, to avoid." Push deceitfulness, false doctrine, and living without the power of the Holy Ghost away. Run from it just like Joseph ran from Potiphar's wife. This kind of powerless life ought to be detestable! The only way to deflect this deceitful way is to embrace what is true in our faith. The Bible says in Hebrews 11:13, "These all died in faith, not having received the promises, but having seen them afar off, and were persuaded of them, *and embraced them,* and confessed that they were strangers and pilgrims on the earth." When you turn away from these perilous last times, be sure that you are turning unto God and His Way!

TOPICS: Authenticity, End Times, Power

DAILY BIBLE READING: Titus 1–3, Philemon

TODAY'S VERSE: Philemon 1: "Paul, a prisoner of Jesus Christ, and Timothy our brother, unto Philemon our dearly beloved, and fellowlabourer."

HERE IN THE BOOK OF PHILEMON, Paul uses family privilege to say things he would not normally say. He claims the right to say them by a close bond with those to whom he writes. As Paul names certain people here, he uses interesting terms in describing his relationship to them. Let's look at these terms today, considering our relationship with others.

We Have a Family Relationship ("our brother"). Paul said that Timothy was "our" brother. If Timothy was Paul's brother and Philemon's brother, then they were brothers as well! A family relationship carries both problems and privileges. You should be able to say some things to family that others might not be able to say. In love for family and a desire to help them, you have a right by relationship to address certain issues that might be off-limits to others. Hebrews 10:24 says, "And let us consider one another *to provoke unto love and to good works.*"

We Have a Fervent Relationship ("our dearly beloved"). Is there any better reason to either compliment or confront an issue than fervent love? Paul employed the principle of Proverbs 27:6a in writing to Philemon on a painful subject: "Faithful are the wounds of a friend." When we love others, we rejoice in their triumphs and we weep in their defeats; we hurt in their pain and we laugh in their joy. Your fervent relationship with another allows you access to his innermost feelings, her misunderstood thoughts, and his life-altering decisions. I find it interesting that the word "bowels" occurs three times in this little one-chapter book, with its older meaning of "deep feeling." This shows us the deep love Paul was expressing to his dearly beloved friend.

We Have a Fellowship Relationship ("and fellowlabourer"). Paul also calls Philemon his "fellowsoldier" in verse 2. Two interesting words are used for these special relationships: "Fellowlabourer" has to do with a *common work.* We are laboring together for the cause of Christ and the work of the gospel. We have a job that needs to be done! We have a harvest that needs to be reaped! We have lives that need to be lived for the glory of God and our Saviour! "Fellowsoldier" has to do with a *common war.* If you have been saved very long at all, you know that we are in a battle. The war is being waged on all fronts, from our homes to our churches. It is so good to have comrades in arms who will help us in the midst of the fight. Some are wounded, some are weary—*fight on!* If you have trusted in Christ as your Saviour, you are my fellowsoldier! Let us pray for one another. Keep fighting the fight! Christ has already won the victory.

TOPICS: Battle, Brotherhood, Fellowship, Relationship

December 19

DAILY BIBLE READING: Hebrews 1–6

TODAY'S VERSE: Hebrews 4:2: "For unto us was the gospel preached, as well as unto them: but the word preached did not profit them, not being mixed with faith in them that heard it."

TODAY WE WILL DEAL with the topic of faith and the Word of God. Our verse gives us a peek into the heavenly economy and the value of the "dollar" of heaven against the world and its standard of prosperity.

The Deposit of the Word of God through Faith ("For unto us was the gospel preached"). Our monetary deposits are very simple: we take money to the bank and deposit it. The more we deposit, the more power we have to make purchases and increase our value. Spiritually, we possess the great value faith in the Word of God, which 1 Peter 1:7 says is "more precious than gold." Isaiah 55:11 proclaims, "So shall my word be that goeth forth out of my mouth: *it shall not return unto me void,* but it shall accomplish that which I please, *and it shall* prosper *in the thing whereto I sent it."* There is no doubt of the potential value of the Word of God! Here in Hebrews we find a necessary element that makes this Word of God not only valuable, but *profitable*—faith! This verse speaks of two groups to whom the Word was preached, but the difference was that *only some had faith.* The Word of God has always been valuable, but it is *profitable* if it is mixed with faith.

The Interest of the Word of God through Faith ("For unto us was the gospel preached, as well as unto them"). In the world system, once our money is in a financial institution, it will begin to accrue interest. Spiritually, the heavenly deposit of the Word cannot accrue interest until faith is placed with it. That is why so many people can hear the Word of God and never do anything with it. It does not grow in value or in volume because it does not have faith with it. Literally, these people have no interest! There is great potential in the Word, but there is no power until faith mixes with it. Once faith is mixed with it, it grows exponentially!

The Reward of the Word of God through Faith ("but the word preached did not profit them, not being mixed with faith in them that heard it"). Second Timothy 3:16 says, "All scripture is given by inspiration of God, *and is profitable* for doctrine, for reproof, for correction, for instruction in righteousness." There are many rewards for making the right investments. Tremendous strength, liberating freedom from debt, and magnificent purchasing power come with prudent management. Credit card companies even have rewards and incentives for their users. But none of these worldly benefits can hold a candle to the rewards that come in a life that has the Word of God mixed with faith. Our money states that it is "Legal tender for all debts public and private." Faith is legal tender for all heavenly transactions, from salvation to obedience and from prayer to miracles.

Today's verse is a great key that will open the great vault of heaven and allow us free access to all divine riches!

TOPICS: Faith, Word of God

DAILY BIBLE READING: Hebrews 7–10

TODAY'S VERSE: Hebrews 7:25: "Wherefore he is able also to save them to the uttermost that come unto God by him, seeing he ever liveth to make intercession for them."

THIS VERSE MAKES ME WANT to shout! It gives us much information about our Saviour. Many have misunderstood the work of Christ at salvation. In doing so, they have also misunderstood the *scope, the security, and the simplicity of their salvation.* How sad it is to misunderstand salvation when it should mean more to us than anything! This verse discusses the desire of our Saviour in His love for man and His eternal work of salvation.

The Reality of Our Savior ("he is able also"). What a precious reality is stated right off the bat and so plainly in this verse—He is able! The word for "able" is the root of our English *dynamite.* I loved the little chorus we learned in Sunday School as children: "He's able, He's able, I know that He is able, I know my Lord is able to carry me through."[3] God is able to *redeem us from sin's power.* He is able to *rescue us with a sacrificial pardon.* He is able to *revive us with a Saviour's passion.*

The Reach of Our Saviour ("to save them to the uttermost, that come unto God by him"). What great news this is for all of us! There is nothing outside the reach of the redeeming hand of God. An old preacher said, "He saves to the uttermost and to the guttermost!" The word for "uttermost" means "full-ended, entire." Whatever needed to be done for us, Jesus was able to do it all! He came all the way for us and paid the debt in full! He opened the door to our sin, went down to its depths, and pulled us out of that horrible pit! He can save whosoever will come unto Him.

The Reason of Our Savior ("seeing he ever liveth to make intercession for them"). This is what gives Jesus joy in living! He "ever liveth" for sinners! He "ever liveth" to continue His work of salvation! The grammatical use of the word for "intercession" is what is called an articular infinitive. It is said to denote purpose. Jesus' reason or purpose in going on is simple—you! He has a great purpose in interceding for you to His Father! Have you thanked Him for His continual love, His continual prayer, and His continual care for you? If not, why don't you do it today?

TOPICS: Christ's Work, Intercession, Salvation

---

3   These words come from the hymn "He Is Able to Deliver Thee" by William A. Ogden.

DAILY BIBLE READING: Hebrews 11–13

TODAY'S VERSE: Hebrews 11:13: "These all died in faith, not having received the promises, but having seen them afar off, and were persuaded of them, and embraced them, and confessed that they were strangers and pilgrims on the earth."

WHAT A WONDERFUL CHAPTER is given to us here! Many have called this the "Hall of Faith" of the Bible. No doubt the saints God has listed for us here can teach us a few things about faith. What a blessing it is to read about the individual challenges they faced and the victories they won! This verse is one of the few in this chapter in which the Holy Spirit does not speak about one person, but speaks about all of them and their faith in God. Faith kept them going. What qualities of faith are able to encourage you to keep going?

Faith's Sight ("but having seen them afar off"). The saints did not see God's promises with their fleshly eyes, but with the eyes of faith. Faith sees things that our physical eyes cannot. That is why we are to walk by faith. Second Corinthians 5:7 says, "For we walk by faith, not by sight." Hebrews 11:10 says of Abraham, "For he looked for a city which hath foundations, whose builder and maker is God." How could Abraham look for something like that here on earth? He was looking with eyes of faith!

Faith's Sureness ("and were persuaded of them"). The word for "persuaded" means "to convince by argument." We should be persuaded of some things in our lives. We need a rock-hard faith that is "steadfast, unmoveable." Hebrews 12:27 says, "That those things which cannot be shaken may remain." We should be persuaded of our salvation, our security, and our surrender. Are you sure of God's love and care for you? Are you persuaded of His continual work in your life? Second Timothy 1:12 says, "For the which cause I also suffer these things: nevertheless I am not ashamed: *for I know whom I have believed, and am persuaded* that he is able to keep that which I have committed unto him against that day."

Faith's Shroud ("and embraced them"). The word for "embrace" means "to enfold in the arms." This is like watching the mother of a newborn babe wrap her child up and embrace him. Nothing can harm that baby without going through the mother's care. Have you ever seen a soldier home from war who takes up his wife and his children and wraps them in a hug of tremendous passion and power? All of his love, protection, care, and power are wrapped around those who mean so much to him. Many people don't understand our fanatic ways and our determined and unswerving dedication to God. I'd love to start a new national phenomenon right here and now, bigger than fish symbols and bracelets with WWJD written on them: ETF! What is ETF? EMBRACE THE FAITH! Enfold it in your arms, wrap it up with your care, hug it with your might, enshroud it with your being!

Faith's Sayings ("and confessed that they were strangers and pilgrims on the earth"). Believe me, your faith will speak! Psalm 107:2 says, "Let the redeemed of the Lord say so"! What does the faith of the redeemed say? It sings the song we love so much: "This world is not my home, I'm just a-passin' through/ My treasures are laid up, somewhere beyond the blue/The angels beckon me from heaven's open door/And I can't feel at home in this world anymore!"[4] The older I get, the fewer things connect me to this ol' sinful earth. As I grow older, I understand more and more the desire of the older saints to go on to the other side. What a glory awaits us there!

TOPICS: Faith, Persuasion

---

4 "This World Is Not My Home (I'm Just Passing Thru)" by Albert E. Brumley. © Arr. Copyright 1936. Renewed 1964 by Albert E. Brumley & Sons/SESAC (admin. By EverGreen Copyrights). All rights reserved. Used by permission.

DAILY BIBLE READING: James 1–5

TODAY'S VERSE: James 5:16: "Confess your faults one to another, and pray one for another, that ye may be healed. The effectual fervent prayer of a righteous man availeth much."

WE WILL CONCENTRATE our thoughts today on the last sentence in this verse. Prayer is perhaps the greatest opportunity to touch heaven that we have upon this earth. Spurgeon said, "I would rather be the Master of the Art of Prayer than MA of both Oxford and Cambridge. He who knows how to pray has his hand on the leverage that moves the universe." We often fail to understand the importance God has placed upon prayer. D. L. Moody pointed out that Jesus never taught His disciples to preach, but He did teach them how to pray. Oh, that we would have people who learn how to pray! More battle is done on our knees than was ever fought at Waterloo, Gettysburg, and the Battle of the Bulge put together. William Cowper once wrote that the devil himself trembles when he sees the weakest Christian upon his knees.

It Is a **Prayer of Heat** ("The effectual fervent prayer"). The word used here for "effectual fervent" prayer means "to be active, efficient." What good is a prayer if it will not do anything? Even the unbeliever can pray such a prayer! The English definition for *fervent* is "to be hot, to boil, to glow."[5] We see this same principle in the tabernacle, where they would make an offering on the golden altar of incense, a picture of our prayers. As the incense was placed upon the fire of hot coals, it would smoke upward to heaven with a beautiful scent. When was the last time the embers of your prayers lit a trail to heaven and entered into God's presence with the sweetest of odors? Moody once said, "Some men's prayers need to be cut short at both ends and set on fire in the middle." We need holy fire to consume our souls with a burden and heart for the things of God. Whenever something is active and moving, there is heat. It is only a cold and lifeless prayer that has no heat and no passion.

It Is a **Prayer of Holiness** ("of a righteous man"). We see this truth in great sincerity in Psalm 66:18: "If I regard iniquity in my heart, the Lord will not hear me." How can we have the audacity to come before the Lord in prayer if our hearts are wandering from Him in presumptuous sin? The promise given in this verse is to the man who respects the character, purity, and holiness of God. This does not imply that God's goodness is earned, but it does teach us of God's desires for us. This man was not righteous in his own eyes, but in God's eyes.

It Is a **Prayer of Heartiness** ("availeth much"). The word translated "availeth" means "to have or exercise force." This is a prayer that has substance to it! Many times I do not feel that my prayers do much at all. But if my prayers come from a sincere heart that is right with God, I am promised that there is much more happening than I realize. There are many times when I feel a burden to pray, but when I kneel, I don't even know what to say! Romans 8:26 helps us understand the true power of prayer: "Likewise the Spirit also helpeth our infirmities: for we know not what we should pray for as we ought: but the Spirit itself maketh intercession for us with groanings which cannot be uttered." When the Holy Spirit starts praying on our behalf, that is a prayer with force! When God prays, He gets answers!

TOPICS: Fervency, Holiness, Prayer

---

5   *Noah Webster's First Edition of an American Dictionary of The English Language* (Chesapeake, VA: Foundation For American Christian Education, 1995)

DAILY BIBLE READING: 1 Peter 1–5

TODAY'S VERSE: 1 Peter 5:8: "Be sober, be vigilant; because your adversary the devil, as a roaring lion, walketh about, seeking whom he may devour."

THIS IS A VERSE OF WARNING to every Christian. This is not some crazy fairy tale about the bogeyman, but the warning of a real and present evil—Satan. If there is a sign in the Bible that says "BEWARE," this is it! Second Corinthians 2:11 gives a similar warning: "Lest Satan should get an advantage of us: for we are not ignorant of his devices." Be warned, child of God! Ephesians 5:15 instructs us, "See then that ye walk circumspectly, not as fools, but as wise."

Our Attention to Danger ("Be sober, be vigilant"). We are commanded here to pay attention. The word for "sober" means to abstain from wine. We must have our wits about us as we live our Christian lives. The word for "vigilant" means "to keep awake, watch." Instead of practicing vigilance, we have become an apathetic people who don't care about what God is doing, much less about what the devil is doing. This is no fable in which God is trying to scare us with false cries of "Wolf!" (or "Lion!"). The word "because" tells us there is a reason for this warning.

Our Adversary the Devil ("your adversary the devil"). The word for "adversary" means "an opponent as in a lawsuit." Though we do have an adversary, we can be thankful that we also have an Advocate! First John 2:1b says, "And if any man sin, we have an advocate with the Father, Jesus Christ the righteous." The devil is a great foe! He is the most powerful of God's created beings. Yet, his power does not even compare to the infinite power of our Lord! Many, however, have assumed they could fight the devil in their own power, only to meet utter destruction. Satan is not just God's adversary, but *your* adversary! He desires to claim you as a trophy.

The Attempt of Deceit ("as a roaring lion"). This very attempt of Satan's to appear as a lion is deceitful because there is only one lion—the Lion of the Tribe of Judah! The devil is just "as" a roaring lion. Everything he has ever done has been a counterfeit of the real thing—he's a fake. He has his own gospel, his own trinity, and his own plan. He wants people to think he is like Christ. He would love for you to think of his badness as equal and opposite to God's goodness. He can roar as loud as he wants, but his bark is much worse than his bite! Do not be deceived by this phony foe.

The Art of Discovery ("walketh about"). There is no doubt that the devil is a hunter. The words for "walketh about" mean "to tread all around." Satan will leave no stone unturned to find a way to destroy his enemies. The grammar here is in the present indicative, meaning that this is occurring as the speaker is making the statement. One thing I have learned is that hunting is an art. Though Satan is not omnipotent in any way, he does have six thousand years of experience in destroying people's lives. Don't take this threat lightly.

The Aptitude to Devour ("seeking whom he may devour"). The word translated "devour" means "to drink down, to gulp entire." Satan is not looking to take a nibble here or there. He does not just want to hurt one part of your life. He wants to consume you! The Bible says that he is "seeking whom he may devour." He is no respecter of persons! He will take whatever and whomever he can. Lest you leave this devotion in fear, let me leave you with 1 John 4:4: "Ye are of God, little children, and have overcome them: *because greater is he that is in you, than he that is in the world*"!

TOPICS: Deceit, Devil, Satan, Victory, Warning

R. CHRIS HANKS

DAILY BIBLE READING: 2 Peter 1–3

TODAY'S VERSE: 2 Peter 1:4: "Whereby are given unto us exceeding great and precious promises: that by these ye might be partakers of the divine nature, having escaped the corruption that is in the world through lust."

TODAY, LET'S FOCUS on one phrase from our verse: "That by these ye might be partakers of the divine nature." Could anything be greater or more precious than God's promises? This little phrase carries with it tremendous truth and has my attention since it explains to me how God's promises can make me more like God.

The Path of the Divine Nature ("that by these"). There are over three thousand promises in the Bible! Better yet, not one of them has ever been broken! Second Corinthians 1:20 says, "For all the promises of God in him are yea, and in him Amen, unto the glory of God by us." How are these promises going to help us become like God? Second Corinthians 7:1 says, "Having therefore these promises, dearly beloved, let us cleanse ourselves from all filthiness of the flesh and spirit, perfecting holiness in the fear of God." The promises are given by God, and they will work in you!

The Partaking of the Divine Nature ("ye might be partakers"). "Partaker" has to do with partnership and companionship. In other words, you will not achieve this of yourself. You will also not continue it by yourself. If I am a "partaker," I must have a companion in the divine nature—God Himself! Let us be reminded that Jesus told us that "My yoke is easy and my burden is light" (Matthew 11:30). A yoke has a place for two! Second Corinthians 6:1 says, "We then, *as workers together with him*, beseech you also that ye receive not the grace of God in vain." Just as Jesus is with us in our service and labor for the Lord, He is with us in partaking of the divine nature. Colossians 1:27 proclaims "Christ in you, the hope of glory."

The Privilege of the Divine Nature ("partakers of the divine nature"). What an honor we have in this verse! When it says "of the divine nature," the word for "nature" means "natural production." Once Christ is in you, it's as if your DNA changes to DDNA (Divine DNA) that will make you into something else. Why is this so hard to believe if the Bible says in 2 Corinthians 5:17, "Therefore if any man be in Christ, *he is a new creature*: old things are passed away; behold, all things are become new." Things begin to change as God takes over our lives. Don't fight the divine nature! Let it run its course and do what it does! It will change you for His glory.

TOPICS: Growth, Maturity, Holy Spirit

DAILY BIBLE READING: 1 John 1–5

TODAY'S VERSE: 1 John 1:1–3: "That which was from the beginning, which we have heard, *which we have seen with our eyes, which we have looked upon, and our hands have handled,* of the Word of life; (For the life was manifested, and we have seen it, and bear witness, and shew unto you that eternal life, which was with the Father, *and was manifested unto us;) that which we have seen and heard declare we unto you,* that ye also may have fellowship with us: and truly our fellowship is with the Father, and with his Son Jesus Christ."

MERRY CHRISTMAS TO ALL my readers today! I trust that God will speak to your heart on this special day and show you His glory. I am blessed to see how we are greeted in our Bible reading today with a passage that speaks of the incarnation and birth of Christ.

First, we see the **Meaning of Christmas** ("which we have seen with our eyes, which we have looked upon, and our hands have handled"). What is the meaning of Christmas? Matthew 1:23 says, "Behold, a virgin shall be with child, and shall bring forth a son, and they shall call his name Emmanuel, which being interpreted is, God with us." That embodies the entire meaning of what we celebrate during the Christmas season—God with us! Praise the Lord for His wonderful works for the children of men.

Second, we see the **Manifestation of Christmas** ("was manifested unto us"). The word for "manifest" means "to render apparent." God made His love and His plan apparent to all of us at the little stable in Bethlehem. Just the fact that God could become man is enough to drive our finite minds wild! What a wonderful manifestation came to the shepherds and the innkeeper. Later, this manifestation was exhibited to wise men who had traveled far, being led by a divine star.

Third, we see the **Message of Christmas** ("That which we have seen and heard declare we unto you"). Now that we understand what Christmas is all about, we must share it with others! Declare it to your family. Declare it to your friends. Declare it to your town. Declare it the whole world over! With Christmas comes the great responsibility of sharing the gospel with others!

God bless you on this special day!

TOPICS: Christ, Christmas, Incarnation

DAILY BIBLE READING: 2 John, 3 John, and Jude

TODAY'S VERSE: Jude 4: "For there are certain men crept in unawares, who were before of old ordained to this condemnation, ungodly men, turning the grace of our God into lasciviousness, and denying the only Lord God, and our Lord Jesus Christ."

ALL OF JUDE SPEAKS of the apostates in the last time. We live in dangerous times as we anticipate our Lord's imminent return. We need our churches to wake up to the wickedness of these traitors to the Word of God and fugitives from the moral code found in God's Word. The problem described in Jude is pervasive today, and because of it, many of our churches are committing doctrinal suicide through the influence of those who have denied the faith. Today's verse in particular is one of warning against certain types of men.

First, it tells us to **Beware of Creepy Men** ("For there are certain men crept in unawares"). These men are **dangerous!** If they have crept in unawares, they are sneaky and stealthy in their character. In the deep south, many of the old-timers used an interesting term when they were talking about a sneaky dog. They would call it "a suck-egg dog." You never took your eye off such a dog, because in a moment's notice, it might try to get into the hen house and suck a batch of eggs dry. We have the same kind of dogs, or "creeps," who are trying to deceive and destroy the flock of God today. God told us about these men in Matthew 7:15: "Beware of false prophets, which come to you in sheep's clothing, but inwardly they are ravening wolves."

Second, it tells us to **Beware of Condemned Men** ("who were before of old ordained to this condemnation, ungodly men"). These men are **damned!** They have one thing left—the wrath of Almighty God! God knew in His foreknowledge that they would reject the way of salvation and choose the way of judgment. Why would the already-condemned try to hurt someone else? They have nothing else in life except to bring others into condemnation! To the spiritual mind, such sabotage makes no sense, but it is all the carnal and deviant mind can know! The word for "condemnation" means "a decision." Their fate without Christ has already been decided. When these men rejected God's way, they condemned themselves to an eternity without God.

Third, it tells us to **Beware of Corrupt Men** ("turning the grace of our God into lasciviousness"). These men are **defiled.** They have no boundaries. They are willing to expand their horizons by taking gifts of God's grace and making them filthy and defiled to other people. Can you think of anything worse than taking God's precious, amazing grace and turning it into something so wicked and fleshly that we might use it for self-gratification? Titus 1:15 explains this well: "Unto the pure all things are pure: but unto them that are defiled and unbelieving is nothing pure; but even their mind and conscience is defiled."

Fourth, it tells us to **Beware of Cursing Men** ("denying the only Lord God, and our Lord Jesus Christ"). These men are **devilish.** This word for "denying" is in the middle voice, meaning that the subject has done this to himself. It means "to disavow, reject." God is not the author of sin, nor does He make man choose the way of wickedness. It is man who has brought himself to this end and has caused himself to reject the gift of God's Son. This is the main goal of the devil himself—to deny, reject, and try to prove that Jesus is not God. Can you not hear that goal in Satan's words when he tempted Jesus in the wilderness? Two out of three times while tempting Christ, the devil said *"If* thou be the Son of God" (Matthew 4:3, 6). Satan is trying to deny Christ today! Don't deny your Lord in these last times, but confess that Jesus is God so that the world might hear!

TOPICS: Apostasy, Defilement, Sin, Warning, Wickedness

DAILY BIBLE READING: Revelation 1-4

TODAY'S VERSE: Revelation 1:17: "And when I saw him, I fell at his feet as dead. And he laid his right hand upon me, saying unto me, Fear not; I am the first and the last."

REVELATION IS THE ONLY BOOK of the Bible that carries an announced blessing for reading it (see Revelation 1:3). There are many interpretations of this book. Many include fallacies, yet there are many truths in the teachings. As we finish this year and close our devotions, let us concentrate on Christ.

The Vision of My Savior ("And when I saw him, I fell at his feet as dead"). What a day it will be when we finally behold Him who gave His life as a ransom for our souls! John exhibited what we *all* will do when we see Jesus. John did not just fall down in humility, but he fell at Jesus' feet as though he was dead. Acts 17:28 says, "For in him we live, and move, and have our being." But John fell at Jesus' feet as *dead!* Every time I hear people speak about what they are going to do once they get to heaven, I shake my head in wonder. If Christ is not the first thing I see when I get there, I will be disappointed. I will find my Saviour and fall at His feet—*as dead!* Yes, the splendors of heaven are numerous and wondrous, but none of them are as beautiful as our Saviour!

The Victory of My Saviour ("And he laid his right hand upon me"). Notice that Jesus laid His *right* hand. This is quite a storied hand we are talking about! Psalm 98:1 says, "O sing unto the LORD a new song; for he hath done marvellous things: *his right hand,* and his holy arm, *hath gotten him the victory.*" I believe it was Jesus' right hand that delivered the death blow upon the head of Satan. The right hand has always had great significance in Scripture. Jesus is presently seated at the right hand of the Father. All of this is a picture of the victory that Christ has won!

The Voice of My Saviour (*"saying unto me,* Fear not; I am the first and the last"). I am so thankful that we have the Word of God today, but I am excited about *hearing* the voice of God in heaven. I want to hear the voice of the sound of His thundering, the voice as the sound of many waters, and the voice that was still and small for Elijah to hear! There is one thing that my Bible cannot give me—*the intonations of God.* We can hear certain things the closer we draw to God, but they are limited. A deaf person can tell you about how their spouse speaks with them, *but they would give everything to be able to hear their spouse's voice!* I would love to hear the voice of my Saviour! To hear Him say, "Well done, thou good and faithful servant" will bless my heart in an eternal way.

TOPICS: Sight, Victory, Word of God

DAILY BIBLE READING: Revelation 5–9

TODAY'S VERSE: Revelation 5:12: "Saying with a loud voice, Worthy is the Lamb that was slain to receive power, and riches, and wisdom, and strength, and honour, and glory, and blessing."

THIS VERSE DEMANDS contemplation today. Seven things are listed for the Lamb to receive: power, riches, wisdom, strength, honor, glory, and blessing. Each one of these things is tremendous and wonderful. The Lamb is not just worthy to receive *some* of each one of those things, but *all* of each one! I would like to look at the beginning phrase: "Worthy is the Lamb that was slain."

The Blessing of the Saints ("worthy"). Strong's says the word translated "worthy" means "deserving, suitable (as if drawing praise)." God alone is worthy of our love, devotion and praise. The Bible says in Proverbs 3:27, "Withhold not good from them *to whom it is due* [or "to those who are worthy"] when it is in the power of thine hand to do it." It would be good for us to learn how to bless God here on earth! It will be our honor to bless Him in heaven, for He deserves our praise!

The Being of Our Savior ("Lamb"). Why not just say that the "Mighty King" is deserving of all these things? Why not call Him strong, glorious—anything but a "Lamb"? There is no power in a lamb. There is no glory in a lamb. But if our Saviour defeated death, hell, and the grave as the Lamb, then we can picture His glory as King of Kings! If our Lord was victorious over Satan, the Beast, and the False Prophet as the Lamb, then imagine His glory as Lord of Lords! What a Lamb we have! This title reminds us of *His submission* (He "became obedient unto death," Philippians 2:8), *His surrender* ("No man taketh it from me, but I lay it down of myself," John 10:18), and *His sacrifice* ("But now once in the end of the world hath he appeared to put away sin by the sacrifice of himself," Hebrews 9:26). Hallelujah for the Lamb!

The Butchering of the Sacrifice ("slain"). The Greek word for "slain" does not just mean "killed," but "butchered." In a picture, Christ was drawn and quartered to atone for man's sin. We should not look at Calvary without seeing it as a butcher shop. Some have sacrificed themselves for others in the heat of a moment or even upon a battlefield. However, when Christ gave Himself, He did so in eternity past, with the full understanding of all that His sacrifice meant. Yes, He is worthy!

TOPICS: Jesus, Praise, Sacrifice, Victory

DAILY BIBLE READING: Revelation 10–14

TODAY'S VERSE: Revelation 11:17: "Saying, We give thee thanks, O Lord God Almighty, which art, and wast, and art to come; because thou hast taken to thee thy great power, and hast reigned."

THIS VERSE COMES BETWEEN the second and third woes of the end times. Some might dare say that the elder's worship was out of place. Giving thanks to God is never out of place! When the woman brought the alabaster box and anointed the feet of Jesus before His crucifixion, some complained that her worship was a waste. You will find that spiritual thanksgiving is never out of style or inappropriate in its offering to the Lord.

We Should Give Thanks for His Perpetual Nature ("Saying, We give thee thanks, O Lord God Almighty, which art, and wast, and art to come"). There is no greater reason to give thanks than the reality of the resurrection. If Jesus was still dead, the twenty-four elders could not have been thankful for His future return! This is the human equivalent of when God said of Himself in Exodus 3:14, "I Am That I Am." It was the very eternalness of God that Satan fought. This phrase also teaches us about God's constancy. He is just as much God now as He ever has been or ever will be! Malachi 3:6a declares, "For I am the Lord, I change not."

We Should Give Thanks for His Powerful Nature ("because thou hast taken to thee thy great power"). Earlier in our verse, God is referred to as "Lord God Almighty." This whole verse is speaking of His omnipotence. The sign of real power is control. God is not tapping His rod of correction to frighten people into obeying Him. God is not some balled-up fist lurking over our heads to crush us in judgment. When it is time, God will use His power as He sees fit. God is secure in His ability, and He is not threatened by man's false ways.

We Should Give Thanks for His Preeminent Nature ("and hast reigned"). Jesus, by His own power and authority, set up His earthly kingdom for His Millennial Reign. This kingdom will be ruled with a rod of iron (Revelation 12:5, 19:15). Jesus Christ will reign! No one can take His kingdom away or remove His crown from His head. He will reign in power and in truth. He will have faithful followers and loyal subjects who obey His will upon this earth. His will be a righteous reign!

TOPICS: Kingdom, Millennium, Power, Reign

DAILY BIBLE READING: Revelation 15–18

TODAY'S VERSE: Revelation 17:14: "These shall make war with the Lamb, and the Lamb shall overcome them: for he is Lord of lords, and King of kings: and they that are with him are called, and chosen, and faithful."

THOUGH WE LOOK with great love and awe upon the Lamb who is our loving Saviour, Jesus Christ, others will try to destroy Him. It amazes me that there are people who hate God so much they would want to end His existence and expunge Him from man's memory. Even today, the world is trying to put God in a box and keep Him there, to take Him out when we need Him rather than include Him in every decision we face. They are trying to take Christ out of Christmas, erase Him from government, restrict Him in church, and deny Him in education. This hatred of God will come to an all-out war one day between man and the Lamb.

The Lamb's Achievement ("These shall make war with the Lamb, and the Lamb shall overcome them"). The word translated "overcome" means "to subdue, conquer." As a matter of fact, this is not much of a fight. This verse sure doesn't give many battle details, does it? That's because there are none to give! Sinful men made war with the Lamb, and the Lamb overcame them! This must be the worst of hopelessness and helplessness. If you spend any part of your day fighting against God, it will be a pointless and fruitless venture.

The Lamb's Authority ("for he is Lord of lords, and King of kings"). There is no person or authority that has any power over Jesus Christ. He is the best! There is none greater than He! This is the real reason why He won the fight. Would you sue Him? He is the judge! Would you accuse Him? He is the law! Would you find wickedness in Him? He is the embodiment of righteousness! The best thing for you to do is to accept Him as the only authority upon this earth and surrender your will to His.

The Lamb's Association ("and they that are with him are called, and chosen, and faithful"). As a child, I enjoyed going places with my father. There were times when we would go into a place of business on an errand. As my father would take care of his business matter, an employee would see me and ask if he could help me with something. My response was simple—"I'm with him." The point is not what we can bring to the table. It is not what we can offer in the battle. We are just "with Him." At the battle of Armageddon, we will follow Christ upon white horses. The Scripture does not say that we will do anything else, for He will destroy the enemy with the sword out of His mouth (Revelation 19:15). The blessing of taking that ride through the heavens is just that we are "with Him."

This verse tells us that those who are with Christ are "called, chosen, and faithful." It tells us first that we had to be *fetched*. Jesus called us out of our sin and put us in His family. It also says that we are His *favorites*—the chosen. The word for "chosen" means "select; by implication, favorite." The last word used to describe us is *faithful*. I am not very faithful now, but when I have been perfected, I shall be!

TOPICS: Authority, Battle, Christ's Victory, Faithfulness

DAILY BIBLE READING: Revelation 19–22

TODAY'S VERSE: Revelation 19:16: "And he hath on his vesture and on his thigh a name written, KING OF KINGS, AND LORD OF LORDS."

WHAT A WAY TO END the year—with Jesus exalted as the Mighty Conqueror and Ruler of All! It seems there is not much to say about what we see in this verse, because the verse itself says it all! Yet, there also seems to be much to say about this verse. We could exhaust pen and paper before ever doing justice to the picture that is painted for us here. The previous verses give us insight in preparation for today. In particular, in verse 13 we see *His redemption,* in verse 14 we see *His return* (we will be with Him!), and in verse 15 we see *His rule* and *His wrath.* **Today, let us look at the garment Christ wears and what it shows us about His person and work.**

The Garment Is a Picture of His Pardon (see verse 13). Ephesians 1:7 says, "In whom we have redemption through his blood, the forgiveness of sins, according to the riches of his grace." The last time Christ was here in Jerusalem, soldiers gambled over His vesture (or robe) while He hung upon the cross (John 19:24). Here in Revelation, we see His vesture that has been dipped in blood, and no man will take it from Him again! My friend, this is no little red parka, nor is Christ a picture of the quaint fairy tale "Little Red Riding Hood." He is wearing a blood-drenched gown that is proof of His divine sacrifice and victory!

The Garment Is a Proclamation of His Power ("on his vesture and on his thigh"). Numerous images and statues from ancient Greek times have been found to have words written upon their thighs, describing a particular conqueror and his power to any who might read it. It is a *conspicuous* message. It is written upon Jesus' thigh as He rides a white horse so that all may see. It is a *comprehensive* message. Everything about Christ is summed up in these words. It is a *conquering* message. He is here to win the victory! For Him, this is no Sunday-afternoon stick fight! This is a war He will win!

The Garment Is Proof of His Preeminence ("KING OF KINGS, AND LORD OF LORDS"). There is no person who can claim this title but our Lord and Saviour, Jesus Christ. This is a name that He has *earned.* It is a name that others *spurned.* It is a name for us to *learn.* This name puts Christ supremely atop all kings and lords of the earth. It also puts Him above every heavenly title and position in the angelic realm. It is a name that demands respect and reverence. Say it aloud right now as you read this devotion! Let its words ring in your ears! Let your heart swell with joy as the words pass over your lips! This is a final victory that will end all wars! This verse at this time of year makes me remember Handel's "Hallelujah Chorus": "King of Kings for ever and ever, and Lord of Lords, Hallelujah! Hallelujah! And He shall reign forever and ever!" *Amen!*

TOPICS: Blood, Power, Sacrifice, Victory

INDEX OF TOPICS

This index corresponds to the topics listed after each devotion. While not an exhaustive index of the book's contents, it serves to highlight some of the key themes and equip you to locate them easily.

R. CHRIS HANKS

Pardon, 50, 61, 69, 192. Parenting, 130, 136, 148, 157, 173, 210. Passion, 44, 132, 156. Passover, 29. Pastor(s), 46, 100, 232, 240, 282, 354. Paths, 234. (See also Old Paths.) Patience, 33, 58, 252, 256, 358. Patriotism, 136. Peace, 30, 97, 105, 127, 145, 192, 221, 234, 241, 264, 274, 309, 326. Persecution, 166, 169, 191, 236, 238, 245, 271, 326. Perseverance, 18, 35, 62, 193, 225, 234, 256, 271. Persistence, 295. Persuasion, 176, 364. Plainness, 283. Possibilities, 176, 230, 243. Power, 93, 127, 129, 159, 199, 216, 230, 239, 244, 265, 291, 329, 360, 372, 374. Power of God, 292. (See also *God's Power*.) Praise, 80, 141, 144, 149, 154, 158, 183, 188, 195, 197, 224, 229, 235, 301, 309, 312, 340, 371. Prayer, 16, 18, 19, 57, 68, 106, 122, 133, 144, 151, 158, 163, 164, 171, 173, 183, 196, 239, 243, 253, 259, 270, 273, 291, 295, 316, 317, 365. Preacher(s), 100, 254, 260, 263, 268. Preaching, 162, 167, 234, 255, 279, 282, 359. Preeminence, 306. (See also *God's Preeminence*.) Preparation, 35, 40, 67, 136, 148, 160, 216, 233, 256. Preservation, 33. Presence of God, 67, 93, 199, 265. (See also God's Presence.) Presumption, 128. Pride, 44, 75, 90, 91, 93, 94, 101, 109, 114, 147, 168, 218, 220, 228, 247, 297, 340. Priorities, 114, 137, 204. Privilege, 70. Promises, 48, 51, 81, 83, 153, 155, 226, 227, 229, 241, 242, 243, 245, 246, 249. (See also God's Promises.) Promised Land, 48. Proof, 91, 307. Prophecy, 176. Prosperity, 61, 79. Prostitution, 205. Protection, 33, 74, 96, 105, 145, 165, 169, 186, 192, 199, 216, 221, 223, 227, 238. Proving, 70. Provision, 70, 96, 118, 145, 166, 227, 232, 264. Punishment, 175, 189, 201, 218, 251, 261. Purity, 35, 41, 132, 170, 173, 179, 205, 208, 256, 268, 270. Purpose, 92, 107, 211, 241, 270, 274.

Rapture, 316. Rebellion, 44, 99, 123, 168, 215, 239. Rededication, 12. Redemption, 69, 192. Refuge, 165. Reign, 372. Rejection, 65, 99, 193, 257. Rejoicing, 50, 172, 229. Relationship(s), 349, 361. Remembrance, 72, 172, 219. Renewal, 266. Repentance, 45, 106, 114, 164, 168, 181, 219, 233, 258, 263, 275. Reproach, 165. Reputation, 140. Resolve, 89. Resourcefulness, 89. Respect, 15, 180, 219, 240, 247. Responsibility, 21, 100, 131, 165, 240, 263, 357. Rest, 127. Restoration, 11, 95, 112, 168, 175, 189, 191, 251, 275. Resurrection, 265, 276, 307, 353. Revelation, 20, 97, 250, 281. Reverence, 49, 317. Revival, 38, 114, 163, 175, 219, 225, 255, 258, 265, 275, 285. Reward(s), 62, 156, 344. Ridicule, 166. Righteousness, 217, 223, 235, 281.

Sacrifice, 29, 41, 47, 117, 166, 177, 277, 318, 335, 371, 374. Safety, 32, 78, 192. Salvation, 34, 42, 60, 69, 72, 80, 110, 118, 134, 135, 171, 217, 223, 230, 252, 280, 288, 313, 325, 340, 351, 363. Sanctification, 43, 294. Satan, 75, 116, 262, 286, 366. Satisfaction, 145, 252. Scorn, 272. Scorners, 182. Second Coming, 267. Security, 32, 145, 153. Seeking, 356. Seeking God, 235. Self, 116. Self-Righteousness, 311. Sensualism, 17. Separation, 48, 294, 349. Servant, 332. Servanthood, 285, 345. Service, 31, 53, 92, 141, 156, 160, 161, 224, 282, 305, 337. Sexuality, 125. Sexual Sin, 169. Shame, 45, 108, 111, 123, 266. Shepherd, 264. Sight, 370. Simplicity, 212. Sin, 10, 21, 42, 44, 45, 46, 64, 88, 89, 95, 111, 128, 132, 139, 140, 147, 151, 168, 175, 182, 191, 200, 201, 206, 215, 216, 228, 236, 280, 311, 340, 369. Singing, 141, 154, 202, 229. Skill, 203. Slavery, 72. Snares, 272. Song, 195, 197. Sorrow, 142, 258. Soul-Winning, 18, 24, 122, 130, 131, 213, 259, 312. Sovereignty, 9, 177. Sowing, 213. Spiritual, 208. Spiritual Desire, 19. Spiritual Growth, 346. (See also *Growth*.) Spiritual Hunger, 308. Spiritual Perception, 20. Stand, 160, 259. Study, 100, 167. Stubbornness, 99. Strange Women, 205. Strength, 27, 84, 127, 148, 159, 166, 203, 225, 274, 352. Submission, 102, 120, 141, 160, 212, 305, 310, 324, 354. Substitution, 170. Subtlety, 350. Success, 78, 79. Suffering, 140, 288, 300, 330. Supply, 127, 223, 226. Support, 31, 78. Surrender, 85, 114, 305, 310, 336. Sustenance, 135, 226.

Taste, 214. Teaching, 173. Temperance, 111. Temptation, 81. Tempting God, 193. Tenderness, 212, 233, 239, 315. Terror, 261. Testimony, 61, 108, 130, 138, 144, 190, 208, 237, 301, 302, 303, 312, 315, 332, 339, 349, 357. Testing, 70. Thanksgiving, 183. Thoughtfulness, 346. Tithing, 318. Tongue, 91, 215. Torment, 218. Training, 203, 304. Trial(s), 27, 245, 253. Tribulation, 16, 326, 330. Trinity, 54, 290. Trouble, 107, 315. Truth, 138, 202, 244. Trust, 27, 58, 67, 113, 140, 153, 185, 187, 199, 219, 221, 230, 242, 246, 252, 322, 334. Trusting, 19.

Unbelief, 193, 292. Uncertainty, 286. Unction, 129. Understanding, 119, 178, 204, 319, 346. Ungodly, 182.

Unity, 31, 242.

Value, 32. **Vanity,** 90, 211. **Vengeance,** 306, 316. **Victory,** 28, 37, 47, 48, 51, 65, 69, 71, 73, 78, 82, 83, 84, 86, 88, 89, 111, 131, 140, 154, 159, 172, 201, 238, 244, 249, 251, 276, 278, 306, 307, 320, 341, 347, 366, 370, 371, 374. **Vision,** 85, 148, 304, 335.

Waiting, 225. **Walk,** 56, 85, 132. (See also Christian Walk.) **Walking with God,** 294. **War,** 56, 71, 75, 82, 83, 89, 92, 111, 162, 165, 203, 238, 248. **Warfare,** 64, 142, 143, 341. **Warning,** 366, 369. **Weakness,** 187. **Wealth,** 299. **Wicked,** 62. **Wickedness,** 125, 128, 205, 369. **Wilderness,** 198. **Will,** 38, 125, 228, 300. **Wisdom,** 39, 81, 94, 103, 119, 122, 136, 178, 180, 182, 184, 204, 212, 247, 350. **Witness,** 92, 102, 106, 122, 126, 130, 144, 293, 299, 302, 303, 312, 315, 329, 331, 332, 335, 336, 357. **Wonder,** 174, 250. **Word of God,** 20, 34, 56, 66, 70, 76, 77, 79, 97, 106, 120, 127, 137, 152, 157, 160, 167, 181, 188, 190, 200, 213, 222, 231, 237, 239, 240, 244, 250, 254, 257, 274, 281, 283, 319, 322, 326, 338, 339, 348, 351, 359, 362, 370. (See also *Bible.*) **Work,** 9, 16, 24, 39, 40, 43, 53, 92, 146, 148, 161, 162, 208, 279, 299. **World,** 71. **Worship,** 12, 16, 39, 44, 49, 55, 56, 87, 106, 111, 121, 125, 143, 148, 149, 150, 154, 155, 157, 164, 166, 171, 188, 197, 202, 214, 215, 217, 224, 234, 250, 293, 296, 299, 300, 317, 328. **Worthy,** 183.